Britain and China, 1967–72

DOCUMENTS ON BRITISH POLICY OVERSEAS
Series III, Volume XIII

DOCUMENTS ON BRITISH POLICY OVERSEAS

Series Editors: Patrick Salmon and Richard Smith

SERIES I (1945–1950)
Volume I	The Conference at Potsdam, July–August 1945
Volume II	Conferences and Conversations 1945: London, Washington and Moscow
Volume III	Britain and America: Negotiation of the United States loan, August–December 1945
Volume IV	Britain and America: Atomic Energy, Bases and Food, December 1945–July 1946
Volume V	Germany and Western Europe, August–December 1945
Volume VI	Eastern Europe, August 1945–April 1946
Volume VII	The United Nations: Iran, Cold War and World Organisation, January 1946–January 1947
Volume VIII	Britain and China, 1945–1950
Volume IX	The Nordic Countries: From War to Cold War, 1944–1951
Volume X	The Brussels and North Atlantic Treaties, 1947–1949
Volume XI	European Recovery and the Search for Western Security, 1946–1948

SERIES II (1950–1955)
Volume I	The Schuman Plan, the Council of Europe and Western European Integration, May 1950–December 1952
Volume II	The London Conferences, January–June 1950
Volume III	German Rearmament, September–December 1950
Volume IV	Korea, June 1950–April 1951

SERIES III (1960–)
Volume I	Britain and the Soviet Union, 1968–1972
Volume II	The Conference on Security and Co-operation in Europe, 1972–1975
Volume III	Détente in Europe, 1972–1976
Volume IV	The Year of Europe: America, Europe and the Energy Crisis 1972–1974
Volume V	The Southern Flank in Crisis, 1973–1976
Volume VI	Berlin in the Cold War, 1948–1990
Volume VII	German Unification, 1989–1990
Volume VIII	The Invasion of Afghanistan and UK-Soviet Relations, 1979–1982
Volume IX	The Challenge of Apartheid: UK-South Africa Relations, 1985–1986
Volume X	The Polish Crisis and Relations with Eastern Europe, 1979–1982
Volume XI	The Unwinding of Apartheid: UK-South African Relations, 1986–1989
Volume XII	Britain and the Revolutions in Eastern Europe, 1989

Britain and China, 1967–72

DOCUMENTS ON BRITISH POLICY OVERSEAS
Series III, Volume XIII

Edited by
Luke Gibbon and Richard Smith

FOREIGN, COMMONWEALTH AND DEVELOPMENT OFFICE

First published 2023 by the
Foreign, Commonwealth and Development Office
King Charles Street, London, SW1A 2AH

© 2023 Crown Copyright

Cover illustration: 'Formal Dinner, June 1972. Anthony Royle, Parliamentary Under-Secretary for Foreign and Commonwealth Affairs, Chiao Kuan-hua, Vice-Minister of Foreign Affairs, John Addis, Sung Chih-kuang, Chinese Ambassador in London.'

Picture credits: Cover and Addis p. viii, SOAS Library; otherwise FCDO.

ISBN 9781905181155 (hardback)
ISBN 9781905181162 (paperback)
ISBN 9781905181179 (pdf)

CONTENTS

Preface		ix
Abbreviations for printed sources		xxiv
Abbreviated designations		xxv
List of persons		xxviii
Document summaries		xxxviii
I	The Cultural Revolution and the burning of the Mission 15 May 1967–18 March 1968	1
II	Clearing the debris of confrontation 21 March 1968–13 February 1970	143
III	Negotiating an exchange of Ambassadors 15 April 1970–13 March 1972	334
Appendix	Joint Communiqué on the Agreement Between the United Kingdom of Great Britain and Northern Ireland and the People's Republic of China on an Exchange of Ambassadors	548
Index		550

British Chargés d'affaires in Peking
Clockwise from top left:
Donald Hopson, Percy Cradock,
John Denson and John Addis

PREFACE

This volume covers Britain's relations with China from 1967–72. It documents attempts by Ministers and officials to formulate policy against the backdrop of the Cultural Revolution and disturbances in Hong Kong. This tense period saw the burning of the British mission in Beijing, the detention of British subjects in China (such as the Reuters journalist, Anthony Grey) and restrictions on diplomatic staff in both countries. With an easing of tensions from 1970 onwards, the volume then charts the negotiations for an exchange of Ambassadors. This involved settling questions relating to Chinese representation in the United Nations, the British consulate in Tamsui and the status of Taiwan. The volume also highlights the consequences for British policy of President Nixon's rapprochement with China. It concludes with the Joint UK-China Communiqué on the Agreement of the Exchange of Ambassadors, signed on 13 March 1972, establishing full diplomatic relations after a break of 22 years. The documents do not cover British reporting on internal aspects of the Cultural Revolution unless this affected relations with China and UK overseas policy.

Britain and the People's Republic of China, 1949–66

On 6 January 1950 the British Labour government accorded diplomatic recognition to the People's Republic of China (PRC), founded on 1 October 1949 following the defeat of Chiang Kai-shek's Nationalist forces by Mao Zedong's Communists.[1] Britain nominated a chargé d'affaires *ad interim*, pending the appointment of Ambassadors, but the PRC proved to be in no rush to exchange representatives with a country responsible for the 'unequal treaties' that followed the Opium Wars (1839–42, 1856–60) leading to China's 'century of humiliation'. Negotiations to establish diplomatic relations fell into abeyance when the Korean War broke out on 25 June 1950.[2] There followed a rapid contraction of British interests in China. Britain's extensive network of consulates closed, and by 1952 Shanghai was the only post remaining outside Beijing. Trading conditions for foreign businesses became progressively harder as the government tried to push them out. Starved of business from the state authorities and facing increased taxes and regulation, most British companies left, handing what remained of their assets to the Chinese Government. The British community in China shrank dramatically after all non-essential British subjects were advised to leave in October 1950. Those who remained were usually either married to Chinese citizens, representatives of the few remaining businesses, or 'foreign friends'—British communist sympathisers working in China. Hong Kong, however, had its uses to the PRC as a source of trade and foreign exchange.

The diplomatic community in Beijing was small, as only a few non-Communist countries had recognised the PRC. The British compound in the old legation quarter, established in 1861 around the former palace of the Duke of Liang to the south

---

1 For the decision to recognise the People's Republic of China see *Documents on British Policy Overseas: Series I, Volume VIII: Britain and China, 1945–1950* (London: Frank Cass, 2002), Nos.105 and 110.

2 For an account of negotiations up to this point see ibid., Nos. 120 and 121.

west of the Forbidden City, had at its peak covered some 30 acres. Although now much reduced, it was still too large for the chargé and his small mission. With no formal diplomatic status their contact with Chinese authorities was minimal. This, along with attempts to keep foreigners in isolation, led Humphrey Trevelyan, the British chargé (1953–55), to think he had been 'admitted to a superior mental home provided with every comfort, but having no contact with the outside world'.[3] Third Secretary, Douglas Hurd, recalled: 'We felt that we lived at the end of the world.'[4] The mission kept up their spirits with Scottish country dancing, amateur dramatics, the occasional film show, and carol concerts at Christmas. In 1959 the mission vacated the old compound for a one-and-a-half-acre site in the new 1st Diplomatic District built by the Chinese. Two two-storey houses set in walled gardens served as an embassy and a residence, whilst staff lived in flats in a nearby compound.[5]

It was not until 1954, at the Geneva Conference on Indochina, that the British presence in China was placed on a firmer footing. Chinese Foreign Minister Zhou Enlai and British Foreign Secretary Anthony Eden agreed to establish diplomatic relations at the level of chargé, with a Chinese official appointed to London. However there was to be no Embassy, only an 'Office of the British Chargé d'Affaires'. The two countries continued to have, in the words of Zhou Enlai, 'semi-diplomatic relations', and further progress stalled because of what the PRC saw as Britain's 'Two Chinas' policy. This included the maintenance of a consulate in Taiwan, where the Nationalists took refuge in 1949, and a lack of support for the admission of the PRC into the UN. From the 1960s the escalation in the Vietnam War provided another obstacle to improving relations, as Hong Kong was used as a rest and recuperation base for US servicemen.

The Cultural Revolution and the burning of the mission

In the summer of 1966 the Cultural Revolution was unleashed on China by Mao Zedong. His attempt to reinvigorate the Communist revolution and reassert his control over the Party plunged the country into a period of social and political turmoil. Students, mobilised into divisions of Red Guards, were encouraged to denounce and punish those displaying 'bourgeois' traits—teachers, intellectuals, party officials. China's internal and foreign affairs became dominated by confused and often murderous factional struggles which brought chaos, violence and widespread economic and cultural disruption. Diplomats described the increasingly Orwellian behaviour of the Chinese (No. 81) and the 'frenzy of emotional self-abuse' that accompanied the cult of Mao (No. 169).[6] Early analysis of the Revolution from diplomats in Beijing concluded that it was 'an essentially internal upheaval' likely to make

---

3 Humphrey Trevelyan, *Worlds Apart* (London: Macmillan, 1971) p. 22.
4 Douglas Hurd, *Memoirs* (London: Little Brown, 2003) p. 105.
5 For the history of the Embassy, and other consulates in China, see Mark Bertram, *Room for Diplomacy: The History of Britain's Diplomatic Buildings Overseas, 1800–2000* (Salisbury: Spire, 2017) and James Hoare, *Embassies in the East: the Story of the British Embassies in Japan, China, and Korea from 1859 to the Present* (London: Curzon, 1999).
6 For recollections of British diplomats during this period, see Percy Cradock, *Experiences of China* (London: John Murray, 1994), George Walden, *Lucky George: memoirs of an anti-politician* (London: Allen Lane, 1999) and FCO Historians, *Witness Seminar: The Role and Functions of the British Embassy Beijing* (2013) www.issuu.com/fcohistorians.

China more isolationist but have little impact on foreign policy.[7] Officials in the Foreign Office were less sure. Bilateral relations would at best stagnate and probably deteriorate. 'The foreseeable future is entirely gloomy', wrote the Assistant Under-Secretary, Arthur de la Mare, 'and there is nothing we can do to make it brighter.'[8] The revolution eventually spilled over into foreign affairs leading to the harassment of diplomats and attacks on foreign embassies.[9]

In May 1967 the Cultural Revolution spread to Hong Kong. A labour dispute at an artificial flower factory in Kowloon led to clashes between workers and the police. It escalated into an eight-month, anti-colonial struggle fuelled by the ideals of the Revolution and inequalities in Hong Kong society. Large-scale demonstrations in Macao during the winter of 1966–67 saw the Portuguese colonial authorities forced to make substantial concessions to the Red Guards. Hong Kong was a tougher nut to crack. With popular support the Hong Kong Government avoided capitulating to communist-inspired agitation and violence. Rioting, inflammatory propaganda and a bombing campaign drew a heavy response from the authorities with mass arrests, detention without trial, and the closure of left-wing schools and pro-communist newspapers. However, the backlash was soon felt by British diplomats in Macao, where the consul was forced to flee, and in China, where staff and their families became hostages for British policy in Hong Kong.[10] The mission was small with just over a dozen diplomats and twice that number of administrative, security and communications staff. On 15 May the Chinese foreign ministry issued a statement castigating the Hong Kong Government for 'fascist atrocities' and made 'five demands' including acceptance of the 'just' demands of the local workers, an end to the arrest and trial of demonstrators, the release of all those arrested and, apologies and compensation for the victims. The British chargé in Beijing, Donald Hopson, concluded that the Chinese Government had decided to risk a direct confrontation on Hong Kong and gave a prescient warning—'We may be in for a very long haul' (No. 1).

In Shanghai British consul Peter Hewitt was summoned by Chinese officials and asked to 'apologise' to a picture of Mao.[11] His house was ransacked and demonstrators burnt effigies of Prime Minister Harold Wilson in the street. Then the Chinese unilaterally announced the closure of the office and Hewitt's family were harassed as they left (Nos. 6, 20). Revolutionary zeal was evident at the Chinese mission in London. When the Foreign Office attempted to make official protests against events in Shanghai, the Chinese chargé refused to accept or convey them to his Government (No. 5). British officials wondered how to deal with those who did not consider themselves bound by existing codes of diplomatic practice. On 21

---

7 FCO 21/26, 'China: Annual Review for 1966', 1 January 1967
8 FO 371/186982/FC 1015/159, Minute by Mr de la Mare, September 1966.
9 Second Secretary John Weston recalled: 'We were often involved in melees and violent arguments on the streets, sometimes surrounded by Chinese who thought we were up to no good, sometimes pursued, sometimes victimised in other ways.' British Diplomatic Oral History Programme, Churchill Archives Centre: DOHP 82, p. 11.
10 For the fate of the consulate in Macao, see Hugh Davies, 'An Undiplomatic Foray: A 1967 Escapade in Macau.' *Journal of the Royal Asiatic Society Hong Kong Branch* 47 (2007) pp. 115–26.
11 As the Chinese declined to recognise the term 'consul' after 1949 he was officially known as: 'Official sent by the British Charge d'Affaires in Beijing to look after the interests of British citizens in Shanghai'.

July 1967, in retaliation for the arrest of New China News Agency (NCNA) staff in Hong Kong, Anthony Grey, the Reuters correspondent in China, was placed under house arrest (No. 24). Grey was subsequently held for 27 months, confined to one room in his house, his only contact with the outside world being three short visits from British diplomats. His detention became a long running source of concern for British officials.[12]

In early August 1967, Mr Hopson cautioned that the Cultural Revolution was making Chinese policy less amenable to reason, less predictable and less inclined to compromise, especially where overseas Chinese communities were concerned. Britain should continue to be patient and firm: 'As long as Chinese xenophobia and administrative persecution do not render life unliveable for the foreign diplomatist in Beijing, we must go on trying to maintain contact as best we can' (No. 27). Later that month the Chinese issued an ultimatum demanding the release of journalists arrested in Hong Kong and the lifting of a recent ban on three Chinese communist newspapers, otherwise 'Her Majesty's Government would be held responsible for all consequences'. Mr Hopson sensed trouble, possibly violent, and warned the Chinese Government of their responsibility for the security of the mission (No. 30). Soon after the ultimatum expired, on the evening of 22 August, a mob broke into the British compound burning the office, sacking the residence, and harassing and beating members of the mission (No. 53). With wireless communications broken, the French Embassy relayed messages to London, whilst staff and their families took refuge with other foreign embassies (Nos. 38). The head of chancery, Percy Cradock, confirmed that it was not an irrational outburst of mob violence, but a carefully planned and controlled operation. The phone lines were cut in advance, the secure zone of the office was deliberately preserved from fire and the People's Liberation Army clearly had orders to ensure the eventual safety of staff 'after a good deal of roughing-up and humiliation' (No. 46).

The British Government protested vigorously. They placed limits on the movement of Chinese Government officials in London, enforced by police and Special Branch surveillance, and required them to apply for exit visas before leaving the UK (No. 40). On 29 August, a manufactured incident occurred outside the Chinese mission in Portland Place, London. Chinese diplomats, armed with clubs and an axe, clashed with police and press, injuring several people—an incident subsequently dubbed 'The Battle of Portland Place'. This gave the Chinese an excuse to impose new restrictions on the movement of British diplomats in Beijing and cancel all exit visas (Nos. 47/48). Mr Hopson was now very wary that any further retaliatory action in London or Hong Kong would have serious repercussions for his staff (No. 51). At the end of August, Foreign Secretary George Brown wrote personally to the Chinese Foreign Minister, Chen Yi, seeking his cooperation 'to bring the situation back to normal and to set both countries on a better course in their relations'. He received no reply, but it was unclear who was actually in charge at the Foreign Ministry (Nos. 52/54). Reviewing relations in September for the Cabinet Defence and Oversea

---

12 In his book *Hostage in Peking* (London: Michael Joseph, 1970), Grey described his house arrest 'as the application, with traditional Chinese subtlety, of a kind of mental thumbscrew, tightened progressively in an attempt to bring an answering twitch of pain and submission from the corporate body of Britain and the British Government in London' (p. 87–8).

Policy (DOP) Committee, the Foreign Office recommended evacuating British women and children from China as soon as possible, replacing male members of the Mission gradually, and warning British businessmen and shipping of the UK's inability to provide them with any protection. The Committee decided not to break off relations with the PRC in the interests of trade, British subjects still in China, and Hong Kong. It was also considered vital for the mission to continue reporting political developments and remain ready to capitalise on any changes (No. 55/56).[13]

The fate of the mission in Beijing was now tied to events in Hong Kong and there were frequent disagreements over the best way to secure objectives, although Chinese intransigence often narrowed differences. The Governor, Sir David Trench, who had spent a large part of his career in Hong Kong, was concerned primarily with local security and adopted a firm line towards China.[14] The mission in Beijing, concerned with the well-being of its staff and with the long-term relationship with China, favoured a more positive and proactive approach. Mr Hopson and his successors argued that the best way to ensure stability for Hong Kong, or to obtain the release of detained British subjects, lay in the general improvement of UK-China relations. The best way to achieve this was to remove as many points of contention with China as possible and to refrain from unnecessarily provocative acts in Hong Kong. The divide reflected the split in the management of British overseas relations during this period. Policy towards China was initiated by the Far Eastern Department (FED) of the Foreign Office in London and implemented by the mission in Beijing. Relations with China always had to take into account the interests of the British colony in Hong Kong, headed by a British Governor and overseen by the Hong Kong Department of the Commonwealth Office. This increasingly anachronistic split in decision-making would end in October 1968 when the Foreign Office and the Commonwealth Office merged to become the Foreign and Commonwealth Office (FCO) with a single Secretary of State. However, a separate Hong Kong Department continued within the new organisation, although jointly supervised along with the FED by an Assistant Under-Secretary.

By the end of 1967 the threat of further physical violence against the mission in Beijing had receded but the Chinese showed little interest in improving relations. Ministers recognised they would have to make the first move. In an attempt to improve the situation they unilaterally ended travel restrictions on Chinese officials in London. Mr Brown argued that the time was right for such a gesture as it appeared that moderates in China, particularly Prime Minister Zhou Enlai, were re-establishing control, whilst relaxing surveillance would also lighten the burden on the police (which the Home Secretary was keen to see) (Nos. 69/70). This policy was vindicated when a week later the Chinese lifted all restrictions on the movement of British staff in Beijing (No. 71).

---

13 The main activity for all foreign missions in Beijing at this time was to read the Red Guard wall posters to try to get a sense of what was going on (see Walden, 1999, pp. 106–8). Second Secretary John Boyd recalled that in gathering such first-hand political intelligence 'we felt our professional life was justified, and the substance was of great interest both to us and Whitehall' (DOHP 60, p. 5).
14 Arthur Maddocks, political adviser in Hong Kong, later said of Sir D. Trench: 'He didn't want to be troubled by any outside influences, whether London or Peking. He didn't really want to hear about China, but he accepted that he had to. I was the instrument through which he was told about China and possible complications' (DOHP 167, p. 31).

Clearing the debris of confrontation: visas, detained subjects and prisoners
In January 1968, Mr Hopson was told that if exit and entry restrictions on Chinese officials in London were lifted there would be 'corresponding gestures'. Mr Brown lamented the fact that 'we always seem to move first!' (No. 77). Mr Hopson was keen to agree terms, seeing a clear opening to settle the visa question for his staff and their dependants, effectively trapped in Beijing, on whom the strain was beginning to tell.[15] He had also been told that the case of Mr Grey was linked to prisoners in Hong Kong and was not a visa question. He recommended keeping the two issues separate as trying to settle both at once would lead to failure (No. 76). However, Mr Grey had been in solitary confinement for over five months, with no firm evidence about his health, and feelings about his situation were running high in Parliament. The Foreign Office decided to grant visas to Chinese diplomats but refuse them for NCNA journalists so long as Mr Grey remained in detention (Nos. 77-79). From Hong Kong, the Governor reported that while public opinion was sympathetic to Mr Grey's plight, there would be 'deep resentment' if any 'substantial Hong Kong interest' were sacrificed for him (No. 80). As Mr Hopson had predicted, the Chinese attitude hardened. He was informed in an interview with Luo Guibo, Vice-Minister for Foreign Affairs, on 8 March 1969, that Hong Kong was 'the crux of Sino-British relations', reintroducing the link between British conduct in Hong Kong and the treatment of the mission, rather than equating British officials in Beijing with Chinese officials in London (No. 83). The mission was disappointed that their advice had been ignored and an opportunity missed.[16] Mr Brown stated that 'before we conclude we must dance to the Pekin' tune I'd like to see the score!'[17] The Government considered further action including economic sanctions, additional restrictions against Chinese diplomats in London, galvanising international action, or a publicity campaign but none were thought to stand much chance of success (Nos. 85/86).

In March 1968 a change of Foreign Secretary brought new impetus. Michael Stewart, who replaced Mr Brown, was more willing to accept Mr Hopson's recommendations and visas were granted to both Chinese diplomats and NCNA staff in London. This risked unfavourable publicity as British subjects continued to be detained in China and held under various pretexts: In February a British journalist, Norman Barrymaine, was arrested in Shanghai; in March George Watt, an engineer with Vickers-Zimmer, was imprisoned for alleged spying; and in April a British sailor, Peter Crouch, was detained in Shanghai. In most cases no explanation was given and consular access was denied. However, as Foreign Office Minister William Rodgers stated in the House of Commons, there was no point 'striking attitudes which, frankly, would yield no results. We must remember that China today is a unique case where none of the normal rules seem to apply.'[18] The hope was that any relaxation would help towards restoring normal diplomatic relations, which might make the Chinese more willing to grant consular access to Britons in detention (Nos. 94/95).

15 As Peking was classed as a 'hardship' post tours were only meant to last two years, with local leave in Hong Kong after six months and home leave after 12 months.
16 Cradock later noted: 'It was about this time that I evolved a rule to which I gave the title of Cradock's First Law of Diplomacy, namely that it is not the other side you need to worry about, but your own' (Cradock, 1994, p. 78).
17 FCO 21/66. Minute by Mr Brown, March 1968.
18 *Parl. Debs. 5th ser., H. of C.*, vol. 766, col. 581, 13 June 1968.

The Chinese responded positively and began granting visas to the British mission. Meanwhile in April, in exchange for special visits to NCNA prisoners in Hong Kong, Mr Hopson and Mr Cradock were allowed a brief visit to Mr Grey, whom they found in good spirits despite his ordeal (No. 101). Mr Hopson and the Governor continued to disagree on the best tactics for securing his release. Trench would only consider the unconditional release of NCNA journalists imprisoned in Hong Kong if they were immediately deported to China, something the Chinese had rejected (Nos. 106-110). Chinese cooperation on visas slowed following a visit to Hong Kong from an American warship, the USS *Enterprise*. The Foreign Office followed the Governor's recommendation to allow the visit to take place, despite Mr Hopson's warning this would antagonise the Chinese (Nos. 112/115). Another issue of contention was the Governor's plan to deregister a left-wing school in Hong Kong. Mr Hopson thought it unnecessary, as the situation was calmer, and only likely to undermine attempts to improve relations (No. 120). In June, Mr Hopson suggested the time had come to use publicity and foreign diplomatic pressure, on the grounds that Chinese actions were contrary to the norms of diplomatic behaviour (Nos. 116/117). Although sceptical of success, officials in London agreed, if only to boost morale in Beijing at a time when it was acknowledged that the Mission had lost confidence in the Office's willingness to accept its advice. Deputy Under-Secretary Peter Wilkinson noted they were 'dangerously out of sympathy', and restoring confidence was of overriding importance (No. 123). On the eve of the campaign, the Chinese resumed granting visas. Mr Hopson was one of the recipients, allowing him to leave in August 1969 (No. 140).

Before he left, Mr Hopson set out his thoughts on relations with China, arguing that the confrontation in Hong Kong needed to end in the best interests of the mission, detained British subjects, political and commercial relations with China, and Hong Kong. He suggested releasing detainees and prisoners not convicted of serious violence in the hope this would lead to further de-escalation. The alternative, he warned, was bad relations for many years, perhaps until 1974 when the last of the confrontation prisoners was due to be released (No. 135). Mr Cradock, the new chargé, saw the ending of the visa issue as vindication of the policy of de-escalation advocated by the mission, whereas restrictions had only led to much harsher counter-measures (No. 163). In February 1969 Mr Cradock was replaced by John Denson, the assistant head of FED, who sent home a familiar message: Hong Kong was the crux of the issue, prisoner release was the key, normalisation of relations was the prize (No. 165). Whilst willing to entertain this approach, London found it hard to counter the Governor's arguments that early release would involve interference in Hong Kong's judicial process and undermine local confidence. Sir D. Trench argued that concessions were likely to encourage further demands rather than stimulate any genuine reciprocity, whilst constant talk of the need to improve relations with China was only raising Chinese expectations. He also warned against encouraging a belief that London was more amenable to pressure than the Hong Kong Government (No. 171). His analysis was in part informed by a back-channel he was running to the Chinese leadership through the Executive Director of the Hong Kong Trade Development Council and a manager in the Bank of China in Hong Kong (No. 145).

Nevertheless, the British Government tried to maintain diplomatic pressure on the Chinese. They gave full publicity to a second visit to Mr Grey made by Mr Cradock and Roger Garside on 26 November 1968. In a press conference afterwards, at which both men were described as 'having difficulty in controlling their emotions', Mr Cradock said of Mr Grey: 'He lives in a void'.[19] Chinese officials were stung by the accusations of 'inhumane treatment' levelled at them by the world's press (No. 160). Periodic releases, within the legal process, of those imprisoned or detained during the 1967 confrontation in Hong Kong did eventually break the deadlock. Mr Grey was released on 4 October 1969, showing 'some natural signs of strain' but 'in fairly good physical shape despite a prison pallor' (No. 175).

During 1970 the British Government continued to seek publicity for the other British subjects detained in China and pressed the Governor to keep the position of prisoners under review. This often led to push-back from Hong Kong. Arthur Maddocks, the Political Adviser, thought the Government ought to be thinking more about Hong Kong and less about China. He found it difficult to take seriously the prospect of a substantial improvement in political relations with China: 'Our inheritance from the last century, the extraordinary dogmatic nature of the Chinese regime, the probable continuation of irritations and problems in Hong Kong and the relative decline of our power in the world set narrow limits to the scope for improvement.' What the Foreign Office hoped to get out of China—more trade, release of British subjects, political influence, better treatment for the mission— he thought seemed small compared with the substantial interests in Hong Kong, 'not only economic, but political, intelligence and human'. Mr Maddocks, an FCO secondee to the Government of Hong Kong, also thought the Foreign Office was conforming to the 'classic criticism' from Whitehall of being too willing to sacrifice genuine British interests, especially of a commercial or financial nature, 'for the sake of smiles and insubstantial generalities' (No. 190).[20] John Morgan, head of FED, thought British Government policy was based on 'hard-headed calculation' and not on 'wishful thinking'. Satisfactory Sino-Hong Kong relations were necessary to preserve the smooth running of the territory, and eventually secure its long-term future (No. 192). Mr Cradock, now with the Planning Staff, believed more thought should be given to, 'on the one hand the declining importance (and increasing embarrassment) of Hong Kong; on the other the increasing importance of China' (No. 192). The issue of confrontation prisoners continued into 1971. Officials and Ministers in London became increasingly frustrated with the Governor's resistance to further measures to normalise relations with China—this time by having the Prison Board of Review reconsider the sentences of confrontation prisoners, with the aim of securing early releases, which might allow a line to be drawn under the issue (No. 215).

---

19 *The Times*, 27 November 1968.
20 Such comments revealed long-standing concerns. On 5 January 1967 Sir D. Trench had written to Sir A. Galsworthy: 'The impression at present which is I fear gaining ground is that she [Hong Kong] is regarded at home not as the loyal supporter she on the whole is, but as a tiresome nuisance, to be slighted and made use of since she cannot be quietly made away with'. *DBEE*, Series A, Volume 5: Part III, No. 333.

Preface

Negotiating an exchange of Ambassadors

During 1970 there were general signs of an upturn in relations. In April Michael Wilford, Assistant Under-Secretary of State, paid a successful visit to China where Denson observed the Chinese 'would like to remove existing difficulties' but the process would be gradual (No. 188). In London, Chinese diplomats started to dine with FCO officials. In June, Deputy Foreign Minister Luo Guibo attended the Queen's Birthday reception at the Beijing mission, where he expressed regret that it had not been possible to exchange Ambassadors (No. 191) The Chinese continued to release other British detainees with the last, David Johnston, a banker arrested on spying charges, freed in January 1971 (No. 218). The election in June 1970 of a new Conservative government with Edward Heath as Prime Minister coincided with this improvement in relations. Whereas the Labour government had latterly spent much energy reacting to events in China and Hong Kong, Heath and his new Foreign Secretary, Sir Alec Douglas-Home, had an opportunity to pursue a more positive engagement. Heath was determined to achieve a rapprochement with China, whilst his pro-European policy was attractive to the Chinese leadership. It was noted by several interlocutors that Zhou Enlai attached great importance to Mr Heath's 1971 Party Conference speech and its references to Britain finding its place in a 'new world', which was taken as evidence of an attempt to move on from its colonial past (Nos. 280/285).[21]

On 15 January 1971 Parliamentary Under-Secretary Anthony Royle, suggested to the new Chinese chargé, Pei Jianzhang, that Britain and China should proceed to exchange Ambassadors (No. 209). On 2 March, Mr Denson was summoned to a meeting with Zhou Enlai who apologised for the burning of the mission and offered to pay for its repair (it had reopened in early 1971). Zhou told Mr Denson that the main obstacles to exchanging Ambassadors were Britain's consulate in Taiwan and its voting policy on Chinese representation in the UN (No. 223). These pre-conditions were affirmed when the Chinese responded officially to the British proposal. Officials now had a clear indication of what the PRC wanted and were relieved that more sensitive subjects, such as the status of Taiwan, had not been raised (No. 226). Of the two issues, the closure of the consulate was the easier to resolve. The consulate in Tamsui, not far from Taipei, functioned under a junior officer with a small staff. Since the UK did not recognise the Nationalist régime, it had no formal contact with the central Taiwan Government but instead dealt with local provincial authorities. The consulate was considered to have only marginal value for political and intelligence reporting but was of some use to visiting British businessmen. Officials were content to recommend its withdrawal on the grounds of economy and removing a source of constant irritation with the PRC (No. 228).

The UN issue was more difficult. The British had consistently voted for the 'Albanian' resolution calling for the seating of the PRC at the UN. They also voted for the Important Question resolution, which stated that as the Albanian resolution

---

21 'It is time for us now to walk out into the light to find a new place, a new Britain in this new world. That is the choice that history offers us today. It is the kind of chance that only comes, if it ever comes, once in a lifetime. Let history record that when we were shown the way we took the way and walked out to meet our destiny.' Mr Heath also mentioned 'China, the awakened giant, taking up its role in the world.' Leader's speech, Brighton, 10 October 1971: http://www.britishpoliticalspeech.org/speech-archive.htm.

was considered 'important' it needed a two-thirds majority to pass. This was largely a procedural device to prevent the seating of the PRC and Britain voted out of support for the US rather than any agreement with the principle involved. The British Government was clear that they would not support the Important Question resolution at the UN in September 1971 but wanted to square their change of stance with the US before informing the Chinese. Officials approached the Americans in January 1971 (No. 212) but they kept stalling, asking the British to hold off from taking any action until they had completed a review of their China policy. The PUS, Denis Greenhill, warned against being misled by the State Department on what would be an important political decision by the President: 'We must keep our ears constantly to the *White House* ground' (No. 195). Anxious to capitalise on the new climate, British officials wanted to inform the Chinese while they could still gain credit for changing their vote. As the months passed, officials became increasingly worried that their negotiating position would be undermined by a US initiative about which they would have little warning. 'It would be deplorable if after we have gone out of our way to assist the Americans, we should find the ground cut from under our feet by a Presidential announcement of this kind,' Mr Wilford warned ominously in May (No. 239). Although frustrated at seeing other countries like Canada and Australia opening embassies in Beijing before Britain, Ministers were cautious about taking unilateral action. The DOP Committee approved the change of stance and the approach to China, but were unwilling to proceed without a clear indication of US views (Nos. 242/246).

This decision to consult rather than merely inform meant that it was June 1971 before the Americans stated there was no need to delay any further (No. 248). This allowed Mr Royle to propose opening negotiations for an exchange of ambassadors on 22 June, nearly six months after his initial approach (No. 251). On 10 July, Mr Denson was informed by Vice Foreign Minister Qiao Guanhua that the exchange should be accompanied by a joint statement, the draft text of which included the phrase 'China's Taiwan Province' (No. 254). By introducing the status of Taiwan into negotiations, the PRC had raised its conditions. The reason for this became clear a few days later when on 15 July President Nixon gave a surprise television address in which he announced that the National Security Adviser, Dr Henry Kissinger, had recently visited China and that he himself was invited to go before May 1972 to discuss normalisation of relations.[22] The British Government had little warning of this announcement. John Graham, private secretary to Sir A. Douglas-Home, lamented to Peter Moon at Downing Street: 'it is legitimate to feel a little hurt that the Americans did not see fit to give us real advance notice of the President's decision particularly in view of the trouble we have taken to keep the Americans informed of the development in the thinking of our own China policy.' In Washington, the British Ambassador Lord Cromer thought a personal message from the Prime Minister to the President on his initiative would be well received, but Mr Heath declined to send one (No. 259).

The Nixon announcement left British officials rueing missed opportunities and believing that a positive response to Chinese overtures in the spring might have

22 Dr Kissinger had visited China for secret talks with Zhou Enlai from 9 to 11 July, the same time the Chinese introduced Taiwan into the negotiations. US documents on the Kissinger visit and the subsequent visit of Nixon to China can be found in *FRUS, 1969–1976*, Volume XVII.

seen an Ambassador in Beijing by now. With entry into the UN looking certain, the PRC now looked to secure its next diplomatic objective—the recognition of Taiwan as a part of China. Mr Morgan argued that if the Government wanted to exchange Ambassadors it would have to sooner or later accept the Chinese phrase 'China's Province Taiwan' (No. 260). The British now faced a dilemma: should they overturn a soundly based and frequently-repeated legal position that they regarded the sovereignty of Taiwan as 'undetermined' or risk the best chance in a generation of re-establishing full diplomatic relations with China and all the benefits it brought? (No. 271). As a signatory of the 1943 Cairo Declaration, Britain had agreed that Taiwan should be returned to China after the war. China had resumed the administration of Taiwan in 1945 and Japan had renounced its title in the Peace Treaty of 1951. However, the Treaty had not transferred sovereignty to China and nor had the PRC ever exercised effective control over the island, by means of which they could have acquired sovereignty. Hence the British contention, announced to Parliament, that the sovereignty of Taiwan remained undetermined.[23] The Foreign Secretary was unwilling to accept any formula which would depart from this long-held British view, so an alternative had to be found (No. 267).

Meanwhile matters came to a head in the UN over Chinese representation. The Americans decided to push for a solution designed to seat both Chinas, something that British officials had already indicated they would find unacceptable. Nevertheless the US looked to Britain to support the inscription of a 'two-Chinas' item, even if they later voted against it, to give an early impression of support for the US position. Mr Denson made it clear that the Chinese would interpret this as 'a breach of faith' (No. 265). The Office was split on tactics: the North American Department not wanting to annoy the Americans and the Far Eastern Department not wishing to annoy the Chinese. However the Foreign Secretary, endorsed by the Prime Minister, agreed to oppose any US 'Two-Chinas' resolution in the General Assembly and vote against inscription of the item in the General Committee (No. 273) much to the Americans' disappointment. In the run-up to the debate the Americans waged, in the words of British diplomats at the UN, 'a no-holds-barred campaign' to get the votes for their dual representation proposal, 'characterised by a surprising degree of emotional commitment and an almost reckless disregard for the longer term consequences' (No. 278). In what Sir Colin Crowe, the British Permanent Representative to the UN called 'a disorderly debate' in October the Americans were defeated, the PRC were admitted and Taiwan expelled. 'I think the main lesson of this debate has been to demonstrate beyond all doubt that no great Power by itself can any longer control events at the United Nations', he added (No. 279). American actions left a lingering bitterness: 'As seen from here the Americans get a good deal and give little in return,' commented Denson (No. 283). Whilst the Embassy in Washington was willing to 'rub in the difficulties caused for us by lack of frankness', they objected to Mr Denson's suggestion of limiting future exchanges of information (No. 293).

---

23 *Parl. Debs. 5th ser., H. of C.*, vol. 536, co. 159W, 4 February 1955.

In September 1971, in an attempt to break the negotiation stalemate, Qiao Guanhua had proposed alternative wording for the joint statement and asked that the Government give an 'oral assurance' that the UK would no longer promote or support the 'fallacy' that the status of Taiwan was 'undetermined'. To avoid further delay British ministers accepted the Chinese draft, which allowed Britain to acknowledge China's position on Taiwan without stating its own, and agreed to give a private assurance; but they refused to give up the freedom, if asked, to tell Parliament that their legal position on Taiwan remained unchanged. In a meeting with English journalist Neville Maxwell on 19 November, Zhou Enlai called the British position 'absurd'. How could the British Government maintain the position that 'Taiwan's status remains undetermined' whilst also acknowledging the PRC position that Taiwan province was an inalienable part of the territory of the PRC. He suspected Britain wanted to 'leave a tail behind' so that it could recognise Taiwan if ever it declared independence. 'Wherever Britain quits, it always leaves some trouble behind' he noted but declared there could be no further progress until the 'tail' was chopped (No. 290).

With negotiations having reached an impasse, Mr Denson left Beijing for medical reasons in November 1971 and was replaced by John Addis, a noted Sinophile who had served in Beijing in the 1950s. It was hoped that a fresh approach could be made once Mr Addis reached Beijing. In the meantime, on 31 December Sir A. Douglas-Home sought the agreement of the DOP committee for a new negotiating position. He recommended a further push based upon the already agreed compromise formula for the joint statement suggested by Qiao Guanhua in September which stated: 'The British Government, acknowledging the position of the Chinese Government that Taiwan is a province of the People's Republic of China, have decided to remove their official representation from Taiwan.' All that remained to settle was the wording for use if questions were raised in Parliament. The Foreign Secretary proposed: 'Both the Government of the People's Republic of China and the authorities in Taiwan maintain that Taiwan is a part of China. We held the view both at Cairo and at Potsdam that sovereignty over Taiwan should revert to China. That view has not changed but we think that it is for the Chinese people themselves to settle this matter.' The Foreign Secretary saw this as legally and diplomatically safe as it did not mention Taiwan as 'undetermined' and made no commitment to present status of Taiwan (No. 296).

On 4 February Mr Addis handed the text of the wording to Qiao Guanhua. The oral statement proved unacceptable to the Chinese who proposed an alternative: 'We think that the Taiwan question is China's internal affair and it is for the Chinese people themselves to settle it'. Qiao stated that if the British believed the question of Taiwan was for the Chinese people to decide, then 'it necessarily and logically followed that the question of Taiwan was China's internal affair'. Mr Addis thought they could now 'clinch the deal at once' by accepting that the Taiwan question is China's 'internal affair'. However Sir A. Douglas-Home insisted that the word 'internal' should be omitted, as it implied recognition of Chinese sovereignty over Taiwan, or the sentence should be rephrased to read: 'We think that the Taiwan question should be settled internally by the Chinese people' (No. 301).

This formulation, again, proved unacceptable to the Chinese, whose position—based on logic rather than legal reasoning—Mr Addis had some sympathy with. He advised London that the choice now was between agreeing to the Chinese wording or accepting an indefinite postponement of an exchange of Ambassadors (No. 303). Joseph Godber, the Minister of State, felt that the latest Chinese demand presented no political, as opposed to legal, problem and that 'having swallowed a fairly substantial political camel it would be a pity to strain at a relatively small legal gnat' (No. 306).

When all seemed lost, Mr Morgan noted that the Chinese wording could also be translated as: 'We think that the Taiwan question is China's internal affair to be settled by the Chinese themselves.' He thought this revised English version would make it easier to argue that the significance attached to 'China's internal affair' must be seen in the context of the sentence as a whole and as meaning 'no more that we regard the question as one to be settled by the Chinese people themselves' (No. 307). This English translation was acceptable to the Chinese and led swiftly to the signing of a joint statement on 13 March. Qiao Guanhua and Mr Addis both agreed that the real achievement of the negotiations was not so much an exchange of Ambassadors 'as an improvement in the state of relations between our two countries' (No. 312). From Hong Kong, the new Governor, Murray MacLehose telegrammed: 'Heartiest congratulations. It was a slow start but a fast finish' (No. 313).

The future of Hong Kong

Shortly after the outbreak of the disturbances in Hong Kong in May 1967, the Cabinet DOP Committee met to appraise the situation. The Commonwealth Secretary, Herbert Bowden, reported that the Cultural Revolution had resulted in a loosening of control by mainland China of the communists in Hong Kong. However, it was not certain whether the ultimate purpose was a propaganda victory, an attempt to achieve British subservience (on the lines the Portuguese had to accept in Macao), or an attempt to drive the British out of Hong Kong completely. 'We could not resist a determined attempt to force us out altogether', he concluded, 'nor could we tolerate a situation similar to that in Macao' (No. 14). In Beijing, Mr Hopson agreed the disturbances were not premeditated by the Chinese Government but a product of local extremists fired up by the Revolution. It seemed likely that the main aim was to make the Hong Kong authorities more responsive to future pressure from Beijing but with minimum damage to China's economic and other interests in Hong Kong. Nevertheless, it brought the future of Hong Kong to the surface 'with a bang' (No. 16). The FED thought that internal struggles amongst the Chinese leadership meant that moderates were under pressure to react more strongly than usual to external situations in which China's interests and prestige were engaged. However, there was no evidence that the Chinese intended to take over the colony and a firm but unprovocative policy remained the best means of helping Hong Kong to ride out the present storm (No. 17).

This view was called into question in early July when hundreds of Chinese demonstrators and militia attacked a police post in the border town of Shau Tau Kok, killing five policemen (No. 22). Other attacks followed and the Cabinet established a Ministerial Committee on Hong Kong to keep the situation under review. The Committee discussed contingency planning for a withdrawal from Hong Kong 'if it were suddenly to become necessary', but the Cabinet was concerned that public confidence would be undermined if it became known that such planning was taking place (Nos. 25/26).[24] In January 1968 the Joint Intelligence Committee examined external and internal threats to Hong Kong and concluded that China could seize Hong Kong militarily at any time but was more likely to use indirect methods—undermining confidence by disrupting government and the economy—if they wanted to make the British position untenable (No. 74).

By March 1969 officials had completed a study of the long-term future of Hong Kong. It provided a comprehensive account of British interests and responsibilities in Hong Kong, China's attitude and intentions, US interests and involvement and, above all, options for withdrawal. The study concluded that Hong Kong's future lay with China and that the main objective was to negotiate its return, at a favourable opportunity, on the best terms obtainable for its people and British interests. It was important to achieve this when not under Chinese pressure and before Hong Kong's economy started to suffer. In the meantime, the Government should demonstrate its firm intent to maintain Britain's position there (No. 166). Ministers did not consider the paper until February 1970. In commending it to the Hong Kong Committee, Mr Stewart reiterated that there was no prospect of reaching agreement about the future of Hong Kong with the present Chinese Government and that any unilateral attempt to work towards some new status for the territories would lead to an immediate loss of confidence. 'We must assume, and be seen to assume, that we shall be there at any rate until 1997' (No. 185). No meeting of the Hong Kong Committee took place before the change of government in June 1970. Meanwhile the FCO undertook to prepare a new paper on the future of Hong Kong which was sent to Mr Royle in June 1971 (No. 252). This then fed into a fresh paper submitted by Sir A. Douglas-Home in December 1971 to the DOP Committee. By this time the heat had gone out of the issue. In October 1971 Zhou Enlai told the former British Commissioner-General for Southeast Asia, Malcolm MacDonald, who was on a private trip to China, that the PRC had no intention of seeking to get Hong Kong back before the expiry of the lease in 1997 (No. 277). The Foreign Secretary recommended maintaining the status quo, and taking preliminary informal soundings with Beijing nearer to 1997 with a view to negotiating an orderly withdrawal (No. 295).

Trade

Although British commercial interests had been largely driven out of China during the 1950s there was great hope for future trade with the country. Whilst UK exports to China in 1966 totalled £31.9 million, only about 0.5 per cent of UK overseas trade, China was viewed as a potential market for British goods, such as the sale of aircraft (No. 13). In 1962 six Viscount aircraft had been sold to China, although there had been some strategic hurdles to overcome (No. 178). The sale of four VC-10s fell through in 1971 (No. 220) but Hawker Siddeley signed a contract

---

24 The need for absolute secrecy made detailed planning impossible, whilst the feasibility of a large-scale evacuation was considered doubtful, leading to the eventual suspension of any planning. *BDEE*, Series A, Volume 5: Part III, No. 337. 'Emergency evacuation of Hong Kong': Commonwealth Office note, 1 Feb 1968.

worth £20 million for the supply of Tridents in the same year (No. 237). Trade was affected by the downturn in relations caused by the detention of British subjects (No. 180) but once this was over, Denson was active in suggesting changes to improve efforts to increase exports to China. This included making the Sino-British Trading Council more representative of major British manufacturing industry rather than the middlemen from old China trading houses, 'the memory of whose privileged position and at times overbearing methods (in some cases at variance with the political aims of HMG) is repugnant to the Chinese' (No. 281). Trade featured in the negotiations for an exchange of Ambassadors: as a lever to put pressure on the British (No. 288) and as an incentive for the British to successfully conclude negotiations. The Chinese import market was expected to grow slowly but Mr Samuel, head of chancery, thought there were good reasons why Britain was in a position to eventually take advantage of it. These included Chinese familiarity with English as a technical language, the good reputation of leading British firms such as Hawker Siddeley, Rolls Royce and ICI, and long experience of the China trade (No. 294).

Acknowledgements

In accordance with the Parliamentary announcement cited in the Introduction to this Series, the editors have had the customary freedom in the selection and arrangement of documents, including full access to all classes of documentation. Where it has been necessary, on a few occasions, to excise words or passages from documents the relevant exemption has been cited.

Documents quoted or cited in footnotes have only been accorded a file reference where it differs from that of the printed document to which they refer. Telegrams have been given the date on which they were sent. Omitted from the headings and formulations at the end of documents are some classifications regarding administration and circulation but the main security classifications are included. The spelling and punctuation of most names in the documents remain as in the original but names in the Preface and footnotes have been modernised. Some minor typing errors have been corrected.

I would like to thank Sir Philip Barton, Permanent Under-Secretary of State, Adrian Blundell, Chief Information Officer, and Stewart MacLeod, head of Knowledge and Information Management Services, for their support. For assistance in providing documents I am grateful to colleagues in the Archives Management Team at Hanslope Park, headed by Martin Tucker, and staff at The National Archives, Kew. For providing general advice I would like to thank Tony Blishen, Hugh Davies and Gordon Barrass. My thanks also go to Linda Lundin for typesetting the volume and to Becky Warren for the cover design. I am grateful to all my colleagues who have helped with the volume, including Patrick Salmon, Gill Bennett, June Walker, Tara Finn and Sue Fleming, and particularly to Paul Bali for his editorial assistance. Above all, I am grateful to my co-editor, Luke Gibbon, who both conceived the volume and undertook the initial archival research before his transfer into the Diplomatic Service.

RICHARD SMITH
December 2022

ABBREVIATIONS FOR PRINTED SOURCES

BDEE, Series A, Volume 5, Part III — *British Documents on the End of Empire*, Series A, Volume 5: East of Suez and the Commonwealth 1964–1971, Part III (The Stationery Office, London: 2004)

FRUS, 1969–1976, Volume V — *Foreign Relations of the United States, 1969–1976*, Volume V, United Nations, 1969–1972 (United States Government Printing Office, Washington: 2004)

FRUS, 1969–1976, Volume XVII — *Foreign Relations of the United States, 1969–1976*, Volume XVII, China, 1969–1972 (United States Government Printing Office, Washington: 2006)

Parl. Debs., 5th ser., H. of C. — *Parliamentary Debates (Hansard), Fifth Series, House of Commons, Official Report* (London, 1909f.)

Parl. Debs., 5th ser., H. of L. — *Parliamentary Debates (Hansard), Fifth Series, House of Lords, Official Report* (London, 1909f.)

Public Papers: Nixon — *Public Papers of the Presidents of the United States: Richard Nixon, 1971* (United States Government Printing Office, Washington: 1972)

ABBREVIATED DESIGNATIONS

ACA	Office of Asian Communist Affairs, Bureau of East Asian and Pacific Affairs, US State Department
AFP	*Agence France-Presse*
APS	Assistant Private Secretary
AUS	Assistant Under-Secretary of State
BBC	British Broadcasting Corporation
BOAC	British Overseas Airways Corporation
BT	Board of Trade
BUA	British United Airways
CAB	Cabinet Office
CBI	Confederation of Business Industry
CC	Cabinet Conclusions
CCP	Chinese Communist Party
CIA	Central Intelligence Agency
CNAC	Chinese National Aviation Corporation
CND	Campaign for Nuclear Disarmament
CO	Commonwealth Office
COCOM	Coordinating Committee for Multilateral Export Controls
CP	Communist Party
CPG	Chinese Government
CPSU	Communist Party of the Soviet Union
CPR	China People's Republic
CRO	Commonwealth Relations Office
CTBT	Comprehensive Test Ban Treaty
DIS	Defence Intelligence Staff
DOP/DOPC	Defence and Oversea Policy Committee
DSAO	Diplomatic Service Administration Office
DTI	Department for Trade and Industry
DTMS	Diplomatic Technical Maintenance Service

DUS	Deputy Under-Secretary of State
DWS	Diplomatic Wireless Service
ECGD	(UK) Export Credits Guarantee Department
ECOSOC	United Nations Economic and Social Council
EEC	European Economic Community
FAD	Foreign Affairs Department
FCO	Foreign and Commonwealth Office
FED	Far Eastern Department, FCO
FO	Foreign Office
GCHQ	Government Communications Headquarters
HE	His Excellency
HM	Her Majesty
HMA	Her Majesty's Ambassador
HMG	Her Majesty's Government
HMS	Her Majesty's Ship
IFT	Immediate Following Telegram
IRD	Information Research Department
JIC	Joint Intelligence Committee
JRD	Joint Research Department
KMT	*Kuomintang* (Chinese Nationalist Party)
LE	Locally engaged staff
LMG	Light Machine Gun
MFA	Ministry of Foreign Affairs
MIFGT	My Immediately Following Guidance Telegram
MIFT	My Immediately Following Telegram
MIPT	My Immediately Preceding Telegram
MOD	Ministry of Defence
MOPBW	Ministry of Public Building and Works
NAD	North American Department, FCO
NATO	North Atlantic Treaty Organisation
NCNA	New China News Agency
OPD	Defence and Oversea Policy Committee

PA	Personal Assistant
PIA	Pakistan International Airlines
PLA	People's Liberation Army
POLAD	Political Advisor
PPS	Principal Private Secretary
PQ	Parliamentary Question
PRC	People's Republic of China
PS	Private Secretary
PUS	Permanent Under-Secretary of State
PUSD	Permanent Under-Secretary's Department
RD	Research Department
ROC	Republic of China
SALT	Strategic Arms Limitation Talks
SEATO	Southeast Asia Treaty Organization
SIS	Secret Intelligence Service (MI6)
Telno	Telegram number
TUR	Telegram under reference
UKDEL	United Kingdom Delegation
UKMIS	United Kingdom Mission
UKREP	United Kingdom Permanent Representative
UN	United Nations
UND	United Nations Department, FCO
UNDC	United Nations Disarmament Commission
USA	United States of America
USSR	Union of Soviet Socialist Republics
WEOG	Western European and Others Group (UN)
WEU	Western European Union

LIST OF PERSONS

Acheson, Dean, US Secretary of State, 1949–53
Addis, John, Chargé d'Affaires, Peking, Jan–March 1972; HM Ambassador, Peking, March 1972–74
Allan, James Nicholas, First Secretary and Head of Chancery, Peking, 1969–71
Allen, Sir Denis, Deputy Under-Secretary of State, Foreign Office (later FCO), 1967–69
Annenberg, Walter Hubert, US Ambassador, London, 1969–74
Appleyard, Leonard, Third Secretary, Hong Kong, 1964–65; Third, later Second, Secretary, Peking, 1966–68; Far Eastern Department, FCO, 1969–71

Barnett, A. Doak, US journalist and academic
Baroody, Jamil, Saudi Arabia's representative to the UN, 1946–79
Barrass, Gordon, Second, later First, Secretary, Peking, 1970–72
Barrington, Nicholas, Assistant Private Secretary to the Foreign and Commonwealth Secretary, 1968–72
Barrymaine, Norman, freelance journalist, detained at Shanghai in February 1968 on charges of espionage
Beamish, Sir Tufton, Conservative MP for Lewes, 1945–74
Benn, Anthony 'Tony' Wedgwood, Labour MP for Bristol South East, 1963–1983; Minister of Technology, 1966–70
Bettencourt, André, French Minister for Planning and Territorial Development
Biggs-Davison, John, Conservative MP for Chigwell, 1955–74
Blishen, Anthony, First Secretary and Consul, Peking, 1965–67
Bolland, Edwin, Head, Far Eastern Department, Foreign Office, 1965–67; Counsellor, Washington, 1967–71
Bottomley, Baron Arthur George, Secretary of State for Commonwealth Relations, 1964–66; Minister of Overseas Development, 1966–1967
Bottomley, Sir James, Assistant Under-Secretary of State, Commonwealth Office (later FCO), 1967–70
Bowden, Herbert William, Secretary of State for Commonwealth Affairs, 1966–29 August 1967
Boyd, John, Third, later Second, Secretary, Peking, 1965–67; First Secretary, Foreign Office (later FCO), 1967–69; First Secretary, Washington, 1969–73
Bray, Raymond John, HM Consul, Tamsui, 1967–70
Brewer, Frank, Research Department, FCO, 1960–76
Brimelow, Sir Thomas, Deputy Under-Secretary of State, FCO, 1969–73
Brown, George, Secretary of State for Foreign Affairs, 1966–16 March 1968
Brown, William, Deputy Director, Office of Asian Communist Affairs, US Department of State, 1970–72
Brown, Winthrop, Deputy Assistant Secretary of State for East Asian and Pacific Affairs, US Department of State, 1968–1972
Bury, Leslie, Australian Minister for Foreign Affairs, March–August 1971

Abbreviated designations

Bush, George Herbert Walker, US Ambassador to the UN, 1971–73
Bush, Ronald Leslie, guard at the British Mission, Peking
Butler, (Frederick Edward) Robin, Private Secretary to the Prime Minister, 1972–74

Cable, James, Head, Planning Staff, FCO, 1971–75
Callaghan, James, Chancellor of the Exchequer, 1964–67; Home Secretary, 1967–70
Carter, William Stovold, Head, Hong Kong Department, Commonwealth Office (later FCO), 1965–70
Cater, Jack, Defence Secretary and Special Assistant to the Governor of Hong Kong, 1967; Deputy Colonial Secretary, 1967–68; Executive Director, Trade Development Council, 1968–70
Chalfont, Lord, Minister of State, Foreign Office (later FCO), 1964–1970
Chang Wen-chin, Head, West European, America and Australasia Department, Ministry of Foreign Affairs, PRC, 1971–72
Channon, Paul, Conservative MP for Southend West, 1959–97
Chen Po-ta (Po'ta) (Chen Boda), Chairman of the Cultural Revolution Group and Member of Politburo Standing Committee, 1966–70
Ch'en Yi (Chen Yi), Foreign Minister, PRC, 1958–72
Chiang Ching (Jiang Qing), Wife of Mao Tse-tung, 1949–76; member of the Chinese Communist Politburo, member of the Cultural Revolution Group, 1966–68
Chiang Kai-shek, President of Taiwan, 1950–75
Chiao Kuan-hua (Qiao Guanhua), Vice Minister, Ministry of Foreign Affairs, PRC; head of the Chinese delegation to the UN, 1971–76
Chi Peng-Fei, (Chi P'eng-fei), Vice Minister, Ministry of Foreign Affairs, PRC until April 1971; Acting Foreign Minister until February 1972; Foreign Minister from February 1972
Chipp, David Allen, correspondent for Reuters in South East Asia, 1953–55; in Peking, 1956–58; correspondent for Reuters in Peking, 1956–58; Reuters management, 1960–68
Chou En-lai (Zhou Enlai), Premier of the People's Republic of China, 1954–76
Cockburn, David, managing director of Vickers-Zimmer, a British company engaged since 1966 in building a polypropylene plant in Lanchow, China
Cradock, Percy, Counsellor and Head of Chancery, Peking, 1966–68; Chargé d'Affaires, Peking, 1968–69; Head of Planning Staff, FCO, 1969–71
Cromer, 3rd Earl of (George Rowland Stanley Baring), HM Ambassador, Washington, 1971–74
Crouch, P. D., second officer of the SS Demodocus, detained at Shanghai on 3 April 1968
Crowe, Sir Colin Tradescant, Chief of Administration, HM Diplomatic Service, 1965–68; High Commissioner, Canada, Sept. 1968–70; UK Permanent Representative to the UN, 1970–73
Crowson, Richard Borman, Assistant Head, Far Eastern Department, FCO, 1971–72

Crozier, T. R. K., employee of the Hong Kong and Shanghai Bank
Darwin, Henry Galton, Legal Counsellor, FCO, 1970–73
Davies, Emrys Thomas, Assistant Political Adviser, Hong Kong Government, 1963–68
Davies, Hugh Llewelyn, Second Secretary, later Consul, Peking, 1969–70
Day, Derek Malcom, Assistant Private Secretary to the Secretary of State for Foreign and Commonwealth Affairs, 1967–68
Dayan, General Moshe, Minister of Defence, Israel, 1967–74
de la Mare, Arthur James, Assistant Under-Secretary of State, Foreign Office, 1965–67
De Palma, Samuel, Assistant Secretary of State for International Organization Affairs, US Department of State, 1969–73
Denson, John, Assistant Head, Far Eastern Department, Foreign Office, 1965–68; Chargé d'Affaires, Peking, 1969–71
Denza, Eileen Margaret, Assistant Legal Adviser, Foreign Office (later FCO), 1963–74
Douglas-Home, Sir Alexander 'Alec', Secretary of State for Foreign and Commonwealth Affairs, 1970–74
Dubcek, Alexander, First Secretary of the Communist Party of Czechoslovakia, 5 January 1968–17 April 1969
Duffy, Thomas, HM Consul, Tamsui, 1970–72
Dulles, John Foster, US Secretary of State, 1953–59
Duncan, John, Head, Personnel (Operations) Department, Foreign Office (later FCO), 1966–69

Elliott, (Thomas) Anthony, Political Adviser, Government of Hong Kong, 1965–68; Counsellor, Washington, 1968, Minister and Head of Chancery, Washington, 1970–72
Evans, Sir (William) Vincent, Legal Adviser, FCO, 1971–73
Ewart-Biggs, Christopher, Head, Permanent Under-Secretary's Department, Foreign Office (later FCO), 1966–69

Finch, John, operator, Diplomatic Wireless Service, Peking, 1967–68
Fuller, Derek Walker, operator, Diplomatic Wireless Service, Peking, 1967–68

Gallagher, M., DTMS, Peking
Galloway, William J., Counsellor, US Embassy, London
Galsworthy, Anthony, Third, later Second, Secretary and Consul, Peking, 1970–72
Galsworthy, Sir Arthur, Assistant Under-Secretary of State, Colonial Office, 1956–66; Deputy Under-Secretary of State, Commonwealth Office (later FCO), 1968–69
Garside, Roger Ramsay, Second, later First, Secretary and Consul, Peking, 1968–1970
Gass, Sir Michael, Colonial Secretary of Hong Kong, 1965–69; Acting Governor of Hong Kong, 1967
Gilmore, Brian, First Secretary, Washington, 1965–68

Gladstone, William, former 19th Century British Prime Minister
Gleysteen, William Henry, Director, Office of Intelligence and Research for East Asian and Pacific Affairs, US Department of State, 1969–71
Godber, Joseph, Minister of State, FCO, 1970–72
Godden, Charles, Private Secretary to the Minister of State (Lord Shepherd), FCO, 1967–70
Gore-Booth, Sir Paul, Permanent Under-Secretary of State, Foreign Office (later FCO), 1965–69; Head of HM Diplomatic Service, 1968–69
Graham, John, Principal Private Secretary to the Secretary of State for Foreign and Commonwealth Affairs, 1969–1972
Grattan, Patrick Henry, Assistant Private Secretary to the Secretary of State for Foreign and Commonwealth Affairs, 1971–73
Green, Marshall, US Assistant Secretary of State for East Asian and Pacific Affairs, 1969–1973
Greenhill, Sir Denis, Deputy Under-Secretary of State, Foreign Office (later FCO), 1966–69; Permanent Under-Secretary of State, FCO, and Head of HM Diplomatic Service, February 1969–73
Grey, Anthony, Reuters correspondent in Peking; placed under house arrest, 1967–69
Griffiths, Eldon, Conservative MP for Bury St Edmunds, 1964–92

Han Nien-Lung, Vice Minister, Ministry of Foreign Affairs, PRC
Han Hsu (Han Xu), Protocol Department, Ministry of Foreign Affairs, PRC
Hart, Judith, Minister of State for Commonwealth Affairs, 1966–1967
Heath, Edward, British Prime Minister, 1970–74
Heath, John, Counsellor and Head of Establishment and Organisation Department, FCO (formerly DSAO), 1966–6
Herries, Michael, Member of Executive Legislative Council, Hong Kong; Chairman and Managing Director, Jardine Matheson & Co. Ltd, 1963–70
Hervey, Roger Blaise Ramsay, Far Eastern Department, FCO, 1970-74
Hewitt, Peter, HM Consul, Shanghai, 1966–67
Hibbert, Reginald, Counsellor, Political Adviser's Office, Singapore, 1967–69
Ho Chi-Minh, Chairman of the Central Committee of the Workers' Party of Vietnam, 1951–69; President of the Democratic Republic of Vietnam, 1945–69
Holroyd, Frank, Vice-Consul, Peking, 1967–68
Holyoake, Sir Keith, Prime Minister of New Zealand, 1960–72
Hopson, Donald (later Sir), Chargé d'Affaires, Peking, 1965–68
Humphrey, Hubert, US Vice-President, 1965–69
Hsieh Fu-chih (Xie Fuzhi), Minister of Public Security, PRC, 1959–72; member of the Cultural Revolution Group
Hsueh, [?], Deputy Head, West European Department, Ministry of Foreign Affairs, PRC
Hsueh Ping, NCNA journalist imprisoned in Hong Kong
Huang Hua, PRC Ambassador to the UN, November 1971–76
Hunter, Alistair, First Secretary (Commercial), Peking, 1965–68

Iliffe, Miss Pat, shorthand typist, British Mission, Peking
Ions, Norman, HM Consul, Macao, 1965–67
Irwin, John Nichol, US Under-Secretary of State, 1970–72

Jamieson, Kenneth, Minister and UK Deputy Permanent Representative to the UN, 1970–74
Jenkins, Alfred, Director, Office of Asian Communist Affairs, Bureau of East Asian and Pacific Affairs, US Department of State, 1971–73
Jenkins, Roy, Home Secretary, 1964–67; Chancellor of the Exchequer 1967–70
Johnson, Lyndon B., President of the United States, 1963–69
Johnston, David, manager of the Shanghai branch of Chartered Bank, arrested on a spying charge on 25 August 1968.
Jones, D. V. Chief Officer of the 'Nancy Dee'; detained in Hsinking on 31 March 1968
Jones, Creech, Secretary of State for the Colonies, 1946–50

Kang Sheng, senior member of the CCP, responsible for internal security and intelligence during the Cultural Revolution
Katzenbach, Nicholas de Belleville, US Under Secretary of State, 1966–69
Kaufman, Gerald, Parliamentary Press Liaison Officer, Labour Party, 1965–70
Kao Shih-k'un, Deputy Director, Consular Department, Ministry of Foreign Affairs, PRC
Kemble, John, Vice-Consul, Macao, 1965–67
Keswick, Sir John, President of the Sino-British Trade Council, 1961–72; chairman of Jardine Mathieson and Company of Hong Kong
Khan, Field-Marshal Ayub, President of Pakistan, 1958–69
Kissinger, Dr Henry, US National Security Adviser, 1969–75
Kosygin, Alexei Nikolayevich, Chairman of the Council of Ministers of the Soviet Union, 1964–80

Laird, Edgar, Head, Hong Kong and Indian Ocean Department, FCO, 1970–72
Laughton, John, Second, later First, Secretary (Commercial), Peking, 1968–70
Levin, Herb, US National Security Council staff member for East Asian affairs, 1970–71
Li Choh-Chih, manager of the Bank of China, Hong Kong
Lin Piao (Lin Biao), military commander and leading CCP member; designated successor to Mao from 1966; died in a plane crash in Sept 1971
Littlejohn Cook, George, Counsellor and Consul-General, Bangkok, 1969–71
Liu Shaoqi (Liu Shao-chi), chairman of the PRC, 1959–68; purged during the Cultural Revolution
Lo Kuei-Po (Luo Guibo), Vice Minister, Ministry of Foreign Affairs, PRC
Logan, David, Private Secretary to the Parliamentary Under Secretary of State for Foreign and Commonwealth Affairs (Mr Royle), FCO, 1970–73
Long, Gerald, general manager of Reuters, 1963–73

Ma Chia-chun, Counsellor and acting Chargé d'Affaires, Chinese Mission, London

MacDonald, Malcolm, retired Labour politician and diplomat. Former Secretary of State for Dominion Affairs, 1935–38 and 1938–39; Secretary of State for the Colonies, 1935 and 1938–40; High Commissioner, Canada, 1941–46; Governor-General of Malaya, Singapore and British Borneo, 1946–48; Commissioner-General for South-East Asia, 1948–55; High Commissioner, India, 1955–60; Leader of British Delegation and Co-Chairman, International Conference on Laos, 1961–62

MacInnes, Keith, Private Secretary to the Permanent Under-Secretary of State, Commonwealth Office, 1965–1968; First Secretary, FCO, 1970–74

MacLehose, Sir (Crawford) Murray, Governor and Commander-in-Chief, Hong Kong, 1971–82

McBain, William, British retiree, arrested in Shanghai in October 1969

McCluney, Ian, Assistant Private Secretary to the Secretary of State for Foreign and Commonwealth Affairs, 1969–71

McKearney, Philip, Permanent Under-Secretary's Department, 1965–68

McKeever, Ronald, HM Consul, Tamsui, 1962–66

McLaren, Robin, Assistant Political Adviser, Hong Kong, 1968–69

McMaster, Stanley, Ulster Unionist MP for Belfast East, 1959–74

Maddocks, Arthur, Political Adviser, Hong Kong, 1968–72

Maitland, Donald, Principal Private Secretary to the Secretary of State for Foreign and Commonwealth Affairs, 1967–69

Makarios, Archbishop, President of Cyprus, 1960–74

Malik, Adam, President of the UN General Assembly, 1971–72

Manac'h, Étienne, French Ambassador, Peking, 1969–75

Mao Tse-tung (Mao Zedong), leader of the Chinese Communist Party, 1935–76; chairman of the People's Republic of China, 1949–59

Martin, Constance, employee of the Hong Kong and Shanghai Bank in Shanghai, arrested in October 1969

March, Derek, First Secretary (Commercial), Peking, 1971–74

Mason, Robert, Assistant Under Secretary of State, FCO, 1968–69

Maurer, Ion Gheorghe, Prime Minister of Romania, 1961–74

Maxwell, Neville, journalist

Melhuish, (Michael) Ramsey, First Secretary, DSAO, FCO, 1968–70

Millard, Guy, Minister, Washington, 1970–71

Monson, Sir (William Bonar) Leslie, Deputy-Under Secretary of State, FCO, 1967–72

Moon, Peter, Private Secretary (Foreign Affairs) to the Prime Minister, 1970–72

Moreton, John, Assistant Under-Secretary of State, Commonwealth Office (later FCO), 1965–69

Morgan, Hugh Travers, HM Ambassador, Peru, 1970–74

Morgan, John Albert Leigh, Head, Far Eastern Department, FCO, April 1970–72

Morphet, David Ian, Assistant Private Secretary to the Secretary of State for Foreign and Commonwealth Affairs, 1966–68

Muirhead, David Francis, HM Ambassador, Lisbon, 1970–74

Mulley, Frederick, Minister of State, Foreign Office (later FCO), 1967–69
Murray, James, Head, Far Eastern Department, FCO, 1967–70

Nixon, Richard, President of the United States, 1969–74
Norman-Walker, Sir Hugh, Colonial Secretary, Hong Kong, 1969–74

Oplinger Gerald G., Second Secretary, US Embassy, London.
Overton, Hugh Thomas Arnold, Head, North American Department, FCO, 1971–74

Palliser, (Arthur) Michael, Private Secretary to the Prime Minister, 1966–69
Parsons, Anthony, Assistant Under-Secretary of State, FCO, 1971–73
Paye, Lucien, French Ambassador, Peking, 1964–69
Peck, Sir Edward, Deputy Under-Secretary of State, Foreign Office (later FCO), 1968–70
Pedersen, Richard Foote, Counsellor, US Department of State, 1969–73
Pei Tsien-chang (Pei Jianzhang), Counsellor and Chargé d'Affaires ad interim, London, 1971–72
Peng Chen (Peng Zhen), leading member of the CCP; major of Peking, 1951–66; purged during the Cultural Revolution
Peters, Theophilus, Counsellor (Commercial), Peking, 1965–68
Pickard, Sir Cyril, High Commissioner, Pakistan, 1966–71
Pope, Captain R.V., Master of the 'Fortune Wind', detained at Tangku on 17 May 1968

Quirie, Miss Mabel Ellis, secretary at the British Mission, Peking

Ray, James, captain of the SS Anchises, arrested in Shanghai on 1 March 1970
Reilly, Sir Patrick, HM Ambassador, Paris, 1965–68
Renwick, Robin, Private Secretary to the Minister of State (Mr Godber), FCO, 1970–72.
Roberts, Christopher, Private Secretary to the Prime Minister, 1970–73
Rodgers, William, Parliamentary Under-Secretary of State, Foreign Office, 1967–68
Rogers, William Pierce, US Secretary of State, 1969–73
Royle, Anthony, Parliamentary Under-Secretary of State for Foreign and Commonwealth Affairs, 1970–74
Rusk, Dean, US Secretary of State, 1961–69

Samejima, Keiji, Japanese Nikkei journalist working in Peking
Samuel, Richard Christopher, Private Secretary to the Parliamentary Under-Secretary of State, 1965–68; Hong Kong, 1968–69; First Secretary and Head of Chancery, Singapore, 1969–71; First Secretary and Head of Chancery, Peking, 1971–73
Satō Eisaku, Prime Minister of Japan, 1964–72

Seaby, John, Head of Security at the British Mission, Peking, 1966–67
Shann, Keith 'Mick', Deputy Director, Australian Department of External Affairs (later Foreign Affairs), 1970–73
Sharland, (Edward) John, Far Eastern Department, FCO, 1967–69
Shen Ping (Shen P'ing), Counsellor and acting Chargé d'Affaires, Chinese Mission, London
Shepherd, Lord, Minister of State, FCO, 1968–70
Sihanouk, Norodom, King of Cambodia, 1941–55; President of Cambodia, 1955–70
Soames, Christopher, HM Ambassador, Paris, 1968–72
Soekarno (Sukarno), leader of the Indonesian independence movement and Indonesia's first president, 1949–66
Spendlove, Peter, First Secretary, Washington, 1967–69
Sterner, Michael, Country Director, Bureau of Near Eastern Affairs, Department of State, 1970–74
Stewart, (Robert) Michael, Secretary of State for Foreign Affairs, 16 March–17 October 1968; Secretary of State for Foreign and Commonwealth Affairs, 18 October 1968–19 June 1970
Stratton, Richard James, Head, UN (Political) Department, FCO, 1971–72
Sykes, Bonor Hugh Charles, Head, Planning Staff, FCO, 1968–70

T'ang Hai-kuang, Deputy Director, West European Department, Chinese MFA
Thomas, George, Minister of State, Commonwealth Office, 1967–68
Thomson, George, Joint Minister of State, Foreign Office, 1967; Secretary of State for Commonwealth Affairs, 29 August 1967–17 October 1968
Tomlinson, Sir (Frank) Stanley, Deputy Under-Secretary of State, FCO, 1969–72
Tregilgas, Mrs J., wife of William Tregilgas
Tregilgas, William, guard at the British Mission, Peking, 1966–68
Trench, Sir David, Governor and Commander-in-Chief, Hong Kong, 1964–71
Trend, Sir Burke, Cabinet Secretary, 1963–73
Truman, Harry S., US President, 1945–53

Walden, George, Second Secretary, Peking, 1967–70
Warner, Frederick, UK Deputy Permanent Representative to the UN, New York, 1969–70
Watt, George, engineer employed by Vickers-Zimmer, detained in Lanchow on 26 September 1967 and sentenced on 15 March 1968 to 3 years' imprisonment for alleged spying
Webb, Norman, Secretary General, Sino-British Trade Council
Webb, Richard, clerk at the British Mission, Peking, 1967–68
Weston, (Philip) John, Second Secretary, Peking, 1967–68; FO, 1969–71
Whitney, Raymond 'Ray', First Secretary, Peking, 1966–68
Wilford, (Kenneth) Michael, Counsellor, also Consul-General, Peking, 1964–66; Acting Political Adviser to Governor of Hong Kong, 1967; Counsellor, Washington, 1967–69; Assistant Under Secretary of State, FCO, 1969–73
Wilkinson, Peter, Deputy Under-Secretary, Foreign Office, 1967–68

Wilson, A. N. third officer on the SS Demodocus, deported from China in 1968
Wilson, Colin, Far Eastern Department, 1969–70
Wilson, David Clive, Far Eastern Department, 1965–68
Wilson, Sir Duncan, HM Ambassador, Moscow, 1968–71
Wilson, Harold, British Prime Minister, 1964–70
Wright, (John) Oliver, HM Ambassador, Copenhagen, 1966–69
Yen Chia-kan (C.K. Yen), Vice-President of Taiwan, 1966–75

DOCUMENT SUMMARIES

CHAPTER I

The Cultural Revolution and the sacking of the Mission
15 May 1967 — 18 March 1968

	NAME	DATE	MAIN SUBJECT	PAGE
		1967		
1	Mr Hopson Peking Tel. No. 480	15 May	The Chinese have decided to risk a direct confrontation with Britain over recent disturbances in Hong Kong.	1
2	Mr Hopson Peking Tel. No. 487	16 May	British diplomats face ongoing difficulties in Peking, Shanghai and Canton over events in Hong Kong.	2
3	Mr. Hopson Peking Tel. No. 490	16 May	Demonstrators have burst into the British compound in Shanghai and made 'humiliating demands'.	2
4	Mr Hopson Peking Tel. No. 492	16 May	A mob has sacked the British compound in Shanghai.	3
5	To Mr Hopson Peking Tel. No. 322	16 May	The Foreign Office protest about 'mob action' in Shanghai and seek guarantees of safety for British subjects in China.	3
6	Mr Hopson Peking Tel. No. 496	17 May	Concerns for the security of Mr Hewitt and his family in Shanghai.	4
7	To HM Representatives Overseas Guidance Tel. No. 106	18 May	Summary and analysis of recent disturbances in Hong Kong, Shanghai, and Peking.	5
8	To Mr Hopson Peking Tel. No. 351	19 May	Mr Brown protests about the treatment received by the British diplomats in Peking and Shanghai.	7

	NAME	DATE	MAIN SUBJECT	PAGE
9	To Mr Hopson Peking Tel. No. 372	22 May	Conveys a message from Mr Brown to Chen Yi protesting at the unilateral closure of the British Office in Shanghai.	8
10	Mr Rodgers Foreign Office	23 May	Minute to Mr Brown suggesting options for retaliatory action.	9
11	To Mr Hopson Peking Tel. No. 385	23 May	Shen Ping delivers an oral démarche on Hong Kong to Mr Rodgers.	10
12	To Mr Hopson Peking Tel. No. 387	23 May	Shen Ping refuses to accept a message from Mr Brown for Chen Yi.	10
13	Board of Trade	25 May	Memorandum on the effect of a rupture of diplomatic relations on UK trade with China.	11
14	Cabinet DOP Committee OPD(67)20th meeting	25 May	Consideration of the situation in China and Hong Kong.	12
15	Mr Hopson Peking	6 June	Despatch: 'Reactions in Peking and Shanghai to the recent Hong Kong disturbances, Part II.'	14
16	Mr Hopson Peking	6 June	Despatch: 'Chinese policy towards Hong Kong.'	17
17	Far Eastern Department	8 June	Summary of a Note on the present situation in China.	21
18	To HM Representatives Overseas Guidance Tel. No. 153	21 June	The Chinese announce the explosion of a thermonuclear device.	24
19	Mr Hopson Peking	21 June	Despatch: 'China: Anti-British demonstrations in Peking, Part III.'	25
20	Mr Hewitt Foreign Office	29 June	Despatch: 'Shanghai: Mob attacks and closure of the Office.'	28
21	Mr Morphet Foreign Office	5 July	Minute to Mr Bolland about an incident outside the office of the Chinese Chargé.	34
22	Sir D. Trench Hong Kong Tel. No. 988	9 July	Account of an armed confrontation at Sha Tau Kok, Hong Kong, on 8 July.	35

Document summaries

	NAME	DATE	MAIN SUBJECT	PAGE
23	To Mr Jenkins Home Office FS/67/59	19 July	Mr Brown proposes retaliatory action against the NCNA in London.	37
24	To Mr Hopson Peking Tel. No. 649	21 July	Mr Rodgers protests about the detention of Mr Grey, the Reuters journalist, in China.	39
25	Ministerial Committee on Hong Kong K(67)1st meeting	24 July	Discussion of an interim interdepartmental report on the prospects of withdrawing from Hong Kong.	39
26	Cabinet DOP Committee OPD(67) 28th meeting	28 July	Discussion of a memorandum by the Commonwealth Secretary on the prospects of withdrawing from Hong Kong.	42
27	Mr Hopson Peking	1 Aug	Despatch on the impact of the Cultural Revolution on China's foreign policy.	44
28	Mr Hopson Peking	8 Aug	Mission staff attempt to remove an effigy of the Prime Minister.	48
29	Mr Rodgers Foreign Office	11 Aug	Minute to Mr Brown proposing retaliatory action against the NCNA in London.	49
30	Mr Hopson Peking Tel. No. 1116	20 Aug	The Chinese MFA issue a 48-hour ultimatum over Hong Kong.	50
31	Mr Hopson Peking Tel. No. 1117	20 Aug	Reports attempts to find out about the current wellbeing of Mr Grey.	51
32	Mr Hopson Peking Tel. No. 1118	20 Aug	Proposes greater pressure on the NCNA in London in light of 48-hour ultimatum.	52
33	To Mr Hopson Peking Tel. No. 774	21 Aug	Shen Ping repeatedly refuses to come to the Foreign Office.	52
34	To Parliamentary Under-Secretary of State Home Office	21 Aug	Minute from Mr Thomson seeking action against the NCNA in light of China's 48-hour ultimatum over Hong Kong.	53
35	To Mr Hopson Peking Tel. No. 1135	22 Aug	Chinese staff at the Mission in Peking protest over Hong Kong.	55

	NAME	DATE	MAIN SUBJECT	PAGE
36	Mr Hopson Peking Tel. No. 1138	22 Aug	Reports large-scale demonstrations outside the Mission in Peking.	55
37	To Sir P. Reilly Paris Tel. No. 2280	22 Aug	Requests the French Ambassador in Peking pass on a report of Mr Thomson's interview with Shen Ping in London.	56
38	Mr Hopson Peking	23 Aug	Three telegrams, transmitted by the French MFA, reporting an attack on the British Mission.	57
39	Mr Denson FED Foreign Office	23 Aug	Minute to Mr de la Mare, received through the Norwegian MFA, on the condition of British staff in Peking.	59
40	Mr Thomas Commonwealth Office	23 Aug	Minute to Mr Wilson reporting the situation in Hong Kong following the attack on the British Mission in Peking.	59
41	Mr de la Mare FED Foreign Office	23 Aug	Minute on possible retaliatory action against the Chinese Mission in London.	61
42	Mr Hopson Peking Tel. No. 1069	23 Aug	Requests assistance from the President of Pakistan for the evacuation of women and children from Peking.	63
43	Mr Hopson Peking Unnumbered telegram	24 Aug	Update on the condition of staff and facilities at the British Mission.	64
44	Mr Hopson Peking Unnumbered telegram	24 Aug	Reports the establishment of temporary accommodation and offices, and attempts to evacuate staff and their families.	64
45	Far Eastern Department Foreign Office	25 Aug	Minute reporting the condition of staff, buildings and communications of British Mission in Peking.	65
46	Mr Cradock Peking	29 Aug	Letter to Mr Denson about the attack: 'not an irrational outburst . . . but a carefully planned and controlled operation.'	67
47	Note of Conversation 10 Downing Street	30 Aug	Mr Wilson and Mr Jenkins discuss a violent incident outside the Chinese Mission in London.	72

Document summaries

	NAME	DATE	MAIN SUBJECT	PAGE
48	Mr Hopson Peking Tel. No. 26	30 Aug	Luo Guibo protests about the treatment of staff in London and places new restrictions on British diplomats in Peking.	73
49	Mr Hopson Peking Unnumbered telegram	30 Aug	Analysis of the meeting in No. 48.	74
50	Mr Hopson Peking Tel. No. 27	30 Aug	Reports demonstrations and protests outside the residential compound in Peking.	75
51	Mr Hopson Peking Tel. No. 28	30 Aug	Discusses the significance of the demonstrations: 'the safety of this Mission is now very precarious'.	75
52	To Mr Chen Yi Peking	30 Aug	Letter from Mr Brown seeking an improvement in relations with China.	76
53	Mr Hopson Peking	31 Aug	Despatch: 'The burning of the British Office in Peking'.	77
54	Mr Hopson Peking Tel. No. 32	2 Sept	Delivers Mr Brown's message (No. 52) to the Chinese MFA.	83
55	Cabinet DOP Committee OPD(67)67	4 Sept	Memorandum by Mr Brown on relations following anti-British activities in China and Hong Kong	84
56	Cabinet DOP Committee OPD(67)29th meeting	5 Sept	Committee's discussion of No. 55.	90
57	To Mr Hopson Peking Tel. No. 18	6 Sept	Reports steps taken to guarantee security of two Chinese diplomatic couriers in hope of reciprocation for Queen's Messengers.	92
58	Sir P. Reilly Paris Tel. No. 903	8 Sept.	In conversation with M. Paye about recent events and UK-China relations.	92
59	Mr Rodgers Foreign Office	11 Sept	Minute to Mr Brown on measures being taken with regard to ship visits and baggage to ensure reciprocity.	94

	NAME	DATE	MAIN SUBJECT	PAGE
60	Mr Hopson Peking Tel. No. 58	16 Sept	Reports lifestyle restrictions on staff at the British Mission in Peking.	95
61	Mr Whitney Peking	15 Sept	Letter to Mr Wilson (FED) exploring whether the attack was deliberate and who in the Chinese leadership was responsible.	95
62	To Mr Hopson Peking	18 Sept	Personal letter from Mr Brown expressing admiration for the courage showed by staff and their families.	98
63	Mr Hopson Peking	19 Sept	Letter to Mr de la Mare discussing the lack of any response to the Mr Brown's letter to Chen Yi.	98
64	To Certain Missions Guidance Tel. No. 238	19 Sept	Reports on the Chinese internal situation and relations with the UK and other countries.	100
65	Hong Kong Department Commonwealth Office	21 Sept	Summary of a meeting with Sir D. Trench.	103
66	Mr Denson FED Foreign Office	21 Sept	Minute on approaching Ho Chi-Minh to intervene with the Chinese on behalf of the British Mission in Peking.	104
67	Mr Hopson Peking Tel. No. 72	22 Sept	Requests that Mr Brown say as little as possible about Chinese actions in his upcoming speech to the UNGA.	105
68	To Mr Hopson Peking	25 Sept	Letter from Mr Bolland proposing certain Chinese diplomats in London be declared persona non grata.	105
69	To Mr Wilson 10 Downing Street PM/67/100	7 Nov	Minute from Mr Brown proposing a unilateral relaxation of restrictions on members of the Chinese Mission, London.	106
70	Mr Murray FED Foreign Office	14 Nov	Minute on improving relations: 'almost all the effort must come from us'.	108
71	Mr Hopson Peking Tel. No. 272	27 Nov	Chinese to lift restrictions on movement of all British Mission staff in Peking.	109

Document summaries

	NAME	DATE	MAIN SUBJECT	PAGE
72	Mr Hopson Peking Tel. No. 298	2 Dec	Reports a setback with the issuing of exit visas to British staff in Peking.	110
73	Mr Murray FED	29 Dec	Minute assessing whether the Chinese worry about their image abroad.	111

1968

	NAME	DATE	MAIN SUBJECT	PAGE
74	Joint Intelligence Committee JIC(68)15(Final)	12 Jan	Report on the internal and external threats to Hong Kong for the next five years.	112
75	Sir D. Hopson Peking	15 Jan	Letter to Mr Murray reporting 'another slight indication' of normalisation in UK-China relations.	118
76	Sir D. Hopson Peking Tel. No. 74	25 Jan	Reports a clear opening to settle the question of exit visas for members of the British Mission.	119
77	To Sir D. Hopson Peking Tel. No. 132	6 Feb	Rejects Sir D. Hopson's recommendation in No. 76 to accept Chinese demands.	121
78	To Sir D. Hopson Peking Tel. No. 133	6 Feb	Resolving the issue of exit visas is secondary to that of securing the release of Mr Grey.	123
79	Sir D. Hopson Peking Tel. No. 114	8 Feb	Sir D. Hopson 'disappointed' with instructions in Nos. 77 and 78.	123
80	Sir D. Trench Hong Kong Tel. No. 186	13 Feb	Argues that concessions to assist in the release of Mr Grey risk stirring resentment in Hong Kong.	125
81	Mr Whitney Peking	27 Feb	Letter to Mr Wilson reporting signs in China that '1984 gets nearer'.	126
82	Sir D. Hopson Peking Tel. No. 174	8 Mar	Luo Guibo states that Hong Kong is 'crux of Sino-British relations'.	126
83	Mr Whitney Peking	8 Mar	Record of a meeting between Luo Guibo and Sir D. Hopson.	127
84	Sir D. Hopson Peking Tel. No. 179	11 Mar	Meeting with Luo Guibo 'a bad setback' but things are 'not as black as they look at first sight.'	131

	NAME	DATE	MAIN SUBJECT	PAGE
85	Mr Murray FED Foreign Office	12 Mar	Note considering options for dealing with UK-China relations after the recent statement of 8 March (No. 82).	134
86	Mr Rodgers Foreign Office	12 Mar	Minute to Mr Brown on a way forward for relations with China.	139
87	Sir D. Trench Hong Kong Tel. No. 33	15 Mar	Responding to No. 84, considers action to be taken to improve relations with China, including unofficial talks.	140

CHAPTER II

Clearing the debris of confrontation
21 March 1968 — 13 February 1970

	NAME	DATE	MAIN SUBJECT	PAGE
88	Mr Murray FED Foreign Office	21 Mar	Submission with policy recommendations on the present state of UK-China relations.	143
89	Sir D. Hopson Peking Tel. No. 229A	21 Mar	An effigy of HM The Queen is burnt during protests outside the office.	149
90	Mr Rodgers FCO	22 Mar	Minute to Mr Stewart commenting on the policy recommendations in No. 88.	150
91	Sir D. Hopson Peking Tel. No. 242	26 Mar	Reports meeting in which the Chinese appear to want an early reply to their statement (No. 82).	151
92	Mr Maitland FCO	26 Mar	Record of a meeting held by Mr Stewart on relations with China.	152
93	Mr Cradock Peking	26 Mar	Letter to Mr Denson giving an update on the state of the Mission and prospects of further turbulence.	153
94	Mr Murray FED Foreign Office	2 Apr	Submission recommending the lifting of entry/exit restrictions on Chinese officials, with accompanying minutes.	155
95	Mr Rodgers FCO	3 Apr	Brief for Mr Stewart on recommendations in No. 94.	159
96	To Sir D.Hopson Peking Tel. No. 338	5 Apr	Mr Rodgers summons Shen Ping to protest about the detention of British subjects in China.	161

Document summaries

	NAME	DATE	MAIN SUBJECT	PAGE
97	Mr Murray FED Foreign Office	10 Apr	Submission to Mr Wilkinson on the reply to the Chinese statement of 8 March.	163
98	To Sir D. Hopson Peking Tel. No. 356	11 Apr	Text of the British Government reply to the Chinese statement of 8 March.	165
99	Sir D. Hopson Peking Tel. No. 302	15 Apr	Sir D. Hopson delivers the British reply which the Chinese find unsatisfactory.	167
100	Sir D. Hopson Peking Tel. No. 304	15 Apr	Analysis of interview between Sir D. Hopson and Luo Guibo.	168
101	Sir D. Hopson Peking Tel. No. 341	23 Apr	Sir D. Hopson and Mr Weston visit Mr Grey under detention at his home.	170
102	Sir D. Hopson Peking Tel. No. 348	24 Apr	Suggestions for improving Mr Grey's conditions of detention and lessening the impact of his isolation.	171
103	Sir D. Hopson Peking Tel. No. 362	29 Apr	Recommendations to help secure the release of Mr Grey.	172
104	Mr Gass Hong Kong Tel. No. 575	7 May	View from Hong Kong on proposals to secure the release of Mr Grey.	174
105	To Sir D. Hopson Peking Tel. No. 459	7 May	Reports discussions with Sir D. Trench on steps to gain further access to Mr Grey and improve his treatment.	175
106	To Sir D. Hopson Peking Tel. No. 460	7 May	Reports discussions with the Governor of Hong Kong on steps to secure the release of Mr Grey.	176
107	Sir D. Hopson Peking Tel. No. 420	11 May	Reply to No. 106: 'I conclude from your telegrams that there is very little you feel we can do at the present time.'	177
108	Sir D. Hopson Peking Tel. No. 443	17 May	Anticipates trouble over the visit of the American warship *USS Enterprise* to Hong Kong and suggests cancelling the visit.	178

NAME	DATE	MAIN SUBJECT	PAGE
109 Sir D. Hopson Peking Tel. No. 453	20 May	Mr Cradock takes up the issue of Mr Grey's treatment with the Chinese MFA.	179
110 To Sir D. Hopson Peking Tel. No. 536	22 May	Rejects Sir D. Hopson's suggestion to cancel visit of USS *Enterprise* to Hong Kong.	180
111 To Sir D. Hopson Peking Tel. No. 561	24 May	Reports an interview between Mr Rodgers and Shen Ping on visas, detention of British subjects and Hong Kong.	181
112 Sir D. Hopson Peking Tel. No. 491	28 May	Luo Guibo protests about the visit of *USS Enterprise* to Hong Kong.	182
113 Cabinet DOP Committee OPD(68)11th meeting	29 May	Discussion over the future strength and structure of the garrison in Hong Kong.	183
114 Sir D. Hopson Peking Tel. No. 526	5 June	Mr Cradock tackles the Consular Department, about exit visas for British Mission staff.	185
115 Sir D. Hopson Peking Tel. No. 527	5 June	Comments on No. 114: 'a distinct setback on visas at a time when we thought we were turning the corner'.	186
116 Sir D. Hopson Peking Tel. No. 558	13 June	Recommends bringing foreign diplomatic pressure regarding the detention of British Mission staff.	186
117 Sir D. Hopson Peking Tel. No. 560	13 June	Recommends publicity on the question of detention of British Mission staff.	188
118 Sir D. Hopson Peking Tel. No. 566	15 June	Proposes he apply for an exit visa.	189
119 Mr Cradock Peking	18 June	Letter to Mr Denson providing an update on the state of the British Mission in Peking since 26 March.	190
120 Sir D. Hopson Peking Tel. No. 577	19 June	Objects to proposals by Sir D. Trench to deregister Chung Wah School.	192

	NAME	DATE	MAIN SUBJECT	PAGE
121	Sir D. Hopson Peking Tel. No. 585	20 June	Proposes using economic 'pinpricks' to warn the Chinese that they ' cannot continue with their present behaviour indefinitely.'	194
122	Sir D. Trench Hong Kong Tel. No. 803	22 June	Agrees to another round of visits for imprisoned news workers in Hong Kong in exchange for access to Mr Grey.	195
123	James Murray FED Foreign Office	22 June	Submission: 'British Mission in Peking: Diplomatic Pressure on the Chinese Government Problem.'	196
124	To Sir D. Trench Hong Kong Tel. No. 1203	24 June	Commonwealth Office doubt whether it is necessary to deregister Chung Wah School.	199
125	Sir D. Hopson Peking Tel. No. 620	2 July	Comments on the proposal to deregister Chung Wah School: the best safeguard for Hong Kong is good relations with China.	200
126	Sir D. Hopson Peking Tel. No. 630	3 July	Reports a meeting on exit visas for senior British staff.	202
127	Sir D. Trench Hong Kong Tel. No. 855	5 July	Provides reassurance over proposals to deregister Chung Wah School.	203
128	Sir D. Hopson Peking Tel. No. 637	5 July	The diplomatic corps in Peking is unlikely to agree to a joint démarche.	204
129	Sir D. Hopson Peking Tel. No. 648	8 July	Seeks clarification on HMG policy to end confrontation with China.	205
130	Sir D. Trench Hong Kong Tel. No. 884	12 July	Sets out main features of current phase of confrontation in Hong Kong.	206
131	Sir D. Hopson Peking Tel. No. 671	18 July	Sets out the benefits expected from ending confrontation with China.	208
132	To HM Representatives Overseas Tel. No. 373	23 July	Instructions to approach host Governments to ask them to lobby the Chinese about the delay in granting visas.	209

NAME	DATE	MAIN SUBJECT	PAGE
133 Sir D. Trench Hong Kong Tel. No. 925	24 July	Raises practical difficulties of taking economic measures against China in Hong Kong.	211
134 To Sir D. Hopson Peking Tel. No. 769	26 July	Prisoners in Hong Kong are the key issue in immediate dealings with the Chinese Government.	211
135 Sir D. Hopson Peking	30 July	Letter and memorandum (dated 29 July) on the prospects for UK-China relations.	213
136 Sir D. Hopson Peking Tel. No. 698	30 July	Argues for the release of detainees in Hong Kong as a key concession to improve relations with China.	222
137 Sir D. Hopson Peking Tel. No. 718	5 Aug	Requests renewing diplomatic pressure over exit visas where Chinese seem more sensitive.	223
138 To Sir D. Trench Hong Kong Tel. No. 1362	8 Aug	Seeks views on releasing detainees as a way of 'de-escalating' tensions with China.	224
139 To Sir D. Trench Hong Kong Tel. No. 1375	9 Aug	Seeks views on possible acts of clemency to assist with the release of Mr Grey.	225
140 Mr Cradock Peking	13 Aug	Letter to Mr Murray reporting on the departure of Sir D. Hopson.	227
141 Sir D. Trench Hong Kong Tel. No. 1007	19 Aug	Responds to No. 139 outlining alternative options to secure the release of Mr Grey.	228
142 Mr Murray FED Foreign Office	20 Aug	Submission to Sir D. Allen re-examining the possibilities of applying economic pressure against China.	230
143 Mr Murray FED Foreign Office	20 Aug	Minute to Sir D. Allen on UK-China relations, with particular reference to Hong Kong, and subsequent minutes.	234
144 Mr Cradock Peking Tel. No. 765	21 Aug	Responds No. 141 and argues for the release of two high profile prisoners to help secure the release of Mr Grey.	243
145 Mr Murray FED Foreign Office	22 Aug	Minute to Sir D. Allen on back-channel communication with the Chinese.	244

Document summaries

	NAME	DATE	MAIN SUBJECT	PAGE
146	Mr Cradock Peking Tel. No. 781	26 Aug	Receives a protest about the deregistration of Chung Wah School.	246
147	Sir D. Trench Hong Kong Tel. No. 1063	9 Sept	Comments on No. 135: pays 'too little regard to the concessions Hong Kong has already made'.	248
148	Sir P. Gore-booth Foreign Office	10 Sept	Minute to Mr Murray reporting a talk with Sir D. Hopson on relations with China.	249
149	Sir D. Trench Hong Kong Tel. No. 2001	20 Sept	Encloses an extract from Mr Cater's report with his Chinese contact relating to Mr Grey.	250
150	Mr Murray FED Foreign Office	23 Sept	Minute to Sir D. Allen recommending a public statement is made about Mr Grey's health.	251
151	Mr Cradock Peking	23 Sept	Despatch: 'The Visa War Part I.'	252
152	Mr Cradock Peking	23 Sept	Despatch: 'The Visa War Part II: Reflections on a Year of Detention.'	259
153	Mr Walden Peking	23 Sept	Letter to Mr Boyd reporting foreign press reactions to the release of Sir D. Hopson.	262
154	Mr Cradock Peking Tel. No. 886	25 Sept	Argues that publicity to assist detained British subjects is not being used as effectively as it could.	265
155	Mr Murray FED Foreign Office	3 Oct	How best to secure Mr Grey's release, following disagreement between Sir D. Trench and Mr Cradock.	266
156	To Mr Cradock Peking Tel. No. 874	9 Oct	Response to No. 154 explaining the Government's approach towards publicity for detained British subjects.	270
157	Sir D. Trench Hong Kong Tel. No. 2180	15 Nov	Reports Mr Cater's discussions with his contact on securing Mr Grey's release and improving relations.	271
158	Mr Palliser 10 Downing Street	2 Dec	Letter to Mr Day reporting Prime Ministerial discussions regarding Mr Grey.	272
159	Mr Maddocks Hong Kong	2 Dec	Letter to Mr Murray suggesting relations could be improved by closing the consulate in Taiwan.	273

NAME	DATE	MAIN SUBJECT	PAGE
160 Mr Cradock Peking Tel. No. 1093	9 Dec	Demands Mr Grey's immediate release and protests against the conditions under which he is held.	275
1969			
161 Mr Cradock Peking	7 Jan	Letter to Mr Murray arguing the closure of the consulate would be of limited value.	276
162 Record of Meeting FCO	10 Jan	Lord Shepherd discusses with Shen Ping the continued detention of Mr Grey.	277
163 Mr Cradock Peking Tel. No. 103	11 Feb	Reports apparent Chinese willingness to improve relations.	280
164 To Sir D. Trench Hong Kong Tel. No. 161	28 Feb	There is little hope of British subjects being released without meeting the Chinese over Hong Kong.	280
165 Mr Denson Peking Tel. No. 170	10 Mar	No chance of the Chinese agreeing to release Mr Grey without a concession in the release of Hong Kong news workers.	281
166 Ministerial Committee on Hong Kong K(69)1	28 Mar	Extract from an interdepartmental study on the long-term future of Hong Kong.	282
167 Lord Shepherd FCO	8 May	Minute to Mr Stewart on securing the release of Mr Grey, without risking the security of Hong Kong.	286
168 To Mr Denson Peking Tel. No. 180	20 May	Reports a meeting with Ma Chia-chun to discuss how to secure the release of Mr Grey.	288
169 Mr Garside Peking	3 June	Letter to Mr Boyd with personal impressions of China.	289
170 Mr Denson Peking	11 June	Despatch: 'China Revisited.'	290
171 Sir D. Trench Hong Kong Tel. No. 588	24 July	Argues firmly against further concessions in Hong Kong and for a firmer line to be taken with China.	295
172 Mr Murray FED FCO	12 Aug	Minute to Sir S. Tomlinson with details of covert contact with the Chinese authorities.	296

Document summaries

	NAME	DATE	MAIN SUBJECT	PAGE
173	To Sir D. Trench Hong Kong Tel. No. 2 Saving	22 Aug	Response to No. 171: need to avoid any impression of differences between Hong Kong and HMG.	299
174	Mr Denson Peking Tel. No. 575	3 Oct	Reports the celebrations marking the 20th Anniversary of the People's Republic of China.	301
175	Mr Denson Peking Tel. No. 586	4 Oct	Confirms that Mr Grey has been released from house arrest.	302
176	Mr Denson Peking	7 Oct	Letter to Mr Murray: Sir D. Trench should resist stronger measures against communists in Hong Kong.	303
177	Mr Denson Peking	14 Nov	Despatch: 'Chinese Foreign Policy.'	305
178	Official Committee on Strategic Exports ESC(O)(69)18	17 Nov	Note by the Ministry of Technology about the export of civil aircraft to China.	312
179	Mr Walden Peking	22 Nov	Letter to Mr Appleyard regarding Chinese attitudes towards the UN.	314
180	Record of Meeting FCO	10 Dec	Lord Shepherd and Mr Keswick discuss prospects for trade with China.	315
181	Mr Allan Peking	30 Dec	Letter to Mr Wilson regarding the problems of pursuing compensation claims against the Chinese.	318
	1970			
182	Far Eastern Department FCO	19 Jan	Note on Chinese foreign policy.	319
183	Mr Denson Peking	27 Jan	Letter to Mr Murray enclosing a paper assessing the current state of UK-China relations.	322
184	Mr Denson Peking	30 Jan	Letter to Mr Murray: Chinese comment they only have 'half relations' with the UK because of Taiwan.	327
185	To Ministerial Committee on Hong Kong K(70)1	9 Feb	Note from Mr Stewart asking colleagues to consider a study on the long-term future of Hong Kong (No. 166).	328

NAME	DATE	MAIN SUBJECT	PAGE
186 Mr Wilson FED FCO	13 Feb	Minute assessing the state of UK-China relations, following a letter received from Mr Denson (No. 183).	330

CHAPTER III

Negotiating an exchange of Ambassadors
15 April 1970 — 13 March 1972

187 Mr Murray FED FCO	15 Apr	Conclusions of a comprehensive review of UK-China relations	334
188 Mr Denson Peking Tel. No. 262	24 Apr	Mr Wilsford visits China: 'it is evident that the Chinese would like to remove existing difficulties'.	341
189 Mr Morgan FED FCO	29 May	Minute to Mr Wilford on whether the UK should support the 'Important Item' resolution at the UN.	342
190 Mr Maddocks Hong Kong	12 June	Letter to Mr Morgan: little chance of improvement in relations with China. Priority should be Hong Kong.	343
191 Mr Denson Peking Tel No. 449	15 June	Reports conversation with Luo Guibo at the Queen's Birthday Party about an exchange of Ambassadors.	345
192 Mr Morgan FED FCO	3 July	Minute to Mr Wilford with general comments in response to No. 190.	345
193 Record of Meeting FCO	29 July	Ma Chia-chun makes clear to Mr Morgan China's strong interest in the fate of confrontation prisoners.	348
194 Mr Morgan FED FCO	11 Sept	Submission to Mr Wilford on whether the UK should take significant steps to place its relations with China on a firmer basis.	349
195 Mr Wilford FED FCO	16 Sept	Minute on No. 194: 'The Chinese will always succeed in finding some stick with which to beat us.'	355
196 Mr Royle FCO	25 Sept	Minute commenting on the proposals in No. 194.	356

NAME	DATE	MAIN SUBJECT	PAGE
197 RECORD OF MEETING Peking	29 Sept	Mr Denson and T'ang Hai-kuang discuss terms for an exchange of Ambassadors.	357
198 MR MORGAN FED FCO	6 Nov	Note on Chinese representation in the UN: some countries could change their position this year.	359
199 MR DENSON Peking Tel No. 752	10 Nov	Recommends no statement is made at the UN on the 'Important Question' resolution.	360
200 MR BOYD Washington	12 Nov	Letter to Mr Morgan reporting on US-China relations and UN representation.	361
201 SIR COLIN CROWE UKMIS New York Tel. No. 2953	20 Nov	Readout of voting on the Important Question and Albanian resolutions at the UN.	365
202 TO MR MOON 10 Downing Street	2 Dec	Letter from Mr McCluney enclosing a note on trade and the UK consulate in Taiwan.	366
203 MR MORGAN FED FCO	10 Dec	Submission to Mr Wilford on the UK's position on Chinese representation at the UN.	368
204 TO MR ELLIOTT Washington	23 Dec	Letter from Mr Morgan to make a formal approach to the US over changing the UK vote on the Important Question Resolution.	371
1971			
205 TO MR HEATH 10 Downing Street	5 Jan	FCO briefing note on UK policy towards China, including scope for initiatives.	373
206 TO SIR D. TRENCH Hong Kong Tel. No. 24	8 Jan	Presses for the early release of Hong Kong confrontation prisoners.	377
207 SIR D. TRENCH Hong Kong Tel. No. 13	9 Jan	Response to No. 206: Argues early prisoner release would risk long-term security.	378
208 SIR D. TRENCH Hong Kong Tel. No. 17	11 Jan	Further observations on No. 206 outlining the potentially destabilising consequences.	380

NAME	DATE	MAIN SUBJECT	PAGE
209 To Mr Denson Peking Tel. No. 29	15 Jan	Mr Royle tells Pei Tsien-chang that HMG would like to proceed to exchange Ambassadors.	382
210 Mr Denson Peking Tel. No. 42	16 Jan	Supports the case for prisoner release.	382
211 Sir D. Trench Hong Kong Tel. No. 36	19 Jan	Response to No. 210 arguing that it underestimates the risks.	384
212 Mr Millard Washington	22 Jan	Letter to Mr Wilford reporting a disappointing meeting about Chinese representation in the UN.	385
213 Mr Denson Peking Tel. No. 58	22 Jan	The Chinese hope some prisoners will be released ahead of the Chinese New Year.	387
214 Sir L. Monson FCO	25 Jan	Doubts whether a prisoner release remains in the long-term interest of Hong Kong.	387
215 To Sir D. Trench Hong Kong Tel No. 82	28 Jan	Argues that stability in Hong Kong is at risk if some confrontation prisoners are not released.	388
216 To Sir D. Trench Hong Kong Tel No. 83	28 Jan	Public opinion in Hong Kong needs to be convinced that prisoner releases are in their interests.	390
217 Mr Wilford FCO	5 Feb	Pei Tsien-chang implies an exchange of Ambassadors is dependent on closing the consulate at Tamsui.	391
218 Mr Denson Peking	9 Feb	Despatch: 'British subjects detained in China: The end of a chapter?'	392
219 To Mr Moon 10 Downing Street	10 Feb	Letter from Mr McCluney providing an update on Sino-British relations for Mr Heath.	399
220 Cabinet DOP Committee DOPO(SE)(71)1	17 Feb	Note detailing the failed attempt to sell VC-10 aircraft to China.	400
221 Sir D. Trench Hong Kong Tel No. 108	19 Feb	Advises that following a Board of Review meeting 24 confrontation prisoners will be released.	401

Document summaries

	NAME	DATE	MAIN SUBJECT	PAGE
222	To Sir D. Trench Hong Kong Tel. No. 164	22 Feb	Will avoid publicly linking confrontation prisoners with better relations, though unrealistic to separate them.	402
223	Mr Allan Peking Tel. No. 183	3 Mar	Reports a meeting between Mr Denson and Chou En-lai to discuss the state of bilateral relations.	402
224	To The Earl of Cromer Washington Tel No. 695	9 Mar	Mr Greene tells Mr Royle that the US hope to reach a decision soon on China in the UN.	405
225	Mr Cook Bangkok Tel No. 136	9 Mar	Mr Denson's thoughts following a conversation with the Sir D. Trench about the meeting with Chou En-lai.	406
226	To Mr Denson Peking Tel. No. 182	26 Mar	Chinese respond formally to the request to exchange Ambassadors, listing two pre-conditions.	407
227	Mr Denson Peking	6 Apr	Letter to Mr Morgan recording views on closing the Consulate in Taiwan.	408
228	Mr Morgan FED FCO	6 Apr	Submission on how to respond to Chinese preconditions to exchange Ambassadors.	409
229	Mr Logan FCO	7 Apr	Mr Royle agrees to No. 228 but does not think Chinese pre-conditions should be met immediately.	413
230	Mr Maddocks Hong Kong	13 Apr	Letter to Mr Wilford with Hong Kong's perspective on developments in UK-China relations.	414
231	The Earl of Cromer Washington Tel. No. 1299	15 Apr	Need to avoid the appearance of presenting the Americans with a *fait accompli* over China and the UN.	417
232	Mr Denson Peking Tel. No. 356	16 Apr	Reports on the embryonic use by the Chinese of 'ping-pong' diplomacy.	418
233	Mr Graham FCO	20 Apr	Minute to Sir A. Douglas-Home summarising policy towards China.	419
234	Mr Darwin Legal Advisers FCO	26 Apr	Minute on the difficulty of finding an argument for changing the UK vote on the Important Question.	420

NAME	DATE	MAIN SUBJECT	PAGE
235 Mr Graham FCO	27 Apr	Reports Sir A. Douglas-Home's discussion with Mr Rogers on the admission of China to the UN.	421
236 The Earl of Cromer Washington Tel. No. 1469	28 Apr	Reports conversation with Mr Kissinger: US review of China policy likely by mid-May.	422
237 Mr Denson Peking	29 Apr	Despatch: 'Trading with China: Review and Prospects.'	422
238 To The Earl of Cromer Washington Tel. No. 1232	30 Apr	Sir A. Douglas-Home, in talks with Mr Rogers, agrees to wait for a US decision on Chinese representation at the UN.	428
239 To Mr Millard Washington	4 May	Letter from Mr Wilford highlighting the risks to the UK of the rapidly evolving US position on China.	429
240 Mr Millard Washington	7 May	Response to No. 239 suggesting it is not too late to take a tougher line with the US on Chinese representation at the UN.	430
241 Cabinet DOP Committee DOP(71) 27	7 May	Memorandum by Sir A. Douglas-Home on proposals to improve relations with China.	431
242 Cabinet DOP Committee DOP(71)11th meeting	26 May	Discussion of No. 241: Ministers wary of making a decision without certainty of the US view.	434
243 Mr Muirhead Lisbon Tel. No. 238	3 June	Reports a meeting between Sir A. Douglas-Home and Mr Rogers to discuss UK proposals towards China.	435
244 Mr Moon 10 Downing Street	7 June	Mr Heath wants to move quickly on China.	436
245 Mr Morgan FCO	8 June	Submission on Mr Rogers' proposal for representation of both China and Taiwan at the UN.	437
246 Cabinet DOP Committee DOP(71)32	14 June	Sir A. Douglas-Home seeks agreement to approach the Chinese for an exchange of ambassadors without further delay.	438

Document summaries

	NAME	DATE	MAIN SUBJECT	PAGE
247	CABINET DOP COMMITTEE DOP(71)12th meeting	16 June	The Committee agrees with the proposals in No. 246, subject to confirmation that the US had no objection.	440
248	TO THE EARL OF CROMER Washington Tel. No. 1671	16 June	Instructions to inform Mr Rogers of the steps the UK intends to take for an exchange of Ambassadors with China.	441
249	MR DUFFY Tamsui Tel. No. 49	19 June	Responds to No. 248: Hopes this does not preclude support for an independent Taiwan.	442
250	MR WILFORD FCO	22 June	Minute to Mr Morgan on Pei Tsien-chang meeting the Governor-designate of Hong Kong.	442
251	RECORD OF A MEETING FCO	22 June	Mr Royle informs Pei Jianzhang, that, having met the two Chinese conditions, the UK would like to exchange Ambassadors.	443
252	MR WILFORD FCO	28 June	Minute to Mr Royle, enclosing a paper about the future of Hong Kong.	445
253	TO MR SOAMES Paris Tel. No. 488	30 June	In the light of Chinese leaks over the exchange of Ambassadors, HMG intend to inform key partners.	451
254	MR DENSON Peking Tel. No. 628	10 July	The Chinese want the principles for an exchange Ambassadors to be put in an exchange of notes.	452
255	MR DENSON Peking Tel. No. 629	10 July	Draft Chinese text for an exchange of notes.	453
256	MR DENSON Peking Tel. No. 636	12 July	Assesses the draft Chinese text.	454
257	MR MORGAN FED FCO	13 July	Submission to Mr Wilford on responding to the Chinese proposal to exchange notes.	455
258	THE EARL OF CROMER Washington Tel. No. 2412	16 July	Reports that President Nixon is about to announce a visit China.	457

NAME	DATE	MAIN SUBJECT	PAGE
259 To Mr Moon 10 Downing Street	16 July	Letter from Mr Graham assessing the consequences of President Nixon's China announcement.	458
260 Mr Morgan FED FCO	21 July	Submission on whether HMG should agree to Chinese wording on Taiwan.	459
261 Mr Denson Peking	27 July	Letter to Mr Wilford suggesting the UK should not rush to exchange Ambassadors if further pre-conditions are made.	462
262 Mr Samuel Peking	27 July	Letter to Mr Hervey giving the background to Dr Kissinger's visit to China.	462
263 Sir S. Tomlinson FCO	30 July	Minute on the lack of expediency in Britain's legal position over the status of Taiwan.	464
264 Mr Overton NAD FCO	3 Aug	Accepting the Chinese formula on Taiwan would contain the seeds of future trouble with the US.	466
265 Mr Denson Peking Tel. No. 743	5 Aug	Qiao Guanhua showed no sign of give in the Chinese position. Considers future tactics.	467
266 Mr Overton NAD FCO	6 Aug	Minute arguing that the UK should delay making a decision on the status of Taiwan.	469
267 To Mr Denson Peking Tel. No. 516	12 Aug	Sir A. Douglas-Home unwilling to accept any formula that would breach UK policy on recognition of Taiwan.	470
268 Sir D. Trench Hong Kong Tel. No. 568	16 Aug	Response to No. 267: 'no hope of progress if the Chinese persist in trying to force us to accept their position.'	472
269 To Mr Denson Peking Tel. No. 532	19 Aug	Directive to see if the Chinese will accept anything less than the wording 'China's Province Taiwan'.	473
270 Mr Samuel Peking Tel. No. 825	26 Aug	Reports a meeting with Qiao Guanhua to discuss possible formula for an exchange of notes.	474
271 To Mr Roberts 10 Downing Street	3 Sept	Letter from Mr Grattan outlining plans to oppose the US 'two-Chinas' policy in the UN.	475

Document summaries

	NAME	DATE	MAIN SUBJECT	PAGE
272	Mr Millard Washington	10 Sept	Argues the US has little grounds for complaint if the UK fails to support them at the UN.	476
273	To Sir C. Crowe UKMIS New York Tel. No. 633	20 Sept	Instructions for informing the US of the UK decision on their item on Chinese representation in the UN.	477
274	To Sir C. Crowe UKMIS New York Tel. No. 644	21 Sept	Slightly modified UN voting instructions issued as a result of Mr Rogers dismay at the UK position.	478
275	Sir C. Crowe UKMIS New York Tel. No. 1112	22 Sept	Reports the outcome of a debate in the General Committee on Chinese representation.	479
276	Mr Stratton UND FCO	7 Oct	Minute to Mr Parsons venting his frustrations at the US tactics at the UN.	480
277	Mr Denson Peking Tel. No. 1076	19 Oct	Readout from a late-night discussion between Mr MacDonald and Zhou Enlai, regarding an exchange of Ambassadors.	481
278	To The Earl of Cromer Washington Tel. No. 2701	21 Oct	US officials try to persuade HMG to vote on a motion for priority for the American Resolution.	482
279	Sir C. Crowe UKMIS New York	26 Oct	Despatch reporting the General Assembly debate on China representation.	483
280	To Mr Denson Peking Tel. No. 772	29 Oct	Reports a discussion between Mr Morgan and Pei Jianzhang, on Hong Kong, Taiwan and a speech by Mr Heath.	486
281	Mr Denson Peking	2 Nov	Letter to Mr Wilford about exports to China and role of the Sino-British Trade Council.	487
282	Sir C. Crowe UKMIS New York Tel. No. 1626	15 Nov	Reports on the Plenary Meeting of the UN General Assembly welcoming PRC representatives.	491
283	Mr Denson Peking	15 Nov	Letter to Mr Wilford suggesting the UK be less forthcoming with the US government over China.	491

NAME	DATE	MAIN SUBJECT	PAGE
284 Mr Denson Peking Tel. No. 1177	18 Nov	Reports discussions over exchange of Ambassadors; also notes recent cordiality from Chinese officials.	493
285 The Earl of Cromer Washington Tel. No. 3854	18 Nov	Reports discussion with Mr Kissinger about British difficulties with China over the exchange of Ambassadors.	494
286 Mr Morgan FCO	18 Nov	Submission on reconsidering the UK position on the status of Taiwan.	494
287 Mr Denson Peking	18 Nov	Despatch: 'China, 1969-71: Mr. Denson's Valedictory Despatch.'	496
288 Mr Samuel Peking Tel. No. 1202	24 Nov	Reports the Chinese are now using commercial relations as a lever in Ambassadorial negotiations.	503
289 Far Eastern Department FCO	24 Nov	Note on the consequences if negotiations fail on the exchange of Ambassadors.	504
290 Mr Samuel Peking Tel. No. 1215	1 Dec	Conveys the text of an interview between journalist Neville Maxwell and Zhou Enlai.	505
291 Mr Samuel Peking Tel. No. 1220	1 Dec	Reports negative comments made by Zhou Enlai on the status of Taiwan and assesses the implications.	507
292 Sir C. Crowe UKMIS New York Tel. No. 1880	1 Dec	Taiwan remains the sticking point to exchanging Ambassadors.	508
293 Mr Elliott Washington	2 Dec	Letter to Mr Wilford responding to No. 283. Lack of frankness with the US on China would harm the UK in other areas.	509
294 Mr Samuel Peking Tel. No. 1233	7 Dec	Argues it would be beneficial for trade if Ambassadors were exchanged.	510
295 Cabinet DOP Committee DOP(71)83	13 Dec	Memorandum by Sir A. Douglas-Home setting out options regarding the future of Hong Kong.	512
296 Cabinet DOP Committee DOP(71)93	31 Dec	Memorandum by Sir A. Douglas-Home seeking agreement to use a compromise formula on Taiwan to reach an agreement.	514

Document summaries

	NAME	DATE	MAIN SUBJECT	PAGE
		1972		
297	Mr Wilford FCO	4 Jan	Minute to Sir S. Tomlinson seeking a readout from No. 10 on Mr Heath's recent discussion with President Nixon on China.	515
298	To Mr Addis Peking Tel. No. 30	24 Jan	Instructions to put forward a compromise formula on the status of Taiwan.	516
299	Planning Staff FCO	2 Feb	Policy paper on 'The Asian Quadrilateral.'	517
300	Sir C. Crowe UKMIS New York	3 Feb	Despatch: 'China's Long March to the United Nations.'	521
301	Mr Addis Peking Tel. No. 77	4 Feb	Reports meeting with Qiao Guanhua to put forwards the comprise formula regarding Taiwan.	534
302	Mr Addis Peking Tel. No. 120	19 Feb	Agreeing language regarding Taiwan is proving difficult.	536
303	Mr Addis Peking Tel. No. 121	19 Feb	Chinese unwilling to accept compromise: choice between accepting Chinese wording or not exchanging Ambassadors.	538
304	To Mr Addis Peking Tel. No. 100	19 Feb	Questions who should take the initiative with the negotiations.	539
305	Mr Addis Peking Tel. No. 123	21 Feb	'The next move is clearly up to us.'	539
306	Mr Morgan Lima Tel. No. 33	23 Feb	Mr Godber feels the Chinese demand presents no political, as opposed to legal, problem.	539
307	Mr Morgan FED	24 Feb	Minute to Mr Wilford suggesting a way forward on the wording of the formula.	540
308	To The Earl of Cromer Washington Tel. No. 469	25 Feb	Instructions to inform the US of the UK decision to accept the Chinese formula.	540

	NAME	DATE	MAIN SUBJECT	PAGE
309	Mr Addis Peking Tel. No. 168	4 Mar	Reports meeting with Qiao Guanhua: Chinese to consider UK proposals.	541
310	Mr Addis Peking Tel. No. 174	6 Mar	Chinese content with UK oral assurance. Formal agreement to exchange Ambassadors will be signed on 13 March.	542
311	To HM Representatives Overseas Tel. No. 269	9 Mar	Advises that an agreement has been reached with China to exchange Ambassadors and provides background briefing.	543
312	Mr Addis Peking Tel. No. 201	13 Mar	Reports the signing of the communique with Qiao Guanhua: Mr Addis formally accepted as Ambassador.	546
313	Mr MacLehose Hong Kong Tel. No. 13	13 Mar	Personal message to Mr Addis: 'Heartiest congratulations. It was a slow start but a fast finish.'	546
	Appendix	13 Mar	Joint Communique on the Agreement Between the United Kingdom of Great Britain and Northern Ireland and the People's Republic of China on an Exchange of Ambassadors.	548

CHAPTER I

The Cultural Revolution and the sacking of the Mission 15 May 1967 — 18 March 1968

No. 1

Mr Hopson (Peking) to Mr Brown, 15 May 1967, 4.20 a.m.[1]
Tel. No. 480 Flash, Confidential (FCO 21/191)

My immediately preceding telegrams.[2]

We must conclude from the Chinese Government statement[3] that they have decided to risk a direct confrontation with us on Hong Kong. The fact they took a relatively long time to reach this decision and then published it in the form of a statement instead of a diplomatic Note may indicate that this decision was reached with some reluctance.

2. On the other hand the Foreign Ministry official who was assisting the Vice-Minister at our interview, when I suggested that a deterioration of the situation in Hong Kong would be bad both for British and Chinese interests there, took me up passionately and declared that we were no longer dealing with the China of even five years ago. Now that the cultural revolution was in full swing the new China would no longer bow to threats. It looks therefore as if the Chinese Government are 'putting politics in command' and may have decided to accept any necessary economic damage.

3. The test will be in Hong Kong itself and in the way the left wing play it there. I should be surprised if a door is not left open for some kind of compromise, though it is difficult see any sign of this at present.

4. I presume it will be your intention to issue an official statement in London and Hong Kong commenting on the Chinese statement. If so, though it will clearly be important to refute the Chinese charges, I hope it will be possible to phrase this in such a way as to avoid provoking the Chinese Government unnecessarily and thus

---

1 Repeated for information to Hong Kong, Singapore and Washington.
2 Not printed. These telegrams contained the text of a statement by the Chinese Foreign Ministry, regarding recent disturbances in Hong Kong, handed to Mr Hopson when he was summoned to see Vice-Minister Luo Guibo early on 15 May. After accusing the British authorities of 'fascist atrocities' the Chinese Government demanded that the British Government instruct the authorities in Hong Kong to: 'Immediately accept all the just demands put forward by Chinese workers and residents in Hong Kong; immediately stop all fascist measures; immediately set free all the arrested persons (including workers, journalists and cameramen); punish the culprits responsible for these sanguinary atrocities, offer apologies to the victims and compensate for all their losses, and; guarantee against the occurrence of similar incidents.'
3 See No. 7.

1

making a compromise (if one is indeed still possible) even more difficult. As seen from here the object should be to bring the temperature down while standing firm on basic principles.

5. It is probable that we shall get some unpleasant demonstrations against this office. I have taken necessary precautions. We may be in for a very long haul.

6. Record of my interview which contained no other points of real interest will be in a following telegram.

No. 2

Mr Hopson (Peking) to Mr Brown, 16 May 1967, 4.45 a.m.[1]
Tel. No. 487 Immediate, Unclassified (FCO 21/33, FC 1/14/A)

Demonstrations against this Mission began on night of 15 May and were resumed on a bigger scale this morning. There is a small static group at the gates of the Office and of my house and a constant procession of demonstrators passing along the road.

2. The walls of Chancery, my house, staff quarters and many other parts of Peking are liberally plastered with posters supporting the Chinese Foreign Ministry statement and condemning activities of British and Hong Kong Governments. Slogans, some in English, include 'Down with Wilson', 'The Debt of Blood Must be Paid'. Loudspeaker vans are also broadcasting continually.

3. The Chinese staff and personal servants have ceased work and joined the demonstrators. Some of the Chinese staff asked me or a member of the Chancery to receive a petition at the main gate. I sent a message to leave their petitions at the Guards' desk, after which one of our interpreters read out the protest in the name of the Chinese staff over the loudspeakers.

4. Peters, who was in Canton for the closing of the Trade Fair walked out of the final reception when Chinese speaker referred to the Hong Kong disturbances in similar terms to the Ministry of Foreign Affairs statement.

5. There are slogans and demonstrations outside the Shanghai Office and Hewitt has received a telephone message from the Shanghai Foreign Affairs Department expressing resolute support of the Ministry of Foreign Affairs statement warning him to expect to receive protests and calling on him to 'show a correct attitude'.

1 Repeated for information to Hong Kong, POLAD Singapore and Washington.

No. 3

Mr Hopson (Peking) to Mr Brown, 16 May 1967, 8.30 a.m.
Tel. No. 490 Unclassified (FCO 21/33, FC 1/14/A)

Hewitt has reported by telephone that he was given an 'ultimatum' to appear at the gates of the Shanghai compound at noon today. When this 'ultimatum' expired a column of demonstrators, numbering several hundred burst into the grounds and marched to the office. Hewitt met them on the steps of the office and then returned with them to the main gate. The demonstrators demanded that he 'apologised' to a picture of Mao which they had stuck in the front lawn of the compound, that he should stand to attention and also made other humiliating demands, all of which Hewitt refused whilst in the compound the demonstrators painted slogans on the paths and the walls of the buildings.

2. Demonstrators have departed and the situation is now quiet. Hewitt is protesting to the Foreign Affairs Department in Shanghai and we have lodged an oral protest here.

No. 4

Mr Hopson (Peking) to Mr Brown, 16 May 1967, 12.01 p.m.[1]
Tel. No. 492 Immediate, Unclassified (FCO 21/33, FC 1/14/A)

Hewitt has just telephoned to say that a mob invaded the Shanghai Compound this afternoon and completely sacked his house, breaking literally everything. They left only after three hours. Hewitt says his wife and three small children were unharmed.

2. I am trying to send someone down to Shanghai as soon as possible. I have also asked for an appointment at the Ministry of Foreign Affairs to lodge a strong protest

[1] Repeated for information to Hong Kong and Singapore.

No. 5

Mr Brown to Mr Hopson (Peking), 16 May 1967, 10.52 p.m.[1]
Tel. No. 322 Immediate Confidential (FCO 21/63, FC 3/3/A)

Your Telegrams 487, 490 and 492 (not to all).[2]

The Chinese Chargé d'Affaires *ad interim*, Shen Ping, was summoned at 7 p.m. this evening. He was seen by de la Mare and asked to transmit immediately to his government a strong protest by Her Majesty's Government against the mob action taken against your premises and particularly those of the office in Shanghai. He was asked to obtain from his government guarantees for the protection of this property and for the safety and wellbeing of all British subjects in China but particularly in view of events in Shanghai of Mr Hewitt and his family.

2. After repeating much of the language contained in the Chinese statement reported in your telegrams 478 and 479,[3] including the reference to 'fascist brutality' which he was asked to withdraw but refused and again repeated several times, the Chargé d'Affaires claimed that the Chinese people were fully justified in expressing

[1] Repeated for information to Hong Kong, Singapore and Washington.
[2] Nos. 2, 3 and 4 respectively.
[3] Not printed.

their indignation as they had done in Peking and Shanghai. He said that our 'so-called protest' bore no relation to the true facts and made black appear white. He rejected it emphatically.

3. Asked whether this meant that he refused to transmit it to his government he replied that this was the case. De la Mare then terminated the interview.

4. For the statement issued to the Press after Shen Ping's call see my immediately following telegram.[4]

4 Not printed.

No. 6

Mr Hopson (Peking) to Mr Brown, 17 May 1967, 6.32 a.m.
Tel. No. 496 Flash, Confidential (FCO 21/33, FC 1/14/A)

My immediately preceding telegram.[1]

I am deeply concerned about the situation in Shanghai and particularly about the security of the Hewitts. Our position there is rapidly becoming untenable and we must urgently consider whether we should evacuate.

2. Evacuation is no doubt what the Chinese want and it goes against the grain to give them a cheap victory. Although we might represent evacuation as temporary it would no doubt turn out to be permanent. We must also consider the position of remaining British subjects in Shanghai particularly the banks.

3. On the other hand we must recognise that the Chinese can make our position untenable (if it is not indeed already so) as they wish. I cannot allow Mrs Hewitt and the children to be exposed to such risks and we must try to withdraw them as soon as possible. If the Chinese would allow us to send members of the staff down regularly to keep Hewitt company it might be justifiable to try to maintain him there alone in the hope that things will calm down. But the Ministry of Foreign Affairs' refusal to allow Weston to go show that we could not hope for this. Hewitt himself has been under great strain (he was walked up and down in the compound for hours yesterday afternoon and manhandled though not actually injured). I do not think he should be asked to stay there alone indefinitely without his family or any support in such circumstances.

4. I have therefore reluctantly come to the conclusion that we must seriously consider evacuating Hewitt and his family together as soon as possible. If we informed the Chinese of our intention (representing it as a temporary withdrawal because they apparently cannot or will not guarantee his security) and requested their assistance in allowing a member of my staff to go down to Shanghai to help pack up, they might agree. If not, the Hewitts would have to come out on their own, provided the Chinese will let them.

5. In this case Hewitt would have to destroy all documents which he could not bring with him.

1 Not printed.

6. On the other hand you may feel that this would be rushing things unnecessarily and that we should instruct Hewitt to hang on (if necessary alone) for a few days to see if things quieten down. But I should emphasise that according to Peters who saw him last week, Hewitt was already showing signs of stress even then. He has hinted over the telephone that he would prefer to come out.

7. I should be grateful for a very urgent decision in this matter and for detailed instructions as to what to do about the compound if you decide on evacuation.

8. I am sorry things have come to this pass. As a possible bonus a cheap victory in Shanghai might make it easier for the Chinese to countenance a slow climb down in Hong Kong, though I doubt it. It might on the contrary encourage them to ask for more. But the immediate issue is the security of the Hewitts.

9. In view of paragraph 6 above please give this telegram suitably restricted circulation.

No. 7

Mr Brown and Mr Bowden to H.M. Representatives Overseas
18 May 1967[1]
Guidance Tel. No. 106 Priority, Restricted (PREM 13/1458)

Disturbances in Hong Kong

Since the Macao incidents[2] of December last year, there has been a new note of militancy in several labour disputes in Hong Kong involving pro-Communist unions. The recent disturbances in Kowloon originated from one of these disputes. After demonstrations and obstructive picketing had led to intervention by the police and arrests, the unions concerned put forward 'demands' for the immediate release of workers arrested, compensation and punishment of the police involved and no interference by the police in labour disputes in the future. The pro-Communist press endorsed these demands and deliberately slanted its reporting to create the impression of unnecessary brutality by the police who had in fact behaved with exemplary moderation. The pro-Communist press has demanded apologies from the Government. (For full details see Verbatim No. 214.)[3]

The Chinese statement and British replies

2. On 15 May the Chinese MFA issued a statement supporting the demands of the pro-Communist press in Hong Kong and castigating the Hong Kong Government for 'fascist atrocities', 'sanguinary suppression of Chinese residents' and 'collusion with the US Imperialists'. The statement included a demand that HM Government should instruct the Hong Kong Government to accept all the demands of the local

---

1 The telegram was sent at 1 a.m. on 19 May.
2 Following riots in 1966 the Portuguese authorities in Macao accepted a number of demands put forward by local communists. These included the dismissal and punishment of the Chief of Police and the Military Commander, the payment of compensation to the victims of police action, the release of all those arrested during demonstrations in Macao, and a published apology by the Governor admitting his 'crimes'. Although the administration of the colony remained nominally in Portuguese hands their authority was much diminished and the communists were able to dictate internal policy.
3 Not printed.

pro-Communists. The statement was the strongest and most abusive about Hong Kong for some years.

3. On the same day the Governor of Hong Kong issued a statement emphasising that the police would only enforce the law when it was broken and were not there to involve themselves in labour disputes. The statement made it clear that the Government of Hong Kong would maintain law and order as impartially and fairly as possible for the benefit of all.

4. On 17 May the Commonwealth Office issued a statement in London (full text in Verbatim No. 214) giving facts about the disturbances, making it clear that the police had shown great restraint and had used minimum force, that the Labour Department in Hong Kong was at all times ready to assist in settling what was essentially a labour dispute and that HMG fully supported the Hong Kong Government in fulfilling its duty to maintain law and order.

Chinese Motives

5. All the available information suggests that the incidents of 6 May and later were not instigated from the mainland. They occurred however partly because control over pro-Communist organisations in Hong Kong from the mainland has recently slackened and local leaders and the rank and file have taken the initiative in acting in a militant fashion which they believe to be in keeping with the present atmosphere within China.

6. It is not yet possible to tell how far the Chinese will go in pressing their 'demands'. There are strong pressures within China tending towards intransigency. Few officials at present will dare to take the risk of being accused of adopting a soft line with the 'imperialists': the Russians have long taunted the Chinese with talking loud but doing little about imperialism on their doorstep and there will be those who argue that extremism in Hong Kong could pay off as well as it did in Macao. The Chinese may also hope that, by putting pressure on Hong Kong, they can prevent the colony being used by American warships and leave personnel.

7. On the other hand the Chinese stand to lose a great deal of foreign exchange if they push matters to such an extent that business confidence in Hong Kong is damaged and the economy is dislocated. They stand to lose even more by a direct bid to take over the Colony. They must also realise that Hong Kong is very different from Macao. Hong Kong has a large and efficient police force as well as sufficient troops to maintain order unless demonstrations reach a very large scale. It is likely also that within the Chinese leadership there are cooler heads who would advise caution and limiting of the present campaign to a war of nerves.

Demonstrations against the British Mission in China

8. Since 15 May there have been large scale demonstrations outside our office in Peking. Images of the Prime Minister have been burnt and slogans plastered over the walls. These demonstrations are likely to continue for some days but have so far been relatively well controlled. In Shanghai the situation has been more serious. The compound occupied by the First Secretary resident in Shanghai (the only British representative there) was invaded by a mob on 16 May and his house ransacked.[4] Neither he nor his wife and children were physically injured. But he was forced by

---

4 See Nos. 3 and 4.

the intruders to march up and down the compound for several hours. There have also been demonstrations at the British Consulate in Macao.

9. On 16 May we made a strong protest to the Chinese government about the demonstrations in Peking and the incident in Shanghai and asked them to provide guarantees for the safety of all subjects and property in China.[5]

The Outlook in Hong Kong

10. Demonstrations organised by the pro-Communists are likely to continue in Hong Kong for some time at least, but it is not possible to tell how much support the pro-Communists will be able to muster nor to what lengths they are prepared to carry them. One encouraging feature has been that non-politically aligned organisations in Hong Kong have been coming out in support of the measures so far taken by the authorities. Morale in the police and auxiliary forces remains extremely high and there is a great proportion of the Chinese population in Hong Kong which has a vested interest in the maintenance of order and economic stability. By firm and unprovocative handling of the situation the Hong Kong authorities should be able to keep the situation under control and ride the present storm.

11. All the above may be used freely (except paras 5 and 6 which are primarily for your own information although they may be used with friendly colleagues and particularly close contacts).

5 See No. 5.

No. 8

Mr Brown to Mr Hopson (Peking), 19 May 1967, 8.20 p.m.[1]
Tel. No. 351 Immediate, Confidential (FCO 21/63, FC 3/3/A)

I summoned the Chinese Acting Chargé d'Affaires on 19 May and delivered a very strong oral protest about the treatment of your Mission in Peking and Shanghai.

2. I said that on 16 May the Chargé had refused to convey a message of protest from me to his government (see my Telegram No. 322).[2] A similar protest made in Peking had been thrown out of the door. No government in relations with another could accept such behaviour.

3. I told the Chargé that my officials in China were being subjected to atrocious treatment. The Commercial Counsellor[3] had been harassed by hooligans and Hewitt in Shanghai literally frogmarched for hours in his own compound. Even more shameful, his wife and young children had been terrorised by a mob of hooligans. Our property had been sacked and defaced and a portrait of the Queen had been smeared and insulted.

4. I made it quite clear to the Chargé that such behaviour would not do. We expected the same treatment for our people and property as was given to the Chinese

1 Repeated for information to Hong Kong, POLAD Singapore and Saving to Washington.
2 No. 5.
3 Mr Peters.

in London. I reserved our right to claim all necessary compensation and told the Chargé to inform his Government that we expected different treatment from now on.

5. I added that I wished to hear no more nonsense about 'fascist atrocities'. I had as long a record of anti-fascism as he had. Such words should not be used to my officials nor should the Chinese Press Office in London abuse our hospitality by publishing these insults here. I asked him to convey my very strong feelings on this matter to his Government.

6. The Chargé attempted to say that it was natural and proper for the Chinese people to express in this way their indignation at the 'bloody suppression' of Chinese in Hong Kong. I said that I would not expect to be allowed to say this kind of thing in China and had no intention of allowing him to abuse my hospitality by using such language here and then terminated the interview.

7. I am making the substance of the paragraphs 1 to 5 above (with the exception of the last sentence of paragraph 2) available to the press.

No. 9

Mr Brown to Mr Hopson (Peking), 22 May 1967, 7.24 p.m.[1]
Tel. No. 372 Confidential (FCO 21/33, FC 1/14/A)

Your Tels. Nos. 544 and 545.[2]

Please pass the following message from me to the Chinese Minister for Foreign Affairs. I am also giving a copy to the Chinese Chargé d'Affaires here for transmission.

Begins.

Mr Hopson, the UK Chargé d'Affaires in Peking, has reported to me that your Government wishes to annul unilaterally the arrangement reached between our two Governments in 1954 whereby we maintain one officer resident in Shanghai. You will understand that an agreement mutually reached between two parties cannot be unilaterally annulled. To do so would derogate from the very basis of the principle of international relations which is that sovereign powers proceed in their bilateral affairs by negotiation and consent. If your Excellency wishes to review the arrangement of 1954 under reference negotiations to that end may take place at any time between our two Governments, whether in London or in Peking. If you would like to propose such discussions I shall be happy to agree.

I further understand that Mr Hewitt, the officer of the office of the UK Chargé d'Affaires resident in Shanghai, has been asked to leave Shanghai within 48 hours. Because of the treatment to which Mr Hewitt and his family have been subjected without any protection being afforded I had already decided to withdraw him from Shanghai at the earliest opportunity. I intend to proceed as planned but this action in no way constitutes my acceptance or acquiescence in a unilateral decision by the

---

1 Repeated for information to Hong Kong, POLAD Singapore and Washington.
2 Not printed. Mr Hopson reported that he had been summoned by Vice Minister Lo Kuei-po and informed that in view of events in Hong Kong the Chinese Government had decided to annul the arrangement where the British had one officer resident in Shanghai.

Government of the Chinese People's Republic to annul an agreement freely reached by both sides. I therefore propose to nominate Mr R. W. Whitney to replace Mr Hewitt and shall be very glad to have your acceptance of this nomination.

Ends.

2. Please report by Flash telegram as soon as you have delivered this message.

3. Please see my immediately following telegram.

No. 10

Minute from Mr Rodgers to Mr Brown, 23 May 1967
Secret (FCO 21/63, FC 3/3/A)

I saw the Chinese Acting Chargé d'Affaires this morning at his request. I thought there was no advantage to be gained by my refusing to see him.

2. The main purpose of his visit was to insist on an answer to the 'five just demands' of 15 May[1] and to engage in some further abuse about Hong Kong. Nothing he said advanced the argument or requires new initiatives from us. Shanghai was not mentioned.

3. The present position on Shanghai is this. We do not expect a reply to your telegram to Ch'en Yi saying that you refuse to accept the unilateral closing of our Shanghai post.[2] This means that Hewitt is likely to leave with his family by about noon our time tomorrow, Wednesday the 24th. Whitney is likely to be forced to leave soon after. The Shanghai post will then be closed and this is likely to be known either by tomorrow evening 24 May or the morning of Thursday the 25th.

4. If we are to take retaliatory action it would best be done without much delay, especially in view of anticipated public reactions here. We will be expected to declare our intentions soon after events in Shanghai are known.

5. The course which most recommends itself is to expel the New China News Agency. This would probably mean asking eight Chinese to leave within 48 hours. We will of course inform Peking and Hong Kong what we have in mind.

6. Expulsion may not be as straightforward as we thought. It looks as if it will require the Home Office invoking powers which they may be reluctant to use. We are however pursuing this at official level, and I will speak to the Home Secretary and if need be to the Attorney.[3]

7. Subject to problems being overcome and to any unforeseen developments, do you agree that we should aim to expel the New China News Agency following the approximate timetable I have indicated? We would of course telegraph Moscow for your approval when we were ready to move.

8. I should make it clear in view of yesterday's uncertainties that I recommend this course with Arthur de la Mare's agreement.

W. RODGERS

1 See No. 1, footnote 2.
2 No. 9.
3 The Attorney-General, Sir E. Jones.

No. 11

Mr Brown to Mr Hopson (Peking), 23 May 1967, 4.54 p.m.[1]
Tel. No. 385 Immediate, Confidential (FCO 21/204, FD 1/6/A)

Hong Kong.

The Chinese Acting Chargé d'Affaires called at his own request at 11 a.m. on 23 May to make an oral démarche about Hong Kong. He was seen by Mr Rodgers.

2. The Chargé referred to his meeting on 19 May[2] with the Secretary of State and said that he had not on that occasion had an opportunity to refute Mr Brown's 'shameful imperialist language'. In addition Mr Brown had on 22 May (presumably on BBC *Panorama*) 'viciously attacked the Chinese people'. He said that large scale 'fascist atrocities' in Hong Kong were the direct result of collusion of US and Chiang[3] clique and referred to the 'beating up and arresting of Chinese compatriots' and 'sanguinary suppression'. The Chinese Government resolutely backed the just action of the people of Hong Kong and stood behind them.

3. The Chargé then said that HMG had not only failed to reply to the five Chinese demands but had allowed the situation to go from bad to worse. He demanded that:

(*a*) Persecution in Hong Kong should cease.

(*b*) HMG should immediately accept the five 'solemn and just' Chinese demands.

(*c*) HMG should make an immediate reply.

4. He concluded by saying that China was determined to continue the struggle. HMG would be responsible for all the serious consequences of their actions.

5. Mr Rodgers said that he was disappointed that the Chargé should talk such arrogant nonsense. He categorically rejected the Chinese allegations about Hong Kong and said the language in which they were couched and the remarks about the Secretary of State were completely unacceptable. If the Chinese had a Note to leave in these terms it would not be accepted. We were always ready to discuss with the Chinese matters of common concern but no discussions were possible if the Chinese used the language not of diplomacy but of propaganda.

1 Repeated for information to Hong Kong, Washington and POLAD Singapore.
2 See No. 8.
3 Chiang Kai-shek.

No. 12

Mr Brown to Mr Hopson (Peking), 23 May 1967, 6.34 p.m.[1]
Tel. No. 387 Immediate Restricted (FCO 21/ 63)

My telegram No. 372:[2] Message to Ch'en Yi.

As it proved impossible to summon a senior member of the Chinese Chargé

1 Repeated for information to Hong Kong, POLAD Singapore and Washington.
2 No. 9.

d'Affaires office on the evening of 22 May, message was delivered to that office, with a Note requesting transmission to Peking.

2. The Note was later returned unopened. I caused the Chinese to be told on the telephone that I wished the message to be transmitted urgently and would send it back for that purpose. They said that the Note and the message had been returned on instruction from the Chargé, and again refused to accept it.

3. It was clear that the Chinese had noted the contents of the message and the action was quite deliberate. No further attempt was therefore made to deliver it.

No. 13

Memorandum from the Board of Trade on United Kingdom Trade with China, 25 May 1967
Confidential (FCO 21/63, FC 3/3/A)

Effect of Rupture of Diplomatic Relations

If a diplomatic break with China were to result in a complete stoppage of our trade in both directions, there would be temporary difficulties for some British industries but no insurmountable problems on a national scale. The longer term effects on our trade prospects in this growing market might however be considerable.

2. UK exports to China in 1965 totalled £31.9 million, and imports from China £33.8 million. China thus accounts for only about ½ per cent of United Kingdom total overseas trade.

3. Unless trade is deliberately restricted by one side or the other, broadly similar figures are expected for 1967. There are no signs as yet of the Cultural Revolution affecting to any noticeable extent the mount of trade currently taking place between this country and China, but future prospects are uncertain.

4. Our exports to China consist mainly of non-electrical machinery (33 per cent of total 1966 exports), iron and steel (19 per cent), electrical machinery (10 per cent), and non-ferrous metals (9 per cent). Principal imports from China were wool, silk and other textile fibres (19 per cent), bristles and other crude animal and vegetable materials (12 per cent), textile yarns, fabrics and made up articles (11 per cent) and vegetable oils (11 per cent).

5. With few exceptions, notably bristles and tungsten, where China is a major supplier and where alternative supplies might be difficult to obtain at short notice, imports from China consist of goods which could readily be obtained from other sources, although possibly at somewhat higher prices. Goods normally supplied to Britain would probably find their way in due course to third country markets, and could be purchased there. More serious from the standpoint of British industry would be any abrupt cessation of our exports. It would for example be difficult and in many cases be impossible to find markets for machinery and equipment being manufactured against specific orders from China, and with iron and steel and non-ferrous metals both in world surplus, it might be difficult to find alternative markets for these too. However, any cessation of shipments of British machinery and equipment

would be even more disruptive of Chinese plans, and it is unlikely that the Chinese would of their own volition interfere with existing orders.

6. While the immediate effects of a break in direct trade could be in time be surmounted, the longer term effects on our exports could be serious. China is a rapidly growing market for British and other Western countries goods. If trade links are once broken, it might be very difficult to regain our position in the Chinese market in face of competition from Japan, West Germany, France and other competitors whose exports to China are already growing more strongly than our own.

No. 14

Extract from the minutes of a meeting of the Cabinet Defence and Oversea Committee, 25 May 1967, 9.45 a.m.[1]
OPD(67)20th Secret (CAB 148/30)

2. *Hong Kong.*

The Committee considered a memorandum by the Secretary of State for Commonwealth Affairs (OPD(67)39)[2] on the situation in Hong Kong.

THE COMMONWEALTH SECRETARY said that, arising out of labour troubles, major disturbances had occurred in Hong Kong linked with hostile demonstrations in Shanghai and Peking and with the expulsion of our representative in Shanghai. It appeared that recent development in China's 'cultural revolution' had resulted in a loosening of control by mainland China of the communists in Hong Kong. It was not known how far the Government of the People's Republic of China, to whom our presence in Hong Kong brought considerable economic benefits, had now decided to go in bringing pressure on us. They might be seeking a propaganda victory as the price for calling off the disturbances, or trying to force us to accept a position of subservience on the lines which the Portuguese had to accept in Macao,[3] or they might even have decided to drive us out of Hong Kong completely. There were no indications, however, that the mainland Chinese were seeking to restrain the Communists in Hong Kong. We could not resist a determined attempt to force us out altogether, nor could we tolerate a situation similar to that in Macao. Our resistance to the latter might compel China to resort to driving us out. A study of the implications of a sudden withdrawal from Hong Kong should now be set in hand. Our immediate responsibility, however, was to maintain law and order and keep up morale and confidence so that Hong Kong's economy could continue to flourish. This would require firm action but we should avoid as far as possible

1 Committee members present at this meeting were: Mr Wilson, Mr Stewart, Mr Bowden, Mr Callaghan (Chancellor of the Exchequer), Mr Healey (Secretary of State for Defence), Mr Jenkins (Home Secretary), Mr Jay (President of the Board of Trade), The Earl of Longford (Lord Privy Seal), Mr Bottomley (Minister of Overseas Development), Mr Wigg (Paymaster-General), Mr Mulley (Minister of State for Foreign Affairs), Mrs Hart (Minister of State for Commonwealth Affairs), Sir R. Hull (Chief of the Defence Staff), Sir J. Grandy (Chief of the Air Staff), Sir J. Bush (Vice Chief of the Naval Staff), Sir D. Fitzpatrick (Vice Chief of the General Staff) and Sir B. Trend.
2 Not printed. Reproduced in *BDEE*, Series A, Volume 5, Part III, No. 334.
3 See No. 7, footnote 2.

action which China would regard as provocative. The commando carrier, HMS Bulwark, was being sent to Hong Kong, and the Governor had already been authorised to neutralise several of the buildings from which the Chinese campaign against us was being conducted by loudspeakers. The Governor should now be given authority to arrest and, if possible deport a few (limited to two or three in the first instance), of the known leaders of the present campaign. The Governor should also be given a general authority to take emergency powers to close down the printing press of the principal communist newspaper in Hong Kong, subject to consulting him (the Commonwealth Secretary) on each individual case. We should also press the Governor to introduce extensive and long overdue improvements in the labour legislation including shortening hours of work of women and young persons. In the background of our difficulties with China lay their irritation at the facilities which the United States Forces in Vietnam enjoyed in Hong Kong. We had recently restricted visits of United States warships to the same number as last year and had suggested that larger ships should not come. We should not however take any further actions at present since it would be claimed by the Chinese as a propaganda victory but we should keep the matter under review. On our latest information the situation appeared to be quieter. Firm though restrained action by the Governor and the police had prevented the disturbances spreading. The strike called by the communist Trade Unions had been only partially successful and public transport would shortly be back to normal. There was no truth in the story being put out by Peking of heavy Chinese casualties.

Discussion showed that the Committee were in general agreement with the views of the Commonwealth Secretary. The actions of the Governor and the police, who had kept control of the situation without having to call upon troops, deserved the highest praise, and in particular it would be appropriate to send a message of congratulation to the police, designed particularly for publication in Hong Kong. The opportunity should be taken of the disturbances to press through urgently improvements in labour legislation, if necessary by use of the official majority in the Executive Council and Legislative Council. The suggestion was made that Mr Ernest Thornton, MP, a former Parliamentary Secretary, Ministry of Labour, accompanied by a leading British trade unionist, might visit the colony to advise on labour relations, but it was pointed out that a report produced in December 1965 by the Labour Adviser to the Commonwealth Office had covered fully and admirably what should be done and it remained only to implement its recommendations. The unofficial members of the Hong Kong Government had up to now resisted these but their attitude might well be different in the light of the recent troubles. In any event, effect must soon be given to the recommendations. In considering the wider problems posed by Hong Kong, the point was made that while Hong Kong was of greater economic value to China than to the United Kingdom, there appeared to be a difference of view within the Chinese Government about whether the present status of Hong Kong should be maintained. An element in Peking appeared willing to sacrifice the economic benefits China derived from Hong Kong to the purity of doctrine of the 'cultural revolution'. We could not rely on remaining in Hong Kong on present terms until our lease of the New Territories lapsed. We should therefore consider what adaptations of the status of Hong Kong might be possible and desirable after the conclusion of the present conflict in Vietnam. We should also consider what steps would be necessary if we were forced to evacuate the Colony.

The Committee:

(1) Approved the recommendations in OPD(67)39 regarding the action to be taken in Hong Kong.

(2) Invited the Commonwealth Secretary, in consultation with the Minister of State for Foreign Affairs, to send to the Governor an appropriate message of congratulation to the Hong Kong Police.

(3) Invited the Commonwealth Secretary, in consultation with the Chancellor of the Exchequer, the Defence Secretary, the President of the Board of Trade and the Minister of State for Foreign Affairs, to arrange for officials to consider our policy in respect of Hong Kong in the long term, on the lines indicated in discussion.

No. 15

Mr Hopson (Peking) to Mr Brown, 6 June 1967
Confidential (FCO 21/64, FC 3/3/B)

Reactions in Peking and Shanghai to the recent Hong Kong disturbances
Part II (23rd May to 3rd June)

Sir,

With reference to my despatch No. 9S of the 24th of May[1] I have the honour to continue my account of events in Peking and Shanghai, in connection with the recent Hong Kong disturbances. The period under review is the 23rd of May to the 3rd of June.

2. On the 24th of May the *People's Daily* published a New China News Agency report which stated that on the 22nd of May 'at least 200 compatriots were killed or seriously injured' in Hong Kong and Kowloon. It seemed that this blatantly inflammatory distortion of facts would almost certainly lead to renewed demonstrations against this Office. Fortunately for us, however, the Chinese discovered from the same issue of *People's Daily* that a new enemy, the Mongolian People's Republic, was now committing 'fascist atrocities' against them; on the 21st of May there had been incidents at Ulan Bator railway station involving the arrest of Chinese teachers and students and the detention of Chinese diplomatic personnel. Accordingly, in Peking the spearhead of the struggle—as Maoist jargon would put it—was turned upon the Mongolian Embassy, which now became the target for several days of demonstrations on the familiar pattern. There was one set-piece mass march-past outside my house and Office on the afternoon of the 26th of May. Unaware perhaps that my staff are now working summer hours, the New China News Agency afterwards commented 'the British officials were so scared they dared not appear'. With this exception and apart from sporadic demonstrations by small groups, we have been spared the attention of the revolutionary masses during the period reviewed in this despatch.

3. Meanwhile in Shanghai my First Secretary, Mr Whitney, who you will recall, Sir, had gone there to relieve Mr Hewitt, was informed by the Foreign Affairs

---

1 Not printed.

Department on the 23rd of May that, as our post in Shanghai no longer existed his function as diplomatic courier would lapse on Mr Hewitt's departure. There having been no response from the Chinese to your message to Ch'en Yi inviting discussion of the Shanghai question, I instructed Mr Whitney to come back to Peking with Mr Hewitt and his family on the 24th of May.

4. Since we have not accepted the formal closure of the Shanghai post, Mr Hewitt informed the Chinese staff that the British Government continued to employ them, and he paid them up to the end of June. The entire Chinese staff then insisted on discussing their future terms of employment (including pensions) with Mr Hewitt and Mr Whitney: talks began at half past six on the evening of the 23rd of May and continued for the next 13 hours. An agreed statement (at Annex A)[1] was eventually signed by Mr Hewitt acknowledging in general terms this Office's responsibility toward the Chinese staff in Shanghai. If and when final closure of the post is accepted by us, there are likely to be difficult negotiations with the Chinese over sale and disposal of the property and severance pay for the staff.

5. Mr Whitney and Mr Hewitt and his family left Shanghai on the morning of the 24th of May. They were subjected to a carefully organised 'send-off' by the Chinese which began when they left the gates of the compound and ended an hour and a half later when they boarded the aeroplane for Peking. This atrocious treatment outdid anything done to the Missions here last February, and occurred despite the fact that the Shanghai Foreign Affairs Department were requested and had undertaken (albeit in a very rude reply) to guarantee their security during departure. Although Mrs Hewitt and the children escaped the worst, thanks to the help of friends including the Polish Consul-General in Shanghai, both Mr Hewitt and Mr Whitney were kicked, struck, had glue poured on them and their clothes torn. One feature of the departure from Shanghai was the remarkable loyalty shown by one or two members of the Chinese staff. With great courage and total disregard for their own position they gave invaluable assistance to Mr Hewitt and Mr Whitney. The rest of the staff followed the mainstream in expressing bitter hostility to the British Government and its representatives, although some of them indicated privately to Mr and Mrs Hewitt that they were very sorry to have to do so.

6. The party, who were even denied the normal courtesies on the Chinese flight arrived in Peking battered but unbowed. I immediately protested to the Foreign Ministry at this gross violation of diplomatic immunity, adding that it was made worse by the fact that Mr Whitney was travelling, as the Ministry was aware, as a diplomatic courier. I sent copies of the Note to the Acting Dean of the Diplomatic Corps and all my colleagues.

7. Our first attempts to get Mr Hewitt and his family out of China on a Russian flight on the 27th of May were obstructed by the Chinese who delayed the issue of exit visas until the airport authorities had informed us that the ticket reservations could no longer be held. They eventually left on a Chinese flight on the 31st of May, safely and without incident.

8. On the morning of the 26th of May none of the Chinese office staff or domestic staff reported for duty. Shortly after opening time they all arrived at the Office and proceeded to demonstrate in the courtyard, chanting slogans, songs and readings from Mao. A small delegation stayed in the waiting room insisting that I should

come out and receive a petition. I nominated a junior member of my diplomatic staff to receive it but this was not accepted. By lunch time, several older members of the Chinese staff appeared to be wilting after some four hours in the sun. I therefore offered to receive a delegation of three in my office provided the petition was presented in the correct manner. This was 'put to the masses' and rejected.

9. The strike continued for the next three days. Each day (except Sunday, which brought welcome respite to both sides) the elaborate charade of negotiations over the terms of handing over the petition was rehearsed for several hours. During the conversations the 'revolutionary masses' (all the Chinese staff except nine representatives engaged in parleying) became increasingly recalcitrant. When their liturgical circumambulations of the Office failed to move Jericho, they resorted to impeding my exit from the compound and then from the Office itself. Tactics became more aggressive and by the morning of the 29th of May it was clear that if we did not achieve some solution I would shortly be faced with a mass sit-in with the Office building itself. After another bout of lengthy negotiations involving a certain amount of give and take I agreed to receive the 'protest' at the front door of the Office flanked by the senior members of my staff. The proceedings were comparatively courteous. After a very short recital from Mao's Thought the 'protest' which was a hodge-podge of previous Chinese statements on Hong Kong (Annex B)[2] was read out in Chinese by one of the Office translators. The spokesman concluded by saying that the Chinese staff wanted a quick reply.

10. I made the concession to receive this protest much against the grain, but in some respects it turned out to be a better solution than it might have been. Originally the Chinese staff had proposed speeches by up to nine of their delegates, to which I was not to be allowed to reply. I insisted that if they spoke I would have to speak too. They rejected this and finally agree that there would be no speeches, just the reading of the protest. On the following day the staff returned to work, no doubt glad not to have been obliged to miss pay-day. Whether they will stay back or whether they will find some pretext for further walk-outs remains to be seen.

11. On the 27th of May the Chinese Foreign Minister Ch'en Yi spoke at a reception given by the Afghan Ambassador in Peking to mark his country's National Day. In the course of his speech Ch'en Yi alleged that the British authorities in Hong Kong were continuing their 'atrocities' against his compatriots and said that the British Government must immediately accept the Chinese demands. At this point I shook hands with the Ambassador and left the reception, accompanied by my wife and members of my staff.

12. The official Chinese Press has continued to publish two or three articles every day on Hong Kong, but it is my impression that, despite the loudness of tone and the extravagance of language employed, the reporting since the 22nd of May has been less blatantly inflammatory and the comment has had more bark than bite. For example, the front-page leading editorial of *People's Daily* on the 3rd of June which was entitled 'Resolutely repel British Imperialist Provocations' contained no reference to the Chinese Foreign Ministry Statement and five demands of the 15th of May. I have none the less taken action to counter some the cruder Chinese propaganda here:

2 Not printed.

on the 29th of May I issued with our daily BBC news bulletin, which is circulated to most other diplomatic missions, a statement of facts and figures about the current situation in Hong Kong. My purpose was chiefly to set the record straight for my diplomatic colleagues on the number of casualties during the disturbances, since it was becoming evident that some of them had no other source of information than the Chinese Press. I also circulated the statement made in the House of Commons by Mrs Hart on the 1st of June.[3]

13. For the present, at least, life in this Mission is almost back to 'normal'. Nevertheless, the Chinese have resorted to a series of 'pinpricks' to harass us, such as refusing to allow diplomatic officers to go to Tientsin to collect shipments from the port of Hsinkang, excluding us from the invitation to spend holidays at the nearby seaside resort of Peitaho and refusing to handle heavy baggage belonging to my staff. However, we are not unaccustomed to such treatment here and are taking our present course of 'acupuncture' with equanimity. A more serious incident, although not directly concerned with this Mission, was the Chinese threat to the Shanghai Branch Manager of the Hong Kong and Shanghai Banking Corporation on the 31st of May, that they would not grant him an exit visa from China until he apologised 'for all the crimes' committed by his Bank since 1949 (the date was later modified to 1955). At present this matter is still unresolved. Meanwhile, also at Shanghai, five British and Australian officers of the British ship *Eastern Moon* have been detained for 'insulting behaviour', and will not be allowed to rejoin their ship.

14. I hope this despatch may prove to be the last in this series, and that at least the more violent phase of this unfortunate chapter in the Sino-British relations is now over. That, however, will depend mainly on what happens in Hong Kong and I fear we may be in for a long period of unpleasantness.

I am sending copies of this despatch without enclosures, to Her Majesty's Representatives at Washington, Tokyo, Bangkok, Canberra, Ottawa and Ulan Bator, to the Governor of Hong Kong and to the Political Adviser to the Commander-in-Chief, Far East, at Singapore.[4]

I have, etc,
D. C. HOPSON

3 *Parl. Debs., 5th ser., H. of C.* 1 June 1967, vol. 747 cols. 266-74.
4 Mr Wilson recommended the despatch be given full Commonwealth distribution: 'There would be no harm if the gist of the contents leaked back to the Chinese through, e.g. the Pakistanis.'

No. 16

Mr Hopson (Peking) to Mr Brown, 6 June 1967
Confidential (FCO 21/204, FD 1/6/A)

China: Chinese policies towards Hong Kong

Sir,
For nearly 20 years the Chinese Communists have been prepared to accept a workable if, at times, uneasy relationship with the Crown colony of Hong Kong.

Now they seem set on a course which will jeopardise this relationship. In this despatch I have the honour to suggest some possible explanations of this development and to examine the question of whether it signifies a change in China's basic policy towards Hong Kong.

2. The point to be made is that the Hong Kong disturbances were almost certainly not premeditated by the Chinese Government. The reports from His Excellency the Governor clearly indicate that the development of the industrial dispute at the San Po Kong plastic flower factory took the Left-wing leadership in Hong Kong by surprise, and that most of the running was made by a group of young extremists. No doubt these people were fired by synthetic enthusiasms of Chinese Cultural Revolution, which had also had the effect of releasing them from the former tight control of the Communist hierarchy. Presumably they were also encouraged by the apparently easy victories gained over the Portuguese authorities in Macao in January and, perhaps, over the Royal Inter-Ocean Line in Hong Kong in a recent dispute concerning the treatment of the Chinese seamen by a master of one of their ships.[1] It is, of course, possible that these extremists received explicit orders from their counterparts in Canton or Peking, but it seems rather more likely that they were acting on their own initiative. Developments in Peking tend to confirm the view that the leadership here was in fact taken by surprise by the escalation of the Hong Kong dispute. The disturbances in Hong Kong began on the 6th of May but it was not until the 15th of May that there was a reaction of any kind from the Chinese authorities. At 6 a.m. on that day the summons came for me to attend the Ministry of Foreign Affairs (as I described in despatch No. 9S)[2] and when I met Vice-Minister Lo Kuei-po I gained the strong impression that he had been engaged in night-long deliberations.

3. The product of these deliberations was the Ministry of Foreign Affairs statement which seemed to mark a significant change in Chinese policy towards Hong Kong. Up to that time the events in the colony were such that, on the pattern of previous years, it would have been possible for the Chinese to have confined themselves to a few hostile clichés in the Press or even to have ignored them altogether. Instead, they produced a strongly worded statement which encouraged the extremists in Hong Kong and made specific and aggressive demands on the Hong Kong Government. Thus it appeared that the gauntlet was thrown down, the collision course set. Either the Hong Kong Government would have to accept demands which would seriously, perhaps fatally, harm its own authority or the Chinese would have to back down. The only certain prospect seemed to be that, whatever the final outcome, the stability, confidence and prosperity of Hong Kong would be bound to suffer.

4. The Chinese action, therefore, indicated that they were ready to put at risk their own interests, which are considerable, in the continuation of the *status quo* in Hong Kong. The exact value of Hong Kong to China in economic terms is impossible to compute with complete accuracy but is certainly very great. In 1966 Chinese export earnings from Hong Kong amounted to £173 million in convertible sterling, about one-quarter of her total export earnings. Earnings in Hong Kong this year

1 For events in Macao see No. 7, footnote 2.
2 Not printed. See No. 1.

are running at a still higher rate (£46 million for the first quarter compared to £36 million last year). Large amounts of foreign exchange also accrue to China from remittances by Chinese in Hong Kong to their families on the mainland. In addition to these economic considerations, it has long been believed that the Chinese also valued Hong Kong for the opportunities it affords for a variety of political contacts and intelligence gathering activities, and even as a kind of safety valve through which those irreconcilably at odds with the régime could be allowed to escape (c.f. the mass defections in 1962).[3] Chinese leaders were reported from time to time as saying in private that the problem of Hong Kong would only be solved at the same time as Formosa, and that meanwhile it was necessary to tolerate the present régime because of the economic benefits it brought to China's reconstruction programme.

5. In previous years these considerations, and perhaps, the fear that any direct action against Hong Kong might provoke an American response, have been sufficient to restrain Peking from using or creating disputes in Hong Kong to bring great pressure to bear on the Government of the colony. In the China of 1967 these considerations apparently no longer apply with same force.

6. The primary reasons for this are all directly related to the effects of the Cultural Revolution. The acceptance of capitalism on the Chinese doorstep, and their willingness to continue to profit from it, may now savour of Liu Shao-chi's 'black line'[4]. In any case the chauvinism generated by the revolutionary ferment in China must have made it much more difficult than it would have been in previous years for the Chinese Government not to come to the support of their 'revolutionary compatriots' in Hong Kong. Still more important, the situation in the colony must have seemed to offer, at least to the extremists in the Chinese leadership, hope of a cheap victory on the Macao pattern. At a time when the Cultural Revolution in China has run into the doldrums, such a prospect must have appeared attractive. It could be held out as another example of the invincibility of Mao's thought and of the value of extreme and uncompromising policies. At the very least, it could serve as another means of uniting the great majority behind the Government. What is more, some kind of success in Hong Kong would admirably compensate for the frustration the Chinese leaders must be suffering in regard to Indonesia, where the Chinese communities are being severely harassed and China is powerless to intervene.

7. There is no doubt that the continued existence of Hong Kong, as an 'imperialist' colony on Chinese territory, is an embarrassing anachronism to Peking. It is a situation about which the Russians, for example, frequently taunt the Chinese and one which is particularly difficult for them to accept at a time when the Cultural Revolution has released such a wave of aggressive nationalism. The movement has also served to heighten the contrast between the frenzy and turmoil on the mainland and the steady progress achieved in Hong Kong. Furthermore, as the war in Viet-Nam has escalated, the increasing number of visits by United States warships to Hong Kong for rest and recreation has been a growing source of embarrassment, particularly *vis-à-vis* their allies in Hanoi.

---

3 In fact, the vast majority of refugees from mainland China to Hong Kong in 1962 were escaping famine and did so without the connivance of the Chinese Government.

4 A reference to the fact that he had been denounced as a 'capitalist roader'—someone who was pulling the revolution in a capitalist direction.

8. Nevertheless the policy advocated by the extremists, or at least the policy accepted by the leadership, probably stops short of a physical takeover of Hong Kong. It seems likely that the main intention is (or was) to humiliate the Hong Kong Government, force it to acknowledge Chinese supremacy and make it more responsive to Peking pressure in the future. This, no doubt, seemed to offer the best hope of a 'success' with the minimum damage to China's economic and other interests in maintaining the present situation in Hong Kong.

9. Another important factor in Peking's decision to aggravate the disturbances in Hong Kong was, undoubtedly the present confused position within the Ministry of Foreign Affairs and the Chinese leadership itself. Nominally, decisions concerning Chinese foreign policy are still the direct responsibility of Ch'en Yi as Foreign Minister and Chou En-lai as Prime Minister, two men who for more than a decade have been the main architects of relatively cautious and pragmatic external policies. However, Ch'en Yi has been severely criticised for some months and it is by no means clear who is actually controlling the Ministry of Foreign Affairs. It is perhaps significant that on the 13th of May, two days before the publication of the Chinese statement on Hong Kong, the Ministry was the scene of serious strife created by 'revolutionary rebels' among its staff. Decisions taken in such an atmosphere are quite likely to disregard the dictates of reason and there are, in fact, grave temptations to those responsible for making decisions to show themselves as real revolutionaries, by acquiescing in adventurist policies over Hong Kong.

10. For some, or all, of the reasons listed in the foregoing paragraphs the Chinese have got themselves into a position where they have challenged British rule in Hong Kong. Their main aim, as I have suggest in paragraph 8 above, seems to be to demonstrate their power to interfere in the colony. There are various indications that they may also have a number of subsidiary objectives; for example, to force us to restrict or completely withdraw the facilities offered to United States ships and servicemen in Hong Kong, to curtail the activities of KMT organisations and to compel us to allow much greater freedom for Chinese propaganda activities in the colony.

11. The latest indications are, however, that the Chinese are beginning to realise that in Hong Kong they are not going to be allowed to achieve a cheap victory on the pattern of Macao. For example, a *People's Daily* editorial of the 3rd of June, although couched in relatively menacing terms, makes no mention of the five demands in the Chinese statement on the 15th of May. If the Chinese were really determined to insist on the fulfilment of their demands one might have expected them, by now, to have stopped their supply of water to the colony or even to have made threatening troop movements on the border. On the contrary, it looks as if they may be preparing to forget their demands, while planning to keep up a steady pressure on the Hong Kong Government by a long campaign of strikes in factories and schools in Hong Kong and by a propaganda offensive. If this campaign does not bring results, it is possible that after a few months, they will drop it. The longer the affair drags on, the better the chances that the more moderate voices in the Chinese Government will be able to reassert themselves.

12. So far in this dispute, there has been no sign that the Chinese leadership has yet decided that the time has come to try to end British rule in Hong Kong. Nevertheless the problem of Hong Kong and its future has been brought to the surface with such

a bang, that we can no longer be sure that the Chinese will feel able to accept the continuation of the present status of Hong Kong almost indefinitely, as we might have imagined until recently. 'The day of reckoning', to use Chinese parlance, has probably come nearer and, as I have tried to show in earlier paragraphs, China to-day is in a very difficult and explosive mood. One cannot be sure that policy decisions will be taken in accord with the logic of the situation. If the extremists in Hong Kong forced the situation there to get out of control or if the leadership in Peking felt badly enough the need for a real victory, there would then be a strong possibility that the Chinese would decide on a physical intervention in the colony.

I am sending copies of this despatch to Her Majesty's Representatives at Washington, Tokyo, Bangkok, Canberra and Ottawa, to the Governor of Hong Kong and to the Political Adviser to the Commander-in-Chief, Far East at Singapore.[5]

I have, etc,
D. C. HOPSON

5 Mr Wilson commented internally: 'Mr Hopson's Despatch is on almost exactly the same line as what we ourselves have been saying. One almost suspects collusion!' In view of the 'great interest' in Chinese policy towards Hong Kong copies were sent for circulation, including through the JIC machinery.

No. 17

Paper by the Far Eastern Department on the Present Situation in China
8 June 1967
Confidential (FCO 21/11, FC 1/1/D)

Summary

Hard evidence on internal events in China is as difficult to obtain as ever. There are, however, clear indications of mounting and serious difficulties for the Maoist leadership who are trying without much success to extend the 'Cultural Revolution' throughout the country and to impose order and discipline on their supporters, the Revolutionary Rebels and Red Guards. There has been much confusion and indiscipline together with some violence and bloodshed. Many provinces are apparently under military rule and others do not seem to be fully controlled by Peking. Official attacks on the Head of State, Liu Shao-ch'i, and unofficial attacks on more 'moderate' Ministers continue, while the cleavage in the leadership between the radical group under Mao Tse-tung supported by the Minister of Defence, Lin Piao, on the one hand, and moderates on the other is still evident.

2. This means that in foreign affairs the second group which includes the Foreign Minister, Ch'en Yi, are under pressure to react more strongly than usual to external situations such as Hong Kong in which China's interests or prestige are engaged. This does not constitute in our view a fundamental change by China to new or 'aggressive' foreign policies but does mean that for Hong Kong we cannot rely to the same extent as in the past on China's recognition of the economic value of this Colony, causing her in all circumstances to maintain the *status quo*. There

is no evidence that the Chinese intend to take over Hong Kong—the latest official Peking pronouncement suggests that they are contemplating a long drawn out struggle. But if large scale disturbances with attendant bloodshed were to occur in Hong Kong or undisciplined elements from neighbouring Kwangtung province broke into the Colony, a situation could arise in which the Chinese leadership in the present overheated and chauvinistic atmosphere of the Cultural Revolution would be impelled to give full support to local pro-Communists and conditions might then be created which the Hong Kong Government would be unable to control. The continuation of a firm but unprovocative policy in Hong Kong and the avoidance of unnecessary retaliatory action against Peking for the treatment of our officials is therefore likely to remain the best means of helping Hong Kong to ride out the present storm.

The Cultural Revolution

3. The main theme of the Cultural Revolution remains the attack in the official press on the Head of State, Liu Shao-ch'i. A mass of historical material continues to be produced in an attempt to prove that he has consistently opposed Mao and his policies for many years, and efforts are now being made to associate him directly with Peng Chen (the ex-Mayor of Peking who was disgraced last year). Many of the charges are obviously nonsense. A lesser victim associated with this attack is the General Secretary of the Party, Teng Hsiao-p'ing.

4. At the same time, the Red Guard press and posters have continued to make unofficial attacks against a number of Vice-Premiers. The most prominent of these have been T'an Chen-lin (an agricultural expert) and Ch'en Yi, the Minister for Foreign Affairs. It is not yet possible to say what the outcome of these attacks will be or whether they will lead to the dismissal of those concerned. The fact that Chou En-lai has taken these Ministers under his powerful and protective wing might well save them.

5. Instructions from the Central authorities in the form of editorials indicate that yet another attempt is being made to impose order and discipline. The *Peking Daily* of 22 May carried a very strong editorial against 'struggle by force'. Although this suggests that the aim of those running the Cultural Revolution is to damp down the campaign and possibly also gradually bring it to an end, it is evident that this policy is running into difficulties. In particular it is proving extremely hard for the leadership to control the activities of Red Guards, who now have a life and momentum of their own, which is often at variance with official policy. It also appears that Peking is having difficulty in imposing its will on a number of provinces.

The situation in the Provinces

6. So far there have only been 6 officially approved 'revolutionary takeovers' i.e. in 4 out of the 26 Provinces and Autonomous Regions and in the cities of Peking and Shanghai—a very poor record after 5 months of effort. In a further 5 Provinces some progress towards a takeover has taken place. According to a report we have recently seen of a speech by the Prime Minister, Chou En-lai, (which was intended for Chinese internal consumption only and appears to be genuine), a majority, probably about 10 of the other provinces (including Kwangtung which borders on Hong Kong), appear to be under the effective control of the Army, which has been striving to restore order

and keep production going. Chou also indicated that in 7 provinces the situation was so unfavourable that no attempt had been made to endorse the local leadership.

7. It is clear, in general, that there is a state of considerable confusion in the provinces and there have been reliable reports of small scale armed clashes in Szechwan (West China) and Honan (Central China). Where order is being maintained this is being done by the Army and by the imposition of control from above rather than the theoretical Maoist method of seizure of power from below.

Foreign Policy

8. The Chinese leadership is clearly devoting its main attention to internal affairs. In foreign policy, China's recent actions have mainly been in the form of responses to external events and not initiatives. But the violent and chauvinistic atmosphere of the Cultural Revolution and attacks on 'moderates' such as the Foreign Minister and senior Foreign Ministry officials have affected the nature of their responses. There is good evidence that a group of revolutionary rebels in the Foreign Ministry exercises much influence, and there was a poster report of an incident on 13 May when groups of Red Guards broke into this Ministry in search of confidential matter to incriminate Ch'en Yi. However Ch'en Yi remains in charge and to some extent has been supported by Cho En-lai. The pressure of Red Guard activities probably means that Ch'en Yi and others under attack are forced to react strongly to external events, such as Hong Kong or the incidents in Ulan Bator involving Chinese teachers, even if they may not consider this to be in the best interests of China's foreign policy.

Hong Kong

9. The pro-Communist leadership in Hong Kong, having suffered a defeat in the first round of their confrontation with the Hong Kong Government, seem now to be reconsidering their tactics. They may well also be waiting for instructions from Peking. Meanwhile, they are organising short token strikes designed presumably to demonstrate their power and to keep up the morale of their supporters.

10. We do not yet know how far the Chinese intend to go in their policy towards Hong Kong. In reaching a decision the main factors will be:

(*a*) the undoubted economic value of Hong Kong to China (about 40% of her foreign exchange earnings come from there);

(*b*) the pressure of extremist opinion which would put 'politics' first and disregard the economic consequences;

(*c*) the Chinese Government's strong commitment to securing acceptance of their five demands.

11. It is reasonable to suppose that the Chinese leadership will be divided in their response to the pressure of (*a*) and (*b*). The 'administrators', who are those most likely to take account of economic consequences, are at the moment under severe criticism and there are therefore strong pressures on them to make concessions towards the 'extremists' in order to save themselves from further attack.

12. The most recent official pronouncement by the Chinese on Hong Kong—an editorial in the *People's Daily* of 3 June—has placed the immediate responsibility for waging the struggle not on China but on the people of Hong Kong, indicated that it should be mainly propagandist and industrial and that it will be a long-term operation. In this way Peking may hope to give the appearance of taking action without necessarily so disrupting Hong Kong as to cause themselves serious economic

damage. We can only hope that such policy will be continued. It is significant in this connection that for over a week now the 'five demands' have not been mentioned in the Chinese press or propaganda.[1]

1 This paper, written by Mr Bolland, was commissioned by Mr de la Mare as 'Ministers will wish to know the extent to which law and order had broken down in China'. Mr de la Mare believed that the situation was probably worse than depicted and thought China had reverted to her 'normal' state of chaos but 'we should keep our toe-hold in China as long as we possibly can'. Mr Brown noted: 'A very good paper'.

No. 18

Mr Brown to HM Representatives Overseas, 21 June 1967, 5.21 p.m.
Guidance Tel. No. 153 Priority, Confidential (PREM 13/1965)

China's H-Bomb
Verbatim No. 280/67

The Chinese Government announced on 18 June the explosion of a thermo-nuclear device. We had foreseen that the next Chinese explosion would be in the megaton range. There is no reason to doubt the Chinese claim that the test on 17 June was a thermonuclear device. We shall not be able to make a detailed assessment until all the debris has been collected and analysed but there has been indications that the yield is between 2-5 megatons. The Chinese are however undoubtedly still some way from an effective nuclear weapons system.

2. There are limitations on the production by the Chinese of a fully-fledged weapons system: fissile material and effective means of delivery. All the Chinese nuclear explosions so far have used enriched uranium. Their supplies of fissile material are believed to be small. Their stockpile of weapons can therefore also be expected to be small for some years.

3. As a means of delivery the Chinese have some light bombers and a few medium bombers, but all are obsolete and would be very vulnerable to a modern air defence system. In the missile field they may have operational medium-range missiles within 2 or 3 years but it is generally believed that they will not have intercontinental missiles until about the mid-1970s.

4. The Chinese nuclear programme has been generally ahead of western estimates and the new test can be expected to increase Chinese prestige throughout the non-aligned countries in Asia. India and Japan will be particularly concerned about the speed of China's nuclear progress. Japan still feels herself protected by her security treaty with the Americans but in India the Chinese test will certainly increase public pressure for an Indian bomb. Such pressure has in any case increased during the past year: but the Indian Government so far have resisted it.

5. It is now more urgent that ever for us to achieve a non-proliferation treaty which India can sign. The Indians attach much importance in this connection to assurance of their security. This concern is understandable, in view of China's development of nuclear weapons. The question of security guarantees by the nuclear powers against aggression with nuclear weapons or nuclear blackmail raises extensive problems which we are studying. No doubt once a draft non-proliferation treaty text can be

tabled in the ENDC [*sic* ?UNDC] at Geneva, these issues will be raised by the non-aligned representatives there. We very much hope a satisfactory solution will be found. This is more likely to be through the United Nations rather than by trying to include a specific clause in the non-proliferation treaty.

6. The Chinese explosion, though it may increase the pressure in America and Russia for a non-proliferation treaty, may well make other arms control agreements even more difficult to reach. It may for instance adversely affect the chances of Comprehensive Test Ban Treaty, and it will no doubt lead to further pressure on the American and Soviet Governments to deploy anti-missile systems which would provide a good defence against China.

7. In order not to lessen the chances of progress towards arms control measures, we consider it best to react moderately to this latest Chinese test. If asked to comment you may draw unattributably on the above to show that the latest test does not in our view radically alter the situation.

No. 19

Mr Hopson (Peking) to Mr Brown, 21 June 1967
Confidential (FCO 21/64, FC 3/3/B)

China: Anti-British Demonstrations in Peking, Part III (7 June–14 June)

Sir,

In my two despatches No. 9S of the 24th of May and No. 11S of the 6th of June.[1] I have already described events in Peking and Shanghai in connection with the recent Hong Kong disturbances, and I expressed the hope that it would not be necessary to continue the series. However, the outbreak of hostilities in the Middle East on the 5th of June[2] led to renewed anti-British demonstrations in Peking. In this despatch, which covers the period from the 7th to the 14th of June, I have the honour to resume my account of events.

2. Large-scale demonstrations against this Mission began again on the 7th of June and continued for three days. The New China News Agency claims that more than 1,200,000 people marched past our premises during this period. The slogans which were shouted and displayed were mostly expressions of China's solidarity with the Arab peoples and condemnations of British and American 'Imperialism' for their alleged support of 'Israeli aggression'. The themes of British 'atrocities' in Hong Kong and the American presence in Viet-Nam were also much rehearsed. The fact that several Arab Embassies are situated in the immediate vicinity of this Office afforded the 'revolutionary masses' an excellent opportunity for complete emotional catharsis; their prescribed route took them from the Embassies of Iraq and the UAR to ourselves, and then off to the Algerian Embassy for a final coda of dervish enthusiasm, before setting out on the march to the other Arab Missions, a mile or two distant.

1 Not printed and No. 16 respectively.
2 The Six-Day War between Israel and Jordan, Syria, and Egypt.

3. A lighter note in all this tumult is provided by the varied assortment of effigies and *simulacra* which find their way to the front gates of my Office and of my residence. As I write, there are half a dozen of these top-hatted straw figures, resembling a detachment of under-fed Guy Fawkes, hanging from a line across the Office front gates and there are several others outside my house. Most of them are labelled: the Prime Minister has been well represented throughout the campaign, but you yourself, Sir, may draw comfort from the fact that you have not been positively identified. The *pièce de résistance* is a three-figure group, modelled a little less than life size in wattle and daub, which depicts President Johnson and 'British Imperialism' (the features of the latter resembling rather an elderly and ailing Gladstone) kneeling, heads a-loll, on either side of a dog, whose epaulettes and black patch mark him as General Dayan and to whom they are attached by a noosed rope.[3] Mr Johnson's wispy straw hair and the bloody sticking plaster on Gladstone's cheek give realistic effect, but the marble eyes of the three statesmen have proved an irresistible temptation to small boys in the neighbourhood.

4. A new feature of this bout of demonstrations has been the violence directed against our property and person by a certain section of the group known here as 'foreign experts', who live in the Friendship Hostel in the western suburbs of Peking and work for the Chinese as translators, teachers and professional fellow travellers. On the afternoon of the 7th of June some 70 of them, of various nationalities including Arabs and English, arrived at our Mission in their luxury coaches. Accompanied by several Chinese photographers, they entered our Mission compound, hauled down and destroyed the Union Jack, threw flowerpots through the ground floor windows and then entered the reception hall of the Office where they smashed the Queen's portrait, before being eventually persuaded to withdraw by my staff. When we protested to the Foreign Ministry by telephone we were informed that 'this action was completely justified'. My written protest was similarly rejected.

5. On the 9th of June the 'foreign friends' returned. As on the previous occasion they walked in through the open front gate unquestioned by the public security sentries. They pelted two of my staff with eggs, threw more flowerpots through more windows and set fire to the car of my Counsellor (Commercial). Immediately afterwards they went to my residence where I and most of my staff were preparing my reception to celebrate The Queen's Birthday. Fortunately I had posted look-outs so I was able to lead a posse of my merry men to confront them at the gate in time. In the encounter which followed, some of my staff were punched, kicked and lunged at with wooden placards, but none of our assailants entered the residence grounds. They left threatening to return the next day to burn my house, and me in it. This has not happened.

6. We learned subsequently through a contact in the Friendship Hostel, that the intruders on the 9th of June were accompanied and directed by members of the Chinese Foreign Ministry. After the incidents I have described above, a discussion apparently took place at which the foreign experts expressed the wish to visit Arab Embassies to show their support, whilst the Foreign Ministry officials insisted that they should go to Chung Nan Hai (Peking's Whitehall) where some of them were required to pose for a photograph with Chairman Mao. This picture was published

---

3 A photograph of this display can be found in Anthony Grey's book, *Hostage in Peking*.

in the *People's Daily* of the 10th of June and has provided us with a useful rogues' gallery for future reference.

7. The Queen's Birthday reception on the 9th of June, therefore, took on a rather special character. Firstly, we did all the work for it ourselves since the Chinese staff of the Office and the domestic staff were again on strike (they returned after four days on the 12th of June). As for Chinese official guests I had decided with your approval, that in view of recent events the farce of exchanging toasts and *politesses* with them would be better avoided. I therefore invited none. It is doubtful in any case whether they would have accepted, but I was glad to have been able to deprive them of the pleasure of declining. The Chinese retaliated by putting my residence under siege by the revolutionary masses throughout the reception and for several hours before and after it. The surrounding area was packed tight with demonstrators including some from the Foreign Ministry and interpreters from the Foreign Language Institute, and all approach roads were sealed off. With the exception of one persevering Dane (who climbed over the back wall) and later in the evening about a dozen French, Dutch, Indian and Yugoslav diplomats, none of my colleagues in the Corps was able to reach my house. Our only company was provided by the Chinese staff, who plodded wearily round my house and garden in yet another funereal demonstration march. The loyal toast was therefore drunk by some 35 members of this Mission and our solitary Danish guest, in champagne which had been intended for 350. The incantations of the mob, which accompanied the burning of numerous effigies at my gate, were thus almost drowned by the popping of corks and later, by the strains of some traditional British songs.

8. During the evening a number of ambassadors telephoned their regrets that they were unable to attend my reception. Some of them also protested in writing to the Foreign Ministry the following day, for example, the French, Swedish, Norwegian and Danish Ambassadors and the Dutch Chargé d'Affaires all did so. I fear that the polished irony of the French Ambassador, whose Note referred to 'des groupes qui, à sa connaissance, n'ont pas reçu officellement mission de régler la circulation dans la ville', was wholly lost upon the Chinese. The Chinese response to the Danish Ambassador's note was probably typical: They adopted an air of bland incomprehension, and said that while they were always careful to respect the proper freedom of movement of foreign diplomats in Peking, the Red Guards and the revolutionary masses had a perfect right to show their righteous indignation at British support for Israeli 'aggression' and British 'atrocities' in Hong Kong.

9. The situation has been quiet again since the announcement of a cease-fire in the Middle East. Such fervour as the masses still retain for anti-foreign demonstrations has recently been directed, on a small scale, against the Bulgarians, for their attitude to Chinese students in Sofia and, with considerable violence, against the Indians in connection with the Raghunath 'spy' affair, upon which I am reporting separately.[4] On the 12th of June, however, I was once again obliged to walk out of an official reception when Ch'en Yi at the Nepalese National Day celebrations repeated the usual charges about British collusion with Israel in the Middle East war. The

---

4 On 4 June 1967, Krishnan Raghunath, an Indian diplomat posted to Peking, was arrested by the Chinese authorities on charges of espionage. On 13 June, a court found him found guilty of spying and he was ordered to leave China immediately.

exodus was soon swelled by my colleagues from the Soviet and most of the East European Embassies, although naturally it was not a case of *post hoc propter hoc*. Nevertheless I was afterwards gratified to hear that my Communist colleagues, for the first time copied my walkout procedure, by going up to thank and bid farewell to the host and hostess, an innovation which I introduced some time ago, to the evident discomfiture of the Chinese.

10. Meanwhile, the Chinese continue to devise more 'pinpricks' against us: for example, the Transport Monopoly are refusing to pack or despatch my personal effects and the office translators will not translate into Chinese our protest Notes to the Foreign Ministry. I am keeping your Department informed of these deliberate inconveniences.

11. It would be rash of me to predict that the present lull in Peking will continue, but one good sign has been the recent departure from the city of large numbers of youngsters to help with the summer harvest. If the Hong Kong situation remains reasonably quiet, it may not be too much to hope that we can occupy ourselves with more productive business than merely keeping our persons and premises intact.

12. I am sending copies of this despatch to Her Majesty's Representatives at Washington, Tokyo, Bangkok and Ulan Bator, to the High Commissioners at Canberra and Ottawa, to the Governor of Hong Kong and to the Political Adviser to the Commander-in-Chief, Far East, at Singapore.[5]

I have, etc.
D. C. HOPSON

5 Mr Bolland commented: 'Mr Hopson certainly seems to have succeeded in keeping up the morale of his staff in very trying conditions.'

No. 20

Mr Hewitt (Shanghai) to Mr Hopson (Peking), 29 June 1967
Confidential (FCO 21/33, FC 1/14)

Shanghai: Mob attacks and closure of the Office

Sir,

My family and I, accompanied by Mr R.W. Whitney, left Shanghai on the 24th of May. I have the honour in this despatch to report the events which led up to our departure.

2. Had I been asked on the 1st of May for an assessment of the Shanghai Office's prospects I would have been cautiously optimistic. The Chinese authorities had been consistently unhelpful over the seven months of my incumbency but this was nothing new; much more important was the fact that they had made no appreciable effort to unseat us. Indeed there were some indications of a slight thaw: over the May Day celebrations we had received an invitation to the same concert as the Polish Consul-General and had received the same courteous treatment as he at the performance; a Mr Wang had replaced Chen Teng-ping in the Foreign Affairs Department and though he gave nothing more away he cloaked his unhelpfulness in more courteous language;

and in recent weeks I had on three occasions been able to visit sick British seamen in the Seamen's Hospital, on the last occasion having actually been asked by the hospital authorities if I could provide a patient with something to read. We had been threatened with invasion by Red Guards some four months previously but the threat was either a hoax or was frustrated by the authorities who had already protected our portals against a group of young people who yearned to gambol on our lawns.

3. When the Hong Kong riots began a few days later the Macao example indicated that the Chinese authorities would whip up mainland sympathy; I drafted a letter for the next Peking bag suggesting a sort of code which could be employed over the telephone to describe harassment of the Shanghai post—one group covered 'invasion' though I never seriously thought that it would be needed. When demonstrations began in Peking on the 15th of May it was obvious that my code would be overtaken by events since Shanghai was sure to see similar manifestations next day.

4. On the morning of the 16th of May my wife had to take one of the twins to the hospital. Unfortunately she was delayed there so that by the time the car got back to the compound the gates were under siege by a large number of Red Guards. They were extremely hostile and although the car contained only the driver, my wife and two small children they beat and hammered it with sticks and fists, painted and postered it and finally jumped on the roof, which partially crumpled. My wife came to my office to tell me of the hooliganism just as Mr Yin our chief translator was taking down a telephone message from the FAD in which they declared support for the demonstrations against the Fascist atrocities in Hong Kong and warned 'Hewitt' (no honorific of any sort) not to provoke the masses. I at once drafted a brief factual report of the car incident and had it telephoned to the FAD whose reply claimed that it was a 'malicious smear'.

5. Shortly afterwards the crowds outside demanded to see me. Yin, in a panic, declined to accompany me to the gates, where I told the demonstrators that if they had any written protests they could hand them to me through the bars. All they did was shout abuse so I withdrew; this pattern was repeated a little later. I then telephoned to Peking to report the car incident and was informed that your office was declining to accept protests personally but had agreed that they could be handed in. The crowds outside our gates then demanded that I should go outside personally within five minutes to receive a protest or 'they would take revolutionary action'; I pointed out that I had already twice fruitlessly been to the gates to receive protests and said that I did not propose to be intimidated by threats. While I was in the house comforting my family the compound was invaded: my staff read out a violent protest, an effigy was burned and a number of persons with paint-pots went into the office where they daubed anti-British and pro-Mao signs on all the walls and daubed the Queen's portrait, our coats of arms and the cinema screen; a lot of books were pulled from their shelves and strewn over the library floor. To get the crowds away from the house I persuaded them to go back to the gates where they demanded that I should apologise for the Hong Kong atrocities and bow to Mao. They were very aggressive and my refusal further incensed them; there were loud demands that I should stand to attention with bowed head—a sort of Davy Crockett fellow with a wooden rifle was particularly demanding in this respect. Eventually, after a lot of jostling and shouting, they all withdrew and we went to lunch unbloody and unbowed.

6. Shortly after lunch a number of youths climbed over the gates with paint-pots, glue and posters and proceeded to write slogans all over the roadways and on the walls of our house. While I was watching this comparatively harmless fatuity I saw the main gates being opened from the inside and the crowds poured in. I went to the gate in a fruitless attempt to stem the tide; I was surrounded by screaming, jostling youths while hundreds more fanned out all over the compound. For the next 3 and a half hours I was jostled up and down between the gates and the house, which was being ransacked, from time to time being thumped and hit with small beflagged sticks and having my neck nearly broken by furious efforts to force my head down in submission to Mao: the heat, the stench and the noise (from large numbers of hand-held loud-hailers) were awful. In an effort to find my wife I managed to force my way into the house but saw only the immense destruction. At about 5 o'clock they decided to have a prayer meeting; they all sat down in a circle, chanting Mao quotations, in which I declined to join, and sang. I was forced to stand on a garden seat and was assailed by more abusive loud-hailers to the point where I thought the least I would escape with would be permanent deafness. I was also invited to comment into a tape recorder on the Hong Kong situation; I did not have any up-to-date knowledge of the exact casualty figures and could only express doubt as to the accuracy of the Chinese ones and regret that relations between China and Great Britain should be strained. Eventually the Red Guard columns vacated the compound, flags flying and in good order, leaving behind a few of their number whose duty it was, they said, 'to watch me'. The house was a shambles, a shell of smashed glass and furniture and torn paper and cloth, but I managed to discover by a whispered exchange with the Number 1 boy that my family were safe. (In fact they had been taken by the *amahs*[1] into the laundry room where the windows were boarded up and the door locked; they sat there for four hours, for most of the time listening to the crash of destruction and the cheers of the wreckers.) As night fell the compound was finally evacuated, we slipped across to House 43 which had escaped unscathed and I telephoned to you, Sir, from the office. We dined that night on strawberries and chianti, but slept little because of a Red Guard-operated loudspeaker of vast volume specially erected on one of the buildings just across the road from our house.

7. The next five days were taken up in salvaging our surviving possessions from the wreckage of House 32, destroying all the sensitive papers in the office and receiving protests from the inflamed citizenry; you are already aware of the drill which was evolved for the last of these. At first we feared that we should be again invaded and that House 43, our only refuge, would be destroyed, but these fears receded as the number of police guards was increased: moreover, we learned from one of the servants that some of the slogan leaders at the protest presentations were in fact Public Security Bureau Officers and that there were plain-clothes officers in the crowds. The weather perhaps helped us in that we had three days of continuous rain, but passions still ran high and whenever I went out Red Guards would do their best to provoke me by flashing their Mao books so close to my face that I felt the draught; one oaf was present at several protest presentations standing beside me and staring, chest puffed out and growling like a mentally retarded bulldog. The noise

---

1 A female employed by a family to look after children and perform other domestic duties.

by day was considerable but fortunately it progressively declined at night and some sleep was possible.

8. Mr Whitney arrived on the 22nd of May, and we began to destroy our remaining files. That evening we received your telephone call to the effect that I was given 48 hours to vacate the post and that no replacement would be permitted by the Chinese authorities. We therefore accelerated preparations for closing the post, and so that the British community could hear of the position from us rather than over Radio Peking, I invited Messrs Self, Johnston and Crozier to the house that night and explained the position to them.

9. The next day was spent in clearing up, packing and making arrangements so that the post's responsibilities for paying pensioners and relief beneficiaries could be taken over by Peking. That evening there began what was perhaps the most bizarre event of the whole period. Understandably the Shanghai staff were concerned over their future and at 6.30 p.m. asked if a deputation could see us to discuss it. We agreed. This 'meeting' lasted until 7.30 the next morning with only an hour's break whilst Mr Whitney and I dined. The staff, led by one Chow Zao-king, a coolie, wanted us to give them 'for their consideration' details of the terminal benefits they would receive were their services to be dispensed with. On your instructions we insisted that they were still in Her Majesty's Government's employ, that it was not possible in the very short time allowed us by the Chinese 48-hour limit to discuss terms but that they could rest assured that they would be reasonably treated. The argument went on and on and on in ridiculous circles; they wanted something in writing but every time we offered a form of words to meet what they asked for they shifted their ground. At one point Mr Whitney and I attempted to walk out but this provoked such a torrent of threats that we thought it politic to remain. All the office and house staff were present throughout this marathon but most seemed to find the proceedings as tediously pointless as we did. Eventually, at 4.30 a.m., a form of words was agreed which gave the staff nothing; you have a copy of the undertaking I signed; its preparation in Chinese and English and its formal sealing took over 1 and a half hours to complete. I then informed the staff that we would pay them their June salary before we left which they graciously declared themselves willing to accept. But they then started another fatuous agitation over arrangements for payment after June, and were only satisfied, after a full hour's argument, with a manuscript note from myself to the effect that the agreement entered into at 4.30 that morning would become operative should arrangements for paying salaries and pensions not be completed by the end of June.

10. We could ill afford the time consumed by this Animal Farm incident. We had arranged that Zee, our driver—whose conduct throughout was first class—should collect as much of our baggage as possible at 5 or 6 a.m. and take it to the airport; he would park the Land Rover somewhere and be at the back gate of the compound at 11.15 to take us to catch the Peking plane. (We had contemplated making a proud withdrawal through the main gates but reluctantly decided against this as the crowds outside might so impede us as to cause us to miss the plane and would in any case further terrify my family.) Bravely, he withdrew from the staff meeting, collected all our baggage and got it out of the compound before the crowds collected. Mr Whitney and I made final preparations for our departure then went to the house to

help my wife with the last-minute packing. The staff were in yet another meeting and we had a tip-off—from the telephone operator who somehow hoped we could take him to Peking with us or ensure his continued employment in Shanghai—that they were proposing to demand that Mr Whitney should hand over a film he had taken of the destruction in our house. There then followed a suspicious message to us that there was a telephone call from Peking in the office. I suspected the staff wanted to shut Mr Whitney and me in my office while they took the film from the camera, so I told the operator to give me the call in the foyer where we could not be confined—there was no call. Meanwhile, M. van Roosbroeck, the Belgian banker who had been sent to China without leave for 20 years, came round to say goodbye and also loaded most of our remaining luggage in his car to take to the airport. By this time the staff had started slinking about the place in a furtive fashion, obviously up to no good and I told Zee to fetch the Land Rover round to the back gate as soon as possible.

11. When we emerged there were a gang of youths in the narrow street some of whom lined up alongside the Land Rover making it impossible to open the doors. In a flash the street filled up from both ends with crowds shouting abuse. Loudspeakers on the buildings opened up and a gang of bill stickers plastered the vehicle with posters. The atmosphere was very hostile and the police studiously avoided our summoning eyes until after about five minutes of the treatment I received an answering nod from a senior-looking officer and knew we would be released in time to catch our plane. The crowds withdrew from the vehicle and let us in but one lout, with glue pot and brush, chucked the latter into the vehicle spattering us with the stuff. They then chased the vehicle down the street hammering on it with fists and sticks. A cine cameraman took films of the whole incident, itself an indication that it was all carefully pre-arranged since the man had shortly before that filmed my final appearance at the front gate to receive protests. Incidentally, cameramen were present at a number of the protest presentations. At one I noticed a woman with a Rolleiflex whom I disconcerted by staring into the camera every time she raised it to take a picture; eventually I tired of this and looked down to read the protest which the spokesman was reading out; click went her camera and she had a picture of me with a bowed head, a position which the crowds frequently demanded I should assume.

12. Our route to the airport was circuitous but since traffic lights invariably changed to our favour long before we reached them, was obviously pre-arranged. The first airport crowd was at the army check post; they hammered on the vehicle and viciously tried to drag the driver out; after Mr Whitney and I had dismounted, been abused and received yet another written protest, we were allowed to proceed. There were very big crowds round the airport buildings and lines of buses and lorries which had brought them. To our pleasant surprise, Mr Ksilsopolski, the Polish Consul-General and M. van Roosbroeck were also present and they stepped forward and took a baby each; my wife and eldest daughter were taken through the crowds to the plane—though they were abused and bruised they were spared the worst. Mr Whitney and I had to run the gauntlet to the aircraft, and even the plane steps were thronged with demonstrators. We were jostled, shoulder charged, tripped and struck with fists and flag sticks, my jacket was torn and my tie pulled into so tight a knot

that it had later to be forced open with a tea spoon. The noise and venom were considerable and we were both hampered by having to carry a heavy crossed bag. When at last we made the plane the stewardesses refused to give us anything to drink, and throughout the flight we were regaled with loudspeaker homilies on the wickedness of the British authorities in Hong Kong.

13. I have no doubt that but for the Red Guard movement we would still be in Shanghai. Indignation against Britain was apparent in every demonstrator's face—given the grossly inflammatory and mendacious propaganda put out by the Chinese this was not surprising—but it was the young people who evinced the real hatred and who smashed our house up. They were at least supported by the Shanghai authorities who made no attempt to meet their obligations to protect our property and persons until too late and whose communications with me were violent and crudely discourteous. I am equally sure that our treatment was not due solely to the Hong Kong situation. Some of the slogans stuck up in our house were exactly the same as those employed against the 'bourgeoisie' in the early, most violent days of the Cultural Revolution, *e.g.* 'people of substance have bad hearts' and the heels were snapped off my wife's higher-heeled shoes. Revolutionary enthusiasm had been waning of late and the authorities had been scraping the barrel for rallying cries; their latest had been celebration of the Revolutionary Workers General Headquarters' first six months of life, a feeble effort which had failed to fire anyone. We provided a splendid target; feelings could be whipped up without internecine strife resulting, and the Red Guards' taste for violence could be indulged in the name of nationalism.

14. The British community were very good in our time of trouble; I must also pay a tribute to M. van Roosbroeck who was particularly helpful and very brave. Closure of the Shanghai office, which I think we must accept if the Chinese insist however much we may object, will have no vital effect on the community since a measure of contact can be maintained by visits and the telephone, and relief payments can be made through such channels as the Bank of China. But their lives will be affected by the loss of the amenities provided in the compound *e.g.* library, films, tennis, badminton and by the removal of the focal point for such social life as was still possible; there will be no more Church services and no more prayers at cremations since it is highly doubtful whether a non-diplomat would be able to take over this aspect of our work. And although it would be idle to claim that we had really been able to do anything in the consular field for the community which could not be done in Peking our presence did provide some slight assurance in their isolated positions. The only consolation that they and we can derive from an unhappy situation is that the Chinese had openly to force the British Office out of Shanghai.[2]

I have, etc,
D. M. Hewitt

---

2 Mr Wilson minuted: 'It is remarkable how 'controlled' the violence was; Mao's booklet's just fanning the face, Red Guards marching out in good order after sacking the house, and the police able to get the Land Rover away to the airport on time after a due period of harassment by the masses. This organised roughing up of diplomats is highly sinister but a striking example of the degree of control which it is still possible to exercise over the Red Guards.'

No. 21

Minute from Mr Morphet to Mr Bolland, 5 July 1967
(FCO 21/64, FC 3/3/B)

Incident outside the Chinese Embassy

The Secretary to the Chinese Acting Chargé d'Affaires rang at 11.35 p.m. last night to say that a few minutes previously what he described as a 'serious political provocation incident' had taken place outside his Chargé's office. He demanded that Mr Shen Ping should see the Secretary of State immediately. I explained that Mr Brown was not yet available after his trip to The Hague and a rather repetitious exchange elicited that anti-Chinese slogans had been shouted, and 'hooligans' had insulted Chairman Mao and the Chinese people. I asked if there had been any damage caused, but the Secretary would not say. I asked if Police protection was adequate and was eventually told that 'the Police stood by with folded arms'. The demand that Mr Shen Ping should see the Foreign Secretary (and later 'any other high official') was repeated several times; and the gist of my reply was as follows: the Foreign Secretary was not yet back from The Hague. Other Ministers and officials were not in the Office. He could, however, take this up in the morning. Meanwhile, was there anything I could do to help, such as increase Police protection? The first exchange ended with a demand that I should ring back immediately to fix an appointment.

2. I then rang Mr Bolland at home who agreed that provided the incident had been a peaceful one, and all was now quiet, there was no need for action until the morning.

3. Meanwhile I had been in touch with the Police (Inspector Thompson at Marylebone Police Station). What happened was this: there was a poster parade organised by CND outside the Chinese office between 10 and 11 p.m. This was entirely peaceful; the organisers tried to deliver a petition. The Chinese would not at first open the door, but when the petition was pushed under it, it was then opened and a certain amount of heated discussion took place. But the total number of people involved was between 30 and 40. At about 11 o'clock only four or five were left and the Police thought that they were extinguishing torches they had been carrying in the gutter outside the office. However, at that point Chinese appeared and captured a book which they had in fact been burning. The Police suppose that this may have been 'The Thoughts of Chairman Mao'. The Chinese then took photographs of the Police officers and reserved the right to complain to the British Government. No arrests were made. The Police were told of the roster parade by CND earlier in the evening. I am assured that the whole parade was properly policed. At the time I rang (just before midnight) all was quiet outside the office.

4. At five past midnight the Chinese Secretary rang back to repeat his demand for an audience for Mr Shen Ping. I told him that there was no-one in the Office to receive him and we would be in touch with his office first thing in the morning. I added that I had ascertained that the office was well protected. That, replied the Secretary, was contrary to the facts. I asked, in that case, what was happening and was told that 'That was not the question.' The Secretary told me that I had 'rejected' the appointment and that every Head of Mission had the right to see the Foreign

Secretary at any time. I replied that I had not rejected the appointment, but explained that there was no-one here to see Mr Shen Ping. I asked if Mr Shen Ping himself [was] there, so that I could explain what was the position to him personally, and received the reply that this was not necessary. The call ended with the demand that I should ring back in 10 minutes.

5. Since the exchange was proving rather fruitless, I asked the switchboard to keep the Secretary waiting for three or four minutes next time he rang back. This he did at 12.55 a.m. The verbatim exchange on this occasion was:

Myself

'Nothing can be done tonight, since no-one is in the Office. We will ring you tomorrow. Meanwhile, I have asked the Police to report any further incidents.'

Secretary

'That means you have rejected the appointment tonight.'

Myself

'No, I have not rejected the appointment but it cannot be arranged till tomorrow morning.'

The Secretary then rang off.

6. It was 7.30 a.m. before the next phone call, in which the Secretary once again repeated the demand and said that Mr Shen Ping was cancelling his trip to Sunderland. Once more I said that there was no-one in the Office and that nothing could be done till 10 a.m. The Secretary appeared to accept this.

D. I. MORPHET

No. 22

Sir D. Trench (Hong Kong) to Mr Bowden, 9 July 1967[1]
Tel. No. 988 Immediate, Confidential (FCO 21/209, FD 3/1/A)

Incident at Sha Tau Kok on 8 July.

Following is more detailed account from police and military sources of yesterday's incident at Sha Tau Kok.

2. From 9.30 a.m. on 8 July demonstrators began to gather in the frontier areas at Sha Tau Kok (Chinese territory). Soon afterwards the shops closed which is normally the precursor of trouble. During the next hour other groups began to gather near the border and anti-British propaganda was broadcast over loudspeakers. A machine-gun mounted on the roof of a shop on the Chinese side of Chung Ying Street, through which the border runs, was manned. Those manning it were not wearing normal border troops uniform. (This seems to be the same machine-gun post as that referred to in my telegram No. 905.)[2]

3. At about 1100 hours the crowd converged on the Sha Tau Kok police post in British Territory (BT) about 50 yards from the border, and a group of 3-400,

---

1 Repeated priority to Peking, FOLAD Singapore and Washington.
2 Not printed.

apparently controlled and well organised, surrounded the police post and threw home-made bombs, normally used for illegal fishing, over the perimeter fence. When the police attempted to disperse the crowd by firing baton shells and tear gas, automatic fire was opened on the post, believed to have come from the machine-gun referred to in paragraph 2 above. At this time a riot company on its way up to support the post was fired upon by rifles and the machine-gun. During this stage two Pakistani policemen in the post were killed by snipers, apparently from Chinese territory (CT) and two policemen in the relieving company were mortally wounded. There were several other casualties including one European officer. At about 1120 hours the Rural Committee offices, where there was a police reserve of two platoons, and which is about 200 yards inside British Territory (BT) was fired at from positions to the north near a village on the British side of the border and rifle (?fire) was reported from another village half a mile inside the border. Attempts were made to blow up the perimeter fence of the forward post and the police opened fire, hitting two men who were dragged away. It is believed that this was the first time the police fired with ball ammunition (carbines) but it has not yet been possible to confirm this. As soon as confirmation is received I shall inform you. By midday snipers were active in STK (BT) at close range pinning down the garrison in the police post and the police in the Rural Committee offices completely.

4. At 1140 hours it was decided to order one battalion of Gurkhas forward to the main police station 2000 yards south-west of STK. These began to arrive about 1300 hours. Meanwhile a party of men in civilian clothes were reported seen carrying a LMG[3] from CT towards high ground in BT overlooking STK from the west. At 1255 hours it was decided to send one company of Gurkhas as soon as possible to eliminate this threat. The area was occupied but nothing was found.

5. At 1330 hours a group of CCA soldiers 50-100 strong were seen moving along the border some 3 miles to the west of STK and at about 1430 hours a further group was seen moving into STK (CT). None of these troops were seen in the immediate area of the border. Shortly after, at about 1500 hours, there were renewed attacks on the police post including the reported employment of a heavy machine-gun from CT. Fire bombs were also used as well as small arms and home-made bombs.

6. At 1500 hours it was decided that a military operation should be mounted to relieve the police in the advanced post. At 1550 hours 1/10 Gurkha Regiment advance with two troops of armoured cars. By 1655 hours the forward police positions had been relieved and the curfew, declared at 1545 hours, brought into effect. There was some sporadic but ineffective firing up to about 1700 hours. The army did not fire their weapons. There were no further incidents. Army with police reinforcements in support took up defensive positions for the night, the armoured cars being withdrawn. On the morning of 9 July, 3 or 4 armed border guards were visible as usual within Chinese territory. Soldiers were observed sandbagging the machine-gun positions referred to earlier and a 107 mm recoilless rifle was also being sandbagged in. At 0930 hours an estimated platoon of soldiers fully armed arrived in two junks at the Sha Tau Kok Pier. The best military estimate is that there are now the equivalent of a battalion of Chinese troops and border guards in Sha Tau Kok. One Gurkha

3 Light Machine Gun.

battalion is in the area on the British side, together with 2 police platoons. Joint patrolling well within British territory is being carried out.

7. Total police casualties were five dead (two Pakistanis and three Chinese) and eleven wounded. No arrests were made and no bodies of civilians were recovered.

8. The men involved in the attack are believed to have been from CT including militia. There is no evidence of any uniformed personnel being involved. Two or three light machine-guns appear to have been used and several rifles. There are unsubstantiated reports of the use of a heavy machine-gun, of grenade dischargers and of mortars. The latter two are thought to be unlikely. The police so far debriefed are convinced that in the opening stages fire came from CT particularly from the machine-gun referred to in paragraph 2. They also believe the heavy machine-gun fire to have come from across the border. There is known to be a heavy machine-gun in the area. The fact that the attacks appeared to be co-ordinated, at least in the early stages, the accuracy of fire and the use of automatic weapons all indicate that many of those taking part had military training. There is no evidence whatever that they were regular or border troops. It is considered that militia were involved who are known to be equipped with small arms including automatic weapons which are not always held in central armouries. Such reactions by the CCA as were seen were defensive in their nature.

9. As soon as our examination is complete a detailed report will be sent by bag.[4]

4 At Cabinet on 11 July concern was expressed at the gravity of the situation and the risk to Britain's position in Hong Kong. They ordered the swift completion and circulation of a report being prepared on action to be taken if the position in Hong Kong became untenable and the establishment of a Ministerial Committee on Hong Kong (CC(67)46th, CAB 128/46/22).

No. 23

Minute from Mr Brown to Mr Jenkins, 19 July 1967
FS/67/59 Confidential (FCO 21/79, FC 3/30/A)

Possible Action against the New China News Agency in London

I have seen Bill Rodgers' record of his conversation with you on 25 May about possible retaliation against the New China News Agency here for the outrages the Chinese have committed against our Mission in Peking and Shanghai.[1] I understand that you are reluctant to take action against the NCNA.

2. The Chinese continue their campaign of abuse against us. With their inflammatory propaganda to encourage violence in Hong Kong. The increasingly firm action the Hong Kong Government are now taking to deal with the situation in the Colony could result at any moment in renewed abuse and harassment of our staff in Peking.

3. If this happens we may have to take action against the Chinese Mission here. There are, however, strong reasons why we should not break off relations with China

1 Mr Rodgers explained that appropriate measures were needed to make clear to the Chinese the Government's indignation at their recent actions, without unacceptable consequences for the mission in Peking or for Hong Kong. Recent NCNA propaganda had been unacceptably abusive and it went far beyond the proper activities of a news agency. The Home Secretary was unenthusiastic about the proposed action stating that the Home Office had never expelled journalists from London for political reasons and the Government would get 'a very bad press' (Note of the meeting by Mr Samuel, 26 May 1967).

if that can be avoided. We could declare certain members of the Mission here *persona non grata*, but I am advised that if we did this the Chinese would certainly retaliate in like or stronger manner and, as we are more vulnerable than they are because we have few Chinese speakers to post to Peking while they have many English speakers to send to London.

4. There is, however, a good case for taking action against the NCNA in London. It is not at all a press agency in our sense of the term but the propaganda department of the Chinese Government. I feel sure that the public and press would support us if we said we had had enough of this organisation. We would have no need to fear criticism that were interfering with the liberty of the press, for we could easily demonstrate that what the NCNA are putting out in this country is not facts and fair comment, but lies, distortion, abuse and vilification of the grossest nature.

5. As you know, our policy is not to seek any quarrel with the Chinese, or to provoke them unduly. But developments in Hong Kong show that our opponents there, having failed in their attempt to rouse the masses against us, are now resorting to increased violence and terrorism. This means that in enforcing law and order we shall clash with them more strongly and perhaps more often than hitherto. This in turns means, on past showing, that the Chinese will attempt to increase their pressure against us wherever they can, whether in Hong Kong or against our Mission in Peking or our ships in Chinese ports. To counter these pressures effectively we ourselves must be ready with our own measures. A committee of officials of the departments concerned is working on this, getting the necessary inter-departmental clearances, etc., so that any given measure, once it is ministerially approved, can be put into effect without delay. The Home Office have so far not been involved in this because up to now the only measure we have in mind which does involve you is action in this country against the NCNA, and on this we need your personal approval before we can go any further. I would emphasise that we are not asking for the immediate expulsion of NCNA—indeed we may not ask for it at all—but we think it important to ensure now that we have agreement, so that we can take decisive action at the psychological moment.

6. That could come soon. At our request your Department are withholding visas for two replacements for the NCNA here. Peking are making threatening noises about the delay and hinting that they may take action against the Reuters correspondent there. If they should expel him it would mean that we had no United Kingdom press agency correspondent in China, for he is the only one. I think it would then be necessary for us, if we are to stand up to the Chinese at all, immediately to expel all the five remaining NCNA men in this country.

7. I hope you will agree that we should clear our lines as much as we can so that we could take promptly any action we may decide on. If you think a discussion would be useful I would be happy to talk this over with you.[2]

GEORGE BROWN

---

2 Mr Jenkins replied on 1 August: 'I see your difficulties, but at the same time I cannot see a clear way through mine.' He stressed that his powers to deport, restrict movement or prevent exit from the country had not been designed as instruments of foreign policy. He would have to be assured that deportation was 'conductive to the public good'. He suggested that officials continue to discuss the matter.

No. 24

Mr Brown to Mr Hopson (Peking), 21 July 1967, 10.55 p.m.[1]
Tel. No. 649 Immediate. Confidential (FCO 21/138, FC 13/8/A)

My Telegram No. 645:[2] Reuters.

Mr Rodgers summoned the Chinese Acting Chargé d'Affaires this evening and protested most strongly about the outrageous treatment of Mr Grey, a British subject, who worked for an international press agency in no way connected with HM Government. Mr Rodgers said that Mr Grey had been summoned to the Press Department of the Chinese Ministry of Foreign Affairs, forcibly detained, driven under police escort to his house and there placed under house arrest. A member of the staff of the Office of the British Chargé d'Affaires had visited the house but had been refused access by the police. There had been no suggestion that Mr Grey was guilty of any offence under Chinese law. He had been engaged only in carrying out his legitimate business as a newspaper correspondent. This was a disgraceful act of which the Chinese Government should be ashamed.

2. Mr Rodgers demanded that Mr Grey should be released without delay and should there be any delay consular access should be granted immediately.

3. After making the protest Mr Rodgers terminated the interview and did not permit Mr Shen Ping to make the prepared protest about Hong Kong which he had clearly brought with him. After Mr Rodgers had left the room, Shen Ping shouted to the four walls that he rejected the protest and condemned our insulting behaviour toward the Chinese Government in refusing to hear what he had to say.

4. For on the record press see my immediately following telegram.

1 Repeated for information to Hong Kong.
2 Not printed.

No. 25

Minutes of a meeting of the Ministerial Committee on Hong Kong[1]
24 July 1967[2]
K(67)1st Top Secret (CAB 134/2945)

Interim report by officials

The Committee had before them a note by the Secretaries (K(67)2)[3] to which was attached an interim report by an interdepartmental working party of officials on the prospects for withdrawal from Hong Kong if it were suddenly to become necessary.

1 In July 1967 the Cabinet set up a small Ministerial Committee to keep a close watch on developments in Hong Kong, chaired by the Commonwealth Secretary.
2 Committee members present at this meeting were: Mr Bowden (in the Chair), Mr Healey (Secretary of State for Defence), Lord Shackleton (Minister without Portfolio), Mr Diamond (Chief Secretary, Treasury), Mrs Hart (Minister of State for Commonwealth Affairs), Mr Rodgers (Parliamentary Under-Secretary for Foreign Affairs) and Lord Walston (Parliamentary Secretary, Board of Trade).
3 Not printed.

THE COMMONWEALTH SECRETARY said that there was no evidence that mainland Chinese were behind the recent disturbances in Hong Kong. We could not be sure of the intentions of either the Government of the People's Republic of China or the local communists in Hong Kong but it appeared that the Chinese Government was reacting to local initiatives rather than instigating them. While the Chinese Government would probably continue to encourage the local communists, it was unlikely that they would directly intervene by sending armed forces across the frontier. This situation might be changed if the Hong Kong Government were to lose control, and developments in the internal struggle in China might also affect the current assessment of Chinese intentions. The report by officials concluded that, with a very large majority of the local Chinese in Hong Kong on our side, we could hold out in the Colony, but there was always a risk of rapid escalation of incidents producing a situation in which the Chinese Government took a decision to expel us. There was also a danger that the disturbances would lead to a decline in Hong Kong's economy and to loss of confidence. Officials therefore recommended that an urgent study should be set in hand of the problems of an emergency evacuation from the Colony, since there was at present no possibility that we could negotiate Chinese acquiescence in an orderly withdrawal, nor could we accept a situation analogous to that in Macao in which, while retaining sovereignty, we surrendered effective control to the communists. It was essential that no hint that evacuation plans were being contemplated should reach Hong Kong, and therefore there could be no local consultations. It was proposed that a small group, including persons with local knowledge, should be established in the Commonwealth Office to produce a plan for the physical evacuation of British subjects and other persons for whom we had a special responsibility. The total numbers whom we ought to evacuate might be between 150,000 and 200,000. The absence of local consultations would reduce the effectiveness of any plan, and it might be necessary for one or two members of the group to visit Hong Kong covertly for personal discussions with the Governor and the Commander, British Forces. At the same time it was suggested that the Treasury should prepare a contingency plan on the emergency action which would be required to safeguard our financial interests in Hong Kong. In the meantime officials proposed to continue with the wide-ranging study, which the Defence and Oversea Policy Committee (OPD(67)20th meeting)[4] had called for, on our policy in Hong Kong and possible adaptation of the status of the Colony in the light of the ending of the lease of the New Territories in 1997.

In discussion there was general agreement with the proposals in paragraphs 20 and 21 of K(67)2 for the immediate preparation of contingency plans for evacuation. The point was, however, made that it would not be possible to rescue physical assets in Hong Kong in the time likely to be available and that planning to safeguard our material interests would have to be confined to the action necessary to prevent the flight of capital and safeguard Hong Kong's sterling assets. The Committee were informed that there had been a recent improvement in the situation in Hong Kong as a result of the firm measures adopted against the local trouble-makers. It would probably be necessary to introduce emergency legislation to enable some of those

4 See No. 14.

arrested to be detained without trial because of the difficulty of bringing evidence against them to court without prejudicing sources of information. In this connection it was suggested that political difficulties would be created by keeping persons in detention for a long time, as had been done in Aden;[5] however, the numbers involved in Hong Kong were very small. The point was also made that we should not cancel planned visits of United States warships to the Colony, since cancellations involved presentational difficulties and could affect local confidence. There was no evidence that these visits provoked the communists to take further action against us. The presence of the United States ships might also be useful if an emergency evacuation became necessary, and could be expected to have some deterrent effect of the actions of the Chinese Government.

On the question of future policy, the point was made that while Hong Kong was indefensible against Chinese military attack, our acceptance of military defeat would have a disproportionate political effect on our influence in the whole of South East Asia and on the position of our friends and allies. In these circumstances consideration should be given to all possible ways of deterring the Chinese from a military attack on the Colony; for example, the stationing in Hong Kong of a small nuclear strike force similar to that stationed in Singapore at the time of confrontation with Indonesia might be studied. We had a direct colonial responsibility to defend the population of Hong Kong which was as large as that of Norway or Berlin. It was necessary to make the Chinese Government believe that we intended to stay in the Colony and that the United States was giving us general support in this intention. Nevertheless we should not at present consult the United States Administration about our plans. A demonstration of our intention to remain would be the most effective way of maintaining economic confidence in the Colony. A high level of investment and economic growth was essential to maintain Hong Kong's prosperity; while there was little evidence that confidence had been shaken by the recent disturbances, in the longer term the level of investment might well decline and there was some evidence that United Kingdom firms were beginning to look elsewhere for goods which they were at present obtaining from Hong Kong.

In further discussion, the view was expressed that the study by officials should include some means by which we might influence the Chinese Government to adopt reasonable policies towards Hong Kong against the background that we could not expect to remain in Hong Kong on present terms until the lease of the New Territories lapsed in 1997. It might be helpful if a note on our relations with the Chinese Government could be circulated to the Committee. The Committee were also informed that the Foreign Office were also discussing with the Home Office the possibility of retaliatory action against the New China News Agency[6] and were considering what advice should be given to British businessmen in China or intending to visit China and to the masters or British ships intending to call at Chinese ports.

Summing up the discussion, THE COMMONWEALTH SECRETARY said that the Committee would wish to keep a close watch on the situation in Hong Kong as it developed. The first task of the group to be set up to consider evacuation plans would

---

5 During the Aden emergency of the 1960s, Britain brought in measures such as detention without trial and set up interrogation centres in an attempt to counter armed insurgents fighting for independence
6 See No. 23.

be to give the Committee a broad indication of the physical problems of evacuation. The study of our long-term policy towards Hong Kong should proceed as rapidly as possible and should cover not only the possibility of political developments but also the means by which pressure could be brought on the Chinese Government to leave Hong Kong alone, including the deterring of military aggression. Attention should also be paid to the need to maintain economic confidence in the Colony. The examination should be conducted in the greatest secrecy. He would report the Committee's conclusions to the Defence and Oversea Policy Committee.[7]

The Committee:

1. Agreed that contingency planning for evacuation should be set in hand as proposed in paragraphs 20 and 21 of K(67)2.

2. Took note that the Chairman would report their conclusions to the Defence and Oversea Policy Committee.

3. Invited the Parliamentary Under-Secretary of State for Foreign Affairs[8] to circulate a note to the Committee on our relations with the People's Republic of China.

7 See No. 26.
8 Mr Rodgers.

No. 26

Extract from the minutes of a meeting of the Cabinet Defence and Overseas Policy Committee, 28 July 1967, 9.45 a.m.[1]
OPD(67)28th meeting Top Secret (CAB 148/30)

Hong Kong

The Committee considered a memorandum by the Commonwealth Secretary (OPD(67)61) covering a report by officials on the prospects of a withdrawal from Hong Kong.[2]

THE COMMONWEALTH SECRETARY said that, at a meeting of Ministerial Committee on Hong Kong earlier that week,[3] it had been agreed that, in view of the current situation in Hong Kong, a study should be put in hand by officials of what contingency plans could be made for evacuation of British subjects and of others to whom we had direct obligations should our position in Hong Kong become untenable and also of what might be done to safeguard our financial interests there is these circumstances. Although evacuation plans would be difficult to make

1 Committee members present at this meeting were: Mr Wilson, Mr Brown, Mr Stewart (First Secretary of State and Secretary of State for Economic Affairs); Mr Bowden (Secretary of State for Commonwealth Affairs), Mr Callaghan (Chancellor of the Exchequer), Mr Crossman (Lord President of the Council); Mr Healey (Secretary of State for Defence), Mr Jenkins (Home Secretary), Mr Jay (President of the Board of Trade), The Earl of Longford (Lord Privy Seal), Mr Bottomley (Minister of Overseas Development), Mr Wigg (Paymaster-General), Mr Mulley (Minister of State for Foreign Affairs), Mrs Hart (Minister of State for Commonwealth Affairs), Sir R. Hill (Chief of the Defence Staff), Sir J. Grandy (Chief of the Air Staff), Sir J. Bush (Vice Chief of the Naval Staff), Sir D. Fitzpatrick (Vice Chief of the General Staff) and Sir B. Trend.
2 Not printed.
3 No. 25

without the kind of information which could only be obtained locally in Hong Kong, it was nevertheless essential that an examination of the possibility of our enforced evacuation of the Colony was taking place should be confined very narrowly and that it should in no circumstances become known in Hong Kong to anyone but the Governor and the Commander-in-Chief; otherwise there would be an immediate and very serious decline in confidence in the Colony which might make it impossible for us to retain control. There had recently been an improvement in the situation in Hong Kong and in particular on the border with China where regular troops had taken over control, but fighting was reported to be taking place in Canton and we could not be sure that the Government in Peking would retain control of Kwangtung Province. In Hong Kong itself the Government had placed about forty people in detention and it had taken powers to detain British subjects who were citizens of Hong Kong. The Ministerial Committee would keep the situation under review and had called for further studies by officials.

In discussion doubt was expressed about the proposal to carry out a study of contingency plans for evacuation from Hong Kong. We should not take the risk that this would become known in Hong Kong when it was already clear that no effective plans could be made beyond those already in existence for evacuation of our own forces and their families and of about 500 other people whether our position became untenable as a result of a direct attack by Chinese forces or because there was breakdown of law and order in Hong Kong. In any event it would be impossible to evacuate the 250,000 people concerned. The key to the situation was the maintenance of confidence in Hong Kong and the continued demonstration to the Chinese that we intended to stay in the Colony, though we must avoid acting in a provocative fashion. Visits by large naval vessels and by aircraft from Singapore were valuable for this purpose and we should also continue to allow recreational visits by United States warships. Although the recent rains had made Hong Kong independent for the present for water supplies from the mainland and the willingness of the Chinese Government to renew normal supply arrangements when these were due to restart later in the year might provide a pointer to their attitude to our position in the Colony.

The PRIME MINISTER, summing up the discussion, said that the Committee recognised the difficulty of carrying out any further contingency planning for a possible withdrawal from Hong Kong and the grave risk that would ensue to our position there should it become known there that such planning was taking place. Nevertheless, they took the view on balance that such planning should be carried out, though strictly within the limits and subject to the restrictions recommended in the report by officials. The circulation of the papers involved should be reviewed and confined within the narrowest possible limits consistent with the work being carried out. Visits by our warships and aircraft and recreational visits by United States warships to Hong Kong should continue on the present basis. The Ministerial Committee on Hong Kong should keep the situation under close review and the Chairmen should inform him if it were at any time proposed to take further measures of importance to deter the Chinese from taking action again Hong Kong.

The Committee—

1. Took note, with approval, of the Prime Minister's summing up of their discussion.

2. Invited the Commonwealth Secretary, in consultation with other Ministers concerned, to arrange for contingency planning for the possible withdrawal from Hong Kong to be carried out on the basis indicated by the Prime Minister.

3. Instructed the Secretaries to review and to limit the circulation of papers on this issue in accordance with the Prime Minister's summing up.

No. 27

Mr Hopson (Peking) to Mr Brown, 1 August 1967
Confidential (FCO 21/52, FC 2/6)

The impact of the Cultural Revolution on China's foreign policy

Sir,

In a speech in the House of Commons on the 20th of July you said the Chinese Cultural Revolution had recently been spilling over into the sphere of foreign affairs.[1] This is an apt description of what has happened. Up till about the end of last year, almost everyone (including myself) assumed that Chinese foreign policy had not been materially affected by the tremendous internal upheaval that was taking place, apart from a general increase in rigidity on Viet-Nam and towards the Soviet Union and an isolated, if ominous, eruption in Macao. This is no longer true, and events in Hong Kong and Burma are there to prove it. Are these phenomena accidental and temporary, or are they symptomatic of a more permanent change in Chinese attitudes to the outside world? It is the purpose of this despatch first to analyse and try to explain what has happened, and then to look at the implications for the future.

2. The 'fall-out' from the Cultural Revolution outside China's frontiers has so far been heaviest in Asia. Chinese attitudes towards the Soviet Union and the United States, the revisionists and the Imperialists have hardened (to the extent that that was possible) but there has been no qualitative change. Here in Asia, on the other hand, the Bandung spirit has been anything but blithe.[2]

3. The Burmese, the good neighbours, the 'cousins', found almost overnight that they now had a 'Fascist reactionary' Government, and that their Communist insurgents were receiving sudden and open encouragement from Peking. In Hong Kong the realistic (though unwritten) *modus vivendi*, based on mutual interest, which the Chinese Government had respected since 1949, gave place within a few days to a full-scale political confrontation. In Nepal the worst has not happened, but the hitherto favoured Government of King Mahendra has been sharply criticised for following 'anti-Chinese policies'. In India a slightly absurd turn of the screw was given by Chinese support for the alleged incipient people's war in West Bengal, to the discomfiture apparently of even the 'orthodox' pro-Chinese faction of the Indian Communist Party. Meanwhile an article published in Peking has finally pronounced anathema

---

1 *Parl. Debs., 5th ser., H. of C.*, 20 July 1967, vol. 750, col. 2500.
2 In April 1955, representatives from 29 Asian and African nations gathered in Bandung, Indonesia, to discuss the role of the developing world in relation to the Cold War, economic development and decolonisation.

on the Indonesian Communist Party's flirtation with Soekarno,[3] so condemned as a Right-wing aberration. A people's war, according to the propaganda organs of Peking, is the only means of salvation for the peoples of Burma, India and Indonesia.

4. All this is a far cry from the *panch shila* and Bandung.[4] What is the explanation? The Chinese, predictably, say that it is the result of an anti-China plot engineered by the 'Imperialists, revisionists and reactionaries'. In fact, although one cannot pretend that it has all happened in the last few months—the Indian and Indonesian incidents have their roots in situations which have existed for some time—these recent phenomena are all in one way or another products of the Cultural Revolution.

5. That this internal struggle eventually overflowed China's frontiers is not in itself surprising. Most revolutionary movements in world history have done the same. Again, it is not extraordinary that the most serious incidents have taken place where there are large communities of overseas Chinese i.e. Hong Kong, Indonesia and Burma. (Conversely, it was probably the absence of such a community in Nepal which kept the dispute down to reasonable proportions.) The important feature of these incidents is not that the overseas Chinese have become infected with the Cultural Revolution bug, but that they have been positively encouraged to participate in the revolution. This represents an important change of Chinese policy, which hitherto has tended to discourage overt patriotic identification with the motherland among overseas communities.

6. Another feature of these incidents which has also been a contributory factor, has been the highly militant behaviour of Chinese representatives abroad, whether diplomatic, consular, or from governmental institutions such as the New China News Agency and the Bank of China. Many of them were brought back for special re-education courses during the Cultural Revolution, and are now determined to win their spurs on return to their posts abroad. In several cases they seem to have gone out of their way to provoke retaliation by the local population or forces of order. In the same way the reports that these people now send back to Peking are probably even more distorted and misleading than heretofore.

7. Meanwhile in the direction of foreign policy from Peking the sheer turmoil and disorder has doubtless played its part. Ch'en Yi, the Minister, has been almost continuously under attack since the beginning of the year, and though he is still apparently carrying out some of his formal functions, it seems doubtful if he still has the same voice in policy decisions. The Ministry itself has been rent by disputes between rival revolutionary groups. On important matters my interlocutor (gramophone-record would be a more apt description) is still the dreary Vice-Minister Lo Kuei-po, but he is now usually accompanied by a representative of the masses, who is clearly there to watch the Vice-Minister and chip in when necessary in a highly

---

3 Leader of the Indonesian independence movement and Indonesia's first president (1949–66). He attempted to use the support of the Communist Party of Indonesia (PKI) to counterbalance the power of the military. The military believed the PKI were behind an abortive coup on 30 September 1965 and killed thousands of communist party members and sympathisers.

4 The Five Principles of Peaceful Coexistence. They included: mutual respect for each other's territorial integrity and sovereignty; mutual non-aggression; mutual non-interference in each other's internal affairs; equality and mutual benefit; and peaceful co-existing. Formally codified in a treaty between China and India in 1954, they were later incorporated into the Ten Principles of International Peace and Cooperation enunciated in the Declaration issued at the Bandung Conference.

disagreeable manner. My personal impression is that the dominant revolutionary group in the Ministry probably takes its orders from the Cultural Revolution Group,[5] and has a decisive voice in discussions, as far as any policy decisions at all are taken in the Ministry. The result is, in any case, to give primacy to extremism, and to make it difficult if not impossible for the 'professionals' to resist pressures to give full support to what are regarded as revolutionary actions abroad, whether these run counter to hitherto well-established Chinese policy or not.

8. Thus far, the factors contributory to these new revolutionary aspects of Chinese foreign policy which I have described might be classified as accidents of the Cultural Revolution, and not the results of conscious, long-term policy decisions. It is, however, possible to detect other factors which may have more far-reaching consequences. I refer to what we usually call the 'struggle for power' element in the present situation, by which I mean the impact of the changes at the top of the Chinese hierarchy, and the implications of the policy criticisms being aimed at Liu Shao-chi.

9. As regards personalities, our Soviet and East European colleagues firmly believe that K'ang Sheng now has a strong voice in foreign affairs, and there is some evidence for this, *e.g.* the Rumanian Ambassador told me he played a prominent part in discussions with Mr Maurer during the latter's recent visit to Peking, though this may have been on the party net. We have had some personal experience of K'ang's influence. In early June he is reported to have complained to Red Guards that not enough people had demonstrated outside this Mission. Shortly afterwards we were visited by over one million people in three days. He is known as fanatically anti-Soviet and pro-Mao. The influence of Lin Piao, Mao's number two, in such matters is not known, but as author of the notorious article published in September 1965 recommending 'people's war' for the under-developed countries, we can assume that he finds the new militancy in the conduct of Chinese foreign affairs entirely to his taste.

10. It is true that Chou En-lai, the architect of Bandung, is still there as Prime Minister, and is said to have taken the Foreign Ministry under his wing, but Chou is something of an enigma. Under the smooth, flexible exterior the core is said to be as hard as flint. In any case his own position is by no means secure. Not only are the Vice-Premiers, including Ch'en Yi, who are usually regarded as his protégés, under continuous criticism, but the charges now being levelled at Liu Shao-ch'i of capitulationism and compromise in foreign affairs, particularly with regard to Burma and Indonesia, must be understood as indirect, if very thinly veiled, attacks on Chou himself, the great salesman of the *panch shila*. While one might suppose, therefore, that his voice would not be raised in support of reason and moderation, he may not in fact, whatever his real inclinations may be, feel strong enough at present to swim against the tide.

11. With the Cultural Revolution still unfinished—as I write the serious situation in Wushan still seems to be unresolved—it would be unwise to dogmatise about the future. Nevertheless, there are certain conclusions we can draw. In the short run, and for at least as long as the present turmoil continues, Chinese policy has become less amenable to reason and prudence, less bound by precedent, and therefore less

---

5 Formed in May 1966 and consisting mainly of radical supporters of Mao, the CRG played a central role in the early years of the Cultural Revolution and for a time replaced the Politburo Standing Committee as the most powerful body in China.

predictable. In Asia, particularly where overseas Chinese communities are concerned, there will be less inclination to compromise with what the Chinese call 'different social systems' merely for the sake of a quiet time on their frontiers. Nevertheless, it is important to note that the overflow across the frontiers has been almost entirely verbal. Encouragement and propaganda, militant diplomatists and indoctrinated 'patriotic compatriots' (overseas Chinese), but no Red Guards, no troops have been launched into neighbouring territories. Furthermore there is no evidence that incidents have been planned ahead and deliberately provoked in order to justify a prepared change of policy. In spite, therefore, of the evident change of attitude towards countries like Burma, I doubt if there is much chance of them deliberately provoking similar crises in the Chinese relationship with say Afghanistan, Nepal or Cambodia. But the latter have been warned that in present circumstances relations with China may be at the mercy of any incident.

12. It is, therefore, I think premature to speak of a strategic change in China's foreign policy. She is still in what I have called the 'strategic defensive stage' (my despatch No. 7S of 14 February, 1966),⁶ though tactically she has become much more offensive. I do not think she is more anxious than she was to intervene directly with ground forces either in Viet-Nam or Hong Kong. The danger is as Mao drives the locomotive of history on regardless, signals may be unrecognised or ignored, and at the vital moment it will be found that the braking system has not be maintained or that the brakesman has been thrown overboard. It is, therefore, of some comfort that the People's Liberation Army is at present fully engaged in trying to sort out the country's internal problems.

13. As for our own policy, I have no new formulae to offer. We must continue to be patient and firm. As long as Chinese xenophobia and administrative persecution do not render life unlivable for the foreign diplomatist in Peking, we must go on trying to maintain contact as best we can. We can hardly hope to exert much positive influence on China, but to appear to yield to her threats over Hong Kong would be the surest way of giving encouragement to the most extreme elements here. We must hope that firmness on the part of ourselves and our allies, and disillusionment with Chinese actions on the part of others, may combine to persuade the future Chinese leaders that their present policies cannot pay.

I am sending copies of this despatch to Her Majesty's Representatives at Moscow, Washington, New Delhi, Wellington, Rawalpindi, Canberra, Bangkok, Rangoon, Vientiane, Saigon, Hanoi, Manila, Phnom Penh, Tokyo, Kuala Lumpur and Singapore, to the Governor, Hong Kong, and to the Political Adviser to the Commander-in-Chief Far East, Singapore.⁷

I have, etc.
D. C. HOPSON

---

6 Not printed.

7 Commenting on the despatch on 15 August, Mr Denson noted that one area not mentioned was the disastrous effect of the Cultural Revolution on China's image in the world. China had deliberately and recklessly damaged her relations with countries of all political persuasions. With no successes in foreign policy over the last 18 months she had sought to compensate for it by 'increasingly childish xenophobia and a still greater turning in on her own resources backed by the fundamentalist creed of Mao.' This had undoubtedly lost China influence in the world, despite impressive performances in the nuclear field and made support for China's entry into the United Nations less likely.

No. 28

Mr Hopson (Peking) to Mr Brown, 8 August 1967
Restricted (PREM 13/1966)

Operation Effigy

Sir,

I have the honour to report that in the late evening of the 5th of August a special operation was carried out by members of my staff which entailed a brief sortie into Chinese territory. The objective was the demolition and, if possible, capture of two groups of effigies and placards which had been erected outside the gates of both my house and this office.

2. The effigies in question, mainly of straw, some dressed in morning-coat and tall hat, were according to their labels supposed to represent our Prime Minister. The plywood placards incited the reader to 'strike down' Mr Wilson, British Imperialism, &c. They were strung on wire a few yards outside our gates, and dangling there since the mass demonstrations of June had finally become a source of irritation to myself and my staff. Casual attempts to interfere with them had been met with a quick objection from the boot-faced police guard (who stands sentinel beneath them) that this was 'Chinese territory'. It was clear that, if they were to be removed, a carefully-organised operation would have to be mounted. I, therefore, authorised the preparation of a plan, christened 'Operation Effigy'.

3. The plan (copy enclosed)[1] devised by my staff provided for two assault groups. The first, to tackle the target outside my house, had a special problem as the wire was stretched about 12 feet from the ground. This was solved by providing them with an old office bus, from the roof of which two members of the group would be able to reach the wire. Both attacks were to be made simultaneously. The only equipment required, apart from the bus, was wire-cutters and hacksaws. Combatants were limited to those with diplomatic privilege. I approved the plan and the necessary briefing, training, and rehearsal began.

4. I selected the night of the 5th of August as a suitable occasion for the operation, as our social club had organised a barbecue in the office grounds that evening; thus those engaged in the operation would be conveniently present, and the noise and festive atmosphere (with the presence of many foreign guests) might be expected to distract the police. By a happy coincidence it was also the official anniversary of the Cultural Revolution (Mao's first big-character poster)[2] and, not so happily for the Indonesians, the afternoon on which the Chinese mob almost burned their Embassy. The Chinese were, therefore, pre-occupied.

5. H-hour was to be 11 p.m., but this was delayed by 15 minutes owing to a rainstorm, which forced the barbecue under cover. By 11 p.m., however, our guests were all happily shaking and jerking on the dance floor (in ignorance of what was being prepared), so I gave the order to proceed, and No. 1 group (under command of Mr Whitney) moved silently off, over the back wall of the office, through the gardens of

---

1 Not printed.
2 Handwritten, wall-mounted posters with large-sized characters used as a means of protest, propaganda, and popular communication.

an Indian house, and over the back wall to my house where their bus and equipment had been parked in preparation. Meanwhile, I had returned to my house to watch, like the Duke of Plaza Toro[3], from my first floor window.

6. At 11.15 p.m. precisely the bus groaned steadily out through my gates and halted. Two prone figures rose from the roof and snipped the wire, while two others had emerged on foot to catch the debris which, after cutting the other end of the wire, they succeeded in dragging inside my garden. Meanwhile the bus had reversed back into my drive. The whole assault had taken about five seconds and there was apparently no reaction from the police guard, under whose nose it all happened.

7. Meanwhile at the office gate, No. 2 group (under the command of Mr Blishen) had simultaneously emerged and cut the wire, which was in arm's reach. There, however, was an immediate reaction from the police guard, who flung himself protectively on the fallen effigies, protesting like a hen covering her chickens that this was 'Chinese property'. Such a reaction had been foreseen, and according to orders No. 2 group then withdrew, leaving the policemen with his pile of wet straw and plywood. After two days it is still in the gutter and rapidly decomposing.

8. The operation, therefore, achieved its main objectives and so far there has been no reaction from the Chinese. I should not have wished to leave these offending souvenirs to haunt my successor, and after sitting in the trenches for three months I think it has done us all good to have a bit of a go. Of course, we may get a new décor provided for us sooner or later. If there is any official complaint I shall reply that 'the action of the British masses was completely justified'. I should like to record that I was much impressed by the skill, enthusiasm and resolution which my 'masses' displayed.

I am sending copies of this despatch and its enclosure to the Governor of Hong Kong and Her Majesty's Ambassador in Washington.[4]

I have, etc.
D. C. HOPSON

3 A fictional character from the 1889 Gilbert and Sullivan comic opera *The Gondoliers* who was reluctant to engage in martial activity.
4 Hopson sent one of the figures back as a souvenir for the Prime Minister. A handwritten note in the No. 10 file recorded: 'Effigy arrived and was sent up to the Private Office.'

No. 29

Minute from Mr Rodgers to Mr Brown, 11 August 1967
Confidential (FCO 21/79, FC 3/20/A)

Retaliation against the Chinese in Britain

I have been discussing with officials what action we can take in retaliation against Chinese nationals in this country bearing in mind the position of the Reuters man in Peking and the possibility of further harassment, for example, of business men, technicians and ships' crews.

2. On the wider issues discussion is continuing with, amongst others, the Board of Trade. One question is whether travel restrictions should be placed on the Chinese

Commercial Office and members of trading corporations. For the present, however, we should pursue the problem of the New China News Agency in the light of the Home Secretary's minute to you.[1]

3. It seems clear that the Home Secretary will not agree at the moment to turning out the NCNA lock, stock and barrel. Since his minute to you, he has confirmed this in private conversation. I suggest, however, that we keep up the pressure in anticipation of a situation arising when there may be a public demand for drastic action.

4. Meanwhile, three other possibilities are open. First, the Home Office can refuse to renew the residence permits of members of the NCNA. Second, the Home Office can refuse re-entry visas for members of the NCNA leaving the country temporarily. Third, the Home Office can refuse visas for newcomers.

5. I doubt whether we can budge the Home Secretary on the first of these (although delay can be used as effective harassment from time to time), but we should go for the second and third. This would run the NCNA down over a period. There might be no publicity for this but we should have a defensible position in Parliament.

6. We also propose a Foreign Office system of exit visas. We can do this on our own but Home Office co-operation would be necessary.

7. I think it would also be wise to discover the whereabouts and activities of the 2,500 Chinese nationals in this country. I would not like to admit that we do not know when our own subjects in China are exposed. Enquiries would also alert them to our interest and represent a mild form of harassment. However, officials are not convinced on this and the Home Secretary might be reluctant to set in motion the considerable administrative action involved.

8. No firm decisions are required at the moment. But a minute to the Home Secretary on the lines attached will enable officials to continue their discussions. We should then have a thorough round-up on your return to the Office after the holiday.

WILLIAM RODGERS

1 See No. 23, footnote 2.

No. 30

Mr Hopson (Peking) to Mr Brown, 20 August 1967, 4.20 p.m.[1]
Tel. No. 1116 Immediate (FCO 21/226, FD 13/8A)

I was summoned to the Foreign Ministry this evening at 10.30 p.m. On arrival we found a crowd at the gates and were diverted to the International Club, where we were received by Mr Hsueh, Deputy Head of Western Europe.

2. He read a Note in the usual form requesting me to forward it to Her Majesty's Government. The Note referred to the arrest of 19 journalists over the last two months, to the suspension of publication of three Hong Kong newspapers, the law

1 Repeated for information to Hong Kong, POLAD Singapore and Washington.

suits against Hong Kong Press owners and editors, and the police action against the 3 banned papers in the course of which 34 further arrests were made. It made a strong protest against these actions and demanded that the British authorities with 48 hours should:

(*a*) cancel the ban on the 3 newspapers;

(*b*) declare all those arrested innocent and set them free, and

(*c*) call off the law-suits against the Hong Kong papers.

Otherwise Her Majesty's Government would be held responsible for all consequences.

3. As language was even more high flown than usual I refused to accept Note and rejected protest.²

4. Note will certainly be published.

2 The text of the rejected note was forwarded in Peking Tel. No. 1124 of 21 August. An extract stated: 'The towering crimes committed by the British authorities in sanguinarily suppressing the patriotic Chinese in Hong Kong and Kowloon have aroused indignation among the entire Chinese people. It is entirely just for the patriotic Chinese press and journalists . . . to report truthfully and expose these Fascist atrocities, as it is their sacred duty to do so. The British authorities in Hong Kong bitterly hate and mortally dread them, and have now concocted various trumped-up charges to carry out all kinds of brutal political persecution against them in an attempt to suppress the patriotic opinion and muffle the voice of justice and truth. This can only serve to thoroughly reveal before the people of the world the British Government's utterly hideous and ferocious features as Fascist imperialism'.

No. 31

Mr Hopson (Peking) to Mr Brown, 20 August 1967, 4.55 p.m.¹
Tel. No. 1117 Immediate Confidential (FCO 21/138, FC 13/8/A)

My immediately preceding telegram.²

I took the opportunity to enquire about the status of Mr Grey of Reuters. I said that for the past two days we had not been able to telephone him and there were reports that Chinese had entered his house. Did this mean there was a change in his status? News Department of the Foreign Ministry had said that Consular access would be granted if official access were granted to NCNA staff detained in Hong Kong. I had given an affirmative response to this suggestion but had had no reply. Where did the matter stand?

2. Hsueh said situation had changed since News Department's offer and this was not the time to discuss it. The masses had struggled by reasoning against Grey and had demanded further measures. The Ministry supported these just demands and further restrictions would be placed on Grey's activities. Cutting of the telephone was such a measure. If we did not change our attitude they would take further measures.

1 Repeated for information to Hong Kong, POLAD Singapore and Washington.
2 No. 30.

No. 32

Mr Hopson (Peking) to Mr Brown, 20 August 1967, 5.20 p.m.[1]
Tel. No. 1118 Immediate Confidential (FCO 21/138, FC 13/8)

My immediately preceding telegrams.[2]

The 48 hours deadline is the first ultimatum we have received over Hong Kong. Clearly this cannot be met. We must therefore be prepared for further action against Grey or this Mission or both which on recent precedents will probably include violence. I am taking the necessary precautionary measures as far as possible.

2. This makes it even more urgent than ever that some severe pressure be exerted on NCNA in London. I recommend that they should be warned immediately that if anything more is done either to Grey or this office their operations will be suspended at once.

1 Repeated for information to Hong Kong, POLAD Singapore, and Washington.
2 Nos. 30 and 31.

No. 33

Mr Brown to Mr Hopson (Peking), 21 August 1967, 5.16 p.m.[1]
Tel. No. 774 Immediate Confidential (FCO 21/64, FC 3/3/B)

My Telegram No. 771: Chinese note of 20 August on Hong Kong.[2]

Shen Ping called at 2.30 pm. Immediately on arrival he attempted to launch into a prepared harangue but de La Mare managed to stop him and make his first point.

2. This was that for the fourth time in the last three months Shen Ping had found excuses for not coming to the Foreign Office when summoned. On one occasion (22 May when we wished to hand him a letter from the Secretary of State to the Chinese Minister for Foreign Affairs) he had not come at all. De La Mare enquired whether Shen Ping thought this behaviour appropriate for a foreign representative and particularly for one whose status was only that of an Acting Chargé d'Affaires.

3. Shen Ping did not answer the actual question but made a statement which seemed to imply that as the representative of his country he had the right to come at his own convenience. De La Mare pointed out that you yourself had been summoned to the Ministry of Foreign Affairs on many occasions at most inconvenient times of the day and night and that foreign ambassadors, if they could not call at the time requested, at least sent suitable explanations. To his knowledge no foreign ambassador behaved in the way Shen Ping did.

1 Repeated for information to Washington, POLAD Singapore and Hong Kong.
2 The Foreign Office reported that they had tried to summon the Chinese Chargé but he had made himself unavailable. Hopson was requested to inform the Ministry of Foreign Affairs of this and state that it was not the first time that the Chargé had acted in this manner.

4. Shen Ping then made his statement which was a repetition of the Note very much as contained in your telegram 1124.³ At the end he insisted that HMG must, repeat must, comply with the Chinese demands within 48 hours. De La Mare told him that you had already rejected the Note and that he did likewise.

5. De La Mare then said that the Note contained a threat that if HMG did not comply with the Chinese demands they 'must be held responsible for all the consequences arising therefrom'. The Chinese had not specified what these consequences would be but de La Mare wished to make it quite clear that HMG held the Chinese government responsible for the safety of your Mission and your staff, for Mr Grey, and for all British subjects in China.

6. Shen Ping concluded by repeating the ultimatum. He said that British Imperialism in Hong Kong would be eliminated (he did not say when) and that the Chinese people always meant what they said.

3 See No. 30, footnote 2.

No. 34

Mr Thomson to the Parliamentary Under-Secretary of State (Home Office), 21 August 1967
FS/GMT/67/74 Confidential (FCO 21/79, FC 3/20/A)

Reuters and the NCNA

We spoke today about the new and urgent situation created for us by the ultimatum from the Chinese Government about Hong Kong which expires tomorrow afternoon. The following are the main points which I said I would put in writing for you.

The Foreign Secretary, in his minute to the Home Secretary of 14 August,¹ asked for your agreement to the withholding of an entry visa for a member of the New China News Agency in London and the withholding of a residence permit for another. I am grateful for the co-operation our officials have had from yours in these particular matters.

The Foreign Secretary also sought your agreement to instituting a system of exit visas for all Chinese officials in the United Kingdom. In the final paragraph of the minute, he asked that consideration be given to taking certain other measures against the New China News Agency if the Chinese took further action against Mr Grey, the Reuters correspondent who is under house arrest in Peking.

As you know an official of the Chinese Ministry of Foreign Affairs on 20 August summoned Her Majesty's Chargé d'Affaires and demanded that all Chinese journalists arrested in Hong Kong be declared innocent and set free, that the ban recently put on three Chinese Communist newspapers be lifted and that law suits instituted against other Chinese newspapers be called off.² If these demands were not

1 Not printed.
2 No. 30.

met within forty-eight hours, Her Majesty's Government would be held responsible for all consequences.

Before this conversation took place 200 demonstrators had already broken into Mr Grey's house in Peking and telephonic communication from the house of the British Mission had been severed. The Chinese Foreign Ministry official indicated to Mr Hopson that if the ultimatum were not met further action was to be expected against Mr Grey. Mr Hopson has reported that in addition he expects action to be taken against the British Mission, probably including violence. Clearly to capitulate before the Chinese demands would besides being legally unmanageable be politically disastrous. The ultimatum expires at about 3.30 p.m. GMT on 22 August.

This is the first time that the Chinese have issued an ultimatum of this kind and we agree with Her Majesty's Chargé d'Affaires that further, probably violent, action is to be expected against Mr Grey and against the British Mission. It was just such circumstances which the Foreign Secretary contemplated when he asked the Home Secretary to reconsider his position on retaliation against the New China News Agency. I am sure you will agree, as the Foreign Secretary pointed out, that if this does happen it would be indefensible before public and parliamentary opinion if we were obliged to admit that we had powers to act against the Chinese in this country but were unwilling to use them.

We have had no indication of the exact nature of the further measures the Chinese will take and on which any retaliatory measures would depend. It is, I think, essential that we should be in a position to act swiftly once the Chinese have acted. I should therefore be glad to have your agreement to inform the Office of the Chinese Chargé d'Affaires in London if necessary that:

(*a*) the New China News Agency should immediately cease functioning and its members should report at stated intervals to the police; or if this was not complied with or if Chinese actions justified it,

(*b*) all members of the New China News Agency should leave the country within forty-eight hours.

I understand that in theory (*b*) might not be possible if any members of the New China News Agency who had been resident in the United Kingdom for more than two years decided to appeal to the Senior Metropolitan Magistrate against a deportation order. In practice, we think that the Chinese would be loath to acknowledge British jurisdiction in this way and would not avail themselves of this right.

We would also be grateful for the co-operation of the Home Office in instituting a system of exit visas which would apply to all Chinese officials in this country including members of the Chinese Diplomatic Mission, the New China News Agency and the Bank of China. We realise that the Home Office does not possess powers to enforce such a system on, for example, Chinese diplomats and that it can be circumvented if the Chinese decide to leave the country by proceeding to Ireland via the West coast. Nevertheless, we consider that the system would be of value and we would be prepared to risk its being circumvented providing that we could count on the co-operation of Immigration officers to inform us if a Chinese tried to leave without an exit visa.

I should make it clear that it may not be necessary to enforce either of the measures referred to in paragraph 5 above. A decision would depend on what action the Chinese take in Peking and we would, of course, consult you before the Chinese Government were officially notified.

GEORGE THOMSON

No. 35

Mr Hopson (Peking) to Mr Brown, 22 August 1967, 6 a.m.[1]
Tel. No. 1135 Priority (FCO 21/33, FC 1/14/A)

Our Chinese office and domestic staff demonstrated outside the office grounds this morning and demanded that I should go out to receive a written protest on the question of Hong Kong. Together with seven members of staff I was surrounded by the demonstrators on the terrace of this office when I went out and demands were made that I should 'Bow my head and admit my guilt' in addition to receiving the protest. I naturally refused. After more than two and a half hours argument and shouting I went to the main gate in sight of the demonstrators outside where the protest Note was read and delivered. The demand for bowing of heads was dropped. I undertook to transmit it to the British Government.

2. Small scale demonstrations have been taking place outside this office since about 1 p.m. Premises are currently well guarded by the police and military.

1 Repeated for information to Hong Kong.

No. 36

Mr Hopson (Peking) to Mr Brown, 22 August 1967, 11.10 a.m.[1]
Tel. No. 1138 Flash Confidential (FCO 21/33, FC 1/14/A)

Demonstrations (now large scale) outside the Mission continue. Police and military have restrained our attempts to leave the office, saying that they could not take responsibility if we do. We are therefore besieged.

2. Our families in the diplomatic compound are so far unmolested.

3. Whitney, the Hunters and Miss Iliffe, who were to go on leave today and had been given exit visas, were told yesterday that no plane seats were available. They were told today that no seats were available on later flights. They are therefore effectively detained.

1 Repeated for information to Hong Kong, POLAD Singapore and Washington.

No. 37

Mr Brown to Sir P. Reilly (Paris), 22 August 1967[1]
Tel. No. 2880 Immediate (FCO 21/64, FC 3/3/B)

As diplomatic wireless contact with Peking is still broken we should be grateful if you would ask the Quai D'Orsay whether the French Ambassador in Peking could convey to Mr Hopson the following account of Mr Thomson's interview this evening with the Chinese Chargé d'Affaires.[2]

Begins

Mr Thomson stated that we had received a telegram from Mr Hopson in the afternoon reporting that a mob had broken into British premises in Peking. Thereafter our diplomatic wireless communications were broken. We subsequently learnt from a friendly power represented in Peking that Chancery building had been destroyed, the Chargé d'Affaires residence and its contents damaged and members of the Mission molested and maltreated. There was no doubt that this attack was deliberately instigated by the Chinese Government despite our reminder to the Chargé d'Affaires on 21 August that his government was responsible for the protection of the British Mission and its staff. This action which violated the immunity of the premises and the personal immunity of HM Chargé d'Affaires and his staff was yet another example of the flagrant disregard of the Chinese Government of the sovereign rights of other governments. It was an outrageous and uncivilised action which would bring the Chinese Government into disrepute throughout the world.

The Chinese Chargé d'Affaires was told to inform his Government that HMG protested most strongly against this outrage. They required an immediate report of what had taken place and an assurance that from now on British premises and British personnel would be protected and that full compensation would be paid for the damage done.

HM Government intended to take the following immediate measures:

(*a*) From now on all Chinese in the United Kingdom holding diplomatic or official passports would be required to obtain an exit visa from the Foreign Office before leaving the country.

(*b*) All members of the Chinese Diplomatic Mission and other Chinese to whom the travel notification system applies would from now on be restricted to travelling within a radius of five miles from Marble Arch unless prior notification had been given forty-eight hours in advance.

(*c*) Permission to operate diplomatic wireless by the Chinese Mission would be suspended until such time as British diplomatic wireless facilities in Peking were restored.

The Chinese Chargé d'Affaires who was probably taken aback by the rapidity and vigour of the protest made a somewhat lame reply in which he blamed British failure to comply with the ultimatum on Hong Kong for what had occurred. He described the actions of the 'Revolutionary Masses' as just and protested against the imposition of restrictions on the Chinese Mission in London.

Ends

1 Sent on 23 August at 10.21 a.m. Repeated for information to Washington, Hong Kong, POLAD Singapore, Moscow, Oslo (for Secretary of State), Bangkok. Tokyo, Canberra, Ottawa, and UKDEL NATO.
2 Mr Thompson spoke to Shen Ping at 11 p.m.

2. Would you please also express our thanks to the French Government for the messages passed this afternoon from the French Embassy in London about our Mission in Peking and say that we should be glad to have any further reports they may be able to send.

No. 38

Telegrams from Mr Hopson (Peking) to Mr Brown, 23 August 1967[1]
(PREM 13/1458)

Pekin Le 23 Août No. 2987/89
Immediat
Je vous adresse ci-après trois telegrammes du bureau du Chargé
d'affaires Britannique a transmettre en immediate a notre Ambassade
a Londres pour le Foreign Office
Citation: to London Immediate
Following for Foreign Office London.

Attack on the mission opened at 10.30 on expiry of 48-hour ultimatum. PLA at gates gave impression of being overwhelmed by sheer weight of numbers of mob but this was almost certainly contrived. There was no previous communication to me, simply violence.

2. Together with the 22 members of my staff, 5 of them ladies, who had been besieged in the office since lunchtime, I retreated to lower confidential offices and then behind sliding metal grill leading to secure zone. Later we retreated behind registry grill since there seemed a chance that the mob might content themselves with destroying the outer and upper section of the office, leaving the secure zone more or less intact.

3. However attack rapidly increased in seriousness with violent assaults on wooden registry shutters and burning of vehicles on the Office garage. Battering ram attack was made on rear door of registry which was our only escape route. Effigies were burned outside registry windows and flames spread to shutters themselves. Smoke was becoming troublesome and escape door was rapidly giving way to outside attacks. There was a danger that it might jam. In view of the risk of our being trapped in burning building I ordered escape door to be opened and all staff went out to meet the mob.

4. Individual suffering at hands of mob varied but general pattern was for beating and kicking followed by rescue by PLA after considerable interval. Some members of staff were compelled by force to bow their heads or kneel and photographed in this posture. Women in our party were treated with slightly less violence. PLA were obviously under instruction to ensure our eventual safety but they had their work cut out. They were at length able to escort us back to flats in the diplomatic compound at 2.30 a.m. where situation had been relatively peaceful.

5. My residence was sacked at about the same time as the Office.

---

1 As wireless communication with the British Embassy was disrupted, the French Embassy in Peking transmitted messages to London on their behalf. The Foreign Secretary wrote to his French counterpart to thank him for the assistance received.

6. Members of staff who went through this ordeal are well, though bruised, cut and shaken.

7. We have received no further communication from the Chinese Government since note of 20 August.

8. Please send all cypher traffic via this channel.

HOPSON

Fin de citation
LUCIEN PAYE

Pekin Le 23 Août No. 2990/92
Citation Emergency
For Foreign Office London
Confidential

I am sending brief summary of last night's events separately. You will be considering whether in present circumstances we should maintain relations with China. My recommendations are as follows:

(*a*) there be no (no) formal rupture of relations.

(*b*) we should close our mission here temporarily and request the Chinese to close theirs in London,

(*c*) in informing Chinese of this decision we should request facilities for immediate evacuation first of all women (including secretaries) and children and then of everyone.,

(*d*) Meanwhile it is vital that we impose stringent measures to prevent members of Chinese office leaving London until it can be synchronised with our departure (glad to hear on BBC of steps taken in this direction). Otherwise Chinese will try to detain us here as hostages against events in Hong Kong. I doubt if Chinese will speak to me here. Démarches should therefore be made in London.

2. I am taking steps immediately to try to evacuate women and children. If no places available on Aeroflot, PIA or Air France it might be necessary to try to arrange special flight. PIA or Air France would have best chance of getting permission. Numbers are 20 adults and 16 children.

3. I have postponed my departure indefinitely.

HOPSON

Fin de citation
LUCIEN PAYE

Pekin Le 23 Août No. 2993
Immediat
Citation
From Peking to Foreign Office
Confidential

We have no first hand information about Grey of Reuter over past 24 hours.

French News agency correspondent went to his house about 10.30 p.m. on 22 August. He said the situation appeared normal from outside. There were no extra police on duty. Lights were visible on first floor.

HOPSON

Fin de citation
LUCIEN PAYE

No. 39

Minute from Mr Denson to Mr de la Mare, 23 August 1967
Confidential (FCO 21/37, FC 1/21/A)

British Mission in Peking

The following message has been received through the Norwegian Ministry of Foreign Affairs:

1. All members of the British Mission are free but some have been hurt. The most seriously hurt is apparently a Chancery Guard, who is being treated by a Czech doctor. The situation does not appear to be critical.

2. Five women and six children are taking refuge in the Norwegian Embassy.

3. A meeting with the doyen of the Diplomatic Corps is to be held in Peking this morning to consider the Chinese action against the British Mission.

4. There are indications that preparations are being made for demonstrations against those foreign Embassies which are sheltering members of the British Mission.

5. The general situation in Peking is reported to be 'out of control'.

We have also received a message from the Swedish Ministry of Foreign Affairs that a number (not specified) of our Mission are sheltering in the Swedish Embassy. We have given the Swedish Government authority to provide them with such money as they require.

J. B. Denson

No. 40

Minute from Mr Thomas to Mr Wilson (No. 10), 23 August 1967
Top Secret (PREM 13/1458)

Prime Minister,

The main features at present in the situation in Hong Kong are as follows:

2. Reports from reliable and extremely delicate sources in Hong Kong indicate that the Chinese ultimatum of August 20th about releasing Communist journalists and stopping legal action against three Communist newspapers was launched in response to an appeal from the Communist leadership in Hong Kong, whose morale is low as a result of the firm measures taken locally, to show more solidarity with their cause.

Although this is the first time the Chinese have issued an ultimatum over Hong Kong, we do not consider that it indicates any basic change in their policy towards the Colony or to recent events there; we see it as a further move to give strong propaganda support to the local Communists without directly intervening on their behalf.

3. We think we probably regard the sacking of our Embassy in Peking as the main Chinese reaction to our rejection of the ultimatum. The authorities in Hong Kong are ready for an intensification of Communist activity in the Colony, which, if it comes, is likely to take the form of a stepping-up of violent incidents on the border. A deliberate stoppage of food supplies is also seen as a possibility.

4. So far, however, there has been little change in the situation in Hong Kong. The frontier remains quiet: there has been no repetition of earlier incidents. Within the Colony, Communist activity has been limited to sporadic 'bomb' incidents and unsuccessful attempts to paralyse the working of the port.

5. A most heartening development of the last few days has been the heavy rainfall which has filled the water reservoirs almost to their full capacity; the existing rationing scheme has accordingly been temporarily lifted. Our plan is to have a total of 15,100 million gallons in storage at the 30th September. This would make it possible to maintain a limited water supply throughout the period of the dry season even if supplies from China are not resumed when they fall due on 1st October (there is no reason at present to believe that the Chinese will not resume supplies on that date in accordance with the Agreement with them concluded in 1964). The amount of water in storage on 22nd August was 14,829 million gallons. This is 5,729 million gallons in excess of the target figure for that date. In addition, there are 6,280 million gallons in the new Plover Cove reservoir although the use of this water may initially be affected by problems of salinity. Despite this currently favourable supply position, contingency planning for an operation to transport water to the Colony by tankers is proceeding and last week a tanker expert from Shell International was sent out from London to assist in this exercise.

6. Although there has been no evidence that the Chinese have at any time made a policy decision to cut off food supplies, conditions in Kwangtung, the closing of the road across the border after recent incidents, and the activities of local Communists engaged in the food trade, have led to intermittent interruptions. Supplies by sea, which normally account for well over 70% of all food from China, have been fully maintained. Investigations are being made with a view to securing supplies from other sources and in this connection Hong Kong has despatched a mission to Japan and South Korea. We are assisting in these investigations and in particular examining the possibility of drawing upon United Kingdom meat stockpiles.

7. July's figures for Hong Kong trade suggest that the immediate economic effects of Communist activity have been small. Exports were 18% up on the same month last year and re-exports were higher by an even greater percentage; imports, because of dislocation in Chinese supplies and the closure of the Suez Canal[1] were slightly down. However, some adverse effect is to be expected, particularly from the very strong Communist pressure being exerted on shipping, and a close watch is being kept on the economic situation which in the long run could prove very worrying.

---

1 Egypt closed the canal on 5 June at the beginning of the Six Day War.

8. Although we do not see this most recent Chinese move as adding to the threat to the Colony, officials are, nevertheless, pursuing the immediate preliminary study authorised by Ministers of the possibility of preparing contingency plans for an evacuation of the Colony should we be forced to withdraw. An interdepartmental team has been set up and is at work on this.

9. You will remember that under the arrangements agreed last December we are planning to withdraw one major unit from Hong Kong by end-March 1968. To achieve this we would have to take preliminary steps now. We feel that in present circumstances it would be impossible to do so. The Commonwealth Secretary will be pursuing this point with the Defence Secretary.

10. I am sending copies of this minute to the Foreign Secretary and to the Secretary of State for Defence.

It was good to see you looking so fit.[2]

GEORGE THOMAS

2 This last sentence was handwritten.

No. 41

Minute by Mr de la Mare, 23 August 1967
Secret (FCO 21/64, FC 3/3/B)

Relations with the Chinese:
Possible further Action against the Chinese Mission

1. We discussed at Mr Thomson's meeting on 22 August whether we should *restrict the members of the Chinese Mission to their premises*. The Home Office objected that if the Chinese chose to ignore the ban and left the building there was nothing that the police could do to stop them. There was also the problem of providing food and other daily facilities. After long discussions it was decided that this proposal should not be further pursued for the time being.

2. According to the reports we have so far our Chancery in Peking has been made completely unusable. We are trying to find out whether the Chinese intend to provide alternative office accommodation. If they do not or if it is inadequate it is for consideration whether we should not deny to the Chinese here their office facilities at 49/51 Portland Place. One difficulty is that these premises are used both as offices and as living accommodation. About half of the Chinese staff of the Chinese Mission live there, although others live in Maida Vale and Gloucester Gate.

We could, however, find administrative reasons for making them vacate the premises. We could say that they are structurally unsafe or that they are urgently required for other purposes. They are not the outright property of the Chinese but are on a lease from Howard de Walden Estates.

If we compelled the staff to vacate the Portland Place premises we would have to find other accommodation for them. Some could no doubt live in the Gloucester Gate and Maida Vale premises but the amount of accommodation there is still being checked.

3. *Use of diplomatic wireless facilities.* In spite of the instruction given by Mr Thomson to the Chinese Chargé d'Affaires last night that his Mission were not to use their diplomatic wireless facilities until such time as ours in Peking has been restored, GCHQ Cheltenham, who monitor the Chinese, tell us that they did use their diplomatic wireless this morning. We are considering technical ways of making this wireless inoperable but the best way to stop it would be to remove the Chinese from the building, ensuring that they did not take their wireless facilities with them.

4. *Rupture of diplomatic relations with China.* There are strong objections to making a complete break. One is that we still believe the internal situation in China to be so fluid that dramatic political changes there could take place quite suddenly and if they did it could be very much to our advantage to have a foothold in Peking. A more immediate objection is that if we break diplomatic relations the Chinese are likely (I think almost certain) to say that the members of our mission in Peking no longer enjoy any diplomatic immunity at all. It is true that as recent events have shown diplomatic immunity in China is virtually worthless. Nevertheless we think that the prospects for the treatment of our staff in Peking are better if they still enjoy even such diplomatic immunity as they now have than if they had none at all.

5. *Withdrawal of mission without rupture of diplomatic relations.* We could tell the Chinese that we for our part are not formally breaking diplomatic relations with them but as they have made it impossible for our mission to function we are withdrawing it. This, in our view, (the Chief Clerk agrees) would be the best course. There are, however, two difficulties:

(*a*) we have no guarantee that the Chinese would allow the members of our mission to leave; and

(*b*) there might be some public criticism if we withdraw the members of the mission, who have diplomatic status, while other British subjects, without diplomatic status, remain hostages in China. These include Mr Grey of Reuters, bankers in Shanghai (five, plus families) and about 20 engineers and technicians (including families) on a construction job in Lanchow in North-West China.

6. *Pressure on the Chinese by friendly powers.* We understand that the French Ambassador has sought to protest at the treatment we have received but as far as we know now he has not yet been able to see the Ministry.

The Scandinavians will almost certainly make their views known to the Chinese in whatever way they can.

The Russians expressed their thanks to us when our mission helped theirs when they were in difficulty but we doubt whether they would want to do very much for us in this instance. This is because the Chinese say that the action they have taken against us is in retaliation for our 'imperialist cesspool' in their own back-yard. The Russians would therefore now find it difficult to protest to the Chinese for having taken action which in fact the Russians have been inciting them to take.

The Pakistanis maintain reasonably friendly relations with China and, subject to the views of the Commonwealth Office which we have not yet sought, would probably be prepared to express concern at our treatment. But they would not, we feel, take very vigorous action, and in any event the Chinese would pay no attention to them.

The Indians, who are themselves the subject of Chinese maltreatment and abuse, are hardly likely to want to stick their necks out on our behalf.

The Dutch, who are represented in Peking, will certainly express their solidarity in any way they can but will be completely ignored.

The West Germans, Japanese, Italians, Canadians and Australians have no diplomatic representation in Peking.

7. *Trade*. Until recently our exports to China had been rising. The last available figures are: half year January to June 1967 inclusive (provisional) exports to China from UK £21,494,000, imports from China to UK £16,500,000.

We have, however, felt bound to ask the Board of Trade to warn business concerns, and particularly British shipping, of the dangers of sending their men or ships to China for the time being. If, however, we break off all commercial and business relations with China it will not cause them very serious harm since they can get elsewhere everything they get from us.

My minute of 23 August to Mr Thomson[3] set out the action against the Chinese in this country which we have already taken. Since it was written *the Security Service have agreed to place all members of the mission and associated organisations (NCNA, Bank of China etc.) under police surveillance.*

A. J. DE LA MARE

3 Not printed.

No. 42

Mr Bowden (Commonwealth Office) to Sir C. Pickard (Rawalpindi)
23 August 1967, 9.40 p.m.
Tel. No. 1069 Secret (FCO 21/37, FC 1/21/A)

Following Personal for High Commissioner.

Please pass urgently the following personal message from Foreign Secretary to President Ayub Khan.

Begins

My Dear Field Marshal,

You must have been as shocked as I have been by the events which have involved our people in Peking. I have been thinking very much about the action I should now take. I wonder whether you could help me at this point.

I do not want to break relations with the Chinese. I am even willing not to play this up. But I need some help. My first requirement is to get our women and children out. These I am told amount to twenty adult women and sixteen children. I would like this to happen straightaway and PIA[1] would clearly be the best way of getting them out.

Secondly, I would replace—since I do not want to break relations—our staff there one for one. Those who have been there have had a pretty rough time. They ought to come home and be replaced. I will of course let the Chinese do exactly the same in this country on exactly the same basis if they so wish.

1 Pakistan International Airlines.

I have as you know to make a speech at the United Nations Assembly towards the end of September. I will clearly have to say something about the way the Chinese have behaved in the light of the situation as it then is. If you can help me I would be very grateful.

GEORGE BROWN

Ends

No. 43

Mr Hopson (Peking) to Mr Brown, 24 August 1967[1]
Tel. Unnumbered Immediate, Confidential (FCO 21/37, FC 1/21)

1. Nobody has been seriously injured or has required more than first aid. My own scalp wound is healing nicely. Mr Seaby who has heart trouble and an old back injury has been suffering from shock but is recovering, though I should probably try to send him out to escort women and children.

2. The office is completely burned out as described in previous telegram and practically all its contents destroyed or severely damaged. The Residence has had all its contents destroyed. An attempt was obviously made to set it on fire but the fireman apparently arrived too soon. All official transport was destroyed except one bus and the heavy lorry.

3. We are at present allowed to visit both buildings. The strong rooms and safe are intact (see previous telegram).

4. Communications by commercial telegram with London seem to be working satisfactorily. We have facilities for limited cypher traffic, but we have not yet tried to send any by commercial channels, and would prefer to reserve this for emergencies for security reasons.

1 A note at the top of the telegram read: 'The following telegram has been received from Peking. The greatest care should be taken not to make known more widely than necessary the fact that such messages are being transmitted on our behalf.'

No. 44

Mr Hopson (Peking) to Mr Thomas, 24 August 1967[1]
Tel. Unnumbered Immediate, Restricted (FCO 21/37, FC 1/21)

All the members of staff and families are now housed in our flats in Diplomatic Compound where they have so far been unmolested. I would not expect further early molestation at this stage; the Chinese probably regard the present round as over. If a threat to these flats were to arise there is a good chance that most women and children could be taken away quickly to houses of friendly Missions, in

1 See No. 43, note 1.

particular French, Scandinavian, Dutch, Indians, Ceylonese, who have been tireless in their kindness.

2. We have established a new office in flat of which you already have address in Diplomatic Compound. Chinese office and domestic staff reported for work as usual this morning. I am trying to set up a small administration office in a separate flat in same compound to utilize services of key Chinese staff, i.e. accountant and administration clerk.

3. I have had no official notification of restrictions on movement. But attempt on 23 August to leave Diplomatic Compound in one of our surviving private cars was stopped by police at gate who said they could not take responsibility for security if we drove out. Our forays so far have therefore been in cars of friendly Missions and confined to visits to ruins of our office. We shall continue probing.

4. We are trying to book seats for thirty-six (thirty-four ladies and children plus two male escorts) in first available flights out, PIA, Air France or Aeroflot. We are also applying for exit visas for same.

5. I have so far had no contact with Ministry of Foreign Affairs though I have sent a Note of Protest for record on sacking of Mission and Residence and notification of our new office address.

No. 45

Minute from Far Eastern Department, 25 August 1967[1]
Secret (PREM 13/1458)

British Mission in Peking

As a result of the attack by demonstrators on the evening of 22 August, the office buildings of our Mission in Peking have been completely burned out and practically all the contents have been destroyed or severely damaged. The strong room containing classified papers remains however intact. It appears that the only important piece of classified material missing is a cypher machine which we must assume has been removed by the Chinese, although there is a remote possibility that it may still be amongst the wreckage of the building. Mr Hopson's house (which was next door to the office) has also been ransacked and all the contents have been destroyed. An attempt was made to set it on fire but this did not succeed. All of the official transport of the Mission has been destroyed except for one bus and a heavy lorry.

2. The mission is now operating from one of our flats in a large compound inhabited also by diplomats from many other missions.

3. Most members of the Mission were pummelled and struck by demonstrators when they finally left the burning office building. No-one however has been seriously injured or has required more than first aid. Mr Hopson himself had a minor scalp wound but this is apparently healing well. Members of the Mission, with the exception of Mr Hopson (whose house has been ransacked) and one second secretary (whose home is in the centre of Peking) have all returned to their own flats in

---

1 This note was provided to No. 10 for the Prime Minister.

the large diplomatic compound mentioned above. They have so far been unmolested since the incident of 22 August, although they have been prevented from leaving the diplomatic compound except when in the cars of members of other Missions. Mr Hopson considers that they are unlikely to be further troubled by demonstrators at the moment and that, if such a threat does develop, it would be possible for women and children to be taken away quickly into the houses of friendly Missions who have all along given a tremendous amount of support.

4. Mr Hopson is now trying to arrange for all the women and children, plus two male escorts, to leave China by the first available foreign flight. He has also asked for immediate exit visas for all these people. We have not so far heard whether either exit visas or plane tickets have been made available but it is almost certain that there will be some delay before any of our people are allowed out of China. At the worst this could last for several weeks or even months. The Foreign Secretary has already sent a message to Ayub Khan asking for his help in getting our people out and suggesting that Pakistan International Airways might be used to do this.[2]

Action against the Chinese Mission in London

5. Immediately after receiving news of the sacking of our Mission in Peking the Chinese Office here was instructed by telephone that all their officials and those of other official Chinese Government organisations in London (i.e. the New China News Agency, the Bank of China and official commercial representatives) would require exit permits from the Foreign Office before being allowed to leave Britain. On the evening of 22 August these instructions were repeated to the acting Chinese Chargé by Mr Thomson and the former was also told all Chinese Government officials in this country would be restricted to an area within a radius of five miles from the Marble Arch unless they had received permission from the Foreign Office to travel further. Permission was also withdrawn for the Chinese to use their diplomatic wireless until our own wireless facilities in Peking were resumed.

6. On 24 August the Home Office attempted to serve a summons on the five members of the New China News Agency Office in London, holding official Chinese passports, requiring them to report twice daily to a police station. This summons was read to a girl from the Office who refused to accept it and said that all such communications should be made through the Chargé's Office. Under the Aliens Order the police are unable to enter the NCNA premises in order to serve the summons. They are therefore guarding the entrance and will serve the summons as soon as any of those concerned emerge. Even if they succeed in doing this it is quite likely that the summons will be disobeyed. If it is, those concerned could be charged, and if convicted sent to gaol. The Home Office are considering what further steps can be taken to enforce their order.

7. The police and security services have put a guard on the Chinese Office and have arranged to follow any member of the Chinese Mission to ensure that they do not infringe the five mile travel ban. So far there have been no such infringements and it is probably unlikely that the Chinese will attempt any. We know however that the Chinese are continuing to use their diplomatic wireless despite the prohibition. We are now examining technical methods of preventing its use. The wireless could be

2 See No. 42.

jammed, but the technical services concerned are reluctant to do so because of possible retaliation against our diplomatic wireless in South East Asia. The only alternative to jamming would be to raid the Chinese Mission and confiscate their wireless but this would be an extremely serious step to take particularly since the Chinese would almost certainly resist. Since our own people in Peking remain virtual hostages we are giving very careful thought to the matter before proceeding any further.

Hong Kong

8. The effect of the sacking of the British Mission on Chinese Communist activities in Hong Kong has probably been to encourage zealots and incite them to greater violence. There is no evidence of any directive by the Chinese Government. Border incursions continue but the Chinese Army seem to be exercising a restraining influence and preventing demonstrations going too far.

FAR EASTERN DEPARTMENT

No. 46

Letter from Mr Cradock (Peking) to Mr Denson, 29 August 1967
Confidential (FCO 21/34, FC 1/14/B)

Dear John,

You have had our telegram of 23 August[1] giving a short account of the attack on our Office and the Residence. You will, I hope, before too long receive a despatch on the subject. We are also collecting some short personal accounts which may be of value to you for details and perhaps eventually to the historians. In the meantime you may find it helpful to have some hasty notes on certain aspects of the affair.

(*a*) The first and perhaps obvious point is that this was not an irrational outburst of mob violence, but a carefully planned and controlled operation. Behind the façade of 'severe action by the enraged masses' (*People's Daily*) there was close co-operation between the PLA and Red Guards. Each had its brief. The masses were given licence at that appointed time to burn and break up most of the premises. But the secure zone of the Office was deliberately preserved from fire and the PLA clearly had orders to ensure our eventual safety after a good deal of roughing-up and humiliation. The Red Guards who made the assault came prepared with all that was needed: the battering ram was in use from the first few minutes and they were seen by the Poles bringing their own petrol. Leaders gave directions by blowing whistles. The signal for the operation just after 10.30 was a red flare (according to the Indian Military Attaché). Cameras were in readiness to record the fun.

(*b*) The operation had the usual qualities of Communist Chinese military tactics: surprise and speed. First surprise. Their intentions were disguised by normal demonstrations (parades and petitions) on Monday 21 August and by the fairly standard, though more violent, protests by our Chinese office staff on the morning of 22 August. From lunch time on 22 August the numbers at the front gate built up slowly

---

1 See No. 38.

but they remained extremely orderly. Shortly after 10 p.m. I stood on the Office terrace listening to them. Someone was introduced as a speaker, made a speech about Hong Kong and withdrew to polite applause. It could have been a political meeting almost anywhere. The search lights and broadcasting equipment by the gate seemed to presage a long siege and less violent demonstrations. Our own egress was stopped from 1.30 pm when the police restrained, rather than positively prevented, our leaving the Office. If we had had a word of warning we could have had everything smashed and been over the wall into the adjoining Indian Embassy houses. But at some point in the evening it seems our telephone lines were cut; no-one could get a warning through. There was also no message from the Ministry of Foreign Affairs on the expiry of the ultimatum.

(*c*) Our own estimate on 22 August was that we were in for a siege like that the Indians had undergone, or the Mongolians about ten days before. Limited incursions, as recently against the Russians, seemed possible. But full scale sacking had hitherto been reserved for the Indonesians who had made violent attacks themselves on Chinese diplomatic premises in Djakarta. If asked we would have forecast all-out attack as the next move but one against us. We also expected a summons to the Ministry of Foreign Affairs at the expiry of the ultimatum.

(*d*) As regards speed, estimates of the length of the attack vary but the longest is three quarters of an hour from the scaling of the compound gates to our emergence from the Registry back door. We were in Registry about two minutes. The preceding weekend we had drawn up a rough plan (called Armageddon) against the contingency of an all-out attack. This envisaged gradual withdrawal behind a series of defensive points: first the wooden door beside the Chancery Guard's desk leading to the stairs and the first floor confidential offices; second behind the sliding metal grille leading to the secure zone; finally behind the Registry grille with the reinforced door at the back of the Registry as our final escape route in case of fire. This plan we followed but it was rather like running a familiar film through at double speed. The points were hardly manned before they were endangered. We were continuously on the retreat. At one point when we were within the Registry it seemed that the attack might be called off; there was a pause and much blowing of whistles. But this was probably only to reorganise and direct the forces against our Achilles heel—the exit door from Registry and its surrounding brickwork.

(*e*) The final break-in took place at the brickwork to one side of the metal door at the back of Registry. The metal door itself was heavily dented but held. I was worried in case it jammed thereby sealing us in the burning building and this was one of the reasons for opening the door. But as it happened the mob had already transferred the battering ram attack to the surrounding brickwork and they had no trouble making a big hole. So that even if we had not opened the door the citadel would have fallen within a minute or two. Examining the rest of the Registry since I see that it held quite well. Registry window bars and riot shutters though only plywood stood up quite well. But even if the steel door and the wall had held the smoke from the burning first floor and from straw at the windows was making the place uninhabitable.

(*f*) Next our sins of omission. The decision against trying to smash cypher machines was taken by Donald Hopson in the later stages of the attack. Frankly we had left it too late. As explained above we had hoped that the mob might content themselves with smashing the outer and upper premises and at one point there was a pause suggesting this. But the final attack on the safe zone then followed fast and it became a question of saving lives. The Registry was smoke-filled and in the dark (the last our own decision to avoid attracting attention). The attack was coming in at a point between Registry and cypher room. At the time it seemed that if we detailed people to open and enter the cypher room we might well lose them altogether.

(*g*) Second, the map of Peking on the speech safe room wall (our telegram of 25 August).[2] This was an oversight. This map was hidden behind curtains on the inner wall of the safe room. I had given general instructions for the removal of all classified papers into the strong room. I had not however made a personal check. General responsibility I think rests with me as post security officer. However its only use to the Chinese would be as 'evidence' if they decided to trump up charges of espionage against us.

(*h*) Those who broke into the secure zone were not indiscriminate vandals. They made for those rooms where the Chinese office cleaners had not been allowed and, as pointed out above, these rooms were largely preserved from fire. They broke into the cypher room by breaking through the wall at the side of the door. They broke into the loft both through the cupboard in the Second Secretary's room and by taking tiles off the roof. As already reported, all really sensitive equipment had been removed to the strong room on 21 and 22 August where it was later recovered and destroyed. One or two items were taken from the loft (Astro and CEI receivers). Little or nothing was taken from room 7A. From beside the speech safe room two cases of DTMS defensive equipment were taken but may have been burnt. A further mark of selectivity; the DWS room with its Piccolo equipment[3] was left alone apart from a perfunctory attempt at burning by flinging in an oil lamp.

(*i*) The strong room was intact and though the Yale key disappeared (torn away with a good part of my trousers) we got in again. Its very considerable contents have now been destroyed in a crash burning programme. No classified paper remains on the premises. It is interesting, and perhaps reassuring, that the PLA at the gates, who must have known what our successive teams using every available burning device were about, did not interfere. According to a Polish source a saloon car carrying a high ranking PLA officer was seen at the Residence on the morning of 23 August. What he was up to is a matter for conjecture. Otherwise there has been no further intrusion, that we are aware of. But there is nothing, according to our estimates, incriminating or of intelligence value to the Chinese left.

2. I enclose an extra 3 copies for distribution to interested parties. In view of the contents we are not retaining a copy. We shall be sending separately photographs of relevant parts of the building.[4]

Yours ever,
PERCY

2 Not printed.
3 A machine used for wireless diplomatic communication.
4 Prior to Mr Cradock's letter staff in London were under the impression that the burning of the Embassy had not been premeditated, supported by an unconfirmed report that Chou En-ai had expressed displeasure at the incident. If this was true then it raised the question of who was in control in Peking (minute by Mr de la Mare, 7 September 1967).

Burnt out and ransacked offices, 1967.

No. 47

Note of a conversation between Mr Wilson (No. 10) and Mr Jenkins (Home Office), 30 August 1967
Confidential (PREM 13/1458)

Incidents outside the Chinese Embassy

The Home Secretary telephoned the Prime Minister at 8.00 p.m. on August 29 to speak about the events outside the Chinese Embassy earlier that day. The *Home Secretary* said that 3 policemen had been injured and that one had been detained in hospital. The *Home Secretary* said that he was worried about what might happen on subsequent occasions. The Chinese had attacked the police and one had been pointing a pistol though it was not known whether this was loaded. Others had axes and iron bars. He had discussed the situation with the Deputy Commissioner of Police who, though confident that police could handle the situation, and that it was not necessary to call for military help, was nevertheless worried about the danger to unarmed policemen. A very difficult situation would clearly occur if an unarmed policeman were to be killed by a Chinese.

The *Prime Minister* agreed and suggested that the Home Secretary should consider whether at least some of the police should be armed. If a policeman were killed by the Chinese the *Prime Minister* thought it would be necessary to consider withdrawing the immunity and taking the Chinese into custody. He asked the Home Secretary to look into how the immunity for Diplomats in London could be withdrawn in circumstances such as this. The *Prime Minister* also suggested that it might be desirable to have a film camera in position outside the Chinese Embassy on the following day so that a complete record of events could be taken in case this was required in any subsequent court proceedings.

The *Home Secretary* said that he would consider this and also whether some of the Special Branch police should be armed. He was, however, concerned about the possible repercussions to Mr Hopson and his staff in Peking if anything should happen to one of the Chinese. He wondered whether it would not be possible to consider some lessening in the harassment policy. He was not sure that the harassment was necessary in order to ensure that the Chinese Diplomats in London were not allowed to leave this country.

The *Prime Minister* said that the present arrangements had been decided upon in discussions with the Foreign Office. He asked the Home Secretary to discuss the situation with the Foreign Secretary to see if any reduction in the harassment could be made which was consistent with the objective of controlling the movements of the Chinese.

The *Home Secretary* said he would discuss with the Foreign Secretary and have a further word with the Prime Minister on the following day if there were any outstanding points.

No. 48

Mr Hopson (Peking) to Mr Brown, 30 August 1967, 10.25 a.m.
Tel. No. 26 Immediate (FCO 21/64, FC 3/3/B)

I was called to the Ministry of Foreign Affairs at 5 a.m. today, where Vice Foreign Minister Lo Kuei Po announced that he wished to inform me about an urgent matter. He then read from a prepared text. Main points were as follows:

2. British police and plain clothes men were surrounding and carrying out various provocations against Chinese Chargé's Office, Commercial Office Hsin Hua and Bank of China in London. On morning and afternoon of 29 August ruffians and police beat personnel of the Chinese Chargé's Office. Ten people were injured and three seriously wounded. The Chinese Government lodged the most urgent, most serious and strongest protest at this barbarous atrocity, and demanded effective measures to prevent recurrence, ensure safety of Chinese personnel, medical facilities, compensation, punishment of culprits etc.

3. This incident followed a number of illegal measures taken against Chinese establishments in Britain on 22 August, which in turn were a continuation of Fascist atrocities in Hong Kong. The Chinese Government asks: where do you want to push Sino-British relations. You must immediately cancel all unwarranted measures and stop your provocations and intimidations otherwise you must face the consequences.

4. The Chinese Government announce that (*a*) from today no personnel of the British Office may leave China without Ministry of Foreign Affairs permission and exit visas already issued are cancelled: (*b*) all personnel of British Office must confine themselves to their office and residences and to movement between them. All other activities require notice of 48 hours.

5. I replied that I was not aware of the alleged incident of 29 August. Perhaps I would have been, if our communications had not been cut in last week's affair. I was surprised that the Vice-Minister had not referred to the appalling events of 22 August when our Mission was burned down and 23 of my staff including myself were manhandled and some injured—one being still seriously ill. That occurred because of inadequate protection from Chinese security authorities, whereas the British police could be relied upon to afford protection and behave correctly. The blame for any incident which may have occurred in London must lie with the Chinese staff.

6. In the ensuing exchange Lo Kuei Po said that what happened on 22 August was the fault of the British Government and Hong Kong authorities. I replied that responsibility for the safety of my staff rested with the Ministry of Foreign Affairs, who had failed to discharge it. I protested at the new restrictions upon my staff, but undertook to report the substance of the interview to you. Lo Kuei Po hastily concluded the meeting and did not attempt to give me the piece of paper from which he had read the statement in paragraphs 1, 2, 3 and 4 above.

No. 49

Mr Hopson (Peking) to Mr Brown, 30 August 1967[1]
Tel. unnumbered Flash, Confidential (FCO 21/64, FC 3/3)

My telegram No. 3119 (sic).

My interview with Vice-Minister could have been much worse.[2] Behind imposition of new restrictions, threats etc. Chinese may be seeking to move into a negotiating position. Following points are of note:

(*a*) Official communications with me have re-opened and at Vice-Minister level;

(*b*) Imposition of new restrictions were related to events in London and not apparently directly to Hong Kong;

(*c*) Requests that Her Majesty's Government should cancel restrictions in London were accompanied by usual threats of dire consequences, but this may perhaps mean just maintaining the new restrictions which have been imposed on us;

(*d*) The new restrictions do not in fact change our de facto situation much except we can no longer visit other Missions though they can visit us;

(*e*) Chinese have now got us in a position where we shall have to negotiate with them for exit visas etc., this may have been their intention.

2. If you agree on this interpretation of events, I hope it may be possible to avoid any action in London which may make the negotiations more difficult. I suppose you may be summoning the Chinese Chargé about yesterday's incidents. I do not think it would help us at the moment to impose any further restrictions on them. They might merely lead to escalation, whereas we want the opposite. You may think the moment has come when we should show our hand to the Chinese and explain that restrictions on them will be lifted as soon as the Chinese agree to allow safe exit with our staff and families. At the same time it would be helpful if you assure the Chinese that their Mission and staff will be given full protection and repeat the demand that we should be similarly treated.

3. I have naturally instructed the staff to observe the new restrictions scrupulously. There are one or two points of obscurity which we will have to test out, though as long as we can maintain access to the grounds of the former office and residence, they should not be insupportable, at any rate for a period.

4. Grateful for earliest possible information about the incidents of 29 August and your thinking. I presume every precaution has been taken against a recurrence as far as this is possible with present attitude of Chinese Diplomatic Staff.

5. I realise other considerations apply in Hong Kong, but I very much hope that the Hong Kong Government may be able to avoid taking further steps which would raise the temperature here.

---

1 See No. 43, note 1.
2 See No. 48.

No. 50

Mr Hopson (Peking) to Mr Brown, 30 August 1967, 12 p.m.
Tel. No 27 Immediate, Unclassified (FCO 21/37, FC 1/21/A)

A crowd of several hundred gathered outside the main gate of the Residential compound at about 10 o'clock this morning shouting anti-British slogans. At 10.30 a delegation claiming to be representatives of Peking revolutionaries arrived at the Office and demanded that within 15 minutes I should appear at the main entrance or suffer the consequences. Members of my staff reminded officers in charge of the body of troops which had appeared around the compound of their duty to guarantee our personal safety and also reported the incident to the Ministry of Foreign Affairs whose reply was that I should accept the protest of the masses. At the expiry of the 15 minutes the masses reappeared and there was nothing for it but to go to the main entrance. Here protests were read and attempts were made to make me and other members of my staff who had accompanied me to bow our heads which we refused to do. There was some manhandling but in the end the soldiers restrained the demonstrators. The whole performance appeared to have been organised by the committee of revolutionary workers in the diplomatic compound. A force of about 100 soldiers are now sitting outside the entrance to the flats where the office is now situated.

No attempt was made to molest the families.

No. 51

Mr Hopson (Peking) to Mr Brown, 30 August 1967[1]
Tel. No. 28 Flash, Confidential (FCO 21/37, FC 1/21/A)

The performance this morning underlines the fact that the safety of this Mission is now very precarious. The new restrictions on our movements prevent our evacuating families to homes of friendly Missions outside the compound. We may expect similar demands in the future for my appearance before the masses and in the hope of reducing risk of violence against the families I will have to make limited compliance, as today.

2. I must emphasise that any further incidents in London or action against left-wing Press in Hong Kong could have very serious repercussions for us here.

3. Please repeat to Hong Kong.

---

1 See No. 43, note 1. The telegram had no sent time but received at 12.13 p.m.

No. 52

Copy of a telegraphic message sent by Mr Brown to Chen Yi, Minister of Foreign Affairs of the People's Republic of China, 30 August 1967[1]
(FCO 21/64, FC 3/3/B)

Your Excellency,

The present state of Anglo-Chinese relations requires that you and I, as the ministers in our respective Governments responsible for our mutual relations, should discuss these relations frankly and dispassionately. I hope that you will take this message as a basis for such discussion.

Our representative in Peking, Mr Hopson was summoned to see your Vice Minister, Mr Lo Kuei-Po on 30 August. The Vice Minister announced the imposition of further restrictions upon the staff of the British Mission in Peking.[2] But, stating that he was speaking on behalf of your Government, he asked: 'where do you want to push Sino-British relations?' I would like to answer this question.

Without reviewing Anglo-Chinese relations in detail I can tell you, as I am sure you already know, that I personally, as well as the Government of which I am a member, have always sought good relations between your Government and ourselves, and in particular we have advocated your membership of the United Nations. We want to continue that support but I must make it quite clear that the actions that have been taken in China in the last months against British subjects there, including our diplomatic mission, are making our task extremely difficult. We have indeed come to the point when many people in this country are asking why continue to maintain diplomatic relations with you at all.

If I judge the sentiment of your Government aright I think that you too wish to maintain diplomatic relations. On this assumption I set out below what I think we should do to preserve them.

I will not rehearse in detail the treatment recently meted out to our diplomatic staff and property and to other British subjects in China. I simply remind you that our Mission and staff both in Shanghai and Peking have been subjected to treatment which would fully justify our rupture of relations with you. The sacking of our Mission in Peking has compelled us to impose certain restrictions on your staff and other officials. These restrictions have never been and are not as stringent as those you have for a long time placed upon our representatives. It was, for instance, only after the events in Peking of 22 August and the steps taken by your Government to prevent members of our staff from leaving China that we placed any restriction at all upon the free movement of your diplomats and officials into and out of this country. It is being represented that your staff in London have been subjected to intolerable harassment. I do not ask you simply to believe me when I tell you this is not so: please seek the views of any impartial observer in London during this last week.

1 This personal message was sent to Peking on the evening of 30 August with instructions that it be personally delivered if possible. In London, the Chinese Chargé was summoned and had the message read to him but Shen Ping left without accepting the text. The message was sent to missions in Copenhagen, Oslo, Stockholm, Helsinki, Berne, New Delhi, Rawalpindi, Colombo, Nairobi, Canberra, Ottawa, Wellington, The Hague and Washington for transmission, in confidence, to the foreign ministry in those countries.
2 Nos. 48 and 49.

I now seek your co-operation to bring the situation back to normal and to set us both on a better course in our relations. You may think that these would be best served if, while maintaining diplomatic relations, both sides withdrew their mission and personnel from each other's capital for the time being. If you thought this would help I would be prepared to allow all members of your diplomatic mission and other official organisations with their dependents and staff and any other citizens of the People's Republic of China in the United Kingdom who wished to leave this country to do so, on the clear understanding that you would allow all British subjects in China, diplomatic, official or others, who wished to leave to do so at the same time. This would include, among others, Mr Grey, the representative of Reuters in Peking, who you now hold under house arrest. If you give me your assurance that you agree to this, but the Chinese newspapermen and news agency personnel recently sentenced in Hong Kong pose a problem for you, I may be able to arrange their departure from Hong Kong for China.

The total, but I hope temporary, evacuation of our mutual personnel might be the best means to ensure that no further incidents develop to make a breach inevitable. But if I could get your personal and official assurance that a British diplomatic mission in Peking would be permitted to function in the normal way and that the safety and dignity of its personnel would be respected I would be prepared to replace the present staff by a new but smaller diplomatic mission to you. It naturally follows that we would accept a Chinese mission in London on similar terms and with similar guarantees.

I think that I for my part have answered the question which your Vice Minister put to Mr Hopson. I repeat that my Government wish to maintain friendly and fruitful relations with you. There is no problem between us which is not susceptible to settlement between men of goodwill. May I therefore ask you, in the spirit in which I sent this message, to let me have your answer to that same question. In particular I would welcome your reply to the alternative suggestions which I have set out above. In the meantime you may rest assured that all your officials and nationals in this country are being given the fullest possible protection.

GEORGE BROWN

No. 53

Mr Hopson (Peking) to Mr Brown, 31 August 1967
Confidential (FCO 21/34, FC 1/14/B)

Sir,

The burning of the British Office in Peking

At 10.30 p.m. precisely on the 22nd of August a mob of several thousand Chinese broke into our compound and destroyed the British Office in Peking. They also sacked my house. In this despatch I have the honour to give an account of that event.

2. Two days earlier on the 20th of August I had been summoned at 10.30 p.m. to the Ministry of Foreign Affairs to receive the Chinese Ultimatum demanding

the release of Chinese journalists in Hong Kong and the lifting of the ban on three Communist newspapers within 48 hours. Actually the meeting took place in an ante-room of the International Club, whither we had been diverted from the Ministry where some unspecified fracas was in progress. Mr Hsueh, the gentle deputy director of Western Europe, when I rejected the Note because of its offensive language, was at pains to press it on me, emphasising the great importance of the time-limit. Whether he was privy to the Red Guards' plans or merely expected something of the kind, he looked a worried man as I took my leave. I shared his feeling of concern and took the opportunity that night to put the signed photograph of The Queen, as well as portraits of my wife and daughter, into the safety of the Office strong-room.

3. We were never in doubt that the Ultimatum was to be taken seriously, in that the Chinese would surely do something on its expiration. It also seemed clear to us that we were the most likely target. What form the action would take (a Chinese order confining us to the compound, massive demonstrations, prolonged siege, or sudden attack) or how far they would go it was impossible to guess, but we prepared for the worst. Mattresses and food were stocked in my house and the Office and instructions issued for all contingencies.

4. On the 21st of August signs of impending Chinese action became manifest. There were small-scale demonstrations and troops (unarmed) reinforced the policemen at our gates which, for the first time, they asked to be closed. On the morning of the 22nd I and my senior staff spent an unpleasant three hours surrounded by our own Chinese employees. I had agreed to receive a protest from them, but then rashly allowed ourselves to be trapped on the terrace where they insisted I must 'bow my head and admit my guilt'. This I naturally refused to do. So we stayed there until years of clock-watching finally had its effect. The numbers (over 50 to begin with) began to thin a little and as closing-time (1.30 pm) drew near and there was a smell of compromise in the air. Finally we were pushed to the main gate, where a crowd of demonstrators had by now assembled, and had the protest presented to us there, with no insistence on bowing of heads or other frills. From that time none of us who were inside the Office compound (18 men and 5 girls, including the wife of Second Secretary Weston) were allowed to leave it, and we were effectively besieged.

5. As night fell the crowd outside increased rapidly in numbers (the official Chinese report put it as 10,000). They were quiet and orderly, sitting down and packed tight in their ranks, while the preparations for the drama were made. Searchlights and loudspeakers were beamed at our building, and a sort of proscenium was rigged up over our gateway. There were speeches, recitations, songs and a rather festive atmosphere prevailed. We did not know that the audience were later to take over the role of actors in the grand finale.

6. Although we were prepared for the worst, we were not in fact expecting it at that particular moment. I thought I might be summoned to the Foreign Ministry as the ultimatum expired, to be given notice of official measures against the staff, *e.g.*, confinement to quarters, &c. We dined together in the office hall off a dinner of tinned sausages and peas, claret and biscuits and cheese, prepared by our ladies. After dinner I went to the first-floor to play bridge, while those of the staff who were not at work watched Peter Sellers in a film entitled, not inappropriately, 'The Wrong

Arm of the Law'! (The last reel was still running when the mob broke in, but we do not know if any tarried to watch.) Mattresses had been laid out in the various rooms for the staff to sleep.

7. At 10.30 p.m. I had just bid 'Three no-trumps', when I heard a roar from the crowd outside. I ran to the window, which looked over the main gateway, and saw that the masses had risen to their feet and were surging like an angry sea against the small cordon of soldiers, who linked arms three deep before the gates. It was an extraordinary sight which will remain imprinted on my memory. I saw at a glance that the cordon could not hold. I gave the alarm which was immediately echoed by our look-out downstairs. Card-players, film-goers and all moved at speed into the area on the ground floor leading to the secure zone. I only had time to throw on my jacket and look again through the first floor window to see the cordon break at one end, and the mob pour through and over the gates like monkeys. We locked the communicating wooden door of the hall leading into the confidential offices and as we pushed a piano against it, we heard the mob enter and begin hammering on the door. We then all withdrew behind the sliding metal grille at the entrance to the secure zone, locked it, and stacked filing cabinets against it.

8. For 10 minutes or so we listened to the noise of breaking of windows and smashing of furniture, and watched the glare outside as the official cars were overturned and set on fire. Steady hammering at a side door warned us that they would soon be through the rather weak grille which protected it. So I gave the order for everyone to withdraw into the inner sanctum of the registry behind another stronger grille. We were hardly in before we heard the other grille give way. The wireless operators had managed to get a final message through reporting that the mob was breaking in.

9. We were now in our last refuge, and in darkness so as not to attract attention. Outside the crowd broke the glass of the windows, but the bars and plywood shutters held. Liquid suddenly started spurting in through the gaps at the sides of the shutters. We thought it might be petrol, but Mrs Weston tasted it and announced it water. This stopped as suddenly as it began, and the mob then started to burn straw at the windows. We threw water through the gaps but the room began to fill with smoke. Meanwhile we could hear heavy blows, apparently from a battering-ram, being directed at the steel door which was our only emergency exit, giving access to the courtyard.

10. Then there was a brief lull and we hoped that perhaps the mob might withdraw, satisfied with the considerable destruction which they had already wrought. This hope proved vain, and with much blowing of whistles the offensive began again with a determined attempt to penetrate the wall at the side of the emergency exit. It was not long before a small hole was made, which was being rapidly enlarged. Smoke in the room was making breathing difficult, we could see the glare of many fires, and as it was now clear that the mob would soon be through the wall and there was a danger that we should be burned alive if we stayed, I gave orders for the emergency exit to be opened. This was done and, as the heavy door swung inwards, the mob began to surge through. I told them we were coming out, so their leaders pushed them back as I stepped out into the glare of the fires and searchlights followed closely by my staff. The mob greeted us with howls of exultation and immediately set about

us with everything they had. The time was then about 11.10 p.m., barely 40 minutes since the attack began.

11. From that moment we were split up, except the girls who all had one or two men with orders to stick by them. We were hauled by our hair, half-strangled with our ties, kicked and beaten on the head with bamboo poles. I do not know how long this lasted but I found myself eventually more or less out on my feet, by what turned out to be the side gate of the compound, though I had little idea where I was at the time. A tall man in scruffy white shirt and trousers grabbed me by the arm and dragged me out of the gate. 'Taipan, taipan (Chargé d'Affaires) come quickly' he whispered, and took me off at a run down the side road to the gate of one of the Indian houses behind our compound. He took me in and hid me behind the porter's lodge. A few seconds later he came back and, after a quick word with the police on duty there, pushed me into the police-box at the gate and told me to sit down and keep quiet. (I presume my deliverer was a police agent in plain clothes.) Shortly afterwards a medical orderly arrived who pointed out that I was bleeding copiously from a head wound, which I had not realised as in the darkness I mistook the blood for sweat. He bandaged it with a field dressing, which on later examination proved to have 'this side to the wound' printed on it in English. Needless to say he had applied the wrong side.

12. I was kept in the police-box for about two hours, from where I could see the glare of the fires a few yards away and hear the general hubbub of the mob and the noise of the fire-engines which by now had arrived. I was visited regularly by police and army officers from whom I asked news of my staff. After some time they said they were safe close by but were unwilling to let me join them at that juncture. Eventually at about 1.15 a.m. I was taken out of the box and about 50 yards up the side road I found the majority of my staff surrounded by large numbers of soldiers. Happily none of them was seriously injured. Of those not present I was told that four were known to be in the Finnish Embassy. Four others were unaccounted for at that stage. I glanced over the wall at my house and saw that it was not on fire, it had obviously seen sacked. We were then told to advance, bending down as low as possible between ranks of specially chosen tall soldiers in order to remain hidden from the mob, some elements of which were still on the rampage. Fifty yards further on we climbed into a military lorry, where again we crouched between ranks of standing soldiers. Preceded by a large black car we were then driven to the rear gate of the international diplomatic compound, about a quarter of a mile distant, where nearly all the staff reside. There we disembarked, and to our joy found the missing four, who by some miracle (and a little help from the army) had found their way back on foot.

13. Most of us then repaired to one of the staff flats for welcome refreshment. One of several members of friendly missions who joined us there remarked on the strange fact that of all the British present none asked for tea. We discovered there that, as soon as the assault on the Office was known to have begun, Mr Hunter whom I had designated to remain in charge of the families in the diplomatic flats had immediately arranged their evacuation by car to friendly Embassies. The French and Norwegian Ambassadors, and the Chargé d'Affaires of the Netherlands, Sweden, Denmark, Ceylon and India had all personally helped in the evacuation, together with members of their staff and some from other missions. The Finnish Ambassador

then appeared with the four who had taken refuge in his Embassy, so we could ask our colleagues to report to you that everyone was safe and comparatively sound.

14. We lingered over our drinks swapping stories and receiving visits from friendly Heads of Missions. Most of the staff who had been at the Office had had similar experiences to my own. Some were paraded up and down, forced to their knees and photographed in humiliating postures. All were beaten and kicked and the girls were not spared lewd attentions from the prying fingers of the mob. Most of those who were wearing wrist-watches had them removed, and shirts, trousers and knickers were torn. So much for the morals of the Red Guards. Mr Blishen had a fine black-eye. He and Mr Seaby, the Head Guard, who already suffers from an old war-time back injury, seemed to have received particularly heavy blows. Most of the staff were eventually rescued by the army and plain-clothes police agents and put temporarily in police-boxes as I was. Those put in the boxes at the entrance of the Albanian Embassy, which is opposite the Office, noted that its staff were watching the performance with considerable glee. Five of the staff managed to reach the Finnish Embassy (opposite my house), but of them only four managed to gain access, Mr Whitney who was putting up a gallant rearguard action being dragged back by the mob before helping hands could reach him. The four who managed to reach the international compound, where the staff flats are located, were followed in by Red Guards who continued to molest them in the courtyard. This was only stopped by the courageous intervention of Dr Fokkema[3], the Dutch Chargé, who eventually persuaded them to desist. Chinese army men then chased them out and there was no further trouble that night within the international compound.

15. So ended our 'Armageddon'. Looking back it is clear that the whole operation was carefully planned by someone, though by whom and at what level we may never discover. The Indian Military Attaché, who was watching from his house nearby, says a red flare was fired at 10.30 p.m. to give the signal for the assault. I myself heard continuous hooting of motor-horns at the same time. The assault teams were well-organised, with special equipment to effect entry, and they knew exactly where to go. Some even brought their own petrol with them. The unarmed cordon at the gate was obviously much too small to resist pressure from such a huge crowd. The rescue arrangements, with special police-agents mingling with the mob, had clearly been prepared beforehand. It is true that posters have since reported Chou En-Lai as denouncing the attack, but his influence has been in doubt for some time. My own guess is that the attack was planned by members of the cultural revolution group with the connivance of the security authorities, whose instructions were to save us from the worst. It is possible that in setting fire to the Office the mob exceeded its instructions.

16. We have reported separately on the damage. The Office is a total loss, though the strong room was untouched. All official transport was destroyed except the heavy lorry and one bus which we kept for emergencies in a garage in the international compound. My house was sacked and its contents including my clothes destroyed. The signed photograph of The Queen, which I had earlier placed in the security zone of the Office, survived though slightly singed.

---

3 Douwe Wessel Fokkema.

17. This has necessarily been mainly a personal account. I have asked all members of my staff involved to write their personal stories, and those I intend to send you in a later despatch. Meanwhile I enclose a list of staff who were in the Office at the time of the assault. I should like to pay a tribute here to the coolness, courage and fortitude which they all, particularly the girls, displayed. There was no sign of fear, all accomplished their appointed tasks without hesitation.

18. I must also mention the whole-hearted and immediate assistance rendered by our diplomatic colleagues as described above. Without this we should have been in much poorer shape and their co-operation is still an essential element in our survival as a Mission here to-day. I hope appropriate messages of thanks may be addressed to the Governments concerned.

19. This is not the place to dilate on the future of this Mission. I was glad that my recommendation that there should be no formal rupture of diplomatic relations has been accepted. Now we are concentrating on trying to arrange the evacuation of our women and children as a first step. So far we have made no progress. Our position here is still precarious and I feel obliged to ask that for the time being no use be made in publicity of the details of Red Guard behaviour described in paragraph 14 above.

I have, etc,
D. C. HOPSON

ENCLOSURE

List of those present in the Office of the British Chargé d'Affaires during the assault of 22 August.

D. C. Hopson (Chargé d'Affaires)
T. Peters (Commercial Counsellor)
P. Cradock (Counsellor/Head of Chancery)
R. W. Whitney (Chinese Secretary)
A. O. Blishen (First Secretary and Consul)
L. V. Appleyard (Second Secretary)
P. J. Weston (Second Secretary)
Mrs Weston
F. B. Holroyd (Administration Officer)
M. Cox (Archivist)
D. W. Fuller (DWS)
G. Mather (DWS)
J. Finch (DWS)
P. J. Talbot (DTMS)
M. Gallagher (DTMS)
G. H. W. Morgan (Clerk)
R. Webb (Clerk)
Miss M. E. Quirie (PA)
Miss A. V. Macdonald (PA)

Miss P. L. Iliffe (Shorthand Typist)
Miss E. J. Pilgrim (Shorthand Typist)
J. Seaby (Head Guard)
R. L. Bush (Guard)

No. 54

Mr Hopson (Peking) to Mr Brown, 2 September 1967, 7 p.m.
Tel. No. 32 Immediate (FCO 21/64, FC 3/3)

Your telegram No. 792.[1]

Having asked to see Ch'en Yi I was given an interview this afternoon with Mr Hsueh, Deputy Director of Western Europe. I read him your letter which he undertook to transmit to Ch'en Yi. He then made some 'personal' comments.

2. He said that the principal reason for the deterioration in relations between our two countries was the 'Fascist atrocities' being perpetrated in Hong Kong. This question had been completely avoided in the letter and only minor matters relating to the staffs of diplomatic Missions in London and Peking had been mentioned. In his view these minor problems could only be solved if the main problem was dealt with. We had received the Chinese Government's five demands in their statement of 15 May[2] and these represented the minimum. The British Government must accept them.

3. I said your letter spoke for itself but that you had proposed a discussion and would naturally take into account any suggestions that the Chinese might have as to what should be discussed. We await Ch'en Yi's reply.

4. I then raised the question of the withdrawal of our women and children from Peking on which subject I had requested a talk with Vice-Minister Lo Kuei-po. We had already applied for exit visas, had he any news? He repeated several times that Lo Kuei-po's statement to me on 30 August[3] was quite clear and he had nothing further to say. I then asked him to look at the problem from a humanitarian point of view, the women and children had been through a very trying ordeal and many of the children were waiting to go back to school in England. He again mentioned 'Fascist atrocities' in Hong Kong and asked whether these could be considered humanitarian. I then said 'is the Chinese government therefore treating our women and children as hostages?' he replied that was a decision for the Chinese government. He had nothing further to say on the subject.[4]

1 Not printed.
2 See No. 1, note 2.
3 See Nos. 48 and 49.
4 In Peking Tel. No. 4 of 2 September, Mr Hopson thought the fact the Chinese had accepted the letter and promised a reply was slightly encouraging, but the continued insistence on the Five Demands as a 'minimum' indicated how hard their position was likely to be.

No. 55

Memorandum by Mr Brown for the Cabinet Defence and Oversea Committee, 4 September 1967
OPD(67)67 Secret (CAB 148/33)

Relations with China

This paper considers what United Kingdom relations with China should be in the light of anti-British activities in China and Hong Kong, culminating in the sacking of the offices and residence of HM Chargé d'Affaires, Peking, on the night of 22 August.

2. *Recommendations*

(*a*) We should not take the initiative to break diplomatic relations with China.

(*b*) British women and children still in Peking should be evacuated as soon as possible.

(*c*) Male members of staff in Peking should be withdrawn gradually but we should attempt to replace some of them with other officers, so that the Mission is in a position to function effectively as soon as conditions allow. To the extent possible and subject to further review, officers proceeding to Peking should be unaccompanied by wives or children.

(*d*) Unless the situation worsens British businessmen and shipping should not be banned from visiting China but the warning already given [to] them of the possible dangers and of our inability to give them diplomatic or consular protection should stand.

(*e*) We should again vote for the admission of China to the United Nations, subject as last year to the 'important question' (which means that a two-thirds majority is needed for the resolution to be passed) but we should take no further action (e.g. lobbying) to promote Chinese admission, and our speech on the resolution should reflect the deterioration in Anglo-Chinese relations brought about by recent Chinese actions.

Action already taken

3. We have enlisted the aid of the President of Pakistan, who still maintains good relations with China, for the evacuation of our women and children and for the eventual orderly transfer of the male staff. The President has caused action to be taken with the Chinese but we do not know yet the result.

4. Lest our people in China be held as hostages, action has been taken to ensure that no citizen of the People's Republic of China, whether diplomatic or other, leaves the United Kingdom without permission.

5. Businessmen and shipping interests have been warned of the dangers to their personnel and ships visiting China, but such visits have not been prohibited. The latest reports from shipping interests indicate that, even in the last week, British ships visiting Chinese ports have not been subjected to the harassment with which they were met a month ago.

6. The Hong Kong authorities have been instructed that, though they must continue to take whatever steps are necessary to maintain law and order, any further measures they may contemplate which could lead to reprisals against British subjects in China must be referred to London before being put into effect.

Arguments on Recommendations

7. (*a*) *That we do not take the initiative to break relations.*

(i) *Trade*

For the first half of 1967 our exports to the Chinese People's Republic amounted to £21½ million and our imports from China to £16½ million. How these figures fluctuate will depend not so much on anti-British feeling in China, which seems hardly to have affected trade at all, but rather on the internal political state of China. If the present chaos and anarchy continue trade is likely to drop. Nevertheless the trend over the last year has been for it to increase and for the balance to increase to our advantage. It is true that countries without diplomatic representation in Peking (e.g. Japan and the Federal German Republic) manage to trade successfully with China, but we believe that if we, who do have diplomatic relations, were to break them off our trade might well be adversely affected. In view, however, of the unsettled conditions in China we cannot say with assurance that the maintenance of our very tenuous diplomatic relations is at present a major factor in any assessment of our future trade prospects.

(ii) British subjects still in China

If we broke off relations completely we would be publicly admitting our inability to do anything for the British subjects still resident in China. At least one of these, Mr Grey, the Reuter representative, is held there under duress and difficulties have also been put in the way of the departure of others. The total number of British subjects in China is small, and some, who sympathise with Mao's policies, would not wish for our protection or assistance in any case; nevertheless HMG might meet with adverse criticism if they appeared to be more concerned with the welfare of our diplomatic staff than with that of other British subjects who enjoy no diplomatic immunities, of doubtful worth though these may be in China at present.

(iii) The uncertain political future of China

We cannot tell how the Chinese revolution is going to develop. It may be that, whether under Mao Tse-tung or those who purport to speak for him, or under some other fanatic and xenophobic leadership, the present phase of violent hostility towards foreigners will continue or even intensify. If that happens there is no hope of any useful and effective diplomatic contact with China for the foreseeable future, and the presence of a mission in Peking will be a waste of money and a hostage to fortune. But opposition to the present regime is increasing all over the country. This opposition, as far as we know, is still based on factional, personnel and local rather than national interests, and it appears to lack cohesion or firm ideological motivation. It may lead to a fragmentation of the country into regional areas, virtually autonomous, under local leaders and warlords as in the 1920s. This would not necessarily be an entirely welcome development from our point of view, for our ability to exploit it would depend on the nature of the regime or faction which held the two areas of China of prime concern to us—the national capital in Peking and Kwangtung province, contiguous with Hong Kong. If the factions which held these areas were Maoist, or otherwise hostile to foreign interests, we would be no better off than we are now. But we should not overlook the possibility that one or other of these factions, or both, may tend towards 'revisionism' and peaceful co-existence. Here again it would not be of great practical help to us in the day-to-day problems of Hong Kong if the faction that held Peking were more friendly towards us but that which held Kwangtung, with which in practice we would have to deal with on

Hong Kong affairs, remained hostile. Nevertheless, a more tractable regime in either Peking or Kwangtung might offer us openings for exercising some diplomatic leverage, whether in relation specifically to Hong Kong or more generally.

So far we have discussed the possibility that either Mao's regime may be followed by one equally xenophobic and exercising greater nation-wide control than Mao's does at present, or that China may break up into virtually autonomous regions; and we have concluded that the first of these possibilities would offer us little or no opening for diplomacy and that the second, while less gloomy, would also be a very dicey proposition from our point of view. But there is a third possibility. There are good grounds for believing that the violent phase of the Chinese revolution may have reached its climax and may from now on blow itself out. This could be either a slow or a sudden process. If it is slow there is little a diplomatic mission in Peking can do but to watch and report. But if the process is swift dramatic changes can take place in China which, in the context of Hong Kong, we may want to exploit without delay. This would require the presence in Peking of a fully operative diplomatic mission.

(iv) *Hong Kong*

Hong Kong is our main residual problem with China. Between now and 1997 when the lease on the 'New Territories' expires we shall want to seek a peaceful settlement with China to incorporate Hong Kong into the Chinese political community with proper safeguards both for our interests and for the livelihood of the Hong Kong Chinese. There is no prospect of our being able to reach such a settlement with the present Chinese Government. At present our choices are limited to:

(*a*) holding out as best we can in the face of implacable Chinese hostility; or

(*b*) evacuating the Colony (if we can) leaving our loyal Chinese subjects there to face the consequences of their loyalty; or

(*c*) being kicked out by force.

None of these solutions is what we want. We want to negotiate the future of Hong Kong in a peaceful, sensible and humane manner. An opportunity to do this—perhaps by a declaration by us at the appropriate time that we are willing to discuss the peaceful transfer of sovereignty with a Chinese Government that gives satisfactory evidence of its adherences to the principles of the United Nations Charter—may come suddenly and if missed may not recur. To try to ensure that we do not miss such an opportunity it is most desirable that we have a diplomatic mission in China both to warn us of opportunities as they may arise and to advise us of the Chinese personalities with whom we might be able to do business.

8. If the recommendation in paragraph 2 (*a*) is accepted, recommendations (*b*), (*c*) and (*d*) will follow automatically and need only administrative action. There remains recommendation (*e*), that we still vote for China's admission to the United Nations. The argument for support of this recommendation is contained in the first annex to this paper. The second annex deals in more detail with the position in Hong Kong.

G.B.

ANNEX 1

Chinese Representation in the United Nations

Problem

In view of recent events should we now change our policy towards Chinese representation at the United Nations?

Recommendation

2. We should continue to vote for China and also for the 'important question' resolution. The speech by our representative supporting this policy should however reflect the deterioration in Anglo-Chinese relations brought about by recent Chinese actions.

Background and Argument

3. Our policy at last year's General Assembly, and for some years before that, was to vote for the Chinese People's Republic on the substantive resolution about Chinese representation. At the same time we voted for a resolution that this question is 'important' as defined by Article 18(2) of the United Nations Charter and therefore requires a two-thirds majority. Over past years the 'important question' resolution has been passed on each occasion. The highest point of support for China on the substantive resolution was reached in 1965 when there was a tie between those voting in favour and those voting against. In view of events in China and changes in Chinese foreign policy during the last year it is highly unlikely that there will be a majority of votes in favour of China on the substantive resolution this year and it is certain that there will be a majority in favour of the 'important question' resolution.

4. Since last year the Chinese have broken practically every rule in the diplomatic book and it could be argued that we should change our policy and either vote against her or abstain. The previous policy was however based not on approval of the actions of the Chinese Government but on the existence of China and the need for universal representation in the United Nations. However unpalatable the actions of the Chinese Government, the existence of China remains a fact and its Government should be represented in the United Nations. We have never been under any illusion about the disruptive effect the Chinese are likely to have if voted into the United Nations but we have always believed that the long term effect of attendance at a world assembly would help towards removing China from her present dangerous, though largely self-imposed, isolation.

5. There is however no good reason why we should this year make any great efforts to ensure that China is seated in the immediate future. We should stick to our present policy of voting in favour of the 'important question' resolution. In speaking on the Chinese representation resolution, our delegate should refer to recent attacks on our Mission in Peking and state that, in spite of these events, we still believe that China should be seated in the United Nations because her continued exclusion will serve only to exacerbate her relations with other countries. The interests of world peace will, we think, be better served in the long run by bringing China into the world organisation rather than in keeping her outside.

ANNEX 2

Hong Kong

There is reliable evidence from Hong Kong sources that the Chinese Government's 'ultimatum' of 20 August to Her Majesty's Government about action against the local communist press was in part a response to an appeal made to Peking by local communists for a demonstration of greater solidarity. There had earlier been increasing evidence of low communist morale in Hong Kong and indications that the communist leadership considered that they had no hope of obtaining the support of the population as a whole. The ultimatum itself and the attack on the British Mission in Peking will however have boosted morale in local communist organisations and will have encouraged supporting demonstrations on the other side of the frontier. Already there has been increased local communist activity and further border incidents.

2. Before the ultimatum was issued the local communists had resorted to the use of more powerful and sophisticated devices resulting in death and injuries to civilians. There is also evidence e.g. the murder of an anti-communist radio commentator with a petrol bomb, that a campaign against selected persons is to be expected. The continuation of firm measures by the Hong Kong Government, including action against the communist press, makes it likely that violence will increase rather than diminish. Three Chinese communist sympathisers, connected with publishing and printing of the independently owned newspaper the 'Afternoon News', were each sentenced on 28 August to three years imprisonment and a court order was made for the suppression of the newspapers for six months. One locally engaged employee of the New China News Agency, an official Chinese Government organisation, and another communist journalist are serving two-year sentences of imprisonment and proceedings have been instituted against five other reporters, one of whom is a member of the New China News Agency.

3. In addition to repercussions in Hong Kong, the firm measures taken by the Hong Kong Government, particularly against the pro-communist press, may result in still further retaliatory action against the British Mission in Peking and against British subjects in China. The acting Governor has been asked to take this into consideration when deciding on further measures. He has agreed to do so but has pointed out that in the course of necessary action against Chinese demonstrators it may be impossible to avoid the arrest of further communist journalists. One such arrest has already taken place. It would clearly be wrong to modify the policy of firmness in Hong Kong, for this would be the first step towards the abdication of our authority and the creation of a Macao-type situation.[1]

4. Any attempt to negotiate with the present Chinese leadership over Hong Kong either on the basis of a return to the *status quo* or on the basis of a British withdrawal from the colony under conditions acceptable to both sides would be out of the question. Any sign that we had such a negotiation in mind would be interpreted by the Chinese as weakness and would probably result in still greater intensification of pressure. When it became known in Hong Kong and outside it would also result

---

1 See No. 7, footnote 2.

in a rapid loss of confidence which would have serious economic consequences and make our exercise of control in the colony still more difficult.

5. It cannot be excluded however that, even during the current anarchic phase of the Cultural Revolution or more likely afterwards, some of the regional areas might break away from control by Peking and pass under the leadership of more rational Party or Army groups. If this occurred in Kwangtung, the province bordering on Hong Kong, it might be possible to arrange a *modus vivendi* which would relieve some of the pressures on the colony. So far, however, the evidence available shows that the Army remains in control along the frontier and subject to Headquarters in Peking. Further back, however, in Canton there has been considerable disorder and this could conceivably spread throughout the whole province.

6. Looking beyond the Cultural Revolution, which is at the root of all the present troubles, and which is likely to end or, at least, lose much of its present fury and irrationality when Mao leaves the political scene, it is possible that a more orthodox and pragmatic government will emerge. Its first task would be to end the present confusion and re-assert central control to enable it to deal with China's pressing internal problems. It would be unlikely to reverse China's general policy of hostility towards the West. But over a period it might modify this attitude, as did the Soviet Union, and revert to China's earlier policy of accepting the *status quo* in Hong Kong. At this stage, if we were prepared to move quickly we might be able to negotiate a gradual handover to China of a viable Hong Kong and to arrange for our orderly withdrawal. With our present hindsight, it would be most unwise to wait again until the situation once more deteriorated in China before considering how we would best divest ourselves of the colony. This and other aspects of the long-term future of Hong Kong are now being studied in detail by the Defence Review Working Party which will be reporting soon to the DOPC.

7. Meanwhile we do not consider that, in the short term, the Chinese intend to launch a military attack on Hong Kong nor even that they wish to create an internal security situation which would offer them a pretext to intervene to restore law and order. Their maximum objective seems to be the creation of a Macao-type situation in which we would continue to exercise nominal control but they would be in a position to dictate all major decisions and at the same time continue to reap substantial economic benefits from the colony. There is however, a danger that if the situation in China, particularly in the Kwangtung province (where there have been persistent reports of unrest and armed clashes), deteriorates still further there might be a sudden influx of a large number of Chinese refugees into the colony which in itself could lead to immense problems both of security and of general administration (i.e. food). In present circumstances the Chinese Government might be unwilling or unable to control such an exodus. Their ability to do so would depend largely on the attitude of the Chinese Army in Kwangtung province. Up to now the Army, while permitting Red Guards and others to carry out incursions across the Hong Kong border, has in general exercised a restraining influence and eventually taken action to prevent getting out of hand.

Conclusions

8. The present firm policy to curb the activities of terrorists and of communist organisations and press and information media should continue. While the British Mission and other British subjects remain in China account should, as far as possible,

be taken by the Hong Kong Government of possible repercussions in China of specific actions against the communists in Hong Kong. Meanwhile, we should watch the internal situation in China very closely to ensure that, as it evolves, we do not miss any opportunity which may present itself to open negotiations for a peaceful transfer of sovereignty of the colony.

No. 56

Extract from the minutes of a meeting of the Cabinet Defence and Oversea Policy Committee, 5 September 1967, 10.30 a.m.[1]
OPD(67)29th Meeting Secret (CAB 148/30)

3. *Hong Kong*
The Committee considered a memorandum by the Secretary of State for Foreign Affairs (OPD(67)67)[2] on the nature of United Kingdom relations with China in the light of recent anti-British activities in China and Hong Kong.

THE FOREIGN SECRETARY said that it was still impossible to diagnose the situation in China with accuracy or to predict how it would develop. The immediate problem was to evacuate women and children from the Office of British Chargé d'Affaires in Peking and gradually to replace the present staff of the Mission. To break relations with China would not help to extricate our staff and their dependents and, if conditions in China become somewhat more normal, it would in any case be useful to have our representatives in Peking, even though the importance of maintaining a Mission was not substantial in the contexts of our trade with China or the protection of British subjects. He had sent a letter in relatively friendly terms to the Chinese Minister for Foreign Affairs and we had enlisted the aid of the President of Pakistan in seeking the evacuation of our present staff and their dependents. At present the situation seemed a little calmer. The British Chargé d'Affaires has been received by an official of the Ministry of Foreign Affairs in Peking, but the latter's reaction to the suggestion that women and children should be allowed to leave had not been very favourable: he had reverted again to British behaviour in Hong Kong. The Foreign Office was examining, in conjunction with the Treasury, Board of Trade and Department of Economic Affairs, what financial and economic pressures could be exerted on China in cases of need, and the results of these deliberations would be put to the Committee in due course. For the present we should not take initiative in breaking off diplomatic relations, we should take the consequential action recommended in his memorandum and we should again vote for the admission of the People's Republic of China to the United Nations, while taking no action to promote it.

1 Those present were Mr Wilson (in the Chair), Mr Brown, Mr Stewart, Mr Callaghan (Chancellor of the Exchequer), Mr Crossman (Lord President of the Council) and Mr Jenkins (Home Secretary). Also attending were Mr Marsh (Minister of Power), Mr Prentice (Minister of Overseas Development), Mr Wigg (Paymaster-General), Mr Reynolds (Minister of Defence for Administration), Mr Thomas, Sir G. Cole (representing Chief of the Defence Staff) and Sir B. Trend.
2 No. 55.

In discussion, some doubt was expressed about the possibility of reconciling the need to take firm measures in Hong Kong with the undesirability of taking any action which might provoke reprisals against the Office of the British Chargé d'Affaires in Peking and it was urged that the former should where necessary prevail. The general view was however that the attempt should be made to hold the balance between these two factors and to keep the situation as calm as possible, though it was essential that we should take such action as was required to maintain full control in Hong Kong. It was also noted that the present police surveillance of the Chinese diplomatic mission in London created a considerable strain on police man-power and some reduction would be desirable by the following week if the situation then allowed.

With particular reference to Hong Kong, the point was made that action was essential in the near future against the so-called 'mosquito broad sheets' (containing threats of death against leading personalities). Since these were printed on presses belong[ing] to the Government of the People's Republic of China the problem of how to deal with them was a particularly awkward one, but the Officer Administering the Government was convinced that firm action must be taken if the Hong Kong authorities were not to lose the confidence of the population. Equally, action was necessary against persons carrying bombs and the view had been expressed that the death penalty might be prescribed in such cases. No action would be taken on any of these points without reference first to Ministers. Apart from this aspect of the situation in the Colony, there was the question of the strength of forces to be maintained there. Despite the long-term plans for the reduction of the garrison, which had been agreed in the course of the recent defence expenditure studies, it had been necessary recently to increase the forces in the colony by one battalion and two RAF flights. It would probably also be necessary to send reinforcements to Hong Kong to cover the period of early October, when the traditional Chinese celebrations might lead to further disturbances.

THE PRIME MINISTER, summing up the discussion, said that the situation must be kept under close review by the Ministers concerned and by the Ministerial Committee on Hong Kong as necessary. Any proposals for action in Hong Kong must be considered in relation to its possible effects on the staff of the office of the British Chargé d'Affaires in Peking and their dependants, though clearly we must do whatever was essential to enable the local Government to maintain order. In the meantime, it would be dangerous if our plans for reducing the garrison of Hong Kong the following spring were to become known. Work on these plans should therefore be abandoned for the time being though our long term plans to that end should remain in force.

The Committee:

(1) Approved the recommendation in OPD (67) 67.

(2) Invited the Minister of Defence (Administration) to cancel any further action on planning for the ultimate reduction of the garrison of Hong Kong on the basis indicated by the Prime Minister.

(3) Invited the Foreign Secretary and the Minister of State, Commonwealth Office, to keep the situation under close review and to consider action to maintain order in Hong Kong including the reinforcement of the garrison during the Chinese celebrations in early October, on the basis indicated by the Prime Minister.

No. 57

Mr Brown to Mr Hopson (Peking), 6 September 1967, 12.33 p.m.[1]
Tel. No.18 Immediate, Confidential (FCO 21/65, FC 3/3/C)

On 4 September the Chinese Mission telephoned to say that two diplomatic couriers would be arriving at London airport at 1300 hours on 6 September, that they intended to send a driver and two other members of the staff to meet them and escort them to the office and that they demanded we take steps to ensure the security of their personnel and diplomatic bags.

2. When we pointed out that they were required to notify us in advance in writing about travel outside the 5 mile limit they drew attention to their protest about this 'illegal' imposition. In the interests of smoothing the way for the Queen's Messengers travelling to Peking and as the Chinese had, in practice, complied with our rules, we told them the journey would be permitted, adding that we would expect members of our mission similarly to be allowed to meet any courier we might send. A police escort will accompany the Chinese car to and from the airport and we are arranging for the immigration authorities to clear the couriers with the minimum delay.

3. Unless you see objection, please inform the Ministry of Foreign Affairs of the action we have taken and say that you assume similar facilities will be given to you and our Queen's messengers.[2]

1 See No. 43, note 1.
2 Mr Brown minuted: 'I can't help wondering why we didn't make this conditional on agreed reciprocity. Especially as we are taking that attitude on other matters. Also because of the fact that they are not complying with our regulations on wireless communications. What was the counter argument that justified what we did?' Mr de la Mare noted on 7 September: 'If as we believe, our couriers will be allowed to go to Peking on Sept 15 and members of our Mission there are allowed to meet them we shall have established reciprocity and, at least on this one issue, done so by relaxing, not by tightening, our controls. Reciprocity by mutual relaxation is, I submit, what we should aim at.'
Mr Brown commented: 'Yes: so long as we get it! But we are always "assuming", "believing", "hoping"!!'

No. 58

Sir P. Reilly (Paris) to Mr Brown, 8 September 1967, 6.28 p.m.[1]
Tel. No. 903 Priority, Confidential (FCO 21/85, FC 3/24)

British Mission in Peking.

The French Ambassador in Peking, who has just returned for a fortnight's consultations, and his wife lunched with me today. I took the opportunity to thank him formally for all the help and support which he and his staff have given to Hopson and his staff, and to assure him that great care would be taken not to compromise the French Embassy nor to overburden it with messages.

2. M. Paye who paid a very warm tribute to the courage and resolution of Hopson and of all the members of his staff and their families, gave me a graphic account of

1 See No. 43, note 1.

the events of 21 August[2] and the following days. He made it clear that as we had already gathered in a letter from Hopson which his wife read to a member of my staff on 6 September, the bestialities suffered by the members of the mission went much beyond what Hopson had allowed himself to report. All the men had been severely beaten with sticks and the women had suffered every kind of indecent assault short of actual rape. When M. Paye first saw Hopson that night not only his face but all his clothes were covered in blood.

3. M. Paye was very pessimistic about the prospects of getting the members of the Mission out. He had no doubt that the Chinese regarded them as hostages, and that they linked their treatment closely with Hong Kong. The incidents in London had clearly been provoked in order to justify what was being done in Peking. I asked whether M. Paye meant hostages for the Chinese journalists in Hong Kong, or something more. He said that he feared it was something more.

4. M. Paye said that he was sure that the Chinese were now unconcerned about the economic advantages to them of the present status of Hong Kong. They needed an external success to distract attention from the regime's present trouble and mistakes. They would not attack Hong Kong directly or risk war with the UK. He was sure, however, that they would increase the pressure by all means and especially by subversion from within and he thought that by intimidation and propaganda they would within the next year produce a situation in which virtually the whole Chinese population would be effectively under their control. They would probably not insist on a transfer of sovereignty for the present but would be content with a situation comparable to Macao, in which they would control Hong Kong while still obtaining foreign exchange from it.

5. On Chinese foreign policy generally, M. Paye said that thought that the Chinese would do all they could to prevent any negotiations over Vietnam. Everywhere else they would be intransigent and would make no concession to governments but would continue their support for revolution in the Third World and especially in Africa by addressing themselves to the people. The greater the gap between the rich and poor countries, the stronger would be their appeal. He thought that this threat should be taken very seriously.

6. Returning to the subject of our Mission in Peking, M. Paye said that the first thing was to get the women and children out. He clearly regarded this as urgently necessary. For Hopson and his staff he thought that an exchange with the Chinese Mission in London might be possible, but it would need precise formulation. The Chinese might for instance be sent to Hong Kong and the exchange arranged on the frontier there. But he feared that something more might be necessary, probably at least the release of the Chinese journalists in Hong Kong. It was evident, however, that he thought that even this might not be enough, and that our mission might be detained indefinitely unless we could offer some further concession over Hong Kong. He thought that since the Chinese could make our position there untenable, we would be wise to consider seriously taking the initiative in making some offer about the status of Hong Kong. We made it clear that HMG were not contemplating anything of the kind.

2 The attack took place on 22 August.

7. It was also clear that M. Paye thought that if we succeeded in getting out the present members of the Mission, the wise course was not repeat not to replace them, but to leave Mission closed without breaking relations. He was not in favour of the idea of reinforcing the Mission with new staff who would remain when the present staff would leave. He believed that this would actually be bad for the morale of the present staff who would consider it pointless to send in more hostages to be kept as confined and inactive as they were themselves.

8. M. Paye thought it possible that there would be no formal reply to your personal message to Marshal Chen Yi. The latter was under very heavy criticism. A photograph had just appeared in a local broadsheet showing Chen Yi bowing to the waist in submission of a meeting of Red Guards.

No. 59

Minute from Mr Rodgers to Mr Brown, 11 September 1967
Confidential (FCO 21/80, FC 3/20/B)

Secretary of State,

At the end of our Ministers Meeting this morning we touched on a question of reciprocity concerning our relations with the Chinese. In particular you expressed concern that members of the Chinese Mission should not slip through our fingers.

2. This arose from my reference to a visit of a Chinese ship, the 'Hangchou', to Liverpool. The position is that we were informed on 5 September that three members of the Chinese Commercial Office intended to travel to Liverpool to visit the ship. We made clear that permission would be granted only if we received a prior guarantee that British officials in Peking would be allowed to visit British ships in Chinese ports. They made the strongest protest against this and repeated their intention of sending three officials to Liverpool.

3. However, they did not do so, and we later intercepted a message that suggested that three members of the crew would come to London. In fact five members of the crew travelled to London on Friday night and returned to Liverpool on Saturday. They were under police surveillance all the time and the police are satisfied that the same Chinese re-joined the ship as left it.

4. The 'Hangchou' is due at London Docks towards the end of this month. We shall follow the same procedure on this occasion and with any other Chinese ships. Members of the Mission will not be free to visit them until we are given an undertaking about the same freedom for our people in Peking. We shall also continue the strictest surveillance of any crew members who visit the Chinese Mission.

5. On one matter there has been a slight relaxation in reciprocity. On 18 August we approached Customs and Excise in order to impose 'administrative delays' on Chinese baggage in view of difficulties experienced with consignments addressed to our Mission in Peking. Since then there has been an effective delay which appears to have caused the Chinese some considerable irritation.

6. However, we have made a small gesture by releasing the baggage that we have been delaying in the hope that this may lead to some slight relaxation in Peking. If

this does not of course happen, we can quite easily impose longer delays on the next Chinese consignment.

WILLIAM RODGERS

No. 60

Mr Hopson (Peking) to Mr Brown, 16 September 1967, 6.30 a.m.
Tel. No. 58 Unclassified (FCO 21/65, FC 3/3/C)

Movements restrictions.

I have been refused permission to take my weekly Sauna bath at Finnish Embassy, and also to dine out and play bridge. All other applications have been granted this week.[1] So far I have not been allowed to dine out at all.[2]

1 Members of the British Mission were confined to the International compound, where the residential flats were located, and to the old Office and Residence, and the 400 yards of road leading there. They had to ask permission 48 hours in advance to travel outside these locations, measures far more restrictive than the 5-mile limit imposed on the Chinese in London. (Hopson to Mr de la Mare, 20 September; FCO 21/37).
2 Mr Brown minuted: 'This is getting worse. Do we still play it soft?'

No. 61

Mr Whitney (Peking) to Mr Wilson, 15 September 1967
Confidential (FCO 21/65, FC 3/3/C)

Dear David,

One of the most important questions arising from the sacking of the Mission on 22 August is the extent to which it represented a deliberate act of policy on the part of the Chinese leadership. This was briefly dealt with in our despatch of 31 August[1]. There is, of course, no doubt that the affair was far from being a spontaneous action by the revolutionary masses and was in fact a well planned and executed operation which must have been sanctioned at the highest level. The problem is to discover who in the Chinese hierarchy was responsible.

2. During the past three weeks there have been a number of indications that the top Chinese leaders wish to deny responsibility for the events of 22 August and even that they regret and deplore them. Some of these we have reported by telegram but it will probably be useful if I summarize them all here.

3. Perhaps the first point to note is the restrained way the episode was treated in the Chinese official and, as far as we know, the unofficial press. The *People's Daily* and NCNA of 23 August went no further than saying that Peking revolutionaries

1 No. 53.

'took strong action' against our Mission. Since then the only mentions of Britain and Hong Kong in the Chinese press have been references to the 'Battle of Portland Place'[2] which appeared on 30 August and to the meeting and demonstration in support of China by 'progressives' in London on 5 September. (NCNA has had fairly regular pieces on Hong Kong). We half-expected that some of the many photographs of the burning building and of ourselves in the hands of the masses which were taken on 22 August would appear in the Red Guard newspapers. So far we have seen none. If they had been published it is likely that we should at least have got to hear of them.

4. Then there are the considerable number of posters which have appeared reporting that various Chinese leaders have condemned the sack of the Office. Both Chou En-lai and Chiang Ch'ing are said to have deplored what happened. Chou is reported to have asked his audience if they really believed such a thing was in accordance with Mao's wishes and, according to one account, Chiang Ch'ing denounced in particular the attack on the Chargé d'Affaires. Another poster says that 'at the time of the burning of the British Office' Chiang Ch'ing and Ch'en Po-ta issued a directive by telephone that the action taken against us should not 'overstep international norms'. If in fact there was such a directive one would like to know at precisely what stage it was issued and what are the 'international norms' it refers to. It is interesting to compare this with a story which was volunteered to a member of staff by a Chinese servant to the effect that Chiang Ch'ing, Ch'en Po'ta, Hsieh Fu-chih and possibly, although there is some doubt about this, Kang Sheng, arrived on the scene in a large car during the attack on the Office and had to intervene personally to stop the revolutionaries going on to set fire to the two British block of flats in the diplomatic compound.

5. Other posters quote unspecified Chinese leaders as saying that the State Council had not authorised 'the incidents of August'. This rather curious formulation appeared to refer to the attacks on us and the Mongolian Embassy and perhaps, on the Indonesians. We have also had reports that many posters now to be seen in Peking say that it is strictly forbidden to enter foreign missions or to molest foreigners in the streets.

6. Finally, we have just been told by a foreigner who works at the Foreign Languages Institute that a rumour is circulating that some people have been imprisoned for the part they played in the burning of our Office.

7. It is certainly difficult to know what to make of all this. It might well be that it is merely a smoke screen deliberately created by the leadership to cover up their role in what was in fact a considered act of policy. After all, whoever authorised the 48 hour ultimatum, with which we were presented on Sunday, 20 August, probably knew what was planned when the ultimatum expired. Another possibility is that the higher leadership was aware that demonstrations were planned but not how serious the attack would be. If true this would be an alarming reflection of the lack of central control of events in Peking. Another possibility is that between the Chinese leadership and those who organised the sack of our Mission there might have been a relationship very similar to that between the Manchu court and the Boxers; they might first have sanctioned and encouraged the revolutionaries but then, after a

---

2 See No. 47.

certain point decided it was wise to disavow them. The parallel with the events of 1900 is temptingly close in so many respects.

8. The most likely explanation, however, seems to be that the whole episode reflects something of the differences within the Chinese leadership itself. Up to 23 August, it appears that the extremists were able to make the running in foreign policy. The long series of incidents in the previous two or three months was a clear reflection of this state of affairs. The thesis is that the attack on us was the point where they overplayed their hand. Immediately after this the relative moderates, represented by Chou En-lai, were able to reassert their influence both in foreign affairs and, because of the precarious situation inside China, in domestic matters as well. Those leaders now in the ascendant are concerned generally to lower the temperature and, as part of this, to reduce or remove the threat to the security of foreign diplomats in Peking. They must be concerned (and with reason) that our holocaust should not lead to a general diplomatic exodus from Peking. If we are to believe the evidence of the posters, Chou En-lai has now been joined by two somewhat more unlikely advocates of moderation in the persons of Chiang Ch'ing and Chen Po-ta. Should this be the case, one is tempted to speculate that Kang Sheng, who in recent months has been seen to be playing a prominent role in the harassment of foreigners, may have suffered something of an eclipse. Other lesser figures who have been advocates of 'revolutionary' policies towards foreigners have certainly been in serious trouble during the last few weeks (I am dealing with this in more detail in a separate letter).[3]

9. Whatever may have been the various degrees of connivance and complicity on the part of the Chinese leaders in the sack of the Office on 22 August, the salient fact of the present situation seems to be efforts at some moderations in treatment of foreigners and possibly, by extension, in foreign policy. The latest incidents on the Sikkim border may belie that statement but one of the interesting points is that only the most carefully controlled demonstrations have so far taken place against the Indian Embassy here.[4] Had the affair occurred a month ago they would have been much more in serious trouble. This development gives grounds for hope that it will be possible to come to some sort of terms with the Chinese leaders ourselves. We can still expect them to be extremely tough in their dealings with us but there is now some prospect that in the future they will be more prepared to base their policies on the dictates of reason. This would be a great advance over the situation we have [been] faced with since May.

I am sending copies of this letter to Emrys Davies in Hong Kong and Brian Gilmore in Washington.

Yours ever,
RAY

---

3 Not printed
4 In September 1967, Indian and Chinese troops fought for four days at Nathu La alongside the border of Sikkim, then an Indian protectorate.

No. 62

Letter from Mr Brown to Mr Hopson (Peking), 18 September 1967
(FCO 21/34, FC 1/14)

Dear Hopson,

We think a lot about you and all your people—and wonder how we can help.

The purpose however of this note is to say that I have just tonight read your despatch of Aug. 31 describing the events you had to put up with on the 22nd of August.

Please tell everybody how impressed we are by the story of the courage they all showed. I only hope I would be as good in such a situation as they all were.

In particular tell the girls how much we all sympathise and admire them.

We shall continue to try hard to get you all home—and be guided by your advice. God Bless and Good Luck.[1]

Yours,
GEORGE BROWN

1 The letter was handwritten. In a reply dated 28 September, Mr Hopson said it was 'a great encouragement to know that you take a close interest in our fate'.

No. 63

Letter from Mr Hopson (Peking) to Mr de la Mare, 19 September 1967
Confidential (FCO 21/37, FC 1/21/A)

Dear Arthur,

It is now over two weeks since I delivered the Secretary of State's message addressed to Ch'en Yi. Although Hsueh then promised that a reply would be forthcoming, I am not particularly surprised or concerned that we have heard nothing so far.[1] It may be that the reply anyway will be given more by actions than by words. This in itself would not be a bad thing (provided, of course, that the actions are helpful), as in a formal reply the Chinese would certainly feel obliged to strike an uncompromising attitude. I am hoping therefore that eventually the Chinese will just start unfreezing the situation and that any suggestions from them will be given orally rather than by an official communication.

2. It is, of course, irritating that there is no sign of movement yet from the Chinese side, but I think we must be patient. They have, after all, some plausible reasons for temporising and no particular cause for hurry. It is possible, of course, that they intend to keep us here indefinitely as hostages, in one way or another, for Hong Kong, as Hsueh rather hinted when I gave him the Secretary of State's letter. It is, however, by no means certain that this is the case. In present circumstances when Ch'en Yi himself has more or less disappeared from view and Chou En-Lai, even if he is formally supervising the Foreign Ministry must have a great many other

1 See Nos. 52 and 54.

things to do, it must be a terribly slow business trying to get difficult decisions out of anyone. Furthermore, the Chinese must have sensed the danger that there might be general *sauve qui peut* in the Diplomatic Corps here, with Missions closing down and women and children being sent home. As you know, the Russian wives and children left earlier this year. Since then, the wives and children of the Indonesians, the Mongols, the Burmese, the Kenyans and the Indians have followed suit (or are in the process of doing so). Now the Kenyans, and the Indonesians (the Cambodians seem to have decided to stay on after all) are apparently trying to close down their Missions altogether. This must obviously be unwelcome to the Chinese since it gives them generally a bad name, so that they might well calculate that to let out all our wives and children now would create such a splash in the world press that the risks of a general diplomatic exodus from Peking would be seen as an admission that something very unpleasant had happened, when their line may well be to pretend as far as possible that the burning has never been.

3. We were encouraged when the Chinese let out the five school-children who were on holiday. Since then, as you know, we have put in another special application for three families and two individuals on medical grounds. So far we have had no reply, but we are hoping that the Chinese may be ready to feed people out in this way, rather than by general evacuation, so we shall just have to wait a little longer to see if they react. If not, we shall have to consider whether there is any further initiative which we can take which would help to break the ice. I rather doubt if there is in fact much that we can do as, if there is going to be a thaw, I would expect that Chinese agreement to let the women and children go would be the first sign. There is, however, one other ploy which we might try, in order to test out Chinese intentions generally, and that is to ask to send in replacements for one or two people who are already time-expired, on the understanding that the people concerned here would be let out, i.e. on applying for visas for the replacements we should have to explain to the Chinese that the new people would only come when the exits of their predecessors had been guaranteed. The person who comes first to mind in this category is Miss Iliffe (Commercial Counsellor's Personal Assistant), but I doubt if we should want another girl as replacement, at any rate at present. Are there such things as male shorthand-typists? The next person who might come into this category is Cox, who came here as a floater to replace Goodwin, the Archivist, during the latter's leave. His residence permit here expires at the end of this month, and the Chinese may then let him go. If, however, they keep him here it will be for consideration whether Goodwin should be asked to come back (without his family) to replace Cox, or whether a new man should be appointed. Or there may be an opportunity for replacing a Security Guard before long. Lastly, there is Theo Peters, but in present circumstances a Commercial Counsellor is such a luxury that I doubt whether we should be justified in asking for a replacement unless, in fact, it proves to be the only way of getting Theo out. The better course in this case may be to ask for Theo's release on the grounds that he has completed his tour, possibly adding that the question of a replacement is under consideration. (I am excluding myself from these manoeuvres as I must obviously stay here for the time being).

4. The Chinese seem to be making great efforts to give an impression among the Diplomatic Corps and foreigners generally that the attack on our Office was a

mistake. There is also, as you know, a general attempt to calm things down, partly, no doubt, with First of October celebrations in view. If the Canton Fair is held this will be an additional reason for keeping the temperature down in Hong Kong. It looks, therefore, as though we may be in for a fairly quiet two months or that, at any rate, this is the intention of the Chinese leaders. One can only hope that the calmer atmosphere will be more conducive to a solution to our problems. I am coming more and more round to the view that we should, in fact, try to maintain some kind of presence here, on a much reduced basis. For one thing, I think the Chinese probably want this and it might therefore facilitate the departure of the present staff.

5. Incidentally, have the Chinese Office in London been asking for any exit visas? I should be grateful if you will ensure that we are kept immediately informed of this kind of thing. If, for example, the Chinese have any exit visas outstanding, I suppose they may have been expecting some kind of return gesture from us for the departure of our school-children, though the latter were a very special case as they were only temporary visitors not residents like the rest of us.

6. To sum up, I think our course for the present will have to be to lie low and be patient, in the hope that the Chinese themselves will want to get the situation back to something like normality. The prerequisite for any such slow thaw is of course the absence of any further upsets from Portland Place or, as far as possible, from Hong Kong. For the moment we shall not do more than remind the Chinese that we have outstanding the special application for visas on medical grounds. If you have any comments on the above, or thoughts on how the game should be played, I should be grateful for them.

I am sending copies of this to Elliott in Hong Kong, Wilford in Washington and to Jock Duncan, as personal matters are involved.

Yours,
DONALD

No. 64

Mr Brown and Mr Bowden to Certain Missions and Dependent Territories, 19 September 1967
Guidance Tel. No. 238 Confidential (PREM 13/1964)

China.
See Guidance No. 196 of 4 August for an earlier assessment.[1]
The Internal Situation
2. There continue to be many reports of disturbances and confusion from almost all the provinces of China. The areas which appear to be the worst affected are Szechwan, Yunnan, Tibet and Kwangtung. These three former provinces belonged to the South West bureau of the Communist Party, of which the First Secretary Li Chingch'uan, has been under attack for some months, but whose present

1 Not printed.

whereabouts is unknown. Kwangtung (capital: Canton) is part of the Central South bureau of which the First Secretary, T'ao Chu, has also been under attack and whose whereabouts is also unknown. It seems likely that the disturbances in these areas are connected with residual support for the two formerly powerful Party leaders. In none of these provinces has an officially approved 'Revolutionary Committee' yet been established. Even in the few areas where officially approved Committees have been established, the situation is far from stable. Over the past month there have been a number of reports of disturbances in Shantung province, which was one of the earliest to announce a 'takeover' on 3 January.

3. The leadership in Peking remains confined to a small group round Mao and Lin Piao in which Chou En-Lai plays an active and to some extent moderating part. Ch'en Yi, the Foreign Minister appears to be in complete disgrace and has not attended any official functions since August. His ceremonial duties are at present being carried out by Li Hsien-nien (the Minister of Finance) and there have been reports that the Ministry itself has now been taken under the wing of Chou En-lai after an attempted revolutionary take-over between 19-23 of August. The position of the military leadership is not clear but differing reactions to the role the army should play at both provincial and central level may be reflected in the apparent eclipse of Hsiao Hua and the General Political Department of which he is the chief.

4. The Central authorities and Cultural Revolution Group continue to make efforts to bring the situation under control and direct the Cultural Revolution along what they consider to be correct lines. All students have been told to return to their own areas, fighting has been condemned frequently and the Army has been told to maintain order and ensure that there is no looting or theft of weapons. There have also been several carefully staged mass trials and executions of those said to have committed criminal acts. It seems that great efforts will be made to try to restore order and to set up new revolutionary alliances before the National Day celebrations on 1 October. Some progress has apparently been made in that preparatory groups have been formed in the provinces of Kiangsi (E. China), Kansu (N.W. China) and Honaria and Hunan (Central China). In all four cases the formation of Committees and preparatory groups appears to have resulted from initiatives by the People's Liberation Army.

5. These efforts are however only being partially successful. The main reasons for this are that indiscipline is rife and has been encouraged by the Cultural Revolution itself, while the rivalry between factions of Red Guards and other 'revolutionary' organisations is now extremely serious. Doubtless this rivalry is also encouraged by different leaders for their own ends. As a result of the confusion and disorder, transport has been severely affected in many parts of China, as has industrial output, although it is not yet possible to assess the exact degree of damage to the latter.

6. The Cultural Revolution itself is clearly far from over, though it may prove possible to achieve a pause during the National Day celebrations. The Central authorities still have reserves of power, which have not yet been used: they could for instance give more specific orders to the Army to re-establish order if they so wished. They are however reluctant to admit the failure of the Cultural Revolution experiment and are therefore trying to guide rather than end the campaign. If this policy is continued there is likely to be confusion throughout China for several more months and it is extremely hard to foresee what the final results of the campaign will be.

Sino-British Relations

7. Our mission in Peking continues to operate from a make-shift office in one of residential flats. Wireless contact has been resumed but on a very limited basis using book cypher. The Queen's Messengers have also managed to visit Peking. There has however been no progress in obtaining exit visas for resident members of the staff and their families though the Chinese did issue exit visas to five children, who had been in Peking for the school holidays.

8. Mr Anthony Grey, the Reuters correspondent in Peking, is still under house arrest and incommunicado although, so far as we know, he has not himself been harmed. Other British subjects in or visiting China have so far been unaffected with the exception of one member of a Vickers team building a plant in Lanchow for the Chinese, who has been prevented from returning to Lanchow from Peking while the Chinese investigate papers which were taken from his wife on her departure from China.[2] A German member of the Vickers team has also been arrested for alleged espionage, although we do not yet have full details. (Neither of these two cases is yet public knowledge and they should not be referred to unless the story has been leaked to the Press.) We are warning British businessmen of the risks of visiting China at the moment but are not advising them against doing so if they have good commercial reasons for going.

9. In London, police surveillance of the Chinese Mission continues (see Guidance 223 (not to all)).[3] There have been no serious incidents since the 'Battle of Portland Place' on 29 August, although members of the Chinese staff have made one or two unsuccessful attempts to create incidents.

Chinese Relations with Other Countries

10. We are not alone in our troubles with the Chinese. The Indonesians (whose Embassy was ransacked by demonstrators on 5 August) have decided to withdraw all their staff from Peking but have not yet obtained exit visas. The Kenyans have also decided to withdraw their two man Mission and facing similar delays about exit visas, while the Cambodians first announced that they intended to withdraw all their staff except for a junior caretaker, and then (after Sihanouk had received a conciliatory message from Chou En-lai) changed their minds. The Burmese have withdrawn their Ambassador and have left their Mission in charge of a Counsellor. The Russians have also been in serious trouble. Their Embassy was raided by demonstrators on 17 August, consular buildings ransacked and some cars burnt. The Mongolians too had their Embassy raided by demonstrators on 9 August after an incident involving the Ambassador's chauffeur although no damage seems to have been done.

11. The above is primarily for your own information but with the exception of points in paragraph 6 about wireless communication and in paragraph 7 about Vickers personnel, it may be used freely with reliable contacts with the caveat that our information about internal developments about China is at present very limited.

---

2 George Watt, an engineer employed by Vickers-Zimmer, was detained in Lanchow on 26 September 1967 and on 15 March 1968, he was sentenced to 3 years' imprisonment for alleged spying. A reply to an enquiry from the Prime Minister noted: 'Our friends [SIS] are in no way involved'.

3 Not printed.

No. 65

Note for Mr Wilson (No. 10) by Hong Kong Department (Commonwealth Office), 21 September 1967
Top Secret (PREM 13/3180)

Meeting with Sir David Trench, Governor of Hong Kong, at 5.30pm, Thursday 21 September 1967

Sir David Trench was appointed Governor of Hong Kong in 1964, after serving as High Commissioner, Western Pacific. He is more than halfway through his five-year term of office which expires in 1969.

2. He arrived in the United Kingdom on leave at the end of June, in a poor state of health. He had not had a proper leave for about three years; and a fairly serious sinus operation in early May, coupled with the strain of the early and more violent phase of confrontation with the Communists, had brought him to a low pitch. He has made a good recovery. Although in normal circumstances, we might have felt it desirable for him to have had a further month's leave in this country in order to consolidate his recovery, the consequences of such a delay would have been such that in his view (which was shared by us) the right course was for him to return to the colony on 23rd September.

3. Points stressed by Sir David in recent talks with Ministers and officials are:

(*a*) Ministers should be in no doubt about the seriousness of the situation for Hong Kong if China should exert strong pressure to achieve its proclaimed intention to humiliate us and drive us out of Hong Kong. We have assured him that there is no disposition here to underestimate the gravity of the Chinese threat.

(*b*) The United Kingdom must take positive steps to help maintain confidence in Hong Kong (including Hong Kong's confidence in our intentions towards, and support for, the Colony). This is the key to our ability to hold the situation there. This is not only a question of giving some tangible assistance towards Hong Kong projects, but of making other gestures of goodwill and support (i.e. generating some warmth in our relations with the Colony). We have been examining a number of projects and ideas with the Governor in this connection and will be reporting some of them to a meeting of the Hong Kong Ministerial Committee tomorrow, which the Governor is to attend.

4. As regards future policy on Hong Kong, we have summarised our present thinking as follows:

(i) HMG's policy is to maintain our position and authority in Hong Kong until China returns to some measure of stability and a Chinese Government emerges with which it would be possible to discuss Hong Kong's future, including the possibility of an orderly British withdrawal from the Colony. No negotiations or even discussions with China are possible at present.

(ii) Meanwhile, although any proposals for action against the Communists in Hong Kong must be considered in relation to its possible effects on the staff of the British Chargé d'Affaires in Peking and their dependants, we must nevertheless do whatever is essential to enable the Hong Kong Government to maintain law and order in the Colony.

(iii) If the situation in Hong Kong deteriorated to the extent that the Hong Kong Government ceased to be able to maintain law and order, an emergency evacuation would have to be carried out of those who would be in particular danger of Communist retaliation. In these circumstances it might only be possible to evacuate some 2000 people, mainly Chinese.

(iv) If it became clear beyond any reasonable doubt either that we were heading for a situation in which we could no long maintain control in Hong Kong, or that the mainland Chinese authorities firmly intended to establish effective authority in Hong Kong and were prepared to take any steps necessary to this end, including armed invasion, at that point we should plan to evacuate Hong Kong at the earliest possible moment.

(v) Our objective is to weather the present storm with a view to seeking a favourable opportunity to open negotiations with a stable Government of China about the future of Hong Kong. This could take several years.

The Governor accepted this.

No. 66

Minute by Mr Denson to Mr Bolland, 21 September 1967
Secret (FCO 21/34, FC 1/14/B)

Mr Bolland,

Mr Ewart-Biggs telephoned today to say that our friends[1] had been giving further consideration to the proposal that Ho Chi-Minh should be asked to intervene with the Chinese on behalf of our Mission in Peking. Though Mr Loseby[2] was dead, his daughter who is a lawyer in Hong Kong, still had some contacts with North Vietnam. She had visited that country in 1960. She had received a message of condolence from Ho Chi-Minh on the death of her father. In replying to this message or separately, if she had already done so, Miss Loseby might be willing to raise the question of our Mission. If we thought this idea worth trying, our friends would be willing to get in touch with Miss Loseby through an intermediary in Hong Kong.[3]

J. B. Denson

---

1 SIS.
2 Francis Loseby was a Hong Kong based British solicitor who defended Ho Chi Minh when he was detained by Hong Kong authorities, 1931-3 and helped him avoid deportation to French Indochina. Loseby, his wife and daughter, Patricia, visited Ho Chi Minh in Hanoi, as official guests, in 1960.
3 In a minute of 25 September, Mr Bolland doubted whether an intervention by Miss Loseby on their behalf would be successful. He preferred to see the outcome of a request made to the Pakistan Foreign Minister for their Minister of Information to approach a Chinese leader when he was in Peking on 1 October.

No. 67

Mr Hopson (Peking) to Mr Brown, 22 September 1967, 6.40 a.m.[1]
Tel. No. 72 Immediate, Confidential (FCO 21/65, FC 3/3/C)

You have no doubt been considering whether to say anything new in your speech to United Nations General Assembly about China in the context of events in Hong Kong and here. I am sure it would be wise to avoid saying anything which might oblige the Chinese to make some public comment which in present circumstances would be bound to be uncompromising and thus make any thaw in their present unyielding attitude less probable. From this post's point of view therefore the less said the better.

2. I realize that after all that has happened it may be difficult to maintain exactly the same attitudes and formulae. You hinted as much in your letter to Chen Yi[2] to which you may still get a reply. If our purpose is to facilitate normalisation of relations with China however, it will not be served in my view by any apparent attempt to bring public pressure to bear. A real effort is being made here at highest level to bring things back under control. Chinese leaders are letting it be known that attack on our Mission was a 'mistake' and they would clearly like to forget it. We should help them in this as far as possible as it represents our best chance of getting back to normal.

3. As seen from here the same considerations apply as a result of which the Chinese are also playing down in publicity at present.

4. I hope therefore that if any change in traditional formula about Chinese representation is thought necessary it might for example be confined to introduction of such a qualifying phrase as 'in spite of recent events which have seriously affected Anglo-Chinese relations'.

1 Repeated for information to UKMIS New York and Hong Kong.
2 No. 52.

No. 68

Letter from Mr Bolland to Mr Hopson (Peking), 25 September 1967
Confidential (FCO 21/80, FC 3/20/B)

Following the 'Battle of Portland Place' on 29 August we made attempts to identify from photographs those members of the Chinese Mission who were most seriously involved in the violence against the police. We have been able to identify nearly all those concerned and to pick out six who were particularly vicious. The most 'revolutionary' and adept axe swinger was Lu Tsung-min, a clerk from the Chargé's Office, who has also been a leading light in other mass quotation sessions on the steps of the Chinese Office. All those involved in the violence were, like him, junior officials and the only Chinese of diplomatic rank to be present through the 'Battle' was a Second Secretary, Chao Tse-min, who stood most of the time with his arms folded and a mandarin expression on his face.

2. It is not of course possible to take legal actions against any of those involved since all were covered by personal immunity at the least and there can be no doubt that, even were this not so, it would in practice prove impossible to bring them before a court. We did, however, consider the idea of declaring at least some of the six PNG[1] in the hopes that the Chinese would retaliate and that we would thus ensure the exit of some of your staff. One possible complication of such a course would be what to do if the Chinese then refused to leave this country and took shelter in the Mission. Their diplomatic immunity would of course have been removed and the police could grab and expel them by force if they left the Mission building. Should this happen, however, it is all too likely that the Chinese would similarly remove the immunity from some of your staff and I suspect that their subsequent action, which would not necessarily end in expulsion, would be a great deal more unpleasant.

3. We are not following up the PNG idea since we think it better for the moment to keep things as cool as possible in the hope that the Secretary of State's message may yet achieve some results and that the more moderate influences which may now be at work in the Foreign Ministry, will operate to our advantage. We still have it in mind however as a possible future ploy if the freeze on exit permits continues or things get worse for you in Peking. I should be very interested to have your views on the idea and its possible repercussions on you in Peking. Perhaps the way in which the Chinese react to the expulsion of two of their people in Djakarta will give a few pointers.[2]

E. BOLLAND

[1] Persona non grata.
[2] Hopson replied, in Peking Tel. No. 109 of 2 October, to say that the idea should be kept in reserve for the time being. It was only likely to bring about the release of a limited number and give the Chinese the chance to select for expulsion key members of Mission staff. Hopson preferred to take advantage of a period of relative calm both generally and in Hong Kong to solve 'problems connected with our representation here as we may find ourselves back in chaos in the New Year.'

No. 69

Minute from Mr Brown to Mr Wilson (No. 10), 7 November 1967
PM/67/100 Confidential (PREM 13/3180)

Prime Minister,

China: Relaxation of restrictions

You will recall that as a result of the sacking of our Office in Peking last August we imposed additional restrictions on the members of the Chinese Mission here. They were forbidden to travel more than 5 miles from Central London without advance notification, and required (by an Order-in-Council)[1] to have exit permits for leaving the country. These restrictions were enforced by police surveillance. The Chinese,

[1] Orders in Council are made by The Queen acting on the advice of the Privy Council and are approved in person by the monarch. Although they are drafted and their substance is controlled by the government.

who even before the sacking of the Office had by administrative means prevented some of our people from leaving, riposted by confining our Mission to the very limited areas of their dwellings and offices, and by refusing exit permits. Since then only schoolchildren and two pregnant wives have been allowed out.

2. On 20 October the Chinese Ministry of Foreign Affairs indicated to our Chargé d'Affaires, Mr Hopson, that there would be no easing of the present Chinese restrictions until we had lifted our August restrictions. Completely disregarding the sacking of our Mission, they perversely argued that since we were the first to impose additional restrictions, we must be the first to relax them. Mr Hopson is convinced that the Chinese will not budge from this position and that they could not be brought to negotiate a procedure of reciprocal relaxations. He thinks, however, that if we were to decide on a unilateral and substantial relaxation and give the Chinese advance notification, they would respond with action on their part; and that this was what they were in effect conveying to him.

3. Our sanctions against the Chinese were not, and cannot be, of such severity and effectiveness as to force a change in policy on the Chinese. They could sit things out indefinitely. We cannot. We cannot reasonably ask our Mission to put up indefinitely with their present trials. One of the wives has already had a severe breakdown—and been refused an exit permit. Moreover, as long as this issue persists, we cannot hope to progress towards more normal dealings with the Chinese on e.g. trade. I think, therefore, that we should now make some relaxation of our restrictions unilaterally. Now would seem a good time for an attempt towards a mutual dismantling of restrictions: the 'moderates' seem to be gaining control in Peking, and would presumably welcome some show of a return to normality in time for the Canton Trade Fair which opens on 15 November.

4. We must clearly retain the requirement for exit permits. We could, however, relax the travel restrictions either:

(*a*) By returning to our pre-August 35-mile travel limit: or

(*b*) By imposing a 12 ½ mile limit, this being the pre-August limit for our Mission in Peking.

Course (*b*) would give us the satisfaction on insisting on extra reciprocity. But Mr Hopson has pressed strongly for course (*a*), arguing that, since course (*b*) would not represent a full return to the *status quo*, it would be unlikely to elicit a full response from the Chinese. Albeit reluctantly, I have come to the conclusion that this is correct. If we were to relax the travel restrictions, we would also dispense with the police surveillance.

5. A unilateral relaxation would of course be an act of faith as we cannot be sure that it would produce results from the Chinese side. But standing pat will not produce results either; and I think our action would be defensible both in Parliament and elsewhere if we made it clear that if there was no response from Peking or more trouble there, we should again impose the restrictions. We might also say that our best hope of settling other outstanding issues with the Chinese, e.g. the detention of the Reuters correspondent, lay in the general improvement of atmosphere which a mutual relaxation of restrictions might bring about.

6. If you agree, I propose to put these views orally to my colleagues in Cabinet on 9 November.

7. The Home Secretary has already drawn to my attention the burden which surveillance of the Chinese is placing on the Metropolitan Police Force and expressed the hope that there will be some early relief from the strain.[2]

G.B.

[2] The Prime Minister agreed with the proposed action. On 21 November, the travel restrictions reverted to the pre-22 August 35 mile radius and the extra police and Special Branch guard were withdrawn. The requirement for Chinese officials in Britain to apply to the Foreign Office for exit visas remained. Mr Hopson had informed the Chinese Ministry of Foreign Affairs on 14 November.

No. 70

Minute from Mr Murray to Mr de la Mare, 14 November 1967
Confidential (FCO 21/65, FC 3/3/C)

Internal developments in China

The Secretary of State has asked how the latest developments in China, as assessed in a JIC Note of 9 November (attached),[1] affect our own relations with China and in particular the position of our Mission in Peking.

2. There is no doubt that the tendency towards discipline and a greater moderation in the Cultural Revolution campaign, which has been apparent since early September has and will continue to have an effect on our own relations with China. The main factors which will affect us are:

(*a*) Violence in general has been condemned by the Chinese leaders more strongly than before and violence against foreign missions in particular. The practical effect of this has been that, since early September, our Mission has not been bothered by Red Guard activities and members of the staff are in much less personal danger than during August. If the present trend continues, I think it is reasonable to assume that members of our Mission will not again be in physical danger.

(*b*) During the heat of the Cultural Revolution, and particularly when the Foreign Ministry was split into several conflicting groups and very much under the influence of the extremists, it was impossible to discuss any problem with the Chinese or even to expect reasonable answers to everyday problems in Peking, such as transporting baggage, or making repairs to the Mission buildings. Since the Cultural Revolution campaign has been toned down it has become slightly easier to deal with these everyday problems and there have been some signs of a more reasonable approach to international problems.

3. It is against this background that Ministers agreed to an attempt to improve the situation of our Mission in Peking by making a unilateral removal in London of some of the present restrictions on the Chinese Mission. Two months ago such a move would have been worthless. Now there is hope that it may succeed. We should not, however, be too optimistic about improving relations with China. Although some of the recent extremism and indiscipline is now being condemned,

[1] Not printed.

there is no particular reason why the Chinese should go out of their way to try to improve relations with us, and many reasons why they should not do so. Our policies are still regarded as basically inimical and we have given no ground on the most important and immediate of our difficulties: Hong Kong. In brief, we have moved from a highly dangerous period during which members of our Mission, and even other British subjects in China, were liable to suffer personal harm at the hands of undisciplined mobs and any incident could quickly snowball into a major crisis, to a time in which this danger is not so great but in which the Chinese are still not willing to make an active effort to improve relations. This being so, almost all the effort must come from us. We must calculate our moves carefully so that they create a possibility for the Chinese to move slowly towards a practical improvement in relations without publicly having to give the impression of compromising with the 'British imperialists'.

JAMES MURRAY

No. 71

Mr Hopson (Peking) to Mr Brown, 27 November 1967[1]
Tel. No. 272 Immediate, Confidential (FCO 21/65, FC 3/3/C)

My telegram No. 269[2] (not to all): Restrictions.

I was summoned by Deputy Director Western Europe this afternoon, who informed me as from 29 November all restrictions on movement of staff of British Office in Peking would be removed and that we should revert to normal limits for Diplomatic Corps.

2. I asked him if this measure included normal issue of entry and exit visas and he confirmed that applications would be dealt with in normal way by Ministry of Foreign Affairs. I take this to mean that visas will in fact be issued.

3. After informing me about lifting of restrictions, Mr Hsueh went on to say the root cause of abnormal state of Sino British relations was the suppressed Chinese citizens in Hong Kong and that until this stopped and British Government accepted Chinese Government's demands and released all prisoners, there could be no improvement or normalisation of relations.

4. I forgot to enquire whether Chinese Government intended to make any announcement about lifting of restrictions. I doubt if they will and unless they do I strongly recommend that we wait to inform Press until we see what happens on 29 November. See my immediately following telegram.[3]

1 Repeated for information to Hong Kong, Washington and POLAD Singapore.
2 Not printed.
3 In telegram No. 273, Mr Hopson reported raising various cases of British subjects who were in trouble in China.

No. 72

Mr Hopson (Peking) to Mr Brown, 2 December 1967[1]
Tel. No. 298 Immediate, Confidential (FCO 21/65, FC 3/3/C)

My immediately preceding telegrams.[2]

This is a bad setback. It is possible Chinese have been double-crossing us from the beginning but I doubt that. Kao did not deny that Hsueh had given some kind of an assurance on 27 November and made it pretty clear that it was subsequent events, or at any rate the impact of recent events, which had led to a hardening in Chinese attitude. At one point he even admitted that it was Chinese Government's wish to normalise relations. This thesis is supported (grp. undec.) last minute substitution of Kao for Hsueh who had given me assurance and would therefore have been in an embarrassing position. The cancellation of Chipp's (sic) interview with Bank of China in Hong Kong is also added support.

2. As usual the Chinese were not forthcoming in any specific suggestions as to how we can get out of this situation except for saying that the British authorities must 'stop suppressing Chinese compatriots in Hong Kong'. Nor did he give me any indication as to how long the ban on visas will last.

3. My preliminary assessment is that a certain amount of time must be allowed to elapse so that these events may be forgotten. Meanwhile it is obviously essential from our point that punitive action in Hong Kong should be kept to the minimum conducive with maintenance of order. The lenient treatment of scholars and children at present awaiting sentence would obviously help. There is one other action which might do the trick. Would it for example be possible for plaintiffs in libel action against *Wen Hui Pao*[3] to say they are satisfied with judgment which has cleared their reputations and that they waive their claim for damage? If it were possible to make a gesture of this kind fairly soon I believe it might provide excuse needed by Chinese Government to get things moving again. I suspect that action against Communist newspaper is most sensitive issue and may have been last straw.

4. An important question which immediately arises is that of desirability of publicity. As you will have seen from my immediately preceding telegram I made some harsh remarks about the Chinese Government's holding us to ransom.[4] They would I presume be sensitive to publication of this. Nevertheless I feel for the moment it would be better to hold this weapon in reserve. Certainly if there is any hope of making a gesture to them about *Wen Hui Pao* as suggested above, it would be easier for them to act if public posture had not already been adopted. It would also be easier

---

1 Repeated for information to Hong Kong, POLAD Singapore and Washington.
2 Not printed. In a meeting with Mr Hopson, Kao stated that owing to recent events in Hong Kong (raids on Chinese schools and an adverse decision against a pro-Chinese newspaper for libel) the Chinese government 'had reason to doubt the sincerity of the British Government's expressed wish to normalize relations' and visas would not be forthcoming. Mr Hopson 'made various pleas on grounds of international law and humanity' but to no avail.
3 A pro-Chinese newspaper based in Hong Kong.
4 Mr Hopson had said that what the Chinese were doing 'was not diplomacy but gangsterism'. Kao protested that it was the British, not the Chinese, who were the gangsters and referred to the long and aggressive history of British imperialism in China (Peking Tel. No. 297, 2 December).

for us to make gesture. For the time being therefore I strongly recommend that no official statement be made and that if anything has to be said it should be confined to a statement that no visas have yet been issued.

No. 73

Minute from Mr Murray to Mr Wilkinson and Mr Samuel
29 December 1967[1]
Confidential (FCO 21/146, FC 13/14)

Do the Chinese worry about their image abroad?

At our meeting on 21 December with Mr Rodgers when we touched on the question of publicity for the plight of our Mission in Peking, it emerged that one of the points at issue was likely to be whether or not the Chinese really mind about the 'image' they present to the outside world. After further consideration, our conclusion is that there are signs that they do mind.

2. Although official propaganda never indicates that the Chinese are worried by the interpretation put by the outside world on events in China, we know from Red Guard newspapers and posters that this bland nonchalance hardly represents their true feelings. An opposite case is that of remarks made by Chinese leaders about the destruction of the British Mission on 22 August. The following are examples:

(*a*) On 5 September Mao's wife, Chiang Ch'ing, made a speech to delegates from Anwhei province, which was never published in the official press, though the whole nation was called on to study the text. From Red Guard newspapers we know that in one section of this speech she said: 'Some people went to foreign embassies to make trouble and the Office of the British Chargé d'Affaires was burnt down. We are of course determined to crush the US imperialists and reactionaries but we must not make trouble at foreign embassies and we must not go aboard foreign ships. It would be childish for good people to do so and if bad people do this they want to ruin the reputation of the country.'

(*b*) Paris telegram no. 917[2] reports that Chou En-Lai also condemned the burning of the British Mission.

(*c*) The former Chinese Chargé d'Affaires in Indonesia, Yao Teng-shan, who is being accused of trying to take over the Ministry of Foreign Affairs and organising action against foreign missions, has been blamed in Red Guard papers for taking steps which had 'irreparable influence on China's national reputation and foreign relations'.

3. We also know from experience of Chinese protests that the Chinese are highly sensitive to anything printed in Western newspapers about China which could remotely be construed as derogatory. The Chinese have complained about unfavourable comments on Chinese internal affairs in many other countries besides our own. They are also very quick to condemn as forgeries any black propaganda activities

1 Copied to Mr C. Wilson, Information Research Department.
2 Not printed.

(generally carried out by the Americans) which put China in a bad light such as e.g. the forged article allegedly from the New China News Agency saying that Chinese diplomatists had been instructed during the Cultural Revolution to return to Africa to foment revolution, and the forged letter allegedly from the Canton Fair Committee saying that Red Guards would vet the activities of visitors before granting exit permits.

4. I think all this means that the Chinese are indeed sensitive about the way in which foreigners regard them, even if this sensitivity is not always the predominant factor in their decision making. They are, I believe, particularly sensitive about being called 'barbarous' or 'uncivilised' and about comment from countries with which, for political reasons, they wish to have good relations, such as Pakistan, Cambodia, Tanzania, etc. Although propaganda is a tricky weapon, my view is that its use should certainly not be excluded if no further progress is made on exit visas for the Mission within the next few weeks.

JAMES MURRAY

No. 74

Report by the Joint Intelligence Committee, 12 January 1968
JIC(68)15(Final) Top Secret, UK eyes only (CAB 158/69)

The threat to Hong Kong

In the report at Annex we examine the external and internal threats to Hong Kong for the next five years as far as circumstances in China permit any realistic assessment.

Conclusions

2. Our conclusions are:

(*a*) China could seize Hong Kong militarily at any time and we might have no effective warning, but on present indications she does not intend to do so in the near future. The economic and other arguments (e.g. possible United States reactions) against a takeover are likely to play an important part in Chinese policy towards Hong Kong;

(*b*) no alternative to Hong Kong as a source of foreign exchange seems available to China in the next few years, but as the Chinese establish more direct trading contacts and improve their own shipping and marketing facilities—and there are already some signs of this—China's dependence on Hong Kong should decline relatively. If this trend continues, the economic restraints on a Chinese takeover of the Colony can be expected to lose some of their force;

(*c*) in any case Peking is likely to watch carefully for any opportunity to acquire Hong Kong should the economic disadvantages of doing so no longer appear so important and it would be unwise to assume that Peking will allow the lease of the New Territories, which expires in 1997, to run its full course. One factor Peking will have in mind is that any British decision to reduce the size of the garrison or to accelerate the reduction of the British military presence in the Far East could have an acute effect on local, and in particular police, morale and thus on the position of the Hong Kong Government;

(*d*) in the event of a decision to take over Hong Kong, China is likely to use methods other than direct aggression such as a co-ordinated and systematic campaign of terrorism aimed at undermining public confidence and at disrupting the machinery of government and the economy to an extent that would make the British position untenable. There is at present no sign of such a decision but there will continue to be a risk of action on these lines. We are likely to get at least some warning;

(*e*) the lack of success achieved by the local communists in their confrontation with the Hong Kong Government and their obvious failure to win popular support reduced their will and ability to gain a quick victory over the Security Forces;

(*f*) with more realistic elements in the ascendant in Peking and some signs that the lull in the Cultural Revolution is to be prolonged, Peking at the end of 1967 ordered a major policy change calling for the abandonment by the local Hong Kong communists of violence and the continuation of the struggle by political means;

(*g*) though a period of uncertainty can be expected, with the recurrence of isolated cases of violence committed by militants, the majority of Hong Kong communists are likely to accept the new line, concentrating on anti-government propaganda and the exploitation of social and industrial discontents. The object will be to achieve a steadily growing influence in the Colony in the hope that ultimately, as in Macao, the communists can virtually dictate internal policy while the commercial and other benefits of the *status quo* are preserved;

(*h*) if during the next few years confrontation were again raised to the level reached during the summer of 1967 and were maintained for a prolonged period, it could have a very severe effect on the economy and the confidence in it on which Hong Kong's viability depends; Peking would therefore try to ensure that such a campaign were regulated so as to avoid the disadvantages attendant on serious economic collapse;

(*i*) a policy of moderation could quickly be reversed, particularly if the Cultural Revolution flared up again with a resurgence of extremism, although this seems unlikely. But if it did, it could create a heightened danger of direct action against Hong Kong either deliberately or by miscalculation.

DENIS GREENHILL
Chairman, on behalf of the Joint Intelligence Committee

ANNEX TO JIC(68)15(FINAL)

The threat to Hong Kong

Background

1. The Chinese Government (CPG) has always had as one of its long-term aims the recovery of territories which it regards as Chinese, and the continued colonial status of Hong Kong remains a particularly distasteful reminder of the concessions forced on pre-revolutionary China by foreign governments. From 1950 to 1965 the policy of the CPG was to tolerate the existence of the Colony, while local communist leaders in the main limited their actions to extending their influence among the people of Hong Kong, particularly through the Chinese-owned banks and other

business concerns, the New China News Agency, the communist-owned press and a section of the trade unions. From 1965, however, certain conditions for tolerating the existence of the Colony were made known. These were that it should not be used as a base for aggression against China or to support United States action in Vietnam and that local communists should not be suppressed.

2. In late-1966 a new situation arose with the 'overspill' of China's violent Cultural Revolution into the foreign policy field. In the neighbouring colony of Macao local Chinese communists mounted a campaign to undermine Portuguese authority and succeeded in obtaining *de facto* control. In Hong Kong the local communist leaders in conformity with the doctrines of the Cultural Revolution allowed 'the masses', i.e. local union officials and workers, to pursue a more militant policy in the industrial field. Open confrontation between the unions and the government inevitably followed and the leadership was obliged to come out in support of its 'patriotic compatriots'. After a short delay the CPG seem to have decided that they must show solidarity with the Hong Kong communists in their attempt to create a Macao-type situation.

3. To this end a series of campaigns in direct challenge to the colonial government was launched. These included demonstrations and riots; strikes aimed at wrecking the economy, particularly by workers in essential services and key industries; street violence, mainly the indiscriminate use of home-made explosive devices and the planting of hoax bombs; and incidents on the border.

4. This has from time to time created a very tense situation, not only in the urban areas but also on the border, and in July border control in Hong Kong became mainly the responsibility of the armed forces. But it is clear that the communists over-rated the extent to which they could gain mass support in their assault on public security, and greatly under-rated the loyalty and abilities of the Hong Kong Security Forces, whose whole emergency structure has been tested and strengthened where necessary. Moreover Peking's assistance, apart from a financial subvention to communist trade unions, has been limited to propaganda support, diplomatic pressure on the British Government to accept their demands and direct action against the British Mission in Peking. In the event the Security Forces have not so far been over-stretched; communist terrorist methods have to a large extent proved counter-productive and have antagonised potential supporters; strikes have failed to disrupt the economy; and the firm attitude of the Hong Kong Government has succeeded in maintaining public confidence.

Factors affecting Communist policy towards Hong Kong

Social

5. The population of Hong Kong now amounts to 3.8 million. Most of it is concentrated in an area of about 33 square miles where despite large-scale building schemes housing conditions are in many parts over-crowded and unsatisfactory. In these circumstances even comparatively minor incidents in the densely populated area are liable to grow rapidly into major riots in which mass excitement and unrest can spread quickly. We can be sure that the local communists would exploit such disturbances and, if they succeeded in gaining wider support from the mass of the population, the disturbances could well be considerable.

Political

6. The present status of Hong Kong benefits China by providing it with easy access to a world from which, through its actions, it has increasingly isolated itself, and by serving as a forward base from which to mount commercial, intelligence and subversive activities. A Chinese take-over would deprive China of these political advantages, but would yield certain clear compensations. It would remove a distasteful legacy of the past and a major inconsistency in Peking's Marxist-Leninist posture. It would also put an end to the activities of the KMT in Hong Kong. As a dramatic anti-colonial gesture it might do something to restore China's somewhat fly-blown image in the 'third world', and a 'conquest' of this sort could be held up as yet another victory for Mao's thought over British imperialism.

Economic

7. China also clearly benefits economically from British tenure of the Colony. During the last few years Hong Kong has been China's largest single source of foreign exchange (which is necessary for imports of grain and capital goods), and no alternative source seems possible for several years to come. Were China to take over the Colony the loss to the Chinese economy would be severe, while the economic problems in having to absorb and support Hong Kong, suddenly cut off from most of its markets and sources of raw materials, would be considerable. However, the loss would in some measure be offset by the acquisition of a large industrial city. Economic factors may not weigh heavily with extremist elements in Peking, but the more realistic leaders, at present in the ascendant, must take a more serious view of the economic consequences of a take-over, and while they retain influence such considerations are likely to play an important part in Chinese policy towards Hong Kong (the economic value of Hong Kong to China is set out more fully at Appendix 'A').[3] But it should be noted that if active confrontation at the June 1967 level were renewed and continued over a prolonged period, this could have a very severe effect on the economy and the confidence in it, on which Hong Kong's viability depends.

8. In the longer term, as the Chinese establish more direct trading contacts and improve their own shipping and marketing facilities—and there are already some signs of this—China's dependence on Hong Kong as a trans-shipment and commercial link should decline relatively. Should this trend continue, the economic restraints on a Chinese take-over of the Colony can be expected to lose some of their force.

The Cultural Revolution

9. Present indications are that the CPG intend to prolong the present lull in the Cultural Revolution, and there is at least a chance that China will in the longer term revert to more normal behaviour both internally and externally. The fact that talks were held towards the end of 1967 between the Chinese border authorities and representatives of the Hong Kong Government was perhaps a sign of this. It is doubtless because more realistic elements are in the ascendant in Peking that the CPG has recently ordered a major change of policy in Hong Kong (see paragraph 13 below).

10. The CPG could quickly reverse a policy of moderation towards Hong Kong, and this would be more probable if the Cultural Revolution again flared up with a

---

3 Not printed.

resurgence of extremism, although the latter seems unlikely. But if it did, this could create a heightened danger of direct action against Hong Kong, either deliberately or by miscalculation.

Views of British Intentions

11. Peking may well consider the appearance of diminished British interest in the Far East as grounds for hoping that Britain will give up Hong Kong voluntarily well before the lease of the New Territories expires in 1997. There is no sign at present that either Peking or local leaders are proceeding on such an assumption. We believe Peking will watch carefully for any opportunity of acquiring Hong Kong should the economic disadvantages of doing so no longer appear to be so important and it would be unwise to assume that they will allow the lease of the New Territories to run its full course. As to the local population in Hong Kong, they could become increasingly inclined to insure against the future, a process which could be expected to work to the communists' advantage.

12. Within Hong Kong doubts about future British intentions in the Far East could well create anxiety about Britain's determination to defend and retain the Colony. Many people in Hong Kong are well aware that Britain's ability to reinforce the Colony in the event of an emergency would be seriously hampered if there were no longer a back-up position in Singapore or Malaysia. In the Colony itself any actual or rumoured changes in military strength would have an acute effect on local confidence which is indispensable to Hong Kong's economy and political visibility. The morale of the Police, which recent events have shown to be a most important factor, owes much to the presence of the British troops. Thus any decision to reduce the size of the garrison or to accelerate the reduction of the British military presence in the Far East could have far-reaching effects on the position of the Hong Kong Government and it would not be surprising if communist propaganda in due course fostered rumours of such decisions.

Possible Developments

Political Action

13. The failure of the local communists in their confrontation with the Hong Kong Government and their obvious lack of popular support reduced their will and ability to gain a quick victory over the Security Forces. Until recently the local communists were nevertheless seeking to keep the Hong Kong authorities under pressure through increasingly selective bomb incidents and propaganda while at the same time working to broaden the base of their general support and, in the longer term, to achieve a steadily growing influence within the Colony. However Peking at the end of 1967 ordered a major policy change calling for the abandonment by the Hong Kong communists of violence and the continuation of the struggle by political means. Though a period of uncertainty can be expected with the recurrence of isolated cases of violence committed by militants, we believe that the majority of Hong Kong communists are likely to accept the new line, concentrating on anti-Government propaganda and the exploitation of social and industrial discontents. The object will be to achieve a steadily growing influence in the Colony in the hope that ultimately, as in Macao, the communists can virtually dictate internal policy which the commercial and other benefits of the *status quo* are preserved.

Renewal of Tension

14. The new policy could quickly be reversed. But if at any time in the next few years the active confrontation of the Hong Kong Government were raised to the level reached during the summer of 1967 and were maintained for a prolonged period, there could be considerable ill effects for China. Given the dependence of the Colony's highly industrialised economy on capital investment from abroad and therefore on confidence in its future, confrontation, if pursued too ruthlessly, could gradually reduce the economy to stagnation. Though this might aggravate internal discontent and give rise to specific industrial grievances which the local communists could exploit, it could hamper their broad efforts to gain mass support. Moreover it could seriously reduce the economic benefits of Hong Kong enjoyed by China. Thus, if such confrontation were renewed, Peking would probably seek to regulate it so as to avoid these disadvantages.

15. Hong Kong will in any case remain exposed to pressure by Peking in various forms. These could include, for example, interference with food and water supplies, constant border incidents and harassment of shipping and air routes. These sanctions, if applied simultaneously, would be difficult to resist without external assistance to match the severity of the action against the Colony.

Take-over by Means Other Than Direct Aggression

16. Were the local communists and Peking to decide to work for the overthrow of the Hong Kong Government, the ability of the local communists to achieve this without substantial support from China is for the present questionable. But in these circumstances any Chinese government, or even a powerful faction in China, could at any time initiate a systematic campaign of terrorism in Hong Kong against senior British officials from the Governor downwards, against prominent Chinese officials and businessmen collaborating with them, or primarily against the Police. To this end they could smuggle in arms, explosives and experts in their use (the CPG have already developed a sophisticated training organisation for terrorists) to cause a breakdown in Hong Kong.

17. A campaign on these lines would probably not alienate the population in general provided the violence was not indiscriminate. Indeed, they might be increasingly inclined to give their support to the communists. It would be ideologically consistent with the Maoist creed of 'liberation from within' and would carry little risk of international reaction.

18. Other possible methods could include the swamping of the Colony's Security Forces by a massive release by China of refugees, although these refugees could not be controlled once over the border and would be difficult for the CPG to deal with both politically and in the propaganda field; or even an invasions of Hong Kong by Red Guards with the connivance of Peking or the PLA; the latter have so far been a restraining influence in the border area.

19. Before deciding to take over Hong Kong by means other than direct aggression, Peking would have to weigh very carefully the political advantages of a take-over against the considerable economic as well as political disadvantages described in paragraphs 6 and 7 above. They would also have to assess the risk of their campaign provoking such a vigorous British reaction that the local communists had to appeal for direct and overt Chinese intervention in their support. This would

put Peking in a difficult position since China's intervention could entail the danger of United States involvement.

Direct Aggression

20. Finally the Chinese will continue to have the capability to over-run Hong Kong militarily at any time and it is clear that no local military action could deter or repel a resolute attack. The Chinese have sufficient adjacent land forces to carry out an immediate attack on Hong Kong and the New Territories frontier in overwhelming number. Over 350 jet fighters, which could operate in the ground attack role, and up to 15 light bombers are immediately available and these could rapidly be reinforced. Coastal craft including a large number of junks are available in the Canton and Pearl River areas for an amphibious operation. A summary of forces available for an attack is at Appendix B.[1]

21. We believe that China will not use direct aggression to take over Hong Kong. It would violate the ideological principle that revolutions must be indigenous rather than externally imposed. Moreover the Chinese may fear that such action might prompt the United States to come to the assistance of Britain and might even involve the threat of nuclear retaliation. The present relative proximity in the Vietnam area of massive United States air and naval forces, together with the fervent advocacy by some United States politicians and sections of the press of direct action against China may reinforce Peking's fears. The Chinese might calculate that by swift action Britain and her allies would be presented with a fait accompli which would reduce the scope of possible reaction; but this would not completely eliminate the risk.

Warning

22. We would expect some but not much warning of both a Red Guard 'invasion' and the release of refugees in large numbers. We would hope to get warning of a major campaign of terrorism; similarly we are likely to get at least some warning of a Chinese Government decision to sponsor such a campaign. No firm indications of a decision to take the Colony by military force are likely and the tactical warning we might receive of a military attack would depend on the manner in which the attack was mounted: the Chinese could mount an attack in such a way that we would have no effective warning.

No. 75

Letter from Sir D. Hopson (Peking) to Mr Murray, 15 January 1968
Confidential (FCO 21/65, FC 3/3/C)

Dear James,

I think that it is just worth recording that at the Cuban National Day reception at their Embassy, Ch'en Yi clinked glasses with me. I was standing between the French and Swedish Ambassadors, but slightly to the rear, when he came up toasted the Frenchman and the Swede and then me. He knows me perfectly well by sight (and in

---

1 Not printed.

any case was told who I was afterwards by the Protocol official who was with him), so he probably realised what he was doing, though he may merely have decided that it would look too rude to cut me in public. Anyway, though we should hardly read too much into this, it is another slight indication of a return towards normality.[2]

DONALD

2 Mr Murray noted: 'How low have our relations sunk that we record every clink of a glass!'

No. 76

Sir D. Hopson (Peking) to Mr Brown, 25 January 1968[1]
Tel. No. 74 Immediate, Confidential (FCO 21/65, FC 3/3)

My immediately preceding telegrams.[2]

We now have a clear opening to settle the visa question for the staff of this Mission on a purely bilateral basis (i.e. not bringing in Hong Kong) and on all our reasonable terms (i.e. a reversion to pre-August arrangements). I recommend most strongly that we take this opportunity and settle at once.

2. As regards exit visas at the moment we have, as predicted in my telegram No. 3, a deadlock.[3] We have now had the Chinese Government's considered reaction to interview of 2 January with Mr Ma and we can be sure they will continue to insist on reversion to pre-August treatment and that attempts to make them comply with our exit visa requirements will merely lead to a prolonged stalemate. On the other hand, lifting the requirements would probably do the trick as far as exit visas for our staff are all concerned. Nor, for reasons given below, would it entail any real risks, it would also give the Chinese the sort of face-saving sop which they need before signing-off. I notice that final paragraph of your Note of 23 August refers to possibility of lifting restrictions if the Chinese assured free movement to our officials.

3. I suggest we reply to the Chinese that as proof of our wish to restore normal movement we are prepared to suspend exit visa requirements on the clear understanding that the Chinese would then grant exit visas now and in future without impediment to our officials and that if this was not done situation would have to be re-examined and control re-imposed. I do not know whether suspension would be a legally complicated operation but if, as I hope, the Order in Council simply gives us powers, it should be possible to suspend exit visa requirement as a fairly simple administrative act and without publicity. We would retain powers in reserve. Nevertheless if no other course were possible I would certainly recommend revocation of Order in Council.

1 Repeated for information to Hong Kong.
2 Not printed. These telegrams reported a meeting Mr Cradock had on 24 January where the issue of restoring staff movements was discussed. The Chinese requested that the exit visa requirement for Chinese officials in Britain be removed and outstanding entry visas for members of the NCNA and the Bank of China be granted. If these demands were met the Chinese would 'certainly make corresponding gestures' (Peking Tel. No. 72, 25 January 1968).
3 Not printed.

4. Suspension would probably be better than the idea of granting visas or endorsing passports at airport as suggested in my telegram No. 3 paragraph 3.[4] It would be administratively easier and more clear-cut. The Chinese might well jib at stamping of their passports with exit visas. If of course the Chinese showed signs of reprisals making a mass exodus without granting us any visas (I think this unlikely and it would soon become apparent) and if they just continued refusing visas to us (again, I think unlikely) control would be re-imposed and we would be no worse off.

5. As regards entry visas, I recommend we grant the Chinese requests immediately and for both Bank of China and NCNA. Attempts to bargain with these would merely hold up thaw and might even mean opportunity would slip. For reasons given in paragraph 3 of my telegram No. 31[5] attempts to impose prior conditions in this way would probably lead to a deadlock. Moreover by granting entry visas we are adding to our potential hostages and making it even less likely that Chinese will all decamp from London. I think that if Bank of China visas are granted and our exit visa requirement lifted the Selfs would have a good chance of visas. In any event improvement of general situation would be bound to influence their problem favourably.

6. I appreciate that there may be reluctance to grant entry visas for NCNA while Grey case is unsolved. But as pointed out in my telegram 48[6] Grey's case turns on prisoners in Hong Kong, not (repeat not) on NCNA in London. Mr Kao underlined this point when he said that Grey's was not a visa case. I am most anxious to do everything possible for Grey but I think that by trying to bring him in on this deal and to solve all our problems at once we shall fail to solve any. Moreover, if this works and Mission's visa problems are solved without involving Hong Kong, Grey's chances should improve since he would become first and perhaps only charge on Hong Kong prisoners. It might be possible to grant only short residence permits, say 3 months, to new NCNA men when they arrive in London; this would increase our opportunities for pressure over Grey. In any event it would still be possible for us to act as suggested in paragraph 5 of your Saving telegram No. 76[7] if by then we had made no progress over deportation.

7. A further argument in favour of acceptance is that if we can solve this Mission's movement problems without bringing in Hong Kong, the Governor's hand should be much strengthened in dealing with local Communists. The Grey problem would remain, but Hong Kong would not have to look over their shoulders at us so much as hitherto.

8. I recommend strongly against delay or attempt to haggle over this offer or to whittle down Chinese terms. They are much better than we might have expected and it is in our interests to seek solution quickly and in a bilateral context if we can. If the Chinese attitude changes or if Hong Kong situation deteriorates the price might be raised or chance lost for good.

9. I accept that this is once more something of an act of faith. But as in the case of the lifting of government restrictions in London in November (which produced corresponding result) we have to move first. We have taken up clear terms and, in Kao's final remarks, as near an assurance on corresponding Chinese gestures to come as

4 Not printed.
5 Not printed.
6 Not printed.
7 Not printed.

we are likely to get. The Chinese may of course change their ground, or even be deliberately deceiving us. But I think this risk is small. In any event with our need for free movement we stand to gain everything. And since our exit visa requirement could be reactivated and further entry visas refused if needs be, we would lose little if gambit did not work. Even if, on the worst hypothesis, the move did not produce a final thaw on our movements we should know where we stood and would still retain the Chinese in London.

10. May I, therefore, seek your urgent agreement to inform the Chinese:

(*a*) That we are prepared to suspend our exit visa requirements on the clear understanding that they will remove all impediments on our movements;

(*b*) That we are ready to grant their entry visa applications at once.

We could go on to add suitable references to watching for signs of progress not only as regards our own staff but also as regards British subjects' problems generally.

11. I earnestly hope we shall not let this chance slip.

12. May I also stress the importance of Hong Kong doing what they can (always consistent with the need to maintain public order) to avoid any untoward incident during the period while the Chinese demands are under consideration.[8]

8 Commenting on the telegram, Mr Brown noted: 'But we always seem to move *first*! This is an important telegram. I'd like to see the considered views *soon*. Grey—what do we know of his conditions? Anybody at all seen him? Previous Commonwealth Secretary was ready for a Hong Kong deal. Is this one?'
Sir D. Hopson, in Peking Tel. No. 82 of 27 January, offered to remain in post to avoid giving the impression that the Foreign Office had secured exit visas for its staff but not other British subjects, if this made it easier to get his recommendations accepted.
In a submission of 31 January, Mr Murray recommended not providing entry visas for members of the NCNA until there has been progress over Mr Grey. Commenting on the submission, on 1 February, Mr Wilkinson said: 'The Chinese have us over the proverbial barrel, and we must make the best of this humiliating posture. I see no scope for a package deal and fear Sir D. Hopson may prove right, namely that unconditional acceptance of the Chinese terms may in the end prove inevitable. But Ministers may feel we owe it to public opinion in the UK to make a special effort on behalf of Grey, particularly since all we look like risking is further delay'. Mr Brown agreed. (FCO 21/66, FC 3/3).

No. 77

Mr Brown to Sir D. Hopson (Peking), 6 February 1968[1]
Tel No. 132 Priority, Confidential (FCO 21/66, FC 3/3/)

Your telegrams numbers 72, 73, and 74: Exit and Entry Visas.

It is encouraging that the Chinese have now dropped the point about Hong Kong and have at last stated what appear to be their terms. Their side of the bargain is tiresomely imprecise but we agree that we are unlikely to get clearer assurance that they will reciprocate if we make the first moves. The fact that Kao was prepared to commit himself even as far as he did, suggests that some high level decisions have now been taken about the treatment of your mission (though not necessarily about Grey).

2. Our views on the individual points at issue are as follows:

(*a*) We are prepared to suspend the exit visa requirement here completely on the clear understanding that the Chinese will make no difficulties about exit visas

1 Repeated for information to Hong Kong.

for your mission. We need not revoke the Order-in-Council, and we would have to revive the system if the Chinese made no move to release members of your mission.

(*b*) We are also prepared to tell the Chinese that entry visas for London will in future be dealt with 'in the normal way' on a basis of reciprocity, although we would of course reserve our right to refuse individual visas. In practice this would mean that we would grant outstanding visas for the Bank of China (on the understanding that there would then be progress on the cases of the Selfs and Croziers)[2] although the officials concerned would only be given residence permits valid for three months at a time until the problem of our own bankers in Shanghai had been solved.

(*c*) The NCNA presents greater difficulties. We really cannot justify here any move to increase the activities of NCNA in London while Grey is still under house arrest and incommunicado. We are prepared to grant the outstanding NCNA entry visas if the Chinese make it clear that they intend to release Grey and we are also prepared to make official the offer already made by you on a personal basis that Grey should be exchanged for Hsueh P'ing (and, if there is no alternative, Lo as well). We are not (repeat not) prepared to give entry visas for NCNA if the Chinese make no move over Grey.

3. You have authority to put these suggestions to the Chinese in the form you think most likely to achieve results. If the Chinese indicate that they will make no reciprocal concessions unless we accept all their 'demands' you should make it clear that we shall have to reconsider the whole position including the concessions at (*a*) and (*b*) above.

4. As seen from here it appears unlikely that you will be able to get much constructive response over Grey during the course of one interview. A possible line of approach might therefore be:

(*a*) You might tell the Chinese that HMG had studied their proposals, found much in them that was constructive and had various concrete suggestions to make in return about improving conditions for both missions. There was however one point that HMG found highly unsatisfactory: No positive suggestion had been made about solving the problem of Grey. How could HMG make any moves to reinforce the activities of NCNA in London whilst Grey was still under house arrest? British public opinion would consider that reinforcing the activities of NCNA was a political and not just a visa matter, and they would not understand. You had already made a personal suggestion about ways of achieving progress over Grey and were now authorised to say that this had the blessing of HMG. You would like to call again in 48 hours to hear what the Chinese had to say about this.

(*b*) If the Chinese subsequently gave insufficient assurance that the Grey problem would be settled quickly providing that NCNA visas were granted, you could then agree to the visas but add that residence permits would only be issued for periods of one (repeat one) month initially until the problem of Grey was finally settled. You could add that the present expired residence permits for members of the NCNA office would also be renewed, but again for periods of one month at a time.

(*c*) If the Chinese made no advance about Grey you could nevertheless put the proposals at paragraph 2(*a*) and (*b*) only, saying that we were prepared to isolate the question of Grey and entry visas for NCNA for the time being in order to allow some progress on the question of the diplomatic missions.

---

2 Mr Self and Mr Crozier were bankers waiting for exit visas.

(*d*) If the Chinese make it clear that it was all or nothing, you could then say that you would have to refer for instructions.

5. We would of course inform the Chinese here that the exit visa requirement had been lifted as soon as we heard from you that you had said as much to the Chinese.

No. 78

Mr Brown to Sir D. Hopson (Peking), 6 February 1968
Tel. No. 133 Priority, Confidential (FCO 21/66, FC 3/3/D)

My immediately preceding telegram: Exit and Entry Visas.[1]

We much regret not being able to accept your recommendations in their entirety. We realise that by insisting on what may turn out to be ineffective terms over Grey we are running the risk of diminishing the prospects of an early release for members of your Mission; and this is a risk we faced only with the greatest reluctance. However, feeling about Grey is high, both in Parliament and in the Press world, where our handling of the case has up until now received general endorsement. Anxiety is the greater in that Grey has now been in virtually solitary confinement for over five months; and we have no firm evidence about his health, or indeed his sanity. We took full account of your argument that the best hope for progress over Grey possibly lay in the improvement of Sino/British relations which complete acceptance of the Chinese 'demands' might bring. But there would be much disquiet in this country if, without making any headway at all about Grey, we allowed conditions for the Chinese officials in this country to return completely to normal and in particular if we permitted the reinforcement of the New China News Agency. However judiciously we argued the case there would be some who would think, however unjustifiably, that we had allowed ourselves to be unduly influenced by our very real anxiety over you and your staff.

2. We very much hope, however, that your present instructions are sufficiently flexible to allow you to make progress on both exit visas for your Mission and on Grey.

1 No. 77.

No. 79

Sir D. Hopson to Mr Brown, 8 February 1968[1]
Tel. No. 114 Immediate, Confidential (FCO 21/66, FC 3/3/D)

Your telegram Nos. 132 and 133:[2] Exit and entry visas.

I was naturally disappointed by these instructions. They risk casting away a splendid chance to settle our staff movement problem cleanly, quickly and on reasonable terms. By linking NCNA entry visas with Grey we may find we have forced Chinese

1 Repeated for information to Hong Kong. This version includes amendments to small mistakes later rectified by the Communications Department.
2 Nos. 77 and 78.

to bring Hong Kong back into what could have been a purely bilateral settlement without helping Grey himself. And we do this while apparently remaining unwilling to make decisive concessions on key factors for Grey, i.e., Hong Kong prisoners.

2. I am however grateful for efforts made to meet my recommendations on all other points and for flexibility allowed by instructions. We have prevented [sic] package as persuasively as we could and must now await Chinese reply.[3] I will not try to forecast what this will be. We do not know what importance Chinese attach to a return to normality in our relations. But by withholding NCNA visas, introducing Grey into the equation, and asking for prior assurances, as we had to, given form of your instructions, we have made operation much more difficult for the Chinese. This will certainly cause delay and may, as admitted in your telegram No. 133, prejudice chances of an early solution. I should not (repeat not) be surprised if Chinese continue to insist that their demands be met in full before reciprocal concessions are made, while asking a high price for Grey in terms of Hong Kong prisoners. What do we do then?

3. I should like to make some comments on points raised in your telegram No. 133. The first, which I have tried to make repeatedly in telegrams, and which has been confirmed by our exchanges with Chinese, particularly those of 31 December, 28 January and 31 January is that Grey's case is linked directly with Hong Kong prisoners and until we are ready to make substantial concessions in this sector we shall not have Consular access to him or procure his release. It is for this reason among others that I have argued for acts of clemency in Hong Kong and for concession to meet Chinese terms over prison visits. These recommendations were rejected. Withholding the entry visas for NCNA while remaining tough in Hong Kong, will not help Grey and may merely prevent us settling our own movement problem. I understand the anxiety about Grey's state of health, or indeed his sanity. I am surprised however that these anxieties were not put to the Governor when last week we could have assured ourselves of immediate access to Grey by allowing special NCNA visits to twelve more men in Hong Kong (in the light of our anxieties not a massive concession). The conclusion that might be drawn is that we are not prepared to ask the Governor for further concession in a sector which would vitally affect Grey while we are prepared to ask for further, and as I see it irrelevant, sacrifices from staff of this Mission.

4. I have done my best in correspondence hitherto to avoid burdening you with references to human problems of our staff and families still unable to leave this country after a very trying year. But they are considerable particularly for those with divided families. The staff have taken it all splendidly but if this deal falls through it will be hard to explain to them their continued detention when a clear chance for settlement has been offered, as they are well aware, and we have failed to clinch the deal on grounds which I cannot with the best will in the world see as convincing. There will not only be gloom but resentment.

5. I understand your anxieties on above mentioned opinions but if as we agree pretext for favourable treatment for this Mission and disregard for Grey is unjustifiable I cannot see where the difficulty lies. It should be possible to explain that our best

---

3 Mr Cradock delivered the reply on 7 February as instructed. Sir D. Hopson judged it best to continue the discussion at Counsellor level where politics was less likely to feature (Peking Tel. Nos. 112 and 113, 8 February).

chances of helping British subjects lies in re-establishing more normal diplomatic relations which we now have the chance to do. If on the other hand it turns out that we now have spoilt our chances by refusing to grant NCNA visas while Grey is in custody, I cannot see how it will help us vis-à-vis public opinion to have all our staff detained in China as well as Grey.

No. 80

Sir D. Trench to Mr Thomson (Commonwealth Office)
13 February 1968
Tel. No. 186 Immediate Confidential (FCO 40/64, HWB 3/2/C)

My immediately preceding telegram.[1]

Following personal for Galsworthy.

I am afraid there is a further important factor which must not be overlooked. Public opinion here is sympathetic to Grey's plight, but there would be deep resentment if what was considered to be any substantial Hong Kong interest were sacrificed for him.

2. A second point is that unofficial members and the local Press, although sometimes a little watchful and suspicious, broadly still trust us in these matters and have not sought to probe into what we may or may not be up to in attempting to obtain an amelioration of his condition; although it is not difficult for them to guess that we are not simply acquiescing in his imprisonment. If we once did anything in Grey's interests that was regarded as too much of a kowtow, the Press would seize upon it and it might thereafter become extremely difficult for me to operate without having to parry incessant demands for full and constant disclosure of what was being considered and discussed between London, Peking and here. While the Press could perhaps be held off, unofficial members might start to demand a say in these matters which could be extremely embarrassing and unhelpful in future manoeuvres over both Grey and the position of the Peking Mission.

3. This is not to say that we cannot do something to help Grey, but whatever we do must be able to show either that it is a reasonably normal procedure and that we have not unduly bent to CPG demands (remembering that the smallest concession will be trumpeted by the Communist Press as a humbling of us) or that the move is in Hong Kong's interests (e.g. deportation). The concessions proposed for these prisoners come very close to the border line of what might be acceptable to local opinion, and I should have to consider very carefully whether or not we unduly risk raising a storm if we make them.

4. I have not copied this to Peking but leave you to send an appropriate version there if you think it necessary.

1 Not printed.

No. 81

Letter from Mr Whitney (Peking) to Mr Wilson, 27 February 1968
Confidential (FCO 21/13, FC 1/1/FC)

Dear David,

1984 gets nearer. Since Sunday the guards in front of the diplomatic missions in Peking stand at their posts clasping the little red book to their middles. When they change duties they perform a little ceremony of waving the red book at each other and shouting 'a long, long life to Chairman Mao' (*Mao Chu-hsi wan-shou wu-chiang*).

2. There is a parallel development among the telephone operators. Both the switch boards serving the two main diplomatic compounds (Wai Chiao Ta Lou and San Li Tun) now frequently, although not yet invariably, answer incoming calls with the same magic phrase. The time and weather telephone enquiry services now say 'Long live Chairman Mao' (*Mao Chu-hsi wan-sui*) before giving the information required. At least 'Heil Hitler' was shorter.

I am sending copies of this letter to Colin Wilson in IRD, Frank Brewer in RD, Leslie Smith and Emrys Davies in Hong Kong, Roy Spendlove in Washington, Reg Hibbert in Singapore and McKearney in PUSD.

R. W. WHITNEY

No. 82

Sir D. Hopson (Peking) to Mr Brown, 8 March 1968[1]
Tel. No. 174 Immediate, Confidential (FCO 21/66, FC 3/3/D)

I called on Vice Minister for Foreign Affairs Lo Kuei-po at his request this morning when he made a statement on instructions from Chinese Government. The essence of his statement was that Hong Kong situation was crux of Sino British relations and that British Government must reply to various demands put forward by Chinese Government on this subject. Only after that would it be possible to discuss other problems e.g. restoration of normal movement for staff of missions, trade, cultural etc. There was no (repeat no) concrete reply to proposals we made on visas and Grey on 7 February.

2. We must therefore consider 'offer' made by Mr Kao on 24 January as dead and we are right back where we began. The 2 visas issued yesterday should be seen, as Blishen visas in December, as a Chinese attempt to present a slightly less inhuman image.

3. Full report and comments below.[2]

---

1 Repeated for information to Hong Kong, Washington and Singapore, and saving to Paris.
2 For a report of the meeting see No. 83.

No. 83

Record of a meeting at the Chinese Ministry of Foreign Affairs
8 March 1968, 11 a.m.[1]
Confidential (FCO 21/66, FC 3/3/C)

Lo said he had asked the Chargé d'Affaires to come to discuss various questions about current Sino/British relations. In response to a question from Sir Donald Hopson he said that he was making an oral statement. On 7 February Mr Cradock in an interview with Consular Department of the Ministry of Foreign Affairs had put forward certain proposals to restore normal movements for the staffs of Chinese and British diplomatic missions for the settlement of the affair of Mr Grey of Reuters. Lo said that he had now been authorised to make a statement of the Chinese Government position on the question of Sino/British relations which he requested Sir Donald Hopson to convey to the British Government.

2. *Lo* said that both the Chargé d'Affaires and the British Government clearly knew that the grave deterioration in Sino/British relations since last May had been the result of the massive suppression and persecution of Chinese residents of Hong Kong by the British authorities. The British Government should therefore be held solely responsible for the deterioration in relations, the interference in the free movement of diplomatic missions and trade between the two countries. The Chinese Government had exercised restraint in Hong Kong and had taken positive steps to relax the situation on the Shumchun border and to alleviate tension but even today the Hong Kong Government have still not completely stopped its suppression. Many Chinese compatriots were still unjustifiably held in jail and there had been no compensation for the loss of lives and property caused by the British authorities. Nor had the British made the necessary arrangements effectively to guarantee the rights of Chinese residents of Hong Kong including their right to study the thoughts of Chairman Mao and to engage in other patriotic activity.

3. The Chinese Government, Lo continued, had clearly pointed out on many occasions that the Hong Kong problem was the crux of Sino/British relations and there could be no talk of normalisation of relations if the Hong Kong problem were left aside. In his letter to Ch'en Yi of 2 September 1967[2] Mr Brown had expressed the willingness of the British Government to seek good relations with the Chinese Government and the hope that the question of relations between the two countries could be discussed frankly and dispassionately. Now the British Government had put forward various proposals concerning entry and exit of Chinese and British personnel and over the question of Mr Grey. The Chinese Government had noted these proposals and were prepared to put forward their views. It must be pointed out however that these were only secondary matters in the general question of current relations and, as the British Government had admitted, the Hong Kong question was both directly and indirectly linked with the whole problem. If the

[1] Present were Mr Lo Keui-po (Vice Minister for Foreign Affairs), Mr Hsueh (Deputy Head of West European Department), a member of the Consular Department and two interpreters; Sir D. Hopson, Mr Cradock and Mr Whitney.
[2] No. 52.

Hong Kong problem were brushed aside it would be difficult for discussions to be fruitful.

4. To this day, the British Government had failed to reply to the various demands put forward by the Chinese Government in connection with the Hong Kong problem. This could not but raise doubts about them sincerely wishing to normalise relations between the two countries.

5. Mr Lo said that was all he wished to say today.

6. *Sir Donald Hopson* said he would like to clarify the Chinese Government's position. Mr Lo had referred to proposals made by Mr Cradock on 7 February but he had not said whether the Chinese Government were prepared to act on them. These proposals had originally been put forward by Mr Kao of Consular Department of the Ministry of Foreign Affairs, in an interview with Mr Cradock on 24 January.[3] Sir Donald Hopson asked if Mr Kao's statements on 24 January still represented the Chinese Government's position and whether they were prepared to accept the proposals put forward by Mr Cradock on 7 February.[4]

7. *Mr Lo* replied that he had just said clearly that the Chinese Government had noted the proposals of the British Government including those of Mr Cradock and those in Mr Brown's letter of 2 September 1967. He had also said clearly that the Chinese Government was ready to put forward its views. The Chinese Government considered that the two questions put forward by Mr Cradock were only secondary matters in Sino/British relations and that they were directly or indirectly linked with the Hong Kong problem, as the British side had admitted in the past. Mr Lo said it was necessary to reiterate here, as the Chinese Government had clearly pointed out on many occasions in the past, that the Hong Kong problem is the crux of present Sino/British relations, and there can be no question of normalisation of relations if the Hong Kong problem is left aside and it would be difficult for discussions to be really fruitful.

8. *Sir Donald Hopson* said he agreed with the Vice Minister that the free movement of diplomatic staff was a secondary matter but it was important that the two missions should be able to function normally and to do their work properly if they were to make a contribution to the solution of the larger problem. Mr Kao had said on 24 January that if the British Government lifted its requirement for exit visas for the Chinese diplomatic staff in London, granted entry visas and returned to normal in the issue of entry of visas the Chinese Government would make reciprocal gestures. Sir Donald again asked if this still represented the Chinese position.

9. *Mr Lo* said that Mr Kao had made such a statement but at the same time he had made it clear that the Hong Kong question was the crux of the problems resulting from the deterioration of Sino/British relations. There could be no solution of these problems if the Hong Kong question were brushed aside.

10. *Sir Donald Hopson* asked if he was now to understand that the British side had misunderstood the Chinese position as set out by Mr Kao. Was Mr Lo saying that even if the British Government lifted the exit visa requirement in London and granted entry visas that there would be no reciprocal action by the Chinese Government unless the British Government took further measures in Hong Kong?

3 See No. 76, note. 2.
4 See No. 79, note 3.

Mr Lo claimed that this question had been answered already. He had said that the Chinese Government had noted the British proposals and was prepared to present its views. He had also made it clear that the solution of these problems would be difficult if the Hong Kong question were left aside because to this day the British Government had failed to reply to any of the previous demands of the Chinese Government in connection with the Hong Kong problem. *Sir Donald Hopson* said it was still not clear to him what steps the Chinese Government envisaged as leading to a solution of the Hong Kong question. Were the Chinese Government reviving the so-called demands of May 1967? Did they wish the British Government to make proposals to discuss the Hong Kong question? *Mr Lo* repeated that the British Government had still not replied to the various demands of the Chinese Government in connection with the Hong Kong question. If the British Government had a sincere desire to discuss these questions this should be backed up by actual deeds.

11. *Sir Donald Hopson* said he now had a clearer idea of the Chinese Government's position and would like to make some comments on Mr Lo's statement. He had said that the trouble in Hong Kong had been caused by the suppression of the Chinese inhabitants by the Hong Kong authorities. Sir Donald Hopson could not accept this view which stood truth on its head. The violence had been caused by the Chinese and the Hong Kong Government had the right and duty to maintain law and order. He was pleased to note the Vice Minister's remark that the Chinese Government had taken steps to relax tensions in Hong Kong and pointed out that the Hong Kong Government had taken steps in the same direction. Those newspapers which had been suppressed had been allowed to re-open publication before the date they were legally entitled to do so and no action had been taken against them. An amnesty had been declared to allow people to hand in illegally held explosives and weapons. There had been other small actions which showed the goodwill of the Hong Kong Government. The Vice Minister had referred to the study of Chairman Mao's thought. It had long been the position of the Hong Kong Government that they had no objection to Chairman Mao's thought. Sir Donald Hopson emphasised that the British and Hong Kong Governments had a sincere wish to return to normal and were taking concrete steps to relax tension in Hong Kong. He would like to ask again if it were a fact that there could be no question of restoring normal movement of the diplomatic missions until the question of Hong Kong was solved or action taken towards its solution. If this were the case he felt bound to say he thought this was a mistaken policy. His experience had been that if faced with a set of problems it was better to solve the easier ones first and then move onto the more difficult. Both missions would be in a much better position to make a contribution to the solution of the major problem if the restrictions on their movement, which at present hampered their work, were removed. Sir Donald Hopson also asked if the Chinese intended to publish a report of this meeting.

12. *Mr Lo* said that the Chinese side would not do so. He repeated that the serious deterioration in Sino/British relations had been caused by the large scale oppression of Chinese inhabitants of Hong Kong which had still not stopped. For example, there had recently been another incident in K'uant'ang, Kowloon. Another example concerned the proposal recently made by the Chinese authorities in Kwantung province to send 5,000 tons of rice to be distributed in Hong Kong and 1,000 pieces of winter

clothing for compatriots in Hong Kong prisons. The Hong Kong authorities had subjected this proposal to a variety of harassments.

13. *Sir Donald Hopson* explained that Hong Kong prisoners had a balanced diet of 3,000 calories a day. This had been carefully worked out by dietetic experts and was fully adequate for prisoners not engaged in manual work and most prisoners in fact gained weight in prison. Similarly, clothing was issued on a scale which covered all winter needs and special privileges could not be allowed for certain categories of prisoners. Clothing sent in for the prisoners would be kept in store until they were released. None of the 1,000 suits of winter clothing donated by the Kwangtung Support Committee had been handed in although 400 suits addressed to individuals had been handed in over the Chinese New Year. It had been made clear to NCNA Hong Kong that any suits handed in should be addressed clearly to individuals and not sent in bulk. The Hong Kong Government had told the China Resources Company that the 5,000 tons of rice supplied by the Kwangtung Support Committee could be brought in under the Hong Kong quota system and that the Government were in fact prepared to allow 300 tons to be brought in outside the quota. The China Resources Company had sent in an application for a licence to import rice but since the language was objectionable the licence had been refused. Subsequently the Hong Kong Government had offered to allow rice to be imported by registered rice stockholders in a way which would not impair the rice control scheme and the company would lose no import entitlement under the quota system. The Hong Kong Government still awaited a reply from the China Resources Company.

14. Sir Donald Hopson pointed out that prisoners in Hong Kong were allowed regular monthly visits by relatives and also visits by employers. Many such visits had taken place to Communist prisoners. He also referred to the offer he had made in an interview with West European Department on Friday 1 March for special visits to NCNA and other patriotic journalists to which there had been no reply or reaction.

12. [sic] *Mr Lo* said that the Chargé d'Affaires had attempted in his remarks to justify himself but much of what he had said did not accord with the facts. For example, reports from various organs in Hong Kong and families who had visited relatives in prison showed that the prison diet was far from sufficient and that the amount of clothing and bedding given to them made it difficult to prevent getting cold in present weather conditions. On the question of rice, Mr Lo said that the demand of the Kwangtung authorities to send rice to relieve the suffering of their compatriots in Hong Kong was entirely reasonable. The rice in question was not marketable rice but rice for the relief of compatriots and so the Chinese side could not agree to make the rice marketable. Mr Lo said that the Chinese had noted that there had been a little easing of the restrictions on visits to prisoners but the British authorities still were obstructive from time to time.

13. [sic] Mr Lo said that if the British were really sincere in their desire to restore normal relations between the two countries there would have to be a concrete reply to the demands raised earlier and they should substantiate their desire by actual deeds. He suggested that the British Government should not miscalculate the situation.

14. [sic] *Sir Donald Hopson* said that on 28 January Mr Hsueh had said that if certain special visits could be arranged to NCNA and other journalists in Hong Kong the Chinese Government would consider granting consular access to Mr Grey. We

had replied to this proposal on 1 March and Sir Donald Hopson asked what action had been taken. *Mr Lo* said that the Chinese Government could only agree to a visit to Mr Grey after they had had reports from their own organisations in Hong Kong that satisfactory arrangements had been made for visits to Hong Kong prisoners. *Sir Donald Hopson* said that as agreed in the meeting with Mr Hsueh on 2 March we were not waiting for the NCNA in Hong Kong to make contact with the Political Adviser there to make the necessary arrangements. *Mr Lo* said that the information had been passed on to NCNA in Hong Kong but they had received no reports so far and he was therefore not in a position to say any more. *Sir Donald Hopson* emphasised that unless someone took action nothing would happen. NCNA in Hong Kong should pass the names of the prisoners to be visited and make the other arrangements with the Political Adviser. *Mr Lo* said he thought that as long as the Hong Kong British authorities made suitable arrangements instead of raising obstructions then the Chinese Government would certainly receive reports about them. *Sir Donald Hopson* concluded by pointing out that he and many members of his staff had now been detained in China for over six months. He raised the strongest protest against this situation which was contrary to all international usage. It was bound to come to the notice of world opinion which would undoubtedly condemn it. *Mr Lo* said he categorically rejected Sir Donald Hopson's protest and it was the actions of the British which would be condemned by world opinion.

R. W. WHITNEY

No. 84

Sir D. Hopson (Peking) to Mr Brown, 11 March 1968[1]
Tel. No. 179 Immediate, Confidential (FCO 21/66, FC 3/3)

My telegram No. 174[2] and immediately following telegrams:[3] Sino/British Relations.

As regards visas this is a bad set back and we must now dig in for phase 2. As regards Sino British relations generally there are features which may not (repeat not) be quite as black as they look at first sight. The fact that the Vice Minister for Foreign Affairs Lo called me (for the first time in over six months) shows that the Chinese regard their statement as important. Lo referred to your letter of 2 September[4] and statement is the nearest thing to a reply that we have got so far. Our proposals of 7 February[5] were said to have been 'noted'; they were not (repeat not) rejected; and Chinese were prepared to put forward their views, though discussions could not be 'fruitful' if Hong Kong were brushed aside. On Hong Kong we were asked not (repeat not) to accept Chinese demands but to 'reply' to them. Finally Chinese do not

1 Repeated for information to Hong Kong, Washington and POLAD Singapore.
2 No. 82.
3 Not printed.
4 No. 52.
5 See No. 79, note 3.

intend to publish their statement. These are hopeful features and indicate that there may be considerable room for manoeuvre. One, though not necessarily the only one, interpretation of issue of visas to Finch and the two wives is that it is a sign to us that they are not completely intransigent.

2. It is I think necessary to ask ourselves whether the Chinese proposals of 24 January[6] were genuine and whether if we had accepted them they would unwarrantably have made reciprocal gestures. In the course of discussion Lo confirmed that Kao had made these proposals, though he alleged (quite falsely) that he had at the same time pointed out that Hong Kong was the crux of our problem. It seems probable that they meant what they said at the time and that if we had settled quickly we would have got at least some people out even if not a complete thaw. Our attempt to bargain and reference to Hong Kong via Grey probably threw question back into the melting pot. Lo therefore changed record which is not first time Chinese have done this. Whether if we now just went ahead and took all action requested by Kao on 24 January including the issue of NCNA visas we would now get full reciprocal treatment seems doubtful. In any case it hardly seems practical politics in the present circumstances.

3. The central question now is what are Chinese objectives? There can be broadly two theories:

(*a*) They are bent on achieving a Macao-like situation in Hong Kong by maintaining pressure on this Mission and British subjects in China and will not settle for less;

(*b*) That they will settle for much less but cannot close the book and return to normal relations without some reference on our part to Hong Kong and their demands which would allow them to claim a 'victory' or at least preserve face.

4. On a priori grounds [? grp. omitted] is much to be said for (*a*). It is however by no means the only possibility. Many features of interview some of which I have already mentioned above suggest (*b*). The statement was oral and not published. There have been no accompanying Press articles against Hong Kong or signs of a reversion to the violent Communist policy there or of other pressure [grp. undec ? against] [grp.undec. ? this] Mission (though these may come). The tone was calm much more so than would be expected if Chinese were going all out for a Macao situation. The statement referred to Chinese steps to alleviate tension and in conversation Lo admitted that Hong Kong Government had also taken some steps. Your proposals in your letter 2 September and our proposals on visas were not rejected: the Chinese noted them and said they were ready to put their views. In conversation Kao's statement on visas was confirmed though Hong Kong rider was added. The Hong Kong demands of last year were not reiterated though referred to. We were asked to reply not to accept them and reminded we could not brush Hong Kong aside. I might add more general point that detention until (*a*) is achieved would seem out of line with current trend in Chinese foreign policy and efforts to restore picture of correct diplomatic behaviour.

5. Vice Minister's statement therefore, although it set us well back on visas, may not be entirely retrograde on wider issue of Sino-British relations and it may be in our interests to explore the possibility of a face saving formula on Hong Kong. The

---

6 See No. 76, note 2.

Chinese may be indicating that they are willing to embark on a general discussion provided Hong Kong is included. The difficulty of course is to find a formula which does not compromise vital interests in Hong Kong and also to avoid any impression of weakness on basic issues, which may only encourage the Chinese to ask for more. I am fully aware that area for manoeuvre in Hong Kong is small. Acceptance of Chinese demands of last year is out of the question. They have asked us to 'reply' to their demands and by this as Lo implied under questioning their meaning by actions as well as words. As regards action the most we can probably do is to try to keep the situation calm and push on with deportations. If the Chinese Government are prepared to accept deportees this may prove to be the key to the problem. It might be possible to offer immediate release to China of a large number of deportees as a preliminary to talks. I also hope that at some point remission of sentences for certain prisoners can be considered. I understand the Governor's problems on this but it is possible that some at least of our present staff and other British subjects, will be refused permission to leave until the majority of the Communist prisoners are deported or released.

6. On the nature of a verbal reply we should consider whether we might make a statement in Parliament on Hong Kong which reaffirmed our intention to maintain order in Hong Kong but recognised that Hong Kong's policies naturally took account of its geographical position, Chinese race of the vast majority of the inhabitants and close links via trade and other channels with the mainland. The statement could reaffirm Hong Kong's wish to maintain friendly relations with China, the fact that political freedom was enjoyed there and that there was no repeat no ban on the peaceful study of Mao or anyone else, and the fact that within the framework of the law the Chinese inhabitants were certainly not [? grp, omitted] from patriotic activities. Statement might refer to the number of last year's prisoners already released, deny any reports of ill treatment in jails and invite inspection by a neutral observer. We should also consider giving Chinese a formal reply to their statement of 8 March[7] preferably orally in order to avoid public commitment. These are only first thoughts and statements would need most careful wording. But it may be in our interests to attempt something on these lines. It would help to narrow down the area of uncertainty about Chinese intentions; it might also advance understanding of Hong Kong's position and thereby assist in any diplomatic or publicity pressure on Peking.

7. As regards this Mission, we have no alternative but to make the best of it and prepare to sit it out. The Chinese treatment, in respects other than our detention, is generally correct and we must hope will continue so. It is possible that we may be allowed a trickle of exit visas on compassionate or health grounds. We shall try.

8. I do not repeat not think we have yet reached a point where we should consider suspending relations. In any case it would not help us; we should still be kept here and should probably be deprived of our diplomatic status But we must now look more closely at our contingency planning (my letter to Wilkinson of 19 December).[8] My first thoughts are:

7 See No. 83.
8 Not printed.

(*a*) I think that the time may have come for immediate diplomatic action on as wide a scale as possible.

(*b*) I think I should sooner or later initiate publicity among diplomatic corps here by writing to the Dean, copying to my colleagues, giving a statement on detention.

(*c*) I think there is also a case for wider publicity i.e. in the world Press. This is however a two-edged weapon. It is arguable that since the Chinese have already chosen to be stubborn we would lose little by publicising the fact. But publicity might cause them to make living here much more uncomfortable, which they could easily do, or might encourage them to cook up some story against member of our staff justifying stringent measures. Our capacity to sit this out depends on some restraint on their part. Also if we publicise the fact that they have told us we must reply to their 'demands' we commit them more firmly to this requirement (we should also have to be careful about this point in diplomatic action). Publicity could also lead to pressure at home for undesirably strong action. I would therefore prefer to withhold this publicity for the moment though it may be impossible to hold position long.

(*d*) We should also urgently examine what other means of pressure we can bring to bear on the Chinese e.g. economic.

(*e*) I strongly recommend against retaliatory action against the Chinese officials in London e.g. restriction of movement or expulsion of NCNA. We would certainly come off worse in any straightforward contest and chances of getting access to Grey would be lost.

9. To sum up I think our policy should now be twofold:

(*a*) To explore what gestures whether practical or verbal we can safely make at present depends on the Chinese requirement for a face-saving formula on Hong Kong and would in any event reduce the area of uncertainty about their intentions. This should be coupled with firmness on all really vital points for Hong Kong.

(*b*) When we have decided what we are going to do on (*a*) we should with due regard to timing, which will be very important, begin to bring diplomatic and perhaps eventual publicity pressure on the Chinese over our detention.

No. 85

Note by Mr Murray, 12 March 1968
Confidential (FCO 21/66, FC 3/3/D)

Sino-British relations after the Chinese statement of 8 March

The statement made by Vice-Minister for Foreign Affairs Lo Kuei-po to the Chargé d'Affaires on 8 March (Peking telegram No. 176)[1] was a very significant shift from the position adopted by the Chinese at interviews on 1 and 2 March at which they had indicated that progress over our Mission in Peking depended on the acceptance of Chinese 'demands' that all restrictions on the entry into and exit from this country by Chinese officials, including officials from the New China News Agency (NCNA) should be removed; and progress over Mr Grey on suitable

---

1 Not printed but see No. 83.

concessions over communist prisoners in Hong Kong. The latest statement means that the Chinese have reintroduced the link between our conduct in Hong Kong and their treatment of our Mission. We had congratulated ourselves that we had succeeded in getting them to shift from this earlier position, and to equate British officials in Peking with Chinese officials in London. It also seems that any initiatives we may decide on with respect to their Mission in London can no longer be 'on the clear understanding of reciprocal treatment by the Chinese'.

Chinese Motives and Intentions

2. Why have the Chinese shifted their ground? The shift might seem to suggest that the extreme 'cultural revolutionaries' are once again in the ascendency in Peking. But we have no other evidence to support this; rather the contrary. A more likely explanation is that there may have been a drop in morale among the communist cadres in Hong Kong as a result of their having more or less to admit publicly that their last year's campaign was a failure; and Lo's statement is intended as a booster to demonstrate to the cadres (who may well have been informed of the statement although it has not been published) that they still have the active support of the Chinese Government. The Local Intelligence Committee in Hong Kong see the statement as a reminder to us that the Chinese Government will continue to support communist action in Hong Kong with diplomatic pressure whenever necessary. The Chinese may also think that our recent financial difficulties, our decision to accelerate our withdrawal from Malaysia and Singapore, and the American difficulties in Vietnam may have weakened our resolution to resist pressures in Hong Kong.

3. What interpretation are we to put on the Chinese statement?

(*a*) I agree with Sir D. Hopson (Peking telegram No. 179)[2] that it may not be as black as it appears at first sight. By Chinese standards it is moderate in tone. It asks us, not to accept, but to 'reply to' the Chinese demands. It includes the first reference to the Secretary of State's letter to Ch'en Yi of last August, which it does not specifically reject. It might therefore conceivably be that the Chinese statement is intended to put on record that their stand of principle over Hong Kong remains, but that while paying lip-service to that principle they may nevertheless be prepared to make some progress on 'secondary matters'.

(*b*) On the other hand the statement is quite uncompromising in content. It would be imprudent therefore not to face up to the possibility that the Chinese may mean exactly what they say and that they fully intend to hold our Mission as hostages until we make concessions in Hong Kong. If so, we are in for a long siege; and it may be many months before exit visas are granted in other than very exceptional cases.

4. What do the Chinese hope to gain by this latest move?

Their decision not to publish Lo's statement (Peking telegram No. 175)[3] would seem to indicate that they have not ruled out the possibility that we may in fact be prepared to make concessions in Hong Kong. Lo did not confirm to Sir D. Hopson that they were still insisting on their 'five demands' which he himself put to us last May.[4] (These were: 'Immediately accept all the just demands put forward by Chinese workers and residents in Hong Kong; immediately stop all Fascist measures; immediately set

2 No. 84.
3 Not printed.
4 See No. 1, note 2.

free all the arrested prisoners; including workers, journalists and cameramen; punish the culprits responsible for these sanguinary atrocities, offer apologies to the victims and compensate for all their loses; guarantee against occurrence of similar incidents.')

But Lo's language as reported in the second half of paragraph 2 of Peking telegram No. 176 reflects the 'five demands'. It seems unlikely that they will be expecting us to make a complete 'kow-tow'; but they may hope to push us some way towards a Macao-type situation by insisting that we release considerable numbers of prisoners (and, no doubt, in the process recognise a special status for the various Chinese official and semi-official organs in Hong Kong).

The Case for Lifting Restrictions on the Chinese in London

5. How should we react to Lo's statement? Initially, I think there is something to be said for mildness while we make one further effort to get the Chinese to deal with the problem of the Mission in isolation from the other outstanding issues in our relations, and thus further probe Chinese intentions. This would mean that, despite the lack of any assurance to reciprocity, we would take the steps recommended in my submission of 7 March i.e. lift the exit permit requirements for all Chinese officials in London, and grant entry visas in the normal way, including visas for the Bank of China and NCNA. I would be in favour of doing this by deed rather than by further discussion; we might simply notify the Chinese Mission here of our decisions. Once we had done this, Sir D. Hopson might tell the Chinese in Peking that we were disappointed that they were once more insisting that progress on all outstanding issues depended on Hong Kong; that we attached prime importance to a return to normal working conditions for both our Missions since this should provide the best hope for progress on all other outstanding issues; and that we had decided to play our part by removing the remaining restrictions on Chinese officials in London, and we hoped that the Chinese would respond by removing the remaining restrictions on our Mission in Peking. The Chinese would be unlikely to give Sir D. Hopson any formal satisfaction; but with the requirement for exit visas in London removed, they might conceivably be prepared in practice to grant exit visas for the Mission in Peking. This is a matter of some urgency, since Sir D. Hopson has recently for the first time introduced the question of staff morale, pointing out that although the situation is not yet desperate, the strain on those divided from their families and those who ought to leave China for medical reasons is beginning to tell.

Mr Grey

6. We have so far made no progress whatsoever towards the *release* of Mr Grey. The Chinese have not yet taken up the question of an exchange although it has been raised with them twice. This is not surprising as Mr Grey represents a valuable card and we may not find out precisely what *quid pro quo* the Chinese want until they have played the game further. On the other hand Sir D. Hopson has thought that there is a reasonable chance that we will be granted *access* following our agreement to special visits to NCNA staff and other 'patriotic journalists' imprisoned in Hong Kong. It would appear from Lo's remarks (Peking telegram No. 178)[5] that the Chinese may still be prepared to go ahead with arrangements covering access.

Hong Kong

7. Sir D. Hopson suggests in his telegram No. 179 that it may not be in our

---

5 Not printed.

interests to explore the possibility of a face-saving formula on Hong Kong. We have so far felt that the Governor, while not being over-rigid, should take only such measures of relaxation as were desirable in the context of bringing things in Hong Kong back to normal; and that if we started to make concessions under Chinese pressure in order to alleviate the lot of Mr Grey or of our Mission, we should be on a very slippery slope indeed. It is clear from Lo's remarks (Peking telegram No. 177)[6] that prisoners are a key issue. The Governor has always been prepared to deport (or 'release to China') considerable numbers of communist prisoners; but understandably he is very reluctant to release them in Hong Kong. The difficulty has been doubts as to whether the Chinese, who have always challenged our right to deport to China, would receive deportees. A test case is being carried out with two communist film starts [*sic*] this week, and we should clearly do our best to push on with this matter. As for face-saving formulae over Hong Kong in general, the trouble is that any statement that satisfied the Chinese seems bound from that very fact to be such as to compromise our position. If we made a statement which failed to satisfy them, we would run the risk of being dragged into discussions which might take us some of the way towards a Macao-type situation. We might, however, explore with the Governor the feasibility of a statement which simply recorded the progress that we had made since the emergency towards bringing things back to normal in Hong Kong, with a passing reference to the number of prisoners already released.

Measures for the Longer Term

8. If lifting of the restrictions on the Chinese Mission here and such conciliatory steps as we feel able to take in Hong Kong do not in the event result in exit visas for our Mission, what then? We are short of effective bargaining counters.

(a) *Withdrawal of the Mission*

It is for consideration whether any useful purpose is still served by retaining the Mission whose very existence inhibits our action in Hong Kong. On the other hand the Government of Hong Kong do find it useful that there should be a direct channel of communication with Peking and that they do not have to deal directly with local communist representatives on major matters. In any case it is very doubtful if the Chinese, given the attitude they have adopted, would be prepared to agree that we should withdraw our Mission. They would gain nothing; and they probably also attach some importance to maintaining their own activities here.

(b) *Rupture of Diplomatic Relations*

We could of course try to force the Chinese hand by formally breaking relations. But I agree with Sir D. Hopson that this might simply deprive our Mission in Peking of such protection as they derive from their diplomatic status, while the Chinese continue to keep them as hostages. Moreover, as a matter of face, the Chinese would be practically bound to try to make serious trouble for us in Hong Kong. A secondary objection to a rupture would be the loss of trade which would certainly be involved.

(c) *Economic Sanctions*

Threats to stop British trade would not modify the Chinese attitude, and loss of trade would be harmful to us here. Economic measures in Hong Kong directed against China would hurt the Colony as much as the Chinese.

6 Not printed.

(d) *Action against the Chinese Mission in London*

The only restriction (apart from normal 35-mile travel limit) still imposed on Chinese officials in London is that they must ask prior permission for leaving this country. They profess to regard this restriction as illegal and refuse to apply for permission. There is thus a self-imposed bar on their leaving the country. (In addition we have refused entry visas to two Bank of China and four NCNA officials.) Sir D. Hopson argues strongly against further action against Chinese officials in London e.g. restrictions on movement or expulsion of NCNA. I agree with him that we would certainly come off worse in any straight-forward contest in nastiness, and the chances of getting access to Mr Grey would be lost. We might of course try expelling members of the Chinese diplomatic Mission (as distinct from NCNA). The risk is that if the Chinese were to retaliate by expelling any of our people from Peking, it would probably be those that the Mission least wanted to lose at this stage.

(e) *International Action*

By any standards the Chinese are behaving monstrously in holding a diplomatic mission as a means of exerting pressure over policy matters and many countries not generally sympathetic to us would nevertheless disapprove of such tactics. I agree with Sir D. Hopson that there may sooner or later be advantage in his initiating publicity among diplomatic missions in Peking by writing to the Dean and his colleagues giving a statement on detention. We shall certainly have to consider what pressure we might bring to bear on the Chinese through intermediaries. The Pakistanis would seem to offer the best prospect, and there might be advantage in asking President Ayub Khan to intervene with Chou En-Lai. But our past experience with the Pakistanis does not offer encouragement that we shall have much success.

(f) *Publicity*

There are two aspects to be considered:

(i) The possibility of *adverse publicity in the United Kingdom* if we lift the remaining restrictions on the Chinese Mission here in advance of any progress on Mr Grey or our Mission, particularly if this were to coincide with publication by the Chinese of Lo's statement. In these circumstances we should simply have to take the line that the Chinese had insisted that the prerequisite for a return to normal diplomatic relations was the removal of the requirement of exit visas for their diplomatists here and normal treatment in the matter of entry visas for the NCNA whom they regard as full members of their Mission. In view of the importance which we attached to the return to normal diplomatic relations which we thought might help Mr Grey, other British nationals in China and our Mission, we had accepted this, and hope the Chinese would match our gesture.

(ii) *An international publicity campaign* designed to show how badly the Chinese are behaving. It is our view that the Chinese may be sensitive to international publicity suggesting that they are behaving in a thoroughly 'uncivilised' fashion. But publicity is a two-edged weapon. If we make it widely known that the Chinese are holding our people until their 'demands' are met in Hong Kong, we commit them even more firmly to that position. They might also react to publicity by making life difficult in Peking for our Mission. Finally we must bear in mind that publicity would lead to increased public pressure here to 'do something' and the preceding paragraphs indicate that possibilities for effective action are limited. Nevertheless dissatisfaction over Mr Grey may in any case bring the whole issue out in the open and we must be ready, despite the difficulties, with carefully-prepared publicity measures.

(g) Steadfastness

To the extent that public opinion here allows it, our best policy may in fact be to play things quietly both in Hong Kong and Peking, remaining firm on issues of principle; and thus hope to convince the Chinese that their hostage policy is not going to lead to concessions in Hong Kong and is therefore not worth the complications that it seems bound to entail for them in the long run.

A Reply to the Chinese Statement of 8 March

9. Our interim reply to the Chinese statement might refer only to normal working conditions for both our Missions (see paragraph 5 above). We might wait until we see whether the lifting of restrictions on the Mission here has any result before giving the Chinese a substantive reply. It would seem dangerous for any substantive reply to go further on the main point than a reiteration of our desire for good relations with the Chinese over Hong Kong. There might be advantage in putting our reply in the form of a message from the Secretary to State to Ch'en Yi, but we should bear in mind Sir D. Hopson's point (paragraph 6 of Peking telegram No. 179) that an oral reply might be preferable in order to minimise public commitment.

JAMES MURRAY

No. 86

Minute from Mr Rodgers to Mr Brown, 12 March 1968
Confidential (FCO 21/66, FC 3/3/D)

Secretary of State,

Until Sir Donald Hopson's interview with the Chinese Vice-Minister for Foreign Affairs last Friday, 8 March,[1] we had in mind to relax all entry and exit restrictions on the Chinese Mission, the Bank of China and the New China News Agency. We hoped that, as a result, we would get our people out of Peking. We had reluctantly concluded Anthony Grey's release depended upon action in Hong Kong, although there was the prospect of some progress on access to him.

2. Our problem now is, first, to judge whether Lo's statement slams the door; and, second, to decide on alternative courses open to us. Our best hope is that the moderate tone of Lo's statement and the reference (for the first time) to your message to Ch'en Yi mean that the Chinese wish to remind us that Hong Kong remains the crucial issue even although they are prepared to deal with 'secondary matters', i.e. the Mission. In this case we should go ahead with relaxation, assuming reciprocity but prepared to clamp down again if need be. The worst possibility is that Lo means what he says and that we are in for a long siege in Peking. But in this case also we cannot lose by testing the water as we have no easy remedy for Chinese intransigence, and none that need be prejudiced by cautious relaxation.

1 See No. 83.

3. As a first stage, therefore, I recommend that we inform the Chinese of our intention to relax restrictions, ignoring as far as possible Lo's statement. This could be done within the next few days.

4. But as a second stage we should consider a three-pronged diplomatic initiative. This might involve a further letter from you to Ch'en Yi (as it can be argued that you have now received a reply to your August message); an approach to the Chinese through the Pakistanis (although they have failed to help so far); and a carefully orchestrated publicity campaign abroad about the uncivilised way the Chinese are behaving (there is evidence that they are sensitive to criticism of the excesses of the Cultural Revolution). There is certainly no guarantee of success but there is no other course open.

5. The plain fact is that there are no effective sanctions we can put on the Chinese. We have more to lose by a trade embargo or by breaking off diplomatic relations (which in any case might well leave the Mission as hostages to Hong Kong). They seem better able to sit it out in London than we are in Peking—there is, perhaps, a lesson here about the size of character of Missions in exposed places.

6. Whatever course we follow I do not anticipate too much press or Parliamentary difficulty. The weakness of our position (for which the Government is not responsible) is well understood. Up to the present there has also been a certain veiled pride in our gallant men and women in a distant outpost. Handling interest in Anthony Grey is more difficult. Here we must rely on the evidence of all we (and Reuters) have tried to do, the link with 'normalisation' as a whole and the advantages to Grey of trying to keep the temperature down.

7. There remains the question of Hong Kong. I am sure that we should continue to try to reach an arrangement by which a number of Chinese prisoners are deported. We should also consider very fully with the Governor all the options open to us which might help in Peking without allowing a Macao situation to arise. It does seem to me however that there is grave danger in going further, or in giving any hint to the Chinese that we might be prepared to move. In this respect a visit to Hong Kong and to London by Sir Donald Hopson (assuming the Chinese would let him out) would seem to me to be dangerous in raising the very expectations on the part of the Chinese which could lead to us sliding into disaster.

WILLIAM RODGERS

No. 87

Sir D. Trench (Hong Kong) to Mr Thomson (Commonwealth Office)
15 March 1968[1]
Tel. No. 330 Immediate, Confidential (FCO 40/65, HWB 3/2)

Peking telegram No. 179[2] to Foreign Office: Sino-British relations.

I agree with much of the analysis in the first four paragraphs of the telegram under reference. There are admittedly some disquieting factors of which account

1 Repeated for information to Peking, Washington and Singapore.
2 No. 84.

should be taken. In Hong Kong the incidents at Kwun Tong and North Point reported in my telegrams Nos. 88 and 93[3] to Peking have provided renewed evidence of the militancy of the Communist rank and file, although they have been reported in a relatively restrained fashion by the bulk of the Communist Press. In China itself the Vickers Zimmer case[4] and possibly also the affair of the *Demodocus*[5] may be a warning that tougher policies can be used against us.

2. We ought not to exclude the possibility that important elements in the Communist leadership in Hong Kong and Canton at any rate would favour, even in the short term, the tougher policy towards Hong Kong set out in paragraph 3(*a*) of the telegram under reference (nor can it be excluded that it is the long term aim of the Chinese Communists as a whole). Nevertheless, I agree that the tone and circumstances of the communication by the Vice Minister suggest that the present aim of the Foreign Ministry at any rate is to pursue the softer policy set out in paragraph 3(*b*). My immediately following top secret telegram[6] (not to all) contains a further indication that the milder policy is at present favoured by Chou En-lai himself. It is, of course, impossible to be sure that our source has given us a wholly accurate account of what he has been told by his influential contacts here. But in general his story rings true: and it seems to fit in neatly with Her Majesty's Chargé d'Affaires impression of what the Ministry of Foreign Affairs were trying to get across in their statement to him. It would be not at all unlike the Chinese to brandish the big stick of more rigid treatment for our Mission in Peking while offering the carrot of negotiation in Hong Kong.

3. What action we should now take obviously requires most careful thought. In general, of course, our aim must be (as it has been) to try to keep the situation calm in Hong Kong. Obviously, however, we cannot do this at the expense of a failure to maintain law and order, and if the communist rank and file continue e.g. to mount disturbances outside the police stations, we shall have to deal with them as firmly and swiftly as in the past. The question is, however, whether there is any action that we could take simultaneously to give the Communist leadership a chance to claim that their moderate policies are paying dividends and thus to strengthen their control over the more militant rank and file. The prospect of 'releasing to China' a substantial number of prisoners or detainees would certainly be attractive from our point of view, but I am afraid that our experience with the film stars[7] up to the time of drafting this shows that it is most unlikely that it will be acceptable to the Chinese. It is hard to think of other ways in which we could make any overt moves in the direction of a settlement with risk to Hong Kong, though I agree that the idea of a public statement on the lines indicated in paragraph 6 of the telegram under reference is worth consideration.

3 Not printed.
4 See No. 64, note 2.
5 Mr P. D. Crouch, 2nd Officer of the SS Demodocus was detained at Shanghai on 3 April 1968.
6 Tel. No. 331 reported that a banking contact had informed them that the Communist government realised a Macau-type victory in Hong Kong was impossible and they wished to settle the issue to their best advantage. Chou En-lai favoured using intermediaries to sound out the Hong Kong Government about a settlement rather than instituting formal talks.
7 On 14 March Chinese officials refused to accept at the frontier two communist film stars previously held in prison in Hong Kong whom the authorities were trying to deport or 'release' to China.

4. This does not mean however that it would not be useful to try to discover more clearly what the Chinese mean by asking us to 'reply' to their demands. There are obvious dangers in embarking on discussions of the matter through official channels, either here or in Peking; we could only too easily be drawn into a Macao-like situation. But I do not think that we need to be too frightened of exploratory discussions through an unofficial intermediary. The approach by the source indicated in paragraph 2 does provide us with a means of testing out the ground that is less risky than most. He has undeniably close contacts with the Communists; but he has taken a firm anti-Communist line during the disturbances; and he would have a good deal to lose if he tricked us or let us down. On the other hand anything that we said to him could, if necessity arose or negotiations went sour, be disowned or repudiated much more easily than communication through official channels.

5. So far we have done no more in response than to express interest in the implications of what we have been told and to say that it would take us some days to consider it. But, if we are not to ignore the approach completely, we should be prepared to give a general indication of our reaction not later than say next Tuesday (19th). Subject to your views, I would propose that a fairly senior official should meet the source and speak on the following lines:

(*a*) We were considerably interested in his message. It is certainly our aim to reduce tension in Hong Kong: though of course we could not do so at the expense of maintaining law and order.

(*b*) If we were to enter on any talks with him they would be entirely on an unofficial, exploratory and confidential basis and we would not regard ourselves as committed by anything said in the discussions.

(*c*) There would be no/no question of our entering into anything in the nature of a written agreement with him or anyone else in Hong Kong.

(*d*) Initially, we would be interested to know what was implied by the suggestion that the discussions be conducted on the basis of the Chinese 'demands'. We had already made clear many times that the demands as we interpreted them were unacceptable to us. But we would like to hear his views on the point.

6. The final question is who should represent us. A possibility would be the Political Adviser or alternatively Cater, who is already in personal contact with the source and who, though still acting as Deputy Colonial Secretary, has also now taken up his duties as Executive Director of the Trade Development Council, and therefore would have the advantage of semi-unofficial status.

7. Grateful for your views.[8]

On 16 March 1968 Mr Brown resigned as Secretary of State for Foreign Affairs and was replaced by Mr Michael Stewart.

---

8 In Peking Tel. No. 211, of 18 March 1968, Sir D. Hopson supported the Governor's recommendations, including probing Chinese intentions via unofficial channels (FCO 21/66). In CO Tel. No. 506 to Hong Kong, of 19 March 1968, the Governor was informed that Ministers had agreed to the course of action proposed in para. 5 with Mr Cater as the representative.

CHAPTER II

Clearing the debris of confrontation
21 March 1968 — 13 February 1970

No. 88

Submission from Mr Murray to Mr Wilkinson, 21 March 1968
Secret (FCO 21/67, FC 3/3/E)

Sino-British relations

The Secretary of State is to hold a meeting on 26 March to review Sino-British relations.[1] The purpose of this minute is to describe the present state of relations, set out the principal problems (many of them inter-connected) for decision, and make preliminary recommendations. Supplementary detail is given in Annexes.[2]

Introduction

2. The Chargé d'Affaires in Peking was summoned by Vice-Minister for Foreign Affairs Lo Kuei-po on 8 March to receive a statement to the effect that the Hong Kong situation was the crux of Sino-British relations; that the British Government must reply to various demands put forward by the Chinese Government on this subject; and that only thereafter would it be possible to discuss 'secondary matters'.

3. The *'secondary matters'* which we now have at issue with the Chinese are:

(*a*) The detention, without consular access, since last July of Mr Grey, Reuters correspondent in Peking.

(*b*) The refusal of exit visas (and also of entry visas) for our Mission in Peking, except in a few very special cases.

(*c*) The detention, with consular access, in north-west China since last September of Mr Watt, an engineer from Vickers-Zimmer, and his sentencing on 16 March to three years imprisonment for espionage.

(*d*) The arrest from a Polish ship in Shanghai about 23 February of Mr Norman Barrymaine, a freelance journalist.

(*e*) The detention of the Blue Funnel ship s.s. 'Demodocus' in Woosung anchorage outside Shanghai since about 26 February.

(*f*) The refusal of exit visas for a British banker and his wife in Shanghai.

Problems for decision

4. There are, broadly speaking, three sets of problems on which decisions are required:

---

1 See No. 91.
2 Not printed.

(*a*) What steps can we take to try to reach a *modus vivendi* over Hong Kong with the Chinese without dangerously eroding our authority there?

(*b*) Since any such arrangement is bound to take time, what can we do meanwhile to persuade the Chinese to make progress on the various secondary issues? In particular, should we make a further effort to get the Chinese to deal with the question of the Mission in isolation from other issues? In practice this would mean removing the remaining restrictions on Chinese officials in this country.

(*c*) If we fail to make any progress whatsoever, what means have we of bringing pressure to bear on the Chinese? What action, if any, should we take against Chinese officials in London; what other sanctions are available; what are the prospects for a diplomatic offensive to try to persuade intermediaries to bring pressure on the Chinese; and what are the advantages and disadvantages of a publicity campaign?

Recommendations

5. My *preliminary recommendations* are these:

(*a*) It would be premature to decide on tactics over Hong Kong until we have had some results from the informal exchanges which the Governor may now be able to have with the Chinese in Hong Kong. (The Secretary of State will no doubt wish to have an early discussion with the Commonwealth Secretary on the long term aspects of the Hong Kong problem.)

(*b*) We should make one further effort to get the Chinese to deal with the question of the Mission in isolation from other outstanding issues; and to this end we should remove the remaining restrictions on Chinese officials in this country as regards both exit permits and entry visas.

(*c*) If within about a month we fail to make any progress, we should consider international action to put pressure on China (concentrating on the Pakistanis) and well organised international publicity.

(*d*) Action against Chinese officials in London would be inadvisable.

(*e*) Economic sanctions would be ineffective.

(*f*) An interim reply should be given orally to the Chinese statement of 8 March, referring only to the importance of normal working conditions for both our Missions. A substantive reply should await Chinese reactions to this, and to further development in Hong Kong.

(*g*) We should be ready at some stage to advise the Secretary of State to send a personal message to Ch'en Yi. But the timing will present problems; and it would probably be premature now.

Argument

Background (See also Annex A)

6. Our present round of troubles with the Chinese Government dates from the overspill early last year of the 'Cultural Revolution' into Hong Kong. This involved firm police action in Hong Kong, the arrest of troublemakers and the suspension of some communist newspapers. The Chinese Government in May presented us with a Note requiring us to accept 'Five Demands', notably the release of all political prisoners. In July, Mr Grey, the Reuters correspondent, was placed under house arrest in Peking in retaliation for the arrest of a New China News Agency (NCNA) journalist in Hong Kong. In August relations reached their nadir when our Mission in Peking was attacked after our failure to respond to the Chinese ultimatum about the suspension of

communist newspapers. This led to our placing additional restrictions on Chinese officials in London and the Chinese retaliated by imposing additional restrictions on our Mission in Peking and withholding exit visas. On 31 August, Mr George Brown wrote to Ch'en Yi urging efforts at re-establishing normal relations and proposing exchanges of nationals (including NCNA journalists in Hong Kong for Mr Grey) and, if no other course was open, the withdrawal of our respective Missions. No reply has ever been received; but there was some slight improvement in relations. Though the Chinese made it clear that our Mission was being held as hostages for our behaviour in Hong Kong, some exit visas were given on health grounds.

7. By November it was evident that the communist campaign of violence in Hong Kong had been a failure, and it was abandoned. The local communists maintained, however, that this was no more than a change of tactics and that it was still their intention to keep up the pressure on the Hong Kong Government by other means. But the atmosphere in Hong Kong greatly improved. In November we removed the 5-mile travel restrictions on Chinese officials in London and the Chinese matched this by putting our Mission back on the same footing as other domestic missions in Peking in the matter of travel. By the beginning of February, we thought that we had succeeded in getting the Chinese to drop the link between our conduct in Hong Kong and our Mission in China and to equate British officials in Peking with Chinese officials in London.

8. Thus Lo's statement on 8 March (Peking telegram No. 176),[3] insofar as it reintroduced this link, represented a setback; but its significance is not entirely clear.

(*a*) By Chinese standards it was moderate in tone (Peking telegram No. 179).[4] It asked us, not to accept, but to 'reply to' the various demands made to us. It included the first reference to Mr Brown's letter to Ch'en Yi. It is just open to the interpretation that the Chinese intended to put on record their stand of principle over Hong Kong but that, while paying lip service to that principle, they would nevertheless be prepared to make some progress on 'secondary matters'.

(*b*) On the other hand, it was quite uncompromising in tone. It would be imprudent therefore not to face up to the possibility that the Chinese meant exactly what they said, and that they are fully ready to hold our Mission as hostages until we make concessions in Hong Kong.

9. Meantime the position has been further complicated by various acts of unfriendliness on the part of the Chinese: the sentencing of Mr Watt; the refusal to accept at the frontier two communist film stars previously held in prison in Hong Kong whom the Hong Kong authorities, as a test of Chinese intentions, were trying to deport or 'release to China'; the continued detention of the 'Demodocus'; and the arrest of Mr Barrymaine.

10. Against this background of uncertainty, the Governor of Hong Kong has had an informal approach, through delicate but normally reliable intermediaries, purporting to have originated with Chou En-lai. According to this approach, the Chinese authorities would like to discuss ways and means of bringing the troubles in Hong Kong to an end; they were, however, having difficulties with their own activists; the basis for the discussions would be the previous 'demands' of the Chinese

3 See No. 83.
4 No. 84.

Government but the majority of these would be insisted on in token fashion only; the most difficult problem was likely to be the release of the political prisoners in Hong Kong, but there was nothing that could not be solved by negotiation. On the recommendation of the Governor of Hong Kong (Hong Kong telegram No. 330),[5] we have authorised him to follow up this approach with due caution and using a representative who can, if necessary, be disowned.

Hong Kong (See also Annex B)

11. We have so far held that the Governor, while not being over-rigid, should take only such measures of relaxation as were desirable in the context of bringing things in Hong Kong back to normal; and that if we started to make concessions under Chinese pressure, we should be on a very slippery slope indeed. Sir D. Hopson has suggested that it may now be in our interest to explore the possibility of a face-saving formula on Hong Kong, and the informal approach referred to above would seem to provide us with a means of doing so that is less risky than most. The trouble is that any statement that satisfied the Chinese seems bound from that very fact to be such as to compromise our position. It is clear from Lo's remarks and from the informal approach that prisoners are a key issue. The Governor has always been prepared to deport (or 'release to China') considerable numbers of communist prisoners, but understandably he is very reluctant to release them in Hong Kong. The Chinese, however, have always challenged our right to deport to China and when a test was carried out with two communist film stars last week, the Chinese refused to accept them and formally protested to our Mission in Peking. It is too early to say what the Chinese hope to achieve from us in Hong Kong in the immediate future. It seems unlikely that they can seriously expect us to accept a 'Macao-type' situation (i.e. a situation in which, while we hold nominal control, our actions are in fact dictated by the Chinese Government through various local communist organisations). But they may hope to push us some way towards such a situation by insisting that we release considerable numbers of prisoners and in the process recognise a special status for various Chinese official and semi-official organs in Hong Kong. For the present we must await the Governor's assessment based on a further probe of the Chinese position.

Restrictions on Officials (See also Annex C)

12. The present position is this:

(a) The British Mission in Peking (20 men, 6 single girls, 17 women and children) is subject to normal travel restrictions inside China. Exit visas are in general being withheld, except for several which have been granted on medical grounds. Entry visas are also being withheld.

(*b*) The Chinese officials in London (about 50 in number) must seek permission of the Foreign Office before leaving the country. If exit permits were applied for, we would give them. But the Chinese regard our requirement which is not imposed on other Diplomatic Missions in London as 'illegal' and discriminatory and refuse to apply for permission. Thus there is a self-imposed bar on their exit. We are also refusing entry visas for two Bank of China and three NCNA officials.

The Chinese will certainly not deal with exit visas for our Mission on a normal basis until we have lifted our requirement for exit permits. They have argued

---

5 No. 87.

somewhat speciously that, as we were the first to impose restrictions on missions (see paragraph 6 above), we must be the first to dismantle them. I think that despite the lack of any assurance of reciprocity, we should lift the requirement for exit visas and grant entry visas to Chinese officials in the normal way. It is highly desirable that the Chinese should be left with no formal pretext whatsoever for withholding visas from our Mission. When informed of such a decision the Chinese would be unlikely to give us any formal satisfaction; but they might conceivably be prepared in practice to grant exit visas for the Mission. This is a matter of some urgency since Sir D. Hopson has recently for the first time introduced the question of staff morale, pointing out that although the situation is not yet desperate, the strain for those divided from their families and those who ought to leave China for medical reasons is beginning to tell. We would not be giving away any significant bargaining counter. What is important is not the requirement that the Chinese should have to ask for permission to leave—which stems from the Foreign Office Note without regular juridical basis. What is important is that if in the event too many Chinese try to leave, the Security Services and the Home Office should be ready to co-operate in effective means to prevent them from doing so.

British Subjects detained in China (See also Annex D)

13. (*a*) *Mr Grey*

Since his detention last July, the Chinese have made it abundantly clear that Mr Grey is linked to developments in Hong Kong. It is for that reason there never has been any hope of achieving his release by pressure on NCNA in London. We have so far not made any progress towards the *release* of Mr Grey. The Chinese have not yet taken up the question of exchanging him against NCNA journalists in Hong Kong, although the offer has been made with them twice since the beginning of the year. This is not surprising as Mr Grey represents a valuable card and we may not find out precisely what the Chinese want in return for him until they have probed our intentions a good deal more. On the other hand there now seems a reasonable chance that we will be granted *access* following our agreement to special visits to NCNA and 'other patriotic journalists' imprisoned in Hong Kong, on the clear understanding of reciprocal visits to Mr Grey.

(*b*) *Mr Watt*

Mr Watt's offence has probably been taking photographs in breach of Chinese regulations and attempting to smuggle them out. His sentence to three years imprisonment came just after the Managing Director of Vickers-Zimmer had concluded unsuccessful talks in Peking with the Chinese authorities. Vickers-Zimmer, who are constructing a synthetic fibre plant, have had commercial difficulties with the Chinese clients, probably on account of bad planning errors by the Chinese authorities and the confusion caused by the Cultural Revolution. There is the possibility that the Chinese are using the Watt case in an effort to thrust on Vickers-Zimmer formal responsibility for delays in the contract. The Chinese statement about Mr Watt accused Vickers-Zimmer of 'fraud in economic and technical fields'. Vickers-Zimmer are writing to the Chinese once again in reasoned terms about fulfilment of the contract. Until there is a reply, it is difficult to assess whether or not the Chinese, having made their gesture, might be prepared to expel Mr Watt in the coming months.

(c) *Mr Barrymaine*

Mr Barrymaine was probably taking photographs in unauthorised places. So far our Mission in Peking have been unable to obtain any details. Mr Barrymaine is known to the Office as an unreliable and slightly unbalanced character.

(d) s.s. 'Demodocus'

The crew of the 'Demodocus' includes 42 British subjects (citizens of the United Kingdom). A Chinese representative of the shipping line's agents in Hong Kong has been to Shanghai and from his reports it would appear that one or more of the officers are under investigation for alleged espionage. The Mission in Peking have been unable to obtain any information. Blue Funnel are holding up sailings to Chinese ports for the time being; and if the affair drags on it could clearly assume very serious proportions.

Measures for the longer term

14. If, despite a conciliatory attitude in Hong Kong and lifting of restrictions on the Chinese officials here, we do not make progress on exit visas for our staff on British subjects in trouble in China, what then? We are short of effective bargaining counters.

(a) *Withdrawal of the Mission*

It may be asked whether any useful purpose is still served by retaining the Mission, the very existence of which inhibits our action in Hong Kong. Apart from domestic political considerations here, it is very doubtful if the Chinese, given the attitude they have adopted, would be prepared to agree that we should withdraw our Mission. They would gain nothing; and they probably also attach some importance to maintaining their own activities here. From the point of view of the Government of Hong Kong there is some advantage in a direct channel of communication with Peking which avoids the necessity of dealing directly with local communist representatives on major matters.

(b) *Rupture of Diplomatic Relations*

We could of course try to force the Chinese hand by formally breaking relations. But this might simply deprive our Mission in Peking of such protection as they derive from their diplomatic status, while the Chinese continue to keep them as hostages. Moreover, as a matter of face, the Chinese would be practically bound to try to make serious trouble for us in Hong Kong. A secondary objection to a rupture would be the loss of trade which would almost certainly be involved.

(c) *Economic Sanctions*

Threats to stop trade from the United Kingdom would not modify the Chinese attitude, and loss of trade would be harmful to us here. Economic measures in Hong Kong directed against China would hurt the Colony more than the Chinese.

(d) *Action against the Chinese Mission in London* (See also Annex C)

Our Mission in Peking are strongly opposed to further action against Chinese officials in London, e.g. restrictions on movement or expulsion of NCNA. We agree with them that we would certainly come off worse in any straightforward contest in nastiness, and the chances of getting access to Mr Grey would be lost. We might of course try expelling members of the Chinese diplomatic mission (as distinct from NCNA). The risk is that if the Chinese were to retaliate by expelling any of our people from Peking, it would probably be those that the Mission least wanted to lose at this stage.

(e) International Action

By any standards the Chinese are behaving monstrously in holding a diplomatic mission as a means of exerting pressure over policy matters and many countries not generally sympathetic to us would nevertheless disapprove of such tactics. There may sooner or later be advantage in initiating publicity among diplomatic missions in Peking by having Sir D. Hopson write to the Dean of the corps and his colleagues. We shall certainly have to consider what pressure we might bring to bear on the Chinese through intermediaries. The Pakistanis would seem to offer the best prospect, and there might be advantage in asking President Ayub Khan to intervene with Chou En-lai. But our past experience with the Pakistanis does not offer encouragement that we shall have much success.

(f) Publicity

An international publicity campaign designed to show how badly the Chinese are behaving will have to be considered. It is our view that the Chinese may be sensitive to international publicity suggesting that they are behaving in a thoroughly 'uncivilised' fashion.[6] But publicity is a two-edged weapon. If we make it widely known that the Chinese are holding our people until their 'demands' are met in Hong Kong, we may commit them to even more firmly to that position. They might also react to publicity by making life difficult in Peking for our Mission. Finally we must bear in mind that publicity would lead to increased public pressure here to 'do something'—and the preceding paragraphs indicate that the possibilities for effective action are limited. Nevertheless the whole question of British subjects in China is likely to become a matter of increasing public concern in this country and we must be ready, despite the difficulties, with carefully-prepared publicity measures.[7]

JAMES MURRAY

6 See No. 73.
7 Mr Wilkinson noted that he supported the recommendations.

No. 89

Sir D. Hopson (Peking) to Mr Stewart, 21 March 1968[1]
Tel. No. 229A Unclassified (FCO 21/66, FC 3/3/D)

About one hundred foreign experts, students and journalists held demonstration outside this office this afternoon. They carried placards and shouted slogans in the usual way but were kept under control by police. They were protesting at the 'shameless and hypocritical stand of the British Government' over Rhodesia and against the Smith Regime. After burning Her Majesty The Queen in effigy they read out and handed over a protest statement which I received from them at the front gate.

1 Repeated for information to Lusaka, Hong Kong, Singapore and Washington.

No. 90

Minute from Mr Rodgers to Mr Stewart, 22 March 1968
Confidential (FCO 21/67, FC 3/3/E)

Secretary of State,

The key to Sino-British relations is the Chinese attitude to Hong Kong. Our best hope is that as the Cultural Revolution dies away, they will be prepared to accept a stalemate. Only at that point are we likely to see our relations get back on to a tolerable basis (although continuing uncertainty is inevitable).

2. I agree with the preliminary recommendations in paragraph 5 of the attached submission.[1] Our best hope is that the informal approach made to the Governor of Hong Kong is genuine, and that there is now a possibility of reaching an understanding. Meanwhile we should investigate the possibility of making progress on 'secondary matters'. The plain fact is, however, that the Chinese have almost all the cards in their hand. There are no effective sanctions which we could bring to bear. We have more to lose than they do from a sharpening of the conflict and a return to the harsh exchanges of last summer.

3. Until Sir Donald Hopson's interview with the Chinese Vice-Minister for the Foreign Affairs on 8 March, we had in mind to relax all entry and exit restrictions on the Chinese Mission, the Bank of China and the New China News Agency. We hoped that, as a result, we would get our people out of Peking. We had reluctantly concluded Anthony Grey's release depended upon action in Hong Kong, although there was the prospect of some progress on access to him.

4. Our problem since 8 March is, first, to judge whether Lo's statement slams the door; and, second, to decide on alternative courses open to us. Our best hope is that the moderate tone of Lo's statement and the reference (for the first time) to the previous Secretary of State's message to Chen Yi mean that the Chinese wish to remind us that Hong Kong remains the crucial issue even although they are prepared to deal with 'secondary matters', i.e. the Mission. In this case we should be able to go ahead with relaxation, assuming reciprocity but prepared to clamp down again if need be. The worst possibility is that Lo means what he says and that we are in for a long siege in Peking. But in this case also we cannot lose by testing the water as we have no easy remedy for Chinese intransigence, and none that need be prejudiced by cautious relaxation.

5. As a first stage, therefore, I agree that we inform the Chinese of our intention to relax restrictions, as in paragraph 5(*b*) of the submission, ignoring as far as possible Lo's statement.

6. I agree also that as a second stage we should consider a three-pronged diplomatic initiative. This might involve a letter from you to Chen Yi (as it can be argued that we have now received a reply to George Brown's August message); an approach to the Chinese through the Pakistanis (although they have failed to help in the past); and a carefully-orchestrated publicity campaign abroad about the uncivilised way the Chinese are behaving (there is evidence that they are sensitive to criticism of the

---

1 No. 88.

excesses of the Cultural Revolution). There is certainly no guarantee of success but there is no other course open.

7. Whatever course we follow I do not anticipate too much press or Parliamentary difficulty. The weakness of our position (for which the Government is not held to be responsible) is well understood. As far as the Mission is concerned, up to the present there has been a certain pride in our gallant men and women in a distant outpost. Handling interest in Grey, Watt, Barrymaine and the 'Demodocus' is more difficult. Here we must rely on the evidence of all we have tried to do and are still doing, especially on Consular access, the link with 'normalisation' as a whole and the advantages of trying to keep the temperature down.

WILLIAM RODGERS

No. 91

Sir D. Hopson (Peking) to Mr Stewart, 26 March 1968[1]
Tel. No. 242 Flash, Confidential (FCO 21/66, FC 3/3)

My immediately preceding telegram:[2] Sino-British Relations.

The Chinese insistence in this interview and in that with Ts'ui on 22 March (my telegram No. 232)[3] on the need for an early reply to the Vice-Minister for Foreign Affairs Statement is interesting. On the whole I would regard this as a hopeful sign indicating a wish to settle outstanding problems with us though of course on terms acceptable to them. They might well have simply restated their demands on Hong Kong and left us to stew. This impression of a wish to push on towards a settlement was borne out by tone of both interviews.

2. It would also seem that the Chinese are not content to let discussion be conducted solely via informal channels referred to in Hong Kong telegram No. 331.[4] They seem to want to have some exchange of views on two levels. I would not see any great danger to us and possibly some advantage in falling in with them on this issue.

3. It is also just possible that the Chinese would consider a reply to Lo's statement as an adequate reply to their demands providing some kind of formal bow was made in this direction. In any event it is in our interest to give a reply which if nothing else would probably help to smoke out the Chinese position.

4. On reflection it would seem better for us to attempt as first priority a reply to the Ministry of Foreign Affairs in what could be a confidential communication rather than a statement in Hong Kong or in Parliament as suggested in paragraph 6 of my telegram No. 179.[5] My immediately following telegram contains a tentative draft of

[1] Repeated for information to Hong Kong.
[2] In this telegram, Sir D. Hopson reported a meeting with the deputy head of the West European Department where it was repeated that Hong Kong was the crux of Sino-British relations with all other issues being secondary, and Britain had yet to respond to the series of demands made by China. If the British were sincere, they should 'hurry up and make an early reply on the main question'.
[3] Not printed.
[4] See No. 87, note 6.
[5] No. 84.

a possible reply which might be best delivered as an oral statement by me to Ministry in Peking. The object would be to acknowledge Lo's statement, show willingness to bring Hong Kong into the discussions and make some gestures in direction of Chinese demand without conceding anything on the essential Hong Kong issues.

5. Our reply would also be an opportunity to point out the difficulty of discussing Sino-British relations when normal diplomatic machinery is not functioning properly. We could re-affirm our wish to restore normal movement and I strongly recommend that we should make the complete offer of reciprocity for visa for officials as argued last in my telegram No. 159.[6] It makes our negotiating position much clearer than if we continue to exclude entry visas for NCNA. It would also strength our position in any subsequent diplomatic or publicity campaign and it might conceivably produce some response in terms of visas from the Chinese before a complete settlement is reached over Hong Kong. See my immediately following telegram.

6 Not printed.

No. 92

Record of a meeting between Mr Stewart and officials, 26 March 1968
Confidential (FCO 21/67, FC 3/3/E)

Sino-British Relations

The Secretary of State held an Office Meeting this morning to discuss Sino/British relations.

2. Mr Stewart began by asking whether the proposition was right that we would make no progress on secondary matters unless we said something to the Chinese on the main issue. The Meeting thought this was probably correct. The danger was that by saying something on the main subject we might get ourselves onto a slippery slope. The Secretary of State then asked whether our position would be strengthened by a statement on the main subject. The Meeting thought there was no clear answer to this in that the Chinese had probably not yet made up their minds on their next step. The point was also made that the Chinese would probably be more interested in action by us rather than words. At the same time in any statement we made we would have to point out the difficulties of meeting Chinese demands. We would have to argue that in Hong Kong the law had to take its proper course and that it should apply impartially to all.

3. Mr Stewart asked whether the Chinese still stood by their original demands. The Meeting thought they probably did, but they might now be looking for a way of retreating from them without losing face. They were also undoubtedly keen to discover how much they could get out of us. There was also the consideration that they probably needed to show their supporters in Hong Kong that they were able and willing to do something for them.

4. The Meeting thought that we were faced with three possible courses of action:
   (*a*) to disengage from Hong Kong;
   (*b*) to accept a Macao-type situation;

(*c*) to hold fast.

5. Mr Rodgers thought that as a first step we should see whether the informal contacts now being arranged in Hong Kong produced any result. Then we might deal with the secondary issues and at a later stage reply on the main question.

6. The Meeting then considered what our policy should be on secondary measures and there was some discussion of the mechanics of preventing the Chinese from removing their whole staff from their Mission in London. The questions of economic sanctions, eventual publicity for Chinese misbehaviour and the recall of Sir Donald Hopson for consultations were also raised.

7. The Meeting reached the following conclusions:

(*a*) we should allow the informal contact in Hong Kong to proceed;

(*b*) we should say something to the Chinese on Hong Kong; Peking telegram No. 243[1] provided a useful first draft for a statement of our position. This would be examined urgently in consultation with the Commonwealth Office and the Governor of Hong Kong;

(*c*) there should be no economic sanctions, but we should examine the question of quota increases;

(*d*) the question of publicity about Chinese conduct should be left over to a later stage;

(*e*) a paper should be submitted to the Secretary of State on contingency plans for dealing with a threat to Hong Kong;

(*f*) we should examine with the Home Office how members of the Chinese Mission should be prevented from leaving this country;

(*g*) Mr Rodgers would discuss the question of shipping visiting Chinese ports with Mr Keswick.

D. J. D. Maitland

1 Not printed. See No. 91.

No. 93

Letter from Mr Cradock (Peking) to Mr Denson, 26 March 1968
Personal and Confidential (FCO 21/37, FC 1/21/A)

Dear John,

Since my last letter to you of 10 February[1] on the state of the Mission there have been a number of important developments affecting our situation, most of them bad I am afraid.

2. The most important was of course the Lo Kuei-po interview of 8 March which set us a long way back on visas, making this as well as other issues dependent on Hong Kong. As we have pointed out in our telegrams, there had been no mention of Hong Kong in the interviews with Kao on 24 January,[2] 7 February or 2 March and in claiming that he referred to Hong Kong as the crux of the situation the Chinese were

1 Not printed.
2 See No. 76.

simply falsifying the record. We have naturally asked ourselves whether Kao meant what he said on 24 January. It is possible to argue that it was all a trick from the start but I think that this is a very unlikely explanation. What seems much more probable is that the offer was genuine at the time and had we clinched the deal quickly we should have got at least some of the staff out. Even a few exit visas would have been a great gain. The failure to settle and the reintroduction of Hong Kong via Tony Grey, complicated the issue and probably meant reference to higher authority on the Chinese side. The effect was that they changed their ground and we were back where we began in December. The plain conclusions, I am afraid, is that a chance was let slip and it is cold comfort to us to know that our repeated warnings (against delay in clinching the deal and against bringing back Hong Kong into the equation) were proved correct. I only hope that when this comes up again, and it is still a live issue, we shall not make the same error and shall be prepared to accept the offer of January 24.

3. The sequel to this was the failure to deport our two film stars from Hong Kong with the conclusion that for the present at least this way to a relatively quick solution of the problem of Hong Kong prisoners is going to be much more difficult. As a result of this, for the first time for a while we had anti-Hong Kong publicity in the Chinese press.

4. The next unwelcome development was the announcement about poor George Watt. We had realised since last September that something unpleasant was likely to happen in this case and it could be argued that the outcome could have been worse and that given the charges of espionage, three years is not so very heavy a sentence in China. Cockburn and Parry also managed to get away after an uneasy week and some of the publicity given to espionage and sabotage may have mainly internal relevance, as an excuse for setbacks in production arising from the Cultural Revolution. Nevertheless the news was bad by any standard and the considerable coverage given in the Chinese press to alleged British espionage has done nothing to improve the atmosphere. We move about even more cautiously in consequence and for the time being carry no cameras.

5. Finally we had on 21 March the first demonstration of the 1968 season, when over 100 African and Arab foreign friends with a sprinkling of Chinese demonstrated at the Office gate about Rhodesia. It was small beer by our usual standards and the police maintained full control. But the placards, posters, shouting and burning effigies were not enjoyed. Donald Hopson, John Weston and I went out to receive the petition with an unpleasant feeling of having been there before and there are inevitably questions in our minds whether this was perhaps only the overture to another lively summer. It happened to coincide with a recent rise in the Peking political temperature: more posters, some rallies, more noise, the outer evidence of some internal struggle. I think this may be merely an eddy in a current flowing steadily in the direction of greater order and control but one can never be completely sure and we would all be a little more comfortable if the political temperature were to fall to its winter level.

6. Against this background you will understand we are all fairly subdued; making personal adjustments to the prospects of a long stay and doing what we can to make ourselves comfortable for the summer, the autumn and perhaps later. I have written to James Murray on some of the welfare problems this raises and again to

John Heath this week on some of the financial aspects. I am sure you will do what you can to support our case. Although some of our Chinese staff have been less cooperative recently (possibly because of the Watt case) we have managed to make some progress over practical matters. Craftsmen have finally turned up from the DSB to repair the broken windows and the burned woodwork in the ground floor rooms of our Office. We have manage to get agreement to install air conditioners in the flat Donald Hopson now occupies—a small thing, you may say, but in the Peking context a major achievement. We are also getting on with improving the grounds and garden in the old office where we are likely to spend a good part of our leisure time this summer. We shall be reporting separately that the new leases for Nos. 5 and 7 Kuang Hua Lu have been signed, with the amendment included that No. 7 may be used as an office or residence. This has taken a weight off my mind.

7. We also push on with requests for individual visas on health or compassionate grounds. Mrs Tregilgas and John Finch left on 11 March. We were particularly relieved John Finch could get away. Mrs Holroyd has decided in the changed situation to stay with her husband and have her baby in Peking. I called on Consular Department on 22 March to press for a visa for Mrs Peters and I think there is an even chance that she may be allowed to go.

I am sending a copy of this letter on a personal basis to Anthony Elliott in Hong Kong and to Ramsey Melhuish in Personnel Department.

Yours ever,
PERCY

No. 94

Submission from Mr Murray to Sir D. Allen, 2 April 1968
Confidential (FCO 21/67, FC 3/3/E)

Sino-British Relations: Restrictions on the Movement of Chinese Officials Problem

At the Office meeting on 26 March[1] the Secretary of State, in discussing the arguments in favour of lifting the restrictions on movement of Chinese officials in this country, directed that we should examine with the Home Office the measures which we could actually take to prevent Chinese officials from leaving the country should the need arise. In addition, he agreed that Sir D. Hopson had provided a useful first draft for a statement to the Chinese on Hong Kong and other issues. (This draft included a reference to readiness to settle the movements problem immediately on the lines suggested by the Chinese, i.e. the removal of the remaining impediments on exit from and entry into the United Kingdom for Chinese staff.) A survey of restrictions has now been conducted with Home Office officials; the results are embodied in the Annex.[2] A decision has now to be taken about the lifting of restrictions.

1 See No. 92.
2 Not printed.

Recommendations

2. I recommend:

(*a*) The requirement for exit permits should be lifted forthwith. A draft Note to the Chinese Chargé d'Affaires is attached.[3]

(*b*) We should ask the Home Office to grant entry visas to the two Bank of China and three New China News Agency (NCNA) officials in respect of whom applications are outstanding.

(*c*) The Secretary of State should write to the Home Secretary informing him of what we are doing. A draft minute is attached.[4]

(*d*) The oral statement which Sir D. Hopson is to make to the Chinese Ministry of Foreign Affairs in due course about Sino-British relations will provide a suitable opportunity for us to tell the Chinese that we expect our gestures to be matched. But we should not hold up the lifting of restrictions while the exact terms and timing of the statement be decided upon.

(*e*) We should explain to Mr Gerald Long, General Manager of Reuters, what we are doing about restrictions.

The Legal Adviser concurs in the Annex and the drafts.

Background

3. The background is in my submission of 21 March[5] and in the Private Secretary's minute of 26 March recording the Office meeting.

Argument

Consultation with the Home Office about restrictions on the Exit of Chinese Officials

4. We have examined once again with the Home Office officials concerned the whole problem of preventing Chinese officials from leaving this country. I attach an annex setting out the present position with regard to restrictions; the implications of lifting the requirement for exit permits; and possible measures if the Chinese were to attempt to withdraw large numbers of their staff without reciprocity for our Mission in Peking. It was this last aspect that most concerned the Secretary of State at the meeting on 26 March. I think that the contingency is an unlikely one. The Chinese undoubtedly attach considerable importance to their activities here. If, however, the attempt were made, the position in brief would be this. We should have to rely on the Security Services for advance warning of Chinese intentions. They have served us well in this respect up to now. Our first step would be to reimpose the requirement for exit permits. If there were indications (again from the Security Services) that this was not going to be enough, we should have to reimpose the travel limit to 5 miles (or indeed less) and ask the Home Office to arrange the police surveillance necessary to enforce it. We should then be in a position to keep a constant physical check on all movements. (We should have to accept, however, that an immediate result would be measures of harassment against our Mission in Peking.) If thereafter, despite the exit permit requirement, Chinese officials actually tried to leave, officials not actual members of the Mission—who are in any case subject to the Aliens Orders—could be prevented by immigration officers under the terms of the Aliens Orders; members of the diplomatic mission would have to be kept from boarding particular aircraft or

---

3 Not printed.
4 Not printed.
5 No. 88.

ships by the imposition of administrative delays. The reason given to the Chinese diplomatic staff for the delay would be that their papers were not in order in that they lacked a Foreign Office exit permit.

5. Home Office officials have been sympathetic about our problems in the past, and have assured us that they will continue to be so in the future. There might, however, be advantage in the Secretary of State writing to the Home Secretary now, explaining what we are doing, and putting on record that his sympathetic co-operation would be expected, if need arose. In exercising our restraints, we must of course try to minimise the possibilities for the Chinese to create a fracas which might inexorably lead to arrests. Such arrests could have painful repercussions for our Mission in Peking. The Metropolitan Police and the Immigration Services are well aware of this aspect.

Restrictions on the Entry of Chinese Officials

6. We are at present withholding entry visas for two Bank of China officials (in retaliation for the refusal of exit visas to a British banker and his wife in Shanghai) and for three NCNA officials (in retaliation for Mr Grey). We have never foreseen any particular difficulty about letting the bankers in when the time seemed right. But we have had serious doubts in the past about granting entry visas for the NCNA officials when Mr Grey was being held incommunicado in Peking. We had thought that we might be criticised by the press here, on the grounds of paying more attention to the welfare of our staff than to that of Mr Grey. This risk still exists. Only with some difficulty has publicity about Mr Grey been kept to its present low level. We know that the National Union of Journalists are going to raise the matter with us again shortly. There are both negative and positive arguments for granting visas to NCNA. The negative argument is that the Chinese have made it abundantly clear that withholding visas for NCNA in London is useless as a bargaining counter in the case of Mr Grey whom they link firmly to conditions in Hong Kong. The positive argument—and one which has been put forcefully by Sir D. Hopson on several occasions—is that the Chinese will certainly not return to normal exit and entry conditions for our staff until we on our side have taken the initiative in returning to normal, i.e. pre-August, conditions here of exit and entry for Chinese officials. Admittedly, if there continues to be no progress over Mr Grey, pressure will certainly further increase for action to help him, possibly in the form of tough measures against the NCNA. In such an event, Sir D. Hopson suggested that we should take the line that denying entry visas to NCNA (or any other positive action against them) would not assist Mr Grey's chances—and that there was no question of sacrificing Mr Grey to the interests of our Mission because we were not intending to withdraw our Mission but merely hoped to replace staff. I think that these arguments will hold up. But I also think that we should take Mr Gerald Long of Reuters into our confidence. Reuters are not merely very concerned about Mr Grey, but also sensitive because of past criticism to the affect that they have been playing down the affair to avoid jeopardising their long terms interests in China.

Timing

7. If we accept—as we do—that there can be no progress over exit visas for our Mission until our own restrictions on exit and entry have been lifted, there is a great deal to be said for lifting our restrictions forthwith. The morale of our Mission is

clearly a factor that has now to be taken into account. Sir D. Hopson has recently pointed out that although the situation is not yet desperate, the strain for those divided from their families and those who ought to leave China for medical reasons is beginning to tell. Admittedly we can have no confidence that our gesture will be matched by the Chinese. When informed of our decision the Chinese would be unlikely to give us any formal satisfaction; but they might conceivably be prepared in practice to begin granting exist visas. We would thus get the most urgent cases out.

8. The oral statement which we are in due course to make to the Chinese about Hong Kong and other issues in reply to Lo Kuei-po's statement of 8 March[6] will provide a suitable opportunity to emphasise to the Chinese that we expect reciprocity. But it may be some days yet before agreement is reached on the terms of this statement. (We have just received the comments of the Governor of Hong Kong on the draft in Peking telegram No. 243, and Sir D. Hopson may wish to return to the charge.) Moreover, the timing of the statement may to some extent depend on progress in the delicate informal talks in Hong Kong which are getting off to a slow start. I do not think, therefore, that we should hold up the lifting of the restrictions until the wording and timing of our statement is finally agreed. Moreover there would be some advantage to the Chinese Ministry of Foreign Affairs in Peking being aware, some time in advance of the statement that we have lifted the restrictions, since this may influence helpfully their initial reactions to it.

Publicity

9. I recognise that by lifting the restrictions now, we could be risking unfavourable publicity along the lines that we are making concessions to the Chinese at the very time the Chinese are multiplying their acts of unfriendliness (cf. the sentencing of Mr Watt, the 'Demodocus' affair). But if we believe that the relaxation may not only help the Mission to obtain exit visas, but might conceivably also help towards a return to more normal diplomatic relations, which might make the Chinese readier to grant consular access to Britons in detention, adverse publicity should not be the decisive factor. But it does mean that the publicity aspect requires careful consideration. Fortunately the terms of our Note to the Chinese of 23 August imposing the exit permit were never published. It is not public knowledge therefore that it made the lifting of the restrictions conditional on the receipt of formal assurances from the Chinese Government about free exit for our Mission. We would not publish our Note lifting the requirement; thus the relaxation need not become public knowledge unless we are directly questioned by the press or in Parliament. The grant of entry visas to NCNA may not become public knowledge until the officials actually arrive in this country—if then. On the other hand the Chinese may choose to publish details of Sir D. Hopson's oral statement in Peking after it is made, or otherwise try to take propaganda advantage from our gestures on movement restrictions. In such circumstances we might explain our decisions publicly here on the following lines. The Chinese insisted that the prerequisite for the return to normal diplomatic relations was the removal of the requirement for exit permits for their staff here and normal treatment in the matter of entry visas for members of the NCNA whom they regarded as full members of their Mission.

6 See No. 82.

In view of the importance which we attached to a return to normal diplomatic relations which we thought might help Mr Grey and other British nationals in China, we accepted this and expressed our strong hope that it would be matched by reciprocal treatment on the Chinese side. (We could add unattributably that if the Chinese did not reciprocate, restrictions could always be reimposed.)

JAMES MURRAY

The action now proposed is as previously recommended by the Department and supported by Mr Rodgers (see Flag E).
On balance I am persuaded that it would now be right for us to relax our restrictions as proposed and I agree with the recommendations and draft note and minute. I accept that we should take this action shortly before Sir Donald Hopson makes the proposed oral communication about Hong Kong affairs. But I think the Secretary of State may wish to consider the wording of that communication, which will shortly be submitted, before actually setting in motion the relaxations now recommended.

DENIS ALLEN

This is an unpalatable course.
But given that we have no means of pressure at all (Chinese are basically expendable in present circumstances) the policy recommended is probably the only one which has any hope of getting results (i.e. releases of exit visas).
The question therefore becomes of political tolerability here.

F. S. Tomlinson

I think that we should now go ahead with relaxation as soon as possible. There will be no publicity but I do not think that we should hide what we have done should the general question of relations with China arise in the House of Commons. On the contrary this modest gesture towards 'normalisation' can be defended as an initiative on our part in a situation where it is patently obvious that these are very few options open.

W. T. R[odgers].

No. 95

Minute from Mr Rodgers to Mr Stewart, 3 April 1968
Confidential (FCO 21/67, FC 3/3/E)

Secretary of State,
You will be receiving tonight a full submission on the removal of restrictions on the movement of Chinese officials in London. This follows our discussion the other day when you agreed in principle on this modest step towards the 'normalisation' of relations. I hope very much that you will accept the recommendation and that the

Chinese Chargé d'Affaires can be informed, if possible tomorrow, that exit permits will no longer be required by members of the Chinese Mission and others.

2. There is a second question on which I think we should also move without delay. As you will have seen, the 'Demodocus' has now sailed from Shanghai but her Second Officer, Mr P. D. Crouch, is under arrest and her Third Officer, Mr A. N. Wilson, has been sentenced to be deported from China. The 'Demodocus' is due off Hong Kong on Friday and I do not think that it will be possible to avoid the news breaking for long. In addition Mr D. V. Jones, Chief Officer of the 'Nancy Dee' has been detained in Hsinking. The news of this will certainly break in due course either through Chinese sources or when the ship reaches port.

3. In these circumstances I think I should see the Chinese Chargé on Friday and deliver a strong protest about detention of British subjects in China. This would include Watt and Barrymaine, and of course Grey, about whom I saw the Chargé last summer.[1]

4. It is most unlikely that a protest here will do much good but at least we shall have it on record. There are presentational advantages also. I made clear in the House of Commons last Thursday in the debate on the Consular Relations Bill[2] that in practice we have found Peking to be the best channel of communication with the Chinese. I think the point was well taken. Nevertheless to make no representations whatever in a situation which is clearly getting worse may be difficult to defend. We should use every channel open to us, even if we are sceptical about its effectiveness.

5. There is the additional question of informing the House about Crouch, Wilson and Jones. I was asked specifically last Thursday whether there were any other British citizens known to us to be detained in China. I said there were none—the 'Demodocus''s position was sufficiently obscure—and added that we had not consciously withheld information from the House. I think there is a strong moral obligation on us to act in the spirit of my reply. We will certainly get into difficulties unless we do so.

6. My conclusion from this is that I should hint to the Members of Parliament who have been principally concerned with British subjects in China—Eldon Griffiths, Anthony Royle, Stanley McMaster, Paul Channon—that we would see no objection to their raising the question on the adjournment for the Easter Recess next Thursday. I would not be specific at this stage about further British subjects detained but would give the information if the debate took place. If in fact the Speaker agreed to provide time for such a debate, it might avoid awkward Private Notice Questions if the news broke meanwhile.

7. I hope you will therefore agree that:

(*a*) We should proceed at once in removing restrictions on the movement of Chinese officials;

(*b*) I should see the Chinese Chargé on Friday to protest about the detention of British subjects;[3]

(*c*) I should take steps on the lines indicated above to ensure that we are not accused of withholding information from the House; while at the same time avoiding

---

1 See No. 24.
2 *Parl. Debs.*, 5th ser., H. of C., 28 March 1968, vol. 761 cols. 1843-64.
3 See No. 96.

discussion in terms which would be embarrassing and possibly damaging to the cause of those we are seeking to help.[4]

WILLIAM RODGERS

4 Mr Stewart noted: 'I am sure this is right.'

No. 96

Mr Stewart to Sir D. Hopson (Peking), 5 April 1968[1]
Tel. No. 338 Immediate Confidential (FCO 21/67, FC 3/3E)

Sino-British Relations

Parliamentary Under-Secretary summoned the Chinese Chargé d'Affaires at noon today.

2. Mr Rodgers said that we had noted Mr Lo Kuei-po's statement of 8 March about Sino-British Relations. We too attached importance to the settlement of outstanding problems in Sino-British relations. We had been considering the terms of the reply to Mr Lo's statement which would make this clear. But our task has been made much more difficult by information that had reached us in the meantime about certain acts of the Chinese Government which seemed to suggest that the Chinese were pursuing a policy of deliberate hostility towards British subjects in China. We had in mind the sentencing of Mr Watt of Vickers-Zimmer to three years imprisonment for alleged espionage: the arrest of Mr Norman Barrymaine a British journalist who was passing through Shanghai; the affair of the S.S. 'Demodocus', at Shanghai, in particular the arrest of the 2nd officer, Mr Crouch and the deportation of the 3rd officer Mr Wilson; and the detention of the Chief Officer of the 'Nancy Dee', Mr Jones at Hsinkang.

3. These were matters which despite Mr Lo's statement, Her Majesty's Government could not regard in any sense as 'secondary'. They were the more disturbed in that in each case the Chinese government failed to reply to our requests for information about why the people had been detained and had refused consular access.

4. Mr Rodgers then dealt in more detail with the various cases mentioning also those of Mrs Epstein and Mr Shapiro. Mr Rodgers referred separately to the case of Mr Grey which, he said, Her Majesty's Government had always viewed with the utmost gravity. Despite our repeated request he had not been released nor had we yet succeeded in gaining Consular access to him.

5. Mr Rodgers next dealt with Chinese failure to grant exit visas to Mr and Mrs Self of the Hong Kong and Shanghai Bank in Shanghai and to members of your Mission. On the latter he pointed out that apart from the few visas granted on medical grounds, you and your staff and their families were being held virtually as hostages. This was in direct contravention of accepted diplomatic practice. It had prevented the return to normal conditions for our Mission in Peking and for the Chinese mission in London and thus inhibited the discussion of outstanding problems. For our

1 Repeated for information to Hong Kong and saving to Washington.

part, we had now removed all restrictions on the exit of Chinese officials from this country as a demonstration of our desire to return to normal relations. We hoped that the Chinese government would immediately play their part and grant outstanding exit visas to our Mission.

6. Mr Rodgers said finally that his main purpose in summoning Shen P'ing was to protest vigorously against the persistent refusal on the part of the Chinese authorities to give information about or consular access to British subjects under detention. Such conduct by the Chinese government was neither civilised nor humane and was in total contravention of the accepted international practice. The conduct of the Chinese authorities must call seriously into question the professed desire of the Chinese government to deal with outstanding issues on a reasonable and sincere basis. We for our part reaffirmed our desire to improve Sino-British relations. But this would be very difficult to achieve if the present Chinese policy with regard to the detention of British subjects was maintained.

7. Shen P'ing replied that of the persons said to be in detention he knew only about Watt and could not discuss the other cases. Watt had been convicted of espionage: stealing intelligence on military, political and economic matters, and on the Cultural Revolution. He had taken photographs in prohibited areas, gravely endangering security and undermining Socialist construction. He had confessed his crimes and the local authorities in Lanchow had published information about the case. He had now to serve his sentence in accordance with the Chinese law. It would be 'inappropriate' to make a request to see him in view of his grave crimes. The British government were already fully aware of the position. Recently a 'big fuss' had been made in the British press and in Parliament about Watt and the alleged detention of other British subjects. The aim was to stir up anti Chinese feeling and threatening language had been used. This could only worsen relations between the two countries. Shen P'ing flatly rejected our protest.

8. As regards Grey, we were fully aware that the Chinese government had 'restricted his freedom of movement' only after representatives of the New China News Agency and other 'patriotic journalists' had been arrested in Hong Kong. NCNA in Hong Kong had applied to arrange visits to their colleagues and other journalists in prison. As the Chinese had already made it clear, if these were satisfactorily arranged, they would consider allowing a member of our Mission in Peking to see Grey.

9. The complaint about failure to grant exit visas for our Mission and for bankers in Shanghai was unjustified. It was clear that the grave deterioration in Sino-British relations was due to Hong Kong where the authorities had not yet completely stopped the suppression and persecution of Chinese residents, large numbers of whom were still in prison. Others who had suffered loss of life and property had not been compensated nor had their cases been properly dealt with. Chinese compatriots in Hong Kong had the right to study and spread the thoughts of Mao Tse-tung and to carry on other patriotic activities. Their right to do so was not being properly and effectively ensured. For their part, the Chinese government had adopted an attitude of restraint and taken certain steps to relax tension in the border area near Shum Chun. The crux of the abnormal state of relations between the two countries was Hong Kong. If the British government wished to improve relations they should take positive action to resolve problems there.

10. Reverting to the exit visas Shen P'ing said that he had that morning received our note cancelling the requirement of exit permits for Chinese Office officials. He would report this to his government. It was, however, wrong to assert that the British mission and other British subjects in China were being held as hostages since the totally unjustified and discriminatory action against Chinese officials had only just ceased. Moreover a number of exit visas had been granted in Peking 'in accordance with the specific conditions of the applications' and this was proof that the conduct of the Chinese government was neither uncivilised nor inhumane.

11. Mr Rodgers, in reply pointed out that whatever the circumstances of the Watt case our mission should have been given information at an early stage. We should have been allowed to make a consular visit and to attend the trial. We simply wished now to repeat our demand for consular access. On Grey, Mr Rodgers again emphasised that we wished to make progress in order that a visit would be possible. He also asked the Chargé d'Affaires to obtain information about Barrymaine, Crouch and Jones and take a very early opportunity to inform us why they were being detained and to arrange consular access. Mr Rodgers concluded by saying that we recognised the importance which the Chinese attach to matters concerning Hong Kong. We wished to deal with outstanding problems in a civilised way and resolve them to our mutual advantage. Press and parliamentary interest in British subjects in China was not an obstacle to progress provided that we approached our problems in a practical and co-operative spirit. But before progress could be made there must be a clear response on the matters which he had raised today.

12. Shen P'ing repeated that any request to see Watt could not be entertained and that positive action to resolve problems in Hong Kong remained a prerequisite of any improvement in relations.

13. The tone of the meeting was quiet and polite and the ritual references to Hong Kong were made without particular conviction.

14. We are informing the press that Mr Rodgers summoned the Chargé d'Affaires to raise the question of consular access to British subjects in China. If questioned we shall add that particular attention was paid to the cases of Watt and Grey.

No. 97

Submission from Mr Murray to Mr Wilkinson, 10 April 1968
Secret (FCO 21/67, FC 3/3/E)

Sino-British Relations: Reply to the Chinese Statement of 8 March
Problem

At the Office meeting on 26 March the Secretary of State agreed that in reply to Lo Kuei-po's statement of 8 March[1] to the Chargé d'Affaires about Sino-British relations (the principal point of which was that the Hong Kong situation was the crux of the matter), we should say something to the Chinese on Hong Kong; and that Sir Donald Hopson had provided a useful first draft. He directed that it be examined

1 See Nos. 83 and 84.

urgently in consultation with the Commonwealth Office and the Governor of Hong Kong. This has now been done. Approval is therefore required for the timing and terms of our reply to the Chinese.

Recommendation

2. I recommend that:

(*a*) Sir D. Hopson should now be instructed to make an oral reply to the Chinese;

(*b*) the reply should be in the terms of the latest proposal put forward by the Governor of Hong Kong, amended to take account of recent developments in London.

Draft telegrams to Peking on these lines are attached. A parallel submission is being made by the Commonwealth Office.

Background

3. Sir D. Hopson was summoned by Lo Kuei-po, Vice-Minister for Foreign Affairs, on 8 March to receive a statement to the effect that the Hong Kong situation was the crux of the Sino-British relations; that the British Government must reply to various demands put forward by the Chinese Government on this subject; and that only thereafter would it be possible to discuss 'secondary' matters (Peking telegram No. 176)[2]. The Chinese on two occasions since then, in interviews with the Mission, have insisted on the need for an early reply. Sir D. Hopson regards this as a hopeful sign indicating a wish to settle outstanding problems with us, though of course on terms acceptable to them (Peking telegram No. 242). Sir D. Hopson put forward a draft of a proposed statement (Peking telegram No. 243). The Governor of Hong Kong commented (Hong Kong telegram No. 397); Sir D. Hopson replied Peking telegram No. 267); the Governor commented again (Hong Kong telegram No. 437) and produced a redraft (Hong Kong telegram No. 398 of March).[3]

4. The only point of substance on which the Governor has not been prepared to meet Sir D. Hopson is whether or not the Chinese should be allowed a say in the eventual return to Hong Kong of persons now in prison in Hong Kong, who may, before the termination of their sentences, be 'allowed to reside in China' (i.e. deported). I am sure the Governor is right in this; and since Sir D. Hopson has not returned to the charge, we can take it that he acquiesces.

5. Sir D. Hopson has defined our objective succinctly: to avoid giving anything away on vital Hong Kong issues while avoiding a reply so narrowly worded as to give the impression of a rebuff. Understandably the Governor has tended to lay more emphasis on the first aspect and Sir D. Hopson on the second. The result of their exchanges seems to strike the right balance. The statement in its present form does not compromise us on any vital Hong Kong issue. On the other hand the Chinese will find it difficult to construe it as a rebuff—unless of course they are resolutely set against any real improvement in relations with us. We have made a real effort to deal with the release of communist prisoners—the most important issue for them—and by a reference to 'the agreement of Chinese Government' have implied a willingness to discuss the matter further. In assessing their likely reaction to the statement we should bear in mind the informal approach that the Hong Kong authorities have recently received through delicate channels from the Chinese (Hong Kong telegram

2 Not printed.
3 None of these telegrams are printed.

No. 331).⁴ If we are to assume that the approach is genuine, we must take account of the remark that 'the Chinese did not want to institute formal talks in either Peking or London because they did not wish to appear to be seeking a solution'.

6. There remains the matter of timing. Earlier on, it had seemed that there might be some advantage in waiting to see whether the informal approach in Hong Kong might give us a more precise indication of Chinese attitudes. The exchanges are now under way in Hong Kong (Hong Kong telegram No. 440);⁵ but it is evident that progress is likely to be slow. Further delay on this score in our reply to Lo would not be justified. Indeed it seems to me that a reply would be particularly timely now, since it would round off the recent series of exchanges we have had with the Chinese:

(*a*) On 3 April the Hong Kong authorities reached agreement with the New China News Agency about additional visits to communist journalists in prison in Hong Kong (which we hope will lead to access to Mr Grey in detention in Peking);

(*b*) On 4 April we informed the Chinese Mission here that we were lifting the requirement for exit permits;

(*c*) On 5 April Mr Rodgers saw the Chinese Chargé d'Affaires and firmly took him to task on all the issues concerning detention of British subjects.⁶

The Chinese Ministry of Foreign Affairs have now had a little time to take account of our relaxation of movement restrictions and of the successful prison visits in Hong Kong (which took place on 9 April); and this may influence them helpfully in their reaction to our reply to Lo. I recommend therefore that there should be no further delay. Moreover, now that we have accorded the additional prison visits in Hong Kong it is desirable that the Chinese should be reminded as soon as possible that we expect them favourably to fulfil their undertaking to consider access to Mr Grey.

JAMES MURRAY

4 See No. 87, note 6.
5 Not printed.
6 No.96.

No. 98

Mr Stewart to Sir D. Hopson (Peking), 11 April 1968[1]
Tel. No. 356 Secret, Immediate (FCO 21/67, FC 3/3/E)

MIPT: Sino-British relations.[2]

The British Government have noted with interest the statement which Vice-Minister for Foreign Affairs Lo Kuei-po made on 8 March and have instructed me to make the following reply:

As the British Government have already made clear, they attach much importance to bringing about an early improvement in Sino-British relations, and recognise the importance of Hong Kong in this context. It is their desire in particular that China

1 Repeated for information to Hong Kong.
2 This telegram instructed Sir D. Hopson to make an early oral reply along the lines set out in this telegram.

and Hong Kong should in future enjoy the especially close connexions and economic ties that have existed in the past to their mutual benefit.

The British Government are well aware of the special position of China with relation to Hong Kong, subject to their overriding responsibility for administration, order, and economic development within the territory, they have always taken account of the view put forward by the Chinese Government about Hong Kong. A stable and prosperous Hong Kong is in the interests of all parties concerned and its stability and prosperity depend on the maintenance of an orderly and peaceful society. With particular reference to the more recent views expressed by the Chinese Government on Hong Kong, the British Government wish to make their policies completely clear. It has been the consistent policy of the British Government to ensure that all sections of the Hong Kong community enjoy the right to live and work freely within the normal framework of law and order. The British Government do not favour, discriminate against, or persecute any section of Hong Kong society, and they recognise the right of all Hong Kong residents to freedom of expression within the law. This includes the personal right to study the works of Chairman Mao Tse-Tung and the right to engage in activities associated with this study provided that they are within the framework of the law, which provides protection of the rights of all persons without discrimination.

The British Government recognise that in the light of recent events the position of certain categories of persons now serving prison sentences in Hong Kong may be of special interest to the CPG. The release of prisoners before the normal expiry of their sentence would present serious difficulties. These difficulties would be especially great in regard to the release in Hong Kong of the persons concerned. However, the British Government are prepared to consider the possibility of allowing certain of these prisoners with the agreement of the Chinese Government, to go to China to reside.

The British Government also take this opportunity to point out that it is always open to individuals who believe themselves to have been wrongfully injured or their property to have been wrongfully damaged to seek redress by normal legal process.

The British Government do not share Chinese views that in the absence of a settlement of differences over Hong Kong other problems in Sino-British relations cannot in the meantime be profitably discussed. On the contrary, the British Government believe that failure to approach other questions in a constructive spirit can only obstruct fruitful consideration of present difficulties in Hong Kong. For example, the continuing failure to restore normal movement for diplomatists, which is contrary to international diplomatic practice, can only throw doubt upon the likelihood of achieving results in negotiation on other matters and seriously impede the regular diplomatic intercourse which is necessary for that purpose. The British Government are ready to settle the movements problem on the lines suggested by the Chinese Government in January and to this end have already lifted the requirement for exit visas from the United Kingdom. Outstanding applications for entry visas have been granted, and future applications for entry visas have been granted, and future applications will be dealt with in the normal way. They hope that this will be matched by early action on the part of the Chinese Government. They also take this opportunity of recording yet again their grave concern at the position of certain British subjects detained in China, as expressed by the Parliamentary Under-Secretary of State for Foreign Affairs to the Chinese Chargé d'Affaires in London on the 5th of April.

In conclusion, the British Government reaffirm their interest in and sincere desire for a full normalisation of Sino-British relations. They are of the opinion that this can be achieved by goodwill and good faith. Failure to achieve it can only be to the loss of all parties concerned.

No. 99

Sir D. Hopson (Peking) to Mr Stewart, 15 April 1968[1]
Tel. No. 302 Confidential, Immediate (FCO 21/67, FC 3/3/E)

I obtained an interview with Vice Minister for the Foreign Affairs Lo Kuei-po on 13 April. Following is summary of the interview.

2. I began by reading out our statement. I went on to point out since the prison visits in Hong Kong had been arranged successfully we expected to obtain early access to Grey. I also handed over outstanding Chinese entry visas at the same time, since Chinese had failed to collect them.

3. In reply Lo Kuei-po expressed profound dissatisfaction with 'arrogant language' and lack of substance in our statement which he said evaded the real issues. This was no help in solving the problems in Sino-British relations. It showed that the British Government was not sincere in its expressed desire to normalise Sino-British relations, furthermore the statement was not a real answer to demands put forward by the Chinese Government on many occasions in the past. Hong Kong was the crux of the present abnormal relations between Britain and China and until this problem was solved it would be difficult fully to normalise relations. Looking at our statement as a whole we had failed to reply to Chinese statement of 8 March.

4. Lo Kuei-po went on to describe our proposal to allow certain prisoners to go to reside in China 'a disguised form of deportation'. The Chinese Government could not agree to this. The Hong Kong Authorities must immediately and unconditionally release these compatriots since they were innocent of any crime. They had the right to live normally in Hong Kong or to return to the Motherland.

5. In my reply I pointed out that our statement had taken up most of the questions raised in Lo Kuei-po's statement of 8 March including the issues of Mao study, prisoners and compensation and had made positive suggestions. We wished to continue discussions and would be interested in having positive suggestions from [the] Chinese side. We had demonstrated our goodwill by lifting exit visa requirement by granting Chinese entry visas and allowing prison visits in Hong Kong. I also rebutted his accusation that language of our statement was arrogant.

6. Lo Kuei-po said he had by no means ignored the questions I had referred to, but our statement was not a satisfactory answer to Chinese demand[s] and that the Chinese Government could not accept our proposal on the prisoners. He went on to say that the right to study Mao was a basic one, which all South East Asian

---

1 Repeated for information to Hong Kong.

citizens should have. The Chinese Government had noted the measures which we had taken on movement of diplomats and on prison visits. As soon as the Chinese Government had received confirmation from Hong Kong that visits had taken place, and from London that visa requirement had been lifted the Chinese Government would 'make its own arrangements in accordance with normal procedures to settle these problems'. But these were minor issues. Hong Kong was the crux. If this was evaded it would be difficult for Sino-British relations to be really normalised.

7. After some exchanges on gifts of rice and clothing and on treatment of prisoners (see my separate telegram) Lo Kuei-po ended by posing three questions:

(*a*) Did the British Government recognise that Hong Kong was the crux of Sino-British relations?

(*b*) Was the British Government prepared to reply to demands put forward by the Chinese Government on many occasions in the past to settle the Hong Kong problem?

(*c*) Did the British Government have sincere desire to hold discussions on the restoration of normal Sino-British relations and on solving the Hong Kong problem?

8. In reply to (*a*) I repeated the opening sentences of our statement about the importance which we attached to the Hong Kong problem, but emphasized that we did not agree that other problems could not be discussed profitably in the meantime. On (*b*) I said that our statement had isolated most of the specific points raised by the Chinese. In answer to (*c*) I reminded Lo Kuei-po that Mr Brown in his letter to Ch'en Yi had expressed our readiness to enter into discussions at any time. I then asked whether the Chinese wanted a public answer to their so called demands or an answer in the same form as our present statement. Lo Kuei-po said the question of the form of our reply could be discussed. When I asked whether we could expect to hear more from the Chinese side Lo Kuei-po replied that the present discussions should be concluded at that point but that if the Chinese Government considered that further approaches were necessary these approaches would be made.

9. It was agreed mutually that these discussions should remain confidential.

No. 100

Sir D. Hopson (Peking) to Mr Stewart, 15 April 1968[1]
Tel. No. 304 Immediate, Confidential (FCO 21/67, FC 3/3/E)

My immediately preceding telegram.[2]

The interview lasted nearly 2 hours and Chinese comments were not always very clear. Lo gave impression of not having mastered his brief, particularly on such subjects as Grey and visas. Tone was mild. On the whole I would regard meeting as giving us some slight grounds for encouragement. The fact that Vice Minister for Foreign Affairs received and was prepared to spend so long with me indicates that Chinese are surprisingly interested in a settlement.

1 Repeated for information to Hong Kong.
2 This referred to discussions about rice, clothing and the treatment of prisoners.

2. As regards Hong Kong, some of Lo's opening remarks e.g. on arrogance and emptiness of our reply, should be regarded as prefatory abuse of a standard Chinese kind and need not be taken too seriously. The original charge that we had failed to reply to the Vice Minister for Foreign Affairs' statement of 8 March was later modified to one that we had not given a satisfactory reply. On the question of Mao study and compensation, Lo did not deny that we had taken account in our reply of some of Chinese demands. However on central issue of prisoners he made it clear that our proposals at least in their present form are unacceptable. It is just possible that in subsequent discussion, and if we were to introduce the idea of released prisoners residing in China temporarily until term of their sentences had expired, we might get agreement. I think we must be ready [gp undec] this idea at a later stage. But on the face of it the Chinese seem likely to insist on release in Hong Kong.

3. Lo's concluding questions and remarks strongly support our earlier impression that the Chinese wish to continue discussions on the question of Hong Kong. It is not clear whether they intend further discussion in Peking or possibly some separate and specific negotiation on Hong Kong question. But they seem to wish to settle the matter though of course on terms advantageous to them. I realise that the question of entering into discussions with the Chinese about Hong Kong is a highly delicate matter but from our point of view it would seem important to continue the dialogue. It is for consideration whether we should give some kind of official reply to Lo's three questions and affirm our wish to continue discussions. On balance I think it would be wiser for us to wait, for a while at least, to see if the Chinese will make the next move. This may allow us to obtain further information on Chinese position via channel referred to in Hong Kong telegram No. 331.[3] It should also give us a chance to see whether anything is forthcoming on visas.

4. As regards visas, Lo's remark that on receipt of confirmation from London (i.e. that there was no barrier to free movement) the Chinese would make their arrangements on exit/entry visas in accordance with normal procedures is obscure and we shall have to wait and see what it means. It could mean a limited thaw. It is relevant that Lo failed to repeat his remark of 8 March about difficulties of discussing visas fruitfully while the Hong Kong question remains unsettled and merely said that Sino-British relations could not really be adequately served if the Hong Kong question were avoided. There might therefore be some tendency to move back to bilateral dealing on visas. The Chinese may realise that our removal of exit visa requirements and granting of entry visas to Chinese officials puts them in a potentially weak position in any diplomatic or publicity campaign. But their officials may sit tight in London and avoid travelling from Peking to London for some time yet.

5. As regards Grey it seems Peking are awaiting a report from NCNA Hong Kong that visits pass off satisfactorily. There was no tendency on their part to jib at the idea of access but I think we should expect a short delay before we achieve it.

3 See No. 87, note 6.

No. 101

Sir D. Hopson (Peking) to Mr Stewart, 23 April 1968[1]
Tel. No. 341 Immediate, Confidential (FCO 21/139, FC 13/8/B)

My telegram No. 334.[2]

Weston and I saw Grey for 20 minutes this afternoon in his home. He was clearly overjoyed to see us. (He had been given only half hour's notice of our visit) and though he was naturally under some emotional stress there was no obvious change in his physical appearance and he looked quite well. He said in fact that he was in good health and had only had one stomach disorder in the first three months for which he had received medical attention at his home.

2. After greetings, I read him message from his mother, Mr Long and Reuter [sic] staff. I then told him of constant efforts which had been made both to see him and to obtain his release. I also gave him some general idea that situation had calmed down both in China and in Hong Kong and that prospects for solving Sino-British difficulties appeared better now than they had for a long time. I assured him that Her Majesty's Government, Reuters and ourselves would continue our constant efforts to obtain his release.

3. In reply to questions, he said he was confined to one room on ground floor of his house to which had had [sic] moved following Red Guard incursion on 18 August, an event he was unwilling to discuss. He said that his food was now normal, implying it had not been so during the first few months. He continues to have services of his domestic staff. He is permitted to exercise twice daily for forty minutes each time in his courtyard. Although he is not free to use his personal books and belongings e.g. chessboard, in other rooms of his house, he has persuaded the guards to bring down a few books from upstairs and also received one parcel from us in December which included books. He is allowed to see the weekly *Peking Review*, and has also purchased books from foreign languages Press. He is not permitted a radio. He is therefore starved of news and did not know for example of the burning of our office last August.

4. As regards mail he has received regular letters from his girlfriend for the past three months and also spasmodically from some friends in Peking. He said he has only received two letters from his mother over past nine months. Although he has sent an occasional telegram i.e. one to his mother a week ago he has not (repeat not) yet tried sending letters out. I have therefore encouraged him to do so. I also suggested that he should try writing to the Press Department of Ministry of Foreign Affairs occasionally requesting that the telephone should be reconnected.

5. He said he had seen no (repeat no) Chinese official since his detention began. He had three guards on standpoint none of whom will converse with him in English. He said that the isolation was complete and terrible. At times he had felt on the verge of a nervous breakdown. In reply to my question he said he had not (repeat not) been accused of committing any offence nor had the Chinese

1 Repeated for information to Hong Kong.
2 Not printed.

discussed conditions for his release with him. In fact as stated above he had no contact whatever with Chinese officials.

6. There has been apparently no effort to brainwash him apart from a natural nervousness of his behaviour and conversation was quite normal. He made a particular point of asking that his mother should be informed that he is in good health and that she should be asked to write more often.

7. I shall give gist of this to Western Press representatives when I see them later this afternoon. In view of his request in paragraph 6 above I shall omit any reference to his nervousness.

No. 102

Sir D. Hopson (Peking) to Mr Stewart, 24 April 1968[1]
Tel. No. 348 Confidential (FCO 21/139, FC 13/8/B)

My telegram No. 341: Grey.[2]

Visit to Grey showed that worst aspect of his condition is his isolation. I therefore suggest our immediate efforts should concentrate on securing improvements in this respect.

2. Clearly best thing would be if we could get Consular access on a regular, say monthly basis. I therefore recommend that I should ask Chinese for another visit to Grey in May, pointing out that isolation he suffers is very much worse than that of Communist prisoners in Hong Kong who in any case enjoy privilege of regular monthly visits. I might refer to and rebut complaints from Lo Kuei-po and NCNA Hong Kong on alleged isolation of Communist prisoners and contrast their regime with complete isolation in which Grey has been kept.

3. It is of course unlikely that we shall get what we want as easily as that. I hope therefore I may at the same time be authorised if and when Chinese turn down this request immediately to offer another round of special visits to Communist newspaper workers in Hong Kong prisons in return for a further visit to Grey. I might offer these visits on similar conditions to last time.

4. I would also propose to ask that Grey should be allowed other comforts such as more books and magazines and letters in and out. In these respects also his condition is worse than that of Communist prisoners. As a longer shot I would also ask for a gramophone and records, a wireless and a telephone.

5. I shall telegraph separately on the question of possible moves to secure release of Grey.

---

1 Repeated for information to Hong Kong.
2 No. 104.

No. 103

Sir D. Hopson (Peking) to Mr Stewart, 29 April 1968[1]
Tel. No. 362 Priority, Confidential (FCO 21/141, FC 13/8/D)

My telegram No. 348: Grey.[2]

I hope approach as recommended in support of my telegram under reference may succeed in bringing about some improvement in Grey's condition. We must however also give further consideration to moves that might lead to his release.

2. We have had no official reply to our proposal to release Hsueh P-ing to China in exchange for Grey but in view of Lo Kuei-po's negative responses to our offer of 13 April that Communist prisoners might be released to reside in China we must assume that a renewal of offer of release to China whether of one or both of NCNA prisoners would be rejected by Chinese.

3. It might be possible to get Chinese to accept an arrangement whereby Hsueh P-ing and Lo Yu-ho would be released and would 'ask' to reside in China until their sentence expires on the understanding that they would be free to return to Hong Kong afterwards.

4. We must accept however that the Chinese may well insist on unconditional release in Hong Kong of one or both NCNA men and it is worth noting that in discussions last week with Bargmann the West German correspondent, Hong Kong Communist leaders are alleged to have stated price for Grey was for both to be released in Colony. In last resort unless we are to abandon our efforts to obtain Grey's release I think we shall have to be prepared to agree to this.

5. I therefore recommend that I be instructed to approach Ministry for Foreign Affairs officially and inform them that you wish me to initiate negotiations for the release of Grey. As part of this first approach I suggest I should refer to our previous offer to deport Hsueh P-ing, to Lo Kuei-po's rejection in general of such procedure, and hint that a compromise satisfactory to both sides might be reached if it were agreed that Hsueh P-ing should be released on clear understanding that he would 'volunteer' to visit China (perhaps in response to an invitation from the Chinese Government) and stay there until his sentence expired, after which date he could return to Hong Kong if he wished. Offer would be made initially for Hsueh P-ing but could be increased to include Lo Yu-ho as a later concession if necessary. We should have to get a firm understanding from Chinese on simultaneous release of Grey. Only in the last resort would we consider offering simple release in the Colony. We should also have to resist attempts by Chinese to include all their 'patriotic' newspaper workers in the deal, though I presume that if Chinese accepted our compromise on 'deportation' the objection to increasing the numbers would not (repeat not) be so great.

6. I recognize these proposals are open to considerable objections:

(*a*) To discriminate again in favour of NCNA prisoners raises obvious difficulties for Government of Hong Kong.

---

1 Repeated for information to Hong Kong.
2 No. 102.

(*b*) Further approach by us might be read (? grp. omitted) by Chinese as a sign of weakness and encourage them to insist on a higher price e.g. release in Hong Kong or other newspapers employees and possibly other confrontation prisoners. On the other hand they have sometimes responded favourably on the limited occasions when we have made conciliatory moves.

(*c*) The Chinese might refuse to treat on Grey in isolation from other Hong Kong issues. This seems to have been their (grp. undec.) coolness in response to our proposals of 7 February on visas. We might therefore find that we were initiating further discussions on Hong Kong at a time when we would prefer to leave it to the Chinese to make the next move.

7. As against this there are the following considerations:

(*a*) Our concern about Grey's well-being. It seems highly likely that until the two NCNA men are contacted Grey will remain in custody. Unless we make some move the earliest date he might expect to be released would be September 1969 (earliest date by which both NCNA men would be free allowing for normal remission).

(*b*) It is just possible that the Chinese who may find publicity on Grey embarrassing particularly the new wave which will presumably follow the news of my visit would be prepared to deal with his case in isolation from other Hong Kong issues.

(*c*) Even if they insisted on bringing in other issues, in the end they might regard the release of the two NCNA men as providing them with 'victory' that they need to sign off in Hong Kong, accepting the release to China of the other prisoners in whom they are interested.

8. This leads on to the question of a larger act of clemency affecting other confrontation prisoners, as discussed first in your telegram No. 2047 to Hong Kong and Hong Kong telegram No. 1501 of 1967 and more recently in correspondence ending with Hong Kong telegram No. 92 of 19 January.[3] I should be glad to have your views and those of the Governor on whether the prospects of such a step are now any brighter and what our longer term plans are for dealing with confrontation prisoners. Even if we are fortunate enough to return to normal movement for staff of this office and for bank staffs in Shanghai we cannot expect to get back to anything like normal relations with the Chinese until the issues of prisoners is dealt with and this is bound to affect the whole range of issues, in particular the treatment of British subjects in detention in China.

9. I should be grateful for your early comments on the proposal about Grey. We shall for example have to decide whether to combine such an approach (should you approve it) with one about visits etc. (my telegram No. 348) or to keep them separate.

3 Not printed.

No. 104

Mr Gass (Hong Kong) to Mr Thomson (Commonwealth Office), 7 May 1968[1]
Tel. No. 575 Immediate, Secret (FCO 21/141, FC 13/8/D)

Peking Telegram 362:[2] Grey.

From the Hong Kong point of view these proposals clearly raise real difficulties. The fact is that the position of Grey is not a matter of immediate concern to the people of Hong Kong; and this imposes very strict limits to the extent to which we could justify locally concessions made here on his behalf.

2. As our telegram 1909 of 26 December to CO[3] indicated, the idea of releasing the two NCNA men to China in return for Grey's release would probably be acceptable here. But there is in fact no legal or moral parallel between Grey's position and that of the two convicted NCNA prisoners; and to release the latter here unconditionally, could not really be justified locally on any reasonable grounds. In principle it would provide an extremely awkward precedent. If the Chinese knew that we were prepared to remit the sentences of those two convicted prisoners and release them prematurely in Hong Kong in order to strike a bargain with the Chinese, it would be foolish of them not to press us to release many more prisoners than two. In the long run, having conceded the point of principle, we might find it impossible to resist demands for the premature release of all the convicted prisoners here. An early move in this direction would risk gravely undermining public confidence and suggest that we were being pushed along the path of acceptance of the communists' demands.

3. The compromise suggested in para 3 of the telegram under reference might just be palatable to public opinion here, provided that the Chinese kept their part of the bargain. But if they did not and we were obviously tricked, public reactions could be very critical and we might face something like a crisis of confidence. For this reason it would seem very desirable at least to test out the ground with Choi (our Top Secret telegram 496)[3] first, before starting to bargain on the much more difficult problem of Grey's release.

4. Of course there are strong humanitarian reasons for doing as much as we can to get Grey out as soon as possible. But it seems doubtful in any case if taking a very early initiative on his problem in isolation will necessarily produce this result. I agree with Para 6 (*b*) of the telegram under reference that it might instead be taken as a sign of weakness and encourage the Chinese to raise their bids. We went some way in our statement of April 13th[4] to make our position clear to the CPG and to give them openings if they really want to negotiate about the major outstanding Hong Kong issues. There is some reason to think that they may still be considering how to deal with the problem; at any rate Li Choh-Chih (our telegram 440)[3] left here on April 23 allegedly for talks in Peking and has not yet returned to Hong Kong. There does seem to be a real risk that an early approach about Grey on the lines of para 5 of the telegram

1 Repeated for information to Peking.
2 No. 103.
3 Not printed.
4 No 98.

under reference could cut across our other lines of contact; and that by suggesting we were prepared to make major concessions in order to deal with this particular case, we would draw attention to a major weakness in our bargaining position.

5. Our feeling is therefore that for the moment it would be best to concentrate on relatively minor moves to alleviate Grey's position; and not to press ahead with negotiations for his release until we have had more time to see whether there is a response (either through the MFA or our own local lines of contact) to the openings provided in our statement of 13 April.

6. As regards the point in para 3 of the telegram under reference about 'clemency' for convicted prisoners, this is the most difficult end of the problem from the political, moral and legal point of view. If we are thinking of entering into some sort of bargain about the release of prisoners, the position of the detainees would provide us with a much easier field in which to manoeuvre, since their release would involve no interference with the due process of law.

7. You will no doubt wish to discuss these problems with the Governor while he is in London.

No. 105

Mr Stewart to Sir D. Hopson (Peking), 7 May 1968[1]
Tel. No. 459 Priority, Confidential (FCO 21/140, FC 13/8/C)

Your telegram Number 348:[2] Grey.

We have discussed with the Governor of Hong Kong what steps might now be taken to gain further access to Grey and to improve the conditions of his detention.

2. To gain further consular access we may indeed in the final instance have to offer another round of special visits to 'journalist prisoners' in Hong Kong but we are very reluctant to take an initiative at this stage. We agree however that we should put on record as soon as possible our dissatisfaction at the conditions in which Grey is detained. We think therefore that your first step should be to test whether the Chinese would accept non-diplomatic visits (e.g. by friends in the Foreign Press Corps) to match monthly visits by relatives and friends enjoyed by prisoners in Hong Kong. We suggest that, as soon as the next monthly visits to the two NCNA journalists have taken place, you should ask for access on behalf of one or more of Grey's friends.

3. We hope that you now have sufficient ammunition on prison conditions in Hong Kong to press for improved conditions for Grey. In doing so it would be advisable to avoid so far as possible discussion of NCNA complaints about Hong Kong prison conditions. You will no doubt wish to make the point in paragraph 2 of your telegram under reference.

4. We considered whether there was any step that could be taken in Hong Kong to back up your efforts to improve Grey's conditions. The possibilities are very limited

1 Repeated for information to Hong Kong.
2 No. 102.

since the treatment of prisoners in Hong Kong is so liberal. The Governor did suggest the possibility of putting the two NCNA and other journalists into an open prison. There may, however, be practical difficulties and it is arguable that certain possible consequences (e.g. prisoners may be less accessible to visitors and liable to heavier work) may more than cancel out any presentational advantages of such a move. We would welcome Hong Kong's comments on this suggestion.

5. MIFT deals with the question of negotiating the release of Grey.[3]

3 No. 106.

No. 106

Mr Stewart to Sir D. Hopson (Peking), 7 May 1968[1]
Tel. No. 460 Priority, Confidential (FCO 21/140, FC 13/8/C)

MIPT: Grey.[2]

The Governor expressed his full understanding of the dilemma we face over Grey's release, and agreed that it was unfortunately likely that this could not be achieved until the question of the two NCNA reporters has been settled to Chinese satisfaction. The Chinese price would probably be the unconditional release of all journalists and newspaper workers under detention. The Governor emphasised that though the situation in Hong Kong had greatly improved the communists were constantly seeking ways to undermine the government's authority and that there were therefore severe limitations on concessions which could be made at this stage.

2. The Governor made it clear that he would be happy to release all 'journalist prisoners' and any number of other left-wing prisoners, provided that they immediately left the colony and there was no commitment to allow them back at any stage. But he emphasised that the release in the colony of the NCNA reporters or other prisoners in circumstances in which it could not be guaranteed that they would leave still presented very great difficulty: if they did not leave, there was no way in which they could again be detained. Unfortunately experience over the attempted deportation of the film stars suggested that the Chinese would be unwilling to accept anything short of unconditional release. We agreed, however, that it would be worth testing Chinese intentions again in the way suggested in paragraph 2 of Hong Kong Telegram No. 530 to the Commonwealth Office.[3]

3. The Governor saw difficulty in the proposal to release prisoners to China on the understanding that they would be allowed to return after the date when their sentences would have expired. This would be regarded in Hong Kong merely as disguised release and taken as a sign of weakness. There was also the problem that Chinese normally only left the colony if they were in possession of a re-entry permit which would allow them to go back freely. He agreed that the authorities in Hong

1 Repeated for information to Hong Kong.
2 No. 104.
3 Not printed.

Kong should be asked to examine the possibility of issuing post-dated re-entry permits in the event of a solution on the above lines becoming feasible at some stage.

4. As regards a general amnesty, the Governor thought that this was not yet on the horizon, at any rate in the case of major offenders (those who had committed trivial offences would be in any case released fairly soon.) The amnesty would be exploited by the communists as compliance with one of the Five Demands and would do great damage. It was agreed that it would be unwise to inject the idea of an amnesty even indirectly into discussions of Grey's possible release.

5. We regard the Governor's arguments as unassailable though we recognise that our inability to make a concession of substance blights any prospect of Grey's early release.

6. In the circumstances, we think it would be wise to keep the matter of visits and release quite separate. We should be glad to have your views on this; and on whether you think there would be any advantage in a further effort at this stage to negotiate his release, hinting to the Chinese that the quid pro quo would be the release to China (without guarantee of return) of the two NCNA journalists and possibly the other journalists and newspaper workers also.

7. Since this telegram was drafted we have received Hong Kong telegram No. 575[4] to Commonwealth Office which is closely in line with the above. We shall discuss it with the Governor when he is in London on 13 May and should welcome your comments by then

4 Not printed.

No. 107

Sir D. Hopson (Peking) to Mr Stewart, 11 May 1968[1]
Tel. No. 420 Immediate, Confidential (FCO 21/140, FC 13/8/C)

My immediately preceding telegram.[2]

On the question of Grey's release I conclude from your telegrams that there is very little you feel we can do at the present time. As your telegram 460[3] recognises this blights any prospect of Grey's early release, with all the attended risks to his physical and mental health which continued solitary confinement entails.

2. I saw only disadvantage in returning to the charge with proposal that NCNA men and other newspaper workers might be released to China in return for Grey without any of them being able to come back to Hong Kong. After clear rejection of this offer by Lo Kuei-po on 13 April, its reiteration now would merely irritate. We must however explore whether there is any amendment to this offer that might make it more acceptable to Chinese. The proposal to release prisoners to

1 Repeated for information to Hong Kong.
2 Not printed. Sir D. Hopson agreed that it was better to keep the question of visits and conditions of confinement separate from that of release. On conditions, he proposed to arrange a meeting with the Chinese (see No. 112). Meanwhile he hoped Hong Kong would explore the possibilities of putting the NCNA and other journalists under as liberal regime as possible, though no action should be taken until the outcome of the meeting was known.
3 No. 106.

China until their sentences in Hong Kong expire seems to me much the best line to investigate. I do not see why it must be regarded in Hong Kong as a sign of weakness (paragraph 3 of your telegram 460). The effect would be to release the prisoners in Hong Kong no sooner than if they had served their full sentence and were then released in the Colony as will happen if we do nothing. I agree that we should test Chinese attitude over releasing Choi (Hong Kong telegram No. 454 paragraph 3).[4] We should also examine possibility of post dated re-entry permits (your telegram 459 paragraph 3).[5] If there appears to be some scope for putting an amended proposal about release to China the best course may be to try this out with Li Chou [*sic* ?Choh]-chih' (Hong Kong telegram No. 454 paragraph 4).

3. If none of this works, are there any legal devices which might be employed to grant greater than normal remission to NCNA and other journalist prisoners? This would accelerate date at which Grey might expect release and would have the advantage of avoiding publicity.

4 Not printed.
5 No. 104.

No. 108

Sir D. Hopson (Peking) to Mr Stewart, 17 May 1968[1]
Tel. No. 443 Immediate, Confidential (FCO 40/57, HWB 2/1/B)

Hong Kong telegram No. 615:[2] Visit of Enterprise.

This NCNA article reads like a warning shot across our bows. As Hong Kong points out in their telegram No. 560[3] previous visits by the Enterprise has elicited protests from Peking. We should therefore expect at least that this time. There may, however, be other disagreeable consequences. The Enterprise has become a kind of symbol. In the context of our recent exchanges with the Chinese on Sino-British relations it is possible that a visit by the Enterprise would be interpreted by the Chinese as final proof of our insincerity when we talk about desiring improvement in relations. It would certainly be seen as provocative. A visit might also have repercussions in the Colony as it has I think been suggested in Communist circles that some revolutionary energies should be diverted to anti-United States and anti-KMT themes. And it could of course affect the position of this Mission just as we are hoping for improvement.

2. I realise it may be difficult to ask Americans to cancel the visit now, but from the point of view of this Post I hope this may be urgently considered. It would not (repeat not) be the first time that we have felt obliged to do this.

1 Repeated for information to Hong Kong, Washington and POLAD Singapore.
2 Not printed. The telegram gave details of an NCNA article, given prominence in the local communist press, critical of the fact that Hong Kong was being used by US warships and service personnel involved in the Vietnam War.
3 Not printed.

No. 109

Sir D. Hopson (Peking) to Mr Stewart, 20 May 1968[1]
Tel. No. 453 Priority. Confidential (FCO 21/141, FC 13/8/D)

My telegram No. 419:[2] Grey.

At our request Cradock was granted an interview with Press Department of Ministry of Foreign Affairs on 18 May. He was seen by Miss Chang, Deputy Section Head.

2. Cradock began by expressing our strong dissatisfaction at Grey's present treatment. He pointed out it was clear from Grey's conditions of confinement in approximately the first month after his detention on 21 July, 1967, that the Chinese statement on that date announcing measures against him was intended only to mean that Grey was not free to leave his house. Since 18 August, however, his treatment has been much more severe. He was confined to one room, deprived of using the rest of his house and personal belongings, his telephone and radio and normal postal facilities. He was denied contact with his friends and with this office. This was inconsistent with [the] only official statement the Ministry of Foreign Affairs had made about Grey. This treatment of an innocent man was both inhumane and uncivilised. Cradock requested that Grey's situation be restored at least to what it was before 18 August, and specifically that Grey be allowed full use of his premises and personal possessions, normal inward and outward mail facilities, radio and telephone; also that he be permitted informal visitors from among his friends in Peking on regular basis of at least once a month.

3. Chang described our requests as ridiculous and groundless and went on contrasting Grey's treatment favourably with that of Hong Kong journalists taken prisoner who, she (? gp. omitted) were treated like wild beasts. She denied flatly that there was any inconsistency between Grey's present treatment and the Chinese statement of July, 1967. She claimed that the issue raised by our requests was very simple. We should consider the question of the patriotic journalists and news-workers in prison in Hong Kong and we would find the answer ourselves. The Grey question was not an isolated one but part of the Hong Kong problem. In any case, Grey was on Chinese territory. His treatment was therefore the business of the Chinese Government and no one else had the right to interfere.

4. Cradock rebutted Chang's charges on Hong Kong prisoners in detail, drawing on the material supplied by the Governor. He contrasted Grey's treatment in the matter of visits, isolation, mail facilities and recreation with that received by the Hong Kong prisoners. He pointed out that Grey, as a British subject, was the legitimate object of our concern. The question affects Sino-British relations. Moreover, the treatment of Grey, a foreigner in China, was noted not only in Britain but by other foreign countries.

5. In reply Chang, amidst some general abuse about Hong Kong, said that as regards visit of Legal Adviser the British had so far arranged only one visit in Hong Kong. Anything else was only what was provided for usual prisoners. Grey's alleged isolation was because he was the only correspondent under restraint. By contrast the

---

1 Repeated for information to Hong Kong.
2 Not printed. See No. 107, note 2.

British had arrested many in Hong Kong (? gp. omitted) Grey's condition had not deteriorated. They were better than before. He was allowed to use his personal possessions and could go upstairs to get his own things. All along he had been allowed to write letters to his family. Not long ago Grey had written a letter home.

6. Lengthy exchanges followed in which Cradock repeated our request and asked that very serious attention be given to them, particularly in the relation to the nature of Grey's confinement, which could gravely affect his physical and mental health. The interview ended at Chang's request after two hours.

7. Full record to follow by bag.

8. See my immediately following telegram.[1]

[1] Not printed. In Peking Tel. No. 452, dated 20 May, Sir D. Hopson noted: 'This was a long and abrasive interview. Our points were registered, but the Chinese attitude was unyielding and I would not (repeat not) expect us to succeed in bringing about much change in Grey's situation in this way. It was fairly clear that the Chinese link further visits to him to further special visits to News workers in prison in Hong Kong.'

No. 110

Mr Stewart to Sir D. Hopson (Peking), 22 May 1968[1]
Tel. No. 536 Priority, Confidential (FCO 40/57, HWB 2/1/B)

Your telno. 443[2] and Hong Kong telno. 630:[3] USS Enterprise.

We have considered very carefully the possibility of cancelling the visit. We agree that we must expect a formal protest from the Chinese and that the other disagreeable consequences which you mention could result from the visit. On balance, however, we doubt they will. It seems to us that the press campaign is more a manifestation of Chinese disapproval of the Vietnam talks in Paris than a move directly related to Sino-British bilateral relations. The Chinese have recently shown some disposition to separate the affairs of your Mission from Hong Kong. We have given them no reason to believe that we are prepared in any way to abdicate our authority in the colony as a price for improved relations. If they wished to find a pretext for reverting, for example, to the previous policy of standstill on staff movements, there are other issues in Hong Kong (notably prisoners and the gift of rice) which would appear more appropriate.

2. Apart from adverse American reactions, there are other more compelling reasons against cancellation.

(a) You and Hong Kong authorities are agreed that the Chinese have got wind of the actual visit by the 'Enterprise' and that the NCNA protest was aimed deliberately at it. To cancel in these circumstances would, as Hong Kong have pointed out, encourage Chinese pressure in the future against US Naval visits and would be a dangerous step in the direction of allowing the Chinese to dictate our policies in the Colony.

[1] Repeated for information to Hong Kong and Washington.
[2] No. 108.
[3] Not printed.

(*b*) Cancellation, which would certainly become public in Hong Kong, would go some way to undermine the robust statement put out by the Hong Kong government (Hong Kong telegram number 622)[3] and could be damaging to confidence.

3. As naval visits are a subject to which the Chinese are clearly again turning their attention and since, subject to maintaining authority in Hong Kong, we certainly wish to do nothing to reverse or retard the present trend towards the normalisation of working relations with the Chinese, we shall wish to review the whole question with you and Hong Kong—and also the Americans—after the present visit has taken place, in the light of these and any further Chinese reactions to it.

No. 111

Mr Stewart to Sir D. Hopson (Peking), 24 May 1968[1]
Tel. No. 561 Immediate, Confidential (FCO 21/68, F 3/3/FC)

Sino-British relations.

The Parliamentary Under-Secretary summoned Chinese Chargé d'Affaires *ad interim* at 11 a.m. today. The interview lasted one hour.

2. Mr Rodgers reviewed developments since the last meeting on 5 April[2] and noted that there had been some progress regarding visas for staff in Peking and access to Grey. He hoped there would be no further delay in granting remaining visas. He described the continued solitary confinement of Grey as barbaric and expressed the deep concern of HMG. He asked for a quick improvement in Grey's conditions as prelude to his release.

3. Mr Rodgers went over all the cases of British subjects known to be detained by the Chinese, including that of Captain Pope.[3]

4. Shen P'ing said that since his last interview HMG had failed completely to reply to demands of Chinese Government, although we had made an oral statement that was 'quite unrealistic'. Shen P'ing said Watt had been convicted of 'counter-revolutionary espionage' and must serve the sentence imposed by Chinese law. Access was inappropriate. On other British subjects Shen P'ing had 'nothing to say at present'. Cases were under investigation and HMG would get details in due course.

5. Regarding visas Shen P'ing recalled that Lo Kuei-Po had said on 13 April,[4] that the Chinese would make their own arrangements and act according to normal procedures: But he went on to argue that entry and exit visas were only a minor part of Sino-British relations. Normality could not be resumed until the Hong Kong problem was solved. This was the crux. Shen P'ing said Chinese arrested and persecuted in Hong Kong had still not been released. He also raised the issues of gift rice and clothing for prisoners. He said the case of Grey related to Hong Kong. Treatment of Grey was lenient in comparison with that meted out to 'patriotic

---

1 Repeated for information to Hong Kong, Washington and POLAD Singapore.
2 See No. 96.
3 Captain R.V. Pope was the master of the SS Fortune Wind detained at Tangku on 17 May 1968.
4 See No. 99.

journalists' and 'patriotic countrymen'. The Chinese people were 'completely outraged' about Hong Kong.

6. Mr Rodgers said he did not believe that questions of the British Mission or British subjects were minor matters. He thought Shen P'ing's response cast doubt on the willingness of the Chinese Government to solve the major matters of Sino-British relations. He found Chinese attitude to these cases shocking and asked again for early information.

7. The interview continued in similar terms. Shen P'ing ended by expressing hope that HMG would expeditiously show genuine sincerity and give a realistic answer to demands on Hong Kong.

8. Though Shen P'ing's language was uncompromising, his general tone was quiet.

9. Full report by bag.

No. 112

Sir D. Hopson (Peking) to Mr Stewart, 28 May 1968[1]
Tel. No. 491 Immediate, Confidential (FCO 40/57, HWB 2/1/B)

My telegrams Nos. 487 and 488:[2] Enterprise.

We can take some comfort from the fact that the protest concentrated on the issue of America's use of Hong Kong. As expected Chinese describe visit of Enterprise as a provocation and proof of insincerity. But they did not, either in Note or subsequent exchange, make so much of these points as they might have done.

2. It remains to be seen what other effect this visit will have. Much will depend on the reactions in Hong Kong and I should be grateful for immediate information of any development there.

3. For the future it should be noted that Lo emphasised that the use of Hong Kong by warships of a 'hostile country' represented a 'political and military threat' to China and that the United States found Hong Kong a useful 'base of operations and logistic centre' for its military effort in Viet Nam. Given Chinese attitude on Viet Nam, quite apart from other factors involved, it seems likely that Chinese will continue to make trouble on this issue. In view of this and the very strained Sino/British relations I hope we shall conduct an immediate review of question of United States Naval visit, as promised in your telegram No. 536.[3] I shall reserve any further comment until then.

4. I await instructions on whether to return Chinese Note.

1 Repeated for information to Hong Kong, Washington and POLAD Singapore.
2 Not printed. On 27 May, Sir D. Hopson was summoned by Lo Kuei-Po to receive a note concerning the activities of US warships in Hong Kong. It called on the British government to immediately order the USS Enterprise to leave Hong Kong and cease 'offering Hong Kong to US imperialism as a base of operations and a logistics centre for its war of aggression against Vietnam.'
3 No. 110.

No. 113

Record of a meeting of the Cabinet Defence
and Oversea Policy Committee
29 May 1968, 10 a.m.[1]
OPD(68)11th Meeting, Secret (CAB 148/35)

1. *Hong Kong Garrison*
(Previous Reference: OPD(67)29th Meeting, Item 3).

The Committee considered a memorandum by the Secretary of State for Defence (OPD(68)32)[2] on the future strength and structure of the garrison in Hong Kong.

THE DEFENCE SECRETARY said that there were two main reasons for keeping a garrison in Hong Kong. The first was to guard the land and sea frontier and identify possible aggression from China; the second was to preserve internal security in the Colony. After our departure from Singapore and Malaysia by the end of 1971, we should no longer be able to reinforce the Hong Kong garrison as quickly as present. Nor could we provide temporary replacements from Singapore for equipment and vessels withdrawn from Hong Kong for maintenance. This situation would entail keeping a higher level of forces in the Colony. On the naval side, we should need one additional frigate, three additional mine counter-measures vessels and a small increase in naval support facilities. We should have to maintain the level of land forces at seven and two-thirds major units, which had been their strength following last year's troubles. From the military point of view it was unnecessary to station fighter aircraft in Hong Kong, but the Governor strongly recommended that, for political and psychological reasons, we should do so. After 1971, the cost of the proposed forces which would have internal security as their primary role would amount to £14 million, of which about £8 million would be in foreign exchange, and some further expenditure might be necessary on buildings. The cost of those forces with external defence as their primary role would be £11 million, of which £5 million would be in foreign exchange. On the basis of an understanding reached in 1966, the Hong Kong Government were contributing £5 million a year in cash and kind for four years ending 31st March 1971. This broadly covered the foreign exchange costs of that element of the Army garrison whose role was primarily that of internal security. After 1971 it should be the responsibility of the Hong Kong Government, or failing this of the Commonwealth Office, to meet the full budgetary costs of the forces with an internal security role.

---

1 Committee members present at this meeting were: Mr Wilson (in the Chair), Mr Stewart (Secretary of State for Foreign Affairs), Mr Jenkins (Chancellor of the Exchequer), Mr Crossman (Lord President of the Council), Mr Callaghan (Home Secretary), Mr Healey (Secretary of State for Defence), Mr Peart (Lord Privy Seal), Mr Thomson (Secretary of State for Commonwealth Affairs), Mr Crosland (President of the Board of Trade), Mr Wedgwood Benn (Minister of Technology), Lord Shackleton (Paymaster-General), Mr Prentice (Minister of Overseas Development), Sir Elwyn Jones (Attorney-General), Marshal of the Royal Air Force Sir Charles Elworthy (Chief of the Defence Staff), Admiral Sir Varyl Begg (Chief of Naval Staff and First Sea Lord), General Sir Geoffrey Baker (Chief of the General Staff) and Air Chief Marshal Sir John Gandy (Chief of the Air Staff). Also present were Sir B. Trend, Mr Rose, Mr Lawrence-Wilson, Mr Trench, Mr Facer and Major-General Gibbon of the Cabinet Secretariat.
2 Not printed.

THE COMMONWEALTH SECRETARY said that the increased level of forces after 1971 proposed by the Defence Secretary was the absolute minimum required. He strongly supported the Governor's proposal for a permanent fighter presence in the Colony. The political arguments in its favour were cogent. Some years ago an aircraft from Formosa had intruded into the airspace of Hong Kong. This might happen again and Peking might seize the opportunity to say that Hong Kong constituted a gap in the Chinese air defence which they would have to fill. In such circumstances, we should either have to reinforce Hong Kong or suffer a political setback which would have severe effects on the morale of Hong Kong. The Hong Kong Government were discussing with the Ministry of Defence the possibility of arranging for a flight of aircraft to be manned and serviced from local resources. As regards costs, he considered that the distinction which the Defence Secretary had drawn between forces required for the external defence and the internal security of the Colony was artificial.

In discussions, there was general agreement with the force levels proposed by the Defence Secretary for Hong Kong. It was also agreed that it would be premature at this time to attempt to decide on where the costs of these forces should be borne. The long-term costings which the Ministry of Defence had recently prepared for the new force structure did not take account of any defence contribution from Hong Kong beyond 1971; to the extent that such a contribution was received, it would have to be taken into account in deciding on the size of the defence budget after 1971. There would be great difficulty in assessing accurately the full cost to us of the Hong Kong commitment in terms that would show what savings would result if the commitment were dropped, since this would involve a reassessment and costing of forces structure and support which we should need without the commitment. Nevertheless, it would be worthwhile to attempt to reach agreement on a bracket of costs within which the full cost of the Hong Kong commitment might lie even though this bracket might well be wide. As regards long-term policy for Hong Kong, a study was in preparation and would shortly be submitted to the Ministerial Committee on Hong Kong who would report in due course to the Committee.

THE PRIME MINSTER, summing up the discussion, said that the Committee approved the proposals of the Defence Secretary for the future strength and structure of the naval and army elements of the Hong Kong Garrison. They also approved the proposal to station Hunter aircraft in the Colony, subject to further examination of the possibility of these aircraft might be manned and serviced from local resources. Consideration of where the costs of the garrison should be borne should be deferred but the Defence Secretary, in consultation with the Chancellor of the Exchequer, should arrange for the best assessment possible to be made of the full cost to us of the Hong Kong commitment. The Committee also took note that it was not yet possible to reach a decision whether or not units stationed in Hong Kong should be accompanied by their families.

The Committee—

(1) Approved OPD(68)32, subject to the points made by the Prime Minister in his summing up of their discussion.

(2) Invited the Defence Secretary, in consultation with the Chancellor of the Exchequer, to arrange for the best possible assessment to be made of the full cost to us of the Hong Kong commitment.

No. 114

Sir D. Hopson (Peking) to Mr Stewart, 5 June 1968[1]
Tel. No. 526 Immediate, Confidential (FCO 21/68, FC 3/3F)

Since more than two weeks had passed since last issue of exit visas and that for Peters in particular was long overdue, Cradock obtained an interview with Ni (Section Head of Consular Department) on 4 June.

2. Cradock referred to Chinese failure so far to issue visas to Peters and to those for whom visas were requested on 8 and 13 May i.e. Whitney, Gallagher, Webb, Tregilgas and Miss Quirie. He noted the issues of entry visas but said that new personnel could not come in until some people had been permitted to leave.

3. In reply Ni said that since Lo Kuei-po and Kao had given assurance that visa applications would be dealt with according to normal procedure, the issuing of visas had proceeded in basically normal way. But abnormality in movement of personnel was caused by Hong Kong suppression of Chinese people there. Abnormal phenomena such as the case of Peters, Whitney and others, were the result of this. Recent vicious acts by the British in Hong Kong had led to difficulties. Movement of personnel was not an isolated question, without a final solution to Hong Kong question other problems could not be solved completely.

4. Cradock said that this statement was in conflict with assurance given earlier e.g. by Kao on 22 April. Ni denied the contradiction, and referred to Chinese issue of visas since April. He said that the movement difficulties had been caused by vicious actions in the period since assurances were given. When asked to specify these acts, Ni referred to protest Note about visit of 'Enterprise' (my telegram 487).[2]

5. Cradock asked whether Ni in the present circumstances meant that visas e.g. for Peters would not (repeat not) soon be issued. Ni said that so far he had no news on this. Cradock said that if visas were not issued very soon we might be forced to the conclusion that British diplomatic agents were being detained in China because of political events. This would be a very serious matter. Ni replied that to draw such conclusion would be to distort his meaning. Detention of diplomats was contrary to Chinese diplomatic practice.

6. Cradock said that in that event he looked forward to the issue of visas in the next few days. This would prove that he had drawn the wrong conclusion. The solution of these difficulties was simple and lay with Consular Department.

7. Cradock then reminded Ni of visit applications on the behalf of Selfs, Croziers and Johnstons in Shanghai. Ni made no direct reply, but reiterated need for British to show sincerity in solving Hong Kong questions. Until this was done there would be difficulties in movements of Chinese and British personnel. Cradock reminded Ni that there were no restrictions on movement of Chinese personnel to or from Britain. We had informed Chinese of this and we kept to our word.

1 Repeated for information to Hong Kong, POLAD Singapore and Washington.
2 No. 112.

No. 115

Sir D. Hopson (Peking) to Mr Stewart, 5 June 1968[1]
Tel No. 527 Immediate, Confidential (FCO 27/68, FC 3/3F)

My immediately preceding telegram (not to all).[2]
This was a much tougher interview than has been usual recently. In contrast with earlier occasions Ni made long direct references to Hong Kong, he also added serious qualifications to Kao's assurances of normal treatment on visas given [gp undec] are to once again we have the hard line [*sic*].

2. This is therefore a distinct setback on visas at a time when we thought we were turning the corner. How serious a set back remains to be seen. It is hard not to see it more as a warning (that we cannot continue to disregard Chinese susceptibilities over Hong Kong and continue to get visas) than a complete change of course, and would expect a delay before any new exit visa once issued rather than a total freeze. But this is always provided that there is no new incident to inflame relations.

3. Ni made it crystal clear that immediate cause of this set back is the visit of Enterprise. I think it a great pity this visit was allowed, but I hope that at least we shall be able to take full account of its consequence in present review of United States Naval visits.

1 Repeated for information to Hong Kong, POLAD Singapore and Washington.
2 No. 114.

No. 116

Sir D. Hopson (Peking) to Mr Stewart, 13 June 1968[1]
Tel. No. 558 Priority, Confidential (FCO 21/68, FC3/3)

In the light of the latest interview on visas (my telegrams Nos. 526 and 527)[2] I think the time has come for us to bring diplomatic pressure on the Chinese on the question of the detention of members of this mission and also to arrange for a limited amount of publicity on the same subject.

2. As regards diplomatic pressure, my main grounds for this recommendation are as follows:

(*a*) Although we have had a strong case on detention since last August, until April we have been to some degree inhibited by the fact that we ourselves applied certain controls on the movements of the Chinese officials to and from Britain. However our own slate had been clean since 13 April when I informed Lo Kuei-po of the granting of outstanding entry visas and the lifting of exit visa requirements.

(*b*) Though the situation on visas is still blurred and a trickle of exit visas may continue the Chinese so far have granted no exit visas to senior staff (except for

1 Repeated for information to Hong Kong.
2 Nos. 114 and 115 respectively.

the First Secretaries Blishen and Whitney which were both requested on medical grounds) despite repeated applications since April, e.g. in the case of Peters.

(*c*) In any event in the interview of 4 June the Chinese apparently went back on assurances of normal treatment given on 13 April and 22 April. They implied that political pressure over Hong Kong would continue to affect the granting of visas until Chinese obtain some kind of satisfaction in settlement of Hong Kong problem. If we remain inactive we condone this treatment which outrages all diplomatic practice and encourages the Chinese in their present course.

(*d*) In the interview of 4 June with Consular Department and previously the Chinese have shown themselves sensitive to suggestions of detention of diplomats. The Chinese are at present trying to reconstruct the image of correct diplomatic behaviour upset by the Cultural Revolution and are being very correct with other Western Missions, of course the Africans and Asians. Various official visits here by Foreign Ministers and Heads of State, have taken place or are impending. The Chinese may also hope for diplomatic relations with Canada and perhaps even Japan. They would not enjoy attention being drawn to their treatment of this mission.

(*e*) Although Hong Kong is not an issue likely to engage support of e.g. Afro-Asian Governments, provided representations are confined to narrow points, interference with movement of diplomats and infringement of diplomatic standards, we should have an issue in which all countries represented here will have considerable self interest.

3. There are possible drawbacks to this course which we should take into account:

(*a*) It is possible that concerted diplomatic pressure might stiffen Chinese at any rate in the short term.

(*b*) Interview of 4 June can be interpreted in several ways, e.g. as show of Chinese displeasure over 'Enterprise' rather than complete change of course. It would be unwise to leap to conclusions and there may be something to be said for continuing with our present low posture at least for a short time.

4. Nevertheless I think that considerations in paragraph 2 above are overriding. Diplomatic pressure would on balance help rather than injure us. As regards 3(*b*) above, a diplomatic campaign could be called off if visas to senior staff were granted and in any event I doubt if expressions of concern to Chinese could do any real harm. You will recall that when Netherlands Chargé d'Affaires[3] was detained here in 1966 representations were made to Chinese by several Western Governments and this may in fact have hastened his release. Even if your reply finally gets visas normalised their treatment of us has been monstrous.

5. We should try for representations in as many countries with Chinese missions as possible. In addition to Western countries, who are likely to be cooperative, we should try the Commonwealth (Pakistan, India, Ceylon, Zambia and Kenya), African and Asian countries generally. Africans may be particularly important in view of current Chinese interest there.

6. Representations should be to Chinese in capitals concerned rather than here in Peking. They are likely to be clearer and stronger if done that way. I am afraid that many colleagues in Peking are lacking in spirit and solidarity.

7. I recommend that we should instruct our representatives in Capitals concerned

---

3 G. J. Jongejans.

to seek the diplomatic support of Governments to which they are accredited, asking them to summon the Chinese Representative and convey to him expression of concern at situation for our Mission here, in particular the failure to grant exit visas to staff attempting to get political preconditions for release. This treatment violates diplomatic practice, thereby raising questions for all countries with representation in Peking.

8. We should try to keep representations to the narrow point of interference with free movement of diplomatic agents. Although there is splendid material available from last year about our treatment it brings in Hong Kong too quickly. Moreover, although it should be pointed out that we have been effectively detained since last August, it will be necessary to concentrate on the period since April when there have been no restrictions to Chinese movement to and from London.

9. The above representations, based on breach of diplomatic usage, would necessarily be confined to detention of staff of this Mission. We could not bring in the cases of other British subjects held in China without raising other issues, e.g. espionage or Hong Kong, thereby blurring the case. Moreover, while we can expect other Governments to exert themselves on behalf of diplomatic practice, which affects their own missions in Peking, we cannot hope to engage them on behalf of British subjects generally.

10. I would not (repeat not) recommend that we make further protests to the Chinese before launching this exercise. Such action would merely raise the temperature.

11. We shall also need to forearm other Governments concerned against the probable immediate Chinese response e.g. references to Hong Kong; restrictions imposed by the British Government; and the granting of entry and exit visas by the Chinese since August last. In order to convey this briefing I suggest our representatives should give the Governments concerned a memorandum which would set out the basic facts and serve as background for representations to the Chinese. My immediately following telegram contains suggested text.[1] A further telegram deals separately with the question of publicity.[2]

1 Not printed.
2 No. 117.

No. 117

Sir D. Hopson (Peking) to Mr Stewart, 13 June 1968[1]
Tel. No. 560 Priority, Confidential (FCO 21/68, FC 3/3)

The arguments [word omitted] publicity are similar to those in paragraph 2 of my telegram No. 558.[2] There are however additional disadvantages:

(*a*) It would put the Chinese more publicly on the spot so that any concessions on their side might be seen as response to pressure of world opinion. The Chinese might become more intransigent in consequence.

(*b*) There is a risk that in order to justify themselves they might engineer some incident or trump up charges against the staff of the Mission. In the present

1 Repeated for information to Hong Kong.
2 No. 116.

circumstances espionage is an obvious possibility, though we must hope diplomatic status would protect us from the full consequences of this.

(*c*) Publicity would be more difficult to control than diplomatic pressure. It would be harder to confine it to the question of interference with the movement of diplomats. It would readily extend to the question of Hong Kong, which in Press of certain countries would get involved with issues of colonialism and so on.

(*d*) Publicity could also generate pressure in the United Kingdom for undesirable action against the Chinese officials, e.g. renewed restriction on movements. It is fundamental to proposed exercise that we should at all costs avoid any such action against the Chinese at this stage. It would completely stultify diplomatic or publicity campaign, would provoke Chinese retaliations and counter-restrictions from which we have just escaped. I hope therefore it can be taken as firm ground that we shall not (repeat not) take such action at this stage whatever Press or public in general may suggest.

2. Despite these considerable risks I think we should arrange for at least one informed Press article to coincide with the diplomatic campaign. I suggest we try for a leader in the *Times*. It should confine itself to the same points as in the diplomatic campaign though it might add some reflection on the uncivilized nature of Chinese conduct. Such an article would not necessarily spark off a great deal of comment in the United Kingdom or abroad. It would on the other hand serve as warning to the Chinese of possibility of a wider Press campaign and give us an opportunity of judging their reactions.

3. I think we must also begin planning now for wider Press campaign which may have to follow later in the game if Chinese remain unresponsive to pressures proposed in these telegrams. Such a campaign would cover wider issues, e.g. British subjects in China and needs careful planning and control once launched.

4. Above recommendations for diplomatic and some publicity pressure involve distinct risks. However I think that the time has come when these risks have to be accepted if we are not to remain entirely passive in Chinese hands. I should add that chances of success of this exercise will be virtually destroyed if at the same time we are completely disregarding the Chinese susceptibilities over Hong Kong, e.g. on such questions as visits by heavy or nuclear-powered United States warships. In fact to give the operation the best chance it should if possible coincide with some conciliatory gesture e.g. accelerated release for some prisoners in Hong Kong which would allow the Chinese to claim that they were responding only to gestures in Hong Kong and not to outside pressures.

No. 118

Sir D. Hopson (Peking) to Mr Stewart, 15 June 1968
Tel. No. 566 Priority. Confidential (FCO 21/68, FC 3/3FC)

My telegram No. 558.[1]
Following for Wilkinson.

---

1 No. 116.

If it is decided to launch this Diplomatic offensive it occurs to me that our case might appear stronger if I myself had applied for an exit visa. In the unlikely event of it being granted before e.g. one for Peters, we could decide in the light of circumstances at the time whether I should use it or not. If you agree I would propose to apply to leave say on 1 July. Our exit visas are normally valid one month. Grateful for your views.[2]

2 See No. 123.

No. 119

Letter from Mr Cradock (Peking) to Mr Denson, 18 June 1968
Personal and Confidential (FCO 21/38, FC 1/21/B)

Dear John,
Since I last wrote to you on the state of the Mission on 26 March,[1] a great deal has happened to us, both good and bad. If we had a situation or morale graph it would show a rise to a new point from March to May, then a sharp drop over the last month since 27 May.

2. First we had the unexpected and happy news from you that the exit visa requirement for Chinese officials leaving the UK was lifted, followed by the grant of outstanding Chinese supplications for entry visas. I say unexpected since although we had asked for this in the context of our draft reply to Lo Kuei-po, in the light of our debates from January to March we had not dared to hope that we would obtain your agreement. The lifting of restrictions produced rapid and good results. The discussion with Lo Kuei-po on 13 April[2] was discouraging on Hong Kong but contained a vague and opaque statement about visas, which on subsequent Chinese exegesis turned out to have been crystal clear and to the effect that the Chinese would now deal with visas in a normal way. A week later four entry visas were granted in London and this was followed by the surprising interview with Mr Kao on 22 April at which we were told that exit visas should not take very long. Kao I have always thought of as a fair-weather man, put on to make the encouraging statements, but shut up again whenever the wind turns chilly. From 22 April to 27 May the wind blew fair and warm and after further haggles the exit visas began to flow. We had six within a month. The Chinese interpretation of 'normal' was of course very odd and it was interesting that the thaw did not apparently extend to senior staff, e.g. Theo Peters. Nevertheless the progress was immense and during the month in question the whole scene with the Office changed. Pat Iliffe, who was to have left on 22 August last year, was appropriately the first to go. As her small figure crossed the tarmac someone asked 'How many telegrams has that cost?' I shudder to think but all were worth it.

3. The flow of exit visas and the grant of entry visas in London made the period up to 27 May an exciting one for everyone here. There remained considerable doubts

1 No. 93.
2 See No. 99.

about the senior staff but it seemed reasonable to hope that after a suitably long delay we might get even those away. The situation changed, however, with the visit of Enterprise to Hong Kong, which we tried unsuccessfully to avert.[3] On 27 May we had the expected protest and on 4 June the not unexpected statement that our exit visas were also affected.[4] We remain uncertain how serious the stoppage is, but with a further visit by a US aircraft carrier in Hong Kong this week we cannot entertain much hope of a resumption. Ray Whitney's visa, though we are delighted he got it, does not signify in this context since he had strong medical grounds.

4. The new interruption in visas hit staff hard. They began to believe that they had turned the corner and planning for homeward bound journeys was well under way. They have all along understood that we and other British subjects here would have to take the consequences of our inability to make concessions over really vital issues in Hong Kong. But since Enterprise it has seemed that the doctrine has been extended and that they must also pay for our unwillingness to make concessions on lesser matters, not bearing directly on Hong Kong's security, e.g. the current level of US naval visits. We have been in active correspondence with you on this issue and on further steps we might take to ease our situation, i.e., diplomatic pressure and some degree of publicity.

5. This setback in our prospects has coincided with alarming news from Shanghai, the disappearance of Frank Van Roosebroeck and our realisation of the fear this must have spread among the British community in Shanghai, for all of whom he was a close friend. Van Roosebroeck, held for some 20 years because a foreign bank would not meet Chinese blackmail, has always been a *momento mori*, a reminder to foreigners in this country of the length to which the Chinese will take the hostage game. His actual disappearance is a reminder also of the intensity of the current spy mania. The arrest in Peking on 8 June of the Japanese correspondent, Samejima, taken from his home at one in the morning in the best Stalinist style, has driven this last point home. These are sinister events and the atmosphere in consequence has suffered.

6. On the credit side we have had some new arrivals and it has been pleasant to see new faces. All seem to be settling in well and slowly acquiring the necessary Peking neuroses. On practical matters too we have made some progress. The repair and repainting of the damaged rooms in our present Office has been completed. At the old office the swimming pool functions well, we have new trees planted and all looks pleasant, apart from the central ruin. The tennis courts are now ready and in use. The Diplomatic Services Bureau have been cooperative over these repairs and indeed gave some indications that they would like us to carry on with the work and repair the old office itself (I am writing separately on this point).

7. In March I wrote to James Murray on a number of welfare problems arising from our detention here and received very helpful answers. I hope that the supply of films and the provision of special bag facilities will continue. On certain financial aspects of our problem I had a sympathetic though negative reply from John Heath. I accept that there is not much we can do about the questions I raised with him, though I have had to point out that the effect is to add some financial hardship to the other rigours staff here have had to sustain.

3 See No. 108.
4 See Nos. 112 and 114.

8. We have had one other great success during this period, namely access to Grey, following an immensely long telegraphic controversy and finally a round of special visits to prisoners in Hong Kong. We were all deeply relieved to find him in reasonable physical condition and not too seriously affected by his isolation and the immense mental strain. Since then, however, our discussions with you and Hong Kong have indicated that the future is not at all bright for him and this has added greatly to our sense of frustration and worry on his behalf. We shall be telegraphing proposing another round of special visits to Hong Kong as a means of another consular visit to Grey.

I am sending copies of this letter on a personal basis to Ramsey Melhuish in Personnel Department and to Robin McLaren in Hong Kong.

Yours ever,
PERCY

No. 120

Sir D. Hopson (Peking) to Mr Stewart, 19 June 1968[1]
Tel. No. 577 Priority, Confidential (FCO 40/88, HWB 9/12/A)

Hong Kong telegram No. 765:[2] Chungwah High School.

The proposal to deregister the school at this stage raises issues on which I should like to comment.

2. First as regards Peking's reaction, we can be sure that it will be sharp. They will see this as a new political persecution, a move against Communist schools in Hong Kong and a breach of assurances given in our statement of 13 April (see paragraph 5 below).[3] As I have pointed out in earlier correspondence, they are specially sensitive about moves against them in the propaganda and education fields. I agree there is likely to be a protest, there may be demonstrations in Hong Kong and the position of this Mission and British subjects in China are likely to suffer in consequence.

3. The Chinese reaction will be sharper because of timing of deregistration. The Executive Council's advice was given in early December at a time of violence. It is now 7 to 8 months since the incident occurred during which time Communist tactics have changed. After so long an interval attempts to present deregistration as something other than a new attack on Communist education and to explain it in terms of an incident last November will not carry much conviction.

4. There are three outstanding arguments advanced for this move. The first is a retrospective argument i.e. that bombs were manufactured on the premises last November. But the persons involved were punished at the time. We cannot surely maintain that guilt attaches permanently to the school; on this principle a large number of institutions in Hong Kong would be permanently banned. Nor are teachers and pupils likely to

---

1 Repeated for information to Hong Kong.
2 Not printed.
3 See No. 98.

make bombs now; the campaign of violence is over. I would have thought it in our interests to avoid digging up the past and to concentrate on possibility of peaceful coexistence with Communists inside Hong Kong now and in the future.

5. The second argument is that deregistration would strike at plans for Communist education in Hong Kong. This raises the question of whether our object is to stop or obstruct Communist education in the colony. My understanding of our policy is that we do not object to Communist schools as such; our objection is to violence. We state there is freedom of speech and education in the Colony and have informed the Chinese, on 13 April in our reply to Lo Kuei-po, that we do not object to study of Mao, or anyone else, provided it remains within the frame-work of the law. If we are now to attempt suppression of Communist schools as such, we make nonsense of these assurances and embark on a new and dangerous policy which we probably lack the power to enforce and in which we can expect all-out opposition from Peking.

6. The third argument is that the reopening of a major Communist school will be a bad blow for public morale. As I have said in correspondence on Naval visits, I find it hard to believe that the Hong Kong public as a whole would wish to have a further battle with local Communists or China or that they would react badly to measures which suggest a return to normality. The return to normal life in Hong Kong, which is our object, must involve reopening of schools, the release of prisoners and restarting of Communist newspapers. All these, according to one interpretation, might be represented as defeats for us and victories for the Communists. But I must repeat that I see the presentation of issues in this form as over-simplified and in-applicable to Hong Kong situation, where the future depends not on attempts to supress Communists but on the achievement of some kind of peaceful coexistence. Provided always order is obtained resumption of normal life is only to our benefit, both in Hong Kong and in the wider context of Sino-British relations.

7. I have set out these comments at some length since I find the proposals in telegram under reference and assumptions behind it extremely disturbing. I do not discount the extreme difficulties of the Hong Kong problem. But as seen from here it is essential to avoid getting into a position where any conciliatory gesture or adjustment to take account of Peking sensitivities is to be rejected automatically as a surrender to Communists. If we are to adopt this viewpoint, and it strongly [gp undec ? upsets] telegram under reference, then we are in effect changing policy hitherto pursued over Hong Kong and makes the prospect for improvement in Sino-British relations and in the treatment of British subjects in China virtually non-existent.[4]

---

4 In Hong Kong Tel. No. 832 to the Commonwealth Office, dated 29 June, the Governor responded that he did not want the Communists to regain a position of strength similar to that held prior to April 1967: 'At present, it is clear that local Communist morale here is very low in all fields except education and possibly the press. I see no reason to do anything to help them bolster it up again, unless there is clear advantage to us to be gained in so doing and I see every advantage in undermining them still further if we can do so discreetly or on good grounds'.

No. 121

Sir D. Hopson (Peking) to Mr Stewart, 20 June 1968[1]
Tel. No. 585 Secret (FCO 21/68, FC 3/3)

My telegram No. 558.[2]

Apart from considering diplomatic and publicity campaigns against the Chinese, we should also be giving further thought to the possibility of other types of pressure, in particular economic pressure. Earlier exchanges on this (resting with my telegram No. 257)[3] have been inconclusive, and I suggest that we now need to study more urgently and in detail the various possibilities in this field.

2. Hitherto we have been considering only fairly drastic economic measures. I still think it important to make a thorough study of these now, since we may eventually need to use those measures that seem practicable. My immediately following telegram[4] contains a list of questions relating to such measures to which it would be useful to have the answers.

3. I suggest, however, that these measures are not what we need at present stage. Our immediate aim is to try and force the Chinese to soften their attitude on Sino-British relations, and measures such as freezing of funds and closing of banks would be likely to have opposite effect. What we need to discover for our immediate purposes are ways in which we might indirectly warn the Chinese, that we are not prepared to allow them to get away with their present behaviour indefinitely.

Two particular methods occur to me:

(*a*) *Pin Pricks*

Could we for example start on introducing slight 'administration signs' into transactions with the Bank of China or with other organisations connected with the Chinese trade? These would of course be unexplained but it would not take long for their purpose to become clear to the Chinese. We should of course have to consider carefully the likelihood of Chinese making administrative difficulties for this mission in retaliation.

(*b*) *Veiled Threats*

An example which occurs to me concerns British import quotas for Chinese goods. Representatives of British companies to whom the Chinese customarily allot a large part of quotas (e.g. Cave of Biddle Sawyer)[5] might be summoned, and requested that because of the persistent bad state of Sino-British relations it might not be possible to maintain those quotas much longer. This would certainly get back to the Chinese before too long.

---

1 Repeated for information to Hong Kong.
2 No. 116.
3 Not printed.
4 Not printed. Hopson asked whether the Chinese could be prevented from chartering ships in London, or if an embargo could be placed on British ships calling at Chinese ports, whether Chinese funds held in London could be blocked and if the Bank of China in London could be closed. However, Mr Rodgers was unconvinced and thought that if these measures carried risks then they should only be used in response to a clear escalation by the Chinese of present antagonisms (note by R. C. Samuel, 25 June).
5 Company specialising in imports.

4. I should be grateful for your urgent views on this, and for any other suggestions you may have about the ways in which we might gently but firmly bring our point home to the Chinese.[6]

6 See No. 133 for the Governor of Hong Kong's view.

No. 122

Sir D. Trench (Hong Kong) to Mr Thomson (Commonwealth Office)
22 June 1968[1]
Tel. No. 803 Routine, Confidential (FCO 21/140, FC 13/8/C)

Peking Tel. No. 587 to Foreign Office, paragraphs 1 and 2.[2]
Grey.
While I still think we ought to try to press for non-consular visits by a friend first (my telegram 536, para. 2 refers).[3] I would now be prepared to consider another visit here to the news workers on or about 15 July. This would have to be:
(*a*) On the same basis as before, i.e. on not more favourable terms, and provided
(*b*) We can be reasonably sure access to Grey results
(*c*) The situation here is still reasonably quiet
(*d*) The climate of public opinion is much as at present. While I have some apprehensions, I think another visit here in July would be accepted for Grey's sake.

2. While it is not for me to assess, I still wonder how wise we really are in continuing to demonstrate our concern for Grey so very clearly. Are we sure that we are not merely convincing the Chinese by our sensitivity to his plight that he has a real value as a hostage and are thus running the risk that they will be even less ready to let him go eventually? It seems to me the essential thing is to ensure that nothing is done which will persuade the Chinese that it would be worth their while to continue to hang on to him even after the NCNA men are eventually released.[4]

1 Repeated for information to Peking.
2 Not printed. In this telegram, Sir D. Hopson noted that it had been two months since they saw Mr Grey and almost a year since his detention. As it was clear that further access would not be granted without a further round of special visits to prisoners in Hong Kong, he requested permission to arrange another round of visits with the Foreign Ministry in exchange for access to Grey (FCO 21/140).
3 Not printed.
4 Replying in Peking Tel. No. 596, dated 24 June, Sir D. Hopson confirmed that a non-consular visit had already been requested without success. He also thought it 'much too late in the day for us to delude [the] Chinese about our anxieties on Grey even if we in this mission were now instructed to feign disinterest nor could we expect Parliament and United Kingdom public opinion to maintain such a pretence.'

No. 123

Submission from Mr Murray to Mr Wilkinson, 22 June 1968
Confidential (FCO 21/68, FC 3/3/FC)

Mr. Wilkinson,

British Mission in Peking:
Diplomatic Pressure on the Chinese Government

Problem

In an interview accorded to the Counsellor of the Office of the British Chargé d'Affaires in Peking on 4 June,[1] a Section Head of the Consular Department of the Chinese Ministry of Foreign Affairs made it clear that the Chinese authorities regarded the issue of exit visas to certain senior members of the British staff in Peking as a matter closely related to events in Hong Kong. Although the Section Head asserted that the detention of diplomats was 'contrary to Chinese diplomatic practice', he contradicted himself by admitting that the withholding of exit visas from certain senior officers was a retaliation for events in Hong Kong. He instanced the decision to permit the United States carrier USS 'Enterprise' to visit the Colony from 24-30 May (Peking telegrams 526 and 527).[2] Since we removed the remaining special restrictions on the Chinese mission in London last April, no visas have been issued to senior members of the British staff, except for the First Secretary, Mr Whitney; but he was permitted to leave specifically on medical grounds. (Since April visas have been issued to junior members of the staff—but not since the interview referred to above.)

2. In the light of this interview Sir D. Hopson has expressed the view that the time has come for us to bring diplomatic pressure to bear on the Chinese on the question of detention of members of the Mission; and also to arrange for a limited amount of publicity on the subject (Peking telegram 558).[3] Sir D. Hopson proposes that representations be made to Governments in whose capitals both we and the Chinese are represented, asking them to tackle the Chinese on our behalf. He has put forward a draft speaking note for our representatives in those capitals (Peking telegram No. 559).[4] He has also discussed the handling of attendant publicity which must be carefully controlled (Peking telegram No. 560).[5] Sir D. Hopson has further proposed that we might strengthen our hand by authorising him to apply for an exit visa (which will almost certainly be refused by the Chinese) and we have agreed.

Recommendation

3. I recommend that we give close scrutiny to the possibility of undertaking the campaign recommended by Sir D. Hopson. However we should not move to put it into effect until we have seen the Chinese response to Sir D. Hopson's own applications for an exit visa; and (assuming that it is refused) have sought further clarification of their attitude from the Chinese in Peking and in London. A draft telegram to Peking is attached.[6]

1 See No. 114.
2 Nos. 114 and 115.
3 No. 116.
4 Not printed.
5 No. 117.
6 Not printed.

Background and Argument

4. We share Sir D. Hopson's concern about the implications of the line the Chinese took with the Counsellor on 4 June. The Chinese position is ambiguous, but they have come the nearest yet to admitting that they are holding senior staff deliberately as hostages for our behaviour in Hong Kong. We had it in mind to instruct Sir D. Hopson to approach the Chinese at the highest level available to request them to dispel this ambiguity and make it absolutely clear whether or not they had specifically adopted a hostage policy (FO telegram No. 668).[6] Sir D. Hopson has commented that he thinks little is to be achieved by this course and we can elucidate Chinese intentions most clearly by seeing whether they are prepared to grant him a visa to leave China. If the Chinese fail to grant visas he could then seek a formal elucidation (Peking telegram No. 580).[6] We have already agreed on this. Clearly if we decide to make representations to other Governments they will carry more weight if Sir D. Hopson himself has applied for a visa and had his application refused. If the application is granted we shall be faced with a new situation, possibly one in which representations are no longer required.

5. Sir D. Hopson has set out the following grounds for recommending a diplomatic offensive:

(*a*) As regards the detention of Chinese officials, our slate has been clean since 13 April when Sir D. Hopson informed the Chinese we had lifted all restrictions of their movements (the Chinese Chargé d'Affaires in London was informed on 5 April).

(*b*) Although some visas have been granted to British staff, none have been granted to senior members (except for two special cases on grounds of illness).

(*c*) On 4 June the Chinese implied a continuing connexion between the events in Hong Kong and the issue of visas to British staff. By remaining inactive we condone this treatment and encourage the Chinese.

(*d*) The Chinese are sensitive to suggestions that they make a practice of detaining diplomats. They may be particularly sensitive at a moment when they are endeavouring to reconstruct the image of correct diplomatic behaviour and normal foreign policy.

(*e*) The issue engages interest of all Governments represented in Peking.

6. Sir D. Hopson admits that there are two disadvantages to the course proposed:

(*a*) It is possible that concerted diplomatic pressure may stiffen the Chinese, at any rate in the short term.

(*b*) The interview of 4 June may represent a brief show of Chinese displeasure over the visit of the USS 'Enterprise' rather than a completed change of course on visas. If so, attempts to bring pressure to bear on the Chinese may make it harder for them to revert to their policy of issuing at least a trickle of visas to junior staff.

7. To these objections we may add a third. Publicity for the link between the treatment of our mission and our policies in Hong Kong—on which we have avoided specific public comment in the past—may import considerations of face for the Chinese. They may be more reluctant to grant visas even to junior staff, lest this be interpreted as approval of our conduct in Hong Kong.

8. Over all, there is the difficulty of making a diplomatic campaign effective. Such a campaign will only be effective if the Chinese find themselves tackled from many quarters. However, we fall very far short of being able to guarantee this. The

Governments which have standing in the eyes of the Chinese and whose goodwill, in the context of Chinese foreign policy, they are anxious to retain, are those least likely to put their relations with China at risk on our behalf. On the other hand the countries most likely to stand by us are those likely to cut least ice with the Chinese. Furthermore the Governments we approach will doubtless do nothing until they have sought the views of their own representatives in Peking; and on past form there can be little doubt that a good number of these representatives will draw attention to the habitual Chinese resentment at third-party meddling and will advise their Governments to have nothing to do with the scheme. We have made a provisional estimate (at Annex A)[7] of the likely reactions of the Governments in whose capitals both we and the Chinese are represented.

9. In less extreme circumstances those objections might be overriding. On balance, however, I doubt whether the exercise proposed by Sir D. Hopson would do much to worsen our already difficult situation in Peking; and it is just conceivable that it may have some effect. An important consideration is the morale factor in Peking. I suspect that Sir D. Hopson occasionally feels we do not attach sufficient weight to the plight of his Mission. This is a matter in which we can at least show willing, even if it does not produce significant results. However, I am sure we should not act on Sir D. Hopson's recommendation until we have proved to our satisfaction that the Chinese intend to withhold an exit visa from Sir D. Hopson himself; and until we have sought in Peking and in London further elucidation of their intentions.

10. The following timetable would seem suitable.

22 June: Sir D. Hopson applies for exit visa w.e.f. 1 July.

2 July: (If the visa has not been granted) Sir D. Hopson asks for an interview with the Chinese MFA.

5 July: (If the interview has not been granted or its terms are unsatisfactory) Mr Rodgers summons the Chinese Chargé d'Affaires in London.

15 July (If there has been no progress), instructions sent to missions abroad to begin the diplomatic offensive.

11. Meantime the Department will get ahead with the preparation of instructions for posts abroad.[8]

JAMES MURRAY

---

7 Not printed.

8 Mr Wilkinson minuted on 24 June that he was not hopeful that this 'grand remonstrance' on behalf of the Mission in Peking would be successful, fearing that those Governments which had influence with the Chinese would be unwilling to intervene. He added however that 'the Mission in Peking have unfortunately lost confidence in our willingness to accept their advice, for example in respect of Chinese relations with Hong Kong, where consideration other than those affecting Peking have to be taken into account. In fact we are dangerously out of sympathy at the moment, and to restore confidence seems to me of overriding importance. Therefore, although the proposed initiative may seem futile or even harmful, I should like to act on Sir D. Hopson's recommendation unless he changes his mind when, for instance, the Chinese have replied to his application for an exit visa'. Mr Allen and Mr Denson also had reservations but were willing to proceed.

No. 124

Mr Thomson (Commonwealth Office) to Sir D. Trench (Hong Kong)
24 June 1968[1]
Tel No. 1203 Routine, Confidential (FCO 40/88, HWB 9/12/A)

Your telegram No. 765[2] and Peking telegram No. 577.[3]

Chung Wah Middle School.

It is quite clear that the incidents which occurred at the school last year fully justified its deregistration, but we are dubious about the proposal to deregister it so long after the event. There is no doubt that to do so at this stage would be regarded by the communists as a provocative act unassociated with last year's events and would provoke a sharp reaction from them in one form or another. We would be quite ready to run this risk if we were satisfied that there was sufficient justification for doing so, i.e. that failure to deregister would have a really substantial affect [sic] on public morale and confidence in the government.

2. You have said that failure to deregister would have a very adverse effect on public morale and would be interpreted as a sign of weakness on the part of government. We agree that this might well be the case if it were public knowledge that deregistration had been seriously considered or earlier decided upon or there were a general public assumption that the school would not be allowed to reopen. But against the background of the abandonment of violence by the Communists and having regard to the time lag, is there not a possibility that public opinion might regard failure to deregister as no more than a gesture by government to encourage return to normality?

3. It would also be helpful to know whether there are any alternative courses open to us, e.g. whether it would be possible to cancel the registration of present staff and management, leaving it possible for the school premises to reopen under fresh (Communist) auspices. If this particular course were feasible, would it not in public eyes constitute sufficient punitive action against those who so clearly overstepped the acceptable limits and provide some insurance that they could not again indulge in similar activities? It would certainly enable us to maintain that we do not object to Communist schools as such (paragraph 5 of Peking telegram under reference).

4. Before reaching any final view we should be grateful to receive your further observations.

---

1 Repeated for information to Peking.
2 Not printed.
3 No. 120.

No. 125

Sir D. Hopson (Peking) to Mr Stewart, 2 July 1968[1]
Tel No. 620 Immediate, Secret (FCO 40/88, HWB 9/12A)

Hong Kong telegram numbers 831 and 832:[2] Chung Wah School.

I should like to comment on the important questions of principle raised in these telegrams.

2. The Governor states in telegram No. 832 that it is not enough to return to the situation as in April 1967 and that we must try to improve our position while undermining that of the Communists. If that is so, much of our correspondence since the Autumn of 1967 has been proceeding on a misunderstanding. I understood, and it has been stated in your telegrams, that we wished to get back to a *modus vivendi* and to normal working relations with the Chinese. On this understanding [the] very best we can hope for is a return to April 1967 conditions. The Governor, however, apparently envisages continuing confrontation and measures of attrition directed against the Communists in an effort to get our position in Hong Kong to one which he would consider as suitable strength.

3. We must be clear about the implications of this. If it is accepted it means a basic change in our policy hitherto (so far as I have understood it); it is inconsistent with what we have told the Chinese, in particular Her Majesty's Government's statement on 13 April,[3] which was agreed in Hong Kong; and rather than providing the basis for improving Sino-British relations it is likely to lead to even greater deterioration.

4. Even last December (see Hong Kong telegram No. 1820[2] of 5 December 1967) the Governor explained that his policy was to suppress violence, rather than interfere in instruction in Thoughts of Mao, and to avoid provocative action. Now, when atmosphere is very much easier and opportunity seems to present for a return to normality, we are asked to accept that we must move on to action which will certainly be provocative.

5. It is not clear what strength in Hong Kong would be considered satisfactory, e.g. how many Communist schools should be closed first. There will never be a really safe level. In any event to think purely in terms of our strength in Hong Kong is misleading. The underlying safeguard for Hong Kong is not our strength in the Colony, which will always be minute in relation to Chinese forces arrayed against it, but Chinese Government's current unwillingness, mainly for economic reasons, to push matters to extremes. But this agreement to live and let live requires two to make it work. If we show we are not interested by pressing for a position of illusory strength in Hong Kong, we endanger the main prop of the Colony which is Peking's tacit agreement to maintain co-existence.

6. In paragraph 8 of Hong Kong telegram No. 831 it is stated categorically, that no practicable concessions in Hong Kong will ever do any good locally (though it is later stated that no one can be absolutely sure of Communist reaction). There is no account taken here of the wider aspects of our relations with China. But even in the narrow context chosen, the assessment seems to me wrong. Surely it is

1 Repeated for information to Hong Kong.
2 Not printed.
3 See No. 98.

contradicted by the Border Agreement of November 1967, which involved concessions but brought distinct benefits for Hong Kong and was generally welcomed by public opinion there? It neglects the attitude of the Peking Government, which since December last year, has sought to restrain and control the Hong Kong Communists. If we show that the only result of Peking ending violence and controlling extremist forces in Hong Kong is that we increase our pressure on the Communists in the Colony, then we give a clinching argument to the extremists, whether in Canton, Peking or Commonwealth. We should remember that there are probably also people on the Chinese side arguing that no concessions are of any use. It is, or should be, our object to ensure that they do not take complete control. The policy now advocated by Hong Kong seems certain to worsen our general relation with China and may even risk provoking renewed violence in Hong Kong itself.

7. In telegram No. 831 paragraph 6 it is stated that while there is no objection to reasonably well conducted Communist schools, in fact there are none. The implications seem to be that we are to engage in a fight against Communist education as such and will take the necessary measures, beginning with the deregistration of Chung Wah. I must repeat my warning in telegram No. 577[4] paragraph 5 that this is a new policy which conflicts with our assurances of co-existence to Chinese and which will bring us into direct collision with Peking. It is clear that one thing Peking will insist on is the 'sacred right to study Mao's thoughts'. It is also clear from latest Hong Kong Department's report (for quarter ending 31 March) that situation in Communist schools is quietening down. It is surely in our interests to encourage this.

8. As regards likely reactions in Peking to deregistration, paragraph 9 of telegram No. 831 suggests some misunderstanding of the situation. My prediction of likely immediate effect is in paragraph 2 of telegram No. 577. I do not expect violence against this office as a result. I feel sure on the other hand that if we act in this way we shall prolong indefinitely our present impasse as regards this Mission and other British subjects in China and in the longer term prejudice any hope of restoring *modus vivendi* with China on which the continuing existence of Hong Kong must depend. It is the wider implications of the Governor's proposal of Sino-British relations that I am principally concerned with. No reference to these occurs in the telegrams under reference.

9. I am afraid that these two telegrams from Hong Kong confirm the fears expressed in my telegram 577. Hitherto I had thought that there was underlying agreement that we wished to end confrontation and restore normal relations and that our arguments were only about best means. It is now clear that we are not all agreed about the ends and that Hong Kong in fact are seeking an altogether different and tougher policy with serious implications. I should be grateful for clarification and I hope reassurance on Her Majesty's Government's policy. It is essential we should know where we stand.

10. On particular question of Chung Wah School, I maintain the recommendation in my telegram No. 577 i.e. that we should not repeat not deregister now, since this will be seen by Chinese as provocative and inconsistent with our professed intentions. I do not regard this as a concession to them but as common prudence in not going out of our way to stir up additional trouble.

4 No. 120.

No. 126

Sir D. Hopson (Peking) to Mr Stewart, 3 July 1968[1]
Tel No. 630 Priority, Confidential (FCO 21/68, FC 3/3/FC)

Your telegram No. 696[2] (not to all): Exit Visas.

As there was no news of my exit visa by 2 July, I requested an interview today with Vice Minister Lo Kuei-po but was told he was busy, so accepted one with Mr Kao Deputy Director of Consular Department instead. I spoke along the lines suggested in your telegram No. 668[2] (not to all).

2. Kao claimed that the abnormality in the question of visas was only a reflection of abnormality of our relations for which we were entirely responsible. Outstanding applications for exit visas for members of British Office, including my own, were all 'under consideration'. It was therefore slanderous for me to suggest that we were being detained here as hostages, though if we wished to put this interpretation on the position this was our own affair.

3. I said that abnormality in visa question was all on the Chinese side as the Chinese staff in London had complete freedom of movement whereas we had 12 people who wished to leave, detained in China. This is a flagrant breach of international practice. Kao had implied that this was due to political differences between our two countries. I would therefore have to report to my government that our worst suspicions were well founded in that we were being kept in China as a means of pressure, and protested strongly against this.

4. Kao said almost exactly what we expected him to say but he was noticeably on the defensive, particularly in claiming that there was no 'detention'. He stressed that visa applications were 'under consideration' and mentioned twice that my own was being 'handled' and that I would be informed when there was any news. One feature of the discussion was that although he referred in general to abnormality in our relations he never mentioned Hong Kong by name once.

5. Although my interview was at a relatively low level and one can hardly regard the outcome as 'satisfactory' nevertheless it serves its purpose and I therefore see no particular point, although no strong objection, to Chinese Chargé d'Affaires being summoned for similar treatment in London.

6. At the same time I should be grateful for confirmation that recommendations in my telegrams Nos. 558,[3] 559[2] and 560,[4] including those about publicity have been accepted.

7. Meanwhile has the position about the medical reasons for Whitney's visa been made clear to the Press?

---

1 Repeated for information to Hong Kong, Washington and POLAD Singapore.
2 Not printed.
3 No. 116.
4 No. 117.

No. 127

Sir D. Trench (Hong Kong) to Mr Thomson (Commonwealth Office)
5 July 1968[1]
Tel. No. 855 Priority, Secret (FCO 40/88, HWB 9/12/A)

Peking telegram 620:[2] Chung Wah School and policy in Hong Kong.

Rather than comment in detail on this telegram, I think it would be more helpful if I made one or two general points.

2. The telegram under reference seems to me to disclose some misunderstandings, and I am sorry if my recent telegrams on this and related subjects, ending with my telegram 832,[3] left any false impressions.

3. It was not my intention to propose any major changes in policy. Our basic attitude here since 1949 has always been to be flexible whenever (word omitted) Chinese communist susceptibilities have been involved, and to endeavour to accommodate ourselves to them so far as we could see our way to doing so. Deliberate and unnecessary provocation has always been avoided. But equally, we have always resisted firmly and to the very best of our ability attempts at grossly unreasonable or oppressive actions on their part. We have always held that to be over-pliant in such circumstances was only likely to lead to additional pressure: But that opposition, when necessary and to whatever degree was possible in the current situation, even in the face of some risk, was more likely to lead to a modification of communist attitudes. Over the years, and on numerous issues, some fairly trivial, some less so, we have I think proved the validity and effectiveness of this policy: Even though it has always been the case, as it is now, that the CPG could overpower us on any pretext whenever they liked and however conciliatory we were.

4. Last May we were faced with a deliberate assault. We could have either given way, in which case it would have been better to do so straight away, or we could have put up a token resistance and been forced into gradual subservience, or we could have followed our normal policy and subdued the Communist assault as firmly and effectively as possible having regard to the danger of CPG intervention and the exposed position of the Mission in Peking. You will recall that following Sir Arthur Galsworthy's visit in May 1967, this last course was confirmed by Ministers. It has at least temporarily paid off—whatever the reason for this may be.

5. We are still faced locally with unreasonable pressure and a continuing threat in both the long term and in the short—although the short term threat may not currently be too severe. I consider it should still be our policy to continue to oppose this threat and reduce it by whatever means lie in our power, while also continuing of course to have regard to the dangers of CPG intervention and the difficulties of Sino-British relations generally as we have always done. In my view, if we now followed any other more markedly submissive course we would then be changing our policy.

---

1 Repeated for information to Peking.
2 No. 125.
3 Not printed.

6. Naturally, the policy described requires care and the avoidance of excessive provocation and in this as in many other situations here over the years fine judgements are required as to how far one can safely go. There can be several opinions on this in any particular set of circumstances, but it is a balancing act in which we are not inexperienced.

7. It is perhaps here, I think, that my telegram 832 may have given a false impression. I continue to think that in present circumstances we can safely deregister Chung Wah, where we are on fairly strong ground, that we ought on the whole to do so, and that we can face any music there may be locally. Only the possible repercussions on the general position of the mission deters me and this is not for me to assess. I am quite ready to reconsider it if it is thought clearly necessary.

8. Apart from this, however, the measures I intend to take to hamper the Communists in their attempts to regain their former strong positions are only those of minimum prudence. Confidence here in our determination to resist must be maintained: it is our chief bulwark against a gradual or not so gradual dissolution of our position. We must try to outflank the Communists' attempts to win adherents and regain strength by improved administrative and similar methods, by better organization to meet the threat, by better public instructions and counter-propaganda and so on. When we have good grounds, such as when the law has been openly breached, we must openly oppose them, especially if the latitude otherwise given would cause public scandal or loss of confidence. In many ways we have had to be over-lenient in this already and it may not be fully understood how many and how flagrant are the abuses we have patiently put up with.

9. But the preceding telegram does not mean that I am proposing to go so far as the Peking telegram under reference seems to fear. Anything we can do must be done carefully and as discreetly as possible. I am not at present intending to close existing schools, or take any similar sort of directly hostile action without obvious grounds for it, although in fact I have ample justification for so doing. Nor do I mind the peaceful propagation of the thoughts of Mao per se but I do object to standing aside and doing nothing to inhibit, even in the rare cases where I can do so, the spread of a system which concentrates on the training of youth in hatred and violence. Nor could I readily acquiesce in any policy of going substantially further passively to allow them to dominate us, unless and until this becomes our considered policy.

10. Finally, the Chargé can be assured that the situation of the Mission is very much in my mind at all times, and whatever I can do to help I certainly will.

No. 128

Sir D. Hopson (Peking) to Mr Stewart, 5 July 1968[1]
Tel No. 637 Priority, Confidential (FCO 21/68, FC 3/3/FC)

Berne telegram No. 124:[2] Exit Visas Peking.

I must emphasise that there is no (repeat no) possibility of a joint approach by all or the majority of this spineless corps. Nearly all Ambassadors are away on holiday

1 Repeated for information to Berne.
2 Not printed.

and in any case there has never been the faintest possibility of organizing such a joint demarche on any subject whatever at this post. Perhaps it could be pointed out to the Swiss Government that although the approaches which we are suggesting would be individual, they would we hope be carried out by several Governments at about the same time. The Swiss would therefore not be making themselves conspicuous. As regards publicity, I have never contemplated that any publicity whatever would be given, at any rate at this stage, to the fact that diplomatic representations are being made by other Governments. Any publicity should be confined to stating the facts of our case and making appropriate comments.

2. I was surprised to see paragraph 2 of Berne telegram under reference about Rossetti's instructions. I know for certain that he never attempted to carry them out. He was in fact notorious for forbidding his staff to have any contact with us during the weeks after the attack on this Mission. He is at present on holiday.

No. 129

Sir D. Hopson (Peking) Mr Stewart, 8 July 1968[1]
Tel. No. 648 Priority, Secret (FCO 40/88, HWB 9/12/A)

Hong Kong telegram No. 855:[2] Policy in Hong Kong.

I am grateful for this clarification. I am, however, sorry to see no reference in this telegram to the ending of the confrontation or the measures which might lead to this or at least explore its possibility. In view of this and the clear statements in Hong Kong telegram No. 832,[3] I should like to repeat my request for clarification from you on Her Majesty's Government's policy: in particular are we seeking to get Sino-British relations back to normal understanding this to be the situation obtaining in April 1967? Do we wish to end confrontation? Are we prepared to consider the possibility of measures in Hong Kong which could lead to this improvement?

2. I am also grateful for the Governor's expression of concern for the fate of this mission. While this is naturally much in my mind, I do not wish it to be thought that we here argue only for our own skins. In fact I find our personal involvement a rather inhibiting factor. The situation of other British subjects here, not only the appalling case of Grey and those held on espionage charges, but also the [?grp. omitted] to expose the British community in Shanghai, gives us in this mission much concern. Take also the less tangible but very important wider aspects of our relations with China, not only political but also commercial. Our export trade has suffered and is bound to continue to suffer while present circumstances persist. To represent the equation solely in terms of this Mission balanced against Hong Kong may be misleading.

---

1 Repeated for information Priority to Hong Kong.
2 No. 127.
3 Not printed.

No. 130

Sir D. Trench (Hong Kong) to Mr Thomson (Commonwealth Office)
12 July 1968
Tel. No. 884 Priority, Secret (FCO 40/88, HWB 9/12/A)

Peking telegram No. 648:[1] Policy in Hong Kong.

I suggest the main features of the current phase of confrontation are:

(*a*) The CPG at a high level have already instructed influential local communist leaders to drop violence and concentrate on broadening the base of communist support. This attempt to win over adherents is of course a policy of many years standing and is obviously one which will never be abandoned. To this limited extent we are already back to normal. With confrontation in Hong Kong largely over for the time being but the propaganda attack is more overt and more bitterly prosecuted than pre-1967, and

(*b*) Whatever we do, active confrontation could start up again at any time if the balance of influence within the CPG shifts.

(*c*) The policy in (*a*) has generally speaking been successfully imposed and, partly as a result, morale in labour circles particularly is low: but there remains a hard core of the militantly minded. This militant hard core will always seek to make trouble, and are certainly not interested in any accommodation with us except wholly on their own terms. The authority of the moderate leaders in the CPG and here is not so complete that they can entirely disclaim the militants. They cannot avoid some bending to militant views, nor avoid giving them some ostensible support. It is indeed arguable that the communist leadership here is at present really quite glad to see us occasionally take a firm line with these people.

(*d*) The present poor state of Sino-British relations, with all the ill-effects which flow therefrom, result essentially from a compound of Chinese feelings over lack of success in Hong Kong; the generally over-excited emotional atmosphere in China; the necessity to tar us with the brush of our American connections; and the ritual need to be both anti-Colonial and anti-Capitalist.

(*e*) As far as Hong Kong is concerned, the joker in the pack is (*b*) this is what we must guard ourselves against, and be in a better position to meet if it happens.

2. Where in this mixture do further substantial concessions on Hong Kong's part, or a search here for measures to end confrontation, come in? Such measures could not help to modify the general state of mind of the Chinese nor undo the events of last year. We cannot expect to persuade local communists to stop or substantially mute their attempts to gain adherents and strengthen their influence: concessions would only help them in this. Neither the militants here nor the moderates will ever be persuaded to be anything but basically hostile towards us. Concessionary moves would not be helping the communist leadership to enforce their present tactic of avoiding militancy, which would only be encouraged by prospects of 'victory'.

3. Possibly a highly concessionary attitude might strengthen the hands of the moderates in the CPG and thus avoid the hypothetical eventuality of a change in

---

1 No. 129.

policy leading to militancy again (the paragraph 1(*b*) situation). But it is just as arguable that we would only be providing ammunition for the militants who would claim that pressure had brought results. If this occurred we would have weakened our position for no gain, and irretrievably. Unless the benefits to be obtained are very certain, therefore, I cannot see much sense in risking it.

4. In all the above I am referring to major concessions and their effect in Hong Kong. Small concessions, if not too damaging to public confidence and to our position, generally, can sometimes help to mute the stridency of the communists by cutting the ground from under them. Such concessions can always be cautiously attempted to test reactions and to match either concessions on their part or tougher action by us in some other sphere, when such action is necessary. The search for suitable minor concessions has continuously engaged our attentions. It is however an ad hoc business, in which day-to-day changes of situation play a considerable part. The extent to which they can be comprehensively planned is limited.

5. But minor concessions, while they have their place here are undeniably unlikely to result in any substantial improvement in Sino-British relations generally. In any case, the scope for real improvement seems small, whatever we do. As mentioned in paragraph 1(*d*), we are unalterably opposed on several basic issues and indeed the Chinese may well not care very much what their general relations with the UK are.

6. Would major concessions here in Hong Kong, then, have this last effect? Perhaps: if we virtually surrendered our authority unconditionally. I do not believe anything much less would do, nor do I think that even this would be any guarantee of proper behaviour in the future. Having squeezed us through the Mission and British subjects successfully once, they would always be tempted to try again for any new purpose that suited them. I therefore believe our best hope lies in trying to find means of persuading them that, in the long run, it is not advantageous to continue to behave like yahoos: and that not until this lesson has been learnt will there be any change on them behaving decently in the long term. There must be elements in the CPG who feel the same way. I do not doubt also that the fortitude of the Mission staff has in itself partly taught this lesson, that they are embarrassed by what they did and would like to undo it if they knew how without too much loss of face; 'demands' in Hong Kong now being in truth partly designed to cover their embarrassment. If we can find ways to drive home the lesson that ill behaviour does not pay by means e.g. of an effective diplomatic offensive of the kind now contemplated, by publicity, or by any other similar means we can think of—and preferably even more telling ones—then, and only then, do we have a chance of being able to establish a relationship of reasonable respect, which is the only kind that can perhaps endure.

No. 131

Sir D. Hopson (Peking) to Mr Stewart, 18 July 1968[1]
Tel. No. 671 Priority, Secret (FCO 21/68, FC 3/3)

Hong Kong telegram No. 884:[2] British Policy toward China.

I think it might assist to set out the benefits we could expect to follow from an ending of 'confrontation'. I use confrontation here to mean the specially bad relations obtaining since May 1967. Basic Chinese hostility, attempts to undermine our position and gain adherents will, as Governor says remain permanent features, but they do not amount to confrontation within terms of this debate.

2. The benefits we could expect are:

(*a*) better treatment generally of British subjects in China, including the release of Grey;

(*b*) normal treatment, in particular over visas, for this mission;

(*c*) improved opportunity for our export trade and reasonable safety for British businessmen visiting this country;

(*d*) reduced tension on Hong Kong Border and a better political atmosphere in Hong Kong.

We could not of course expect Sino-British relations to be good and Chinese hostility would remain but it would not be expressed in the forms it has taken over the past year. Within these limits the scope for improvement is considerable.

3. It should, I think, be our object to achieve this improvement if we can do so without excessive cost. On Chinese side, as para 6, of telegram under reference points out, there is no doubt but that Chinese would like to get off the hook if they knew how to do so without too much loss of face. Our object therefore should be to facilitate this disengagement by showing that we are willing to draw a line across the book and by offering the makings of the face-saving victory they will require.

4. The difficult questions arise when we consider the sort of concessions we might be prepared to make in hope of achieving this. It is axiomatic that we should avoid, whenever we can, acts likely to appear provocative to the Chinese or make their climb-down more difficult. But the nub of the problem is the convicted prisoners and key concession would be the release of some at least before conclusion of their terms. There are two questions to ask about concessions:

(*a*) Will they do any good? And

(*b*) Can we afford them?

On (*a*), it is possible to argue, as telegram under reference does in para 3, that concessions will clearly strengthen the militants on the Chinese side by allowing them to argue that pressure brings dividends. This, however, is strictly an argument against any concession, e.g. release of detainees, which I think centre of Governor's position. For example the telegram states in paragraph 6 that concessions might do some good but that they would have to be very large ones and paragraph 4 allows that minor concessions are supervening this, by cutting ground from under militants'

1 Repeated for information Priority to Hong Kong.
2 No. 130.

feet. Moreover, I think the argument neglects that militants in Hong Kong have suffered open defeat in their policy of violence and since December 1967 under CPG control. Concessions now several months after the abandonment of violence would strengthen the hand of those responsible for December directive against violence. Conversely, refusal of any conciliatory gestures may only weaken these moderates by allowing militants to argue that there is nothing to lose by a resumption of tough line in Hong Kong. Our experience so far e.g. the Border Agreement, visits to Grey, lifting of movement restrictions in London last November (even to more limited extent lifting of exit visas requirement in April) suggest that carefully judged concessions do bring certain dividends. There is little doubt for example the release of news workers in Hong Kong would bring release of Grey.

5. The key question therefore is (*b*) whether we can afford relevant concessions. This will always be a difficult decision and timing will be one factor. I would not, for example, advocate any earlier release of prisoners until we have had time to see effects of diplomatic and publicity campaign (see paragraph 7 below) but I hope we shall examine possibilities of an earlier release of some prisoners, say at the end of 1968, most carefully. We ought to ask whether release at that time, after some (almost two thirds) of convicted prisoners have served their full terms, and a year after violence was renounced, would very much injure prestige of Hong Kong Government.

6. We must also reflect that refusal of any substantial concessions may well mean prolongation of the present bad relations, with their effects, for a number of years. The Chinese may let matter drop before 1974 but that is date all confrontation prisoners will be released and therefore our terminal date. Grey could expect to remain in confinement at least until September 1969 perhaps longer until all news workers have been released. The above assumes that there will be no new deterioration and no arrests in the meantime, which will always be more likely while confrontation persists.

7. As regards diplomatic and publicity campaign we must certainly give this all the backing we can but we should not be too hopeful that it will solve the problem of itself. The means at our disposal are limited and in present circumstances Chinese are probably even less sensitive than usual to this kind of attack. The situation of this mission might be improved thereby but other sectors, e.g. Grey, trade relations etc. are unlikely to derive benefit unless there is some gesture in Hong Kong.

No. 132

Mr Stewart to HM Representatives Overseas, 23 July 1968[1]
Tel No. 373 Priority, Confidential (FCO 21/68, FC 3/3)

My telegram No. 358[2] to Berne: British Mission in Peking.
You should now approach the Government to which you are accredited at the

---

1 Addressed to Berne, Sofia, Budapest, Bucharest, Prague, Warsaw, Copenhagen, The Hague, Helsinki, Oslo, Paris, Stockholm, Belgrade, Cairo, Colombo, Kabul, Kathmandu, Delhi, Rawalpindi, Kampala, Nairobi, Lusaka, Rabat, Vientiane, Khartoum, and Mogadishu. Repeated for information to Peking, Hong Kong, Dar-Es-Salaam, Washington and Moscow, and Saving to Baghdad
2 Not printed.

highest level readily accessible to you and ask them to intervene with the Chinese on behalf of our mission in Peking. Your representations should take the form proposed in paragraph 2 and 3 of the telegram under reference. You should leave a *bout de papier* giving background, and in this you should make it clear that we regard all the exit visas applied for as overdue (details of dates of applications are in my immediately following telegram).[3] Applications to which we attach particular importance include those of the commercial counsellor made three months ago and the Chargé d'Affaires who applied on 22 June to leave on 1 July. For the Chinese to claim as they have done to our Mission that the visas are 'under consideration' and are not therefore being withheld is disingenuous.

2. You have discretion to leave an aide memoire setting out your substantive representations in whatever form you consider likely to be most effective, if you think this desirable for ensuring that subsequent action with the Chinese is on the right lines. On the whole however we would prefer the Chinese not to be presented with a number of nearly identical pieces of paper. We think that varied approaches to them, which had a greater appearance of spontaneity, might be better.

3. The Chinese do not claim to be beyond the diplomatic pale. They claim to behave correctly themselves and are ready to invoke diplomatic rules when it suits them, e.g. last year against the Indonesians, the Indians, and the Burmese: and even against ourselves in respect of our special travel restrictions of last August. (Supplementary material is in my second immediately following telegram).[3] The Chinese Foreign Ministry have also denied in two recent interviews with our mission that they detain diplomats.

4. As Governments may be reluctant to engage in what might appear to be a joint demarche in Peking, you should say that in our view it might be preferable to summon Chinese representatives in the capital, but this is of course a matter for Governments themselves to decide.

5. You should inform the Government to which you are accredited that we are in general approaching all Governments with which we and the Chinese are in diplomatic relations but we should prefer that any consultation should be carried out directly between Governments and not through us as an intermediary. If this seems useful, you may say that we thought it might be appropriate because of their very strained relations with the Chinese to ask the Russians to intervene, but that we have informed them about the action taken with other Governments. (We are not in fact taking action in Ulan Bator and Algiers. Action may be delayed for local reasons in Baghdad and Prague. In the case of Tanzania, we hope to use Mr Malcolm MacDonald as an intermediary with President Nyerere in about ten days time).

6. You should assure the Government to which you are accredited that there will be no, repeat no, publicity about our approach to them or about the reactions to our request. You should add, however, that if knowledge of our general diplomatic offensive became public we would merely confirm that we had informed and sought the co-operation of certain Governments in this matter. You may also say that we may initiate some limited general publicity about the plight of the Mission to coincide with this exercise.[4]

3 Not printed.
4 In Tel. No. 383 to Berne and certain other posts, dated 29 July, this diplomatic offensive was suspended in light of reports from the Chinese Ministry of Foreign Affairs that all outstanding applications for exit visas were to be issued (FCO 21/69).

No. 133

Sir D. Trench (Hong Kong) to Mr Thomson (Commonwealth Office)
24 July 1968[1]
Tel. No. 925 Priority, Secret (FCO 21/69, FC 3/3/G)

Peking telegrams 585 and 586:[2] Sanctions against China.

I regret the time it has taken, but we have been anxious to examine the possibilities suggested by Peking in paragraph (*e*) of telegram 586 as carefully as we could.

2. It would be possible to do very little in Hong Kong against Chinese trade without legislation. Moral pressure upon individual firms is unlikely to achieve much in this free competitive society.

3. Legislation would have to be either specifically directed against China or non-discriminatory. If it were specifically directed against China on trade matters, it could obviously be made very effective but dependent as we are on cheap Chinese foodstuffs (50% of our imports from China are of food) and to a lesser extent water, the risks of retaliation against Hong Kong by China in the face of even minor economic restrictions would be quite unacceptable.

4. If legislation were non-discriminatory it would be relatively ineffective against China depending upon the precise methods used and it would be much resented by all non-communist enterprises. I have been unable to identify any measure which would be sufficiently effective against Chinese trade and earnings to justify the outcry which would arise from non-communist firms and the damage to Hong Kong's prosperity.

5. As regards use of external sterling, it would be technically possible to refuse Bank of China, Hong Kong permission to convert its resident sterling into external sterling. If this were effective, it would destroy China's incentive to supply Hong Kong. But it could in any case be substantially circumvented, probably to our detriment, by changes in Chinese trading practices.

6. I regret therefore, that there appear to be no economic measures or sanctions against China that I can recommend to be taken in Hong Kong.

1 Repeated for information to Peking.
2 No. 121 and not printed respectively.

No. 134

Mr Stewart to Sir D. Hopson (Peking), 26 July 1968
Tel. No. 769 Priority, Confidential (FCO 21/69, FC 3/3/G)

Personal for Hopson from Murray.

Sino-British Relations.

Now that the diplomatic offensive is under way, we must try to secure the approval of Ministers for the principles which should guide our immediate dealings with the Chinese—and incidentally reply to the questions in your telegram No. 648[1] [of 8 July].

1 No. 129.

2. In doing so, we shall of course give full weight to the case which you have argued in recent correspondence, the main elements of which I take to be broadly these:

(*a*) We cannot hope to move the Chinese to a more reasonable position over the whole field of Sino-British relations if we simply set the problem of Hong Kong aside.

(*b*) If our position in Hong Kong is to be tolerable to us, there must be some tacitly agreed *modus vivendi* with the Chinese Government.

(*c*) There are certain particularly sensitive areas where the limits of possible tacit agreement on the *modus vivendi* are narrow, notably education and the Press.

(*d*) If, in attempts to reduce the mischief-making potential of the local Communists, we go beyond these limits, we risk creating more problems than we solve.

(*e*) The Chinese leaders must see themselves as having gone some way on their side towards re-establishing a *modus vivendi* after last year's troubles, and therefore expect positive steps on our side.

(*f*) We must be seen to be seeking ways of re-establishing a *modus vivendi*. Otherwise we risk not merely stalemate, but a further deterioration in Sino-British relations.

(*g*) We should not be too pessimistic of our prospects of success, since some features of recent Chinese policy are most readily explicable on the basis that the Chinese are prepared to move towards a *modus vivendi*.

(*h*) The key issue is prisoners.

3. In our recommendation we shall be expected to take account of possible evolution of events inside China. The old *modus vivendi* in Hong Kong was upset not by action by us, but by the overspill of the Cultural Revolution. We shall therefore have to argue whether it is now time to make a determined effort towards a *modus vivendi*, and whether conditions for a 'settlement' are likely to improve or deteriorate.

4. While there seem bound to be differences of opinion here about the definition of principles and about timing, I am sure that there will be complete agreement that the prisoners are the key issue. I am much relieved that the Governor now considers it feasible to begin releasing detainees, and I hope that the process will continue. But this in itself will not be enough. The central issue to which we shall direct the attention of Ministers is whether, and if so when, some acts of clemency in respect of convicted prisoners will be feasible (I know that you consider that the Governor may be over-anxious about the effects of clemency on public opinion in Hong Kong, and I was particularly impressed by Whitney's arguments on this aspect. But you will understand that on an issue of this kind it is not easy to have the man with local executive responsibility over-ruled).

5. We were very much interested by the presentation of the argument in the notes attached to Cradock's manuscript letter of 16 July to Denson.[2] However, Peter Wilkinson, with whom I have fully discussed all this, suggest[s] that it might be better not to put it in the form of a despatch, which would inevitably have wide distribution. In the form of a letter it would however very usefully reinforce our brief for some fairly delicate manoeuvres here without the risk of anyone feeling obliged to take up an entrenched position.[3]

---

2 Not printed.
3 See No. 135.

No. 135

Letter from Sir D. Hopson (Peking) to Mr Wilkinson, 30 July 1968
Confidential (FCO 21/69, FC 3/3/G)

Dear Peter,

In accordance with the advice tendered in Murray's very helpful telegram No. 769[1] of 26 July, I enclose in the form of memorandum (I am sending six extra copies separately to Murray for internal use if necessary), our analysis of the prospects for Sino-British relations. We have all worked hard at this and, though it was drafted before the recent breakthrough on visas, I think the arguments are still valid and I would not want to change anything.

2. I doubt if there is any single, simple explanation of why the Chinese have suddenly decided to let us out—providing, of course, that they do, as I think they will. I think that first and foremost the Governor's action in beginning to release detainees in Hong Kong may have provided the Chinese with the occasion to show us that all this is the kind of gesture they want, in the hope of getting more. Secondly I believe they must have got wind of our diplomatic and publicity campaign. (I had always hoped that it might work out like this and for that reason had not kept it a closely-guarded secret here). The impending visit of the Pakistan Foreign Minister at the end of this week may have stimulated the Chinese to regularise the position before his arrival.

3. If all goes smoothly and we get out, I hope the Governor will respond by accelerating the rate of release of detainees. For once it will be the Chinese who have taken the initiative, and we who shall be responding. If he could manage say as many as ten to twenty in one fell swoop, or in fairly rapid succession, I am sure this would be interpreted by the Chinese as a conciliatory response on our part and might produce further dividends for British subjects in China e.g. exit visas for our Shanghai bankers, release of some of those under arrest, and perhaps even something for Grey. I am, also telegraphing about this suggestion.

Yours ever,
DONALD

ENCLOSURE IN No. 135

Sino/British Relations: The Prospects

On the 13th of April this year on instructions I communicated to the Chinese Foreign Ministry an oral statement by HMG on Sino-British relations.[2] This statement declared that HMG 'attach much importance to bringing about an early improvement in Sino-British relations, and recognise the importance of Hong Kong in this context.' This memorandum explores some of the implications of this proposition as seen from this post.

1 No. 134.
2 No. 98.

Present State of Sino-British Relations

2. The past year has brought relations between Britain and China to their lowest point since we embarked on regular intercourse with the present Chinese Government. Any of the larger objectives we set ourselves in establishing relations with Communist China are inevitably denied. We have no chance of representing to the Chinese a more balanced view on world political issues. At a time when a solution of the Vietnam conflict is at least conceivable, and our Co-Chairmanship of the Geneva Conference may assume a new relevance, we are cut off from any access to Chinese leaders. It is true that the Cultural Revolution and the current intransigence of the Chinese Government would probably make such contacts rare and unrewarding in any event; but as a result of our dispute with the Chinese we suffer an additional and basic disability. If any opportunity for diplomacy were to occur we certainly could not seize it. This damage has also taken more tangible forms affecting our interests. The volume of British exports to China will fall sharply this year and this is attributable in part at least to the events of the past year. No British businessman is entirely safe visiting this country. Cultural exchanges between the two countries are non-existent. British subjects are arrested or detained in China: not only Mr Grey of Reuters, now under solitary confinement for a year, but British merchant navy officers taken from their ships, and the British community in Shanghai, denied permission to leave and living under harassment and fear. Virtually all British subjects in this country are under some form of restraint, and we are unable to exercise the most basic consular functions for their protection. Meanwhile we in this Mission, operating from makeshift quarters in what was my house, beside the shell of our former Chancery building, exist in a sort of diplomatic limbo. We are fed and housed and no longer particularly harassed in our daily lives, but we are (and have been for over a year) excluded from any official Chinese function, and are denied exit visas or even permission to move outside Peking. Thus we approach the end of our first year of detention as political hostages. In Hong Kong violence has ceased and tension both in the colony and along the frontier has receded, but the Communists continue to show an attitude of open and militant hostility towards the Hong Kong Government.

Origins of the Crisis

3. Before proceeding to explore possible ways and means of attaining that 'early improvement' in Sino-British relations, which we have told the Chinese we desire, it would be salutary to ask ourselves why and how they have reached their present pass. This phase in our relations is sometimes described as 'confrontation', which is a not inconvenient term, providing we realise that there will always be, even at the best of times, a persisting clash of interests between Peking and Hong Kong, as the former strives to improve its position within the colony at our expense.

It is most unlikely that in the foreseeable future our relations with China will ever be characterised as 'good'. 'Confrontation' should, therefore, be understood in this paper to mean the state of abnormal tension in our relations which has obtained since May, 1967.

4. The origins of this situation do not require detailed rehearsal. Last summer during a particularly violent phase of the Cultural Revolution the Chinese Government, no doubt encouraged by their earlier success in humiliating the

Portuguese in Macao and possibly led on by their extremist supporters in Canton and Hong Kong, gave open backing for a communist campaign of demonstrations and violence designed to intimidate the Hong Kong Government. Though the campaign failed, thanks to the firmness and flexibility of the Hong Kong Government, and violence was called off last December, confrontation continued and the various Chinese demands addressed to the Hong Kong Government have not been withdrawn or allowed to lapse. The dispute now centres around the communist prisoners (some 700 in all) held as a result of last year's disturbances, whom the Chinese Government wish to see released. Exchanges between the British and Chinese Governments in March and April have not led to any progress. The present state of our relations is the result.

Will Confrontation End of Itself?

5. It is important here to dispose of the theory that confrontation is a merely temporary aberration, a reflection of the more violent phase of the Cultural Revolution, and that as more restrained counsels come to prevail among Chinese leaders we may expect a return to the comparatively quiet co-existence which characterised Hong Kong's and therefore Britain's relations with China in the late 1950s and early 1960s. This theory is reassuring but mistaken. It ignores the fact that more than six months after the communists called off their campaign of violence in Hong Kong, Sino-British relations have not in fact improved to any significant degree. I have no doubt that China's policy towards Hong Kong last year was partly the result of extremist counsels prevailing during the turmoil of the Cultural Revolution. It is certainly true that much of this turmoil appears to have ended and that in recent months the Chinese have been at some pains to restore their badly damaged reputation in international diplomacy. If, therefore, confrontation were a purely temporary aberration, we could expect by this time to be able to point to specific improvements in Sino-British relations which had come about with the passage of time. This is not the case. Even such small concessions as the Chinese have made (for example on the question of visas for some junior members of the staff of this Mission, or the Hong Kong border agreement of November 1967) have come only in return for concessions from our side.

6. Furthermore, we have had it officially and explicitly from the Chinese, at many interviews during the past months, that there can be no 'normalisation' of Sino-British relations so long as the question of Hong Kong is left on one side. While careful not to dissent from the aim of improving relations between Britain and China, they have repeatedly said that they are waiting for concrete actions from us in Hong Kong as an earnest of our good intentions. Nor must we overlook the fact that the Chinese Government have taken up a public stand on confrontation which they can hardly abandon without great loss of face both at home and abroad.

They are smarting from the defeat they sustained after the failure of the communist campaign of violence in 1967. Moreover they may well still have some difficulty controlling their Hong Kong supporters. In present circumstances, therefore, unless they are provided with some device that will allow them to claim, however implausibly, that their demands in Hong Kong have been satisfied, the Chinese cannot be expected to drop their confrontation policy. We must also remember that while this situation persists there is continuing danger that some incident, whether fortuitous or deliberately provoked, may lead to a renewal of violence in Hong Kong, which would not only prevent an improvement in Sino-British relations but would lead to a further deterioration.

Chinese Attitude and Objectives.

7. At this juncture in the argument it would be useful to make some estimate of Chinese attitudes and objectives. Are the Chinese authorities interested in co-existence, or the end of confrontation on terms we might consider tolerable? What would they expect to get out of it? It would be a mistake to dismiss China in its present state as a kind of mad giant, to conclude from the turmoil in Canton and the corpses floating down the Pearl River that any reasonable converse is possible, that all we can do is, therefore, to strengthen our defences, political and military, in Hong Kong, and add a prayer for the British subjects in China. In fact a striking feature about the trouble even last year is that much more could have been done by Peking to make our position difficult or impossible in Hong Kong, e.g. no arms were sent in and the bomb campaign was obviously disapproved of. Since then the wish of the Chinese Government to get back to some sort of co-existence has been evident from e.g. the calling off of violence, the reduction and threatened withdrawal of financial support for Hong Kong communists on strike, the maintenance of order on the frontier, the control shown recently over reinstatement delegations when they threatened to become disorderly. All this proves a positive wish to keep the tension down and live and let live. It is all done quite naturally from selfish motives. China's large foreign exchange earnings in Hong Kong are a vitally important factor for her foreign trade plan—particularly important now after the disruption in her exports caused by the Cultural Revolution and with the prospect of a poor harvest this year. Economically, China has a vested interest in a considerable degree of stability in Hong Kong.

8. It is therefore unrealistic to argue that no kind of dialogue is possible with the Chinese. Nevertheless it may still be said that the Chinese terms for a settlement would be extravagant and unacceptable, that while eschewing violence they are bent on achieving a Macao-like situation in Hong Kong by means of quiet pressure on British subjects in China and that they will not settle for less. Although it is impossible to be quite sure of Chinese objectives, I greatly doubt whether this is the case. Chinese behaviour points rather to the need to emerge from the struggle with something to their credit, rather than to the theory that they are conducting an all-out offensive for a success along the line of Macao. The abandonment of violence, the reduction of financial support for strikers and the concentration on the question of prisoners all suggest an essentially defensive tactic. Their need to rebuild a following in Hong Kong and their current united-front tactics point to the same conclusion. We have to bear in mind the immense loss of face the Chinese have already suffered in having to call off the campaign of violence and admit that the struggle in Hong Kong cannot be won in the immediate future.

Their statement to us in March and April[1] seem to be requests in disguised form for some suitable response on our part. They have not asked for their demands of 1967[2] to be fulfilled, but for a 'reply' and have indicated that they expect 'con-

---

1 See Nos. 83 and 99.
2 See No 1, note 2.

crete actions' in Hong Kong as an earnest of our good intentions. We have also had through unofficial channels a strong hint that the Chinese Government do not seek another Macao and realise that that is out of the question. It is true that the Chinese authorities have rejected our proposals of immediate release to China, i.e. deportation, of the confrontation prisoners, and it may be argued that this indicates that they are uninterested in a settlement. But deportation to China (without permission to return) of a large number of Hong Kong citizens who have been active in their cause would almost certainly be seen by Peking as a further and public defeat rather than the concession they need to get themselves off the hook. We have offered them so far nothing they will regard as meaningful. To sum up, the evidence may not be conclusive but it points strongly to the possibility of a settlement on tolerable terms. On the most gloomy interpretation there is a considerable area of uncertainty which it would seem greatly in our interests to explore in order to determine the price of a settlement.

What Can Be Done? External Pressure on the Chinese Government

9. Given that both we and the Chinese Government seem to have an interest in bringing confrontation to an end, how can this be achieved? The Chinese, in an attempt to extract the best possible price from us, try to exert pressure by holding the staff of this Mission (and some other British subjects) as hostages. Have we any means of countering this blackmail? We are currently planning to bring various pressures on the Chinese Government, e.g. by diplomacy and publicity, possibly also in the economic field, to persuade them to conform to more civilised standards of behaviour. We must recognise, however, that the means at our disposal are limited and that the Chinese are less sensitive than most Governments to these types of pressure. Moreover it is clear for the reasons set out earlier in this paper that these pressures of themselves are unlikely to restore Sino-British relations to normal, though they may perhaps help to bring about an improvement in the limited sector, e.g. treatment of this Mission. There is also the question of retaliatory action. We could, if necessary, control the exit of members of the Chinese Office in London by re-imposing the exit visa requirement. But this would be a backward step rather than the de-escalation we need. Moreover experience with the Chinese over the last year has shown that this kind of retaliation would only be counter-productive. It would almost certainly lead to a further tightening of the screw here, and in this kind of competition the Chinese, by the nature of their political system and moral attitude, will always win. Such retaliatory measures would, therefore, at any rate in present circumstances merely serve to prolong the argument and delay a solution. In any case it is important from the point of view of publicity that we should present, in contrast to the Chinese, a blamelessly liberal image to world opinion.

Avoidance of Further Friction If Possible

10. What other means have we at our disposal? It is always unpleasant, and usually unwise to surrender, or even appear to surrender, to blackmail. As I have stated earlier the Chinese, while not seeking another Macao, will try to get as good a price as they can (in terms of concessions in Hong Kong) for ending confrontation and normalising our relations.

On the other hand, it is also true that they have their own reasons for wanting a settlement, but need a face-saving gesture before they can afford to climb down. Before we investigate this possibility, however, I must mention what is an obvious pre-requisite to moving towards an accommodation with the Chinese: the avoidance meanwhile, as far as this is consistent with security or other vital interests, of any action in Hong Kong likely to provoke the Chinese, feed their distrust of our intentions, or make it more difficult for them to appear to be taking a soft line with us. I wish to emphasise the importance of this, because there has been some suggestion recently that what we must aim at is not a return to pre-confrontation co-existence, but something more, namely the attainment of a position of greater strength in the colony, which would improve our defences against the next communist attack. This seems to be a dangerously unrealistic course which disregards the hard facts of our situation in Hong Kong, quite apart from jeopardising any chance of improving Sino-British relations. The main condition for our continued control of Hong Kong is no longer our own strength, which nowadays will always be minute in relation to the Chinese forces arrayed against it, but Peking's tacit agreement, largely for economic reasons, to co-exist. If, by seeking to increase our own strength at all costs, we make it less worthwhile for Peking to maintain their co-existence, we do ourselves more harm than good. Moreover, if we show that the only effect of Peking exercising control and restraint over the local communists is that we not only fail to move towards settlement, but even adopt tougher measures, then we provide a clinching argument for extremists, whom we may be sure exist, whether in Peking, Canton or Hong Kong. The line we have taken hitherto, that we will not tolerate violence and disorder in the colony, is one which I think is understood and broadly accepted in Peking. If, however, we go on from there to attempt to cut down on communist positions, giving the impression that, for example, we are attacking communist education as such, then we endanger the basis of our co-existence and risk a new and more violent confrontation. Obviously we have no intention of assisting the communists in their present state of convalescence in Hong Kong, but there is a great difference between that and measures which will seem to Peking as signalling an offensive on our side.

11. This need to co-exist means not only taking account of Chinese sensitivities but recognising that they have become much sharper than two or three years ago. Much has happened since then—the Cultural Revolution, communist success in Macao, confrontation in Hong Kong, setbacks to Chinese policy over Vietnam—and it is no longer possible to argue, in defence of a course, that it was followed two or three years ago without trouble. This attention to Chinese sensitivities is not to be regarded as a surrender, rather as the adjustment to a powerful neighbour which ordinary prudence would dictate.

Moves to End Confrontation: The Negative Argument

12. Is it possible to go beyond this negative policy of avoiding further friction and to take positive steps to end confrontation? Is there a gesture which we can concede to the Chinese in order to enable them to climb down without losing too much face but without compromising our essential interests? At this point it may seem reasonable to object that any worthwhile concessions to the Chinese would be dangerous, in that it would encourage extremists to ask for more and undermine our position in Hong Kong.

The argument might run that the release of confrontation prisoners (which would probably have to be the nub of any settlement) would be a fatal blow to public confidence and the prestige of the Hong Kong Government and would encourage the communists to make new and more outrageous demands leading eventually to humiliation on the Macao pattern. The communists, it might be agreed, have shown no real readiness to reach a settlement. Alternatively, if they really do want one, we have only to sit tight and wait for them to climb down. Our only course therefore is, while avoiding provocation, to maintain a firm front to Chinese pressure, to make no discrimination in favour of communist prisoners and to let them serve their term. The majority would be released in the normal way in 1968 and 1969 (though some 80 to 90 will remain in prison after that date, some until 1974). Until then the corresponding injuries to Sino-British relations in terms of detention of British subjects and decrease in British exports to China will have to be reluctantly accepted as a necessary evil. We should of course bring all possible external pressure on the Chinese, e.g. by diplomacy, publicity and economic measures to compel them to conform to more civilised standards. But there should be no concessions in Hong Kong.

13. This argument has at first sight a certain force, though I think that on examination it proves open to overriding objections. In the first place it assumes that any concessions to the Chinese are likely to lead only to further demands and that they will not stop short of a Macao situation. I think this is a false assumption for the reasons given in paragraph 8 above and that, while communist intentions are by no means entirely clear, the balance of evidence suggests that they would favour a settlement in terms we might accept, or at the worst that there is sufficient uncertainty to justify exploration on our part. Nor has our experience over the last year been that meeting Chinese terms has always led to new demands. So far when we have come to an agreement with them the bargain has usually been honoured (e.g. the visit to Grey). These arguments also assume that the release of communist prisoners would gravely injure public morale in Hong Kong. With respect, I wonder if this is a reasonable assumption. Surely it is just as arguable that public opinion is worried at the continuation of confrontation and would welcome acts indicating a return to normality? The border agreement of November 1967 involved concessions to the communists but brought considerable benefits and was broadly welcomed by Hong Kong opinion. Special prison visits in April this year were adroitly presented as a sign of diminishing tension. The press reaction in Hong Kong from both right and left to the recent release of four detainees has been encouraging (quite apart from the possibility that it produced four exit visas for this Mission). The release of prisoners more than a year after the crisis and seven months after violence ended, at a time when the Hong Kong Government is under no great pressure, might be seen by the people of Hong Kong and by British opinion as an act of statesmanship coming from strength. Communist propaganda would, no doubt, claim a victory (this would be an essential part of the exercise) but it would be wrong to conclude that we would thereby have suffered a real defeat. If tension were reduced in Hong Kong and there were consequential improvements in Sino-British relations we should in fact have made important gains.

14. The policy implied in the argument in paragraph 12 seems to me to be one of great pessimism, for which a heavy price, human, political and perhaps economic, would have to be paid probably over several years. It rejects at the outset the possibility of continued detention for British subjects in China and abandons hope of restoring Sino-British relations even to anything like their old level. Nor, I believe

would such a policy necessarily protect Hong Kong against further communist disturbances. The failure to make the gestures needed to end confrontation might sooner or later provoke further unrest, which as the Governor has recently stated is ever a latent threat. Further unrest could mean further arrests. It would not then be just a question of sitting tight until 1970, or 1971 or 1974. We would have the makings of a self-perpetuating crisis. Meanwhile for the reasons given in paragraph 9 above, it would be unrealistic to expect that external pressures e.g. by diplomacy, publicity or economic measures (if we can find any) will of themselves restore Sino/British relations to a normal level.

The Argument for Earlier Release of Some Prisoners

15. The alternative course is that, while we should of course, keep up external pressure on the Chinese authorities to behave better, we should accept the need for moves on our part in Hong Kong that might lead to an end to confrontation. This will always be a delicate matter and the likely cost in Hong Kong terms would have to be carefully weighed; but we should be actively exploring possibilities. The release of the fifty detainees now held under emergency legislation seems the obvious first step and in view of the encouraging reaction (or lack of it) from the communist press in Hong Kong to the releases already effected, I hope it may be possible to push ahead with that as fast as possible. I think, however, that careful consideration should also be given to the possibility of arranging earlier release of prisoners convicted in the courts; for example those not convicted of serious violence and those in sectors of particular interest to the Chinese, such as newspaper workers. I am aware that this idea of an amnesty was considered premature when it was mooted some months ago.

Nevertheless, more than a year has elapsed now since the confrontation campaign began and more than six months since violence ended. Has not the time come to take another careful look at the amnesty idea, and make sure that we are not, in rejecting this out of hand, denying to British policy the very flexibility that is most needed at the present time?

16. What general advantages could we expect to draw from declaring some kind of amnesty for confrontation prisoners in Hong Kong? Suppose that it was decided to release in the colony, say at the end of this year, on condition of good behaviour, a substantial number of those convicted for offences connected with confrontation which were not serious acts of violence. By that time almost two-thirds (422 out of 655) of the confrontation prisoners at present in jail will have served their full terms. At a time when the Government of Hong Kong has proved beyond doubt its ability to maintain law and order and is under no direct threat from the Chinese, we should be demonstrating in a concrete way our readiness to reach an accommodation with the Chinese over Hong Kong. We should be allowing the Chinese Government to claim that there had been a response to their 'demands', thereby enabling them to close the book on last year's events and to disarm any of their number still advocating more extreme counsels in respect of Chinese policy toward the colony.

It seems unlikely that those released would resort to violence, any more than their communist colleagues now at liberty, or the communist prisoners already released after completing their sentences, are doing. Such an act on our part would probably be followed by a significant easing in our relations with China. I would expect the release of certain British subjects under detention in particular Anthony Grey, as well as more reasonable treatment for the staff of this Mission and our Shanghai bankers. We should at least improve the prospects of early release or deportation of other British subjects imprisoned or under house arrest in China. The Chinese verbal response would probably remain grudging or offensive; nevertheless there is a good chance that their acts as opposed to their words would be helpful and that we should have laid the foundations of a more relaxed phase in our relations.

17. This course, like any other, would be subject to disadvantages and risks which I do not wish to discount. It can be argued that any such act as an amnesty would be widely regarded by public opinion as an abject surrender to the communists and would thus encourage further Chinese pressure against Hong Kong. I am sure that the Hong Kong Government Information Services are capable of presenting, and the Hong Kong public of understanding, an amnesty as a responsible act of good government: the fact that it also coincides with communist interests is not sufficient reason, particularly in the special circumstances of Hong Kong, for it to be automatically condemned. For the reasons given earlier, it seems to me highly improbable that those releases would be followed by reversal of present communist policy, a new offensive and new demands. In the worst possible case, the making of such a gesture would hardly have impaired the Hong Kong Government's capacity to take any necessary measures, as it has so successfully done in the past. We should have lost nothing but our illusions and we would have a clearer understanding of the Chinese position.

Conclusion

18. No course is without its risks; but the arguments I submit are overwhelmingly in favour of a flexible rather than rigid policy. We are faced with a serious situation; the continuance of confrontation is the cause; sitting tight in Hong Kong will not suffice because things are unlikely to improve themselves whereas the situation could well deteriorate; it is therefore in our interest not only to keep the temperature down and to avoid action in the colony likely to inflame Sino-British relations further, but also explore the possibility of gestures that could lead to an end to confrontation; and we must do this not just in the interests of this Mission, but for the sake of other British subjects in China, our political and commercial relations with China and also, in the last analysis, the best interests of Hong Kong itself. I am not suggesting that it would necessarily be right to declare an amnesty here and now. I would have thought that next New Year's Day (by which time the great majority of the prisoners will have been in any case released after serving their full terms) might be an appropriate time. The detainees, on the other hand, will I hope be released continuously from now on.

19. It will be seen from the above that I am not suggesting a negotiated settlement, but rather a series of acts of de-escalation on each side. I think it most unlikely that the Chinese would enter into specific negotiations with prior undertakings. I doubt whether it would be to our advantage either.

20. It might also be argued that in the present turmoil of the Cultural Revolution now is not the time to seek even a tacit agreement with the Chinese Government, and that we should therefore wait in the expectation that a more moderate and reasonable regime will emerge. It is impossible to forecast the future course of events in China, but we have no reason to expect that a more moderate regime will emerge, at any rate in the next few years. Then chances are that Maoist extremism will remain in full strength. On the other hand we have had clear indications that the Chinese

would like to move now towards a settlement of our difficulties. In short we cannot bank on conditions improving, and there is therefore no point in waiting in the expectation that they will.

21. I realise that these recommendations contain unpalatable elements but the alternative is the prolongation of our present very bad relations for a number of years. The Chinese may possibly let the matter drop before 1974 but that, the date when all confrontation prisoners will be released if they serve their full terms, is strictly our terminal date. Even this assumes that there is no new deterioration in the situation, as will always be more likely while confrontation persists. To resign ourselves therefore to a policy of waiting for things to get better, when they may well get worse, seems very much a policy of despair. I must, of course, on behalf of my staff and myself declare a highly personal interest in the solution of this problem. I hope this fact has not overcoloured some of the arguments in this memorandum, in which I have tried to present the problem, in terms of our wider interests, as objectively as possible.[3]

D. C. HOPSON

---

3 When officials in the Commonwealth Office finally saw a copy, Mr Galsworthy thought the memorandum persuasively argued but it oversimplified the main issue of amnesty and underestimated the difficulties this would create for the Hong Kong government. Mr Mason found the argument that the Chinese were looking for a way of getting off the hook unconvincing (minutes of 19 August; FCO 40/68). However, the Commonwealth Office had already been persuaded to approach the Governor regarding the release of prisoners and the issue of clemency (see Nos. 138 and 139).

No. 136

Sir D. Hopson (Peking) to Mr Thomson (Commonwealth Office)
30 July 1968[1]

Tel. No. 698 Priority Confidential (FCO 40/68, HWB 3/2G)
Hong Kong telegram No. 928:[2] British policy towards China.

The key concession to bring about the benefits of better relations and therefore the concession on which we should concentrate is the release of Chinese in custody (detainees and prisoners convicted in Court). In this telegram I shall deal with the detainees. My immediately following telegram[2] deals with earlier release of some convicted prisoners and general points raised by Hong Kong telegram under reference.

2. Detainees seemed [sic] to be the sector in which we can with relatively little difficulty make gestures bearing on key issue. We have the flexibility. The detainees have not been sentenced to a set term so that there is no question of 'premature release'. The release of four so far has gone smoothly and Press reaction has been encouraging.

3. As regards dividends from such release, Hong Kong telegram No. 850,[2] paragraph 3, agreed that tangible results were not very likely from a trickle of detainees,

---

1 Repeated for information to Hong Kong.
2 Not printed.

so it can hardly be a matter of complaint now if we have not yet seen any obvious dividends from the release of four (paragraph 1(*a*) of telegram under reference). In fact, however, I think there may well have been dividends since this release has probably been a factor in the resumption of exit visas for this Mission.

4. This leads me to recommend strongly that urgent consideration be given to the possibility of releasing a sizeable number of detainees in response to the granting of exit visas to the staff of this Mission, if, as we now expect, the Chinese carry out their promise of 27 July (my telegram No. 691).[2] It is very much in our interest to show them that acts of de-escalation on their part are very likely to be followed by suitable response on ours. In this case we should for once not be making the first move. The effect might also be to encourage the Chinese to make further concessions e.g. over British subjects detained in China in the hope of further response from us. I very much hope, therefore, that if the current outstanding exit visas are granted the Governor would be prepared to release, say, 10 to 20 detainees at once.

No. 137

Sir D. Hopson (Peking) to Mr Stewart, 5 August 1968[1]
Tel. No. 718 Immediate, Confidential (FCO 21/69, FC 3/3/G)

My telegram No. 691.[2]

No further exit visas were issued last week despite several telephone reminders to Consular Department. In response to Consular Departments request on 29 July I submitted on 30 July a further note giving details of my visa application. In it I asked for issue not later than 2 August of an exit visa valid for one month.

2. Since this date passed without result Counsellor has asked for urgent interview with Consular Department. Meanwhile I have indicated to Mr Hsueh on 3 August that I wish to leave here on 10 August and have since confirmed this by Note.

3. It seems that either the Chinese will issue all or some of the visas (Mr Hsueh said he knew mine was being 'dealt with') or that they will merely repeat their statement on 27 July without giving any indication of when they will issue them. They possibly calculate that their assurance of 27 July plus issue of 4 visas on 29 July has been sufficient to fend off further pressure for the time being (which to a considerable extent it has).

4. I do not think we can afford to let them get away indefinitely with this continued flagrant breach of diplomatic practice. Foreign Governments will be already reluctant to bring diplomatic pressure on Chinese until interval of perhaps some weeks has passed after the 27 July assurance without significant results in the shape of further visas for senior staff. But I do not think we should wait too long before reactivating the diplomatic campaign, and in the meantime we should initiate further publicity. Experience over the last weeks has indicated that the Chinese are more

---

1 Repeated for information to Hong Kong.
2 Not printed.

sensitive to diplomatic and publicity pressure on subject of detained diplomats than we first thought. Having found a nerve we must press hard.

5. I therefore propose that if Counsellor's interview proves unfruitful News Department should immediately issue a statement (which I hope the BBC Overseas News would carry) saying that the Chinese on 27 July promised to issue the outstanding 18 visas. On 29 July they issued four but there have been no more since then, although repeated requests have been made. Despite the assurance therefore the 14 staff including myself are still unable to leave China. I would circulate a copy of this statement amongst diplomatic colleagues here. If timing allows it would be useful if this statement (if it is made) could coincide with Pakistan Foreign Minister's[3] presence in Peking i.e. be made no later than 6 August. This would not preclude a further statement if and when the Chinese have failed to issue my exit visa by 10 August.

6. This telegram is in the nature of contingency planning only. I will telegraph firm recommendation in the light of events today or tomorrow.

3 Mr Mian Arshad Hussain.

No. 138

Mr Thomson (Commonwealth Office) to Sir D. Trench (Hong Kong)
8 August 1968[1]
Tel. No. 1362 Priority, Confidential (FCO 40/68, HWB 3/2G)

Peking Telegram No. 698:[2] British Policy towards China.

As we view the situation from here, and subject of course to your views as regards the Hong Kong end, we see force in Sir D. Hopson's arguments in favour of the release of a significant number of detainees as an act of 'de-escalation', provided the Chinese implement in full their undertaking to grant all outstanding visas for the Mission. You have already indicated broad agreement with the study on detainees (your telegram 802)[3] which recommended that consideration be given to the unconditional release within the Colony of a small group of the less important Communists and—depending on Communist and public reaction—to a phased release programme based on the general principle of releasing, first, those who are less important and have been detained the longest. Communist reactions to the first four releases seem to have been minimal and satisfactory from our point of view. We see advantage therefore in making further releases as Hopson proposes. The Chinese leaders no doubt regard this latest shift on visas in Peking as a contribution on their part to re-establishing a *modus vivendi* with us, and expect recognition of this on our part . If they do fulfil their undertaking on visas, it may well signal the beginning of an improvement in Sino-British relations which we would naturally wish to encourage as much as possible and which we could reasonably expect to be reflected in the Chinese attitude towards Hong Kong. Speeding-up of releases could therefore reasonably be presented not as a concession

1 Repeated for information to Peking
2 No. 136.
3 Not printed.

to Chinese pressure, but as an active contribution on our part to return to some degree of normality in our relations. We agree that the releases would not necessarily yield direct results but they would in our judgement improve the atmosphere of Sino-British relations, and such an improvement should yield some dividend in Hong Kong.

2. We have considered the point that by the release of detainees in the way proposed, we would be underlining unduly the link between British subjects in China and our policies in Hong Kong, and that this might encourage the Chinese to try to bargain further and larger releases of detainees against the release of British subjects in detention in China. However, the significance of Hong Kong is now so clear that there seems little advantage in trying to play it down. Moreover, we are sure that the Chinese would not consider the release of detainees as an appropriate *quid per quo* for the release of Mr Grey, and we doubt very much whether it would directly influence their attitude towards other British subjects either.

3. We recognise that there is no moment which from the Hong Kong point of view could be regarded as ideal for making concessions, but since neither we nor you would judge releases of this sort to be a major concession, we would hope that they could be made at a time when the situation *vis-à-vis* the local Communists is 'not unfavourable' (your telegram 928).[4] If you were to see strong objection to the simultaneous release of the number of detainees Hopson proposes, we think that the release of several small groups over a period of weeks would also be beneficial. But in the light of the foregoing considerations, as seen here we believe there could be substantial advantage in a larger gesture involving a minimum of ten persons.

4. We should be most grateful if you would consider these suggestions and let us have your views.

5. If the Chinese honour their undertaking on visas and we match it by a gesture on release of detainees, this might create the sort of atmosphere in which we could work towards a solution to the intractable problem of Grey. We shall be telegraphing separately about this.

4 Not printed.

No. 139

Mr Thomson (Commonwealth Office) to Sir D. Trench (Hong Kong)
9 August 1968[1]
Tel. No. 1375 Routine, Confidential (FCO 40/63, HWB 3/2G)

Our Telegram No. 1362.[2] Anthony Grey.

The continued detention of Anthony Grey is causing increasing concern in this

1 Repeated for information to Peking. The wording of this telegram was a compromise between the Foreign Office and the Commonwealth Office. The latter did not want to convey the impression that the concerns of the Governor were not being considered, given Sir D. Trench had previously voiced his opposition to the premature release of prisoners and asked London to show understanding of his difficulties. The Foreign Office wanted to underline the pressure the Government was under from public opinion to assist Mr Grey (minute from Mr Murray to Mr Allen, 12 August 1968; FCO 21/140).
2 No. 138.

country and there is likely to be mounting criticism of the ineffectiveness of our efforts to secure his release. This criticism may well become sharper if the conditions of movement of our Mission in Peking are seen to have returned to normal. Gerald Long of Reuters has formally raised with the Foreign Secretary the question of an act of clemency in Hong Kong. Even if Long has to be informed that an act of clemency is for the present at any rate still out of the question, we shall no doubt hear more of this.

2. When the matter was discussed with you here last May, there was general agreement that the minimum price which the Chinese were likely to exact for Grey was the release in Hong Kong of Hsueh and Lo but that they might initially try to insist on the release of all Communist newspaper workers now in prison. Both you and we saw objection to the premature release of these persons, not merely because of the juridical difficulties, but because of the boost this would give to local communist morale and the blow it might strike at public confidence in Hong Kong. Since May however your reports have indicated that the position of the Government *vis-à-vis* the local Communists has improved and we should be grateful for your views on whether you would now consider an act of clemency in relation to Hsueh and Lo to be possible, or whether the objections to any premature release of either or both of them are still overriding. It would be helpful if you could give us our assessment in relation to:

(*a*) A continuation of the present situation following upon the grant of an exit visa to Hopson, i.e. on the basis that this action does not herald any further visible improvement in relations, and

(*b*) A situation in which the Chinese grant all our exit visa applications and this, with any matching gestures we may be able to make, produces a significant improvement in relations.

In November in any case a decision will have to be taken about the remission of Hsueh's sentence. Even if Grey had not been released by then, there would appear to be strong arguments in favour of letting Hsueh out with full remission. There is possibly therefore something to be said for trying to make some use of him as a bargaining counter while we can.

3. There would of course be the problem of ensuring that any act of clemency on your part covering Hsueh and Lo alone would in fact achieve the desired result of Grey's release. Unfortunately it seems unlikely that we could obtain any firm undertaking from the Chinese. If we were to ask the Chargé d'Affaires in Peking to put the proposition to the Chinese that Hsueh and Lo be released immediately in Hong Kong in return for the release of Grey, the most we would expect would be some vague form of words indicating that they might be prepared to consider this but it is almost certain they would not be prepared to go further. We imagine that, like us, you would be reluctant to use NCNA in Hong Kong to probe Chinese intentions, particularly when members of their own staff were directly involved. The covert channels which have been tried in the past, whatever the results they might yield in the long term, are unlikely to enable us to reach any quick assessment of the Chinese attitude to this particular transaction.

If therefore you felt that the situation in Hong Kong is now such that you could contemplate an act of clemency our present inclination would be to instruct the Chargé d'Affaires to put a proposition on the foregoing lines to the Chinese, explaining that, in addition to our concern for Grey, our purpose was to demonstrate that we wanted to return to normal Sino-British relations.

4. We should then have to consider the next step in the light of the Chinese reply. We should therefore be most grateful if you could consider this matter on two hypotheses:

(*a*) That—unexpectedly—we were able to secure some sort of understanding with the Chinese;

(*b*) That the Chinese reply, although not completely negative, nevertheless fell far short of anything that could be regarded as an understanding.

Looking at it from most angles other than the effect in Hong Kong itself, we would incline to the view that, even in the case of (*b*), an act of faith for the sake of Grey would, on humanitarian grounds, be worth taking. But of course we recognise that the paramount consideration must be the likely effect in Hong Kong and we can well see that it might be much easier to reconcile Hong Kong public opinion to an act of clemency in the circumstances at (*a*) than in those at (*b*). But we should like your assessment on whether, in the situation as you now see it in Hong Kong, it would be at all possible for you to contemplate an act of clemency on an 'act of faith' basis, i.e. in the circumstances envisaged at (*b*) above.

5. While we have felt it right to ask you to review this matter once again in the light of developments since last May, there is of course no question of our seeking to persuade you to take any action which in your considered judgement would entail unacceptable risks in Hong Kong.

No. 140

Letter from Mr Cradock (Peking) to Mr Murray, 13 August 1968
Confidential (FCO 21/69, FC 3/3G)

Dear James,

Donald Hopson left Peking this morning with a very solid turn-out by diplomatic colleagues, and of course all UK staff, at the airport to wish him well and wave him goodbye.

2. His visa was splendid news. The purpose of this letter is to add what I am sure will be a supererogatory note of caution, namely that we should not draw too large and hopeful conclusions from this single very happy event. We should not suppose that the situation has fundamentally changed.

3. The precise reasons for the Chinese softening on the subject of this Mission in the last few weeks will probably always remain obscure. But we can safely say that the three main factors have been:

(*a*) The continued absence of any restrictions on their officials in London. We did not, as they may have expected, reimpose control when the flow of visas for us dried up in June and thereby provide them with an excuse for maintaining their restrictions on us;

(*b*) Complementary to this, the other prong of the pincer, there was the increasing publicity and the threat of a diplomatic campaign;

(*c*) Finally, there was the release of 4 detainees in Hong Kong.

Under these pressures the Chinese have abandoned, or more strictly are withdrawing from one exposed position (detention of diplomats). But it would be wrong to conclude that they will not hold firmly to their remaining strong points. There has been no change of heart or general policy. Our reception at Protocol Department yesterday was proof of that, if further proof were needed. If therefore we wish to make progress on the other sectors, where the need has all along been more acute than in our own, we shall need to make the appropriate moves in Hong Kong. I am greatly encouraged by the recent telegrams on the subject of releases of detainees and on Tony Grey, which suggest that such progress may be possible before very long.

4. Even as regards the Mission it would be wrong to assume that we are altogether out of the wood. Garside's interview yesterday confirmed this. The Chinese may in fact consider that by granting the Head of Mission's visa they have bought time and spiked the diplomatic offensive and can therefore afford to play very slowly with the remaining outstanding applications and any in the future. There is also the possibility that the final news of the deregistration of Chung Wah will adversely affect visas for a time. I do not rate these dangers too highly and feel that with luck the remaining visas should come along in the next few weeks. It will now be much more difficult to bring diplomatic pressure to bear. But it is most important that we make sure of things by keeping up the publicity pressure. The Chinese are obviously more responsive to this than we at first thought; for those going in for the business of detention and blackmail they are curiously sensitive. Donald Hopson's appearance over the next few weeks are likely to be the occasions for considerable publicity and should provide excellent opportunities for emphasising any continuing Chinese malpractice in this matter. August 22, the anniversary of the burning, might also be used as a peg on which to hang a reminder.

I am copying this letter to Arthur Maddocks in Hong Kong.[3]

Yours ever,
P. CRADOCK

[3] In a reply dated 22 August, Mr Murray was also puzzled to know why the Chinese had decided to let Sir D. Hopson out at this particular time but thought it wrong to conclude that they would not hold firmly to their remaining strong points. The plight of Mr Grey, he added, 'raises much more complex difficulties which are causing us a good deal of concern.'

No. 141

Sir D. Trench (Hong Kong) to Mr Thomson (Commonwealth Office)
19 August 1968[1]
Tel. No. 1007 Priority, Secret (FCO 40/68, HWB 3/2G)

Your Telegram No. 1375:[2] Grey.

I realise that concern over Grey is increasing and is likely to go on increasing, and

[1] Repeated for information priority to Peking.
[2] No. 139.

that it may become more and more difficult to resist pressure for some action of a kind that can be publicly disclosed. I hope however that we shall be able to avoid action for its own sake, and can continue to base our tactics on what will most surely assist Grey without too greatly jeopardizing Hong Kong's long and short term interests.

2. I think we should now seriously consider the desirability of encouraging a carefully timed publicity campaign about Grey. I recognize that one (illogical) consequence may be to increase pressure on me to release prisoners but possibly the Chinese Government, embarrassed to some extent as they may well by now be over Grey, might be becoming susceptible to pressure of this kind.

3. From Hong Kong's point of view, I would prefer to do nothing else until Hsueh is released on 18th November (he has not been deprived of good conduct marks and his release then will be automatic and not a matter requiring decision). We could then wait a week or two after his release and see whether the Chinese responded by releasing Grey as a consequence of Hsueh's release and publicity pressure over Grey. We will thus at least have indicated to some degree that we are not readily susceptible to retaliatory action which is an important point to uphold in the long term.

4. If they did not respond, however, I would then be prepared to suggest to them (using the same channels in paragraph 6 below) that we were ready to release Lo in the very near future, if they for their part were prepared to release Grey. I would be prepared to do this in either of the situations in your paragraph 2(*a*) and (*b*).

5. But if you consider that something more than a publicity campaign is unavoidable before November, I would be prepared to accept what I regard as the second best course of action, i.e. to enter into secret discussions fairly soon with the Chinese and try to bargain the release of Hsueh and if necessary Lo for the release of Grey. I realise this could not be disclosed and might therefore not help much to relieve the pressure for action but it could at least be said in confidence that something was being done.

6. I consider that if we were to enter into such a discussion it should be started through Cater and his contact (my telegram No. 996).[3] Cater could say that he was acting on his own initiative, but believed he might be able to obtain my approval for the early release of Hsueh if the Chinese Government were prepared to release Grey. He could say that this offer was being made in the light of Peking's apparent desire to improve relations, and that he was prepared to seek official reactions to his suggestion only if his contact could produce some reasonable assurance that Grey would be released.

7. This offer would no doubt, after a certain delay, produce either a cryptic response (whose intention we would have to assess as best we could or ask for further elucidation), or no response, or a demand for more. If the last, Cater could then reply by saying that he was prepared to suggest that Lo too should be released at the same time, but that in order to obtain agreement he would have to have more specific assurances about Grey.

8. If the reply from the Chinese was that the release of Hsueh and Lo was not enough, and that we must also offer the release of all the news workers, I would see very great difficulties in agreeing, and I hope that it will not be contemplated. In this event, I would wish Cater to say that he regretted he could not pursue the matter on that basis.

3 Not printed.

9. I realise that there are bound to be some hesitations about using the Cater channel, especially since we have not tried to do any serious business by that means. But it has the advantage that the Government would not be officially committed and it would provide a useful test of the value of this channel. The alternative informal channel via NCNA here has the disadvantages that the NCNA is likely to be intransigent on this issue and it would commit the Governor more clearly. The disadvantage of an approach in Peking is that both sides might find themselves committed officially to irreconcilable attitudes. This might be positively damaging to Grey's chances of release, and I would advise against it.

10. I am therefore now prepared if necessary to contemplate an act of clemency limited to Hsueh and Lo on the hypothesis in paragraph 4(*a*) of your telegram, but I would much prefer to see the matter handled as in paragraph 3 above. I do see difficulties on the hypothesis in paragraph 4(*b*) but so much depends on what the Chinese actually say that it would seem better to leave a firmer answer until their reply can be evaluated.

11. I discussed this telegram with Hopson before departure. His firm view is that the best chance of getting Grey released is to release Hsueh and Lo unconditionally now. If however this was to be decided against, he would regard his proposals in this telegram as the next best course.

12. Hopson may, of course, be right, but it remains a matter for conjecture.

My objections briefly are:

(*a*) Whether successful or not, to release these two men unconditionally now would not only be an act of faith but an act of submission. As such, it might be swallowed locally once, but having submitted once it becomes harder to resist further submissions with progressively more damage to confidence.

(*b*) If unsuccessful, our action would be that much more open to criticism locally, and the possibility of being able to help Grey would be greatly receded.

No. 142

Submission from Mr Murray to Sir D. Allen, 20 August 1968
Confidential (FCO 21/101, FC 6/12)

Economic Pressure against China

Problem

Some weeks ago, when no progress was being made in the matter of exit visas for the Mission, Sir Donald Hopson raised the question of applying economic pressure on the Chinese, should diplomatic pressure and publicity campaign fail to move them to more reasonable policies (Peking telegram No. 585).[1] He went on to suggest possible forms this pressure might take (Peking telegrams 586 and 672).[2] Ever since the sacking of the Mission, we had been keeping the question of economic sanctions under review. However, we re-examined the matter in the light of Sir D. Hopson's suggestions.

1 No. 121.
2 Neither printed.

2. Since the proposals were made, the situation has been transformed, and we hope that exit visas will now be issued in a more or less normal fashion. Nevertheless, it seems worth putting on record the conclusions of our latest review of the possibilities of economic pressure—particularly since, as long as Mr Grey and other British subjects remain in detention in China, we shall always be under pressure from some sections of public opinion here to take strong measures against the Chinese.

Conclusions

3. The conclusions of our review are these:

(*a*) A policy of economic pressure is likely to prove an ineffective instrument for bringing the Chinese to more moderate policies; it would encounter strong opposition from other Government departments; and it could be considered only if Ministers were to think it essential to demonstrate to public opinion in this country that we were taking firmer action against China.

(*b*) In the present circumstances, any attempt to apply economic pressure would not be right.

Background and Argument

4. From the outset of the present crisis in our relations with China, we have kept the possibility of economic pressure under continuous review. But we have always come to the conclusion that such pressures would be ineffective against the Chinese. My submission of 21 March on Sino-British relations[3] summarised the position in the following terms: 'Threats to stop trade from the United Kingdom would not modify the Chinese attitude, and loss of trade would be harmful to us here. Economic measures in Hong Kong directed against China would hurt the Colony more than the Chinese.' This was approved by the Secretary of State at an Office meeting on 26 March.

5. The possible forms of economic pressure suggested by Sir D. Hopson were these:

(a) Prevention of the Chinese from chartering ships in Britain

The Board of Trade have informed us that they have no legal powers effectively to prevent the chartering of ships. They could, however, ask the Baltic Market and those companies which arrange the charters, not to charter to the Chinese. Such a request would be most unsympathetically received. The companies concerned would stand to lose a considerable amount of money and would argue that by withholding their services they would simply be handing over the China chartering trade to their foreign competitors. Many of the ships are not British, and if they were not chartered through the London market, they could be chartered elsewhere.

(b) Prevention of British ships visiting China

As the Board of Trade have no power to prevent such visits, they would be obliged to rely on requests to the companies concerned. The companies are however well aware of the risks involved, and are nevertheless anxious to continue trading. They would no doubt point out that some of the incidents leading to the arrest of ships' officers were of the latters' making and that some ships (Glen Line) are calling regularly at Chinese ports without incident. They would not be sympathetic to a request to curtail ship's visits as a means of political pressure while it still remained

---

[3] No. 88.

our policy to encourage trade. It would, however, be possible to force the ship owners' hands by means of a formal warning to the effect that we considered Chinese ports dangerous to British vessels and seamen, and visits to China dangerous for British subjects. This would have the effect of inflating insurance rates and making the China shipping trade unprofitable. Such action would be strenuously opposed by the Board of Trade as well as by the 'China Trade' lobby, and would not in any case affect all companies as some carry their own insurance.

(c) Harassment of Chinese ships in British ports

Few Chinese vessels call at British ports (not more than one a month). They could be subjected to considerable delays since there are a number of international agreements on safety regulations to which the Chinese Government are not a party. Harbour authorities could, therefore, insist on thorough inspections of the ships, and could refuse clearance until they were satisfied that all was in order. The objection to such action is that the Chinese have ample scope for retaliation against British vessels in China, and are not necessarily constrained in their behaviour by civilised or humanitarian considerations, as we are.

(d) Action to reduce imports from China

No powers exist to compel importers to boycott a specific country. The only recent peacetime precedent would be Rhodesia, where HMG are implementing a Security Council resolution. Exhortations to restrict imports would be ineffective in the absence of some public declaration that trade with China was not in the national interest. Action could be taken to reduce the Chinese share of goods whose importation is regulated by quotas, but this would be open to objection by traders for the same reason. (Some discrimination against China has already been shown in that the quota increases agreed for some other Communist countries were not applied to China.) In any case, as less than 10% of our imports from China consist of items on quota, the effect of action would be minimal.

(e) Action to freeze Chinese assets in London

This is theoretically possible, although its effectiveness would be doubtful as the Chinese sterling balances held in London are now estimated to be less than £10 million. The wider implications of such action at a time when we are trying to prevent depositors withdrawing sterling from London are obvious.

(f) Action against the Bank of China

(i) Staff

The expatriate staff of the Bank of China could be refused extension of permission to remain in the United Kingdom, or could be deported. The latter would be the only effective sanction. If it were resorted to, any official with more than two years' lawful residence here would have the right to make representations to the Chief Metropolitan Magistrate. The Home Secretary already has the necessary powers to take the above action, but would need to be persuaded that it was 'conducive to the public good' under the terms of the Aliens Order. Our experience over trying to move the Home Secretary to act against the New China News Agency does not suggest he would be cooperative over the more innocuous Bank of China. Action against the staff of the Bank would also run the risk of retaliation against the expatriate staffs of the two British banks in Shanghai, and would be contrary to our Mission's known views about avoiding restrictions on persons.

(ii) *Banking Facilities and Financial Sanctions*

The Bank of England, acting in conjunction with the Treasury, has wide powers to regulate Banks, and powers under the Exchange Control legislation. It would be possible to remove the Bank of China, and other Chinese banks with the branches in the United Kingdom, from the list of authorised banks. This would have the effect of forcing them to do much of their foreign business through an intermediary. The Board of Trade could also revoke their registration as banks. Such action would have the effect of driving the banks concerned speedily out of business. In addition, the Bank of England could decree that payments to China could only be authorised by itself, and could then impose such administrative delays as it thought fit. Both the Treasury and the Bank of England would however be strongly opposed to such action. They would claim that, even though we could argue that the Chinese provided us with ample justification, the City's reputation, and thus its usefulness and profitability, would be damaged if it were seen that these pressures were being applied for political reasons.

(g) *Action in Hong Kong*

In Hong Kong telegram No. 925,[4] the Governor reported that, after a detailed examination of the possibilities, there were no economic pressures that he could recommend to be taken in Hong Kong. In view of the obvious vulnerability of Hong Kong to Chinese pressures, his arguments are unassailable.

6. Sir Donald Hopson in making his recommendations sought to differentiate (Peking telegram No. 585) between what he called 'pinpricks', and serious economic pressure (Peking telegram No. 586) which would come later and would inevitably provoke retaliation. I am not convinced that such 'pinpricks' would have the desired effect or—more important from a practical point of view—that we should ever secure the agreement of other interested Departments, the Bank of England and British firms in such a course of action. It would certainly require a decision at the highest level that as a means of political pressure to secure better treatment for British subjects in China, everything possible should be done to discourage commercial contact with China regardless of the consequences.

7. Thus, even had there been no progress in the matter of exit visas, I doubt if a convincing case could have been made out for economic pressure. In the new circumstances, there is certainly nothing to be gained by attempting such a policy.

8. However, I see some advantage in discreet publicity directed at the commercial reputation of the Chinese. The unilateral annulment of the Vicker-Zimmer contract and various other recent actions suggest that the Chinese may be engaging in something near sharp practice to minimise liabilities which are becoming onerous and contributing to the shortage of foreign exchange. This might with due discretion be exploited to demonstrate that China's former excellent commercial reputation is becoming tarnished (Peking telegram No. 572).[5] We might also try to persuade representatives of the Sino-British Trade Council and other British businessmen to be a little less sycophantic in their dealings with the Chinese in London and, in particular, to indicate to the Chinese that their treatment of British

---

4 No. 133.
5 Not printed.

subjects in China and their conduct over Vickers-Zimmer cannot fail to damage trade with this country.

9. Even if we need not pursue the question of economic pressures now, there is of course always the possibility that Sino-British relations may in future take a violent turn for the worse and we shall once again be under pressure to take drastic economic action against the Chinese. Such drastic action is bound to generate ill-will in commercial circles, particularly when HMG are urging unremitting efforts towards increase exports. It will be necessary—as before—to take account of:

(*a*) the likelihood of influencing the Chinese in the direction of greater reasonableness by other means;

(*b*) the difficulty of enforcing forms of economic pressure; cf. paragraph 5(*a*) and (*b*) above;

(*c*) the likelihood that Hong Kong will remain the key issue determining the state of our relations with China.[6]

JAMES MURRAY

6 Mr Allen indicated he agreed with the paper and its conclusions. Mr Murray forwarded a copy of the paper in a letter of 22 August to Mr Cradock, and advised that there was no intention of carrying matters further at this stage (FCO 21/99).

No. 143

Minute from Mr Murray to Sir D. Allen and subsequent minutes
20 August 1968
Confidential (FCO 21/69, FC 3/3G)

Sino-British Relations, with particular reference to Hong Kong
Problem

At the time when the flow of exit visas for our Mission in Peking had been interrupted, Sir D. Hopson produced a memorandum dated on 29 July on the prospects for Sino-British relations (attached).[1] It was prompted by the conviction, arising out of a protracted exchange of telegrams with the Governor of Hong Kong, although it was generally acknowledged that Hong Kong was the key to any general improvement in Sino-British relations, the Governor was being too inflexible in his reluctance to take measures which might result in an accommodation locally with the Chinese. Since the memorandum was written, the situation has been transformed to the extent that the flow of visas was resumed, including visas for two senior members of staff. Even so, Sir Donald Hopson has commented (Peking telegram No. 692)[2] that this does not invalidate the argument in his paper which is concerned with Sino-British relations generally: he says that he will feel in a strong position to argue on these lines, now that he lacks so personal an interest. The purpose of this minute is to draw attention to the main issues which we

1 See No. 135.
2 Not printed.

shall wish to discuss with Sir D. Hopson—who in turn has now had an opportunity to review them personally with the Governor.

Conclusions

2. The debate between Sir D. Hopson and the Governor illustrates the difficulty of drafting any general principles for governing Hong Kong. However, principles are important only insofar as they offer guidance for various troublesome practical decisions with which the Governor and ourselves are likely to be faced in the next few months. These will relate to the desirability of action of two kinds: measures of firmness against local Communist malpractices, and measures of conciliation:

(*a*) As for the first, both the Governor and Sir D. Hopson would agree that if our position in Hong Kong is to be tolerable to us, there must be some tacitly accepted *modus vivendi* with the Chinese Government. Sir D. Hopson lay stress on avoiding provocative action in sensitive areas. The Governor places equal emphasis on the need for firmness in dealing with the Communists, lest they be encouraged to think that sufficient pressure will bring us to an accommodation on their terms. But this is not a matter which can be settled in abstract. In each particular set of circumstances, a balance will have to be struck—as in the past—between firmness and excessive provocation.

(*b*) The only measure of conciliation which is likely to have any considerable impact on Sino-British relations is the premature release of convicted prisoners. The central issue to which we shall have to direct the attention of Ministers is whether, and if so when, some acts of clemency in respect of convicted prisoners would be feasible. (Foreign Office telegram No. 769 of 26 July.)[3]

Argument

3. The main argument in Sir D. Hopson's memorandum are these:

(*a*) Sino-British relations are now worse than at any time since the Communists took over. We can exercise no political influence on Chinese policies, and we are suffering commercial loss. British subjects are being detained and arrested.

(*b*) The cause of trouble is the continuance of 'confrontation' in Hong Kong: this is not a temporary aberration which will correct itself in time; unless we take steps it will persist, and the situation may deteriorate further.

(*c*) The turmoil of the Cultural Revolution does not mean that reasonable converse with the Chinese authorities is impossible. They have already exerted restraint on their followers in Hong Kong and retain a clear appreciation of their economic interests there.

(*d*) The Chinese will need a face-saving gesture for ending confrontation, but are not seeking another Macao. A settlement on tolerable terms is not impossible.

(*e*) External pressure on the Chinese by diplomacy, publicity and possible economic measures may help, but are unlikely of themselves to ensure a return to 'pre-confrontation coexistence'. Retaliatory measures on our part in London would only be counter-productive.

(*f*) As a first step, we must try to avoid further frictions in Hong Kong, taking account of currently heightened Chinese sensitivities.

3 No. 134.

(*g*) It could be argued that the necessary concessions would cost us too much in Hong Kong in terms of public confidence there and encouragement to the local Communists to ask for more; and that we should simply stand firm against Chinese pressure. But the cost of such a policy in human and political terms would be high, lasting over years. In Hong Kong it would be more likely to prompt than preclude further unrest. Moreover, the assumptions about public opinion in Hong Kong and about Chinese intentions on which this policy would be based are questionable.

(*h*) The alternative course calls for positive steps in Hong Kong to end 'confrontation' both by the release of detainees and the early remission, say at the end of 1968, of convicted prisoners not involved in serious violence.

(*i*) There are of course risks in this course also, but the balance of advantage is strongly in its favour. What is proposed is not a negotiated settlement but a series of acts of de-escalation on each side.

(*j*) We cannot bank on conditions improving inside China and there is therefore no point in waiting or hoping for a better climate for this de-escalation.

(*k*) The alternative is bad relations with China, with their effect lasting some years and possibly until 1974 (when the last 'confrontation' prisoners will be due for release in the normal way).

4. There are some general observations to be made on this thesis at the outset.

(*a*) Whatever the larger objectives we set ourselves in establishing relations with the Chinese in the first place, we (in common almost certainly with all other countries with established relations) have never been in a position to exercise any political influence. Nor indeed have we been able to do much to protect the interests of our nationals in difficulties. The same has applied to a greater or lesser extent to other countries; and this is not a phenomenon peculiar only to the period of the Cultural Revolution.

(*b*) Even were we able to reach an accommodation with them over Hong Kong, the Chinese are unlikely to wish to have good relations with us. While we maintain our present posture in foreign affairs, in particular our general support for American policy in Vietnam, as well as our attitude towards Formosa, the Chinese will not consider any real improvement in relations possible.

(*c*) Trade might increase if relations became less acrimonious: but the current drop in British exports is due more to the Chinese shortage of foreign exchange and destructions caused by the Cultural Revolution than to active discrimination against us.

(*d*) Again, if relations became less acrimonious, our Mission might be able to do more for British subjects in trouble in China. But concessions in Hong Kong are unlikely themselves to secure the release of Mr Watt or of the British Merchant Navy officers.

(*e*) As a result of a recent review, we have concluded that a policy of economic pressure on the Chinese is likely to be neither feasible nor effective.[4]

5. A copy of the memorandum has not so far gone to the Governor of Hong Kong for his comments. But we are well aware of the Governor's views as a result of the interchange of telegrams between the Governor and Sir D. Hopson in July,

---

4 See No. 142.

arising out of the issues of the Chung Wah School and the release of prisoners. The Governor's views are to be found in cogent form in Hong Kong telegrams Nos. 855 of 5 July,[5] 884 of 12 July[6] and 928 of 25 July.[7] His thesis, which the Commonwealth Office has endorsed, can be broadly summarized as follows. Our objective is indeed a return to reasonable working relations with China over Hong Kong, if that can be achieved. (In the anomaly of Hong Kong, things have never been normal.) On the Chinese side, this postulates, if not acquiesces, at any rate, toleration and respect for our position and authority in the Colony. On our side it means that we continue (as we have done since 1949) to accommodate ourselves to Chinese susceptibilities wherever possible, provided always that we stop short of undermining the authority in the Colony; and it means also that we continue to avoid unnecessarily provocative actions, while reacting firmly to unreasonable Chinese pressures. But there is, in the Governor's view, no clear evidence that the Chinese are interested in placing relations with Britain over Hong Kong or other issues on a basis which we would regard as normal. Their present aim in Hong Kong appears to remain one of increasing their influence by exploiting the activities of their local supporters. On present indication, their price for the return to 'normality' in Sino-British relations is concessions in Hong Kong so substantial as inevitably to undermine our position. Therefore we must firmly maintain our position and authority in Hong Kong; to do otherwise would indicate weakness which would encourage Chinese designs and seriously damage public confidence in the Colony on which our policy basically depends. In taking the necessary measures in Hong Kong, due regard must of course be paid to the exposed position of our Mission and of other British subjects in China. But it would be most dangerous to give any impression to the Chinese that this consideration was of overriding importance to us since they would only be encouraged to increase their demands on us in Hong Kong without necessarily improving the lot of British subjects in China. For so long as we have reason to believe that the Chinese are concerned primarily to exploit the present situation with a view to weakening our position in the Colony and extending their own influence, there can be no one-sided gestures or damaging concessions of substance on our part, (The Governor admits the possibility that *some* concessions might be made without danger; but emphasises that it is a matter of judgment.) Moreover, it is a matter of prudence in this situation to take such measures as are open to us to prevent the Communists in Hong Kong reestablishing a position from which they could mount a repetition of last year's events. (On this account it has been right to resist the reinstatement of dismissed strikers in the essential services.) This does not mean that we should fall back on a policy of suppression for local Communist activities; but it does mean that we should deal firmly with such activities as are flagrantly illegal. Meantime, the present situation in Hong Kong is not unfavourable, with the active phase of 'confrontation' ended and Communist morale generally low.

6. Between these two approaches the divergencies are perhaps not so much of an aim as of method, and above all, of timing. Essentially, they seem to me to pose the following questions:

5 No. 127.
6 No. 130.
7 Not printed.

(a) Do the Chinese leaders in Peking seriously want an accommodation with us over Hong Kong?

Sir D. Hopson argues that they do, if only the necessary face saving formula can be found; and that gestures and concessions by us towards that end will be matched by corresponding Chinese action. I think however that it must be acknowledged that there is no really convincing and comfortable evidence to support this. But any debate about Chinese intentions is bound to be inconclusive and I doubt if there is great profit in pursuing it. It seems to me that it must be the object of our diplomacy to probe—through the admittedly very inadequate channels at our disposal—what the Chinese price for an accommodation would be, always however recognising that the price may in the event turn out to be unacceptably high.

(b) Is it now the right time to make a determined effort towards an accommodation with the Chinese over Hong Kong; are conditions for a 'settlement' likely to improve or deteriorate?

It is of course quite impossible to give any accurate forecast of future events in China over the next months or years. Sir D. Hopson is right to insist that we cannot bank on conditions improving for a settlement. Nevertheless, the possible effect on Sino-British relations of changes within China must not be underestimated. It is still unclear why the Chinese eventually decided to grant exit visas to senior staff, but it is at any rate arguable that it was the result of a high-level decision by the more pragmatic members of the leadership that a policy of blackmail was neither benefiting the national reputation of China nor extracting concessions from us in Hong Kong. The timing of concessions is clearly important in that ideally we should wish to make them at the time when we considered that the attitudes of the leadership were such as to make it likely that the Chinese would respond. But this is a counsel of perfection. From the practical point of view, all that can be said is that the Chinese decision on exit visas can be taken as an indication that the leadership are in a reasonably pragmatic frame of mind and that they are as likely to respond now as at any time in the immediate future to any attempts to accommodate that we may make.

(c) What are the risks that policies of firmness against the local Communists in Hong Kong will provoke another outburst of violence?

It seems to me that if the Government of Hong Kong are to maintain their authority and prestige among the population as a whole, they must continue—as they have done in the past—to take firm action against Communist activities when these show any signs of getting out of hand. (Hong Kong telegram No. 832.)[8] Admittedly, there are particularly sensitive areas, notably education and the press, where attempts to reduce the mischief-making potential of the local Communists might well create more problems than they solved; and Sir D. Hopson has very rightly drawn attention to the risks (Peking telegram No. 620).[9] But the Governor is well aware of this. (He told me privately that in deference to Chinese susceptibilities he has connived at sedition on the part of the Communist press to a considerable greater degree than he has thought strictly desirable from the point of view of the local Hong Kong situation.) Moreover, such is the Chinese interest in the economic viability of Hong Kong

8 Not printed.
9 No. 125.

that they would probably have to be greatly provoked before sanctioning a further recourse of violence. All this is very much a matter of judgement in particular sets of circumstances; and, as the Governor pointed out in Hong Kong telegram No. 855, it is a balancing act in which the Hong Kong Government are not inexperienced.

(*d*) *What measures are open to us in Hong Kong to promote an accommodation?*

In recent months, the Chinese have been pressing us for action with varying degrees of insistence in the following matters: prisoners, the reinstatement of workers, and gift rice. (I exclude education because their present complaints about the closure of Chung Wah School do not yet seem to amount to a campaign against the Hong Kong Government's educational policy in general; and also US naval visits, because I doubt if we shall hear a great deal more about this for the time being—provided we keep the 'Enterprise' out of Hong Kong!)

7. We have long accepted that the Communist prisoners in Hong Kong are the key issue. If the Chinese Government are to retain the respect of their local followers, they must keep up some form of pressure on us as long as over 600 of these followers are in prison in Hong Kong for what the Chinese certainly regard as political activities. The Chinese probably do not differentiate between convicted prisoners and detainees, since they regard all as having been 'illegally' detained.

(*a*) The detainees present the lesser problem since they are being held under emergency administrative arrangements and can be released at any time. At present there are 43 in number, nine having been released in recent weeks, the last three as a tacit acknowledgement on our part of Sir D. Hopson's exit visa. The Governor now intends to follow a policy of releasing further batches in step with the grant of exit visas to those members of our Mission who are still due to come out. This seems satisfactory; and I do not think that it would be desirable to press the Governor to do more at this stage.

(*b*) Convicted prisoners present a much more serious problem. They could be released prematurely only by acts of clemency or by a formal change in the regulations governing the remission of sentences. On 25 July (Hong Kong telegram No. 928), the Governor stated that there were still in his view serious objections to release before sentences less remission were completed. His reaction to a further attempt by Sir D. Hopson to press him on the matter (Peking telegram No. 699)[10] was to send a personal telegram to Sir A. Galsworthy (Hong Kong telegram No. 960)[10] asking to be excused from making further comment. We have now asked him to reconsider the position in the case of the two NCNA journalists, the release of whom we reckon to be probably the minimum required for the release of Mr Grey. His reply with detailed views on how the matter might be handled has just arrived. Until it has been settled how we should proceed in this matter, it would be premature to pursue the question of clemency for other convicted prisoners.

8. Reinstatement of workers and gift rice are in comparison minor matters.

(*a*) Though the reinstatement by the Government and private employers of workers dismissed during the troubles for political strikes is clearly an issue of importance for the local Communists in Hong Kong, it has not attracted a great deal of support from Peking. The Governor reported on 25 July (Hong Kong telegram No. 928) that the Communists were on the point of admitting that this campaign had failed and

10 Not printed.

that he thought that no concession seemed useful or in practice at all feasible. In a matter of such local complexity, I think we must accept his judgement.

(*b*) *Gift rice*. The Chinese wanted, for propaganda purposes, to bring into Hong Kong outside the normal quota system, 5,000 tons of rice for free distribution. Although the Hong Kong authorities have not stood on the letter of the existing regulations and were prepared to grant the necessary permits if the Communists made a more or less token application through the normal channels, the Communists appear to want only a substantial propaganda victory. In the face of the refusal of Hong Kong authorities to give them this, they seem to have more or less dropped the idea in recent weeks. I doubt therefore if there is much to be gained by making a gesture to China over this—even if we could bring the Governor to agree to it.

JAMES MURRAY

MINUTING ON NO. 143

This is a useful summing up of a difficult and contentious subject. We shall need to discuss it with Sir D. Hopson but preferably after he has had some leave and perhaps also—as regards at any rate the longer term aspects of the Hong Kong problem—after 'merger'.[11] It can be misleading to talk of 'ending confrontation over Hong Kong' and of 'normalising our relations with China'. Our relations with China will never be normal so long as Maoist Communists are in power and confrontation of one kind or another will continue so long as we stay in Hong Kong.

But we shall have to go on working to ensure that in the shorter term we do not miss chances of gradual de-escalation, e.g. though well timed release of detainees and even convicted prisoners in Hong Kong; and in the longer term we keep open the possibility of our eventual accommodation with China about the future of Hong Kong and prevent a collapse of confidence among the younger Hong Kong Chinese before our departure. Indeed the time is coming when a policy of simply hanging on in Hong Kong is not enough and we shall need to try to chart a navigable course towards our final exit.

DENNIS ALLEN
21 August 1968

After discussion with Far Eastern Department, the Planning Staff recently prepared a draft Planning paper on Sino/British relations and Hong Kong. I attach a copy.[12] Briefly, the conclusion is that limited conciliatory gestures to the Chinese in Hong Kong could be made without significant risk but need to be carefully calculated, and that our general guidelines should be flexibility without excessive expectations, bearing in mind doubts about our ability to maintain our military commitment in Hong Kong over the next thirty years.

---

11 In March 1968, the Prime Minister announced that the Foreign Office and the Commonwealth Office would merge. This took place on 17 October 1968.
12 Not printed.

2. On reading Mr. Murray's submission in conjunction with the Planning paper it is brought home how severely limited is our room for manoeuvre. In the short run at least we are very vulnerable both in Peking and Hong Kong. It is unlikely that we could get out of either Peking or Hong Kong even if we wanted to. We are open to continuing blackmail and the chances of influencing Chinese policy through our Mission are pretty small. However, applying the general conclusions on our Planning paper to the short term, the right course would seem to be not only to make further releases of detainees (*pari passu* with the easing of visas for our Peking Mission) but also to prepare the ground for selective, limited releases of convicted prisoners (c.f. action in train in connection with Grey). The success or failure of such a policy of gradual and limited de-escalation would become evident as we went along. The trend could be accelerated or reversed depending on Chinese reactions.

3. As to the longer term—charting the course towards 1997—I wonder if there is really anything we can do beyond trying out the policy suggested above. Whether this course is really navigable will depend on circumstances largely outside our control, e.g. Chinese irrationality, the outcome in Vietnam and comparative British weakness in the Far East. Indeed, in the light of Chinese irrationality one is bound to be a bit sceptical about the application of our own type of rational assessment to such a situation. It is a glimpse of the obvious to say that whatever we do there is a risk of grave trouble for us; but, if ever we get a chance to get out of Hong Kong in good order, we should clearly seize it.

4. As regards our Mission in Peking, the sensible pragmatic course seems to be to maintain it on a reduced scale, bearing in mind that while the advantage of maintaining it are small in the short run, they may increase and it would in any case probable not be possible to withdraw it completely.

5. In terms of procedure, I wonder whether longer term aspects (with which Planning Staff are mainly concerned) might not be best be looked at after the merger when our draft paper could be used to help focus discussion in the combined Office perhaps first at a meeting of the Planning Committee, which we would hope Sir D. Hopson could attend.

B. H. C. Sykes
26 August 1968

While I see no option for Hong Kong to continue for the time being with a tight-rope policy, it must be borne in mind that the balance of educated Chinese opinion will, for pragmatic reasons, move progressively against us as time goes on. For instance the Governor said on his visit home earlier this year that with 29-years to go, he could no longer offer a full career to civil servants; and similarly for other professions. Furthermore Chinese capital, originally seeking refuge from Shanghai, is now slipping on from Hong Kong to Singapore where it will be of greater benefit not only to its owners but also to British interests generally. Thirdly, our defence effort in Hong Kong cannot be sustained at its current strength for the next 29 years; I myself have doubts whether, when we withdraw from Singapore, the garrison can be effectively and credibly maintained at the end of such a long line of communication.

For these and other reasons there is an optimum point in time between 1972 and 1997 at which we should seriously think of negotiating our way out of Hong Kong; but short of that point it is worth hanging on in case the Chinese attitude changes.

It would be useful to argue this all out at a Planning Committee, and there would be advantage in confronting Sir D. Hopson and a member of Hong Kong Government on 'neutral' ground. The Governor is unlikely to be back this autumn, but would the Chief Secretary or Political Adviser be available. Could we aim for this in early October?

EDWARD PECK
27 August 1968

If I may venture to say so, I entirely agree with the conclusions in your submission about Sino-British relations. I have not seen Sir D. Hopson's memorandum, but on his first point that Sino-British relations are now worse than at any time since the communists took over he forgets the period during the Korean War when, though we were represented in Peking, the Chinese had no representation in London; when we had no access to the policy levels in the Chinese Ministry of Foreign Affairs; when the very considerable British establishment which then existed in China was being destroyed and when there were some really tricky situations in Hong Kong such as the handing over of the CNAC aircraft to the Formosans and the requisitioning of the 'Yung Hao' It is, I suggest, a mistake to look at the Hong Kong situation simply in the immediate context.

2. In my own view, the Chinese do not want any 'accommodation' over Hong Kong. If at a given point they are prepared to stop their probing it will only be because it does not suit them to go on pushing at that particular point of time. If we were to try to reach some sort of agreement with them they would only use it as a platform from which to make additional demands when the situation changed. Any Chinese government of whatever conviction is bound to try and undermine our position in Hong Kong and *a fortiori* a revolutionary government must do so. The only thing that will restrain them is their assessment of the balance of their interest in letting Hong Kong be or disrupting it. While therefore we need to avoid doing things which might provoke the Chinese our object must surely be to exercise sufficient firmness so that the Chinese reckon that if they press on with any particular line it will either be defeated or cause such a degree of disruption as to harm their own interests. The policy of the Government of Hong Kong seems to fit in very well with this.

3. Perhaps I am stressing the obvious but, in contrast to what seems to be the drift of Sir D. Hopson's memorandum, I feel sure that a dialogue with the Chinese over Hong Kong is not and is never likely to be a practical proposition.

C. T. CROWE
22 August 1968

No. 144

Mr Cradock (Peking) to Mr Stewart, 21 August 1968[1]
Tel. No. 765 Immediate, Secret (FCO 21/140, FC 13/8)

Hong Kong telegram No. 1007:[2] Grey.

The telegram under reference considers three possible courses of action:

(*a*) a publicity campaign until November and then, if Hsueh's release does not produce results, secret discussions with the Chinese on the release of Lo in return for Grey;

(*b*) secret discussions with the Chinese now, bargaining the release of Hsueh and if necessary Lo, in return for Grey;

(*c*) unconditional review of Hsueh and Lo now.

2. To take these in order. On course (*a*), a publicity campaign unaccompanied by any concession in Hong Kong is most unlikely to procure Grey's release. We must distinguish his case from that of the staff of this Mission. On the latter the Chinese were to some extent on the defensive as a result of removals of restrictions on the movement of their officials in London and the imminent diplomatic campaign. We had made the relevant concessions. Grey on the other hand has been explicitly linked by the Chinese with the Hong Kong prisoners and we cannot expect progress until we have made some move in that sector. By waiting until November for any such move we would deprive ourselves of the chance of making a gesture over Hsueh since he would be released then in any event. We would add another three months to Grey's solitary confinement. I am not convinced by the argument in paragraph 3 of telegram under reference that by waiting until 16 November we would give a greater impression of strength. Acting now fifteen months after the trouble began and eight months after the violence ended would not be seen to be acting from weakness. If the earlier release of NCNA men at this stage is, however, to be equated with weakness we would still incur the charge in November as a result of our readiness to release Lo.

3. On course (*b*), we face the problems we have encountered repeatedly over the last year: how to assure ourselves in advance the concession we contemplate will produce the desired result. The short answer is we cannot. I greatly doubt whether we shall get any reliable prior undertaking from the Chinese on the release of Grey. Something cryptic after a long delay, or no answer at all, is more likely. The delay involved is important both for humanitarian reasons and since the longer we wait the less of a concession we have to offer over Hsueh. We must assume that some months would be taken up by this probe, particularly if we use the channel referred to in paragraph 6 of the telegram under reference. There is also the danger that by putting this proposal beforehand we shall encourage the Chinese to go for higher stakes, e.g. all news-workers, or to widen the discussion in other ways. To sum up I do not consider the chance of the extra [gp. undec]s this course may produce on Chinese intentions is worth the delay and the [*sic*] raising their sights involved in the probe.

4. As regards channels to be used if discussions were nevertheless decided on, we must balance the 'deniable' nature of unofficial channel against the greater obscurity

1 Repeated for information priority to Hong Kong.
2 No. 141.

and delay. It is arguable that, if we are clear up to what price we will go, it would be better to put proposal officially in Peking on grounds that our chances of a quick and reliable answer would be higher there. But I hope discussions by whatever channel can be avoided.

5. On course (*c*), unconditional release now would carry an obvious danger: we might find we had released two men without getting Grey out. On the other hand for reasons given above I doubt this risk can be greatly reduced however we approach the matter. We know we are making relevant concessions, whether they are decisive or not we shall only discover by making them. As regards the appearance of an 'act of submission' (paragraph 12 of telegram under reference) any premature release, successful or not, or indeed any concession, might conceivably be interpreted this way. But at this interval after last year's violence and in the present more favourable political climate the risk seems slight. The earlier release of young convicted prisoners, which I understand occurred in April, June and July, has not been seen in this light. The release of Hsueh and Lo could be readily presented to the public as an act of humanity to assist Grey's release. If the Chinese failed to respond they would be much more vulnerable to publicity. [gp. undec.] I do not agree that the possibility of helping Grey would have greatly receded (paragraph 12 of telegram under reference).

6. I should add that the immediate release of Hsueh alone, followed by the possible release of Lo if the Chinese reaction is encouraging, would not be a satisfactory compromise. If we are prepared to release the two we should do so in one act. Instalments will encourage the Chinese to ask for more instalments and would have the many disadvantages of course (*b*). Nevertheless if it came to the choice, I would prefer this to course (*c*).

7. My recommendation is strongly for course (*c*).

No. 145

Minute from Mr Murray to Sir D. Allen, 23 August 1968
Top Secret (FCO 40/70, HWB 3/2)

Sino-British Relations

Hong Kong telegram No. 996[1] to the Commonwealth Office reported a meeting between Mr Cater and an intermediary of the Chinese Communists. Since there has recently been discussion in the context of Mr Grey of ways in which a dialogue might be opened with the Chinese, you may care to be reminded how this channel was established and of the exchanges which have taken place to date.

2. In early March this year the Manager of the Bank of China in Hong Kong, Li Choh-Chih, approached Mr Jay, a British businessman and a former manager of the same Bank, allegedly on instructions from Chou En-Lai and proposed that there should be discussions on an entirely confidential basis to 'settle the Hong Kong question' to the advantage of both the United Kingdom and China. Li indicated that

1 Not printed.

the basis of the discussion should be the 'demands' put forward by the Chinese in May, 1967, but the majority of these would only be insisted on in a token fashion. The most difficult problem was likely to be the release of political prisoners in Hong Kong. On the recommendation of both the governor and the Chargé d'Affaires in Peking, Ministers agree that we should respond to the Chinese initiative (my submission of 18 March).[2]

3. It was accordingly decided that Mr Cater, formally Deputy Colonial Secretary who now holds the para-governmental appointment of Executive Director of Trade Development Council in Hong Kong, should be the Hong Kong Government's representative and treat with the contact, but not direct with Li. The first meeting took place on 27 March (Hong Kong telegram No. 387).[3] The contact repeated that the Chinese considered the demands as 'token' and had no intention of trying to bring about a 'Macao-type' situation in Hong Kong. There was some further discussion about the release of prisoners and Mr Cater indicated that the discussions must be two-way, i.e. the British side would have requests to make such as an undertaking that the local Communist press would be kept under control, that British nationals in China should be properly treated, and that events in Hong Kong should be accurately reported by the New China News Agency.

4. A second meeting took place on 3 April at which the contact said the Chinese were disappointed at the slowness of the Hong Kong government's initial response. However some of the urgency has gone out of the situation as the approach had been made in the first instance because at some unspecified date in the recent past Chou En-Lai had learned that 'a Chinese army to the North of Hong Kong had been making preparations to go to the assistance of the patriotic compatriots' and had thought it necessary to open a dialogue without delay, (nothing more was subsequently heard from the contact about the army). Li had added that after being informed of the Hong Kong government's slowness to respond Chou En Lai had issued instructions to the local communists that the struggle with the Hong Kong government should cease, that local patriots must be informed 'that the enemy is not Britain but the United States' and that the Chinese are keen to have good relations with Britain. There was some further general discussion but no real progress was made.

5. Li went to China on 18 May and the next meeting did not take place until 10 July. On that date the contact claimed that Chou En-Lai personally had approved the channel of communication between him and Cater on the assumption that it was the only channel and should be kept very secret (Hong Kong telegram No. 895).[3] Of the points put by the contact, the most specific was that the Communists in Hong Kong were concerned mainly about prisoners both convicted prisoners and detainees and strikers but in the long run both might turn out to be of minor significance and the most difficult problem would be the question of saving face. The contact gave it as his advice that it would be wrong to make concessions or to start discussions on specific points at this stage. It would be sufficient (*a*) to confirm this channel of communication, (*b*) to agree it should be kept secret, and (*c*) to reaffirm our desire to have peaceful relations with China while maintaining law and order in Hong Kong.

2 No. 88.
3 Not printed.

6. The Governor commented after this meeting that he suspended judgement on whether the Chinese government would in the end try to use this channel of communication for serious business but saw advantage in keeping the channel open. He accordingly authorised Mr Cater to proceed on the lines suggested. Since then there have been further meetings on 16 July and 2 August (Hong Kong telegram 996). In the course of these Mr Cater has been able to clear up a misunderstanding about an alleged Hong Kong Government's circular concerning reinstatement of strikers and to give the Communists advance warning of the release of detainees. He has also explained Government policy over Chung Wah School and this elicited the reply that Li (presumably reflecting the local Communist opinion) realised that the Hong Kong Government had no real alternative to deregistration. The question was not of serious concern to the local Communists but they had to make a fuss.

7. It is still unclear why the Chinese decided to open this channel assuming that it is genuine. Some of the views attributed by Li to the communists are hard to swallow (end of paragraph 4 above) and may only be intended as bait to encourage us to swallow demands for concessions. After the initial haste to start discussions, meetings have been well spaced. Nothing has apparently been achieved, nor has there been any perceptible softening of the local Communist attitude, e.g. in the press, though Li has claimed there has been. There seems however every advantage in keeping the channel open as discussion with the Chinese through other channels, e.g. in London and Peking, has so far not proved very productive; while there are obvious objections to using NCNA in Hong Kong. We shall have an opportunity to test the value of this channel if it is decided to pursue one of the Governor's proposals on negotiating an exchange of Mr Grey for the two imprisoned NCNA correspondents. I am submitting separately on this question.[4]

JAMES MURRAY

4 Mr Allen minuted on 27 August that the contact was worth maintaining.

No. 146

Mr Cradock (Peking) to Mr Stewart, 26 August 1968[1]
Tel. No. 781 Immediate (FCO 40/88, HWB 9/12A)

I was summoned to the Foreign Ministry this afternoon to receive a protest from Hsueh (Deputy Director of Western Europe) about the deregistration of Chung Wah School.

2. In an oral statement Hsueh said the British authorities had disregarded the stern warning of the Chinese Government of 3 August and on 14 August had announced their decision to cancel registration of Chung Wah School. This was a grave incident which amounted to wilful persecution of Chinese Patriotic Educational undertakings and could only lead to renewed tension in Hong Kong. The Chinese government had

1 Repeated for information to Hong Kong.

long ago made clear that compatriots had the inviolable right to study and propagate Mao's thought in Hong Kong and carry out related activities. In November 1967 the British authorities had closed the school on a pretext about an explosion, arrested the Headmaster and deprived hundreds of teachers and students of the right to teach and study. Now the British authorities were deregistering the school upon the specious pretext. This was a great new political provocation. Hsueh said that the Chinese government was very indignant and that he was instructed to lodge a serious protest. The British side were always talking glibly about their desire to ease Sino-British relations and to settle outstanding differences. However in fact they indulged in repeated brazen provocation against the Chinese people and their compatriots. The British authorities would be fully responsible for the consequences.

3. In reply I said we had already explained our policy fully on Chung Wah at the 3 August interview. The school was closed and deregistered as a result of a violent incident which took place there last November. The Hong Kong government had made it clear that although the school was deregistered, they were prepared to consider an application to open a new school on the same premises with a different name and different staff, in accordance with the normal criteria. This was an important gesture by the Hong Kong Government towards the cause of peaceful education. I pointed out that there were plans in hand to open 25 new Communist schools in Hong Kong: 9 applications to open new schools had already been submitted and were being dealt with in the normal way: 2 new schools had already been registered. This proved that the Hong Kong government were not against peaceful education. I said I could not accept the protest because it was without foundation and reiterated the British Government's desire to improve Sino/British relations. I repeated that if an application was made to open a new school there was a good chance it would be accepted. But I emphasised that if, without applying to have a new school registered, an attempt was made to continue to run an unregistered school on the Chung Wah premises, then that would be illegal, and the Hong Kong Government would not hesitate to apply the law.

4. In the subsequent exchange, Hsueh said that opening new schools and closing a long existing one were two different matters and we were double faced trying to compare them. If we had a genuine wish to ease Sino-British relations we should prove this by our acts. Since May last year 4 or 5 thousand compatriots had been arrested, of whom several hundred were still in gaols and concentration camps. Moreover, the question of economic losses to patriotic Chinese and patriotic undertakings have not yet even been raised. The British side said that they ensured the right to study and propagate Mao's thought, but their persecution of patriotic schools including Chung Wah belied their words. If the British side wanted to ease relations and solve outstanding differences they must give serious consideration to the various just demands of the Chinese government.

5. I said there was no contradiction in the Hong Kong government's policy towards education. We could accept peaceful education but we would not tolerate violence. As for easing relations, our acts did not belie our words, as Hsueh would know if he studied the Hong Kong situation closely. I repeated that if an attempt was made to carry on education in Chung Wah School without registration this would be contrary to the law and the Hong Kong Government would have to apply the law.

6. In answer to my question Hsueh confirmed that the Chinese statement would be published, see my telegram No. 783.²

2 In this telegram Mr Cradock commented: 'By Chinese standards this was a fairly restrained protest which they probably felt obliged to make for the record'. It was couched in generalized terms and did not make specific demands.

No. 147

Sir D. Trench (Hong Kong) to Mr Thomson (Commonwealth Office)
9 September 1968
Tel. No. 1063 Priority, Secret (FCO 21/69, FC 3/3G)

Following personal for Galsworthy.
Your letter of 23rd August: Hopson's despatch of 29th July.¹
Most of the ground of this despatch has already been covered in the series of telegrams on Sino-British relations. I accept a good deal of what Hopson says although from the purely Hong Kong angle I would often wish to vary the emphasis and to dispute some at least of his assessments.

2. In particular, I think the despatch pays much too little regard to the concessions Hong Kong has already made and continues to make for no appreciable return. We have recently sent you a paper assessing the concessions on both sides but here I would especially emphasise our restraint in relation to the seditious press and to Communist schools.

3. I naturally agree that we should aim to avoid further friction wherever we can but in the ordinary course of maintaining law and order clashes inevitably continue to occur and militant Communists [?continue] to get prison sentences.

4. The despatch lays its main emphasis on the need for further positive concessions in the form of the release of detainees and as amnesty for convicted prisoners. As regards detainees I shall continue the present policy of releasing them as and when I am able to satisfy myself that the security risk of doing so is acceptable. This must be overriding and needs to be appreciated that, while at present we have a number of lesser risks whom we can afford to release, as these go we get down to the hard core. These it may be preferable to retain in custody for some time yet rather than to risk releasing them and then have to re-arrest them.

5. As regards the convicted prisoners (apart from the two NCNA prisoners for whom special arrangements are under consideration) it would be recommended that virtually all the lesser confrontation offenders will be freed with full remission by the end of this year. Those for whom Hopson recommends an amnesty are in practice those convicted for serious violence or other serious crimes and sentenced to more than two years. Although their crimes were committed as part of a politically inspired Communist campaign, they were not political offences and to make them the subject of a political amnesty as a gratuitous act on our part could, apart from other objections, have a most serious effect in Hong Kong.

1 No. 135.

No. 148

Minute from Sir P. Gore-Booth to Mr Murray, 10 September 1968
Confidential (FCO 21/465)

Sino-British Relations

Thank you very much for this very comprehensive submission as background for my talk with Sir D. Hopson.[1]

2. I did not discuss matters in great detail with Sir D. Hopson but said that his valuable contribution, plus the Governor of Hong Kong's comments (which I showed him) meant in effect that the triangular game of tennis between Peking, Hong Kong and London would continue and that in the immediate future it looked as though we could move a little further and hope that this might lead to some further concessions. This seemed to be the only way in which to proceed, especially as we could never be quite confident about Chinese motivations or procedures. Sir D. Hopson agreed with our own feeling that the Chinese must have got wind of the organisation of the diplomatic move against them and have decided to anticipate it rather than to react to it.

3. Sir D. Hopson was further relieved to find that Sir A. Galsworthy, with whom he had had a long conversation, had agreed that the basic long term aim of policy must be how to disengage ourselves from Hong Kong. He drew a parallel with General de Gaulle's decision over Algeria; I pointed out that it was a stage worse in the sense that the French gave their '*colons*'[2] a chance to get away whereas there was no possible prospect of our evacuating more than an infinitesimal number of Chinese from Hong Kong. Nevertheless I agreed that the objective was inevitable.

4. I think that it would help if the Department would use the Governor's telegram[3] as a basis for an effort to condense doctrine and tactics into a short submission as is practicable distilled from the volume of minutes attached.[4] It could indicate both the consensus of views in the external departments on a number of points and also show where there are still differences of opinion. Subject to your views and those of the Planners this might go up, through Sir D. Allen, myself and Mr Foley, to the Secretary of State; I think it would be timely for him to see the Department's conclusions. The Commonwealth Office may wish to make a parallel submission.

P. H. GORE-BOOTH

1 No. 143.
2 Settlers.
3 No. 147.
4 Not printed.

No. 149

Sir D. Trench (Hong Kong) to Mr Thomson (Commonwealth Office)
20 September 1968[1]
Tel. No. 2001 Priority, Top Secret (FCO 21/142, FC 13/8)

My Telegram No. 2000:[2] Grey.

Following is extract from Cater's Report:

'At this stage I said that we were delighted that visas had now been issued to all the old Peking Mission staff, as indeed contact had promised that they would be. Contact was clearly tickled by this and rambled on at some length to the effect that it was a good thing that all 'the old problems' had now been settled. This gave me an excellent opportunity to say that this was true except, of course, for the outstanding case of Anthony Grey, the Reuters correspondent. I then went on to say that I had been thinking the matter over recently: we were aware that Grey had not been well in recent weeks and in spite of considerable pressures had done our best to curb publicity on this rather emotional matter. Although clearly difficulties were involved, I wondered whether it would be possible to obtain Grey's release if, say, we were to consider releasing Hsueh Ping. Contact reacted very strongly to this and interrupted saying that this would be a very silly thing to do. I tried to continue my explanation but against the greatest of opposition. Contact continually butted in, saying finally this would be quite stupid of us to think in these terms. On asking his reasons, he said without hesitation that it would be an open invitation to grab British people in China and to hold them as hostages in order to force our hand on other matters: that to show interest of this sort would clearly lead to demands for a great deal more than the release of Hsueh. In any event, contact said, Hsueh was not the price Peking want for Grey. When the opportunity arose I said that we had gained the impression in Peking that Grey had been placed under house detention as a reprisal for the arrest and imprisonment of Hsueh and that accordingly Grey would not be released until Hsueh Ping was released. Contact replied that this could well be the sort of answer that Peking might give in response to any enquiry from the Chargé d'Affaires but what else, he asked, could they have said?—they had to have some logical reason for detaining Grey. It was Contact's understanding that Peking in fact were highly embarrassed by Grey's situation, and he believed that it was only a matter of time, and not a great deal of time, before the Chinese would release him. Having said this, he reminded me that previously I had said that as Judiciary and the Administration were quite separate it would not be possible to arrange the release of a convicted prisoner. I said that, whilst clearly there would be difficulties involved, I was confident that I could persuade the Governor to release Hsueh Ping in these rather special circumstance and especially as Hsueh

---

1 Repeated for information to Peking.
2 Not printed. In this telegram, Sir D. Trench stated that his instructions to Mr Cater were to begin by mentioning the possibility of releasing Hsueh for Mr Grey and towards the end of the conversation mention the possibility of releasing Lo as well. However, the conversation moved in a different direction. He added: 'As the Contact has been well informed over other matters such as exit visas for the mission and Chung Wah School, it is possible he will turn out to be right about Grey to.'

Ping had already served over a year of his sentence. After further lengthy discussion on these lines, Contact said that he thought it quite disastrous for us to make an offer of this type. He thought that if anything were to be done at all on this, there should be no mention of making an enquiry but that he should write to Chou En-lai's secretary stating simply that, now that relations were so much better between Britain and China, it seemed a pity that there remained the one outstanding problem of Anthony Grey. He would ask what the circumstances were concerning this and whether anything could be done. I commented that this was certainly one method of approach but would it not take a rather long time to obtain a definitive answer. He immediately said no, that it would not take long, no more than a week or perhaps 10 days. In the circumstances and in the face of his very strong reaction, I accordingly agreed that he should proceed as proposed. He then went on to say that at the same time he would take the opportunity of mentioning Johnston so that it would not appear that there was over-anxiety in regard to Grey. In the circumstances, I of course made no mention of Lo.'

Mr Cater comments in his report that he is only too well aware that he did not carry through your intentions but he considered that by accepting Contact's proposals there should be no great loss of time and there might be substantial advantage.[3]

---

3 In Peking Tel. No. 883, dated 24 September, Mr Cradock expressed his concern at the 'decisive role' the contact seems to have played at the meeting. Instead of acting as a channel of communication for a specific British proposal he had, on the basis of his personal views, made a generalised approach himself to the Chinese.

No. 150

Submission from Mr Murray to Sir D. Allen, 23 September 1968
Confidential (FCO 21/141, FC 13/8D)

Mr Anthony Grey

Problem

In a letter to Miss McGuinn on 5 July, Mr Grey indicated that he was worried about his health (Foreign Office telegram No. 808 to Peking).[1] We therefore instructed the Chargé d'Affaires in Peking to express our concern and repeat the request for access to Mr Grey. The subsequent call of a member of the Mission on the News Department of the Chinese Ministry of Foreign Affairs is reported in Peking telegram Nos. 830 and 831.[1] After further reminders the Chinese eventually said the following on 16 September: 'as we told you before and as you know yourselves, his (Mr Grey's) situation is excellent including his health' (Peking telegram No. 861).[1] Mr Cradock recommended that in view of the unsatisfactory nature of the Chinese reply we should give publicity to the question of Mr Grey's health. We have to decide whether and in what form to do so.

Recommendation

2. *I recommend* that News Department make an on-the-record-statement and

---

1 Not printed. Miss McGuinn was Mr Grey's girlfriend and future wife. They married in 1970.

comment on it unattributably on the lines of the attached draft.¹ Reuters have been consulted and concur.

Background

3. When Sir D. Hopson visited Mr Grey on 23 April he seemed to be in satisfactory health. Since, however, he is confined effectively to one room and only allowed two short exercise periods a day, it would not be surprising if his health had suffered, as he indicated in the letter to Miss McGuinn. (Miss McGuinn has since had a letter dated 3 August in [which] he seems in a more cheerful frame of mind.)

4. I doubt whether the Chinese would allow his health to deteriorate seriously. On the other hand I see considerable advantage in using the Chinese failure to grant access or give any specific information about Mr Grey's health to make some publicity. There have been indications that the Chinese are somewhat sensitive to implications that they are behaving in an uncivilised way. I do not think, however, that we should go so far as Mr Cradock suggests and say that we conclude that the Chinese have something to hide and that Mr Grey may not be in good health. This could give rise to serious public concern here and might very well upset his mother despite any reassurances she receives from Reuters. A plain statement of the facts should be sufficient to show up the extent of the Chinese iniquity.²

JAMES MURRAY

2 FO Tel. No. 859 to Peking, 2 October 1968, reported that a statement was made but received little coverage in the press. It refrained from saying openly that the Government had misgivings about Grey's health.

No. 151

Mr Cradock (Peking) to Mr Stewart, 23 September 1968
Confidential (FCO 21/69, FC 3/3G)

Sir,

The Visa War Part I

On the 22nd of August, 1967, on receipt of the news of the sacking of this Mission, the Foreign Office informed the acting Chargé in London of certain restrictions on the movements of Chinese officials: their radius of free movement was reduced from 35 miles to 5 miles from the centre of London and before leaving the United Kingdom they were required to apply for exit visas. The Chinese responded a week later by imposing much harsher restrictions on the movements of this Mission. A hard and claustrophobic year ensued. Eventually, on the 27th of July this year, a junior official of the Chinese Foreign Ministry informed us, at the close of an interview on another matter and almost as an aside, that the Chinese would grant all outstanding applications for exit visas for our staff. The last such visa was issued on the 13th of September. Though it would be hazardous to assume that the story is over there seems now a good prospect that, unless further tension develops in Hong Kong, movement for staff of this office may return to something approaching normality. This may therefore be a convenient point to look back over the past year of detention, both in order to provide some record of an extraordinary episode in diplomatic history and to consider whether it offers any cautionary experience for further dealings with the Chinese. For convenience I have dealt with the subject in two despatches: the first offers a summary narrative of events since August 1967 as seen from here; the second ventures to draw some conclusions.

2. As with most crises its precise starting point is hard to determine. There had been an ominous example of the Chinese readiness to interfere with diplomatic movement for political purposes in 1966, in the curious affair of the Chinese welders. A delegation of such welders in Holland, who were reasonably suspected of having murdered a member of their delegation, were detained for criminal investigation. In retaliation the Netherlands Chargé d'Affaires here was promptly declared *persona non grata*, but not allowed for a period of some months to leave the country or even his residence. The proper conclusions were not, however, drawn from this incident and though some Western governments, including our own, made representations to the Chinese, the Peking diplomatic corps as a body remained silent and obsequious.

3. In our own case the prelude was the crisis in Hong Kong arising from the Chinese communist attempt, beginning in May 1967, to intimidate the Hong Kong Government. As the summer of 1967 wore on with relations rapidly deteriorating, violent demonstrations against this Mission and the detention of Reuter's correspondent in Peking, there was some interference with free movement of officials. We withheld a reply to applications for entry visas to the UK made by five Chinese officials: two New China News Agency correspondents, a *People's Daily* reporter accompanied by his wife and two officials of the Bank of China. The Chinese were later to make great play with this. The Chinese for their part showed their displeasure at our policies in various ways, but did not interrupt departure from the country until the 21st of August on the eve of the burning, when they prevented three members of our staff and one wife and child who had visas and tickets from leaving China the next day on the pretext that there were no seats on the plane. The visas were not at that time cancelled, however, and it is uncertain how long this obstruction would have been maintained. However we interpret these preliminaries the period of formally restricted movements began on the 22nd of August. I do not know the precise grounds for our decision that day restricting Chinese movements. But the need to respond to the barbarous events of the preceding night was obviously important; a further need, as it seemed at the time, was to prevent Chinese staff from slipping out of the UK leaving this Mission in Chinese hands with equivalent hostages in London.

4. The Chinese response came on the 29th of August in the strange affair of Portland Place when their diplomats, armed with axes and baseball bats, sallied forth to do battle with the police. This fabricated incident was no doubt intended to offset the moral and publicity advantages we enjoyed as a result of our trials on 22nd of August and to provide the prelude for Chinese counter-restrictions. These were duly announced at an interview at 4 the next morning with Vice-Minister Lo Kuei-po. Our free movements were limited to the compound containing diplomatic flats, our former Office and the Chargé's Residence, plus the 400-yard strip of connecting road. Permission to move outside this area required an application made 48 hours in

advance. All existing visas were cancelled. An ugly demonstration at our improvised office involving some personal violence rounded off the proceedings.

5. There was for a time a danger of further physical violence against our staff or our remaining premises. But before long this receded and we were left to enjoy some of the security as well as the restraints of prison life. Movement within the tiny area laid down by the Chinese took place without difficulty. Permission to move outside the area was often refused, or, if granted, made subject to capricious qualifications. We were at all times zealously shadowed by police in cars, on foot or on bicycles. The Chinese in London were also under strict surveillance but had, of course, a very much larger area in which to move. On the issue of evacuating our staff, which was our major preoccupation, we made virtually no progress. Applications *en bloc* for visas for our women and children went unanswered. A letter from your predecessor to Ch'en Yi proposing that staff on both sides should be temporarily withdrawn to their own country or, alternatively, that a smaller staff be left under suitable guarantees, received no reply. Only by drastically lowering our sights did we achieve any results. An application for exit visas for five school children who had come to Peking for the summer holidays was granted in September and an application for two pregnant wives was granted in October. Meanwhile the Chinese officials in London sat tight and made no attempt to leave or apply for visas.

6. It was soon apparent to us that in this exchange of harassments and restrictions we were at a substantial disadvantage. The Chinese capacity to be unpleasant was infinitely greater than our own and their officials, living comfortably in London, were endowed with greater endurance. This Office therefore proposed in October that as a move of deescalation, we should consider lifting the special restrictions on Chinese movement in London while retaining the ultimate sanction of exit visas. It was hoped that this might set in motion a train of events which would extend from movement in the two capitals to travel between the two countries. Here, however, we began to run into problems with which we became familiar as the year went by and which were, I suppose, inherent in the situation. The question was naturally asked, why we, rather than the Chinese, should make the first concession. Was it not too early to do so in the light of the restraints placed not only on our own staff but on other British subjects in China? There was the doubt whether we could safely act without a firm prior undertaking from the Chinese that they would reciprocate. It was also suggested that a more limited deescalation might suffice, perhaps lifting the movement restrictions on a small group of Chinese officials rather than the whole of the Chinese staff. Eventually, however, it was accepted that we must move first if we wished to see any relaxation; that our concession must be substantial enough to have meaning to the Chinese and to point the way to reciprocal concessions affecting this Mission; finally that we could not hope to engage the Chinese in any meaningful prior discussion; we would have to act on hints. The Chinese had given such hints. On the 14th of November we accordingly informed the Chinese Foreign Minister that on the 21st of November restrictions on Chinese movement in London would revert to the normal 35 mile radius. Nothing was said about exit permits, which were retained as a final bargaining counter and safeguard.

7. In words the Chinese reply was grudging and offensive. Mr Hsueh, the Deputy-Director of West European Department, who received us emphasised that any real

improvement in Sino-British relations depended on Hong Kong and we were harangued at some length on that subject. Nevertheless on the 27th of November we were informed that restrictions on our movement in Peking would be lifted from the 29th of November. The date was no doubt dictated by the Chinese wish to maintain their restrictions for exactly as long as ours; ours had antedated theirs by eight days. Duly on the 29th the apparatus of surveillance vanished; the first knot had been untied.

8. In the interview of the 27th November in answer to a question on exit visas, Mr Hsueh had said that applications would be dealt with in the normal way. We ingenuously supposed that this meant that visas would be forthcoming and applied for exit visas and for entry visas for replacements. We were disappointed and on the 2nd of December Mr Kao, the Deputy-Director of Consular Department, informed us that the reason lay in our policy in Hong Kong. Recently there had been raids on 'patriotic' schools there and an 'illegal decision' against a communist newspaper. This had caused the Chinese Government to doubt the sincerity of our expressed wish to normalise relations. He therefore had 'no fresh news' on visas. This was the first appearance of a manoeuvre with which we were to become familiar: concessions given with one hand were withdrawn or qualified by the other on the pretext of Hong Kong. From December, therefore, we were limited to the enjoyment of normal freedom of movement inside Peking. Only one member of the staff and his family succeeded in leaving the country and this was on urgent medical grounds. No entry visas for replacements were granted.

9. In the last days of December there were signs that the Chinese in London were proposing to test our requirement that they apply for exit visas before leaving the country. Two of them were known to be preparing to travel to China but no application for a visa had been made. An unpleasant scuffle at the airport seemed only too likely. The Chinese Chargé was accordingly summoned and warned of our regulation; he protested against it as unjustified and discriminatory and his staff stayed at home. The same point was made at greater length in an interview I had with Mr Kao of Consular Department on the 24th of January. In this the Chinese showed more of their hand. After giving their version of events in the visa war since the summer of 1967 they made two demands: that we should grant all outstanding entry visa applications, including those for the five officials and one wife referred to in paragraph 3 above; and that we should abolish our exit visa requirement. Asked what return we might expect if we conformed with these demands, Mr Kao gave his personal view that the Chinese would certainly make reciprocal gestures.

10. The offensive Chinese language did not conceal the fact that offers were being made. As offers they had considerable attractions: they suggested that the movement problem for officials might be settled on purely bilateral terms without involving concessions in Hong Kong; and the terms proposed, a reversion to the pre-August 1967 arrangements, were not extravagant. Moreover there was a good indication of reciprocity if we accepted. If there was no reciprocal gesture or if there were signs of a Chinese exodus from London the exit visa requirement could always be reimposed. We in this post strongly urged acceptance. Here, however, the stumbling block proved to be the requested entry visas for NCNA correspondents. It was felt that it would be wrong to allow free movement for NCNA officials while Mr Grey, the detained Reuters' correspondent, remained under confinement in Peking,

and that there was a risk that public opinion in the UK might not welcome a return to normal movement on the part of diplomatic staff in Peking if Mr Grey remained in this confinement. As against this it was argued from here that Grey's case was explicitly linked with that of imprisoned communist news-workers in Hong Kong. A Chinese offer made on the 28th of January of access to Grey in return for special visits to these news-workers, an offer HMG had not felt able to accept, illustrated this link. Withholding NCNA entry visas while refusing concessions over news-workers in Hong Kong would not help Grey and might merely spoil the chances of progress over movement for diplomatic staff. These arguments were carefully weighed but it was decided that we must nonetheless try to bargain with the NCNA entry visas in an effort to obtain Mr Grey's release or some improvement in his situation. On instructions I accordingly informed Consular Department on the 7th February that we were ready to dismantle the exit visas requirement and grant all outstanding entry visas apart from those for the NCNA officials. In return I sought an assurance of return to normal movement for our staff. I also made it clear that if we could have some assurance that the Chinese Government intended to settle the Grey problem quickly that would be of great assistance in dealing with NCNA entry visas.

11. The Chinese gave no formal answer for some time although they indicated that they found our reply unsatisfactory on two grounds: we fell short of their proposals; and, although promising to lift restrictions, we had not actually done so. They also repeated the question of Grey was not one of visas; it was linked with that of Hong Kong and was therefore on a different footing from movement of officials and diplomatic staff. On the 8th of March we were eventually summoned for the formal reply by Vice-Minister Lo Kuei-po who, in a general statement on Sino-British relations, said that our proposals on visas, as those on Grey, had been noted but that the key to the problem lay in Hong Kong. The British Government had failed to reply to the various demands made by the Chinese Government on the subject of Hong Kong in 1967. If the Hong Kong problem was brushed aside it would be difficult to hold fruitful discussions on visas and other secondary matters.

12. This was an extremely disappointing answer. It seriously qualified the Chinese offer of the 24th of January and seemed to make any progress on visas dependent not on reciprocal relaxation in London but on concessions in Hong Kong, which were of course of a very different order. The pattern of events strongly suggested that by attempting to bargain with the NCNA visas and by bringing the issue of Grey into the discussions of visas for officials we had widened the debate and introduced much more difficult questions such as release of communist prisoners in Hong Kong. We braced ourselves for a long siege. As regards an answer to Lo Kuei-po, it was decided to make a reply which, while reaffirming our desire for better relations with China and our wish to ease tension in Hong Kong, would make it clear that we regarded the failure to restore normal diplomatic movement as a barrier to any settlement of wider issues. It was also decided finally to meet the Chinese terms of the 24th of January, even though these might have become superseded. Again I do not know the precise reasons for this decision; but it was advocated from this post on the ground that it would make our negotiating position much clearer; it would strengthen our hand in any subsequent publicity or diplomatic campaign; and it might conceivably produce some response in the form of visas from the Chinese before any settlement was reached over

Hong Kong. At an interview with Lo Kuei-po on the 13th of April Sir Donald Hopson accordingly delivered a statement from HMG on Sino-British relations and handed over the outstanding entry visas, those for the NCNA representatives included. The requirement that Chinese wishing to leave the UK should apply for an exit visa had been lifted on the 4th April. Happily at about the same time it was decided to make the concession over special visits to imprisoned communist news-workers in Hong Kong which would lead to access to Mr Grey and we were eventually able to see him on the 23rd of April. Progress was therefore made on both fronts.

13. On the subject of visas the immediate Chinese reply was more than usually opaque. The Vice-Minister, who had clearly not mastered the question and spent most of the interview fumbling at this brief, written on extremely flimsy pieces of paper and kept in a sort of shopping-bag, said that when the Chinese Government had received confirmation from London that the visa requirement had been lifted they would 'make their own arrangements in accordance with normal procedures to settle these problems'. This might mean almost anything and since the Vice-Minister added considerable abuse on the subject of Hong Kong the outlook was not hopeful. However, only a week later a messenger making a routine call at the Office of the Chinese Chargé in London returned bearing four entry visas for new members of our staff wishing to enter China who had applied in December, 1967. On the 22nd April Mr Kao of Consular Department in his most engaging mood stated in answer to my enquiries that his Vice-Minister had made the matter crystal clear; he had stated that the future visas would be granted for British staff according to normal procedure. Nothing could be clearer. Pressed on the subject of exit visas, Mr Kao said the Chinese 'would do their best to grant them' and 'he hoped it would not take too long'. By now wary of these promises we waited and eventually, after further delay and further representations from our side, exit visas for three junior staff were issued on the 7th of May, the first on other than medical or compassionate grounds to be received since August, 1967.

14. Three more visas for our junior staff followed on the 20th of May and a number of entry visas for replacements were issued about this time in London. Meantime there was no sign of a Chinese exodus from London. One or two staff left for home; but new staff entered the country. Here unhappily a further hitch occurred. On the 24th of May the US nuclear aircraft carrier 'Enterprise' called at Hong Kong. The visit of this giant vessel is invariably a matter for a protest from the Chinese Foreign Ministry and we in this Office had for that reason asked that a visit this year should be cancelled. The protest was duly made on the 27th of May and with it came a stoppage in the trickle of exit visas. In answer to our questions the Chinese justified themselves by reference to our 'recent vicious acts' in Hong Kong which, they explained, meant the visit of 'Enterprise'. This seemed to us at the time a particularly threatening move. Hitherto the freeze on our movements could be explained by reference to the restrictions we had imposed in London. But these restrictions had now been totally dismantled. This further Chinese interference with movement on the pretext of Hong Kong was therefore a breach of the assurances of the 13th and 22nd of April and a blatant case of political blackmail. It was accordingly decided to put into action a plan we had drawn up in December and to launch a diplomatic campaign seeking support from as many foreign

governments as possible, asking them to express to the Chinese their concern at the detention of the staff of a diplomatic mission in Peking and the reiteration of political pre-conditions for their release in contravention of all international practice. As a means of filling the cup Sir Donald Hopson applied for an exit visa on the 22nd of June to leave on the 1st of July. At the same time it was decided to give increased publicity in the UK to the predicament of the Mission and we here circulated our diplomatic colleagues with a list of staff who had applied for visas and who had been kept waiting.

15. Sir Donald Hopson's visa was not issued on the 1st of July as requested but the Chinese response to our representations was more defensive than hitherto. Mr Kao of Consular Department maintained that this application, like all the others in the long list, was 'being handled'. It was slanderous of us to allege that we were being detained; nevertheless if we insisted on putting that construction on it that was our affair. There was admittedly abnormality in the question of visas but this was only a reflection of the abnormality of our relations, for which we were entirely responsible. Hong Kong was not directly mentioned in this interview though it hovered in the background. Nevertheless there was no reason for postponing the diplomatic offensive and on the 23rd of July instructions were issued to our representatives in twenty-six posts, including certain East European posts, to approach the governments to which they were accredited at high level and seek diplomatic support. By the next week reports of the *démarche* were coming in, indicating considerable sympathy on the part of foreign governments, much caution and readiness to take action with the Chinese in a number of cases. A statement was also made in the Foreign Affairs debate in the House of Commons on the 18th of July as the prelude to increased publicity at home. No foreign government had had time to make representations to the Chinese, however, when, by an uncanny coincidence, on the 23rd of July the flow of visas for junior staff, interrupted for some two months, was resumed and on the 27th of July we were given the undertaking referred to in paragraph 1 above, namely that if we would submit an up-to-date list of our visa applications they would be granted.

16. Characteristically the Consular Department official at the interview on the 27th of July did not say when the visas would be granted and there remained a period of almost two months, room for much uncertainty and many further representations on our side, before the undertaking was fully honoured. The threat of a crisis over the reregistration of a major communist school in Hong Kong in August added some last-minute complications. Nevertheless visas for senior staff began to be issued; one was granted to the Commercial Counsellor on the 29th of July. There remained the question of Sir Donald Hopson's visa. In order to extract it we informed the Chinese that he been instructed to leave China on the 10th of August. I sought from Mr Kao an assurance that he would be permitted to leave on that date, otherwise the appropriate conclusion would be drawn and the fact could not be kept hidden however much the Chinese would like to do so. Mr Kao in reply insisted that visas were issued when the Chinese chose, not when we asked, and the Foreign Ministry made a point of exceeding the deadline, though only by two days. On the 12th of August the visa was issued. Over the next month the remaining visas followed.

I am sending copies of this despatch to Her Majesty's representatives at Washington, Canberra and Tokyo, to the Governor, Hong Kong and to the Political Adviser to the Commander-in-Chief for Far East in Singapore.

I have, etc
PERCY CRADOCK

No. 152

Mr Cradock (Peking) to Mr Stewart, 23 September 1968
Confidential (FCO 21/69)

Sir,

The Visa War Part II: Reflections on a Year of Detention

In the first of these two despatches[1] I have given a much simplified account of the manoeuvres on movement restrictions and visas which occupied us from August 1967 until September of this year. It remains to see what conclusions may be drawn from this experience.

2. Two main themes can be discerned. The first is the Hong Kong problem. The visa war was only one aspect of the general deterioration of Sino-British relations resulting from confrontation in Hong Kong. The Hong Kong crisis—the communist demonstrations and violence in the Colony and the necessary and successful counter-action by the Hong Kong Government—provided the background to the various Chinese activities against this Mission in the summer of 1967 and the suppression of three communist newspapers in the Colony was the immediate pretext for the climax, the attack of the 22nd of August. Whatever the immediate cause for their imposition, the restrictions applied to our movements by the Chinese at the end of August became a powerful means of bringing pressure for concessions in Hong Kong. Though the campaign of violence in the Colony was abandoned in December 1967 the Peking authorities still had to consider the situation of their followers there, in particular the communist prisoners and detainees, numbering in 1968 between six and seven hundred. Even when the Foreign Ministry promised normal procedure over visas or later assured us that visas would be issued, the need to buy time and let down their Hong Kong followers gently was presumably a potent factor in Chinese calculations. Although diplomatic movement may now revert to something like normality, Hong Kong remains an unsettled problem in Chinese eyes and the main cause for Sino-British discontents.

3. Superimposed on the Hong Kong issue was the bilateral question, restrictions in London as against restrictions in Peking. Our best tactics were to disentangle the question of diplomatic movement from the Hong Kong issue as far as possible and to seek a settlement of the movement problem by bilateral concessions only. The Chinese worked on two levels. At certain times, carefully editing history and omitting all reference to violence against us, they argued that the problem

---

1 No. 151.

was all our doing; their restrictions were merely a defensive reaction to ours. At other times, however, they argued that visas, like any other matter large or small, reflected the state of relations between the two countries concerned; bad relations deriving from Hong Kong meant bad visas. In the end we largely succeeded in disengaging visas from Hong Kong; yet it was throughout not a bilateral question but an ugly triangle; and the recurrent Chinese tactic was to qualify promises made in the bilateral context by falling back on unsettled or new issues relating to Hong Kong.

4. Why did the Chinese release us? Their precise grounds are likely to remain unknown but we can be confident that the following factors were important. First there was the removal of all restrictions in London that could serve as an excuse for Chinese restrictions on our staff. By April of this year there were no special restrictions on the Chinese and our practice had reverted to that of July 1967. Though this did not automatically bring full freedom for us it brought immediate improvements and, though there were to be further setbacks, from April the Chinese were on the defensive. Second was the pressure in July from increasing publicity and the imminence of the diplomatic offensive. It seems likely that the Chinese got wind of the latter; in some ways we hoped that they would. Our circulars to diplomatic colleagues giving a list of detained staff almost certainly came into Chinese hands. Thirdly, beginning in July it proved possible to release in Hong Kong a small number of communists detained since 1967 under the emergency regulations. Out of a total number of fifty-two, two were released on the 6th of July and two more on the 20th of July. This almost certainly had a helpful effect. Fourthly, there was the general factor of greater order in the Chinese internal scene and greater efforts on their side to recreate an image of correct diplomatic behaviour. The hope of Canadian recognition of China may have been particularly influential here. There is some evidence that this became linked in the Chinese mind with our predicament; it may have moved them to try to cover up some of the blacker spots of their diplomatic record.

5. One point the year's experience made clear: that tough retaliatory action against the Chinese in a situation such as ours is unwise. Our restrictions on Chinese movement were mild; in the matter of visas we were merely bringing our practice into line with what theirs had always been. But the result was much harsher counter-restrictions; and the game is one which the Chinese can always play harder than we. Moreover, restrictions it seems acquire with alarming speed a life and supporting philosophy on their own; once erected they are not easy to dismantle; which side is to begin the process? It was often urged, particularly in the early stages of our predicament, that only a tough policy would avail; that relaxations on our side would only be seen as a sign of weakness and prompt the Chinese to even more extravagant demands. In the visa context at least, this was not our experience. The Chinese were adamant that we should make the first move; but once that was made they usually responded, though sometimes needing the help of additional pressure, such as publicity, before giving full reciprocal treatment.

6. The line of progress over the year is worth noting. It was a series of deescalations. It proved impossible to engage the Chinese in any meaningful negotiations on visas. They were fertile in abuse; they formulated demands; they went so far as to hint at the result if their demands were met. But negotiations in the normal acceptation [sic]

of the term proved impossible. We progressed by a series of lurches towards freedom. We had to make the first move, the Chinese then followed; if we had insisted on the reverse order we might well have been waiting still. There was no explicit link between the two acts of deescalation; and, although our concessions were carefully judged and there were preceding hints, we were obliged to take what was in some respects a leap in the dark. I would not claim this a universally valid pattern for dealings with the Chinese but it has relevance in our efforts to reduce tension in the larger issue of Hong Kong and to effect the release of British subjects such as Mr Grey.

7. Since there was no negotiation there was no scope for bargaining. Attempts to beat down the Chinese price got us nowhere. Moreover, within the extraordinary context of violence and blackmail the Chinese showed a certain legalism and pedantry. The price for freedom for our officials was freedom of movement for theirs. At several points in the story we considered whether we could bring into the equation British subjects without official status and insist on concessions for them before removing restrictions on Chinese officials. But the attempt to do so in February in order to help Mr Grey merely put the clock back in our own case without assisting him. The Chinese advantage, of course, was that their NCNA representatives have official status.

8. The Chinese proved themselves to be well adapted for the struggle which they undertook. Isolated, bigoted, ruthless and non-signatories of the Vienna Convention on Diplomatic Relations, they seemed also immune to pressure. Anxious examination on our side of the means at our disposal for persuading them to adopt more civilised behaviour revealed how limited was our armoury. Mob violence of the kind used by the Indonesians in October 1967 in compelling the Chinese to accept a withdrawal of missions was not available to us. The possibility of economic pressure was examined but the conclusion was that any such action would present serious difficulty and could only be contemplated in extreme circumstances. On the other hand the Chinese were not quite so ruthless as we feared. They showed a wish to keep their mission in London. Though there was infinite petty harassment, violence was not used against us after the 30th of August, nor did the other unpleasant possibilities we considered, for example charges of espionage, come to pass. In the hostage game they seemed to recognise certain limits. Moreover our experience suggests that we were not altogether defenceless. The Chinese proved more vulnerable to publicity and the threat of diplomatic pressure than we had hoped. For those going in for the business of blackmail and detention they showed a curious sensitivity. This may not have been true during the more violent phase of 1967, but in the calmer times of this year with the Chinese attempting to recreate an image of better international behaviour and perhaps attract diplomatic relations with new countries, both publicity and diplomatic pressure proved useful weapons. We probably underestimated them.

9. This raises the question whether such weapons might be applied in defence of British subjects without official status who are in custody in this country. This despatch has examined only one small corner of the battle-field which we dignify by the name of Sino-British relations. While the Chinese are apparently withdrawing from one exposed position, the detention of diplomats, they have so far shown no similar readiness to abandon other strong points in the absence of suitable gestures on our part in Hong Kong. The number of British subjects under detention or arrest shows

no tendency to diminish. Foreign diplomatic pressure is unlikely to be available to assist them. Nevertheless the pattern of deescalation described above may be of relevance, with the release of detainees or even convicted prisoners in Hong Kong as our bargaining counters. Publicity for British subjects' predicament, particularly in the foreign press, should almost certainly be of value. It was often feared in our own case that publicity would only drive the Chinese into greater intransigence. This proved not to be true. Publicity is an instrument still not fully applied on behalf of British subjects in this country.

10. To return to the subject of this Mission, we have made great progress and almost all the staff and families who bore trials of the last eighteen months with such fortitude have now left for home. But we are not altogether out of the wood. We must wait to see how future applications for visas are treated. In the matter of travel in China outside Peking we are still the subject of discrimination, denied permission to visit the handful of cities open to other embassies, in particular Shanghai with its long-suffering British community. We still inhabit a kind of protocol limbo, excluded from all functions at which the Chinese Government are hosts. With luck the situation should improve. But we can never be sure of Chinese conduct in the future. Having played the visa game once they may well be tempted to play it again whenever relations become particularly strained. I am afraid that this Mission will always be a potential hostage or whipping-boy for British policy in Hong Kong. This raises questions outside the scope of this despatch. But two points may be made in passing: first, that total withdrawal of the Mission would probably prove extremely difficult; secondly, that though any staff here will always be very exposed, a continued absence of restrictions on Chinese staff in London plus a judicious use of publicity and diplomatic pressure should be able to offer them some shreds of protection.

I am sending copies of this despatch to Her Majesty's representatives at Washington, Canberra and Tokyo, to the Governor, Hong Kong and to the Political Adviser to the Commander-in-Chief Far East at Singapore.

I have, etc,
PERCY CRADOCK

No. 153

Letter from Mr Walden (Peking) to Mr Boyd, 23 September 1968
Confidential (FCO 21/151, FC 13/22)

Dear John,

You may be interested in more details and further comments on the series of articles which appeared in the *Reference News*[1] around the middle of August reporting foreign press reactions to the release of Sir Donald Hopson and other members of this Mission. All these reports were given space on the front page of the newspaper.

2. The first item appeared in the 7th August edition. This was a UPI report of 2

---

1 A press digest.

August on the arrival of Theo Peters in London. Something of the Chinese view of his remarks comes through from the heading, which was: 'British Commercial Councillor Peters attacks our country on his return to London'. The report appeared to give a straight-forward account of Theo's comments, and said that he had been detained in Peking for almost a year. Nor did the Chinese flinch from reproducing his charge that China had 'detained diplomats and their families in violation of all diplomatic procedures and international practice'. By selecting for publication a more flattering passage, where Theo said that the Chinese attitude towards British subjects was now 'normal' and that many ordinary Chinese were perfectly pleasant, the editors were perhaps compensating for the possible unfavourable impact of the report on their readers.

3. Beginning on 15 August, i.e. only two days after Sir Donald Hopson's arrival in Hong Kong, the Chinese printed an almost daily series of reports from the western press concerning the position of this Mission and Sino-British relations. On 15 August the *Reference News* summarised *The Times* leader of 13 August, including a reference to Grey, *The Daily Telegraph* editorial of the same date and the comments of 'reactionary Hong Kong newspapers' on Sir Donald's arrival there. These items appeared jointly under the heading: 'British newspapers attack our country on the occasion of the departure of Sir Donald Hopson from Peking'. The sub-heading stated that 'The Daily Telegraph rants that British should maintain "pressure" on us'. The following day, the bulletin published a Reuter's account of Sir Donald Hopson's press conference in Hong Kong. The sub-title read: 'Reuter's reports a statement that "there are important reasons" for Britain maintaining relations with China'. A smaller item in the same issue noted that Sir Donald had held talks with the Governor of Hong Kong during his stay there. An irrelevant but revealing sub-title read 'he said that during his flight from Peking to Canton he was well treated'. This report, also from Reuters, ended with the puzzling remark: 'the diplomat said "when I left Peking, a Chinese official and diplomats from many countries saw me off"'. (There was, of course, no Chinese official at the airport, and Sir Donald must have been misquoted). On 17 August the Chinese picked out the statement of a Foreign Office spokesman denying that the British Mission in Peking would only have a skeleton staff (this assurance formed the title of the article). The spokesman repeated Sir Donald's remark that the release of the British Chargé was seen as a 'good sign'. He then went on to point out that the arrival of new staff in the Mission was sufficient to demonstrate that it would not be reduced to a skeleton, though he qualified this by saying that the Foreign Office was reluctant to send diplomats with children to this post.

4. A further item on 20 August, quoting British newspapers in Hong Kong, gave brief details of comments made by Miss Smyth and Gallagher on their arrival there, including the latter's remark that his experience in China had been 'unusual'. Both were said to have voiced particular concern at the plight of Grey.

5. The *Reference News* continued to track Sir Donald's progress through to his arrival in London. On 21 August it quoted passages from an AFP report datelined London, 19 August. The Foreign Secretary's congratulatory message of welcome to Sir Donald was reported in this item. Once again the sub-title gave some hint of the Chinese view-point when it singled out Sir Donald's statement on maintaining relations with China.

6. It is difficult to draw clear-cut inferences from the publication of these reports for circulation to Chinese cadres. At the very least we can conclude that NCNA Offices abroad have been directed to report back any criticism of Chinese treatment of British diplomats and subjects in China. It is of interest that this is done so promptly: nearly all the articles mentioned above appeared in the *Reference News* only two days after publication. The Chinese are obviously sensitive to criticism of their behaviour in the press.

7. Grey rarely gets a mention in the bulletin, and it is of some interest that his case was not excised in the process of summarising foreign reports. For purposes of publicity, the Chinese may well see his position as similar to that of diplomats.

8. It is less easy to discern Chinese motives for bringing such pejorative material to the attention of their cadres (we should not forget that the *Reference News* is reputed to have quite an extensive circulation). The facts of China's cynical attitude towards diplomatic practice and international law emerge quite clearly from these reports. Part of their purpose may have been to demonstrate to their readers that the game of detaining diplomats was simply not worth the candle. In this context it is important to remember that the *Reference News* began to carry an increased number of articles on the Hong Kong question around about the time of the British diplomats return from China. In some cases, these articles gained in significance by being printed alongside the reports described above. The reader would not have to be very intelligent to conclude from the Hong Kong reports that the authorities were continuing to take a firm line in dealing with the communists. Nor would it be very difficult to go one step further and deduce that, not only had the detention of diplomats damaged China's prestige, but it had failed in its objective, namely, to put pressure on the British Government to persuade the Hong Kong Government to take a more conciliatory line.

9. The presentation of these reports suggests strongly that the Chinese are still interested in the future of this Mission and Sino-British relations. It is possible to detect some relief in their practice of singling out reassuring statements by Sir Donald and Foreign Office spokesmen on Britain's desire for the maintenance of relations, and her disinclination to run down the Mission to a skeleton staff. One could of course take a more cynical view of Chinese motives in emphasising simultaneously both the sense of outrage as reflected in the British press and the determination of official circles to maintain relations. The more unscrupulous cadres might be tempted to draw the conclusion that, no matter how hard you squeeze the British, they still come back for more! But, on balance, it is unlikely that this was the message readers were intended to grasp. China is in the process of reconstructing her foreign policy. A diplomatic coup of some significance—recognition by Canada—is round the corner. There are signs that the Chinese hope that Canada's initiative will set in motion a chain reaction involving such countries as Australia and New Zealand. As we have pointed out elsewhere, there is evidence that the Chinese are perfectly well aware of the link between the prospects of recognition and China's unconventional diplomatic behaviour.

10. We would therefore conclude from the slight but tangible evidence of the *Reference News* that the Chinese (*a*) are relieved that Britain intends to maintain a fairly high level of representation in China, (*b*) have a realistic appreciation of their

losses in terms of prestige caused by their more flagrant diplomatic outrages, (*c*) will probably be more circumspect in future in attempting to influence our policy by bringing pressure to bear on this Mission.

11. The main lesson for us seems to be that we have probably under-estimated China's sensibility and thus her vulnerability to criticism on this score. It is in our interests and those of other Missions here to make sure that the point is driven home to the Chinese. This might seem belated in relation to Chinese treatment of this Mission. But it would have immediate relevance to her treatment of British subjects who as yet have not felt the benefits of the present better atmosphere and whose needs all along have been greater than ours. It is therefore essential that there should be hard-hitting but not offensive follow-up publicity, particularly in the foreign press. This could draw attention to China's bleak record in the past two years, and warn that the world is watching to see whether her return to a more civilised pattern of behaviour will be lasting.

12. I am copying this letter to McLaren, Hong Kong and Spendlove, Washington.

Yours ever,
GEORGE

No. 154

Mr Cradock (Peking) to Mr Stewart, 25 September 1968[1]
Tel. No. 886 Priority, Confidential (FCO 21/83)

My impression is that we may not be using publicity to assist British subjects detained in China as widely or as effectively as we could.

2. We earlier had doubts about publicity on two main grounds:

(*a*) It might create pressure from public opinion for undesirable action on our part e.g. retaliation. However it now seems accepted that reprisals e.g. against Chinese in the United Kingdom would only do great harm, so that this danger has presumably receded. Moreover, the most useful publicity would be abroad and would not therefore invite such dangers (please see paragraph 5 below).

(*b*) It might drive the Chinese into greater intransigence or into some kind of justification action. This however, has not been borne out by our experience of publicity over visas for the Mission since July. Visas flowed despite considerable critical comment in the UK Press. Publicity almost certainly helped rather than hindered. There is in addition encouraging evidence of Chinese vulnerability from *Reference News* (my telegram No. 843).[2] Conversely our silence on such matters as the arrest of the Merchant Navy officers has brought no obvious dividends.

3. At present, apart from a brief announcement on Johnston we seem to have had little or no publicity on the Shanghai community despite the recommendation

---

1 Repeated for information priority to Hong Kong.
2 Not printed. See No. 153.

in my telegram No. 764.³ Sharland's letter of 12 September to Garside³ suggests we may be deliberately withholding publicity until Simon-Carves⁴ team are out of China. This seems misconceived. Publicity on Shanghai would not prejudice Simon-Carves' chances; it might add slightly to their protection (my telegram No. 809).³ For reasons given in paragraph 2(*b*) above such publicity should assist rather than retard any chances Croziers etc. have of obtaining visas.

4. As regards Grey, public speculation about Hsueh Ping's release in November may not be desirable but publicity on Chinese barbarism in Grey's case would do good. There are indications the Chinese are embarrassed about Grey. Let us therefore pile on the embarrassment. As regards Crouch, Barrymaine, etc., I cannot see that they have anything to lose.

5. The most useful publicity would be articles not in the British but in foreign Press and in suitable cases in commercial circles, emphasising the uncivilised nature of Chinese conduct, secret police methods, hostage-taking, breach of contract, refusal of information and access and disregard of international standards. I hope IRD would feel able to get such pieces planted. Even in the British Press there is scope for publicity on maltreatment of businessmen, Merchant Marine officers, etc., with the objective of getting over to the Chinese that their conduct is likely to damage trade.

6. As pointed out in separate correspondence, the Chinese hope of Canadian recognition offers special additional opportunities.

7. Altogether the Chinese as they improve their behaviour seem to be growing more vulnerable to well-judged publicity. The evidence suggests we may have found an opening. We should exploit it to the full. I appreciate we cannot decide all these matters on our own and that the banks and commercial firms are involved but I am sure if we put arguments forcibly they will agree.

8. I should be grateful for your early comments.

3 Not printed.
4 A British engineering company.

No. 155

Submission from Mr Murray to Sir D. Allen, 3 October 1968
Secret (FCO 21/141, FC 13/8D)

Mr Grey of Reuters

Problem

On 30 August we asked the Governor of Hong Kong to conduct a covert probe of Chinese intentions regarding the price they would exact for the release of Mr Grey, the Reuter's correspondent detained in Peking. The probe has not gone entirely to plan. There is now disagreement between the Governor and HM Chargé d'Affaires in Peking on how next to proceed. The Governor recommends sitting tight until Hsueh P'ing, one of the NCNA correspondents imprisoned in Hong Kong, is released on 17 November. Thereafter, he believes we may hope for the release of Mr Grey before too long. Mr Cradock, on the other hand, recommends the immediate release in Hong Kong without prior conditions of Hsueh and perhaps also of a second NCNA correspondent, Lo Yu-ho.

Recommendation

2. *I recommend* that we authorise the Governor to proceed as he suggests at the same time suggesting the further action which may be necessary if this does not work. A draft telegram is attached.[1] Commonwealth Office concur.

Background

3. In Commonwealth Office telegram No. 1414 of 30 August to Hong Kong, we asked the Governor to conduct a covert probe of Chinese intentions about the price they would exact for the release of Mr Grey. We suggested that from the outset we should be ready to offer the release in Hong Kong of both the NCNA correspondents (Hsueh and Lo) imprisoned there. The Governor at first expressed his broad acceptance of our proposals (Hong Kong telegram No. 1045) but subsequently had second thoughts (Hong Kong telegram 1059). He believed that it might be possible to secure the release of Mr Grey in exchange for that of Hsueh alone. With some reluctance we agreed to let the Governor proceed by stages i.e. offering the Chinese Hsueh alone on the first occasion and reserving Lo, if necessary, for a further meeting (CO telegram No. 1452).

4. The covert probe has now taken place in Hong Kong. It has not gone as we hoped. The Governor had issued instructions to his agent conducting the probe that Hsueh should be offered initially and that Lo might be offered in the same conversation, though at the end. However, in the event the interview on 17 September with the selected Chinese contact took a turn which made it impossible for the Governor's instructions to be carried out in a satisfactory manner. The suggestion even that Hsueh might be released as the price for Mr Grey was not made in definite terms. A tentative approach to the subject provoked the comment from the contact that any offer of an exchange would be disastrous. The contact undertook however to write to Peking and enquire about the possibility of releasing Mr Grey. This was agreed (Hong Kong telegrams Nos. 2000 and 2001).[2] Matters did not end there. At the subsequent meetings held at the request of the contact on 21, 24 and 25 September (Hong Kong telegrams Nos. 2007, 2008, 2030 and 2031), it became clear that he had discussed the matter in depth with a prominent mainland representative in the Colony (Li Cho-chih of the Bank of China) and had also written to Peking about Mr Grey but in the most general terms. This meant that our original intention of making a firm offer for the release of Mr Grey, but in strictly defined terms, had not been achieved. On the one hand we were not forcing the Chinese hand; on the other we were offering them the chance of forcing up the price for the release of Mr Grey.

5. At the meeting on 25 September the contact delivered a return message in the following terms:

(*a*) Chou En-lai was concerned about Mr Grey and would act 'when the opportunity occurred'. He had asked the contact to send an assessment of the situation regarding Mr Grey.

---

1 Not printed.
2 No. 149. None of the other telegrams under reference in this document is printed.

(*b*) The mainland representative, Li Cho-chih, had received instructions that the contact should not press ahead with discussions about an exchange of Mr Grey. In any negotiation of this kind Peking felt they would be bound to ask for more than the release of Hsueh—probably at least all the fifteen news workers imprisoned in Hong Kong in whom they are known to have an interest.

(*c*) Li had said that rather than conduct an exchange, Peking would prefer simply to release Mr Grey, in their own good time. The contact explained that this would be in the fairly near future and in any case by the end of the year. 1 January had been set as the target date for complete return to normality in Sino-British relations. The Governor of Hong Kong had indicated that he accepts this message at face value. The Governor holds that any attempt to proceed with a negotiation for the release of Mr Grey through an exchange would constitute an unacceptable risk to Hong Kong. He feels that the release of Hsueh alone will achieve nothing and only put the present channel of communication at risk. We already know that he is deeply averse to the simultaneous release of Hsueh and Lo, let alone without a prior guarantee that this will secure Mr Grey's freedom.

7. [*sic*][3] The contact's connexions are exclusively with the 'moderate' faction around Chou En-lai and the message will only represent the views of that group. Were they again edged away from power (which we do not now believe likely) the content of the message would at once be without significance.

8. HM Chargé d'Affaires in Peking has watched the progress of the covert probe with an uneasy eye. He has commented on the fact that it is the contact rather than we ourselves who has been playing the tune (Peking telegram No. 883). He has pointed out that the passage of time makes the release of Hsueh increasingly valueless as a concession and had recommended his immediate release (Peking telegram 891) In a further telegram (Peking telegram No. 907) he has reinforced this proposal with the recommendation that we consider releasing both Hsueh and Lo without prior undertakings. He makes it clear that he disagrees with the apparent immobilism of the Governor on the following grounds:

(*a*) humanitarian grounds; the need to get Mr Grey out as soon as possible;

(*b*) the difficulty in defending further delay in public and parliament;

(*c*) giving the Chinese time to release Mr Grey had not worked in the past;

(*d*) while the Chinese have said they do not want negotiations they have not said that they do *not* want the release of Hsueh and Lo. Negotiation may be the slippery path; unilateral release is not (Peking telegrams Nos. 891 and 906).

Argument

9. I see much force in Mr Cradock's case. Ideally there is no doubt that the course most likely at the outset to lead to the release of Mr Grey was unilateral release in Hong Kong of both the NCNA correspondents. This would however have been a gambler's throw. If it had not worked we should have put ourselves in a most awkward and indefensible position. In any case we lost our best chance of bringing the Governor to accept this course when we agreed to let him play the hand his way. As things now stand the unilateral release of both Hsueh and Lo may still in theory be the best way to proceed but there is no chance whatsoever of the Governor agreeing

---

3 A section of this paragraph has been retained under section 3(4) of the Public Records Act 1958.

to this. It would remain a gambler's throw. Moreover the future utility of the Chinese contact is now also thrown into the balance. As the Governor has pointed out the contact is idiosyncratic but he is certainly useful. His reports in the past have generally been reliable. While not of paramount importance, it is certainly to be born in mind that if we now discredit the contact by flagrantly ignoring the advice he has conveyed from Peking he will decline to act for us in future.

10. We had earlier envisaged that, if we had no satisfactory result through the covert channel, we could make a follow-up approach through our Mission in Peking, if this seemed desirable. The Governor would certainly argue against such an approach as flying in the face of the contact's advice. Perhaps a more important objection is that it is all too likely that such an approach would merely encourage the Chinese to name an unacceptable price. Accordingly I am against it.

11. I think we have, reluctantly, to agree with the Governor that in the situation with which we are now confronted it is best to let the case of Hsueh take its course. He will be due for release, with remission (which we do not contemplate withholding) on 17 November. Thereafter the Governor believes Mr Grey may be released quite quickly. I have my doubts, but believe we should go along with the Governor to that stage.

12. Thereafter, if Mr Grey is not released, we shall be under greater pressure than ever either to retaliate against Chinese citizens here (which would gravely prejudice Mr Grey's chances) or to make the appropriate concessions in Hong Kong. Reuters are likely to be among those pressing for the latter solution. Public indignation about Mr Grey will grow rapidly if he is not released shortly after the release of Hsueh, and sympathy on his behalf must be expected to increase with the approach of Christmas. I believe that we should allow no more than about a month for the Governor's method to demonstrate its effectiveness. If by mid-December Mr Grey has not been released we shall have to press the Governor hard to release Lo without conditions. Fortunately he had indicated in Hong Kong telegram 1026 of 28 August that at that point he might indeed agree that this was the only way.

13. The foregoing line of argument was agreed with the Commonwealth Office before the arrival of Hong Kong telegram No. 2051 in which the Governor has commented on Mr Cradock's proposal for immediate unilateral release of Hsueh and Lo. Though the argument that to release Hsueh in the hope of securing Mr Grey's release is in itself trying to strike a bargain and would thus be embarrassing to the Chinese is in my view over-subtle and by no means necessarily valid, the general tenor of the Governor's telegram amply confirms our judgement that he is not to be moved to any unilateral concession now.

14. If the recommendation is accepted, we should tell Mr Long in general terms of the results of our covert probe and explain why we are taking no further action for the time being.[4]

JAMES MURRAY

---

4 Mr Allen supported the recommendation. The decision to await the release of Hsueh and see what happened was conveyed to the Governor in CO Tel. No. 1505 to Hong Kong of 7 October, as 'the least unsatisfactory course of action'.

No. 156

Mr Stewart to Mr Cradock (Peking), 9 October 1968[1]
Tel. No. 874 Priority, Confidential (FCO 21/83, FC 3/21B)

Your telegram number 886:[2] Publicity.

We agree that reticence over the treatment of British subjects under detention does not seem to have done any particular good. On the other hand there is firm evidence that the Chinese at any rate note critical comment about their treatment of foreigners and it is therefore reasonable to assume that some sections of the leadership are aware that this behaviour is damaging internationally. It is for this reason that we have recently been happy to see greater publicity given to the plight of British subjects. It is however not true that public pressures for undesirable retaliatory action have ceased. We receive a steady trickle of letters and some parliamentary questions demanding tough action. As is shown by the recent article in *The Economist* calling for the expulsion of the NCNA from London if Grey is not released soon after Hsueh Ping comes out of prison in Hong Kong, this line is not confined to extremists.

2. We did not attempt to mute publicity about Johnston and the Shanghai community because the Simon Carves[3] team were in China. The terms of the statement on Johnston were agreed with the Chartered Bank who asked that they be restrained in the hope that if the arrest was connected with the affair with the Bank of China in Singapore, [the] matter might be settled quietly. The situation is still obscure and depending on developments it might be advisable to give more publicity to the case later. For the present however we are going along with the Bank's request that pressure be kept up mainly through the diplomatic channel.

3. There is a steady interest in the British press in detained British subjects but recently it has inevitably been muted in face of Czechoslovakia,[4] Biafra[5] and other examples of 'Man's inhumanity to Man'. It is regrettable but inevitable that the British press have become to some extent inured to Chinese behaviour. There are therefore limits to which their interest can be engaged. Interest could always be greatly stimulated if we took retaliatory action but we are all agreed this would be wrong.

4. As regards the foreign press we do what we can to place pieces in newspapers both in Europe and in Afro Asian countries. But foreign readers are not greatly interested in the difficulties of British subjects in China. As we found when the question of publicity for the British Mission was examined last year there are serious difficulties in getting material accepted in government-controlled press of such countries such as Pakistan, Cambodia, Nepal and Tanzania (where the Chinese probably have an interest in cultivating good relations). Opportunities are rather better in Ceylon, Kenya and Zambia and we shall certainly keep up our efforts. As you pointed out,

---

1 Repeated for information to Hong Kong.
2 No. 154.
3 A British engineering company.
4 On 20 August 1968, the Soviet Union led Warsaw Pact troops in an invasion of Czechoslovakia to crack down on growing reformist trends in the country.
5 Biafra was a secessionist state in West Africa that had separated from Nigeria in May 1967, leading to a civil war that lasted until 1970.

apart from charges of hostage-taking etc., Chinese are also vulnerable to charges of commercial sharp practice. The difficulty here is that the information usually derives from sources which cannot be compromised. But we shall explore possibilities further.

5. As you have acknowledged we have to take into consideration before launching any general publicity campaign the attitude of the employers, relatives and others concerned. The group of detained persons is far from homogeneous. Reactions towards them will not be uniform nor will our chance of influencing the Chinese be the same in each case. We are however reviewing the whole question, in particular the case of Barrymaine who has received probably less attention than any of the others. You may be assured that in no case will we lose an opportunity for publicity if other considerations permit it.

On 17 October 1968 the Foreign Office and the Commonwealth Office merged to become the Foreign and Commonwealth Office. Mr Stewart became the Secretary of State for Foreign and Commonwealth Affairs.

No. 157

Sir D. Trench to Mr Stewart, 15 November 1968[1]
Tel. No. 2180 Priority. Top Secret (FCO 21/467, FEC 3/548/1)

My telegram No. 2117.[2]
Cater saw contact again on 13 November.

2. Contact said that on 6 November Li Cho-chih had summoned him urgently and had spoken in an anxious way about Press reports of the discussion here between Murray, Cradock and the Political Adviser. Li feared that new tough measures were being prepared, he wanted contact to pass a message to the Hong Kong Governor to the effect that if we wished to improve Sino-British and Sino-Hong Kong relations, it would be possible to make arrangements on the basis that the Hong Kong Government would take steps to de-escalate and the Chinese would reciprocate, from the Chinese point of view various things could be done including the release of Grey. Cater pressed contact for an explanation of what these various things might be. Contact said he did not know what Li had in mind but thought it might be an improvement in Sino-British trade.

3. Contact said he had pressed Li for further details. Li had allegedly said that an exchange of Grey for Hsueh Ping was not possible because he would be released automatically soon, but an exchange of Grey for all the convicted news workers might be possible. Contact had pointed out that if that were arranged, other groups such as Trade Unions would press to have their members released. Contact nevertheless suggested to Cater that it might be possible for us to release three or four news workers as a special act of clemency. Cater replied that there could be no question of

---

1 Repeated for information to Peking and POLAD Singapore.
2 Not printed.

a deal being arranged on this basis and reminded contact that he himself had previously advised strongly against it (my telegram No. 2001).³

4. Contact's own view was that it was desirable and important for us to make an early response to this approach. He quoted Chou En-lai who allegedly had said that it was typical of British diplomacy to profess great interest at first and then to let the matter fade away.

5. Cater tried to find out whether in contact's view the proposal was Li's own initiative or was made on instructions from Peking and suggested three possible reasons:

(*a*) The reason stated by Li, i.e. that Chinese feared new tough measures following Murray's and Cradock's visits;

(*b*) A rebuff to NCNA who he thought had exceeded their brief in their discussions with Political Adviser about visits to news workers (my telegram No. 2149);⁴

(*c*) The result of an enquiry from Chou or possibly even Chairman Mao about the state of affairs in Hong Kong.

6. Cater asked contact to tell Li that we were pleased to learn of their desire to improve Sino-British and Sino-Hong Kong relations but that we needed first of all to know more about the proposals from Li and in particular whether he had anything definite to suggest. Cater also asked that Li should be informed that there was no possibility of releasing convicted news workers in exchange for Grey.

7. Cater also mentioned contact's proposed China Trade Development Group and said that, although he had given a great deal of thought to the proposal, he found it difficult to understand how it would work. Contact at once replied that there was no hurry about this and that he would raise it again after giving it more thought.

8. Contact said that he was taking action about the Crosiers [*sic*] in Shanghai and expected no trouble in obtaining their release.

3 No. 149.
4 Not printed.

No. 158

Letter from Mr Palliser (No. 10) to Mr Day, 2 December 1968
Secret (FCO 21/485, FEC 13C/1A)

Dear Derek,

The Prime Minister discussed the question of the continued detention in Peking of Mr Anthony Grey of Reuters with the Minister of State for Foreign Affairs (Mr Mulley) when he and Lord Chalfont were with the Prime Minister this evening. He explained that Mr John Beavan of the *Daily Mirror*, with a group of leading journalists, had asked to come to see him to raise the question of Mr Grey.

Mr Mulley explained that Lord Shepherd had held a meeting earlier today to discuss this and other related matters connected with our relations with China. HM Chargé d'Affaires in Peking had been instructed last week to see the Chinese Foreign Ministry to make our position clear to them.¹ It was considered preferable that he

1 See No. 160.

should do this before there was any question of raising the matter with the Chinese Chargé here.² We had however gained the impression from secret sources that there was a chance of Grey being released three weeks after the release of the Chinese journalists imprisoned in Hong Kong, for whose imprisonment his detention was believed to be a reprisal. Although only one of these men has been let out so far, with remission for good behaviour, and the second was not due for release for another 18 months, there seemed nevertheless a reasonable chance that the Chinese might act over Grey unless a counter-productive campaign for his release developed here. In that case the Chinese might continue to detain him.

The Prime Minister said that he had been asked about this at a luncheon given by *The Sunday Times* on November 29. He had warned his hosts against excessive publicity and whipping up anti Chinese feeling, since this might be counter-productive for Mr Grey's own interests.

It was agreed that for the time being it would be preferable not to stir up publicity in this matter; and that we should at least delay for a further week or so to give an opportunity for Cradock to pursue the matter in Peking. The Prime Minister said that he thought that he would see Mr Beavan privately; and, without revealing what Mr Mulley had told him he would give him to understand that it would be preferable, in Mr Grey's interest, to be patient for a little while longer.

I am sending a copy of this letter to Gruffydd Jones (Cabinet Office).

Yours ever,
MICHAEL

2 See No. 162.

No. 159

Letter from Mr Maddocks (Hong Kong) to Mr Murray
2 December 1968
Confidential (FCO 21/535, FEF 25/3)

Dear James,

Representation in Taiwan

Since 'confrontation' began last year we have frequently been told by the Chinese that Hong Kong is the crux of the Sino-British relations and that we cannot expect any improvement until the Hong Kong problem has been 'solved'. One conclusion which emerged from our recent discussions with the Acting Governor and Percy Cradock is that our ability to make the kind of concessions which might satisfy the Chinese is severely circumscribed. We keep on releasing detainees; we tolerate the excesses of the communist press; and we are careful to avoid provocative action; but none of this seems likely to be enough to effect a general improvement in Sino-British relations and to go further is very difficult. Another complication is that Hong Kong pays the price for benefits that accrue partly or even mainly elsewhere.

2. If little can be done in Hong Kong to bring about an improvement we should, I suggest, examine other areas in which our policies impinge on our relations with China. The one which springs to mind is the question of our relations with Taiwan. The Chinese contention that Hong Kong is the crux of Sino-British relations is of recent origin. During the fifties and early sixties we used to be told, with monotonous regularity, that the real obstacle was our pursuit of a 'two Chinas' policy as demonstrated by our attitude towards the status of Taiwan and by our maintenance of the Tamsui Consulate. When we last proposed an exchange of Ambassadors to the Chinese in 1962, they made clear, when refusing, that our attitude to Taiwan was the main cause.

3. During the intervening years nothing has happened to lessen the importance of Taiwan in Chinese eyes. It was only a few months ago that the information of the last provincial Revolutionary Committees on the mainland led to the revival of the 'liberate Taiwan' slogan. We must therefore assume that, although Hong Kong is at present the central issue in Sino-British relations, our attitude to Taiwan remains a serious irritant, and that if we could bring ourselves to make a gesture over Taiwan, the Chinese would recognise it as a major concession. We should, I suggest, give serious consideration to closing the consulate in Tamsui.

4. It is not for me to say how valuable the Tamsui Consulate is. Obviously it has some value or it would have been closed during one of our economy drives. On the other hand its value is limited by the anomalous status of the Consul, the direction of trade to other countries and the relative unimportance of KMT policies. But it is not part of my case that we should lose nothing by closing it. I accept that we should lose something. My argument is that if Her Majesty's Government wants to pay a price for the hope of better relations with Peking, here is a price that would be fully understood in Peking, that is relatively low and that would be paid by the UK not Hong Kong.

5. I imagine that the main problems would be domestic political considerations and the American reactions. But I would have thought that in the present economic climate there would be no difficulty in justifying the closure to British and American opinions as an economy measure. We have after all closed down a number of posts abroad on that ground, and the case would be quite plausible. Whatever justification we used there is no doubt that Peking would take the point.

6. I assume of course that we do wish to achieve an improvement in our relations with the Chinese and that we accept the possibility that at some stage a gesture by us would be appropriate.

7. I am sending a copy of this letter to Percy Cradock in Peking and to Bray in Tamsui.

A.F. MADDOCKS

No. 160

Telegram from Mr Cradock (Peking) to Mr Stewart, 9 December 1968[1]
Tel. No. 1093 Confidential (FCO 21/485, FEC 13C/1A)

My immediately preceding telegrams:[2] Grey.

I began by referring to Chinese statement of 21 July 1967, pointing out that all the Chinese referred to in that statement had now been released and I must therefore ask what were the Chinese Government's intentions in respect of Grey. Yuan replied by reading out a prepared series of points to the effect that the Chinese Government were fully justified in restricting Grey's freedom; [2 groups undec.] was lenient; the British Government were fully responsible for failure to solve the problem; the British Government had done their utmost to spread sinister propaganda on subject of Grey's treatment misleading public opinion in a planned way, but this would be of no avail and would only complicate matters. In particular he instanced your statement of 27 November at Rawalpindi[3] about 'inhuman restraint', saying that this was distortion and slander.

2. I pressed for an explanation of Chinese Government's position, pointing out that if 1967 statement had any meaning Grey should have been released. Yuan repeated his piece, though he said at once that since 1967 announcement the British side had gone further in persecuting and arresting large numbers of patriotic countrymen and press workmen. Solution could only come through act by British Government.

3. I said that I was instructed to demand Grey's immediate release. I also lodged the strongest possible protest against the conditions under which he was held. I dealt with these in detail covering isolation, deterioration in conditions with respect to access to books, mail, visits, access to officials. I stressed our serious concern over effect of his long solitary confinement under these inhuman conditions upon Grey's health and called for proper medical treatment.

4. Yuan rejected the protest and referred to conditions in Hong Kong, though in a somewhat half-hearted way. He said on subject of health 'we know how to deal with the relevant problems of Grey's livelihood'.

5. I rebutted Hong Kong charges, drawing on material supplied by acting Governor and pointing out the many respects in which Hong Kong prisoners were treated better than Grey. I demanded immediate improvement in Grey's conditions and stressed Chinese responsibility for Grey's health. I reminded Yuan that despite Chinese wishes facts could not be hidden from people outside China. Yuan repeated

---

1 Repeated for information to Hong Kong.
2 Not printed. Mr Cradock reported that he had obtained an interview with Mr Yuan, the Deputy Director of the News Department.
3 Mr Stewart's comments, made during a trip to Pakistan, followed a visit Mr Cradock and Mr Garside had paid to Mr Grey on 26 November, the details of which were released to the press. They reported that Grey was confined to a 12ft square room, under near constant surveillance and was denied English reading material. He seemed in reasonable physical health but in a state of 'considerable nervous tension.' In his speech Mr Stewart stated he was distressed to learn of the conditions in which Mr Grey was confined and he hoped for his early release 'in line with the easing of relations which have recently been evident in Peking'. The Prime Minister raised the plight of Mr Grey at the centennial banquet of the Press Association on 27 November, stating that the Government were doing everything possible to obtain his release. *The Times*, 27 November 1968.

his party piece, again stressing that Chinese knew how to look after Grey's health.

6. See my immediately following telegram.[4]

4 Mr Craddock stated that by local standards the meeting was mild. Yuan was defensive in manner and avoided the usual 'blood-curding stories' about Hong Kong prisoners. He was obviously embarrassed and upset by the publicity campaign, and anxious to get over the point that the Chinese would look after Grey's health. But he refused to be drawn into giving an explanation for Grey's continued detention or a price for his release.

No. 161

Letter from Mr Cradock (Peking) to Mr Murray, 7 January 1969
Confidential (FCO 21/535, FEF 25/3)

Dear James,

Representation in Taiwan

I read with great interest Arthur Maddocks' letter of 2 December[1] on this subject. Whilst I agree with the general lines of his argument in paragraph one, two and four, I have reservations as to how much good such action now would do for our relations with the Chinese.

2. As I understand it, his suggestion is limited to the physical closure of the Consulate in Tamsui. He does not propose that we should adopt and announce a change in our view of Taiwan's status ('undetermined'). We should presumably also continue to vote in the same way at the United Nations and take the same line on representation in other international organisations. In other words, as paragraph five of his letter makes clear, we should not present the step as indicating any change in our view of the legalities. Thus, whilst I agree that the Chinese would appreciate the action as a concrete gesture, it would be quite a small gesture, not the major concession suggested in paragraph three of Maddocks' letter. The other, probably more important elements of our attitude to Taiwan which annoy the Chinese would continue to annoy them.

3. Nonetheless, I agree that such a gesture would be worthwhile at a time when other circumstances did not militate against its effectiveness. I think that at present, however, we must take the Chinese at their word when they say that Hong Kong is the crux of Sino-British relations and we cannot expect any improvement until the Hong Kong problem is solved. The question of prisoners and detainees is now the outstanding issue, provided we continue to behave with caution over such questions as schools, ships' visits, etc. And on our side, the remaining problem of British subjects in China is clearly linked with this specific Hong Kong issue. If this issue were settled, I see no reason why Sino-British relations should not revert to something like their pre-'confrontation' state, which was certainly not good but was tolerable. If on the other hand we remain unyielding over prisoners in Hong Kong I do not see the proposed concession over Taiwan having much effect. The Chinese would pocket it and continue to direct their fire on Hong Kong. Its potential good effect would probably be lost.

4. To sum up, I see advantage in this proposal from a Peking point of view, but only limited advantage. I do not think it would offset in Chinese eyes our sins in Hong

1 No. 159.

Kong. I should therefore like to see it held over and given favourable consideration when we are finally able to close the book on the present 'Hong Kong question'. I must hope that in saying this I am not advocating indefinitely suspended action.

I am sending copies of this letter to Arthur Maddocks in Hong Kong and to Bray in Tamsui.

Yours ever,
PERCY CRADOCK

No. 162

Note of a meeting between Lord Shepherd and Shen P'ing, the acting Chinese Chargé d'Affaires, at 11.30 a.m. on Thursday 9 January 1969
Confidential (FCO 21/465, FEC 3/548/1A)

Present:
Lord Shepherd   Shen P'ing
Mr C. Wilson   Interpreter
Mr C. H. Godden

After courtesies, *Lord Shepherd* emphasised the wish of HMG to have normal diplomatic relations with China and expressed the hope that the Chinese would co-operate in this respect. He then went on to draw attention to the serious problem of the treatment of British subjects in China and, in particular, stressed that the failure of the Chinese to release Mr Grey was a major stumbling block to good relations. In speaking Lord Shepherd followed closely the speaking notes prepared by the Department. The only deviations were personal; that he had some 15 years' commercial experience in the Far East where he had attracted a Chinese nick-name meaning 'Good Luck' and that he hoped that this would be a significant omen in his dealing with representatives of China; and that from his own experience of the Chinese he knew how much importance they attach to families and to family life.

2. In reply *Shen P'ing*, speaking from a prepared note, said that the Chinese Government were fully justified in restricting the freedom of movement of Mr Grey. As his Government had repeatedly expressed, their decision to restrict Mr Grey's freedom of movement arose initially out of the savage persecution and arrest by the British authorities in Hong Kong of loyal and patriotic Chinese journalists in the territory. The British Hong Kong authorities had not immediately released the journalists but had gone from bad to worse and continued to make arrests. He added that at present 11 were still in prison. Since the British authorities in Hong Kong continue to keep these patriotic journalists in gaol, the action which the Chinese had taken over Mr Grey was in no way unjustified and was in fact, consistent with the stand on this which China had adopted.

3. *Shen P'ing* then went on to argue that Mr Grey was in fact being treated leniently. He had been allowed to remain on in his house and his conditions were in the main as before his restriction. By contrast, the Chinese journalists unjustly detained in Hong Kong have been kept in prison.

4. *Shen P'ing* accused the British Government of conducting a vicious propaganda campaign over the detention of Mr Grey by distorting the facts and slandering the Chinese people in order to deceive public opinion in Britain. He added that this campaign did not help solve the problem and, indeed, only complicated the situation. As Lord Shepherd himself had said in his opening statement, Mr Grey had been medically examined and declared fit; and the British representatives in Peking who recently visited Mr Grey had to admit he looked quite well. The recent attempt by the British Government to spotlight the conditions of Mr Grey's detention were clearly calculated to stir up feeling against the Chinese. But the British Government would achieve nothing from this. In regard to the other cases mentioned by Lord Shepherd, he had already dealt with these with Mr Foley and, on this he (Shen P'ing) had nothing to add. If Lord Shepherd so wished he would repeat what he had told Mr Foley in this connection; but obviously this would be time consuming. The Minister had expressed strong dissatisfaction about the way in which certain British nationals had been treated in China. But the Chinese had greater cause for dissatisfaction. British subjects in China had violated Chinese law and this had aroused the anger of the Chinese people.

5. The Minister had also expressed the wish of HMG to improve Sino-British relations. But it was deeds not words that counted. He himself had seen no tangible evidence of Britain's desire to improve relations.

6. Responding *Lord Shepherd* said that he had just a few points to make. In regard to persons other than Mr Grey, it was true that this was a matter which had been raised three months ago by Mr Foley. It was also clear that the Chargé was not in a position to give any further information today. But he nevertheless hoped that within the next few weeks the Chargé would look into the matter again and let him know the outcome. In particular he would appreciate information about those people who appear to have disappeared in China—stressing that if only we could tell the families of the people concerned that their relatives were fit and well it would be a marked step forward and would surely cause no local embarrassment to the Chinese Government.

7. *Lord Shepherd* said that he was sure that Shen P'ing would agree that an orderly and peaceful Hong Kong was important to both China (particularly in view of China's trade with Hong Kong) and Britain. The past twelve months or so had seen serious disorder in the territory resulting in loss of life and a good deal of bomb throwing. He instanced the large number of bomb explosions which occurred when he arrived in Hong Kong in October, 1967. Like most people he regretted that it was necessary for arrests to be made. But the men to whom the Chargé had referred were (and he was sure that Shen P'ing would agree with this) tried fairly by the local courts for crimes against the civil law. What was more important was that those imprisoned as a result were visited by their friends and were also able to mix freely with others in the prison. This contrasted sharply with the treatment meted out to Mr Grey, who is held in what can only be described as solitary confinement. As he (Lord Shepherd) understood the position Mr Grey is confined to one small room. The Minister could not really believe that anyone could honestly say that it was right or in any way justifiable that any human being in this modern world should be so treated.

8. *Lord Shepherd* said that Shen P'ing had referred to a vicious propaganda campaign on the part of the British Government, slandering the Chinese Government

and its people. There was no substance whatsoever in this. He would have thought that what his Secretary of State, Mr Stewart, had said recently about Mr Grey was very restrained. *Lord Shepherd* emphasised that the British Government is in no way responsible for what Press, radio and TV commentators in this country say on any subject: certainly their comments do not emanate from the British Government.

9. In conclusion, Lord Shepherd said that he appreciated that Shen P'ing would now wish to report to his Government in Peking and expressed the hope that, when he did so, he would draw attention to the present relaxed atmosphere in Hong Kong. Much of the trouble and strife there had disappeared. Lord Shepherd also hoped that the Chargé would convey to his Government what he had said about the real desire on the part of the British Government to improve Sino-British relations. He was sure that steps could be taken by the Chinese Government to help us—we who genuinely desire to see improved relations between our two countries—achieve this end.

10. *Shen P'ing* said that he had not intended to talk about Hong Kong. However, since Lord Shepherd had referred to the troubles there he felt obliged to comment. The tension in Hong Kong was attributed to the persecution of patriotic Chinese citizens by Hong Kong British authorities. These citizens had been forced to make a stand in their own interests. In this they had the support of the Chinese people. The Chinese Government had taken a restrained attitude towards the Hong Kong question. Yet for the past year or so the British authorities in Hong Kong had persecuted and arrested many Chinese citizens on trumped up charges. At present some 300 Chinese people, including the eleven journalists, were still imprisoned in Hong Kong, some in concentration camps. The British authorities had also dished up a series of so-called emergency regulations. The effect of these measures was to stimulate resistance among the Chinese in Hong Kong and also to arouse strong feelings in China. Even bourgeois British lawyers in Hong Kong had referred to some of the emergency regulations as barbarous. They were totalitarian and represented a reign of terror.

11. *Lord Shepherd* said that clearly these were points on which it was necessary to agree to disagree. But if Britain were as vicious as Shen P'ing had suggested it was strange that Chinese Communist papers were still published in Hong Kong and that more and more Chinese there were able to go to Chinese Communist schools. Surely, if we were as vicious as the Chargé suggested, we would not allow such a state of affairs to continue? If the Hong Kong police had used unnecessary force at any time he would be among the first to condemn it. His belief was that the Hong Kong Government and police had reacted to the recent disturbances in a moderate way. The atmosphere there had now become more relaxed and surely this in itself was a sign that Britain was ready to see a happier relationship between Britain and China. He was sure that if the Chinese Government could only take some of the steps he (Lord Shepherd) had outlined, it would bring about the desired effect.

12. In closing *Lord Shepherd* told the Chargé that he was grateful for his coming to see him and said that he looked forward to meeting him more informally on some other occasion when between them they might explore ways and means to improving relations between the two countries.

13. Concluding *Shen P'ing* said that obviously Lord Shepherd was very familiar with the past history of Hong Kong and present conditions there. Since the subject had been mentioned again he felt obliged to say a few further words. Although Hong

Kong had been under British control for over 100 years, it was nevertheless Chinese territory. The Chinese position on this was abundantly clear. The patriotic Chinese in Hong Kong could not be deprived of their right to run their own newspapers. The Chinese Government were rightly concerned with the Chinese people in Hong Kong.

14. The meeting which lasted about 1¼ hours was conducted in a fairly relaxed atmosphere.

No. 163

Mr Cradock (Peking) to Mr Stewart, 11 February 1969[1]
Tel. No. 103 Priority, Confidential (FCO 21/465, FEC 3/548/1A)

My immediately preceding telegram.[2]

It was an encouraging interview. It was the most relaxed discussion of Sino/British relations I recall. T'ang was polite and very restrained in language throughout.

2. It is of interest that the Chinese 'took note' of our desire to improve relations and even consented to declare their own willingness to do so. They had clearly also taken note of Lord Shepherd's remarks.[3] Naturally the onus for solving remaining problems was again thrust on us, but T'ang implicitly admitted that this was a mutual process by claiming that the Chinese had shown willing by releasing Croziers.

3. It is evident that release of 11 journalists is foremost in the Chinese minds. T'ang picked these out and confined his claims for release to them. His failure to demand the release of all convicted prisoners is significant and it seems the Chinese may now regard the release of journalists as key to further progress not only on Grey but on other British subjects as well.

4. The Chinese sensitivity to publicity on British subjects detained in China again emerged strongly from meeting but I think it would be wrong to conclude from this that all publicity should be dropped. Well-judged items in foreign (repeat foreign) press should still be useful.

1 Repeated for information to Hong Kong.
2 Not printed. On paying a farewell call to the Deputy Director of the West European Department, Mr Cradock noted an improvement in relations over the last six months and hoped this would continue after the arrival of his successor.
3 See No. 162.

No. 164

Mr Stewart to Sir D. Trench (Hong Kong), 28 February 1969[1]
Tel. No. 161 Priority, Confidential (FCO 21/465, FEC 3/548/1A)

Personal for Moreton from Murray.

Cradock's farewell interview with the Deputy Director of the West European

1 Repeated for information to Peking.

Department (Peking telegram No. 102 of 11 February)[2] seems to me to indicate that it might be possible to start a saner dialogue with the Chinese about Sino-British relations. The Chinese may indeed expect that Denson shall shortly have something fresh to say. I am afraid, however, that unless we can show some progress, however small, towards meeting the Chinese over Hong Kong the momentum is likely to die and there would be little prospect of progress over the release of British subjects. Given the difficulties involved over the release of convicted prisoners, the only concession we can at all readily make to the Chinese is the release of the four remaining detainees. If it is likely that they will be released within a few months with expiration and existing warrants, there is something to be said for gaining that political advantage we can *vis-à-vis* the Chinese by releasing them immediately.

2. You may care to discuss this aspect with the Governor.

2 Not printed. See No. 163.

No. 165

Mr Denson (Peking) to Mr Stewart, 10 March 1969[1]
Tel. No. 170 Immediate, Confidential (FCO 21/465, FEC 3/548/1A)

My telegram No. 169:[2] Interview with West European Department of Ministry of Foreign Affairs.

The interview went on predictable lines. The only aspects from which we can draw any comfort are admission that Grey had access to his books and possibly the unsolicited statement at the end that China wanted to improve relations with us.

2. T'ang, who I understand is normally courteous and restrained exhibited signs, whether real or simulated, of considerable irritation while British subjects were being discussed. He said with evident frustration that there could be 'no question of improving Sino-British relations without solving Hong Kong problem'. Despite my pressing him, he refused to make any comment on specific matters I had raised except Grey. He referred again to News workers in context of Grey but did not refer specifically to other prisoners except in a general statement that prisoners were being maltreated, which I was able to refute. He did not choose to pursue the matter.

3. My conclusions are:

(*a*) that Chinese do want to get off the hook but progress will depend on some move by us in Hong Kong;

(*b*) If we make no move, there will be a deadlock; no progress will be made on any cases of British subjects (excluding yachtsmen); the Chinese may soon refuse to discuss British subjects with me at all. Forms of pressure such as publicity, will not move them.

(*c*) The key to the problem remains Grey. If his release could be achieved, we might well be able to work towards a gradual normalization of relations.

1 Repeated for information to Hong Kong.
2 Not printed.

4. I hope therefore that cases of the four remaining detainees can be urgently reviewed. Their release would help to maintain some momentum and might permit a continued dialogue with the Chinese. At the same time I hope that some way can be found whereby we can be seen to have made a concession in matter of news workers' release. I see no repeat no chance of Chinese agreeing to release Grey without it.

See my immediately following telegram.[3]

3 Not printed.

No. 166

Extract from an interdepartmental study for the Ministerial Committee on Hong Kong, 28 March 1969
K(69)1 Top Secret (CAB 134/2945)

Note by the Secretary of State for Foreign and Commonwealth Affairs

I am circulating herewith, for consideration at a meeting of the Committee, a copy of an interdepartmental study by Officials on future policy in regards to Hong Kong.[1]

2. An interim report (OPD(67)61) was prepared in July 1967 on the prospects on withdrawal from Hong Kong if it were suddenly forced upon us. Officials were further instructed (OPD(67)20th Meeting)[2] to examine policy towards our tenure of Hong Kong in the long term, on the basis that we could not rely on remaining in Hong Kong on present terms until the lease of the New Territories lapsed in 1997 and should therefore consider what adaptations of its status might be possible and desirable after the conclusion of the present conflict in Viet-Nam.

3. Responsibility for implementing these instructions was assumed by the Cabinet Office and carried out by a small group of the Defence Review Working Party. The Working Party's report, although substantially the work of the departments of the former Commonwealth Office and Foreign Office, is therefore an interdepartmentally agreed study. It was prepared in consultation (as opportunity offered) with the Governor of Hong Kong and Sir Donald Hopson, former Chargé d'Affaires in Peking. For security reasons, no copy of the report (or of earlier drafts) is held by anyone outside of Whitehall. The outcome represents many months work, hampered by the uncertainty surrounding Chinese attitudes and intentions towards their Colony at the height of the Cultural Revolution and the difficulty of assessing what effects the turmoil in China might have on that country's policy towards Hong Kong in the long term.

M[ICHAEL] S[TEWART]

1 Only the Conclusions and Recommendations (sections I and J) have been reproduced here. The full document can be found in *BDEE*, Series A, Volume 5, Part III, No. 339.
2 See No. 15.

ENCLOSURE IN NO. 166

Long Term Study: Hong Kong

I. Conclusions

British Interests (Paragraphs 3-19)

(*a*) Our present *net* annual expenditure on defence in Hong Kong is of the order of £15 million rising to an estimated £20 million after 1971 (assuming no change in the rate of the Colony's defence contribution). There are no other costs involved in maintaining our position there, and we have a sizeable investment in the Colony and a considerable trade with it. It has accumulated large sterling balances which it is in HMG's interest to see maintained.

(*b*) We derive considerable advantages from Hong Kong as a centre of communications and for intelligence operations, and politically it has some value to us in our relations with our allies, particularly the Americans.

(*c*) But Hong Kong could become a major liability if, as expected, its economy begins to run down towards the end of the lease or as a result of Chinese pressures. If it suffered a period of prolonged economic recession or stagnation, the Colony could become a major liability. Internal pressures and outside criticism may build up because constitutional advance is a point of friction in our relations with China. And we are obliged to maintain a garrison there which would be a serious risk in the event of a Chinese take-over.

British Responsibilities (paragraphs 20-27)

(*d*) We have a general responsibility to safeguard the welfare and interests of the population of Hong Kong and a particular responsibility to about half the population who are British subjects (i.e. to some 2 million, nearly all Chinese). We have a special responsibility to some 100,000-200,000 Chinese who will be particularly vulnerable to Chinese retaliation or to whom we owe a particular debt because of their connection with us. In whatever circumstances we abdicate our position it will be impossible to discharge all our responsibilities to the Hong Kong Chinese or to remove or protect all British and Hong Kong-owned assets (other than a proportion of the moveable assets).

Chinese Interests (paragraphs 28-36)

(*e*) Hong Kong provides China with easy access to the free world—for trade, travel and subversive activities. In our hands it is of considerable economic value to China, accounting for about a third of its total foreign exchange activities; while in Chinese hands it would be almost valueless. However, as China's economy develops the relative value of Hong Kong in this connection could diminish.

(*f*) There is evidence that these economic considerations are still regarded as paramount by the more moderate pragmatic elements who are now extending their influence in the Chinese leadership; but there is always the danger that extremist elements may gain the ascendancy, who would be prepared to sacrifice the economic benefits.

Chinese Attitude and Intentions (paragraphs 37-50)

(*g*) The Chinese regard the whole of Hong Kong (both ceded and leased areas) as Chinese territory to be recovered (although they are on record as saying that they will 'negotiate' its return); and even if they allowed the lease of the New Territories to run its full term, we could not expect to re-negotiate it in 1997.

(h) At the moment they are prepared to accept the continuing existence of the Colony because it brings them economic and political advantages. The campaign of violence has been abandoned for the present and they apparently recognise that it may take a long time to bring the Hong Kong Government, to a position of subservience using the methods of long term 'struggle'. Their immediate aims are to maximise their commercial interests in the Colony and to concentrate on broadening the base of their support among the people. In certain circumstances, however, this policy might quickly change to one of reducing the Colony to a position of subservience or even of taking it over.

(i) We have virtually no means of bringing pressure to bear upon the Chinese to change whatever course of action they decide on. We should nevertheless keep under review the scope for withdrawing services and facilities (e.g. in banking and shipping) in the event of another 'confrontation'.

(j) It is unlikely that the Chinese would wish to take Hong Kong by direct military attack; it would be more in keeping with their theory of indigenous revolution to create, by local action, a breakdown of authority in the Colony.

(k) As 1997 approaches confidence will inevitably drain away with adverse economic and political effects making it increasingly difficult for us to maintain our position. This will raise some tough problems in the spheres of economic and social policy and in the public service; studies of these problems (necessarily conducted within a limited circle) can best be put in hand in Hong Kong.

American Involvement (paragraphs 51-53)

(l) The Americans make great use of Hong Kong and would wish us to stay, at least as long as there is a Communist Government in Peking not recognised by them.

(m) Fear of American retaliation (which we might foster) may inhibit the Chinese from taking any action that could be clearly defined as 'Chinese aggression'. We might consider separately whether we should seek American support and understanding for the policies we desire to adopt.

Withdrawal (paragraphs 54-83)

(n) Hong Kong's future must eventually lie in China. This is likely to become an issue in the 1980s (when confidence and the economy must inevitably start to run down) or earlier if, in the meantime, Chinese pressures carry the indication that China has a serious intention to make our position untenable. But in present circumstances we need not—indeed, we cannot—contemplate action to this end.

(o) When we do decide to withdraw we will face major problems (some insoluble) in the discharge of our responsibilities towards the Chinese section of the community (particularly those that are British subjects or who may be vulnerable to retaliation because of their loyalty to the British connection) and in the maintenance of internal security during the period of withdrawal.

(p) The nature of these problems points to the need for some understanding with the Chinese. We can in any case put out of our minds any thought of an independent status for Hong Kong, under UN auspices or otherwise. We shall have to hand over sovereignty to China.

(q) A unilateral decision on our part to withdraw would be a course of last resort in present circumstances. This would invite severe harassment by the Chinese who would not acquiesce in our withdrawal at our own speed and in our own way; and we could not prevent their interference. At some future date it might be used to bring the Chinese to the conference table.

(r) At present the only solution acceptable to the Chinese would be to gain indirect control over the administration of the Colony. This we must avoid at any time as a step towards ultimate withdrawal.

(s) There might be an opportunity to negotiate withdrawal although we cannot see when this might arise. We should avoid if at all possible any form of joint administration of the Colony prior to handing over since this would give the Chinese an infinite capability for mischief and for frustrating our intentions.

(t) The course best suited to our interests would be an informal and disavowable approach to the Chinese when the time is ripe aimed at reaching a tacit understanding about an eventual withdrawal at a suitable agreed date.

(u) The Chinese response to a formal or informal approach would depend very much whether it suited their policy interests at the time to take the Colony over and on the strength of our position. The chances of a favourable response would be best if the Chinese were genuinely anxious, for economic reasons, to take Hong Kong over with minimum damage to the economy; our negotiating position would be strongest if we sought to withdraw when the Hong Kong economy was its normal buoyant self and there was no Chinese pressure.

(v) Our position is, however, weak in that we have many hostages in the Colony in terms of people and assets and no means of bringing significant pressure to bear on China. Its strength will rest on Hong Kong's economic value to China and on our ability to hand it over with that value unimpaired and its trading links with Western countries kept open. To use this card, changed attitudes towards China on the part of some Western countries will be a prerequisite.

(w) The initiative does not effectively lie in our hands: the Chinese could always frustrate our attempts to negotiate or reach an understanding with them. But on the timing of an approach all the considerations indicate that we should make it as soon as there emerges in China a regime with which we might do business and before the Hong Kong economy starts to run down as it well may in the 1980s.

The Worst Case (paragraphs 34-91)

(x) In the event of a Chinese military attack obviously mounted with the objective of taking over Hong Kong we would surrender the Colony with only a show of resistance. Unremitting Chinese pressure short of a military take-over could render our position untenable and lead us to the conclusion that we must withdraw with or without Chinese co-operation.

(y) In either event China might not accept our renunciation of control but might aim to force us to maintain a puppet British administration under their control. In such circumstances it might be better to co-operate with them rather than to sever, as in a formal way we could easily do, our political and economic connections with the Colony.

(z) However these are decisions which can be taken only in the light of the circumstances at the time. We consider that whatever may happen in Hong Kong the Governor should remain in charge of the civil administration of the Colony and therefore that the Dormant Commission conferring full administrative authority upon the Commander, British Forces, should be revoked.

J. Recommendations

The following are the recommendations of the study.

(1) We should recognise that Hong Kong's future must eventually lie in China and that our objective must be to attempt to negotiate its return, at a favourable opportunity, on the best terms obtainable for its people and for our material interests there.

(2) Withdrawal should not be contemplated while present conditions in China persist. We could not now negotiate terms that would in any measure meet our responsibilities towards the people or our material interests.

(3) We should watch for an acceptable opportunity to negotiate or reach some understanding with the Chinese on our withdrawal, if and when a suitable regime emerges there. It is important to do this when not under Chinese pressure and before the economy of the Colony starts to run down as it well may in the 1980s.

(4) Meanwhile we should show firmly that we intend to maintain our position there, giving no indication that we contemplate withdrawal. To this end we should keep under inter-departmental review what means we have from time to time of countering any renewed Chinese pressure.

(5) We should consider separately whether to seek American support and understanding for the policies we decide to adopt.

(6) The likely effect in the Colony of the approach of 1997 should be discreetly studied locally and policy in Hong Kong reviewed in the light of the results.

(7) At regular intervals and at any time the Chinese regime or attitude towards the Colony change significantly, future policy towards the Colony should be reviewed, in consultation with the Governor.

(8) In the event of an armed attack the Colony should remain under civil control. The Dormant Commission (under which the Governor would in certain circumstances hand over to the Commander, British Forces) should accordingly be revoked.

No. 167

Minute from Lord Shepherd to Mr Stewart, 8 May 1969
Secret (PREM 13/2523)

Secretary of State,

Mr Anthony Grey of Reuters

You will know that I and the department have been giving deep and anxious thought to the problem of Mr Anthony Grey and how best we could obtain his release without risking or prejudicing the security and stability of Hong Kong. I have also had an opportunity of discussing this with Mr Cater and Mr Cradock.

2. Both Mr Cater and Mr Cradock believe that the Chinese are determined that Mr Grey will not be released until the eleven journalists are released from prison.

3. As you will see from the submission,[1] the departmental advice is that in the interests of Hong Kong we should in general stand on our present position whereby the ten journalists would be released in September on the completion of their

---

1 Not printed.

sentences and Wong Chak, the remaining journalist, whose sentence the Review Board has recently shortened, would be released early in October. The official view is that this should meet the Chinese demands and should obtain the release of Mr Grey shortly after Wong Chak's release.

4. In addition to this course, (*a*), there are two other possible courses, (*b*) and (*c*), which I have considered and discussed with the department.

5. Course (*b*) is that the Governor should at his discretion and exercising his prerogative release the ten journalists in July leaving Wong Chak only in prison until October. The official advice in the submission is that I should discuss this with the Governor when I am in Hong Kong when we could take into account the reactions of the Chinese following the announcement of the reduction in Wong Chak's sentence (on May 9 and other local factors). On this possible course I could make the comment that I think that the Governor will be loath to agree. Personally I think it might make it more certain that the Chinese would release Mr Grey although I do not believe they would release him until Wong Chak was released in October. Whilst all the latest information is that the health of Mr Grey is good and we have no reason to believe that he could not withstand confinement until then, particularly if news of steps taken in Hong Kong became known to him. I feel I should mention my misgivings about a course of action that would leave him in detention until October. But I do accept that from the presentational point of view in Hong Kong there is much to course (*b*). It seems to me however that when it becomes known that while we were ready to release ten of the journalists but were insisting that Wong Chak remains a prisoner until October—which means the continued confinement of Mr Grey—we might be confronted with press and parliamentary clamour. So far we have been able to hold this within limits. It may however become so great that the Chinese might either feel that they could not be seen to be releasing Mr Grey as consequence of public criticism, as I suspect might have been the case in 1968, or they may feel that the pressure on us is such that the original price for Mr Grey is too low and make more difficult demands as the price for his release. One does not wish to exaggerate this risk. I am however especially conscious of the proposed petition to be delivered by Mr Grey's family. If, as is likely, this is delivered in the glare of TV and the press, it could well spark of the pressures which we know to be there but which have been deliberately restrained in interests of Mr Grey.

6. Course (*c*) is the earlier release of Wong Chak to coincide with that of the other journalists at the earliest date possible. If this were to be the decision, clearly it would place the Governor in a very difficult position in that he had just accepted the Review Board's recommendation to reduce the sentence to three years instead of five and will be justifying this as a normal review procedure quite unconnected with the Grey case. It would be hard to explain, although not impossible, if the Governor by exercise of his prerogative went beyond the recommendation of the Review Board so soon after he had accepted it and released Wong Chak with the other prisoners at an earlier date. I do not think however there is any doubt that this course provides the best opportunity of getting the release of Mr Grey and will avoid the risks which I have mentioned above of a release by stages as envisaged in course (*b*).

7. Course (*c*), if you agree, could also be discussed by me with the Governor. I am not however due in Hong Kong until about 1 June. And in the meantime circumstances may arise which you may think require a decision before then.

8. To come to a decision on this finely balanced problem in which conjecture must carry as much weight as logic, since there is no firm evidence on how the Chinese may react, is very difficult. This is more so in view of the consistent and well-argued advice of the Governor and officials. My own feeling, which is the one I expressed to you on 3 April when I talked over the submission by the department of that date, is that while we must take no steps which would place at risk Hong Kong, we should ask the Governor to try to devise some procedure to mitigate any risk but ensure the release of the eleven journalists during June or at the latest July.

9. Like Mr Long, I do not believe this step would place at risk the security or stability of Hong Kong though I do see that it would involve difficult and embarrassing administrative problems. I accept however that it would probably be right for us to defer a final decision—if possible—until I have had an opportunity of weighing the issues fully with the Governor and in any case until after we have had the reactions to the reduction of Wong Chak's sentence. The period of delay worries me and if we adopt this course, I think it necessary that I have a directive from you to make a decision so as to avoid further delay which may prejudice Mr Grey's release.

10. In view of the fact that I am leaving for an overseas visit tomorrow I felt it right to record my views, although we may have an opportunity of discussing this matter today.

SHEPHERD

No. 168

Mr Stewart to Mr Denson (Peking), 20 May 1969[1]
Tel. No. 180 Immediate, Confidential (FCO 21/465, FEC 3/548/1A)

My IPT.[2] Call of Chinese Chargé d'Affaires.

The atmosphere of the interview was fairly relaxed. In general Ma was less negative than his predecessor Shen Ping. After rejecting our protest he offered without further probing to pass on our requests for information and consular access.

2. Ma's statement on the price for Grey was the most significant part of his remarks. The offer to release Grey in return for the release of the news workers was stated in unequivocal terms and goes further than the NCNA statement of 28 December. Although Chinese motive in making this offer is undoubtedly to encourage us to release the news workers prematurely, statement was in such terms that we can reasonably conclude:

(*a*) That it is intended to apply irrespective of the actual timing of the release of the news workers

---

1 Repeated for information to Hong Kong, Washington, POLAD Singapore and Bangkok (for Godden).
2 Not printed.

(*b*) That the Chinese will not release Grey before all eleven are released.

The phrase 'Grey's freedom of movement would be restored' is somewhat vague, but we assume that the Chinese would not withhold an exit visas after Grey had been released from house arrest.

3. Ma used phrase 'all patriotic journalists'. In asking him to confirm offer Moreton referred specifically to 'all eleven'. Ma did not contradict this but again used his earlier phrase apparently reading from instructions.

4. We are assessing our tactics further in light of this development and in particular extent to which public use should be made of the offer. For the time being we propose to inform only Long of Reuters, and possibly also Grey's family, in strict confidence.

No. 169

Letter from Mr Garside (Peking) to Mr Boyd, 3 June 1969
Restricted (FCO 21/425)

Dear John,

China: How it hits you

May I, in contrast to the rigorous textual analysis, zealous verbal information gathering and in-depth perspectives usually offered by my colleagues, jot down one or two personal impressions on the way China now hits a Briton returning from leave? I can do so in the knowledge that after four happy weeks reform-through-labour on a Hampshire hillside my feelings about China, however partial, are not influenced by the frustrations and deprivations of Peking life. You will appreciate that I am not in the least attempting to give my considered view of Chinese society.

2. I was looking forward to my return. Then I crossed the border; and not only was I back in the atmosphere of torpor, shabbiness and primitive ineptitude but once again Chinese officialdom was demonstrating its self-destructive talent for mishandling foreigners. One small example: the French Embassy doctor who enjoys diplomatic immunity foolishly brought out a *mah jongg* set to while away the time in the Chinese border rest-room. Before he could start to play it was confiscated, and for an hour he did battle with Chinese customs officials who insisted that they had the right to impound it. although it was a personal possession, on the grounds that *mah jongg* is forbidden in China. Most of the senior hierarchy of the customs post spent an hour or two defending an action which betrayed total ignorance of diplomatic privilege but would obviously cause ill-will without any compensating gain in defence of China's morals for of course the Frenchman would never play *mah jongg* with any Chinese. The set was returned to the doctor the next day.

3. Back in Peking, the immediate impact is of a shabby city, primitive, antiquated and almost without charm, filled with people whose faces betray ignorance, ill-education, and brutalising of the senses; one is struck by an absence from their faces of evidence of self-realisation. In 24 hours in Hong Kong (a society which, heaven knows, has a good many deficiencies) I had seen so many men whose faces, in contrast, seemed to be straining with intelligence and alertness, and women who

were obviously delighting in their own beauty or their families. There is a rat-race cynicism which drains its own line on Hong Kong men's faces and there is a cultural emptiness which leaves blanks under the make-up of Hong Kong women, but even so they are alive and realising their potential far more than the Pekingese.

4. Watching faces on a Peking street may be depressing but cannot evoke a reaction whose intensity can match the horror and disgust evoked by a spectacle which is enjoying almost nightly showings on TV here this week. I mean Mao's personal appearance before 10,000 army men which took place on 19 May. No matter how many times one has seen this standard formula of Mao walking onto, around and off a stage, to the accompaniment of mass hysteria one's stomach is always turned by the crowd's performance. It is animal not human. Like a pack of watch-dogs they strain forward awaiting his appearance. He appears, and 10,000 throats open to bay and yelp, and yelp and bay until he disappears again. Supposedly mature officers of 40 years of age jig up and down in a frenzy of emotional self-abuse determined that they at least shall achieve ecstasy before he is gone. Before one's eyes men turn into animals, but the infinitely self-conscious way in which they do it suggests that awful Liuist[1] scepticism is very near to the surface.

5. After a week back here one tries to think of images which might sum up one's feelings about the place. Perhaps it is a bankrupt Shangri-la, a hideaway world founded and financed by a millionaire who went bust, and now there is no money left for human or physical maintenance; or perhaps it is the East Asian social equivalent of the Ground Nut Scheme: a vast, dream-led project, the monuments to the failure of which are not tangled weeds and rusting tractors on an East African hillside, but people rusting in the dust of Peking streets.

6. I am sending copies of this letter to Miss Draycott in IRD, Brewer in RD, Weston in PUSD, Pierce in DIS, Spendlove in Washington, Hibbert in Singapore, McLaren and Ashworth in Hong Kong, Hewitt in Canberra, and Chancery at Tokyo.

Yours ever,
ROGER

1 Liu Shaoqi.

No. 170

Mr Denson (Peking) to Mr Stewart, 11 June 1969
Confidential (FCO 21/441, FEC 1/16)

Sir,

China: Revisited

It is 16 years since I first came to China as a member of the staff of the Representative Negotiating for the Establishment of Diplomatic Relations—a process which, in the Chinese view, has only been partially completed. In this despatch, I record some first impressions of Peking in 1969 and some of the changes which have struck me since I was last here.

2. The dominant impression for anyone arriving in China is the cult of Mao Tse-tung. Everywhere the eye and ear are assailed. Mao portraits and busts of all sizes and varieties are ubiquitous. The moon face gazes out from every shop window and doorway, from hoardings, from the tops of buildings, from hillsides and from the multiplicity of badges worn on nearly every breast. Cult emblems such as paper sunflowers and red hearts inscribed 'loyal' abound. The little red book is carried everywhere as the passport of orthodoxy. There are morning and evening 'services' before Mao's image in schools, institutions and even hotels There have been reports of Mao 'loyalty altars'. The city is dressed overall with slogans, often in man-high characters: ejaculations of praise, the 'Thoughts', revolutionary exhortations. The name of Mao comes again and again over the loud-speakers in a never-ending litany. The cult has encroached on, and in some cases taken over, those ancient monuments which are still open: the Summer Palace, the Temple of the Sleeping Buddah, the Temple of Heaven, where one of the most celebrated vistas in China, through an archway to the Temple of the Happy Year, tripled-roofed with blue tiles, is now marred by a larger than life size bust of Mao in white plaster.

3. The effect of the cult and other changes brought about by the Cultural Revolution has been to destroy much of the grace and individuality of Peking. Tattered posters and slogans in apparently indelible paint still disfigure the walls. Buildings are falling into dilapidation through neglect. The zeal of the reformers has swept away the legacies of older Peking. Gone are the story tellers, the old men selling birds in cages, the dealers in lamps and lacquer and camphor wood chests, the Peking Opera. The Cultural Revolution has brought a revivalist atmosphere; processions, flags, bugles, cymbals, drums and revolutionary songs. An emphasis on work and prayer and a deliberate fostering of Puritanism. Physical training is encouraged but organised games have apparently ceased. Fortunately a few of the old restaurants remain. Not even Madam Mao has yet dared to reform Peking Duck!

4. On the credit side the roads have been widened and improved and many trees planted. New flats have been built for the privileged. They are red brick blocks of five or six stories. A family appears to get two to three rooms. There is a minimum of furniture, only the one picture, rarely are there curtains and the lighting is for the most part by naked electric light bulbs. Public transport has improved. There are many more buses and lorries, though still no privately-owned cars. The insistence on the old rule of hooting at all intersections, at policemen and adjacent vehicles has produced a deafening cacophony in the main streets. An underground railway is being built following the line of the old city wall almost all of which has now disappeared. There are more bicycles. In a society where self-denial is a fetish, a bicycle must be one of the few status symbols which can safely be acquired. Consumer goods are more plentiful than they were 15 years ago. In the large department store interested groups can always be seen at the counters selling radio sets, cameras and electrical equipment. But not many people seem to buy the higher priced articles. A simple medium-wave radio might, for example, cost £10—a month's wages for the average worker.

5. In less tangible ways the contrasts are equally great. My previous stay coincided with a period of relaxation in the cultural field. It came at the completion of the various 'reform' movements the régime carried out after the coming to power: land

reform, the campaign against counter-revolutionaries, and the campaigns to stamp out corruption and malpractice in Government Departments and in private commerce and industry, known respectively as the Three Antis and the Five Antis. At that time an attempt was being made to revalue China's literature and art in Communist terms. In effect, to justify a continued admiration for Chinese civilisation which in the official view was largely the product of a feudal society administered by a minority *élite*. This gave rise to some strange paradoxes and contradictions but it did mean that history, philosophy and literature, Chinese and foreign were still studied; ancient monuments were preserved; porcelain and bronzes were collected from construction sites and displayed in museums. Novels and plays of some literary merit were still being written. The Cultural Revolution with its emphasis on the extinction of 'bourgeois' influences has resulted, at least for the moment, in China turning its back on its own civilisation, as well as rejecting everything foreign. No objects of traditional art are on display. Classical and pre-Cultural Revolution literature is no longer on sale. Drama has been reduced to a few revolutionary operas. Artistic activity of all kinds is totally political and in most cases dedicated to the Mao cult. The Cultural Revolution has also caused academic pursuits as such to be denigrated and education to be oriented towards labour, even to the extent of workers and peasants 'teaching' in schools. Some corrective to the traditional Chinese tendency to over-emphasise the academic to the exclusion of the practical sides of education might not be out of place. It remains to be seen how far the Chinese will go—already notes of caution are being sounded—and whether some sectors will be excluded from the system. There does however seem to be a real danger that there will be a general lowering of standards which could be damaging to China's longer-term prospects. Already as a result of the Cultural Revolution universities have been effectively closed for nearly four years.

6. For the diplomatist living in Peking life is less gracious than it was. Foreign diplomatic Missions have been systematically moved from the old Legation Quarter in the middle of the city with its unhappy extra-territorial memories for the Chinese. With few exceptions, we now live and work in two insulated diplomatic quarters some miles from the centre. The Chinese draw a distinction between Head of Missions, who are allowed houses with a modicum of convenience and space, and their staffs who are mostly lodged in blocks of Soviet-style flats with all nationalities and political persuasions cheek by jowl: a genuine test of the ability to co-exist with those of 'differing social systems', codes of behaviour, size of families and standards of hygiene. The system enables the authorities to control more effectively contacts with the man in the street. Armed public security guards are at the gates of every Chancery residence and each diplomatic quarter. Even on picnics in permitted areas local children are shepherded away when foreigners approach lest they should be polluted by 'imperialist' or 'revisionist' influence. But when contact is accidentally made with an ordinary person there is usually no sign of hostility, only curiosity and the tendency to stare as if the foreigner were an animal in the zoo. This is of course entirely familiar as are the occasional cries of 'Big Nose' and 'Foreign Devil', though these are now officially frowned on. The Cultural Revolution accentuated the natural chauvinism of the Chinese and their suspicion of foreigners which became for a time 'spy mania' as a number of unfortunate British subjects know to their cost. The

feeling has now abated a little and may do so further, but some of the legacies of the Cultural Revolution are likely to remain. Access to all forms of information is still more difficult than it used to be. Provincial newspapers cannot be ordered or even the local *Peking Daily* is forbidden to foreigners, whose diet is the *People's Daily* and one other newspaper of scant interest. The few contacts with Chinese other than officials formerly allowed to members of this Mission have ceased, though some more favoured colleagues maintain tenuous links with the non-diplomatic foreign community. A number of diplomatic Missions, particularly the Africans, live in a vacuum, bewildered and unhappy in the face of Chinese unwillingness to let them make friends or find out what is going on in the country. They have little knowledge of China, for the most part they have no Chinese speakers, and few have really adequate or secure communications with their own Governments.

7. The concept of reciprocity has always been alien to the Chinese and they still tend to treat diplomats like the representatives of tributary States. The habit has become more frequent of grading countries according to their 'friendliness' and distributing favours accordingly: travel, invitations to official functions, the provision of efficient local staff. After the events of 1967 we find ourselves sharing the bottom of the diplomatic league table with the Russians and the Indians—a striking reversal of fortune for both of them since the days I remember of China's 'unbreakable friendship' with the Soviet Union (now transferred to puny Albania), and the Sino/Indian agreement on Tibet in which the Five Principles were first enunciated. In our case positive harassment may have stopped, but anything approaching courteous co-operation has not yet begun. The burnt-out Chancery stands untouched and we still use the former residence as a makeshift office. The last approach about repairs elicited the classic statement that according to the terms of the lease we would be required, if necessary, to hand it back in the same state as it was taken over! Unfortunately few of those diplomatic Missions whose Governments have no problems with the Chinese, or whom the latter might wish to influence, ever see fit to complain about their treatment, on the contrary they display a childlike pleasure whenever they are thrown a few crumbs from the Imperial table: a Vice-Minister to dinner, a handshake from Chou En-lai, a visit to Nanking. It is often argued that universal recognition of China and China's entry into the United Nations besides being realistic and right are necessary in order that China can be exposed to outside influence and thus induced to behave as a civilised member of the international community. Experience in Peking suggests that if this is ever to happen, and any inroad is to be made into the Middle Kingdom mentality, a much firmer line will be required from prospective educators.

8. The impressions I have recorded are of a situation which may change now that the Ninth Congress of the Chinese Communist Party has taken place and there has been a *de facto* end to the Cultural Revolution. A great deal may happen between now and the 1st of October, when the 20th anniversary of the founding of the Republic will no doubt be celebrated with great éclat. There are already signs of some easing of tension. There have been reports of a much more relaxed atmosphere in certain provincial cities such as Shanghai, Canton, and even nearby Tientsin. There is always a danger in regarding this cathedral city of the Cult as the microcosm of the whole of China. It is particularly difficult to form a just picture fed almost exclusively

on written material in a jargon which is, if possible, even more cliché-ridden and indigestible than before. So far there has been few opportunities to compare the written word with reality, or to judge how much pragmatism, cynicism or just cheerfulness are breaking in to mitigate the frightening rigour of the mass indoctrination programme, the joyless Puritanism, the endless hard work. As always the man in the street seems resilient and fairly cheerful, though at times weary. The young children remain extremely attractive. It is a terrifying thought that they are now being recruited and indoctrinated apparently from the age of five or six. It seems likely that as long as Mao remains on the scene, the attempt to bring about a vast remoulding of society, to create new selfless men and to break down the distinctions between town and country, mental and manual labour will continue, though in a progressively less frenzied way. The creation of new organs of government and the linking of the Party structure to them will of itself create stability and tend to institutionalise revolutionary fervour in the direction of greater common sense. Whatever Mao may say about the evils of bureaucracy, a bureaucracy is bound to grow up again, altered in composition and to some extent in nature, but in the long term dedicated to its own aims and interests. Furthermore there are still those who do not share Mao's notions on proletarian Utopia and they will assert themselves when the time comes.

9. There have already been some signs of a return to normality in foreign relations by the despatch of a few Chinese Ambassadors to their posts and some greater regularity in the administration of the Ministry of Foreign Affairs. We may see an attempt by the Chinese to improve relations with certain countries and to treat others, for example, in Eastern Europe more individually in the hope of widening any differences with the Soviet Union. So far as Sino/British relations are concerned, I am afraid that we cannot expect any flowering such as occurred during my previous stay following the Geneva Conference of 1954, but as Chinese arrested in Hong Kong during the 1967 confrontation are released, we may expect gradual improvement, including, it is to be hoped, the release of British subjects detained.

10. When reflecting on the differences and the similarities of life in China today and 15 years ago, a passage of Lord Curzon's came to mind written after a visit to Peking in the 1890s, 'the frugal, hard-limbed, indomitable, ungracious race, who oppose to all overtures from the outside the sullen resistance of a national character self-confident and stolid, a religious code of incredible and all-absorbing rigour and a governing system . . . still wrapped in the mantle of a superb and paralysing conceit'. It remains a remarkably accurate judgment, and explains the frustration which any diplomatist feels when trying to penetrate the political and psychological wall the Chinese have built round themselves. At the same time, the attempt is worthwhile and it is this which makes life here, despite its limitations and difficulties, endlessly fascinating.

11. I am sending copies of this despatch to Her Majesty's Representatives at Washington, Tokyo, Moscow, Ottawa and Canberra, to Commander-in-Chief Far East, Singapore, and to the Governor in Hong Kong.

I have, etc.
J. B. DENSON

No. 171

Sir D. Trench (Hong Kong) to Mr Stewart, 24 July 1969[1]
Tel. No. 588 Routine, Secret (FCO 21/466, FEC 3/548/1B)

Your telegram 240 to Peking, para 3, Sino/British Relations.[2]

The suggestion in your telegram that further pressure for 'concessions' is likely to be directed against Hong Kong is disturbing. It accords with the knowledge we have had for some time that the local communists, and probably the Peking Government, are telling themselves that further pressure on London and Hong Kong will gradually gain them all they want: although they do seem to recognize a need to pace their demands a little to allow us to preserve our *amour propre* somewhat. They increasingly appear to believe also that HMG in London are more responsive to such manoeuvres than the Hong Kong Government and that differences of view exist between us. See, for example, my telegram 230 of 17 March.[3]

2. In short, I suspect that, as I have always feared, our 'concessionary' actions over the past few months have contributed more to encouraging a belief in our susceptibility to pressure than to stimulating any genuine reciprocation by the Chinese, other than over Grey who was an embarrassment anyway. Indeed, we have been consistently warned to expect ill-effects from giving away too much for insufficient return—see for example my telegram 2001 of 20 September, 1968,[4] para 3 of my telegram 391 of 15 May[5] and others in this series.

3. I feel therefore I must make it clear that there is nothing more of any substance I can do here. I have been unable so far to find any acceptable cover for advancing the release of the news workers. The cases of all remaining long-term prisoners cannot now be taken out of the hands of the Board of Review, and I can do nothing more to speed up releases should this be asked of me. With the last of the detainees released and the emergency regulations put back into cold storage we have come to the end of the positive steps we can take, always assuming the return of prisoners to China remains unacceptable. Moreover, we have taken the public here with us to just about the limits of safety by way of 'concessions' in the interests of Grey; and we cannot go any further to relieve British subjects whose predicament is only connected with Hong Kong events in the sense that they are regarded by the Chinese as a useable lever against us.

4. If therefore we are to avoid the difficult situation which will arise if the Chinese commit themselves to a demand that further confrontation prisoners must be released before their due date, it is essential that we try to make clear to them that we have no more to offer and are calling a firm halt.

5. The question is, how can this be done? Because of their belief that Hong Kong is less amenable to pressure than HMG, I fear that anything we say in Hong

---
1 Repeated for information to Peking, POLAD Singapore and Washington.
2 Not printed. Paragraph 3 stated: '... clearly we are going to hear more about this [prisoners in Hong Kong] in our relations with the Chinese once, as we hope, the Grey affair has been settled in October'.
3 Not printed.
4 No. 149.
5 Not printed.

Kong may not carry quite the same conviction as remarks made in London or by the Chargé d'Affaires in Peking, although they could do no harm. There is also the tactical problem that anything said with authority by us in London or Peking may imply that a demand has in fact been made by the Chinese Government and recognised by us to be such. In other words it is difficult to say anything without appearing to be making the opening move in a negotiation. There may also be problems finding an occasion for an authoritative statement.

6. However, I believe, first, that we should now moderate our references to 'improving Sino/British relations'. The phrase may seem unexceptionable and reasonable to us and to imply that it is up to the Chinese to take steps to bring that improvement, but the Chinese are not likely to be able to discern any field of substantial concern to them which 'Sino/British relations' exist other than over Hong Kong, and no doubt find it difficult to imagine we do either. The phrase, to Chinese minds, and remembering their Brahminical self-righteousness, can only mean that HMG and the Hong Kong Government are suggesting that they would be prepared to offer more. For these reason, I believe reiteration of this phrase is doing more harm than good.

7. Next, I believe that, rather than speaking formally, we should seek opportunities to bring into any conversation phrases which make it clear that we have nothing further to offer. We should couple continued demands for proper access to imprisoned British subjects with firm rejection of any suggestion that Hong Kong is in any way relevant to their cases: pointing out that if they consider it *is* relevant, then they are admitting that the British subjects are innocent hostages. We should represent the situation here as largely satisfactory and normal, apart from misdemeanours by individuals which will be dealt with: taking the line that we have nothing of substance to raise with them over Hong Kong and have no reason to discuss it.

8. Finally I consider it important that we should indicate to them whenever and however we can that the differences of view on 'concessions', which they imagine to exist between us, are illusory; and are not open to exploitation by them. Throughout, our aim should now be forestall further demands before they are made and to do nothing which might encourage them. Once made, an undesirable deadlock will have arisen which is far better avoided.[6]

6 Replying, in Peking Tel. No 440 of 31 July, Mr Denson thought that as little as possible should be said to the Chinese until after Grey's release. He agreed with the Governor that references to improvements in relations should be moderated, as they had amounted to little beyond a relaxation in Grey's conditions and improvements in the treatment of the Mission.

No. 172

Minute from Mr Murray to Sir S. Tomlinson, 12 August 1969
Top Secret (FCO 21/490, FEC 13C/1)

Covert contacts with the Chinese authorities through Hong Kong

From my submissions on the case of Mr Anthony Grey, the detained Reuters correspondent in Peking, you will already be aware of the existence of a covert channel to the Chinese authorities on the mainland through Hong Kong. This may be the moment to set out what we know at greater length.

2. The go-between in Hong Kong is a local businessman of Chinese race, K. C. Jay. He has acted as a point of contact between ourselves and the Chinese authorities on the mainland for a number of years. He is regularly in touch with Mr Jack Cater of the Hong Kong Trade and Development Council, a career Civil Servant of the Hong Kong Government on detached duty. The following is a brief assessment of the advantages and disadvantages of the use of this channel.

Advantages

3. It is clearly useful to have a point of contact in Hong Kong with the mainland authorities through whom messages of a practical, and occasionally of a political character, can be passed. There is of course already one such point of contact. The principal representation of the mainland interest in the Colony is, as in many parts of the world, the New China News Agency. Business of a practical nature has often to be conducted through this body. However, the NCNA has tried for many years to acquire a quasi-consular position as the spokesman of 'progressive' Chinese elements in the Colony vis-à-vis the Hong Kong Government and all business conducted through the NCNA, treated as the *interlocuteur valable* of the Chinese Government in the Colony, tends invariably to enhance the public standing of the organisation. This, for obvious reasons, we are anxious to discourage. Jay's first value therefore is that he provides an alternative to the NCNA.

4. Jay's second point of value is that he is deniable. The Hong Kong public do not know that he is a channel to the mainland and arrangements reached through him have the advantage that they remain without official character unless the Hong Kong Government decides otherwise. An example of this function is offered by the case of Mr Grey. It was possible to conduct with Peking a form of flexible negotiation over Mr Grey (albeit unsuccessful) which could not be done through more orthodox channels, for fear of the consequences for public confidence in Hong Kong. Such a negotiation would be much more difficult to conduct through the diplomatic channel in Peking (or in London) where, given the nature of relations between officials on our side and their Chinese counterparts, it would have to proceed by rigidly formal steps, and where bargaining might in effect be ruled out by Chinese unwillingness to be dislodged from any position which they had formally taken up.

Disadvantages

5. The disadvantages of the Jay channel are, however, considerable. First, like many such go-betweens, he has a tendency to want to be all things to all men. Not content with passing messages to us from the Chinese authorities, he is unable to refrain from embellishing them with personal philosophy and advice and it is often difficult to disentangle the two strands. A second functional disadvantage is his reluctance to work to one master alone on the Chinese side. Jay works in the first instance to the Manager of the Bank of China in Hong Kong, who is known to be a competent and responsible official enjoying the confidence of the Peking authorities. However, Jay also claims to carry on a personal correspondence with Chou En-lai's private secretary in Peking. Based on this latter correspondence he produces assessments of the balance of forces among the leaders in Peking (on the lines of 'extremists' versus 'moderates') which sometimes look like playbacks of assessments by Western 'China-watchers' and consequently liable to be

misleading; and which sometimes seem designed deliberately to make our flesh creep and hurry us into concessions.

The Balance

6. Thus there must be reservations about the reliability of this channel. Nevertheless, we know from discussion last year that the Governor of Hong Kong has some faith in Jay. And our friends,[1] whose experience of Jay goes back some years, have in the past found him to be a reliable contact. I myself favour the continuing use of this channel provided we remember what we are doing; we must continue to treat Jay's messages from China with a large pinch of salt and set out the messages we wish to have conveyed back in a form that is entirely unambiguous. If the Chinese attempt to set a price (in terms of the release of prisoners in Hong Kong) on the British subjects, other than Mr Grey, still in detention in China, we may be glad of Jay's services, if only to try to head the Chinese off.

Recent exchanges

7. Meanwhile the continuing conversations between Jay and Mr Jack Cater provide a certain insight into the thoughts and neuroses of the Chinese leadership vis-à-vis Hong Kong.

8. Mr Cater's report of 20 June provides good examples of mainland thinking. In this conversation Jay purports to express mainland preoccupations about the next incumbent of the governorship of Hong Kong and about the next Colonial Secretary. This simply confirms yet again the anxiety of the Chinese—of which we have always been aware—that these posts should not fall into other than British hands. (It is simply a detailed reflection of the Chinese anxiety that nothing should ever happen that might contribute towards a change of constitutional status for the Colony—whether it be self-government, independence or some form of internationalised status.) Jay then goes on to set out the communist attitude to Hong Kong i.e. that the communists have no love at all for capitalist economics as such and would dearly love to undermine the Hong Kong administration, but that in practice they find Hong Kong too valuable in its present form, both economically and politically, to upset the applecart; and that they are less likely to change their mind if they continue to see that we ourselves are prepared to use considerable firmness to keep the applecart upright. Jay comments interestingly that the date of 1997, when our lease on the New Territories expires, 'really means nothing'. We have already written to the Political Adviser in Hong Kong asking for an exegesis of this phrase. In particular, we have asked for an opinion as to whether Jay was speaking on instructions or simply venturing a personal view. Meanwhile I would only venture the remark that reassuring words about 1997 from the communists are not necessarily an accurate guide to their eventual intentions. For one thing, they will no doubt continue to weigh up the balance of gain and loss that would accrue from a takeover of the Colony, not to mention the balance of forces involved at any one time in any test of wills. Second, there is no interest for the communists in taking over a bankrupt Colony and the only way to preserve prosperity in Hong Kong in the interim is for them to let it be thought that they have no intention of ever taking over.

9. Finally, Jay refers to the possible repercussions for Hong Kong of recognition

---

1 SIS.

of China by the United States. Here we are up against a hypothetical situation. Factors that would modify Jay's warning are the question of physical facilities (i.e. whether the Chinese can develop Shanghai as a viable alternative to the splendid port of Hong Kong) and whether or not United States big business decides to continue to use Hong Kong as its base for the China trade or to abandon it. I do not think we need let ourselves be too alarmed at this stage by Jay's predictions.

JAMES MURRAY

No. 173

Mr Stewart to Sir D. Trench (Hong Kong), 22 August 1969[1]
Tel. No. 2 Saving Secret (FCO 21/466, FEC 3/548/1B)

Your telegram No. 588:[2] Sino-British Relations.

We have taken careful note of the points in paragraph 3 of your telegram under reference. It would indeed be regrettable if the Chinese were to conclude from your policies over the past few months in Hong Kong that we were susceptible to pressure. Seen from here, however, the policies have appeared an effective combination of firmness and flexibility, indeed a successful balancing act of the kind in which, as you rightly comment in your telegram No. 855 of 5 July, 1968,[3] the Hong Kong authorities are not inexperienced.

2. We foresee that we here may well be in for a difficult time over the other British subjects, who are likely to become a matter for increasing public concern if the Grey affair is resolved. While it may be, as you say, that their predicament is connected with Hong Kong events only in the sense that they are regarded by the Chinese as a useful lever against us, nevertheless their relatives have argued that it must be significant that their detention post-dates the conviction in Hong Kong courts of large numbers of Communist offenders. Moreover, the local Communists in Hong Kong must surely hope that the Peking authorities will use the British subjects as a means of speeding up the release of prisoners in Hong Kong. The degree of support that they will receive from Peking in this remains problematical. In any case you may be assured that we are fully aware of the slippery slope on which we would be starting if in the interests of these British subjects we were to hold out any prospect whatsoever of concessions over convicted prisoners in Hong Kong.

3. Indeed there appears to be close agreement among us on the handling of the cases of the long term prisoners. We agree that, on the assumption—clearly still a valid one—that the expulsion of prisoners to China remains unacceptable to the Chinese, there is little to be done without crossing the limits of safety to which you refer. (We are sure, however, that you would agree that it does not follow that we

1 Repeated for information to Peking, Washington and POLAD Singapore.
2 No. 171.
3 No. 127.

should abandon the self-imposed restraint that we have observed in such matters as the Communist Press or education).

4. We agree that a further formal demand by the Chinese for the premature release of prisoners would much increase our difficulties (although it can be argued that such a demand is already inherent in the 'Five Demands'). It is however difficult to see how best to play our hand to head this off. We agree that a formal statement of firmness on our side is as likely as not to drive the Chinese into a hopelessly entrenched position. It would be a pity to prejudice in this way the prospect, however slight, of an improvement in the situation of British subjects after the release of Grey.

5. Both you and the Mission in Peking recommend that we moderate our references to 'improving Sino-British relations'. In our eyes the phrase has had little more than ritual meaning and it is difficult on the face of it to believe that simple repetition of the phrase, in the face of much hard evidence to the contrary, can have led the Chinese to take it as an indication of readiness on our side to capitulate on specific issues. However, we are certainly ready to accept your advice and shall in future play these references down. In addition we shall be careful in briefing the Press and other contacts on the progress of Sino-British relations to avoid giving the impression that Sino-British relations are improving faster than is in fact the case.

6. We accept that conversations of a less formal kind with the Chinese could provide a convenient occasion for putting across the appropriate message about our intentions. We do not dispute the aptness of the points in your paragraph 7. We are concerned only to choose our moment well. The need to head the Chinese off a collision course over prisoners, and the desirability of influencing any broad decisions by the Chinese on relations after Grey's release argue in favour of our taking an early opportunity to speak as you suggest. But the disadvantages could be considerable: the stated basis for the release of Grey (which at present has a look of stability) might well be called in question by a message which the Chinese might choose to believe heralded a change of line on our side; also the chances (slim though they are) of any spontaneous release of other British subjects after the release of Grey would almost certainly be destroyed. On balance therefore we favour silence for the time being.

7. Meanwhile it goes without saying that we must continue to avoid anything which could give substance to the idea that there are differences of view on 'concessions' between the Government of Hong Kong and Her Majesty's Government. To make a statement to the Chinese, whether formal or informal, to the effect that no such differences exist could, we believe, only confirm them in the suspicion. Short of this however we shall redouble our efforts to counter any differences whatsoever between us over the handling of the Grey case or other aspects of relations with the Chinese Government.

No. 174

Mr Denson (Peking) to Mr Stewart, 3 October 1969[1]
Tel. No. 575 Priority Confidential (FCO 21/449, FEC 1/28)

My telegram No. 570:[2] 20th Anniversary Celebrations.

The celebrations were undistinguished, thus confirming our impression that the occasion would be treated in a low key. The parade included slightly increased military contingent. There were no weapons on show except rifles carried by the infantry. The themes of the parade were predominantly civilian.

2. As already reported, Mao appeared fit though some television observers say he looked very stiff and immobile. At the end of the parade he did however walk to both ends of the rostrum and showed himself to the crowds in the stands, including diplomats. Lin Piao seemed paler than ever and his speech, with its somewhat distorted delivery, did not draw a great response from the crowd. Other senior leaders appeared at the parade and on other occasions.

In the normal order though Chiang Ch'ing was absent from the state banquet on 30 September. Senior representatives from the provinces in the politburo were absent, but there were no other senior absentees of consequence.

3. The most interesting feature of the foreign representation was the presence of the president of North Korea who arrived late on 30 September. We had been assured up to the last minute by the Eastern Europeans that there would be no Korean special representative. His presence is variously interpreted as the vicarious Soviet gesture of conciliation and a move of Pyongyang in defiance of Moscow. We favour the first view. The only other visitor of special note was Pham van Dong[3] who has had talks with Chou En-Lai. We attach no particular significance to the presence of a Cambodian and Congo (Brazzaville) Prime Ministers. Albanian and Pakistani representation was at relatively low level.

4. A striking feature of the celebrations and accompanying official statement was the abrupt and steep reduction in Chinese attacks on the Soviet Union. The Joint *Peoples Daily/Red Flag/Liberation Army Daily* editorial of 30 September affirmed Chinese wish to settle border conflicts (in the past Chinese have always referred to border questions) between countries through negotiation. The speeches of Lin Piao and Chou En-Lai strongly emphasised Chinese intention not to attack first and to abide by the five principles of peaceful coexistence. There were at the same time repeated references to nuclear blackmail and the need to oppose a war of aggression especially one in which atom bombs are used as weapons. This and the continuing prominence of the campaign for stepping up war preparations and for vigilance against surprise attacks suggest that the Chinese are still as apprehensive about Soviet intentions. The Anniversary editorial also referred to attempts to organize rebellion in border areas which may well be a reference to Soviet activities in Sinkiang.

1 Repeated for information to Hong Kong, Moscow, Washington, POLAD Singapore, Vientiane, Bangkok, Saigon and saving to Hanoi.
2 Not printed.
3 Prime Minister of North Vietnam, 1955-1976.

5. There have so far been no repeat no references to the Chinese nuclear explosions reported to have taken place in Sinkiang. But the passage in Chou en-Lai's speech on Chinese development of nuclear weapons which reiterates the standard line on Chinese peaceful intentions echoes statements issued after previous nuclear tests.

6. In the familiar references to revolutionary movements, prominence has been given to the Laotians struggle against the US Imperialists and reactionaries of Thailand. In Lin and Chou's speeches, Laos displaced Palestine in third place after Albania and Vietnam, though it was not mentioned in the pre-anniversary slogans. This might reflect Chinese recognition of the brittle situation there and a desire to see it exploited.

7. The Anniversary editorial was un-illuminating on internal developments. There was little emphasis on the urgency of continuing 'great revolutionary criticism'. The familiar themes of increased Mao study and strengthening of the dictatorship of the proletariat were emphasised. There were no indications of further radical reforms in town or country.

8. Statements about the economy were comparatively modest and low key. Bothou's speech and the joint editorial said that China had attained 'initial prosperity'. The pre-anniversary press roundup concentrated on industries where genuine progress has apparently been made e.g. oil. Several passages placed industry ahead of agriculture in the order of priorities with national defence construction third. This together with increased emphasis on science and technology may be in part retrospective as it goes back to the priorities of the 1949 common programme when industrialisation was the main objective. It could however presage some greater emphasis on industry in the fairly near future.

No. 175

Mr Denson (Peking) to London, 4 October 1969[1]
Tel. No. 586 Immediate, Confidential (FCO 21/458, FEC 13C/1E)

My Tel. No. 583.[2]

Grey seemed to be in a very balanced frame of mind though not surprisingly rather keyed up and nervous. The account he has given us of his detention indicates that the Chinese were even more petty and vindictive than we had thought. He is clearly reluctant to deal more than necessary with Chinese officialdom now that he is free and we shall try to shield him as far as possible. It was for this reason that he did not wish to go to the Public Security Bureau this evening about his exit visa. We hope that the Chinese will be willing to arrange the necessary formalities on Monday.

2. Grey was fully alive to the political dangers of passing through Hong Kong and readily assented that he should leave by another route. He has enquired about

---

1 Repeated to Hong Kong.
2 Not printed. The telegram confirmed that Mr Grey was now at the British mission. Earlier that afternoon Mr Denson had been informed that he would be released at 3 p.m. He was met by Mr Garside.

whether the British press have been critical of HMG's handling of his case but has himself so far expressed no view. I have spoken about the cases of other British subjects detained but I have not thought it necessary to draw on the arguments in your Telno 344. I will, however, do so if necessary later. At present Grey's main resentment is directed towards the Chinese.

3. In answer to press enquiries here we have merely confirmed that Grey's freedom of movement has been restored and that he is with us. We are declining to grant interviews to correspondents.

No. 176

Letter from Mr Denson (Peking) to Mr Murray, 7 October 1969
Secret (FCO 21/466, FEC 3/548/1B)

Dear James,

Thank you for your telegram No. 348 of 3 October[1] which I found reassuring.

2. As you probably know, the Governor intends to make proposals for stronger measures against the local communists now that Grey has been released. He wishes in particular:

(*a*) to pursue the cases of the 37 persons for whom warrants are still outstanding since the disturbances of 1967;

(*b*) to arrest further Trade Union leaders who are illegally holding office;

(*c*) to take action against the headmaster of the former Chung Hua Middle School who has been visiting the premises of the Yu Hwa Middle School more than he is technically permitted to do by the Director of Education.

I understand that papers have been prepared in Hong Kong which will form the basis for discussions in London.

3. If these proposals are carried out, they will amount to a very distinct hardening of policy against the Hong Kong communists just at the time when the release of Grey has removed a major obstacle to an improvement in relations with the Chinese. The treatment of the Mission at the National Day celebrations when all the diplomatic staff were invited to the parade in the morning and the fireworks in the evening as against limited invitations to the staffs of the Soviet and Eastern European Embassies is a small indication that we are in greater favour than before. If there is a hardening of policy in Hong Kong it could well effect the treatment of the Mission, not only in things like invitations (which are not of great intrinsic importance) but travel, commercial contacts, co-operation over the repair of the Chancery, and so on. In a word the effectiveness of the Mission, quite apart from the question of a tolerable life for its members. More important than this, it could affect the release of the remaining British subjects detained, remission for George Watt, and the granting of exit visas to British subjects in Shanghai. Sino/British trade has had a very good year so far. But if the all-round trend towards improvement in relations is halted or reversed, this could rebound on trade and make it more difficult to maintain present levels.

1 Not printed.

4. As I have indicated before, I am in no sense a supporter of a weak and indecisive policy in Hong Kong in the interests of, what must remain for a considerable time, a limited improvement in Sino/British relations in general. I entirely approve of the action taken against Chinese nationals from the mainland who try to abduct Hong Kong residents, against unruly minibus operators and the like. I also recognize that once the present series of remissions of prison sentences have taken effect and we are down to the hard core it may be difficult to do anything further without appearing to undermine the judicial process (though I hope the possibility of an amnesty has not been entirely lost sight of). I must however emphasize strongly that I consider the present proposals ill-conceived.

5. I have already written at length about the headmaster of the Yu Hwa Middle School in my letter of 6 May to John Moreton.[2] I understand he is a well known trouble-maker and probably not popular with either the local communist hierarchy or the Central Government here. On the other hand, if the case is pursued and he is eventually brought to court it seems to me almost certain that he will go to prison, in which case he will achieve the status of a martyr and the Chinese might be obliged to take up the cudgels on his behalf. This case and those of the illegal Trade Union officials are to my mind trivial. I can scarcely believe that if they are not pursued, it will make much difference to public confidence in the authority of the Hong Kong Government.

6. Conversely, were they the only cases to be considered, the consequences for our relations of agreeing with the Governor's proposals would be limited. But the Chinese are likely to take a far more serious view of the pursuance of the cases of the 37 for whom warrants are still outstanding. The Director of Special Branch has indicated that about half of those concerned could be arrested if a vigorous enough search were made. At the moment, they are apparently lying low and doing no harm. I can see that if they resume any illegal activities or came fortuitously in the way of the police, it would be difficult not to arrest them. But provided they do neither, surely it is in our wider interest if they should be left alone.

7. In the course of conversations with the Governor, it became clear that apart from his temperamental dislike of 'letting go' and, in his view, allowing the communists to flout his authority, he was being encouraged by reports from secret sources indicating that a policy of toughness paid off. In particular, he was struck by a directive from Peking to local Trade Unions saying that they should not elect as officials persons legally disqualified. It may be true in this case that the policy is correct. But if it is applied across the board, it might well strengthen the hand of the militants in Hong Kong. Though this is strictly speaking outside my province, I derived the impression from the Governor and others of a certain complacency about the dangers of a revival of militancy which might result from cracking down too hard. The assumption seemed to be that, if it revived at all, it would be the result of allowing local communists too much rope. As seen from Peking, this assumption is mistaken. So long as the situation remains quiet and local sympathizers have few serious grievances to exploit, they are likely to receive no encouragement to make trouble, quite the reverse. But if there is a very perceptible hardening of policy, it will enable them

---

2 Not printed.

to enlist the support of any element in the leadership here who are opposed to the present policy of maintaining the status quo. In the long run, pressure could build up for them to be given their head and allow them to act in a way which would oblige the Hong Kong Government to take very strong measures, and thus risk an escalating situation. Unfortunately the advice which we can offer from here about Chinese policy on Hong Kong cannot be based on any precise knowledge. But in so far as a judgement can be made, I think that the Chinese do wish to remove the debris of 1967 both here and in Hong Kong and will control the local militants to achieve this, and that we should as far as possible help them to do so. I hope therefore that you are able to ride the Governor off these proposals.

Yours ever,
JOHN

No. 177

Mr Denson (Peking) to Mr Stewart, 14 November 1969
Confidential (FCO 21/458, FEC 2/6)

Sir,

Chinese Foreign Policy

Lin Piao's Political Report to the Ninth National Congress of the Chinese Communist Party in April this year, on the internal political aspects of which I reported in my despatch of 21st of May,[1] laid down guidelines for Chinese relations with the outside world. Since then there has been some regularisation in the conduct of these relations, but nothing like coherent policy is yet evident. This is partly the result of the slow and painful emergence of China from the Cultural Revolution, and the lasting effects of the campaign, and partly of Chinese preoccupation with the risk of an armed collision with the Soviet Union which has increased since the border clashes in March. In this despatch I offer some general reflections on the likely course of Chinese foreign policy in the light of these considerations.

State of Chinese foreign relations at the time of the Ninth Party Congress

2. If the Chinese took stock of the country's foreign relations at the time of the Ninth Congress, following the hiatus of the three preceding years, they can scarcely have found the picture encouraging. The alienation of Burma in 1967 tightened the ring of States around China which the Chinese choose to regard as implacably hostile. The increasingly noisy condemnation of Soviet/United States 'collusion' has done nothing to diminish the realities of power politics, or to arrest the trend towards East/West *détente*. In Viet-Nam, where Mao's philosophy of People's War is being tested on China's doorstep, the Chinese have been forced into the position of bystanders while Hanoi, stubbornly resisting China's advice, is pursuing its own tactics of fighting and negotiating. (With the death of Ho Chi Minh relations may be in a state of flux and until the new Viet-Namese leadership emerges it will not be

---

1 Not printed.

possible to estimate how China's position has fared.) With the exception of Albania and Rumania, Chinese relations with both the East European and the Asian ruling Communist Parties (apart from North Viet-Nam) have further deteriorated. China's final estrangement from the international Communist movement was symbolised by its absence from the Moscow conference in June at which the Russians, while not securing any formal condemnation of China, were able to ventilate fierce criticism without upsetting the potentially precarious applecart. China's failure to produce even a prompt and authoritative condemnation of the Moscow meeting suggests that the Chinese have opted out of the competition for influence in the Communist movement according to the normal ground rules, though a response is being made piecemeal in a form which may appeal to some Asian nationalists. Lin Piao made it clear, however, in his report that China remains in the movement with the clear implication that China's role is to reform and lead it. This in itself contains the seeds of future difficulty as China's existing appeal, such as it is—to the Rumanians and others—derives from the championing of the complete autonomy of States and Parties. Few would wish to exchange precarious co-existence with Moscow for domination of Peking.

3. In Africa, with a few exceptions, notably Tanzania and Zambia, and amongst most developing countries, China has lost ground since the heyday of 1964-65. China's short-lived expressions of support for Biafra were ill-conceived. They seem to have been largely the result of a desire to take the opposite side from the Soviet Union. They were generally unwelcome to the Organisation of African Unity and the Chinese soon retreated in silence. In South Asia, China has fared somewhat better, maintaining good relations with Pakistan after the change of Government, and receiving a windfall in Nepal as the result of worsening relations between that country and India. But in neither case has the Soviet Union suffered correspondingly. While in the Middle East the inexorable progress of events proceeds largely without reference to the wishes of the Chinese, whose ability to influence the Governments of the area is limited by the quarrel with the Soviet Union and by all-out support given, for ideological reasons, to the Palestine guerrilla organisations. Furthermore China's image as a potentially responsible Great Power has been sullied by the Cultural Revolution, its attraction as the model for developing countries must have declined and the economic disruption of the last few years has further reduced the resources at China's disposal for aid giving, though selective assistance will always remain possible.

Lin Piao on foreign policy

4. Other major impediments to China's re-emergence on the international scene are the domestic preoccupation with finding the elusive balance between permanent revolution and 'normalisation', which is likely to absorb much of the energies of the leadership in the immediate future; and the dogmatic, inflexible and 'revolutionary' nature of Mao's policies which have again come to the fore as the result of the Cultural Revolution. In the external field, this means support for the doctrine of armed struggle as the only valid means of political change; in practice the encouragement of revolutionary movements, particularly in Asia. This doctrine took pride of place in the international section of Lin Piao's report, which also noted with satisfaction the efficient working of the various contradictions in relations between and within the 'imperialist' and 'revisionist' worlds destined to hasten the doom of

China's enemies. Viewed from Peking through the reporting of the New China News Agency and Chinese diplomatic Missions, the seemingly unbroken picture of industrial unrest, financial instability, student and racial discontent, the origins of which are all conveniently over simplified, may well cause some sections of the leadership to take a mistakenly optimistic view of the imminence of, at any rate, Western collapse in the same way as some Western observers predicted the break-up of China in 1967. On the more pragmatic side, the report also contains qualified references to China's 'consistent' policy of developing friendly relations with 'Socialist' countries and to the application of the 'five principles of peaceful co-existence' to relations with countries of different social systems. These scarcely counterbalance the general prognostication of war, revolution and struggle, but they are important, as they serve as the theoretical foundation for an opportunistic diplomacy. Their application can accommodate cordial relations with the Kingdom of Cambodia, as well as the current truce in the propaganda war between Peking and Belgrade. The Chinese have themselves publicly reiterated their readiness (in November 1968) to conduct relations with the United States on the basis of these same five principles. The remainder of this despatch with examine how far the Chinese will in fact seek to enter the lists of diplomacy, and how far they will be content to 'sit on the mountain and watch the tigers fighting', while Mao's inexorable laws of history work themselves out.

Developments since the Ninth Congress

5. During the months since the Ninth Congress a somewhat more flexible and pragmatic approach to foreign affairs and a greater sense of professional direction have become apparent in Chinese policies. This has been accompanied by a welcome return to more normal standards in the treatment of foreign diplomatic Missions in Peking, though, as before, some are more equal than others. To date, 17 Chinese Ambassadors have been appointed to the broadly predictable posts in Asia and Africa (Paris and Stockholm are presumably included because of the Viet-Nam peace talks and the Canadian negotiations with the Chinese on recognition). It is thus true to say that the Chinese are in the process of repairing and lubricating their conventional mechanisms, but this does not, in my view, mean that the clock is merely being put back to 1965. Since the incidents on the Ussuri in March[2] it has become clear that in the estimation of the Chinese leaders the threat from the Soviet Union has become more real and more urgent than from the other principal enemy, the United States. Much of the new diplomatic drive may therefore be dissipated in the obsessive conflict with the Russians, for example in attempts to counter the spread of Soviet influence in areas which have not always been of traditional interest. Paradoxically it is just in these areas, e.g., the Middle East and South-East Asia, that for other reasons China is not well placed to deploy diplomatic strength. Hence no Ambassadors have returned there (except to Syria, Cambodia, Afghanistan, North Viet-Nam and Yemen). With other countries there are no diplomatic relations, or the Chinese Missions are working at a reduced level. These are the targets of 'popular' diplomacy and propaganda assault which in the past have in many cases been regarded as of more importance by the Chinese than diplomatic relations as such.

---

2 The Sino-Soviet border dispute was a seven month undeclared military conflict between China and the Soviet Union. The most serious border clash occurred on the Ussuri River in March 1969.

Eastern Europe

6. The policy, faintly discernible is differentiated treatment of Eastern European countries, the object of which would be to encourage nationalism in order gradually to loosen ties with the Soviet Union, has become entangled in a web of contradictions, and is likely to prove ineffective, at least in the short term. Chinese treatment of the invasion of Czechoslovakia, when they meted out condemnation to all sides—calling Mr Dubcek a 'capitulationist'—demonstrates how they are the victims of their own extremism. As a result they were unable to make any impact on the Czech Government or people, or to exploit the situation in such a way as to slow down the reconciliation between the United States and the Soviet Union. This is very different from 1956, when the Chinese played a role of some significance in the aftermath of the Hungarian and Polish uprisings. Nor will their new-found reluctance to attack the leaders of such countries as Hungary and Poland and their apparent willingness to normalise some aspects of State relations (*e.g* trade) compensate for the affront of fathering rival Polish and Hungarian Communist Parties dedicated to the removal of these same leaders. Given these factors and the tightening grip of the Soviet Union on Eastern Europe, there seems little hope of the Chinese making any inroads on the hardcore members of the Warsaw Pact. They will continue to give all-out support to Albania, to cultivate the special relationship with Rumania and possibly make limited overtures to Yugoslavia.

Western Europe

7. Sir Duncan Wilson in a recent despatch defined one of the Soviet Union's aims in Western Europe as the defusing of political relations so as to avoid involving the Soviet Union in crisis on two fronts. The Chinese conversely have an interest in maintaining tension between NATO and the Warsaw Pact. Some remarks made by a Foreign Ministry official to my Norwegian colleague suggested that the Chinese were content to see NATO continue as a counter-Soviet influence in Europe and as a means of holding down Soviet troops. This may be partly true and partly a rationalisation of China's inability to bring any influence to bear in Europe. A strong NATO would in fact militate against another Chinese aim: to increase friction between the United States and Western Europe and to loosen the cohesiveness of Western Europe itself. In this latter connection it is noteworthy that even when General de Gaulle was in power and there was a definite coincidence of Sino/French interest *vis-à-vis* the two super Powers, the Chinese apparently did little to exploit the situation. They may be now even less sure of the General's successor. Certainly the reception of the new French Ambassador in Peking has not been so cordial as might have been expected. Privately the French are expressing disappointment that relations, particularly in the cultural field, have not developed more quickly and seem genuinely pained that Chinese propaganda should be directed against France's economic and financial difficulties. This is probably a legacy from General de Gaulle's over-estimate of France's world position and also the result of a failure to take adequately into account the fundamental Chinese suspicion and dislike of all 'capitalist and bourgeois' societies.

8. The Chinese also seem uninterested in developing relations with West Germany (which at one time seemed possible) and might have given the opportunity for fishing in troubled waters to the discomfort of the Russians and the Americans. At the moment

West Germany is under heavy attack because of closening contacts with the Soviet Union, even while the latter is still, with apparent seriousness, raising the spectre of Bonn/Peking *entente*. There is no sign that initiatives are likely elsewhere in Europe apart perhaps from some encouragement of anti-American feelings in Scandinavian countries, particularly Sweden, mainly in the context of Viet-Nam. Relations with the United Kingdom probably do not loom large in Chinese calculations, though even limited improvement will be difficult until the Chinese imprisoned in Hong Kong following the disturbances in 1967 are released. China's main interest in Europe will, as before, remain commercial. Here the Chinese, despite protestations to the contrary, are adept at separating politics and economics when they so choose.

United States/Chinese relations

9. An area in which the Chinese might be able to cause difficulty for the Russians is in their relations with the United States. The increased Soviet threat has probably coincided with a realistic Chinese estimate of a reduction of the chances of conflict with the United States, particularly since the cessation of the bombing of North Viet-Nam and the announcement of troop withdrawals—though this in no way affects the reality of power, America's nuclear superiority. Peking is undoubtedly aware of Moscow's sensitivity towards any sign of a Sino/American rapprochement. The Chinese may have been playing on these fears when they offered to resume the Warsaw Talks[3] last November. They could do so again, but this would require some gestures towards the Americans which seem very unlikely in present circumstances. I do not, however, rule out a resumption of the Warsaw Talks, though I see no prospect of any real shift in China's attitude towards the United States within the next few years unless there is a radical American swing away from support for Taiwan. Anti-Americanism is in any case now so inbuilt as to have become something of a necessity for the Chinese. If there were no American military presence in Asia, it might have to be invented.

Sino/Soviet relations

10. There does not therefore seem to be any prospect within the next few years of a Chinese accommodation with either the United States or the Soviet Union. The Chinese will have to continue to stand alone against the infinitely more powerful northern neighbour whose position they are ill-placed to undermine diplomatically in the areas which matter most. Western Europe and the United States. The present Chinese leadership will undoubtedly stand firm but will probably avoid provocative action as they did earlier when there was a risk of collision with the Americans. The Chinese must rate seriously the possibility of a punitive strike. The Russians have recently been brandishing their superior military strength with the intention of unsettling the Chinese and in the hope of heightening any differences which may have grown up in the Chinese leadership about the priority which should be given to improving the defence industries at the expense of other objectives. The risk of Soviet military action is now probably running at an unacceptably high level from the Chinese point of view. It is therefore possible that they may respond to the Soviet offer of negotiations (the conclusion of the agreement at Khabarovsk on river

---

3 On 1 August 1955, China and the USA opened a series of ambassadorial level talks in Geneva to discuss mutual issues of concern, as the two countries did not have formal diplomatic relations. From 1958 the meetings were held in Warsaw, continuing until 1970.

navigation when Sino/Soviet polemics about the border were at their height may be a significant pointer). As this despatch goes to Press, it has been reported that Kosygin has seen Chou En-lai in Peking, which is further evidence of the Chinese (and Russian) desire to lower the temperature. Kept within bounds, however, the dispute, even more than the opposition to the United States, has become almost indispensable to Mao as an internal unifying factor and an ideological bogey. He is therefore likely to continue it in the foreseeable future.

Asia

11. The area where the Chinese might be expected to take the initiative is in Asia, where traditionally they have dominated and where the United States and more recently the Soviet Union have encroached. Slowness and inflexibility characterised China's policy during the period of the Cultural Revolution. While President Nixon, Mr Kosygin and Mrs Gandhi were moving among their friends and associates, the Chinese remained inactive. (Chou En-lai's brief trip to Hanoi after the death of Ho Chi Minh was the first time he had left the country for three years.) During this time significant developments had taken place. Japanese economic power had grown to the point where Japan is virtually the third industrial nation in the world. Despite this the Chinese have pursued an unenlightened policy by subjecting the Japanese Government to an unbroken stream of hostility and abuse, thus playing into the hands of Mr Sato and probably making the renewal of the United States/Japanese security treaty easier rather than harder for him. Had the Chinese pursued a quieter and more subtle policy they might have influenced a great proportion of the Japanese people. They could do so in the future if their policy changed.

12. The inroads made by the Soviet Union in the area include the supply of arms to Pakistan, the establishment of diplomatic relations with Malaysia and Singapore, increased economic co-operation with Japan, a mild flirtation with Taiwan and most recently proposals for an expanded transit trade and for collective security in Asia. To this China has responded like a raucous paper tiger and remained passive apart from servicing existing friendships with Cambodia, Pakistan, Nepal and to some extent Ceylon. There is no sign of any change in this policy.

13. China's room for manoeuvre in Asia is restricted mainly because of the support given to revolutionary movements in Laos, Thailand, Malaysia and Burma and the consequent impossibility of developing useful intergovernmental relations. The same is true with some other Governments which have been written off as reactionary, notably India, Singapore and Indonesia. Though the emergence of the Soviet Union as a *status quo* Power should enhance China's appeal as the revolutionary focus in Asia, in the shorter term at any rate, this is not of benefit. Furthermore, the example of Viet-Nam has not been entirely encouraging. Any form of settlement on honourable terms would in fact be a defeat for the Chinese theory of protracted war however it were presented.

Advantages of a Chinese policy of inactivity

14. The foregoing all suggests that in Asia as elsewhere there will be little change in China's policies in the near future. There may however be more positive motives leading the Chinese to a policy of patience and passivity in Asia. The projected withdrawal of some American military forces from the area and to a lesser extent our own East of Suez policy have been made possible precisely because of China's relative

weakness and inactivity. American intentions, as recently proclaimed by President Nixon, have been denounced as a 'fraud' in Peking but the Chinese must feel some satisfaction at this turn of events. Moreover, they may calculate that a restrained posture in the immediate future will serve their long-term interests more surely. If they were now to adopt a more active policy, by military threats, all-out support of guerrilla movements and a generally more vigorous diplomacy, they might make it more difficult for the Americans to leave. China's private reaction to the Russian proposal for Asian collective security, which has been so loudly condemned as a further move towards the encirclement of China, may be less alarmist than propaganda implies. Like some Western observers, the Chinese may suspect that the Soviet proposals will fall on stony ground and are content to let them die for lack of encouragement. If they showed any signs of getting off the ground, the Chinese would no doubt be able to exploit Asian nationalism to discredit the new 'imperialism', especially if they themselves were adopting a low posture.

Conclusion

15. My conclusion therefore is that in the short term, certainly at least until a much greater degree of political stability has been achieved, the Chinese will be content to 'sit on the mountain'. China is better fitted than most countries to flourish in isolation. Lin Piao's statement that it is 'China's honour' to do so is more than a cry of defiance; it reflects China's fundamental *Weltanschauung*[4]. The Chinese may reckon that without taking initiatives the sheer size of the country, the forces of the national character as well as the growing nuclear capability will exercise a steady pull of attraction. This has already been borne out by the decision in principle of the Canadian and Italian Governments to recognise China (though they were also partly motivated by domestic circumstances), and by the feelers put out by the Indonesians. In the same way the Chinese will make no concessions to gain entry into the United Nations, but wait until the seat which they consider rightfully theirs is handed to them. In the longer term there loom the imponderables of the Viet-Nam settlement and the American posture in Asia afterwards, and the emergence of Japan as a major political (and possibly military) power in the world. It is impossible to predict what accommodations the countries of Asia may make in response or how China will react. In the meantime we can probably look forward to a breathing space when China will not wish or be able to cause serious trouble and the work of building up the political and economic strength of non-Communist countries of Asia and of encouraging co-operation between them can continue.

16. I am sending copies of this despatch to Her Majesty's Representatives in Tokyo, Bangkok, Vientiane, Phnom Penh, Saigon, Hanoi, Manila, Djakarta, Kuala Lumpur, Singapore, Colombo, Ulan Bator, Moscow, Prague, Bucharest, Belgrade, Washington, Ottawa, Paris, Stockholm, Cairo, Lusaka, Dar-es-Salaam, to the Political Adviser to the Commander-in-Chief Far East at Singapore and to the Governor, Hong Kong.

I have, etc.
JOHN DENSON

---

4 German word meaning 'world view'.

No. 178

Note by the Ministry of Technology to the Official Committee on Strategic Exports, 17 November 1969
ESC(O)(69)18 Secret (CAB 134/2801)

Export of Civil Aircraft to China

Introduction

1. It is necessary to give guidance to the British aircraft industry on how to treat the Chinese market. The Chinese Government is believed to wish to modernise and increase its civil aircraft fleet and to allocate funds for this purpose within the next 2 years. Its domestic network of about 30,000 miles serves some 70 cities. Scheduled international services are operated to Rangoon, Pyongyang, Hanoi and Irkutsk. The fleet is believed to be made up of 6 Viscounts bought from BAC in 1961 and obsolescent Russian types, the last purchase of which was made in 1966.

Chinese Feelers

2. Enquiries have been made by the Chinese among British, European and Japanese manufacturers, whose aircraft are almost exclusively powered by Rolls Royce engines. British manufacturers who are in contact with the Chinese have been advised not to enter into negotiations on possible sale of any aircraft or engine before HMG has fully considered the implications. The Chinese, for their part, have indicated that they are not prepared to negotiate purchases without a prior assurance that if the negotiations were successful an export license would be granted.

3. It may be assumed that similar feelers have been or will be put out in other countries. An increasing number of secondhand aircraft—Viscounts, Comets, Britannias, Vanguards, but also in small numbers VC10s, Tridents and BAC1-11s are coming onto the world market and it might be difficult to prevent other countries from exporting them to China.

4. For the more advanced types of aircraft, USA, France and the United Kingdom are the only possible sources, at any rate until Chinese trade with the Soviet Union is resumed. It is considered that the American Government will not permit the sale of American aircraft of any type. The French attitude is likely to be dictated by a similar balance of military and commercial considerations to our own.

Military Implications of Civil Aircraft Sales to China

5. The Joint Intelligence Committee has recently assessed the military implications of re-equipment of the Chinese civil aircraft fleet with certain European and Japanese aircraft powered by Rolls Royce engines. Their conclusions, which are set out in full in the annex[1] to this paper, may be summarised as follows:

(*a*) China's military lift capacity is low and a purchase of large western aircraft would considerably augment it;

(*b*) Suitably converted, any of the large aircraft would considerably increase the range and load capacity of China's nuclear and conventional bombing capability. It seems unlikely, however, that the Chinese are seriously interested in converting civil

---

1 Not printed.

aircraft into nuclear bombers, unless the credibility of their missile nuclear deterrent becomes open to question;

(c) Modern western jet aircraft and engines would give China equipment and knowledge more advanced that she at present possesses. Such engines as the Conway, Spey, RB162 and Tyne would greatly increase China's knowledge of advanced jet engine technology; and China is known to have sought to obtain, by covert means, both civil and military Speys. It would however, take the Chinese 10-15 years to copy the larger aircraft and 5-10 years the smaller.

Reaction of Other Governments

6. Apart from the UK's view of the security implications of exporting certain types of civil aircraft to China, account must also be taken of the likely reactions of other Governments whose security would thereby be more directly threatened and whose views might differ from our own. Any sale which could be considered to improve Chinese military potential would provoke opposition to greater or less extent from USA, Japan, India, Australia, New Zealand and the non-communist countries of south-east Asia. For the time being the USA can be expected to oppose any sale with every means at its disposal, including even interference with exports of British aircraft equipment to the USA.

Strategic Embargo

7. The British aircraft listed in the Annex would be exempt from strategic embargo under COCOM rules provided they were not fitted with certain types of engines or items of equipment. Most of their electronic equipment is, however, embargoed and while we have discretion in most cases to approve exports of such installations in civil aircraft, the approval of COCOM would be necessary for certain items. Until current US attitudes change such approval is unlikely to be granted. Export in 1961 of the electronics in the Viscounts was authorised by HMG in spite of COCOM objections. Similar defiance of COCOM would probably again be needed if sales of these aircraft were to be authorised.

8. Most of the aircraft listed contain American equipment, and under existing US legislation there would be no possibility of obtaining from the US authorities the necessary permissions to re-export. All parts of American origin would therefore have to be replaced with British or other non-American equipment. This effectively rules out the Skyvan, Beagle 206 and Islander, all of which have US engines with no suitable British or European counterpart. For the others the substitution required might significantly increase the cost.

9. There are signs that the US Administration may be easing its attitude towards China and considering whether to trade. A progressive relaxation could reduce objection to sales to China of British components, aircraft with US engines and other equipment. The UK would have ample warning of a policy change of this kind.

Future Prospects

10. Although in the long run, China should be a large potential for aircraft, it is unlikely for the foreseeable future that the Chinese will wish to devote more than a fairly small percentage of their currency earnings to the purchase of aircraft. Many military and industrial projects command high priority. While an early toe-hold for British aircraft in this market might have some value the prospects for substantial sales in the next few years are likely to be limited.

Conclusions

11. In the light of the above considerations, it is concluded that sales of British civil aircraft to China must continue to be restricted. It is recommended that, as far as China is concerned, British civil aircraft should be categorised as follows:

(*a*) those for which export licences will *not* be granted in present circumstances: Super VC10, VC10, Comet, BAC1-11 and Trident;

(*b*) those for which export licenses will be considered on their merits, subject to COCOM and USA approval where necessary: Britannia, Vanguard, Viscount, Argosy, Herald, HS748, Jetstream, Islander, Skyvan, HS125, HS Dove and Beagle 206.

Recommendation

12. The Committee is invited to endorse the recommendation at paragraph 11 above and to agree that British aircraft and engine manufacturers should be advised accordingly. Since the attitude of other countries might change at short notice, this policy should be kept closely under review.[2]

---

[2] The Committee endorsed the general line in the paper and the division of aircraft into two categories but asked that the policy be kept under constant review. A change in China's capability or expertise, or in the attitude of any other potential suppliers of civil aircraft to China, should lead to a reconsideration of policy. Drafting changes were asked for: to avoid suggesting that a decision to supply any case in light of a COCOM objection amounted to defiance COCOM; that COCOM and US approval amounted to the same thing; and that a COCOM objection would not necessarily rule out the possibility, in certain circumstances, of an export licence being granted (CAB 134/2801/ESC(O)(69)5th meeting, 20 November 1969).

No. 179

Letter from Mr Walden (Peking) to Mr Appleyard, 22 November 1969
Confidential (FCO 21/454, FEC 2/1E)

China's attitude to the United Nations

The standard Chinese reflex reaction to this year's United Nations debate on the seating of Communist China has been fairly predictable. There has been some slight moderation of the tone of Peking's familiar denunciations, though it is too soon to conclude that this marks a more positive Chinese attitude to the organisation.

2. The first hint of a more subdued approach came when the Chinese press of 21 October published a summary of the Albanian delegate's speech to the General Assembly on China's representation. This was markedly less virulent than its 1968 equivalent. It emphasised China's adherence to the principles of peaceful coexistence, and in general, seemed more concerned to present China as a suitable candidate for membership. (Presumably the Chinese had some say in drafting the speech).

3. China's perennial riposte to the United Nations debate came this year in a *People's Daily* and NCNA article of 17 November. Although there is no evidence to suggest any fundamental shift in China's view of the organisation, a comparison with the *People's Daily* report of 22 November, 1968 reveals a calmer approach to the problem. The US is again sharply condemned, but there is more emphasis this year on the isolated position of the US *vis-à-vis* other members of the organisation. Though the *People's Daily* does not report the voting results, the Chinese are presumably gratified with the slightly more favourable outcome this year, and this may

account for the increased *schadenfreude* with which they belabour the US: 'It is not China but United States imperialism itself which is really isolated in the world.'

4. This year's article is also a little more restrained (by Chinese standards) in its criticism of the organisation as such. The concluding paragraph in the 1968 article said that US exploitation of its voting machine during the debate to exclude China had again exposed 'the political and moral bankruptcy of this so-called 'United Nations' organisation, and proves that the Chinese people's assessment of this so-called 'international organisation' is completely correct: 'it is merely a tool of American imperialist aggression'. This year, the United Nations is alleged to have been manipulated by the United States all along, and to have become a market place where the US and 'social imperialism' bargain over the redistribution of the world. It was also 'an instrument for these two to carry out power politics, aggression and intervention in other countries'.

5. Diplomatically, the Chinese are also showing a little more interest in the United Nations. The Rumanian Ambassador, who enjoys more frequent contact with the Chinese than most other missions recently assured John Denson that the Chinese had definitely not abandoned the United Nations as hopeless. Chou En-lai expressed his gratitude to the French ambassador for France's support of the Chinese position during his interview several weeks ago. As we have already reported, the Chinese now more frequently take this line in public e.g. at National Day receptions. A Rumanian contact of variable reliability has even told us that in discussion of this year's vote, the Chinese had contrasted the silence of the Russians with the statements of the French and British representatives who had 'sustained' China. We think this just possible, but unlikely.

6. Despite these indications, we doubt whether there has been any change in China's basic attitude. It seems more likely that the more moderate tone with which she states her case is simply a by-product of the incipient normalisation of her diplomatic behaviour. She is unlikely to take a more positive stand towards the organisation while there is still no early prospect of her being admitted. Her reservations about the functioning of the UN have not been entirely abandoned. We can hardly expect her to go much further than she does at present in showing enthusiasm for a club which she is not allowed to join, and whose leading members she execrates.

7. Copies of this letter to go to Miss Draycott in IRD, Brewer in RD, Weston in PUSD, Goss in DIS, Hibbert in Singapore, Boyd in Washington, Hewitt in Canberra, McLaren and Ashworth in Hong Kong, UKMIS in New York and Chancery at Tokyo.

Yours ever,
GEORGE

No. 180

Note of a meeting between Lord Shepherd and Mr Keswick, President of the Sino-British Trade Council, 10 December 1969, 11.30 a.m.
Confidential (FCO 21/475, FEC 6/548/1C)

Present:
Mr Keswick   Lord Shepherd

Mr Webb   Mr James Murray
                                                      Mr C. H. Godden

Mr Keswick opened by referring to the Memorandum on 'UK Commercial Policy for China' prepared by the Sino-British Trade Council [SBTC] in October. The memorandum, he said, anticipated the release of Anthony Grey and pointed to a need to review our trading position and relations with China. There were encouraging signs that the Chinese were adopting a more reasonable attitude towards British traders—though he accepted that there was another side to the coin in that some Britons were still under arrest in China and that insults to British nationals continued. The memorandum had contained nine suggestions designed to stimulate increased Sino-British trade. Of these, five were within the power of HMG to offer assistance. He hoped that such assistance would be forthcoming.

2. On Sino-British trade generally, *Mr Keswick* said that superficially it seemed that trade had been increasing. But this to some extent was attributable to a boost in the export of non-ferrous metals which would not necessarily continue. However, signs for the future were encouraging. The Chinese were sending a Trade Mission to this country shortly. Furthermore, the Chinese Commercial Counsellor in London would be visiting a group of Midland factories in the near future. All this could lead to increased trade.

3. *Mr Keswick* then referred to the first of the nine points in the SBTC Memorandum to which he had drawn attention: the need to improve relations between Hong Kong and Peking. He thought that a key factor here was the choice of Sir David Trench's successor as Governor. We had all good reason to be grateful to Sir David Trench for his firm handling of a difficult situation. But in Chinese eyes, he was associated with the 1967 troubles, and with a bad phase in relations between Hong Kong and China. It was, therefore, important that his successor should be someone known to the Chinese who could establish a personal rapport with Peking. Other than that, he did not see what HMG nor the Hong Kong Government could do in Hong Kong to help improve relations. Clearly, neither HMG nor the Hong Kong Government could, unless there was a general amnesty, release the 120 persons still detained in the Colony.

4. *Lord Shepherd* agreed that the scope for Britain to improve relations between Hong Kong and Peking was limited. We had done our best; but the Chinese had not responded in the same spirit. It was true that they had released Anthony Grey and a number of other Britons. They had, however, now inexplicably arrested another two elderly Britons, McBain and Mrs Martin. We would have to press very hard for their release. In Peking, Mr Denson had sought and was still seeking ways to improve relations but his efforts, too, had met with little response. Indeed, the treatment accorded to him the other day was not particularly encouraging. The Minister of State wondered, however, whether something might be done to improve relations when the Chinese Trade Mission came to this country.

5. At this point *Mr Murray* interjected to say that, on our side, treatment of the Chinese mission in London was back to the pre-1967 situation.

6. Replying to Lord Shepherd, *Mr Keswick* said that because of the Chinese interest in trade, they tended to treat commercial officers better than other diplomats.

Emphasis, therefore, ought to be on greater commercial representation in Peking. He also suggested that the Board of Trade should ask the Chinese for better facilities and treatment for British traders, making our approach at ministerial level to the Ministry of Foreign Trade in Peking through the Commercial Counsellor in London. Parallel action could be taken by the Foreign and Commonwealth Office. He also thought that when the Chinese Trade Mission came here, Lord Brown might invite their leader and possibly the Commercial Counsellor to lunch.

7. *Mr Murray* pointed out that HMG had not been idle in trying to improve Sino-British trade. Both Mr Laughton and Mr Denson, in Peking, had been trying very hard indeed. Yet, while we were anxious to improve relations with China, the recent treatment of McBain and Mrs Martin in particular had been monstrous; and he thought it might be misunderstood in this country if a British Minister were to be seen to entertain Chinese representatives while public indignation was being expressed in parliament and the press about the treatment of these two elderly Britons. Having said that, he was strongly in favour of the SBTC, themselves, establishing close contact with the Chinese Trade Mission when they came here.

8. *Mr Keswick* said that he did not entirely accept Mr Murray's argument. He thought, it would be perfectly reasonable, and not inconsistent, for a senior official or a Minister to invite the Chinese Commercial Counsellor to the Board of Trade—the FCO could at the same time call in the Chargé d'Affaires to deliver a protest about the treatment of British nationals.

9. *Mr Keswick* then touched upon two other points: quotas and the strategic embargo. The question of quotas he said he was taking up with the Board of Trade. (At this point *Mr Murray* intervened to say that he believed that Mr Keswick would get a measure of satisfaction over quotas.) On the other point, he said that he thought our policy over aircraft was much too cautious. In his view it was nonsense to say that the export of the BAC 111 aircraft was unacceptable and yet at the same time urge the sale of the Britannia, which had greater military potential.

10. *Mr Keswick* expressed the hope that Sino-British relations would increase greatly within the next five years or so. He thought that at present we were behind Japan and West Germany—but not too far behind. As Lord Shepherd would appreciate, it was his job to press for greater efforts. He thought that the time was now ripe for Mr Denson to ask the Chinese Foreign Ministry whether a SBTC mission to Peking would be acceptable.

11. *Mr Murray* said that this was something which he had recently discussed with the Board of Trade. Their combined view was that the SBTC could make such an approach direct, through their own contacts, whenever they thought the time was ripe. Timing and the extent of official sponsorship would obviously depend on Chinese attitudes and the progress made in improving Sino-British relations. *Mr Keswick* said that he took the point; but maintained that Mr Denson should nevertheless also put the request to the Chinese Ministry of Foreign Affairs, perhaps after the Chinese Trade Mission completed their visit here.

12. *Mr Keswick* then reverted to the question of the appointing of a Commercial Counsellor in Peking, arguing that we should match the Chinese, who had a similar request in London. Failing that, he suggested that Mr Denson might be designated 'Chargé d'Affaires and Head of the Commercial Section' or some similar title.

13. *Lord Shepherd* said that he would consider, in consultation with Mr Murray and his department, the points which Mr Keswick had raised.

No. 181

Letter from Mr Allan (Peking) to Mr Wilson, 30 December 1969
Confidential (FO 676/555)

[No salutation]

I apologise that we have never written a substantive letter about the problems of claims against China raised in your letter of 16 July[1] to John Denson. You will however have seen that John Denson said in his letter to James Murray of 12 August[2] (about the reconstruction of the old office) that the Chinese are most unlikely to be willing to embark on any negotiation for a final settlement of this matter.

2. The whole history of the communist take-over here and their action over the last twenty years suggests that there can be no hope of them entertaining claims for compensating individual British firms and citizens, many of whom, in their view, were exploiters or enemies of the Chinese people.

3. Ideally therefore we should perhaps be considering finally admitting in public that there is no chance of ever obtaining payment from the Chinese.

4. I appreciate that ministers, particularly in 1970, may feel unable to do this. The question thus arises, should we proceed with the making of an order under the Foreign Compensation Act 1969? I think that what you say on this in the latter part of para 3 of your letter is right.[3] Certainly the Chinese in present circumstances would probably make adverse play both with the timing of the making of the order and with the substance of the matter, and the raising of claimants' hopes would be dangerous for the reasons you give. Parenthetically one can note the dilemma we are always in: i.e. when relations with China are getting better one is reluctant to take action because this might set back Sino-British relations, and when relations are going badly one again is reluctant to take action for fear of this leading to even worse relations. At the moment our view is definitely against making an order.

5. On the question of reserving our rights to submit an omnibus claim (assuming ministers will not take the decision mentioned in para 3 above), this is particularly difficult time to put in a note. However it seems possible that the Chinese would accept it (as they do for example over our notes on British subjects) and would make no adverse comment. There might therefore be something to be said for taking two

---

1 Not printed.
2 Not printed.
3 The Government's public position regarding British claims for property lost in China since the establishment of the People's Republic was to negotiate a general settlement as soon as it became practicable to do so. The passage of the Foreign Compensation Act 1969 made it possible to make a China Registration Order-in-Council, leading over a period of two years to the compilation of a list of claims. However, in paragraph 3 Mr Denson pointed out that the Chinese might well interpret the making of an Order as a provocation at a time when the Government was struggling to improve bilateral relations. Also, as the Government could not back claims up with effective action claimants might be misled into thinking there was a real chance of making progress, and it would inevitably rekindle Parliamentary interest in the subject.

bites at the cherry; i.e. separating the questions of reserving our rights calling for registration. Accordingly we would be prepared to put in such a note, but the timing needs thinking about. There might be advantage in not submitting it until we have completed our discussion over the rebuilding of the chancery building (during which we would of course specifically make clear that this was without prejudice to any claim for compensation).

6. Incidentally, are you yet in a position to give us the total valuation of British Government property in China (see the Chargé d'Affaires letter of 12 August)?

7. Perhaps you could let me know the state of your thinking on this matter.

J. N. ALLAN

No. 182

Briefing note from Far Eastern Department, 19 January 1970
Confidential (FCO 21/654, FEC 2/2)

Chinese Foreign Policy

Present Trends

Though China's basic long-term strategy has not changed, there have been signs over the past year that Chinese leadership are adopting a more flexible approach to international affairs, in an attempt to repair some of the damage caused by the Cultural Revolution.

2. Since the Ninth Party Congress in April seventeen Chinese ambassadors to key posts in Asia and Africa have resumed their duties. Inside the Foreign Ministry itself, professional officials appear to be re-asserting their influence and the treatment of foreign Missions in Peking has returned to something approaching normality.

3. The Chinese have made some effort *to mend their fences with neighbouring Asian countries*. They were quick to restore friendlier relations with *Cambodia and Nepal* after the excesses of the Cultural Revolution and have now begun to work towards a gradual *rapprochement* with Ceylon. *Relations with North Vietnam and North Korea* have also now been improved. *Ambassadorial contacts with the United States* were resumed in Warsaw on 11 December after a break of nearly two years. Since then there has been a further procedural meeting on 8 January, and it is now known that substantive meetings will be resumed on 20 January. Negotiations with Canada and Italy with a view to mutual recognition have been under way for some months, though they seem to be making little headway. Finally, after a year of mounting tension between the two countries, China and the Soviet Union began border talks in Peking on 20 October.

Sino-Soviet Relations

4. The Chinese are still preoccupied to a large extent with their dispute with the Soviet Union. The series of border clashes during spring and summer 1969 brought relations to an unprecedented level of tension, reaching a peak in August. The Soviet leadership began to drop hints that if these clashes continued, the Soviet Union might undertake military action against China either in the form of a limited strike

or even a wider form of attack. The meeting in Peking between Kosygin and Chou En-lai evidently laid the basis for the opening of the border talks in Peking on 20 October. By then the Chinese at least were acutely concerned over the possibility of an uncontrollable conflagration.

5. So far the talks, which have been conducted at Deputy Foreign Minister level, seem to have made little or no progress. They were adjourned for three weeks from 15 December when the chief Soviet delegate, Kuznetsov, went back to Moscow for consultations. His return to Peking coincided with a fierce attack on Soviet policy in the *People's Daily* New Year's Day editorial. The editorial attacked Brezhnev by name and described the 'Brezhnev doctrine' as 'a variation of moribund neo-colonialism'. The Soviet Union was accused of pursuing 'fascist dictatorship at home and carrying out aggression and expansion abroad'. The editorial marked the toughest Chinese attack on the Soviet leadership since the talks began and was followed by an article in Hong Kong Communist newspaper, *Ta Kung Pao* on 8 January which sought to show that the lack of progress at the talks was not the fault of the Chinese. At the same time the Soviet press has been intensifying its own criticism of Chinese policy. The growing bitterness of the polemics between the two sides hardly augurs well for the future conduct of the talks (which have now resumed) and the Chinese clearly see little hope of rapid progress.

6. Even an agreement on border problems would not bring the Sino-Soviet dispute to an end or lead to a diminution in the competition between the two countries in the World Communist movement and the Third World. The ideological and national differences between the two sides run deep, and the Chinese have made it clear their determination to pursue their criticism of Soviet policy. Indeed as long as the present Chinese leaders remain at the helm an accommodation between the two countries does not seem possible.

Sino-American Relations

7. Over the past year the Americans have made a number of cautious overtures to China, mainly in the form of providing increased opportunities for cultural trade contacts. The Chinese response has been minimal so far, but they must have taken these moves into account in their decision to resume ambassadorial contacts. The Chinese have shown considerable interest in re-opening their dialogue with the United States, presumably first of all in order to keep their lines of communication open in case of a dangerous crisis and perhaps also to gain a direct insight into the latest American thinking on Asia in the light of President Nixon's speech at Guam in July last year. They may also aim to exert increased leverage over the Soviet Union in the Sino-Soviet border talks and over the whole range of Sino-Soviet relations, and at the same time to create difficulties for the Russians in SALT. The Russians are extremely suspicious of signs of Sino-American *rapprochement* and no doubt the Chinese will play upon their fears as much as possible.

8. As long as the US Government maintains its support for the Nationalists in Taiwan, any wide-reaching accommodation between United States and China is out of the question. In any case anti-Americanism is now firmly built in to the Maoist philosophy. But the Chinese have shown considerable caution hitherto in avoiding situations liable to lead to a major conflict with the United States, and we expect them to maintain this restraint.

Asia

9. In addition to making efforts to improve relations with North Korea, North Vietnam, Nepal and Cambodia, *the Chinese have also taken care to safeguard their friendship with Pakistan* despite their suspicions of Pakistani intentions towards the Soviet Union and the United States. By contrast, the Chinese have made no response to recent overtures from the Burmese and Indian Governments, whom they clearly regard as beyond the pale.

10. Meanwhile, the Chinese have maintained their efforts to expand *their influence in Asia through support for local insurgency movements in neighbouring* non-communist countries. The Chinese road-building programme in Laos is being extended; co-operation with the North Vietnamese over aid to the Pathet Laos appears to be running smoothly. Chinese assistance to dissident Meo and Thai communist groups in Thailand, the White Flag sect of the Burmese Communist Party in Burma and the Naga and Mizo insurgents in India continues undiminished. The Chinese seem particularly concerned about the growth of the Soviet interest in South-East Asia. So far, while the Chinese have concentrated mainly on supporting local insurgency groups, the Russians have devoted their attention to improving relations with the Governments of the countries concerned.

11. *Relations with Japan remain hostile and the recent electoral victory of Mr Sato's Liberal Democratic Party was a serious blow to China's influence in Japan.* The Chinese have shown no inclination to tap the deep reservoirs of pro-Chinese feeling in Japan; despite Japan's growing political and economic strength, the Chinese seem to have made little preparation to meet the challenge which Japan will inevitably pose to China's hopes for achieving dominant position in Asia.

12. *The Vietnam War is still the crucial factor in Chinese policy towards Asia.* A negotiation settlement on reasonable terms would be a major blow to the Maoist doctrine of protracted war. The Chinese are still urging the Vietnamese to fight on but it must be clear to them by now that the North Vietnamese are determined to conduct the war as they see fit. Much will depend on the evolution of future American policy towards Asia and the rate and scope of US withdrawal. One of China's chief concerns will be to ensure that any vacuum created by American withdrawal is not taken up by the Soviet Union. While a Vietnam settlement would undoubtedly reduce the risk of a head-on collision between China and the US, the focus of competition between the US, Soviet Union and China may simply move to Laos, Thailand and Burma.

Europe, Africa and the Middle East

13. The Chinese have not made any consistent effort to exploit differences between the Soviet Union and her East European allies following the invasion of Czechoslovakia. Albania remains China's lonely outpost in the area and we are inclined to doubt rumours that the Albanians are re-insuring to any significant degree with Yugoslavs. China's special relationship with Rumania has been preserved, but her relations with the other East European countries are bleak.

14. The Chinese have shown growing interest recently in Western Europe. The volume of trade with Western Europe is increasing and the Chinese have shown some concern both over the possible enlargement of the EEC and moves towards a Conference on European security. A powerful factor in Chinese calculations is

doubtless the desire to keep the Soviet Union occupied in European affairs so that the pressure on China is reduced. China's relations with France, which deteriorated sharply during the Cultural Revolution, are now on the mend but the French have still not succeeded in achieving a special position among European countries in Chinese eyes. Meanwhile the Chinese are still persevering in their plans to build up pro-Chinese splinter groups in the West to counteract the orthodox pro-Soviet Communist Parties, but so far these groups have gained little mass support.

15. China's main effort in Africa is directed towards Tanzania and Zambia, where the Chinese are still engaged in discussions about the construction of the costly Tanzam railway. At the same time, the Chinese have maintained their links with Guinea, Mauritania, Somalia and Mali. In the Middle East their propaganda and material support for the Palestine guerrillas has continued, despite the friction which this policy has caused with some Arab governments. However, China's ability to influence events in the Middle East is still only marginal.

Sino-Indian Relations

16. China's main preoccupation in South Asia is India, which she still sees as a dangerous rival for influence. The increasing reliance placed by the Indian Government on the Soviet Union has no doubt reinforced China's hostility towards India. For many years the Chinese effort in India has been concentrated on fostering subversion, especially among the Naga and Mizo peoples. The Chinese presence along the northern borders has also placed a heavy strain on India's national resources in view of the disproportionate share of India's defence effort which has been absorbed by the threat from China. The brief peasant disturbances in Naxalbari in 1967 seemed a golden opportunity for spreading the Maoist gospel, but since the collapse of the uprising the Chinese have had little success in stimulating further outbreaks. Tiny pro-Chinese splinter groups have been formed in India but their effectiveness seems to be severely limited. While the Chinese clearly intend to keep up their support for insurgent movements inside India, in view of the present level of tension on the Sino-Soviet border they could hardly afford to become involved in a major conflict with India. But a resumption of local border skirmishes cannot be ruled out.

No. 183

Letter from Mr Denson (Peking) to Mr Murray, 27 January 1970
Personal and Confidential (FCO 21/715, FEH 2/1)

Dear James,

You had earlier said that you would be letting me have your views on the state [of] Sino/British relations following my interview with the Acting Head of the Western European Department of the Foreign Ministry on 22 December. Since then there have been various developments and I thought that you might like my own assessment in the form of a consolidated paper, which I now enclose.

2. The picture which I paint is bleak, particularly as regards the prospects for the release of detained British subjects. I hope that I am proved wrong, but I think

that the unpleasant possibility of there being no further releases (except on health grounds) for some years must be faced. If, as a result of this, and the lack of any progress towards the release of confrontational prisoners in Hong Kong, our political relations remain soured, it could have a depressing effect in other directions, including trade. But as you will know from recommendations I have made separately, I am certainly not working on this assumption.

3. My views about the need to co-ordinate all aspects of Sino/British relations and to regulate actions in Hong Kong accordingly are already on record and have been well reflected in the paper prepared by Far Eastern Department for the meeting with the Governor of Hong Kong on 25 November last (enclosed in your letter of 4 December).[1] I share your hope that we shall be able to steer the Hong Kong Government away from injudicious policies. If at any rate this should stop the position getting worse, though if the line on prisoners is maintained, I doubt if it will get much better. It is very difficult to argue from here against the view that any further remissions or releases would be damaging to confidence in the Colony and have the various other unfortunate effects which the Governor claims. It is however a fact that everyone in Hong Kong does not share the Governor's view. There are some that think that the Hong Kong Government is now in a position of such strength and the Chinese are so anxious not to rock the boat that the moment is propitious for some political gestures in the interests of relations with China as a whole. They also share my view that the real danger lies in an incident or situation arising in which the Hong Kong authorities would be compelled to take strong action, thus risking escalation. An unabrasive policy would minimise the risk, but the possibility of it happening spontaneously e.g. an incident on the border or in a street market cannot be ruled out. In these circumstances, if a policy of gradual relaxation is not being followed, there will be no fund of local or Chinese Government tolerance and the restoration of order may accordingly become more difficult without repressive methods. I dare say that these are some of the subjects which will come up for consideration when the appointment of the new Governor is made. The main purpose of my paper is to point to the probable consequences of the continuation of the present situation. I fully agree with the statement in paragraph 7 of the Far Eastern Department's paper that Hong Kong is the 'prime element' in Sino/British relations. In this case, we may be justified in sacrificing all other elements in order to maintain the position we want in Hong Kong, using the methods the incumbent Governor considers appropriate. But we should be clear what this sacrifice may entail.

4. I have made certain recommendations of which (*a*) and (*c*) might be examined further, subject to your views. I should in any case be glad to know what you think of my general analysis and the prospects I foresee for the future.

Yours ever,
JOHN

1 Not printed.

ENCLOSURE IN NO. 183

Sino/British Relations

Present Position

After the release of Mr Grey and five other British subjects in October, and even after the subsequent arrest of Mrs Martin and Mr McBain, the Chinese in contact with us laid stress on the efforts they had made to improve relations and indicated that reciprocal measures were expected. Specific mention of confrontation prisoners in Hong Kong was not however made until 22 December when I pressed the Acting Director of the West European Department very hard for information about Mrs Martin and Mr McBain. Reference to prisoners was again made when Mr T'ang protested to me on 5 January about the death of the Chairman of the Taikoo Dockworkers Trade Union and asked that these prisoners should be released. The Chinese representations were made in a low key and were clearly intended mainly to support representations by local communists in Hong Kong. I do not think the death will prove a decisive element in our relations, but the timing was unfortunate. It is clear however that the only measures which the Chinese had in mind are connected with confrontation prisoners. It is highly unlikely that they expect us to release a large number at once; what they are probably looking for is some movement which would enable them to justify to local communist sympathizers in Hong Kong further relaxations, including the release of detained British subjects. It is possible that some element in the leadership, including Chou En-Lai, are keener than others to see an end to confrontation problems in the interests of better relations with us.

2. The Chinese may well have expected that after Mr Grey's release there would be steady progress towards the release of confrontation prisoners or possibly a negotiated settlement of all outstanding problems. They were therefore prepared to release five other British subjects as an earnest of goodwill. They have probably now concluded that further progress is unlikely. They are no doubt also displeased because, except in the commercial fields, we had made no particular effort to court them. On the contrary, there have been very strong protests about Mrs Martin and Mr McBain; increased publicity about the treatment of British subjects now released, as well as those still detained; this Mission has continued the policy of resisting unreasonable Chinese demands in the administrative field, protesting about Chinese discourtesy and so on; and Reuters have decided to suspend their operations.

3. The Chinese have indicated their displeasure by a concentration of anti-British articles in the Chinese Press following up the long article of 26 December on our economic difficulties (reported in my telegram No. 771 of 31 December 1969).[1] In the period 9-26 January there have been fourteen substantive anti-British items on a variety of domestic and external topics, as well as numerous incidental references. From our experience of the Chinese treatment of other countries, it is clear that such a concentration could not be accidental. Furthermore, the Chinese have been totally unco-operative in granting permission to travel to members of the Mission, whereas members of other Missions have been allowed to do so.

1 Not printed.

The Situation in Hong Kong

4. The situation is at present quiet. Local communists appear to be engaged in the slow rebuilding of their position but are under instructions not to cause trouble. The Prisons Board of Review has completed its work and has not recommended the remission of sentences on any further confrontation prisoners. According to the Chinese, there are still 134 left (earlier Hong Kong information had predicted 125 at the end of 1969—see the paper forwarded by the Political Adviser under reference SCR6/2621/67 of 30 October, 1969).[2] The criteria in accordance with which the Review Board work suggests that further remissions are unlikely. If this is so, we shall have to wait until the end of 1974 before the total of prisoners is down to 7 and by the end of 1977 there will still be 2 remaining prisoners as well as 2 others serving life sentences. The question of an amnesty for confrontation prisoners has been ruled out by the Governor. At the meeting with Officials in London on 25 November, the Governor agreed that he would consult in advance before any new measures were taken against communist sympathizers. He was urged to exercise constraint in the interest of British subjects detained and the functioning of the Mission, but gave no undertaking to do so. The possibility remains that certain confrontation prisoners for whom warrants are still outstanding might be arrested and if the sentences they receive are comparable with those in 1967 (e.g. 5-8 years) the list of long-term prisoners could lengthen.

Prospects

5. The Chinese would probably like improved relations with us both as part of the general process of normalisation in external relations and because they wish to maintain their line to the West in the event of increased difficulties, or even hostilities, with the Soviet Union. At the same time, relations are in many respects already satisfactory from their point of view in that trade in and through Hong Kong is being maintained, and they are able to increase their trade with the United Kingdom in so far as they wish, despite the political difficulties. They know that no effective sanctions will be taken against them in the interest of British subjects; indeed it is difficult to see that any form of sanctions is feasible. For these reasons, I do not think that there is any pressure on the Chinese to be helpful towards us in the political field in the absence of movement on our side.

6. The following is my assessment of the probable results of the position we have reached:

(*a*) There is little chance of early release of the remaining British subjects detained except (i) on grounds of health, which might apply particularly to Mr McBain; (ii) if the Chinese became convinced they were gaining nothing by a hostage policy, and that their international image was being adversely affected by the publicity given to it; (iii) in the unlikely event of their wishing at some time in the future to make a gesture towards us. (i) seems the best hope and (ii) just possible.

(*b*) There will be no remission for Mr Watt. (Unless, as seems just possible from his letters, he becomes so brain-washed or mentally unstable that the Chinese decide to deport him.) In the normal course of events, he should be released in September this year but the Chinese might keep him until March 1971, though he was arrested in September 1967, he was not sentenced until March 1968.

(*c*) There may be less administrative co-operation by the Chinese with this Mission, which could among other things affect the rebuilding of the Chancery.

(*d*) Travel by members of the Mission may continue to be curtailed.

(*e*) The Chinese may continue the ban on British businessmen in Hong Kong attending the Canton Trade Fairs, and not extend the list of United Kingdom businessmen whom they allow to go.

(*f*) The Chinese might discriminate against us commercially by choosing to buy certain items of comparable price and quality such as machinery, lorries etc., from our competitors. This could seriously affect our export figures if, as we think, Chinese purchases of non-ferrous metals from the London Metal Market fall off in the coming years.

(*g*) It will become increasingly difficult if not impossible to conduct a dialogue with the Chinese on any general political subject. Though it would be unrealistic to suppose that a Western country, or indeed any country, could have a real influence on Chinese policy, there might be advantage at a time when the Chinese are beginning to enlarge their diplomatic contacts, when there is the prospect of diplomatic relations being opened with other Western countries, and when the Chinese have renewed talks with the Americans, in their hearing a European voice other than the French, and to a lesser extent the Norwegian.

Conclusion and Recommendations

7. If the situation over prisoners in Hong Kong remains unchanged, I think we must be prepared for a prolonged freeze in our political relations. As prisoners are gradually released the Chinese may release British subjects one by one and after a number of years they might decide that the remainder are an encumbrance and release them also, while tacitly accepting the continued imprisonment of a small number of their sympathisers in Hong Kong. This could well take some time as even by the end of 1972 there will still be 44 prisoners left (plus the two with life sentences).

8. My *recommendations* are:

(*a*) We again put to the Chinese the proposal that confrontation prisoners should be 'returned to China'. The chance of their acceptance is slight but the attempt should be made.

(*b*) Publicity about remaining British subjects detained should be maintained at as high a level as possible.

(*c*) The Governor should be pressed to continue the regular review of sentences. If there are any plausible medical or compassionate grounds to release prisoners, the opportunity should be taken to do so.

(*d*) Every opportunity should be taken to emphasize to the Governor the need for restraint in action against communist sympathizers and for full consultation in advance of action.

No. 184

Letter from Mr Denson (Peking) to Mr Murray, 30 January 1970
Restricted (FCO 21/668, FEC 3/548/2A)

Dear James,

In my telegram No. 50 of 26 January,[1] I referred to a remark made by a Chinese Vice-Minister of Foreign Affairs that the United Kingdom was a country with which China had only 'half relations'. The remark was in fact made by Lo Kuei-po, in the course of the dinner which he gave for the French Ambassador on 16 January (reported in my telegram No. 38).[1]

2. The first report which we received of the remark was garbled and we were led to suppose that it was both gratuitous and very offensive. Manac'h has now given me a full account of the conversation, from which it appears that the remark was made at the very end of a long Chinese disquisition on the importance they attached to the Taiwan question (this was obviously intended for American ears). Manac'h had been urging Lo Kuei-po to look at the question in the longer term, to bear in mind American difficulties and take into account the fact that there were few American ground forces on the island, and the present patrolling system of the Taiwan Strait was less rigorous than it had been. This led Lo to remark that there were difficulties with both Canada and Italy over Taiwan and that there were certain countries e.g. the United Kingdom and The Netherlands, with whom China only had 'half relations' because of this question. It does not therefore appear that Lo was being particularly unpleasant though any references to third countries, except China's major friends and enemies, is rare in private conversations. But, it certainly confirms that even if we eventually get over our difficulties in Hong Kong, this is likely to remain an important obstacle to any exchange of Ambassadors.

3. Manac'h asked me whether the formulation was new and I told him that I vaguely recalled its having been used on previous occasions, probably when there had been discussion of a possible exchange of Ambassadors. I think there was some discussion on this in 1954 at Geneva and again later in 1956. I wonder if someone in Research Department could look this up and see also whether there are any other references to 'half relations'.[2]

4. I am sending a copy of this letter to Ray Bray in Tamsui (who did not receive the telegram under reference), John Boyd in Washington and Arthur Maddocks in Hong Kong, and the Chancery in Paris.

Yours ever,
JOHN

---

1 Not printed.
2 The Research Department found a reference in a *People's Daily* editorial of 12 May 1964 entitled, 'China will not tolerate interference in respect of sovereignty over Taiwan', which referred to Britain as 'a country which has established semi-diplomatic relations with China'.

No. 185

Note by Mr Stewart to the Ministerial Committee on Hong Kong
9 February 1970
K(70)1 Top Secret (CAB 134/2945)

Hong Kong: Long Term Study

In the early months of 1969 officials completed a comprehensive study of Hong Kong in the long-term. This is the first occasion in which their report, circulated by me under the cover of a note as K(69)1, has been considered by Ministers.[1]

2. I shall not attempt to draw up a balance-sheet in respect of our continuing administration of Hong Kong. The advantages we derive and the liabilities we could incur in the short or longer term are carefully set out in the study. But this is not the central issue. What is crucial is that we have little freedom of choice about the future discharge of our responsibilities. Hong Kong is a special case in the political evolution of our colonial territories. We cannot attempt to bring it to any form of independent status, since this would be quite unacceptable to the Chinese. We must recognise that it will eventually be returned to China, and that the circumstances of the return are almost bound to be painful, both to the inhabitants of the Colony and to ourselves. The saliently gloomy features of the problem as they emerge from [the] study are these:

(*a*) The Chinese Government have at their disposal (even without the use of military force) the means of making our position in the Colony humiliating and intolerable.

(*b*) In whatever circumstances we abdicate our position, it will be impossible to discharge all our responsibilities to the Hong Kong Chinese, or to remove or protect all British and Hong Kong owned assets; and we shall in effect be abandoning some millions of unwilling inhabitants to Communism (of whom about two million are citizens of the UK and Colonies).

(*c*) If we were to try to withdraw from Hong Kong prematurely, it is by no means certain that the Chinese would accept our renunciation of authority. They might attempt to force us to maintain a 'puppet' British administration under their control.

(*d*) If it is assumed that the Colony will be returning to China not later than 1997 (the termination of the lease of the 'New Territories') there must, as this date approaches, be a decline in confidence in the Colony leading to the possibility of prolonged economic recession. This could be quite a significant factor in the situation by the 1980s, if not before.

3. It would be wrong, however, to concentrate entirely on the negative aspect. The Chinese are for the present clearly prepared to accept the continuing existence of the Colony on account of the economic and political advantages it brings them. There are no signs that an early renewal of the 1967 campaign of violence is likely, and the Chinese apparently recognise that it may take a long time to bring the Hong Kong Government to subservience using the methods which they describe as 'long-term struggle'. Their immediate aims are to increase to the maximum their commercial interests in the Colony and to concentrate on broadening the base of their support among the people. This is a state of affairs which in the best circumstances might

1 See No. 166.

last for some years yet. Moreover, in the meantime a new regime may emerge in China. There is no solid ground for believing that any such regime would be more accommodating. But it would be wrong to assume that it would not.

4. In view of the difficulties which seem almost inevitable for the future, officials in making their study were understandably concerned to ensure that all feasible precautions for forestalling disaster had been considered and that no opportunities had been overlooked for initiating policies now with the Chinese that might make the problem easier to deal with in future. It is, I think, a reasonable conclusion from the report that there are no fresh initiatives that we can take in present circumstances that would make the problems of Hong Kong less intractable in the longer term. There can be no clean-cut, tidy solution to the predicament facing us. Were we to attempt to discuss it with the present Chinese regime we could only expect hostility (even malevolence) and a desire on their part to pay off old scores. The Colony will remain, as the Chinese themselves have put it, the crux of Sino-British relations. Our presence there, despite the advantages they derive, must be an irritant to them. But efforts on our part to extricate ourselves prematurely might well turn out to be a greater irritant. For the present, I am sure that we must continue to show firmly that we intend to maintain our position, giving no indication whatsoever that we might, in certain circumstances, contemplate premature withdrawal. Moreover any sign of weakening resolve on our part would lead to increasing Chinese pressure. It would be no gain if, in an effort to mitigate the long-term difficulties, we were to precipitate an immediate catastrophe.

5. The emergence of more pragmatic regime in China would, of course, introduce a new dimension. If such a regime were to emerge there would be much to be said for attempting to negotiate the return of Hong Kong on the best terms available for its people, or perhaps even for exploring the terms on which the Chinese might envisage an extension of our tenure. But as I indicated above, there is, as yet, no solid ground for believing that such a regime would be more accommodating. Moreover, the whole matter is so hypothetical and subject to so many imponderables, that it is doubtful if anything is to be gained by attempting now a detailed assessment of the possibilities.

6. To sum up, the general conclusions which I should like my colleagues to endorse are these:

(*a*) There is no prospect of us reaching agreement about the future of Hong Kong with the present Chinese Government.

(*b*) Any unilateral attempt on our part *now* to work towards some new status for Hong Kong would lead to an immediate loss of confidence within the Colony and could quickly be disastrous.

(*c*) If a more pragmatic government were to emerge in China we should consider the possibility of negotiating with them new arrangements for Hong Kong. But it would be premature to attempt now a detailed assessment of the possibilities.

(*d*) For the present, in administering the Colony, we must assume, and be seen to assume, that we shall be there at any rate until 1997.

This may seem a somewhat Micawberish policy.[2] As I acknowledged at the outset, disaster could befall us at any time with very little notice. But short of some radical transformation of the situation, e.g. an all-out effort by the Chinese to make

---

2 A reference to the character Wilkins Micawber in the novel, *David Copperfield*, by Charles Dickens who lived in hopeful expectation that 'something will turn up'.

our position intolerable or an expressed determination by them to take over the Colony in the fairly near future, the approach I have outlined might see us through at any rate the next five to ten years—which is perhaps as far ahead as it is prudent to look in dealing with Hong Kong.

7. The conclusions above are broadly in line with the conclusions and recommendations of the report K(69)1. Accordingly, I propose that the Committee, if it shares my views, should give general endorsement to the recommendation that future policy with regard to Hong Kong be reviewed at regular intervals in consultation with the Governor, should direct officials to undertake a further review in the course of this year in time to submit a revised report to the Committee in the first half of 1971 by which time the next Governor should have taken up his post. Amongst the issues to which officials should devote attention are those mentioned in recommendation (6) of K(69)1.

8. I draw the attention of my colleagues on the Committee to the very strict security rules covering the preparation and circulation of this paper and the preceding report.

No. 186

Minute from Mr Wilson to Mr Appleyard, 13 February 1970
Secret (FCO 21/715, FEH 2/1)

Sino-British Relations

This is a somewhat depressing letter from Mr Denson[1] on the prospect of improving Sino-British relations and obtaining the release of the remaining nine British subjects detained. I would agree with him that the chances of their being released in the near future are bleak but it seems over-pessimistic to suggest that there will be no further releases for some years.

2. I think that we would agree in Far Eastern Department that the premature release of at least some of the remaining Chinese prisoners in Hong Kong is unlikely to weaken confidence in the Hong Kong Government's ability to manage its affairs. But we are not going to convince the Hong Kong Government of this at the moment. However, it is not axiomatic that the release of the Chinese prisoners would lead to the release of British prisoners. The Chinese have never directly linked the nine with the remaining Chinese prisoners in Hong Kong. It is well to remember too that the Chinese are displeased with other aspects of our policy towards them and that their internal political scene is also a factor in their policy-making.

3. I do not see how we can avoid the danger that the Hong Kong Government may need to take strong action against local communists if they decided under instructions to court such a reaction. But all the evidence at the moment is that this is unlikely. The local communists are under instruction not to provoke the Hong Kong Government. Mr Denson perhaps puts his finger on our dilemma when he states that in the final analysis it is our position in Hong Kong which counts rather than improved relations with the Chinese.

1 No. 183.

4. It is not entirely clear how much weight the Chinese attach to obtaining the release of the remaining prisoners in Hong Kong. In official exchanges they have only raised the issue twice in recent months and in both instances it is difficult to see how they could have avoided doing so (our representations in December on behalf of Mrs Martin and Mr McBain, and the Chinese protest about the death of a Chinese Trade Unionist in a Hong Kong prison). For the most part there is very little pressure in Hong Kong for the release of the prisoners and the Tang case was fairly quickly dropped from communist propaganda. In general communists in Hong Kong seem resigned to the fact that the confrontation prisoners will serve out their sentences.

5. In his analysis of recent development in Sino-British relations I think that Mr Denson perhaps exaggerates the extent to which they have deteriorated. On the debit side a number of events are known to have displeased the Chinese;

(*a*) our vigorous representations on behalf of Mrs Martin and Mr McBain;

(*b*) the supplement on Taiwan in *The Times*;

(*c*) ECGD cover for the construction of a power station by a British firm in Tawain; and

(*d*) the dispute over the dumping of Chinese alarm clocks on the British market. It is true that there has been a general increase in the amount of space in the Chinese press given to anti-British reports. But the Americans have been similarly attacked at the same time as the Chinese have resumed contacts in Warsaw. It is possible to argue that the purpose of these articles was less an indication of Chinese displeasure than an attempt to demonstrate that we are a weak and insignificant power, racked by political and economic crises and therefore not presenting any significant threat to Chinese interests. This line of argument could well be used to justify Chinese inaction to their supporters in Hong Kong over the issue of confrontation prisoners. The articles are also part of the continuing Chinese attack on imperialist powers.

6. As regards other signs of displeasure by the Chinese cited by Mr Denson, I have seen no evidence that the Chinese are annoyed by the closure of the Reuters office. On the contrary they could have made difficulties for us but were in fact fairly helpful. We have seen no evidence either of the Chinese creating administrative difficulties in other areas. A MOPBW representative is now in Peking discussing the reconstruction of the Chancery building with the Chinese and these negotiations will no doubt provide some evidence of whether we can expect the Chinese to be helpful or not over this question. Since the arrest of Mrs Martin and Mr McBain there has been no further harassment of other British subjects in China. On the contrary the Chinese have returned promptly some yachtsmen who strayed into Chinese waters around Hong Kong and our fears that a British businessman (Mr Crowe) might be detained in Peking before Christmas were not realised. As regards the chances of British businessmen in Hong Kong attending the Spring Canton Trade Fair, the SBTC remain optimistic that the ban will be lifted on this occasion. There are no signs that the Chinese are discriminating against us commercially. On the contrary our commercial relations both here and in Peking are cordial.

7. The main act of discrimination has been the curtailment of travel by members of our Mission outside of Peking. A comparison of the dates of our representations in December on behalf of British subjects and the dates when applications were first refused suggests that this was a direct act of retaliation signifying Chinese

displeasure at the way in which we had deliberately raised the temperature. Mr Denson also suggests that our recent publicity campaign about the treatment of Mrs Martin and Mr McBain would also have irritated the Chinese. In fact this campaign was a flop and I doubt whether the Chinese would have noted any additional effort above the usual coverage given to this subject in the British press. We are not aware that there has been any significant foreign news coverage. On the whole, therefore, my assessment of recent events is that relations remain as poor as ever but that it is difficult to argue that there has been a noticeable deterioration. The Chinese do not want to put the clock back but they seem to have no enthusiasm at the moment to move it forward.

8. Mr Denson concludes with a number of recommendations for future policy.

(*a*) The chance of the Chinese agreeing to the confrontation prisoners being 'returned to China' is virtually nil. If we raised this with the Chinese again it would be largely for the benefit of relatives and possibly Parliament if we were prepared to announce publicly that we had done so. We would have to decide whether the offer should be made through 'Contact' in Hong Kong or diplomatic channels. Timing would also be important if we hoped to attract a not entirely unfavourable Chinese reaction. I doubt whether the present moment is propitious when the Chinese are showing no particular interest in obtaining the release of the prisoners. It would be better to keep it up our sleeves until they return to the charge again as they undoubtedly will at some future date.

(*b*) I agree that we should continue to stimulate publicity but we must recognise that the British subjects are a less interesting item for the press now that Mr Grey has been released. Our publicity campaign for the Martin and McBain cases was a flop. It is also worth considering whether we have reached the point of diminishing returns with the Chinese over negative publicity of this kind and should now concentrate on a more positive publicity line. In this connexion it is perhaps worth considering whether we should not stimulate articles which draw attention to our improved commercial relations, indicating at the same time our willingness to be helpful to the Chinese and hence evidence of our desire to improve Sino-British relations in general. This has its dangers I realise and could well provoke the opposite reaction in Britain from those who are keen to impose sanctions on the Chinese. Nevertheless it is the one area in which we are useful to the Chinese and although one must not exaggerate the leverage which we obtain from this there would seem no harm in the point being underlined in publicity.

(*c*) The letter from Mr Maddocks (attached)[2] on the activities of the Board of Review is unhelpful. The Board's deliberations show no sign of any particular urgency to resolve this problem. It sat only three times since July. On the last two occasions it failed to recommend any of the prisoners in whom we are interested for release. The procedure seems inflexible and apart from supporting Mr Denson's suggestion that offenders who have health problems might be considered for release I cannot see any way of getting round its rather rigid terms of reference. I should be grateful for Hong Kong Department's views on this. It is worth pointing out however, that the courts would now appear to be applying more lenient criteria in

---

2 Not printed.

their judgment of offenders than was the case in 1967 (the head of the Gasworks Union) and it would be reasonable to argue that the Board of Review should take a similar relaxed view when examining these cases. There seems to be one inconsistency in Mr Maddock's letter; in paragraph 5 he reports that the case of eleven young offenders were reviewed twice within the last year although prison rules allow only for annual review. Would it be possible, therefore, to have the long-term prisoners reviewed at less than the statutory interval of every two years? It would be useful if Hong Kong Department could remind us of the criteria used by the Board when considering remission of sentences.

(*d*) It must have been clear from the paper prepared for the talks with the Governor in December and from our discussion with him that we had been irritated by the lack of consultation on cases which had come before the courts during the latter part of 1969. Rather than remind the Hong Kong Government 'at every opportunity of this obligation' which might be counter productive, it would be better to confine it to occasions when we think that consultation might have been swifter, e.g. the recent case involving the arrest and sentencing of a former prisoner who had not observed his supervision order. In this instance it is not clear whether the delay in informing us was deliberate or due to administrative inefficiency.

9. We must conclude that apart from continuing to advise restraint on Hong Kong we are unlikely to persuade the Hong Kong Government to make concessions over the remaining Chinese prisoners substantial enough to evoke a response from the Chinese. Must our relations with the Chinese, therefore, remain in a state of suspense? Mr Denson points out that the Chinese would probably like to improve relations with us as part of their policy of maintaining links with West European countries in the face of Soviet pressure. The importance to the Chinese of European countries as a source of supply has clearly increased during recent months. Hence the increased activity of the Chinese Commercial Office in London. It is true that the Chinese probably realise that they can pocket the commercial benefits without making any political concessions to us. We must therefore not exaggerate Chinese dependence on UK suppliers or our leverage over them. Nevertheless commercial contact is the one aspect of our relations with the Chinese which remains fairly cordial and we should therefore build on this. I referred in paragraph 6 [*sic*] (*b*) to the dangers of appearing too forthcoming to the Chinese in commercial matters, but this should not prevent us from continuing to be helpful and provide facilities in commercial matters in the hope that some of the goodwill generated by our actions will rub off on our political relations.[3]

C. WILSON

---

3 Mr Appleyard agreed with Mr Wilson's assessment and thought that Sino-British trade was the only feasible area in which significant positive steps might be made towards achieving better relations with China. A proposal to release Hong Kong prisoners inside China would only be counter-productive given the Chinese had already rejected this suggestion.
Commenting in a minute dated 2 March, Mr Carter of the Hong Kong Department thought the Governor was fully aware of the need for caution and restraint in handling the local communists. 'Successive Governors have become skilled at treading the narrow path between firmness and avoidance of provocation, and I do not think that Sir David Trench is any less skilful or less discerning in plotting the right course'.

CHAPTER III

Negotiating an exchange of Ambassadors
15 April 1970 — 13 March 1972

No. 187

Minute from Mr Murray on Sino-British Relations, 15 April 1970
Confidential (FCO 21/668, FEC 3/548/2A)

Mr Denson's visit to London before Easter for consultations was made the occasion for a comprehensive review of Sino-British relations. Office meetings were held by the Secretary of State and the Permanent Under Secretary. This minute records the main conclusions reached about future action. It also repeats, in a form revised to take account of the discussions and of subsequent developments, the argument in the departmental paper dated 24 March on 'Prospects for Sino-Soviet Relations', which was prepared for Mr Denson's visit.

Conclusions

2. The main conclusions of the review were these:

(*a*) The intractable problem of the communist prisoners in Hong Kong serving sentences for offences committed during the troubles in 1967 remains central to our relations with China. The Secretary of State agreed that during his visit to Hong Kong he would in private conversation with the Governor express the hope that the Governor would feel able to keep the position of the prisoners under review and to examine whether the small gesture of a premature release could not from time to time be arranged without damage to the interests of Hong Kong.

(*b*) We should continue to seek publicity for the cases of British subjects in detention in China. But this largely negative criticism of Chinese actions might be balanced with a publicity line which spelt out the basis for a more satisfactory relationship between ourselves and the Chinese.

(*c*) Commercial relations would seem to be the most promising area for making progress. The Chinese should be encouraged to send more commercial missions to the United Kingdom.

(*d*) We should do what we can to facilitate sales of British aircraft to China.

(*e*) We should explore with the Royal Society, and subsequently with the British Council, the feasibility of renewing formal cultural relations with China.

(*f*) We should look into the question of restarting the direct telephone link between the UK and China.

(*g*) The time has perhaps come to try to draw the Chinese into dialogue on matters of general mutual interest. We should therefore try to improve our contacts both in Peking and in London.

Argument

3. It is difficult to define with precision the present state of Sino-British relations. Bad though they are in the important matter of the treatment, of British subjects in China, they are in many other respects perhaps as satisfactory as we can realistically expect them to be.

The Present State of Relations

Commercial Relations

4. There is no evidence that the Chinese are discriminating against us commercially. On the contrary, the volume of Sino-British trade in 1969 reached the record level of £89.5m. Relations between our Commercial Secretary and the Chinese Trade Organisations in Peking are reasonably good, and the Board of Trade and the Sino-British Trade Council have given every assistance to members of the Chinese Commercial Office in London; in particular, special visits have been arranged for them to two industrial areas in Britain. With the apparent phasing out of the Cultural Revolution and the return to more stable economic conditions with China, the prospects for a further expansion in Sino-British trade look reasonably promising.

Hong Kong

5. The Chinese continue to behave well over Hong Kong. They have refrained from statements publicly attacking our policies; and in private they have restrained the local cadres. We know that they regard the Communist prisoners still in Hong Kong as a key issue in their relations with us and we must assume that it remains their objective to secure their release. On the other hand it is not always clear how much weight they really attach to this problem. For example during the exchanges with them in London and Peking over the recent detention of the two ships officers in Shanghai, Hong Kong was not referred to. There is little pressure in the Colony from the Communists for the release of the prisoners, and a case involving a prisoner was dropped fairly quickly from local Communist propaganda. In general, the local Communists seem to accept that we are unlikely to make concessions.

Discrimination against the Mission in Peking

6. The Chinese continue to discriminate against our Mission in numerous petty ways. There is an accepted 'pecking order' in which we, together with the Russians and the Indians, come out the bottom. However, the ban on travel outside Peking by members of our Mission, which was introduced in December, has been lifted in that a member of the Mission has now been to visit Tientsin. But the chances of being allowed a visit to Shanghai seem slight at the moment.

Treatment of British Subjects

7. Chinese treatment of British subjects remains the major irritant in our relations. In particular there has been no progress at all in the cases of Mr Crouch the Blue Funnel officer detained in Shanghai since March 1968, and Mr Johnston the Chartered Bank manager detained in Shanghai since September 1968. The Chinese have failed to provide details of the charges against them and continue to refuse access to them by members of our Mission. (Mr Watt serving a three-year sentence is due to end this September or in March 1971 depending on when the Chinese reckon it to have begun, and the group of former 'fellow travellers' in Peking need cause us less concern).

8. It must be significant that Shanghai has been the scene of much of the trouble over British subjects (the detention of Mr Crouch and Mr Johnston and the affairs of Mrs Martin and Mr McBain) and of the major shipping incidents. Shanghai has had a reputation for taking an independent and extremist line during the Cultural Revolution. Two members of the Municipal Revolutionary Committee are members of the Politbureau and are associated with the Radical Group. It is also clear from the 'leftist' line taken by the Shanghai press in recent campaigns against counter-revolutionary tendencies in literature that the city remains the power base of the Radical Group on the Central Committee. This Group has reason to be dissatisfied with the trend of events in China, and, in particular, could be expected to have reservations about 'the revisionist policy' of the Central Government towards Hong Kong. By their behaviour over British subjects, the Shanghai authorities underline their independent position and cock a snook[1] at the Central authorities. Even if the Central Government was so inclined, it is not in a position to bring undue pressure to bear on Shanghai authorities to disgorge captives. Assuming that there are persons within the Ministry of Foreign Affairs who are interested in pursuing more reasonable policies towards us, they clearly cannot afford to expose themselves to the criticism of being conciliatory while their compatriots remain in prison in Hong Kong. Until the Central Government is in a stronger position to exert its authority it would appear that Shanghai will be able to frustrate relations with the UK by arresting other British subjects still resident in the city or seamen visiting the port.

The Balance and the Consequences

9. Before striking a balance, we must be clear in our own minds about the kind of relationship which is possible with the Chinese. Relations with the Chinese will always be prickly while we remain in Hong Kong. Indeed, even if the immediate point at issue, the release of the Chinese prisoners in Hong Kong, is resolved, there are other impediments in the way of an improvement in relations: our attitude towards Taiwan; the role we play in the annual debate in the UN on Chinese representation; and our general association with US policies. There have of course been more cordial moments in relations since 1950. We are still some way from the 'pre-confrontation co-existence' of the mid-1960's, and we are even further from the 'honey-moon period' of our relationship which followed the Geneva Conference in 1954. Nevertheless, it is a very considerable boon that the Chinese have abandoned their policy of violence in Hong Kong and a *modus vivendi* in the Colony's relations has been reinstituted. Our trading relations are as good as we could reasonably expect, given the present state of the Chinese economy and the efforts of our competitors. There is still room for a good deal of improvement in the treatment of our Mission, but restrictions on travel are as much a reflection of Chinese dislike of foreigners travelling about China as of our indifferent relations. In brief, the main factor which distinguishes our relations now from earlier more satisfactory times is the problem of British subjects.

10. Examining the Chinese view Mr Denson has argued from Peking that the Chinese are already probably fairly satisfied with relations in that trade in and through Hong Kong is being maintained, and they are able to increase their trade

---

1 Show a lack of respect.

with the United Kingdom insofar as they wish, despite the political difficulties. They must judge that no effective sanctions will—or indeed can—be taken against them in the interests of British subjects. For these reasons he does not think that there will be any pressure on the Chinese to be helpful towards us in the political field in the absence of movement on our side. He argues that without some such movement we may face a prolonged freeze in our relations. In this case we should have to accept that it may take a long time to secure the release of the British subjects. Moreover we shall remain vulnerable to the inevitable incidents of Sino-British relations (e.g. excessive zealousness on the part of local Communists in Hong Kong, the forthcoming publication of Mr Anthony Grey's book) since the Chinese will not be disposed to co-operate with us in playing them down. And we may be handicapped vis-à-vis over European competitors in efforts to increase trade. In any case it would be wrong to draw the conclusion that our trade will go on expanding regardless of the political climate; and we must accept that further increases may well depend in some measure on political factors.

11. In the longer term we must look at Sino-Soviet relations [*sic* ?British] in the context of the Sino-Soviet dispute. The best prediction we can make is Sino-Soviet hostility will continue. In the light of this the Chinese are likely to be increasingly interested in improving contacts with the West and in keeping in touch with political and military developments in Western Europe. They have shown an interest in the health of NATO and, while they may go through the motions of denouncing the European Economic Community, they may also have an interest in its development. There is also our and Europe's long term interest in improving contacts with China and assisting in her eventual emergence from isolation. The Soviet Union and the United States may be disqualified from doing so. There is therefore a potentially valuable political role we could play in Peking. The present state of our relations disqualifies us from doing so. If anyone, the French derive the advantages of acting as the European interlocutor with the Chinese.

Possible Courses of Action

12. What then is to be done? Since each new Chinese misdeed revives public interest in tougher measures it will be convenient to consider first the limitations on the means of pressure we can exercise on the Chinese. We can then consider ways in which we might possibly be rather more forthcoming.

Sanctions

13. Since 1967 we have had under constant consideration the possibility of applying economic pressures to the Chinese. The sort of measures which have been suggested are a ban on trade with China and the prevention of British ships from visiting Chinese ports. Following the recent incidents in Shanghai the Ocean Steamship Company has announced that sailings to China have been suspended pending clarification of the reasons for the detention of the two officers. In fact the Company has decided not to resume sailings to China in the foreseeable future. The withdrawal of the Ocean Company's ships from the liner trade will considerably inconvenience the Chinese if only temporarily, particularly since the majority of other European shipping companies which specialised in the China trade have now withdrawn. In addition, the Ocean Steamship Company (who are rightly not letting up in their

efforts to secure the release of their officer Mr Crouch) have been seeking the support of seamen's organisations to put pressure on the Chinese. The British Shipping Federation are shortly issuing a warning notice to British shippers which will remind companies of the risks involved in visiting Chinese ports. The general effect of these various actions will be to discourage shipping companies from sailing to China, increase insurance rates, and make it more difficult for the Chinese to charter vessels. We know that the Chinese shipping organisations are well aware of the problems which incidents in Chinese ports cause for their British charterers, and we hope will now draw the appropriate economic conclusions. Although we have given discreet encouragement behind the scenes to the shipowners, it is clearly preferable from a tactical point of view that they should take the initiative in these matters. In our view the Chinese are more likely to be moved towards more reasonable policies in response to market forces than to political pressures. Any attempt to control British trade with China would, in my opinion, be ineffective. We could expect opposition from other government departments and those firms engaged in China trade. In any case the Chinese would quickly switch to other suppliers.

Publicity

14. We should continue to seek publicity for the cases of British subjects, while recognising that it is becoming increasingly difficult to sustain a publicity campaign in the absence of new developments. The initial incident generates wide publicity but, as we found in the cases of Mrs Martin and Mr McBain, press interest wanes quickly. Moreover the Chinese are less sensitive than most other governments to publicity. (The time has perhaps come to balance this largely negative criticism of China's actions with a more positive publicity line which spells out the practical basis for a satisfactory relationship between ourselves and China. Depending on Chinese reactions to the various initiatives proposed towards the end of this paper, such publicity could draw attention to the mutual benefits to be gained from closer co-operation in the technological field, from specialist training and from cultural and commercial relations).

What do the Chinese want?

15. Before turning to the consideration of ways in which we might be more forthcoming towards the Chinese, we must ask ourselves if we are right in assuming that there are persons in Peking (as distinct perhaps from Shanghai) who are interested in pursuing more pragmatic policies towards us? A number of recent pointers suggest that this is a reasonable assumption. The handling at the Peking end of the recent Shanghai shipping incidents and the comparative rapidity with which they were settled are hopeful signs. The Chinese have also approached negotiations for the re-building of our Chancery, burnt down in 1967, in a constructive mood. Furthermore, a delegation from the British shipping brokers, Lamberts, who handle the bulk of Chinese chartering, was given a cordial reception by the Chinese in Peking recently. The importance of European countries to the Chinese as sources of supply has clearly increased as the Sino-Soviet dispute intensified. Indeed, it is possible to argue that the strategic and economic value of Hong Kong to the Chinese has similarly increased. In short, there are sound reasons of self-interest why the Chinese Government should wish to see a continuing improvement in their relations with us. A corollary of all this would be that we should do what we reasonably can to help

those in Peking whom we believe are interested in pursuing more sensible policies towards us to demonstrate that better relations with us are beneficial to China.

Hong Kong

16. As the Chinese have frequently reiterated in the past, Hong Kong is the 'crux' of our relationship with China. There are still some 115 Chinese prisoners in gaol in Hong Kong, sentenced for their part in the disturbances in 1967. By the end of this year a further 35 will have been released provided that they earn full remission of sentence. As long as any substantial number of these 'confrontation' prisoners remains in gaol, the Chinese cannot be expected to accept that the situation in Hong Kong has returned to 'normal'. There can be little doubt that a release of a substantial number of them would have a considerable impact on Sino-British relations. The recent study by Hong Kong Department of the feasibility of accelerating their release, either by means of the Board of Review or by an amnesty, concluded that there is little leeway to make concessions substantial enough to evoke the desired response from the Chinese. Nevertheless, we must keep under review possible ways of easing this intractable problem, which remains central to our relations with China.

17. A further consideration in the context of Hong Kong is the need to avoid provocative actions which revive disputes of the 'confrontation' period or raise new problems in areas where the Chinese are known to be sensitive, e.g. the Chinese press and Chinese schools. The Hong Kong Government have assured us that they see the need to avoid policies which the Chinese might consider unduly provocative. But at the same time they insist, in my view correctly, that they must deal firmly with unreasonable pressure from the local Communists or the Chinese government. The balance is not an easy one to strike.

More forthcoming policies

18. In face of the difficulties of any early gesture towards the Chinese in Hong Kong affairs, is it possible for us to take any steps which might lead to an improvement in our relations with China, or should we sit tight in the hope that the present very gradual trend towards an improvement in our relations might continue and eventually lead to the release of more British subjects? As long as Mr Crouch and Mr Johnston in particular remain in detention there will be difficulties over justifying a conciliatory policy towards China. It might well be argued that a conciliatory policy must inevitably include concessions which might lead to further demands from the Chinese government. There is also the possibility that extremist opinion within the Chinese leadership would argue that this showed that it paid to be firm with the British. The Chinese leadership might also conclude that an attempt at conciliation on our part indicated that we were now less interested in obtaining the release of British subjects. But on balance, I think that, whatever might be the risks of any gesture to the Chinese in the context of Hong Kong, a conciliatory attitude in areas unrelated to our current differences would be less likely to be interpreted as a 'kowtow', and would indicate that we did attach importance to improved relations.

19. We have accordingly sought to identify areas where we can appeal to Chinese self-interest or where the results would be mutually beneficial.

(*a*) As the Chinese are clearly interested in expanding their trade with us, commercial relations would seem to be the most promising area for making further progress. The Chinese should be encouraged to send more commercial missions to the UK.

(*b*) The Chinese are known to be interested in re-equipping their civil air fleet and are negotiating with Pakistan International Airways for the transfer of four secondhand Tridents. British aircraft manufacturers should as soon as possible be authorised to offer aircraft to the Chinese direct within the limits proposed in the recent paper on the matter.

(*c*) In the early 1960s we had a modest cultural exchange programme with the Chinese. At one time 30 Chinese specialists and about 50 students were studying in the UK. This programme came to an end when the Chinese withdrew them during the Cultural Revolution. (The Chinese visitors behaved very badly and caused great distress to their tutors and others who had taken a great deal of trouble over them). The Chinese need for technical training has not lessened during the intervening years. Indeed, we understand the Chinese have already sent some students back to France and also made a tentative approach last year to the Royal Society about a renewal of their previous programme. In the circumstances it seems possible that the Chinese would be attracted by an offer of places. (In view of present conditions in China, we would not want to press for a reciprocal arrangement at present. In any case, the Chinese would probably be reluctant to allow foreigners to live in China until they have finally emerged from the Cultural Revolution.) To make the maximum political impact, it would be desirable for the initial approach to the Chinese to be made through official channels. But detailed arrangements could again best be handled by the Royal Society and the British Council. We must accept however that in view of the bitterness engendered by the previous conduct of the Chinese neither body will be particularly enthusiastic.

(*d*) A recent Parliamentary Question reminded us of the efforts which have been made since 1949 to restore a direct telephone link between the UK and China. The last abortive attempt was made in 1966. As the GPO[2] remain keen to re-establish the link we see advantage in putting the proposal to the Chinese again as evidence of our desire to improve contacts.

(*e*) The time has perhaps come to try to draw the Chinese into a dialogue on other matters of mutual concern. A number of posts have already reported useful exchanges on international affairs with their Chinese colleagues. In Moscow and Ulan Bator members of the Chinese Mission have not allowed our poor relations to inhibit them from talking freely and in non-ideological terms about their relations with the Soviet Union. We should therefore try to improve our contacts with the Chinese in Peking and London.

20. It is possible that the Chinese will be slow to respond to any of these initiatives. They may take the view that there can be no 'normalisation' of Sino-British relations as long as there are important questions unresolved in Hong Kong; and that such minor conciliatory gestures are not the specific actions implied in the oft repeated refrain that they require deeds not words from HMG. This is something which we must be prepared to accept. In putting forward these proposals we would be indicating to the Chinese that we are interested in broadening contacts and improving relations. It would constitute an attempt to return to 'pre-confrontation co-existence'.

JAMES MURRAY

---

2 General Post Office. At this time, it was the UK's postal and telecommunications carrier.

No. 188

Mr Denson (Peking) to Mr Stewart, 24 April 1970[1]
Tel. No. 262 Priority. Confidential (FCO 21/698, FEC 22/3)

Wilford left Peking yesterday for Ulan Bator after a most successful visit. The Chinese having granted his visa at short notice, acceded to all the requests which I made. He was received by the acting head of the Western European Department and the acting Chief of Protocol together on 20 April and they both accepted an invitation to dine with me the following evening (in the event Han Hsu was called away but sent his deputy). On 22 April we saw Vice-Minister Lo Kuei-po for an hour. Discussions with him and T'ang covered much the same ground. Wilford also had the opportunity of speaking to the French Ambassador and some of my other more knowledgeable colleagues.

2. Wilford emphasized to the Chinese our desire to see relations further improved. He referred to the progress already made, particularly in the commercial field and said that we recognised the Chinese had taken some steps on their side; but he added that further progress would require hard work by both sides. The Chinese replied that they also wanted better relations and said they had taken note of the various statements in this sense by British Ministers. If Her Majesty's Government were sincere this was most welcome to them; but practical measures were required as the responsibility for the present difficulties lay with us. The Chinese made it quite clear that the difficulties related to Hong Kong. Lo mentioned it specifically and T'ang referred indirectly to the remaining Chinese prisoners who he said numbered 120.

3. Both T'ang and Lo enquired about your visit to Hong Kong and Wilford spoke on agreed lines.

4. Wilford said that the Chinese Government had taken actions which caused us great difficulty in normalizing relations. He raised with Lo the question of access to and information about detained British subjects. He did not dispute the Chinese right to insist that British subjects living in China should obey Chinese laws or that the Chinese had their own practices as regards access and information, but added that there were cases such as that of Crouch who had been detained for two years without charges being made, which the British Government and Parliament found very difficult to understand. Lo replied on standard lines and referred to the four British subjects recently released whose cases had been dealt with on their merits.

5. I think Wilford's exchanges with the Chinese have been most useful. The atmosphere throughout was relaxed, and the Chinese were clearly making an effort to avoid contentious statements which might raise the temperature. It is evident that the Chinese would like to remove existing difficulties but they recognise that the process will have to be gradual. Lo expressed willingness for discussions to be continued on any matters of common interest either in London or Peking.

6. Full records by bag.

---

1 Repeated for information to Hong Kong.

No. 189

Minute from Mr Morgan to Mr Wilford, 29 May 1970
Confidential (FCO 21/656, FEC 2/4A)

Chinese Representation: The Important Item

I wonder whether we should not take another look at our support for the 'Important Item' resolution at the United Nations.

2. There are three reasons why this could be timely:

(i) the softer line of President Nixon's Administration on Sino-US relations could make them less likely to raise objections to a change in our policy.

(ii) the Prime Minister reaffirmed during the debate on Cambodia on 5 May that:
'The whole House recognises the undeniable very much wider fact, which overlies all conflict in Asia, that the conflict of South-East Asia, and every manifestation of that conflict, cannot be decided on a world scale without the representation on a world scale, at the United Nations, of the Chinese Government and the Chinese people.'[1]

(iii) We have been looking for gestures that we could make to the Chinese to show our willingness to improve Sino-British relations.

3. Our support for the 'Important Item' and for the substantive vote on Peking's admission cannot be justified on the basis of logic. The purpose of the 'Important Item' resolution is simply to facilitate the continued exclusion of Peking and as such the Chinese are right in regarding it as a 'crude procedural device'. Our support for it is based solely on a desire to go some way to meet the Americans.

4. The effect of the 'Important Item' resolution is for the substantive question of Peking's admission to require a two-thirds majority. In practice I am not sure whether even this purpose is tenable. If my understanding is correct the 'Important Item' is something of a paper tiger. If a simple majority of members of the United Nations were in fact determined on Peking's admission they could equally overrule the 'Important Item' resolution as this of itself only requires a simple majority.

5. Last year there was a swing in voting on the Albanian Resolution in the Chinese direction: 56 against, 48 for compared with 58 against and 44 for in 1968. The 'important question' resolution was adopted 71 for, 48 against as compared with 73 for and 47 against in 1968. But the votes in 1968 were unusually unfavourable to China due to the hostility aroused by the Cultural Revolution. Taking the voting over the last decade, the pro-Peking votes on the Albanian Resolution in 1969 represented 38% of the total, as compared with 37% in 1963 and 39% in 1965. Hence last year's increase in the pro-Peking vote was not so much a new swing towards China as a return to more normal voting pattern. The American resolution still commands a substantial majority, and barring unforeseen events, looks like sustaining this majority for some time to come.

6. From Far Eastern Department's point of view now would be a good time to consider altering our stand.

7. I should add that I am under no illusions that a change in our stand would transform Sino-British relations. The Chinese have many other complaints against

---

1 *Parl. Debs.*, 5th ser., H. of C., 5 May 1970, vol. 801, col. 266.

us and their list is headed by our consulate on Taiwan. My main concern is to remove what is from Far Eastern Department's point of view basically an indefensible posture if we are sincere in seeking a vote in favour of Peking's admission. If we are to pursue this we would need to bring in United Nations (Political) Department and ask American Department how seriously the new Administration takes this Item. Before going further I should welcome your view on whether this hare should be started at all.[2]

J. A. L. MORGAN

[2] Mr Wilford, in a minute of 30 May, had much sympathy with Mr Morgan's point of view but he was unsure whether the present Government would 'eat their words' on the Important Question, although he pointed out that the French had done so 'without so much as turning a hair and with impeccable logic.' He also asked when the importance of the Consulate in Taiwan was last assessed. He presumed it had only two assets—to assist British businessmen and service liaison—and asked 'but what of *real value* do we get?

No. 190

Letter from Mr Maddocks (Hong Kong) to Mr Morgan, 12 June 1970
Confidential (FCO 21/715, FEH 2/_)

Dear John,

Sino/British Relations

Thank you for your letter FEC 3/548/2 of 2 June.[1] I look forward to discussing this large subject with you in a few weeks' time.

2. You will find that, having been here two years, I have become a strong advocate of the Hong Kong point of view. I find myself out of sympathy with the argument which starts from the assumption that the UK's political and economic relations with China are capable of substantial improvement and goes on to conclude that it is possible and wise to make some concessions in Hong Kong to achieve those purposes.

3. I find it difficult to take very seriously the prospects of a substantial improvement in political relations between UK and China. Our inheritance from the last century, the extraordinary dogmatic nature of the Chinese regime, the probable continuation of irritations and problems in Hong Kong and the relative decline of our power in the world set narrow limits to the scope for improvement. The present discounted value of our political prospects in China seems to me to be almost zero. If we stay as we are, we shall not do too badly.

4. The economic outlook seems hardly better. Although we know very little about the Chinese economy, it seems likely that her rate of economic growth is very small indeed. Dramatic changes in the total volume of her external trade are not to be expected. The present volume of UK/China trade is low in terms of the UK's trade. It is of importance to a number of firms and pressure groups, but it does not seem to me to make good commercial sense to concentrate much effort or hope on trade with China. The lesson we have reluctantly learned in the '50s and '60s is that

[1] Not printed.

the industrialised countries of the world show the really dramatic increases in trade openings for Britain. We want to do our best in trading also with the under-developed world including China but the real pickings are not there.

5. Of course I accept that we would be well advised to improve political and commercial relations with China if we can. I am simply arguing that we ought to make a very cool, realistic judgement of the probabilities, especially if there is a price to be paid for the chance of obtaining these benefits.

6. On the other side of the equation I should like to emphasise the difficulties of making concessions in Hong Kong. First of all it is a matter of opinion whether making concessions is a sensible way to deal with the Peking government. Secondly there is the particular question whether a concession can be made. If one looks towards the confrontation prisoners in Stanley and Laichikok the Hong Kong view is that it cannot. The subject was examined *ad nauseam* during Grey's detention. There is nothing new to say. I think it would be best to accept that there is no possibility of a concession on that subject. Instead of minuting that the subject should be kept under review, etc. the file should be marked 'BU1974'.[2] The number of prisoners will in the normal course of events have been reduced by then to single figures and it might be worthwhile looking at the subject afresh. But not in 1970 or 1971.

7. In other words what we might hope to get out of China—more trade, release of British subjects, political influence, better treatment for our diplomatic mission—seem to me very small objectives (or if big, have to be heavily discounted because they are unlikely to be gained) compared with the very substantial values we have at stake in Hong Kong, not only economic, but political, intelligence and human. I shall therefore argue that we ought to think more about Hong Kong and less about China (even that we should think more about improving relations with the Hong Kong government than with the Peking government!).

8. Because I am a member of the Diplomatic Service serving for the moment outside the Diplomatic Service I find myself repeating the classic criticism made in Whitehall of 'the FO', which is that 'the FO' tended to be willing to sacrifice genuine British interests especially of a commercial or financial nature for the sake of smiles and insubstantial generalities.[3]

Yours ever,
Arthur

---

2 Bring Up. A diplomatic term meaning to be reminded to look again at a subject in a specified time e.g. by looking at a file with relevant correspondence contained within it.

3 Commenting on the letter in a minute of 3 July, Mr Cradock, now with the Planning Staff, found the letter unconvincing. He thought Mr Maddocks should give more thought to the future: 'on the one hand the declining importance (and increasing embarrassment) of Hong Kong; on the other the increasing importance of China'. He also asked: 'What does HMG gain from Hong Kong? It would be interesting to see a balance sheet'.

No. 191

Mr Denson (Peking) to Mr Stewart, 15 June 1970[1]
Tel. No. 449 Routine, Confidential (FCO 21/668, FEC 3/548/2A)

Lo Kuei-po, Vice Minister of Foreign Affairs responsible for Western Europe attended The Queen's Birthday Party on 13 June accompanied by the acting Head of West European Department, the acting Chief of Protocol, the Director of the Machinery Corporation and twenty or more other Chinese. I proposed the toast to Mao Tse-tung and Lo proposed The Queen. The national anthems of the two countries were played.

2. Lo was relaxed and did his best to make himself agreeable. When the conversation turned to Sino/British relations he said that we had been in 'semi-relations' for sixteen years i.e. since the exchange of Charges d'Affaires in 1954 and that it was unfortunate that it had not been possible for us to exchange Ambassadors. I said I recalled that we had proposed this on a number of occasions but the Chinese had been unwilling to agree. Lo replied that this was because of our attitude on Taiwan and its influence on our vote on the seating of China in the United Nations. I then said that there had nevertheless been some improvement in relations since I arrived and we hoped to see this continue. We were exploring fields in which progress could most usefully be made. Trade was one such field. I should be calling on a Vice-Minister of Foreign Trade next week and would be putting to him various specific proposals and discussing the possible sale of aircraft. Lo showed considerable interest in aircraft and said that in the past we had been willing to sell only small aircraft. We had on one occasion refused to sell the Chinese three Tridents. I said that I was not aware that the Chinese had been interested in such a sale. The British Government was now willing to sell to the Chinese any aircraft in current production. I should be explaining the position in more detail during my call at the Ministry of Foreign Trade.

3. Other Chinese officials present were friendly and the general atmosphere was considerably more relaxed than last year. Letter follows.[2]

1 Repeated for information to Washington and Hong Kong.
2 Not printed.

A general election, held on 18 June 1970, returned a Conservative government with Edward Heath as Prime Minister and Sir Alec Douglas-Home as Secretary of State for Foreign and Commonwealth Affairs.

No. 192

Minute from Mr Morgan to Mr Wilford, 3 July 1970
Secret (FCO 21/715, FEH 2/1)

Hong Kong and Sino-British Relations

Mr Maddocks will be in the office on 6 and 7 July and is booked provisionally to see you on 7 July. One of the subjects he will wish to discuss is the place of Hong Kong within the broader context of Sino-British relations. In anticipation of his discussions Mr Maddocks has written expressing considerable misgivings about what he sees as our policy of bartering material interests in Hong Kong against unreliable and ephemeral expressions of goodwill from the Chinese.[3]

2. Mr Maddocks' views appear to derive from a difference of view on the basic aims of our policy. Since the comments in Mr Maddocks' letter underly [*sic*] some of the telegraphing from Hong Kong (though in a more extreme form), it is important that Mr Maddocks should be reassured that we are under no illusions about the extent of which Sino-British relations can be improved, that we shall continue to pay due heed to the substantial real interests in Hong Kong, and that our policy is based on hard-headed calculation and not on wishful thinking. Most of the points raised by Mr Maddocks have already been discussed at length, but I have some general comments on his letter.

Sino-British Relations

3. No one here is under any illusions that in the foreseeable future we can expect to have close and friendly relations with China, given the present Chinese leadership and its likely successors. There are too many deep-rooted obstacles: history, competing ideologies, our close links with the United States, our votes on the China seat in the United Nations and our views on the status of Taiwan. These impediments will persist even if the short-term problem of British subjects is resolved. The most we can aim for in the long term is a satisfactory working relationship, sufficiently well founded to ensure that the temporary incidents (e.g. events in Hong Kong) do not have a significant lasting effect on relations and are dealt with in a reasonable fashion on the basis of *our* mutual interests. In the short term we can hope for an atmosphere, in which problems like British subjects or potential disagreements can be settled sensibly. In addition of course we want our trade to continue to expand on a sound commercial basis without discrimination against our traders on political grounds. These are very limited objectives, based on a calculation of the possibilities and, we consider, within our reach without the sacrifice of real interests.

Commercial Relations

4. We should agree with much of what Mr Maddocks says in paragraph 4 of his letter. We do not expect our trade with China to outstrip our exports to markets in Europe or under-developed countries. It will always be a small proportion of overall British trade. But the level of business continues to rise and the balance is in our favour. Given that we are not bargaining away our interest elsewhere, and that the trade is conducted on a strictly commercial basis, there is every reason to work for further improvement.

The Place of Hong Kong

5. The crux of Mr Maddocks' case is that we are too ready to make concessions in Hong Kong in the search for a will-o'-the-wisp[4] improvement in Sino-British relations.

6. The long-term study of the future of Hong Kong has shown beyond any doubt that this is bound up with China. We can put out of our minds any idea of independence under UN or any other auspices. Similarly if an extension of the lease in 1997 is out of the question, sooner or later, and possibly long before 1997, we shall have to

---

3 No. 190.
4 Something that is impossible to get or achieve.

come to a settlement with the Chinese over Hong Kong. This is bound to be painful. The most we can hope for is an orderly withdrawal on terms consistent with our moral obligations to the inhabitants and one unlikely to bring international discredit on this country. This presupposes a considerable degree of Chinese restraint and moderation. It follows therefore that it is in the long-term interests of Hong Kong itself that Sino-British and Sino-Hong Kong relations should at least be sufficiently smooth that we can enter into informal talks with the Chinese on this problem with a reasonable chance of success.

7. In the short term it is scarcely necessary to re-emphasise the need for satisfactory Sino-Hong Kong relations to preserve the smooth running of the colony. Accordingly we must continually strike a delicate balance between maintaining confidence in our determination and ability to preserve our position in the Colony, and the long and short-term necessity to preserve sound relations between Hong Kong and China. This means that while we should, and indeed do, pay close attention to maintaining public morale in Hong Kong by showing that we are prepared where necessary to resist Chinese pressure, we should pay equal attention to removing irritants in relations with China where this is possible. This entails a hard look at the practical possibilities available to us, and more particularly at the question of confrontation prisoners No purpose will be served simply by ignoring the problem, even if the Chinese would allow us to do so. Given the oft-repeated Chinese statement that they regard confrontation prisoners as the most important indication of our wish to maintain reasonable relations, we must at least continue to examine the problem as much in the interests of Hong Kong as for Sino-British relations. We may still conclude, as Mr Maddocks suggests, that there is little leeway for action; but this is no reason for not taking up the issue, particularly as the local Communists show no sign of wishing to resume their campaign of violence and the success of the Hong Kong government in preserving order becomes clearer and clearer with the passage of time. In any case we cannot shelve the problem of confrontation prisoners for four years, as Mr Maddocks suggests, since we shall have to decide during next year whether we wish to recommend the Governor to re-activate the special Review Board called in 1969.

8. A further point is that of timing. Moments of 'good' relations with the Chinese are fleeting. They are clearly under instructions to ensure that difficulties should not be raised at present. We should ensure we are not losing a good occasion for extracting benefits from them at a lower cost than might be required at other times.

9. Mr Maddocks touches briefly on the problem of maintaining confidence between Whitehall and the Hong Kong Government. This is one of the questions which Hong Kong Department is keeping under constant review.[5]

J. A. L. MORGAN

---

5 Mr Wilford minuted on 7 July: 'Clearly we have failed abysmally to convince Mr Maddocks and the Government of H[ong] K[ong] what our policy towards China is, or that we have any but the most evil intentions towards Hong Kong. I find this very sad, but we shall have to go on trying. I doubt if I shall make much impression on Mr Maddocks tomorrow.'

No. 193

Record of a conversation between Mr Morgan and Mr Ma, the acting Chinese Chargé d'Affaires, in the Foreign and Commonwealth Office
29 July 1970, 5 p.m.
Confidential (FCO 21/668, FEC 3/548/2A)

Those present:

Mr J. A. L. Morgan
Mr J. L. Stevenson

Mr Ma Chia-chun
Mr Chiang En-chu
Mr L. V. Appleyard

Mr Ma began by saying that he had requested this interview to discuss several questions. He had reported to his Government what Mr Morgan had said during their last interview on 2 July. The Chinese Government had noted Mr Morgan's statement that the British Government wished to improve relations. The Chinese Government welcomed this assurance. The British Government could be in no doubt that the Chinese Government shared their desire to improve relations. The Chinese Government had made quite a few efforts and had taken several measures to achieve this end. The Chinese Government hoped that the British Government would make even more positive efforts to improve relations by releasing promptly the 95 patriotic compatriots unjustifiably detained in prison by the Hong Kong British authorities.

2. Mr Ma went on to say that on 2 July Mr Morgan had said that since 5 May onwards the Hong Kong British authorities had already released over 20 patriotic compatriots with remission of sentences; that is, before the completion of their sentence. Mr Ma said that according to his information this was not accurate. None of the compatriots concerned had been released before the completion of their sentence. The Chinese Government did not take this matter as proof that the British Government had taken concrete measures to improve relations.

3. Mr Ma said that Mr Morgan might already know that the authorities concerned in China had decided to release Mr Watt before he had served his full sentence. During his sentence, Mr Watt had displayed fairly good results in reforming himself. His confession had been satisfactory and he had shown signs of repentance. His behaviour had been good. The authorities had therefore dealt leniently with him.

4. Mr Ma ended by repeating that the Chinese Government wished to improve relations. They welcomed Mr Morgan's assurances that the British Government also wished to improve relations. But the British Government must take even more positive steps to release promptly the 95 patriotic compatriots in Hong Kong before the completion of their sentence.

5. *Mr Morgan* thanked Mr Ma for the news about Mr Watt. He confirmed that we had not received any information about this release. He asked Mr Ma if he could confirm whether the release had already taken place.

6. *Mr Ma* said that Mr Watt would be released in a matter of days.

7. *Mr Morgan* said that he was grateful for the part played by Mr Ma in transmitting to his Government our concern over British subjects detained in China. As far as the prisoners in Hong Kong were concerned, our understanding was that all of the

prisoners mentioned had received remission of sentence. He undertook to clarify the matter. Mr Ma might like to know that by 31 July there would only be 89 prisoners in Hong Kong whom Mr Ma described as 'patriotic compatriots'. He would like Mr Ma to see that the releases were going forward.

8. Mr Morgan went on to say that during their interview on 2 July he had mentioned to Mr Ma the cases of the other six British subjects detained in China. When Mr Royle subsequently spoke to Mr Ma at the Mongolian reception, he described Parliamentary interest in the case of Mr Crouch and Mr Johnston in particular. Mr Morgan asked whether, when he reported his present conversation to Mr Royle, he would be able to tell him anything new about those two cases.

9. *Mr Ma* said that according to his information, what Mr Morgan had said about the early releases of over 20 patriotic compatriots was not accurate. None of these had been released before the end of their sentence. Mr Ma said that as far as other British law-breakers in China were concerned, the Chinese authorities were dealing with their cases in accordance with Chinese law and on the merits of their individual cases.

10. *Mr Morgan* said that provided Mr Ma had no objection he would tell News Department in the Foreign and Commonwealth Office that Mr Ma had informed the British Government of the impending release of Mr Watt and that Mr Morgan had taken the opportunity to enquire about the other six detainees.

11. *Mr Ma* said that he would like to repeat that the Chinese authorities had decided to release Mr Watt before the end of his sentence. As for timing, this would be in a matter of days. The competent authorities were dealing with the cases of the other British lawbreakers in China in accordance with Chinese law and on the merits of their individual cases. If Mr Morgan wished to inform the News Department of this, this was his own affair. Mr Ma ended by repeating his assurance that the Chinese Government wished to improve relations, and repeated his statement that the British Government must take even more active steps to secure the prompt release of the 95 patriotic compatriots in Hong Kong.[1]

1 In Peking, Mr Allen was called to a meeting at the Ministry of Foreign Affairs where he received the same message (see Peking Tel. Nos. 546 and 547 dated 31 July).

No. 194

Submission from Mr Morgan to Mr Wilford, 11 September 1970
Secret and Guard (FCO 21/668, FEC 3/548/2A)

Sino-British Relations

Problem

In April this year it was agreed that we should go ahead with various cautious and limited measures to improve our relations with China. These consisted of approaching the Chinese about a direct UK/China telephone link, exploring the possibility of cultural exchanges, aircraft sales and increased contacts with Chinese officials. Action has been taken on all these points.

2. The Chinese regard the question of the release of the confrontation prisoners in Hong Kong as the most important index of our desire to improve Sino-British

relations and have linked them to the six British subjects detained in China. This is the subject of separate consideration. Meanwhile, given the present gradual improvement in our relations with China and evidence of the American Government's desire for more satisfactory relations with Peking, we should consider whether we are yet in a position to take any more fundamental steps to place our relations with China on a firmer basis.

3. The specific points examined are:

(*a*) Should we change our vote on Chinese representation in the United Nations? At present we vote for an Albanian resolution calling for the seating of Peking and the exclusion of the Nationalists. Alone among those UN members which are in favour of seating the CPR we also vote in favour of an American resolution which defines Chinese representation as an 'important' question under Article 18(2), with the result that any resolution to replace the Nationalists by the CPR requires a two-thirds majority. Should we now change our vote on the Important Question resolution?

(*b*) Should we respond to recent Chinese approaches on the possibility of upgrading our diplomatic representation to Ambassadorial level?

(*c*) Should we continue to maintain our Consulate in Taiwan?

(*d*) Should we maintain our legal position that sovereignty over Taiwan is undetermined?

Recommendation

4. I recommend that:

(*a*) We should not change our vote on the Important Question resolution in the United Nations at the coming Session. But given the more relaxed attitude on the part of the US Administration to the question of Chinese representation, it would be appropriate for us to sound them out about what their reaction would be if we were to change our vote on the Important Question resolution in 1971. If this is agreed I should be able to take preliminary soundings during my visit to Washington next month.[1]

(*b*) We should leave the question of an exchange of Ambassadors until we have come to a decision about our vote in the United Nations. The Chinese have so far refused to agree to raising our diplomatic representation because of our attitude to sovereignty over Taiwan and our voting on the China seat in the United Nations. Clearly no progress is possible on an exchange of Ambassadors until at least we change our UN vote.

(*c*) The question of our Consulate in Taiwan is also linked to the question of our UN vote in terms of Anglo-American and Sino-British relations. We should not consider a change until we have come to a decision over the UN vote. Nevertheless,

---

1 Commenting on a draft of the paper, Mr Cradock, in a minute dated 8 September, proposed taking a firmer approach believing that 'if we go with open minds, we shall soon find ourselves under pressure and reaffirming our present position.' He thought it preferable to approach them with the announcement that the Government had decided to shift its position in 1971. It would be in Britain's interest to shift position whilst there was still some credit to be gained from the Chinese. 'A position of "faithful unto death" will assist us only with the US Administration and perhaps not very much there'. Mr Wiggin of the American Department, in a minute of 14 September, hoped that the Americans would not be presented with a *fait accompli* warning 'it can sometimes be dangerous to try to bounce the Americans on something major and highly political when they seem to be engaged in a process of internal argument and evolution.' He opposed moving on this 'in the face of serious opposition from President Nixon.'

if it were decided to close the Consulate for reasons of economy, we should exploit this in our dealings with Peking.

(*d*) We should not change our line on sovereignty over Taiwan. UN (Pol) Department, American Department and the Planning Staff concur in these recommendations.

Argument

Chinese Representation in the United Nations

5. Our position at present is that we advocate the seating of Peking in the United Nations as one of the long-term objectives of British policy. Mr Warner's letter of 14 July[2] to me states:

> 'As for the overall merits of the case, the views of this Mission are still represented in a passage which we suggested for insertion in the UN policy planning paper. The gist of this was that the arrival of the Chinese in the UN would be the most frightful nuisance and might disrupt everything for the next five or ten years. Nevertheless, they will have to be admitted one day—so the sooner the better. The United Nations does not work so well and efficiently that we should lose very much by a period of instability.'

We have consistently voted since 1961 for the Soviet (later Albanian) resolution calling for the seating of Peking. At the same time we have sought to argue that Chinese representation is obviously 'important', as defined by Article 18 (2) of the United Nations Charter We justify this on the basis of the inherent importance of the question, and the deep division of opinion in the United Nations revealed by the voting on this issue. For this reason we support the American-sponsored Important Question resolution, though we are unique among member states in that we vote for both resolutions.

6. There is an implied contradiction in our position, since we advocate the early seating of Peking, while at the same time voting for a resolution which, by a procedural device, effectively prevents Peking from taking up its seat. While we took our position on the Important Question resolution with due consideration of the legal implications, it is true to say that the reason for our vote on this question was dictated by considerations of Anglo-American rather than Sino-British relations. From 1950 to 1960 we voted for a US-sponsored 'moratorium' resolution (which later became the Albanian resolution) advocating the seating of Peking. As a package deal with the Americans, to soften the impact of our change of policy, we then agreed to vote for the Important Question resolution, which was first proposed in that year. The Americans were told at Ministerial level in 1966 that we would not be prepared to support any other blocking device that might be introduced should the Important Question position crumble.

7. The Chinese have repeatedly objected to our support of what they regard as a crude procedural device.

8. The crux of the problem is the attitude of the American Government of any change. In response to my letter of 3 July, our Mission in Washington report a somewhat relaxed view of the likely American reaction. Their impression of thinking among American officials is that while they will continue to work for the continued presence of the Nationalists, they recognise, and are privately reconciled, that they will suffer an eventual defeat. It is not clear whether President Nixon or his senior

---

2 Not printed.

advisers share this view. The issue has clearly been defused to some extent in the United States. When on 4 June the Foreign Aid Budget was passed in Congress, the customary clause opposing the entry to the UN of the CPR was dropped. The fact that the clause was left out without any serious Congressional or public reaction is a sign that the climate in Washington is changing. Our Embassy has been reporting for the past few months the steady decline in influence and vociferousness of the traditional Taiwan lobby.

9. President Nixon himself has made no bones about his desire to achieve a more satisfactory relationship with China. Indeed some form of tacit understanding may be essential if the US withdrawal from Vietnam and the Guam doctrine are to succeed. Over the past year the US Government has published a series of administrative measures designed to ease trade and cultural contacts with China. Most recently they have authorised the sale of American-made engines to China as part of an Italian sale of trucks. Although the Warsaw talks have been postponed at China's insistence, the Americans have made no secret of their keenness to resume the dialogue. So far the American press and public appears to have welcomed these moves, mainly in the context of US disengagement from mainland Asia. The US Government has given no public indication that its opposition to the seating of the CPR has diminished, but the American press has not been slow to draw this conclusion. All in all, it is now a good time to consider discussing with the Americans a future change.

10. The Chinese have shown renewed interest of late in membership of the UN—on their own terms. These terms vary from time to time. A recent explicit indication came from Mr Ma, the Chinese Chargé d'Affaires, in a conversation with me on 28 May. The terms he then listed were:

(*a*) The UN must declare Taiwan to be an inalienable part of China and the Nationalists must be excluded from all UN organs.

(*b*) The UN must condemn the US for occupying Taiwan.

(*c*) The UN must repudiate the 1950 resolution branding China as an aggressor in the Korean War.

11. It is difficult to say how the Chinese would react if they were given a real chance to enter the UN without prior conditions (assuming the Nationalists had already left). During the visit of M. Bettencourt[3] to China in July the delegation gained the impression that the Chinese were seriously interested in joining and that, on balance, they would decide to go ahead on reasonable terms. Certainly there have been numerous references to China's 'lawful rights' in Chinese speeches of late. In any case, if the Chinese failed to take up their seat on the grounds that their unreasonable demands had not been met, the onus for their continued absence would be placed firmly on their shoulders.

Future of Taiwan

12. While considering the entry of China we should bear in mind the consequence for Taiwan. It seems inevitable, given the opposition of both the Nationalists and Peking to a 'two Chinas' solution, that disenfranchisement of Taiwan would be an unavoidable consequence of Peking's entry. This would be unwelcome in some UN quarters, where the Taiwanese have made themselves popular. But the exclusion

3 M. André Bettencourt, French Minister for Planning.

of 750 million mainland Chinese as against the absence of 14 million Taiwanese seems much the greater of two evils, regrettable though the exclusion of Taiwan would be. There has been speculation that the Taiwanese might conceivably opt for representation as the Government of Taiwan, but this seems unlikely.

13. It is axiomatic that if we are contemplating a change in our vote we must consult the Americans at a very early stage. Our long-term objective of working for the seating of Peking is well known but timing is the essence of the operation. Clearly unless there is a significant change in the situation it is too late this year to alter our vote, since there wouldn't be time to consult the Americans adequately. If, as seems likely, the US administration is now taking a more relaxed attitude to the China seating problem this may well be the moment to broach the subject to them. The Americans believe, for reasons set out below, that by 1971 their procedural fortification against Peking may be crumbling. We agree with them. My visit to Washington next month offers an opportunity for a preliminary sounding out of the Americans about what their reaction would be if we were to change our vote on the Important Question resolution. I would make it clear that we had no intention of presenting them with a *fait accompli* or brushing aside their views. If the American attitude was reasonably calm, we might then review the question early next year by which time the likely voting patterns in the UN for 1971 should be clearer. We could then consider the terms of which any change should be presented. There should be no great difficulty in presenting an eventual shift in Parliament or elsewhere where the conflict in consequence of our voting has been the subject of criticism over the years.

14. The American calculate in any case that by 1971 their position may be crumbling. The Canadians and Italians are still negotiating with the Chinese with a view to mutual recognition. Though there is still some way to go, the Canadians report that 'some progress' was reached in the latest round on 1 August of Sino-Canadian talks in Stockholm. If the Canadians find a mutually acceptable formula the Italians will quickly follow suit. The Canadians could still conceivably reach an agreement before discussion in the General Assembly this year; they may well do so by next year. Belgium, Austria and Luxembourg are reported to be interested in establishing relations with Peking, so that Canadian and Italian recognition could start a slide. The Belgians also recently floated a 'two China' type of resolution, pointless in itself, but indicative of new thinking on their part. The Dutch are also believed to be reviewing their own UN vote. There is speculating among diplomats in Peking that some of the African countries may now change from opposition to the seating of Peking to either abstention or a vote in favour. Moreover, Chinese policy has entered a more active phase since the middle of last year. The xenophobia of 1966/68 resulted in a swing against Peking in the UN voting in 1968, but by 1969 the position had returned more nearly to normal. We can expect Chinese blandishments to have increasing effect, especially in the Third World.

15. Last year the voting on the US resolution was 71 for, and 48 against, and 4 abstentions; on the Albanian resolution it was 48 for, 56 against, and 21 abstentions. To produce a tie on the Albanian resolution again (as in 1965) would require only four straight switches, or four changes from 'abstention' to 'for', plus four from 'against' to 'abstain'. If the current speculation about possible changes in the votes of some African countries turn out to be correct, the voting on the Albanian resolution

this year will be close. The Americans, however, seem confident that they can hold the position this year. A simple majority on the Albanian resolution would not itself bring Peking into the United Nations, since a two-thirds majority is required. But it would be an important effect on voting on the Important Question resolution which in itself only requires a simple majority.

Exchange of Ambassadors

16. For the first time in five years, the Chinese have recently on several occasions expressed interest in raising our respective diplomatic representations to Ambassadorial level. At present both sides are represented by Chargé d'Affaires of Counsellor rank. At the Queen's Birthday reception in Peking on 13 June Deputy Foreign Minister Lo Kuei-po remarked to Mr Denson that we had been in 'semi-relations' since 1954. Mr Denson replied that we had in the past proposed an exchange of Ambassadors and were ready to consider upgrading our Mission. Lo then repeated the familiar Chinese line that this was impossible at present in view of our attitude over Taiwan and its effect on our vote in the UN. Since then we have learned that during the visit of M. Bettencourt Chinese officials made the same points about Sino-British relations.

17. An exchange of Ambassadors is not an end in itself; it is simply a tangible sign of better relations. For present purposes we are adequately represented and we do not believe that other Missions in Peking derive very great advantage solely from the fact that they are represented by Ambassadors. The Chinese do however choose to be protocolaire on these matters and keep the access to Chinese officials for our Chargé at a lower level than, for example, the French Ambassador. At present we obviously cannot meet the Chinese price. We could only begin to do so if we changed our vote on the China seat in the UN. Even then there would be the obstacle of our attitude to the status of Taiwan. We should therefore defer consideration of this issue until we have come to a decision about our vote in the UN next year.

British Consulate in Taiwan

18. We have maintained a Consulate in Tamsui, not far from Taipei, the capital of Taiwan, since the middle of the 19th century. The Consulate functions under a junior officer with a small staff. Since we do not recognise the Nationalist régime, the Consulate has no formal contact with the central Taiwan Government, although for practical purposes it is obliged to deal with certain local authorities. Its presence is an irritant to Sino-British relations, and one to which the Chinese return repeatedly.

19. The Consulate is of some marginal value for political and intelligence reporting. It is of limited use to visiting British businessmen, given the restrictions on its contacts with the Nationalist authorities. In any case exports to Taiwan for 1969 only ran at £4½ million compared with £52.8 million for our exports to China. There may well be grounds at some stage for withdrawing the Consulate for reasons of economy. In which case we should exploit our decision for political ends.

20. It could be argued that withdrawing our Consulate is a gesture which we can make in isolation and without reference to moves in the UN. In my view however, from the point of view of stabilizing our relations with China, we should devote primary attention to our position in the UN. Here again, we should postpone a political decision on the Consulate until agreement has been reached with the Americans on a change in the UN vote.

Sovereignty over Taiwan

21. This is a much more complex problem than the question of the Consulate. The background is as follows.

22. In the Cairo Declaration of 1943 we joined with America and China in declaring our intention that Taiwan should be returned to China after the war. In the terms of the surrender the Japanese undertook to carry out this intention. When the Treaty of San Francisco was negotiated there was already dispute as to which was the *de jure* government of China, and this intention was not carried out. The Japanese therefore only surrendered their own sovereignty over the island, but it was not assigned to another power. For this reason we have always taken the view that sovereignty over the island is still undetermined and we cannot accept the claim of the CPR that the island is an integral part of mainland China. This view has been place on record many times by Ministers, together with the view that the wishes of the inhabitants should be consulted in any final settlement.

23. Our position on the legal status of Taiwan was taken after considerable investigation on the legal issues involved. We cannot abandon it without difficulty both from the legal point of view and in relation to our policy on self-determination. We could hardly advocate that Taiwan should become part of mainland China, when we can be in no doubt that this would be very much contrary to the wishes of the local populace. If on the other hand we were to declare for an independent Taiwan, the mainland Chinese would be deeply offended and would very likely break off relations. For these reasons I recommend that we should not change our legal position on the status of the island.

J. A. L. Morgan

No. 195

Minute by Mr Wilford, 16 September 1970
Secret and Guard (FCO 21/668, FEC 3/548/2A)

Sino-British Relations

My views are very much in accord with Mr Morgan's.[1] *Seriatim* they are:

(*a*) *The important question.* I see no point in going down with the sinking ship. If this year's vote on the main resolution shows that China is likely to achieve a simple majority in 1971 I think we should do as Mr Morgan suggests and tell the Americans that we cannot support their procedural device any longer. Even if there is no certainty of a simple majority in 1971 I would like to see us change our vote. The French had no difficulty in justifying a change and I am sure that our lawyers could produce a respectable arguments.[2]

(*b*) *Ambassadors.* I think Mr Morgan exaggerates the extent of Chinese interest. I regard any change in the status of our heads of mission as quite unacceptable to the

---

1 See No. 194.
2 The PUS, Sir D. Greenhill, noted on 18 September: 'A change on the 'important question' needs great care both with the US and the Australians. At this stage my understanding is that Mr Morgan will merely sound out the Americans. Personally I do not see how the change in our vote can be made with any dignity'.

Chinese in present circumstances and I do not think we should waste time thinking about it. I do think however that we should consider restoring our head of mission at Grade 3 level if relations continue to improve. Mr Denson will be due to leave about this time in 1971. We might consider a more senior appointment say in mid 1972 when the new Counsellor has worked himself in.

(*c*) *Consulate at Tamsui.* I agree with Mr Morgan. If we should decide to close the Consulate for economic reasons we should extract maximum credit from the Chinese for our action. This is a card which should not be thrown away unrequited.

(*d*) *Sovereignty over Taiwan.* Paragraph 22 of the submission is not wholly accurate, but I agree with the conclusion.

2. We must always bear in mind that the Chinese will always succeed in finding some stick with which to beat us. If we give up voting for the Important Question, they will still hold up Taiwan against us. If we close the Consulate they will say we support US 'occupation' of Taiwan, and so on. Nevertheless we should remove as many obstacles as we can.

3. I agree that Mr Morgan should tentatively discuss the future of the UN vote when he is in Washington.[3]

---

3 Reporting on his visit to Washington in a minute dated 29 October, Mr Morgan stated that at no point in discussions with the State Department and the White House was any disquiet expressed about a possible change in Britain's vote on the Important Item Resolution next year, and officials tended to speak in favour of the US itself taking a more positive line to secure Peking's entry. Sir D. Greenhill minuted on 1 November: 'We have to be v. careful not to be misled by the State Dept (or CIA) on what will be a v. important political decision by the President. We must keep our ears constantly to the *White House* ground' (FCO 21/663).

No. 196

Minute from Mr Royle, 25 September 1970
Secret and Guard (FCO 21/669, FEC 3/548/2B)

Sino-British Relations

I have read with interest Mr Morgan's submission on this subject.[1] I agree with the Recommendations although, as will be seen from notes that I have written in the margin, I am not altogether happy with some of the implications of the paper. I would like to make the following comments on the Recommendations:

(*a*) Any approach to the Americans must be very tentative at this stage. I do not feel that we should go as far as Mr Wilford suggests and tell the Americans at this stage[2] that we cannot support their procedural device any longer. I agree with the PUS's comment that any change needs great care with both the Australians and the Americans, and I would go further by underlining that I am not at all certain that there would be no great difficulty presenting an eventual shift in Parliament and elsewhere.

(*b*) I accept this Recommendation with no reservations and agree with Mr Wilford's note.

---

1 No. 194.
2 Mr Wilford noted in the margin: 'With respect—not what I suggested. We shd await the outcome of this year's vote.'

(*c*) I agree with Mr Morgan's recommendation at this time and also with the suggestion that if the Consulate in Taiwan was closed we should exploit this in our dealings with Peking. I feel strongly however that this Consulate should not be closed on any account. I am intending to look carefully into the economic benefits of such a proposed closure but I doubt that they will justify such a decision. As therefore will be seen from the foregoing, I hope that the Mission in Tamsui will be kept going. The recommendation will not therefore apply.

(*d*) I agree with Recommendation (*d*).

ANTHONY ROYLE

No. 197

Conversation after a dinner given by Chargé d'Affaires (Mr Denson) for Chinese officials to meet Mr Morgan, 29 September 1970
Unclassified (FCO 21/698, FEC 22/3)

Chargé d'Affaires	Mr T'ang Hai-kuang
Mr J. A. L. Morgan	Mr Chang
Mr J. N. Allan	Mr Chang Yi-chun
Mr J. D. Laughton	
Mr G. S. Barrass	
Mr H. L. Davies	
Mr A. C. Galsworthy	

In the course of a conversation about Chinese entry into the United Nations, *Mr T'ang* reiterated what he had said during a meeting that morning about Britain's position on the important question resolution; Britain's stand was unwise, and in following American attempts to use the two-thirds majority issue to obstruct Chinese entry, showed an undesirable and blind faith in American power. When asked again whether China would take her seat if voted in on an Albanian-style resolution, he replied that the rumours which had recently been prevalent that China would not enter the United Nations even if the Albanian resolution was passed, were a plot, intended to persuade people to refuse their support. He remarked that he thought that a policy on the important question resolution was a result of mistaken decisions rather than a misunderstanding of the intentions of the resolution. *Mr Morgan* said that he felt that this was an important statement which should be made clear. Was he to deduce from this talk of rumours and plots that China would take her seat immediately if the Albanian resolution was passed? *Mr T'ang* replied that he had made the Chinese position very clear, and it was up to us what conclusion we drew from it. The Chiang Kai-shek clique must be expelled and China's legitimate rights must be restored. Rumours that China would not enter the United Nations even if the motion was passed were a plot. *Mr Morgan* said that this rumour and plot had to a certain extent been spread by the Chinese Foreign Minister in discussions with Japanese journalists in 1965. However, he thought that Mr T'ang had made it very clear that the conditions no longer applied.

Mr T'ang then referred to the question of bilateral relations in particular the level of our representation. He said that it was the responsibility of Britain that relations remained at their present level. If the British Government had a desire to further improve or change them to ambassadorial relations, the British Government should recognise the Chinese People's Government as the only government of China, and also the fact that there was only one China in the world. They should change their attitude in the United Nations. Further, there was still a British Consulate in Taiwan. It was these problems which impeded development of relations. Recognition of the fact of there being only one China and full support for the expulsion of Chiang Kai-shek from the United Nations and the restoration of Chinese legitimate rights would facilitate the further development of our relations. *Mr Morgan* replied that our office in Taiwan was very small, dealing only with provincial representatives; it did not imply any recognition of the nationalist government or have any contact with it. He asked what exactly comprised the list of conditions before the United Kingdom could change the status of her relations. *Mr T'ang* replied that France had not adopted the attitude we had adopted in the United Nations. If the problem of our two Chinas attitude could be resolved then the issue would be simple. However, the question of our contacts with Taiwan was essential to the problem. There would of course have to be talks about this and China would be willing to listen to suggestions made by Britain.

Summing up, *Mr Morgan* said that he now had the following understanding from the conversation:

(i) any thought that China would not enter the United Nations if voted in was a rumour and a plot;

(ii) before any change in the level of our representation we should have to change our attitude in the United Nations and close our office in Tamsui;

(iii) we should recognise that there was only one China. Mr Morgan pointed out that in fact we already met this point by voting for the Albanian resolution.

Mr T'ang replied that his remarks could be interpreted in this way. *Mr Morgan* said that we did not think that questions relating to our Consulate in Taiwan or to the United Nations issue had any bearing on the existence of one China. We had suggested the establishment of diplomatic relations at ambassadorial level in 1950; if the Chinese continued to regard these questions as fundamental to the establishment of ambassadorial relations then we should no doubt continue with relations at Chargé d'Affaires level. In reply to a question from Mr T'ang as to whether the British Government concluded, from the fact that Taiwan was not at present under the control of China, that Taiwan was not part of China, *Mr Morgan* said that we regarded the status of the island as undetermined. *Mr T'ang* said that this view was unacceptable to China and was really simply a 'one China, one Taiwan' theory, which was a variety of the two China theory. Those who held this theory were unfriendly to China. On the improvement of relations China would have to see how far the British Government would go: this was Britain's affair. Mr T'ang would however remind Mr Morgan that present British policy would not in the long run be effective; it was moreover an obstruction to the improvement of relations between Britain and China but China was not impatient.[1]

---

1 In a separate meeting Mr T'ang repeated that further active steps were needed to release confrontation prisoners in Hong Kong before there was any change in the policy of the Chinese Government towards British subjects.

No. 198

Minute from Mr Morgan to Mr Wilford, 6 November 1970
Confidential (FCO 21/657, FEC 2/4B)

Chinese Representation in the United Nations: Background Note

The debate on Chinese representation is expected to begin in the General Assembly on 12 November. Since there are signs that some countries will change their position this year, and there has been speculation about the result of the debate, this background note has been prepared in consultation with UN (Pol) Department.

2. The item on the agenda is entitled 'Restoration of the Lawful Rights of the People's Republic of China in the United Nations'. Since 1961 the pattern has been that two draft resolutions are debated. These are:

(*a*) the American-sponsored 'Important Question' Resolution, which provides for the Assembly to re-affirm its decision in 1961 that any proposal to change the representation of China is 'important' under Article 18(2) of the Charter and therefore requires a two-thirds majority;

(*b*) the substantive 'Albanian' Resolution which calls for the restoration of the 'lawful rights' of the Chinese People's Republic to represent China and for the expulsion forthwith of the representatives of the Nationalists.

3. The Important Question Resolution itself, which is procedural, only requires a simple majority. In the past it has always passed comfortably (71-40-4 in 1969).

4. The voting on the 'Albanian' Resolution has usually been much closer. Although the Resolution has never attained even a simple majority, there was a tie in 1965. Last year the Resolution was rejected, 56-48-21.

5. We are the only country which has consistently voted for both resolutions (Mauritius voted as we did last year for the first—and probably the last—time). This year there are signs that a number of countries will change their voting in Peking's favour. The Canadians and Equatorial Guinea have recently recognised Peking, and Italy will do so today. The Malaysians have stated they will abstain on the Albanian resolution instead of voting against. Other countries, which are reported to be contemplating changing in Peking's favour, are Kuwait, Austria, the Central African Republic, Togo, Sierra Leone, Cameroon, Gabon, Dahomey,[1] Chile, Ireland and Mauritius, while several Latin-American countries may also switch. On the other hand, the Cambodians will almost certainly absent themselves this time. It is still by no means clear how many of these countries will in the end decide to change, but the best estimate we can make at present is that, for the first time, the Albanian Resolution will be carried, possibly 52-51.

6. We estimate that the Important Question Resolution is still likely to secure a comfortable majority this time, so that, even if the 'Albanian' Resolution obtains a simple majority, this will not lead to Peking's entry. But a simple majority on the Albanian Resolution could have an important effect on voting next year, particularly as other countries will possibly recognise Peking in the next twelve months. This will be even more likely if the Chinese maintain their current somewhat more

---

1 Known now as the Republic of Benin.

conciliatory foreign policy. This means that by 1971 there may well be a pronounced swing in Peking's favour.

7. We do not intend to change our vote this year. But we have told the Americans that we shall have to take a fresh look at our vote in 1971. We have also reminded the Americans that, as Ministers have told them in the past, we could not support any new proposal which appeared to be simply a device to prolong Peking's exclusion. For their part, American officials appear to be taking a much more relaxed view of the possibility of Chinese entry. We have reassured the Americans that there is no question of our changing our vote without full consultation with them first.

8. Our Mission in New York have been authorised to let other delegations know that we shall not change our vote this year. We do not intend to reveal to any country other than the United States that we shall be looking again at our vote in 1971.[2]

J. A. L. MORGAN

2 Sir A. Douglas-Home noted: 'Yes. But what will be our attitude to Taiwan in 1971?'

No. 199

Mr Denson (Peking) to Sir A. Douglas-Home, 10 November 1970[1]
Tel. No. 752 Immediate, Confidential (FCO 21/657, FEC 2/4B)

UKMIS New York Tel. Nos. 2772 and 2773:[2] Chinese Representation in the United Nations.

The Chinese made clear during Morgan's visit that they regard our voting in favour of the 'Important Question' as unfriendly and the result of a mistaken decision to follow the Americans rather than a difference in interpretation of the intention of the resolution. While our policy of voting this year both for the Albanian Resolution and for the 'Important Question' does not represent a change on our part, the attitude of the Chinese has changed in that they are showing a much keener interest in entering the United Nations. They appear to have dropped all pre-conditions apart from the expulsion of Taiwan and they have recently been expressing fears to Western Representatives (see records of conversations with the Norwegian Chargé d'Affaires and the Danish Ambassador sent by bag)[3] that if Taiwan is not expelled soon, their entry may be blocked by another device thought up by the Americans e.g. a 'Divided Nations' Resolution.

If, as now seems possible, the Albanian Resolution contrary to earlier predictions is carried, the 'Important Question' will for the first time be the real obstacle to Chinese entry and the argument we used during Morgan's visit that it was a 'paper tiger' will no longer hold up.

1 Repeated Immediate for UKMIS New York, Priority for Washington, Moscow, Paris, and Tamsui.
2 Not printed. These telegrams considered the merits of making a statement explaining the reasons behind the UK's vote and contained a draft text.
3 Not printed.

2. We are certain by supporting the 'Important Question' to damage our relations with China and probably slow down progress which is being made in various fields. I assume that this was taken into account when the decision was made. But I think we shall be compounding our difficulties with the Chinese if we at the same time make a statement on the lines proposed which however defensive from our point of view will be regarded by the Chinese as the ultimate in hypocrisy. We shall in their words be lifting up one hand to knock it down with the other. The last sentence of the draft is likely to be regarded by the Chinese as particularly gratuitous and could, in my view, only cause irritation.

3. While I fully recognize the advantage of a statement in the United Nations context, I recommend that in the interests of Sino-British Relations no, repeat no, statement should be made. The absence of a statement might give rise to speculation but would it not suffice if advance assurance on our voting this year were given in private to our friends and to any countries we judged sensitive on the 'Important Question' Resolution. If we could at the same time indicate that next year we should be reconsidering our position (and this were in due course relayed to the Chinese) it would do something to mitigate the damage of this year's vote.[4]

4 Mr Denson's advice was taken and no statement was made about the vote but only the Americans were told of the intention to take a fresh look at the vote next year (FCO Tel. No. 1693 to UKMIS New York, 12 November).

No. 200

Letter from Mr Boyd (Washington) to Mr Morgan, 12 November 1970
Confidential and Guard (FCO 21/663, FEC 3/304/1)

Dear John,

China/US Relations

You asked for some thoughts on China/US relations by the time of this year's debate on Chinese representation.

2. You will no doubt remember that when you were in Washington Al Jenkins of ACA spoke of the testimony on China given recently by Marshall Green before the Foreign Affairs Committee of the House. Jenkins said that this contained no surprises but was the best recent official summary of US policy. I had hoped to send you a copy of this before Marshall Green's visit to London. However, the State Department tell me that release of a bowdlerised version of the testimony (which was of course given in a closed session) is being held up deliberately until after the China debate. I have asked whether we could be given an earlier sight of the testimony and have been told that this is under consideration. Congressional sensitivities are of course involved; the transcript is technically the property of the House committee. Nevertheless I would not put it past Marshall Green to have pulled a copy from his hat when in London.

China Policy: The approach

3. Pending confirmation of such an eventuality it may still be useful if I attempt to sum up the Washington end of China/US relations. US China policy was recently

described to me by a member of the White House staff as 'whirling around on one spot'. This may be true as of now; but the expression somewhat undersells the efforts towards an improvement in relations that have been made by the present Administration since early 1969. It is hard now to remember how hidebound and for how long the Democrats had allowed themselves to remain on the China question. The nearest they got to an act of modernisation were the trial balloons launched by Humphrey and Katzenbach in the summer of 1968 (on which Far Eastern Department submitted at the time). The reasons for this hesitation were in part domestic; the Democrats were after all, the party which had lost China. But there was also a significant philosophical hang-up.

4. As Dr Kissinger never tires of pointing out, the Democratic approach to foreign policy particularly as expressed in President Kennedy's 1960 inaugural, was both ideological and undiscriminating. Mr Rusk (who learned to deal with the Chinese at the time of Korea) remained consistently resistant to pressures from below in the direction of a more flexible China policy. Notoriously, Vietnam was for him a defensive war against Greater China. In contrast, the present Administration with Dr Kissinger as its spokesman, has stressed the need in dealing with foreign countries to distinguish between issues of primary and secondary importance for the US and between areas of overlapping or conflicting interest. This new approach is supposed to safeguard the essential interests of the US while permitting greater flexibility in diplomacy; and to save the US direct expense of both energy and money, by greater use of traditional balance of power tactics.

5. I make no apology for these remarks on theory. There is ample evidence from Kissinger's off-the-record press briefings that the academic approach, particularly the rather Newtonian view of relations between countries, governs the way the Administration tackles the specific policy problems. As applied to China the Kissinger view of life means first of all that China has become something of a second order problem for the United States. Ideological objections to the Chinese form of government are rarely voiced. China is seen of course still as a potential great power but one which in the meantime remains gravely hindered by internal dissensions and inefficiencies and under serious threat from the USSR. But as a problem for the immediate future it has, I should judge, become of much less urgency to the Administration than Japan, Europe or the Mediterranean. Second, although this has, to my knowledge, never been set out in terms, it seems clear the Administration—having first banished the idea of an overwhelming threat—has no hesitation in identifying the following areas of overlapping interest with China: fear of the USSR; cultural, commercial and technological exchange; biological survival (e.g. the pollution question); US retrenchment in Asia, possibly even stabilisation of South-East Asia after Vietnam. In contrast, the only area of obviously conflicting interest (since in the Kissinger approach not much attention is paid to the simple, ideological prejudices of opponents) is Taiwan. The President's own thinking on these points, as far as it can be identified, seems to be notably 'liberated'. Although the Department does not approve of triangle talk. Mr Nixon has said freely that he sees China as a useful counterweight to the Soviet Union. And although the prickly question of diplomatic relations does not seem—precisely because prickly—to be high on his list of problems, he made a point of speaking recently of the 'Peoples Republic of China'.

The Warsaw Talks

6. In this context Warsaw has been something of a disappointment. The Americans had hoped that the Chinese would be ready to discuss questions falling in the field of overlapping interest, preferably before but at least in parallel with Taiwan. At the meetings which have taken place under the current Administration this proved not to be the case. It is now realised in the Department that the Chinese interest in coming to the table in Warsaw is very much a function of the temperature on the Sino/Soviet border. Nevertheless the Americans remain anxious to continue the meetings. They have made this clear to the Chinese by repeated public statements (most recently on 13 October) and also privately, between Missions, in Warsaw. As Al Jenkins mentioned to you there was, after the events of May in Cambodia, a local theological debate about whether the ball lay in the American or Chinese court. In practice the Americans have taken no chances about this and can have left the Chinese in no doubt about their desire to continue.

7. Meanwhile it would be hard to pretend that the talks had succeeded in bringing the parties closer together. They have been used by the Americans to inform the Chinese officially of the series of moves taken by the Administration to break down the old apparatus of containment on the American side; to stress the desire of the US for better relations; but to underline that the US cannot, in this cause, discard *le minimum*, i.e. its continued political and defence relationship with Taiwan. This approach has, quite rapidly, reached the limits of its effectiveness. There are various further steps the Americans can take, particularly in the field of non-strategic trade. But as Al Jenkins phrases it 'it takes two to tango'. At the recent House hearings notably few reservations were expressed about the desirability of an improvement in relations with China. But there were some doubts about how far it was desirable for the US to continue to take steps unilaterally and unrequited. The Administration can and does make the argument that steps it has taken are, even without a specific Chinese response, in the interest of the US. But in practice it may feel that there is a limit to how far it can go without making itself look slightly ridiculous.

Domestic Pressures

8. At this point it may be useful if I say a word on the domestic climate. Domestic pressures on the Administration in connection with the New China policy are actually few. While there are of course differences within the Administration on specific points (the dispute over the recent sale of truck engines to China is a case in point) no-one in Government appears to dispute the broad direction of policy. In wider Washington, as a member of the CIA remarked to you recently, the China Lobby is dead (there was indeed a most amusing 'obituary' in *The Washington Post* last January which I sent to Len Appleyard). The conservative business interests which stood behind it are now, if anything, looking for greater speed in dismantling hindrances to trade with the CPR; certainly they are no longer pressing the other way. As far as the wider public is concerned Mr Nixon seems to have secured general agreement that China is China; that its government resides in Peking; and that the time is long overdue for an improvement in relations with it. However it is important to draw a line between this position and readiness to concede that, in the interests of better relations with Peking Taiwan can be dumped. At the recent House hearings, for instance, a member of the Committee made the point that he approved of the general direction of Administration policy but

that when it came to a 'sell-out' of Taiwan in the UN there were 'many hard hats in the House'. They would be watching the President very closely on this point. I think that this is a fair expression of the sentiment of the House and the President will think twice before confronting this sentiment directly. Bill Brown of ACA shares this view, so does Herb Levin at the White House.

Chinese representation

9. There is of course no question of a change in the US vote on Chinese representation this year, but Brown confirmed to me once again last week the obvious, that after this year's debate the US will be bound to take a look in depth, as it has not yet, at its whole Chinese representation strategy. Brown himself thinks that the battle within the Administration will be heated. Outside, positions have long been taken up by the liberal academics. People like Doak Barnett argued at the House hearings that time was running out and that the US should take the initiative in working towards some form of dual representation. A letter to *The New York Times* on 28 October signed by the familiar Harvard gang argued that some such effort begin this year. This was all predictable. Of more interest are the various private positions staked out, for next year, by members of the State Department or other agencies. I have so far identified three clear strands:

(*a*) The US should face the fact that there cannot be two Chinas in the UN, it should jump as elegantly as possible on the China bandwagon.

(*b*) The US should maintain its present policy and should go down with at least the appearance of a fight though perhaps with a concealed smile.

(*c*) The US should, while there is yet time, place itself in the van of those working for a Two Chinas solution (by whatever name).

10. I have the feeling that the first of these views may have the support of Al Jenkins. He speaks freely about the impossibility of solving the great international issues without Chinese co-operation. As you know, he was, at the time of your visit, extremely disturbed by preliminary reports that the Vice-President had given an open-ended assurance of US support in the UN to C.K. Yen (Bill Brown tells me that the actual record did not confirm this). He has also told us before now that he thinks that the Nationalists could survive very nicely outside the UN. But it is hard to see how the transformation at (*a*) could be accomplished with a total and inelegant break with Taiwan. Solution (*b*) is supposed to have been dreamed up by Bill Gleysteen in INR who is close to Marshall Green. I can see a lot to be said for it. Solution (*c*) is of course the solution with the greatest theoretical appeal, and is thus much favoured by the academics. We have occasionally (e.g. when John Denson was here) heard members of the State Department toy hopefully with the idea that the Chinese might come round to something of the kind. We never fail to make the point that this seems to us quite unrealistic. The pre-requisite from the US point of view would of course be getting the Nationalists to look at it—a pretty daunting prospect.

11. For the time being the public position of the Administration is consistent with both (*b*) and (*c*) though not with (*a*): the sticking point for the US is the expulsion of Taiwan. Some fuss was made in the press last week following remarks to the effect by the President's Press Secretary. *The Washington Post* claimed that this marked a move to a new Two Chinas policy. In fact there is nothing new in the US position

which was set out very clearly in the annex to the hearings of the Symington Subcommittee on Taiwan, held in November 1969 (my letter 2/9/2 of 29 July,[1] enclosing the transcript refers). The only fear in ACA is that by saying anything at this point the US may become tied to one particular chariot or another, in advance of the forthcoming policy review. Meanwhile the US position is one that you could call 'principled yet flexible'.

12. At this stage there is little point in guessing which, if any, of the approaches (*a*)—(*c*) will appeal to the President who himself is never one to take a decision before he has to. All one can say is that the factors to be weighed will have to include:

(i) Congressional sentiment (and as I say views in the House, of less formal importance in foreign affairs than the Senate; but in a matter traditionally carrying such domestic overtones a pretty good guide to US sentiment, will militate against solution (*a*));

(ii) the effect of the seating of China on the one hand or of too evident a defeat of the US on the other on the rather fragile support enjoyed by the UN among the wider US public (more Americans than ever before, according to Dr Gallup, would like to see China 'admitted' to the UN but still much less than a majority.)

(iii) the repercussions of the choice on the US position both at the UN and elsewhere, particularly in Asia; and finally

(iv) the effect on the organisation itself of the seating of Peking (it can be argued, and some here are ready to do so, that the presence of Peking in the UN would be a more unwelcome distraction for the USSR than for the West).

13. In short, we are making no bets on Chinese representation in 1971 at this point, but can guarantee an enthralling ballgame.

Yours ever,
JOHN

1 Not printed.

No. 201

Sir Colin Crowe (UKMIS New York) to Sir A. Douglas-Home
20 November 1970, 1.15 a.m.[1]
Tel. No. 2953 Priority, Confidential (FCO 21/657, FEC 2/4B)

My IPT:[2] General Assembly: Chinese Representation.

The voting of the Albanian Resolution turned out roughly as expected. The only switches of voting of which we had no previous indication were those of Botswana (from a negative vote to an abstention) and of Mauritius (from a positive vote to a negative one). But it is interesting that as many as nine waverers changed from negative votes to abstentions in spite of heavy pressure both here and in capitals

1 Repeated for information immediate to Peking, Moscow, Washington and Tamsui; and saving to Paris and Hong Kong.
2 Not printed.

from the Americans. The US Mission told us this afternoon that they had hoped to prevent some of the 'defections', particularly those of Ireland and Botswana: virtually their only success was with Mauritius (they say they achieved this by pointing out that in view of Mauritius' abstention in 1968 and a positive vote in 1969 the best way of showing its neutrality would be a negative vote this year).

2. The slippage on the Important Question Resolution was rather greater than we had expected. One reason for this may be that some countries—eager to follow the swing in favour of Peking but reluctant to damage their relations with Taiwan, e.g. Chad, Guyana and Trinidad—may have compromised by withdrawing their support for the Important Question Resolution while maintaining their position on the Albanian Resolution.

3. First reaction amongst delegations are that the psychological effect of a simple majority for the Albanian Resolution plus the heavy erosion of support for the Important Question clearly imply that the latter resolution would fail if it came to the vote next year, i.e. that, if the Assembly was faced next year with the same two Resolutions, the result would be immediate seating of Peking and expulsion of the Nationalists.

4. Against this background and in the light of the abortive moves by the Belgians, Ghanaians (who nearly launched a last minute move to 'sanitize' the Albanian Resolution by asking for separate voting on the clause about expelling the representative of Chiang Kai Shek) and Tunisians in this year's consideration of the problem, there is also a strong feeling that there will be a different scenario next year. The statements in the debate by the sponsors of the Albanian Resolution made clear that they suspect that the United States intend next year to launch a Two Chinas initiative in the hope that this will attract enough votes from the large number of delegations which do not wish to see the Nationalists expelled, to fog the issue and buy more time. The US Mission here confirmed to us that a major review of US policy towards the Chinese Problem will now be undertaken in the light of the result of this year's debate.

5. We shall discuss the situation with the Americans and other friendly delegations and comment further in due course.

No. 202

Letter from Mr McCluney to Mr Moon (No. 10), 2 December 1970
Confidential (PREM 15/196)

Dear Peter,

You wrote on 25 November about the Prime Minister's conversation with Sir John Rodgers, MP, on the subject of Taiwan.[1]

I attach a background note to cover the points raised by Sir John Rodgers. Sir John has recently written to the Foreign and Commonwealth Secretary on the same matter—I attach a copy of his letter and of the Secretary of State's reply.[2] He has now

---

1 Sir John Rodgers, Conservative MP for Sevenoaks, had paid a visit to Taiwan in October 1970.
2 Not printed.

accepted the Secretary of State's invitation to discuss our relations with Taiwan and he and Sir Tufton Beamish are calling on 8 December.[3]

Yours ever,
IAN MCCLUNEY

ENCLOSURE IN NO. 202

Taiwan

On our recognition of the Chinese People's Republic in 1950 we withdrew recognition from the Nationalist authorities in Taiwan, who still claim to be the Government of the 'Republic of China'. We have stated on numerous occasions that in our view sovereignty over the island of Taiwan is undetermined. We have nevertheless maintained our Consulate there; in fact, since the mid-19th century. The Consul is instructed to maintain relations only with officials of the Taipei municipality and the Taiwan Provincial Government. This latter is theoretically one of the many provinces of the 'Republic of China'. As Sir John Rodgers says, he is under instructions not to deal officially, or to mix socially, with officials of the central 'Nationalist Government'. The Consul carries out normal consular functions and does general political and economic reporting to the Foreign and Commonwealth Office. He and his staff are under instructions to promote British exports as actively as possible within the limits set by our non-recognition of the Nationalists.

2. There is no doubt that the Nationalist authorities would be very happy to talk officially with our Consul, and it would make life easier for him to be 'accredited' to them. However we cannot allow British representatives anywhere to treat Nationalist officials as if we recognised their Government. A motive in the Nationalist willingness to improve relations is to discomfort our relations with Peking. Our relations with Peking, despite their vicissitudes, are patently of far greater importance, in both the short—and the long—term, than our relations with Taiwan, and we cannot permit them to be jeopardised for the sake of Taiwan. The Chinese have consistently cited the presence of our Consulate in Taiwan as one of the impediments to an exchange of Ambassadors. The Chinese keep a close eye on our relations with Taiwan. This year they protested to the Foreign and Commonwealth Office because a Nationalist flag was flying at the Do-It-Yourself Exhibition at Olympia.

3. The most tangible and immediate benefit of our relations with Peking is in fact our trade. Last year our exports to China totalled some £52 million, and there is scope for considerable growth. There is in particular a real possibility for substantial sales of civil aircraft. It would be foolish to put this at risk for the sake of our trade with Taiwan, which last year amounted to £4.7 million, less than 10% of that with China.

4. We are considering urgently, nevertheless, ways of improving our share of Taiwan's imports. We are looking at the possibility of strengthening the Consul's local commercial staff. But even if our relations with Taiwan were completely normal, there would frankly be no prospect of British sales becoming comparable with

---

3 In a reply dated 7 December, Mr Moon noted a comment by the Prime Minister that 'our Consul should use every device to increase trade with Taiwan without giving Peking a chance to complain'.

those of the United States or of Japan, whose links with Taiwan are, for differing reasons, far closer than ours could ever be, and who between them now hold 67% of the market; nor could they ever be expected to compare favourably with even our present level of sales to China.

5. Sir John Rodgers mentions as an obstacle to the expansion of British trade with Taiwan the difficulty experienced by British businessmen in obtaining visas for Taiwan. The Free Chinese Centre to which Sir John alludes does to some extent act as a focus for Nationalist sympathisers, but has no official standing. We should certainly not allow it to acquire the function of issuing visas. For Her Majesty's Government to permit the Nationalists, at this stage, to set up in this country facilities amounting to those of a regular consulate would be to invite quite disproportionate trouble from Peking. The Nationalist authorities themselves occasionally make difficulties for British businessmen, by refusing to admit those who have ever visited Communist countries, including even Yugoslavia.

6.[4]

[4] Paragraph 6 has been retained under Section 3(4) of the Public Records Act 1958 and 1967.

No. 203

Submission from Mr Morgan to Mr Wilford, 10 December 1970
Confidential (FCO 21/658, FEC 2/4C)

Chinese Representation in the United Nations

Problem

In the present General Assembly for the first time the resolution calling for the seating of Peking and the expulsion of the Nationalists received a simple majority. In the light of this new development what should our attitude be towards the question of Chinese representation at the next General Assembly and in the Security Council? The Minister of State instructed on 7 December that 'we must adopt a clear and unequivocal attitude on this and should state our position not later than March 1971'.

Recommendation

2. I recommend:

(*a*) That we should now proceed to the next stage in our consultations (at official level) with the Americans (approved by Mr Royle on 25 September)[1] to seek their reaction to a change in our vote on the Important Question resolution if it is again tabled.

Draft letter to Washington submitted.[2]

(*b*) That we should maintain our present instructions to our Delegate at the Security Council.

Draft letter to UK Mission, New York, submitted.

UN (Pol) Department, American Department and Legal Advisers concur.

[1] No. 196.
[2] None of the draft letters are printed.

Argument
Approach to the Americans

3. The simple majority in favour of the Albanian Resolution for the first time has created a new situation. There was a pronounced swing towards Peking in the voting this year. The vote on the substantive 'Albanian Resolution' was 51-49-25, as compared with 48-56-21 last year when it was rejected. Although the Important Question Resolution was again adopted the majority was substantially reduced: 66-52-7, as opposed to 71-48-4 last year. The tide in favour of Peking is gathering momentum and could now be irreversible. The preliminary view of our Delegation in New York is that the Important Question Resolution could well fail next year, if it came to the vote.

4. At present, many members of the United Nations, including the Americans, are reassessing their policies on Chinese representation. We have been given an assessment of our Embassy in Washington of American thinking (Mr Boyd's letter of 12 November).[3] This was prepared before voting took place. It is apparent from Mr Boyd's letter that the Americans were far from clear in their own minds how best to proceed. So far they have been unexpectedly relaxed on the question, although they mounted a lobbying campaign shortly before the vote. Our Embassy believe that American public opinion is disposed to accept the Administration's gradual adjustment to the reality of Peking's existence. There is some pressure from the business community to improve contacts in the hope of opening up a considerable market. Congressional opinion against Peking's entry seems to have substantially diminished, although opposition has been expressed to a move which would exclude the Nationalists.

5. Our Mission in New York have told us that 'a major review of US policy towards the Chinese problem will now be undertaken in the light of the result of this year's debate' (UKMIS telegram No. 2953, paragraph 4).[4] In the context of our relations with Peking, there is considerable advantage in clearing our lines with the Americans as soon as practicable (this is set out in some detail in paragraph 4 of the draft letter).

6. There has been some speculation that the Americans might drop the Important Question Resolution next year, and seek another device to delay Peking's entry. Judging by the debate in the Assembly the most likely proposal is one in which the acceptance of the CPR would be coupled with the separate representation of Taiwan. The US speech gave this impression; Tunisia and Ghana also supported Taiwanese representation. We have consistently opposed a solution on such lines, and we must continue to regard it as unrealistic, given the uncompromising opposition to it by both Peking and the Nationalists. The Nationalists' adherence to their claim to represent the whole of China remains a cornerstone of their policy. It will be most difficult for the Americans or any other country to devise a formula acceptable to them.

7. Sir Denis Greenhill has minuted that we must pay close attention to the views of the White House in all this. It is essential that we should know the President's own thinking; and I have mentioned this point in my draft to Washington.

8. It has been suggested that we should approach certain Commonwealth countries at the same time. But since our voting after 1961 has been based essentially

3 No. 200.
4 No. 201.

upon the agreement which we reached at that time with the Americans, it is more appropriate for us to discuss the question with the American alone in the first instance. If the American reaction would not be unacceptably hostile, and if agreement is secured here to change our vote, then it would be appropriate to inform the Canadians, Australians, and New Zealanders before any public indication is given of the decision.

Chinese Representation in the Security Council

9. We have been asked whether we wish to make any change of substance in the contingency brief, prepared by our Mission in New York, to cover any move to oust the Nationalists from the Security Council and admit the CPR representative. (Mr Parsons' letter of 13 November to Mr Lambert.) The question will have added point next year, when the UK Representative will be President of the Security Council during January, the first month of the newly composed Council.

10. Mr Wilford had minuted that it could be argued that, although the majority of the members of the United Nations wish to see Peking seated at the General Assembly, her admission to the Assembly is frustrated by what amounts to a blocking device (the Important Question Resolution), and that therefore the matter should be pursued elsewhere. For a long time we have publicly maintained that the proper forum for a decision on this question is the General Assembly. We would in any event not wish to change our policy in the Council at least until we have made some headway in our discussions with the Americans.

11. If the necessary votes were found to support the seating of Peking in the Security Council, this would be a legitimate act of the Council and we should have to accept it. Thereafter the CPR representative on the Council would no doubt veto any proposal to admit Taiwan as a new member.

12. It is unlikely that the issue would arise in some other part of the United Nations such as ECOSOC or a specialised agency.

13. It could be that we should end up in the minority on a vote approving Peking's admission. The Chinese would then undoubtedly criticise us. Nevertheless our stand is fully consistent with our frequently stated view that Chinese representation should be decided in the General Assembly. I do not think that possibility of Chinese criticism should deter us.

Background

14. Our overall strategy in the Security Council is to support moves designed to block a challenge to the credentials of the Nationalist representative. If, despite these efforts, a challenge to his credentials is put to the vote, our representation is then under instructions to abstain.[5]

J. A. L. MORGAN

---

[5] Mr Wilford, in a minute of 11 December, agreed matters should be taken forward, following the Prime Minister's forthcoming visit to Washington. Mr Greenhill, on 14 December, also agreed but noted 'I very much doubt if the Americans will be in a hurry to clear this all up so early in 1971.'

No. 204

Letter from Mr Morgan to Mr Elliott (Washington), 23 December 1970
Confidential and Guard (FCO 21/658, FEC 2/4C)

Chinese Representation in the United Nations

We were grateful for John Boyd's assessment in his letter of 12 November of American thinking on China.[1] The situation has now changed, with the new vote on the Albanian Resolution, and we see from UKMIS telegram number 2953[2] that the Americans are undertaking a major review of policy on this issue.

2. You will recall that when I was in Washington I sounded out the Americans tentatively about what their reaction would be to a change in our vote on the Important Question Resolution next year. We gather that this was not touched on in the discussions between the Prime Minister and the President. Ministers have accordingly agreed that you should now make a formal approach to the Americans to seek their considered reactions to a possible change. No decision has yet been taken, and we shall need American views before we submit further. It seems from John Boyd's letter that, at official level, the Americans are fairly relaxed over this issue. This assessment was confirmed in our discussions with Al Jenkins in London last month. At the same time, we think it important that we should also be able to assure Ministers that the views of the White House on this matter are clearly known and have been taken fully into account. We leave it to you to decide at what level the approach should be made.

3. It might help if I go through the factors which dispose us to consider a change in our vote. We have supported the Important Question Resolution now for the past ten years, essentially in the interests of Anglo-American relations. It is obvious that the policy of the American Government towards China is evolving and that the United States would like to achieve at least an understanding with the Peking Government in the interest of their own redeployment in Asia. Judging from John Boyd's letter, this evolution has gained broad support from the American public and has met little real opposition in Congress.

4. At the same time, our own relations with Peking are entering a new phase. The Chinese have in the course of this year released all those British subjects about whom we have expressed particular concern. We should hope to put Sino-British relations on a firm, long-term basis, not only because we believe China should be brought more fully into the international community, but also in terms of essential future British interests, in particular, Hong Kong. If, as is now more possible, Peking secures entry in 1971, we should be reluctant to be seen to be going down with a sinking ship. We should then be left among the small band of countries against whom the Chinese could bear a permanent grudge. As I said to the State Department, we could be in an exclusive doghouse in Peking which could hamper the work of our mission—and its usefulness as a source for the Americans. This would be doubly unfortunate in view of our strong public statements over many years, and notably the Secretary of State's speech this

---

1 No. 200.
2 No. 201.

year, in favour of Peking's admission. For Sino-British relations in the short-term, the sooner we can reach a decision, the better. Our relations have improved markedly over the past six months. We should make the most of the opportunity created by any decision to change our vote, and the present climate of our relations, to win concessions across-the-board, particularly in the matter of trade and the position of our mission in Peking. We might well have to wait a very long time for a more favourable moment.

5. There has been some speculation that the American Government might drop the Important Question Resolution next year in favour of some other stratagem. Ministers have made clear in the past that we could not support any new proposal which amounted to yet another device to delay Peking's admission. The State Department should be reminded of this. There have been increasing reports that the US administration may be turning now to a variant of the 'two Chinas' solution, as some way of securing the continued representation of Taiwan while acquiescing in the entry of the Chinese People's Republic. Once again, we have made clear that we could not support such a tactic. We argued strongly against the Belgian proposal on similar lines earlier this year. We maintain the view that a 'two China' solution remains unrealistic, in the view of the implacable opposition to it of both Peking and the Nationalists.

6. You will have noticed that hitherto in our exchanges we have simply said that we are considering changing our vote. No decision has been reached about whether this might mean abstention or a vote against. This is a difficult problem and the strength of American reactions would certainly be a factor in our decision.

7. Any change in our position will require an explanation, but this is of course not something you need to discuss with the Americans. We do not pretend that this would be easy, but other countries have managed the change without very much difficulty, and the Canadian delegate's statement this year sets their own course by saying: 'I wish to make it clear, however, that if in our judgement continued support of such a Resolution could in the future frustrate the will of the General Assembly, my Government will change its position.' In any case, the adoption of the Albanian Resolution has created a new situation, and we can expect a general realignment of positions on this matter throughout the United Nations. It is true to say that virtually all the Parliamentary Questions we have had for many years on Chinese representation have been based on the proposition that we were not doing enough to secure Peking's admission.

8. You could reaffirm that these are our preliminary views and that no final decision has been taken and that we have not consulted other governments. We are conscious that the Americans might be tempted to delay their reply. We do not wish to appear to be rushing our fences, but, for the reasons set out in paragraph 4 of this letter, we should be extremely reluctant to go along with a long delay. We are under firm instruction by Ministers to reach a clear and unequivocal position by the first months of next year. We therefore hope that the Americans will be able to let us have their views in good time.

9. You will have seen from my letter to Tony Parsons of 21 December[3] that we do not intend changing our attitude to this question in the Security Council.

J.A.L. MORGAN

3 Not printed.

No. 205

Briefing Note on Sino-British Relations, January 1971
Confidential (FCO 21/831, FEC 3/548/1)

Policy and Scope for Initiatives

The Prime Minster has asked for a Note setting out broadly our policy towards China and what scope for initiatives on our part we see for the future. He has also enquired what the Chinese regard as their outstanding problems relating to Hong Kong, and, in particular, whether these are primarily the imprisoned Communists.

Policy and Objectives

2. Our present objectives towards China are:

(*a*) To normalise and improve our bilateral contacts.

(*b*) To increase the share of the Chinese market, in particular, in capital goods.

(*c*) To help to bring China into a healthier relationship with the rest of the world, and, in particular:

(i) to useful membership of the United Nations, and

(ii) to participate in international agreements, such as the Nuclear Test Ban Treaty, which are of limited meaning without her.

(*d*) To maintain the peace and prosperity of Hong Kong.

(*e*) To maintain and improve our presence in Peking, which gives us an exceptionally high level of specialist Chinese expertise. This is of outstanding use in the context of intelligence exchanges with our allies.

Background

3. However erratic China's development, with its vast population and nuclear capability it is bound to occupy a commanding position in the Far East and considerable influence throughout the world. Sino-British relations in the longer term should be seen in the context of the Sino-Soviet dispute. The best prediction is that Sino-Soviet hostility will continue. The Chinese are likely to be increasingly interested in improving Western contacts and learning of political and military developments in Western Europe. They have shown an interest in the health of NATO, and, while they may go through the motions of denouncing the EEC, they may also have an interest in its development. There is also our and Europe's long-term interest in improving contacts with China and assisting in her eventual emergence. The Soviet Union and the United States may be disqualified from doing so. There is, therefore, a valuable political role we could play in Peking. At present it is the French who reap the benefits of acting as the European interlocutor of the Chinese.

Scope for Initiatives

4. All our policy objectives are facilitated in varying degrees by expanding contacts. Our initiatives should take the form of leaving the Chinese in no doubt that we are prepared to normalise and improve relations. During the last few years the Chinese have contracted virtually all their foreign policy activities. We should be ready to respond when they are prepared to take moves towards expansion in any direction of use to us. In the last year we have taken modest steps in such things as agreeing in principle on a direct telephone link between Peking

and London and issuing invitations to scientific congresses (not accepted). The Chinese, for their part, have released all those British subjects detained in China about whom we had expressed particular concern. The remaining four believed to be still detained worked in various capacities for the Chinese Government and had lived there for many years. We should nevertheless continue to ask the Chinese about their whereabouts, but without regarding their detention as a serious obstacle to improving relations. At the initiative of our mission in Peking, the Chinese agreed to a BBC Panorama team paying a visit to China. We should encourage further press contacts. There have been two delegations of British businessmen in the last few months. The Chinese Government now play a full part in the formal functions of diplomatic life in London and have increased social relations with FCO officials.

5. Our role in Peking is limited as the Chinese regard us as being in semi-relations. One option open to us is to send back a Minister to head our Mission as Chargé d'Affaires *en titre*. This we could do at any time and the Chinese are likely to reciprocate. (Both Missions are now headed by officers of Counsellor rank). A British Ambassador would be received at a higher level in Peking and could have a greater influence on Chinese thinking. We have more than once offered to appoint an Ambassador so the Chinese are in no doubt that we should be prepared to raise the level of our representation if they chose to waive their preconditions. These, in the past, have been that we should change our policy on three points:

(*a*) our support for the Important Item Resolution on Chinese representation in the United Nations;

(*b*) our maintenance of a Consulate in Taiwan; and

(*c*) our statements that we consider sovereignty over the island to be undetermined.

We are considering a change in (*a*) (see paragraph 6 below). Nevertheless, the Chinese have been told that we are not prepared at present to change our policies on all three points, indeed to change our position on (*c*) involves tricky legal issues and it is not easy to see who in the future can 'determine' the sovereignty over Taiwan. The time could conceivably come when the importance of good relations with China, for example, over the future of Hong Kong, would be over-riding and sufficient to justify at least closing our small office at Tamsui.

6. As regards the United Nations, since 1961 we have voted in favour of Peking's occupancy of the China seat and the exclusion of the present occupants. Since then, we have also supported the American-sponsored resolution saying that this vote required a two-thirds majority. For the first time, this year, the substantive vote obtained a simple majority and the Important Resolution therefore, for the first time, effectively barred Peking's admission. We are discussing with the Americans whether we should now change our stand on the Important Item Resolution. This would almost certainly have the effect of admitting Peking at the next Assembly. Our relations with Peking would be disproportionately harmed if we were to maintain our support for the Important Item Resolution when that resolution was defeated. The American attitude is now more relaxed and they may well see a change by us as helping them towards a 'soft-fall'. It is important that, before the next Assembly we should ensure that Chinese entry is not seen as a defeat for Western interests. In China's present, more conciliatory mood in foreign affairs,

it could be that the inevitably disruptive effect of her entry will be less than while she was pursuing more polemical and violent policies.

7. We must, however, remember that the three preconditions set out above are by no means the only things which the Chinese hold against us. Support for the US on a host of issues, including Vietnam, has been quoted in the past also. Unless the Chinese wish an exchange of Ambassadors to take place, they could prevaricate endlessly for a variety of reasons

Hong Kong

8. The importance of our relations with China is greater than for other Western European countries because of the existence of Hong Kong. Although the Chinese have repudiated what they regard as 'unequal treaties', they have not specifically questioned the special status of Hong Kong, preferring to say that this is a matter which will be resolved at the appropriate moment. Nevertheless, it remains under British rule because China finds it convenient and profitable. Over one-third of China's foreign exchange earnings come via Hong Kong. The Chinese will always have it in their power to make trouble for Hong Kong, in varying degrees, at any time of their choosing. Over the past twenty years they have complained about a wide range of subjects, from the presence of Nationalist agents to so-called 'oppression' of Communist schools. Of late their most repeated complaint relates to the continued detention of 74 Chinese arrested during the rioting in 1967. At the time 1,832 were arrested, and those remaining in prison are the hard-core committed for acts of violence. The Chinese have linked their detention with that of the 4 British subjects detained in China. They have recently also linked them with the future of branches of British banks in Shanghai. They could conceivably connect them to our export possibilities— even aircraft. There has also recently been some evidence that they intend to demonstrate the indignation of relatives in Hong Kong. Having played their best remaining bargaining card in releasing Mr Johnston, they may feel they need to resort to expressions of popular concern.

9. The attitude of the Governor (who has statutory powers to grant full remission) is that releasing these prisoners now could lead to a reduction in confidence in the firmness of the Government of Hong Kong and be a sign of submitting to Chinese pressure. All but 7 will be released in the normal course of events by 1974. On the other hand, the situation is now calm, three years have passed, and pressures are muted. If the Chinese see themselves as forced to mount a full campaign for their release, tension could increase disproportionately. We are in touch with the Government of Hong Kong about the possibility of further releases, and have suggested that the Prison Board of Review might look particularly at the possibility of changes in sentences which were of an exemplary nature.

10. The Communists are under instructions from Peking to derive as much economic benefit as they can from the Colony and not to engage in disruptive political activity. They are at present avoiding clashes with the Government and the Chinese authorities are being fully co-operative in the provision of food and water. It is possible, within the ambit of Chinese policy, to improve links in modest fields where they are of advantage to us. The Chinese have recently reinstated the Canton/Hong Kong parcel post. We may wish to discuss with them direct

railway and telecommunications links. It is only if friendly workmanlike contacts can be developed that the future of the colony can be discussed. The lease of the New Territories expires in 1997—these comprise of 365 sq. miles of the total land area of 400. Hong Kong Island without the Territories would not be commercially viable.

Commercial Prospects

11. The figures for our exports for January-November, 1970, are approximately £41 million, as compared to £47 million for the same period in 1969. The outlook for trade is nevertheless encouraging. We should be able to hold our share of the China market. We have told the Chinese of our readiness to sell them any British civil aircraft in current production, and they are now assessing the findings of their expert mission which visited the UK in September 1970. They are, in particular, deciding about BUA's offer of four secondhand VC10s and, possibly, additional Tridents to supplement those already bought from Pakistan. If we succeed in further sales, it could give a good opportunity for BOAC to consider routes into China (Pakistan International Airlines and Air France already operate). The Chinese would probably be interested in reciprocal rights involving Hong Kong or other areas such as the Persian Gulf. We are encouraging trade missions from China. We have considered the possibility of suggesting to the Chinese a visit by a Department of Trade and Industry Minister, but believe that such a suggestion would meet with a rebuff while substantial numbers of confrontation prisoners remain detained in Hong Kong. There would be more advantage in inviting a senior official, possible [*sic*] a Vice Minister of Foreign Trade to visit London. We are also considering trade exhibitions in China. Our regular shipping services to China were withdrawn at the time of the Cultural Revolution. Discussions are taking place between commercial interests and the Chinese Mission about resumption. This will depend on the views of our shipping lines on the economic viability. We will ensure that our commercial representation in Peking will be equal to any increase in work.

Future Prospects

12. We have now reached a crucial point in our relations with China. Since the end of the Cultural Revolution the Chinese have adopted a more conciliatory foreign policy—in some respects even more conciliatory than before the Cultural Revolution. They are increasingly confident of admission to the United Nations, and are showing a more co-operative face to the world. We may well have to wait a long time for a more favourable moment to develop our relations.

Conclusions

13. (1) We should exploit the present more conciliatory line to expand trade and contacts with the Chinese in all appropriate fields to help us to bring China into a healthier relationship with the rest of the world.

(2) We should develop friendly and workmanlike contacts over subjects of interest to Hong Kong.

(3) We should pursue with the Government of Hong Kong the possibility of further leniency towards the remaining Chinese confrontation prisoners.

(4) We should pursue more actively the possibility of raising the level of our diplomatic representation—eventually to that of Ambassadors.

(5) We should consider inviting senior Chinese officials to the United Kingdom, possibly in the first instance a Vice Minister of Foreign Trade.[1]

FOREIGN AND COMMONWEALTH OFFICE

1 In approving the paper Sir A Douglas-Home commented that it was possible to overstress the new Chinese friendliness—'they are very certain of their own superiority to other inferior peoples' (Mr Graham to Mr Moon, 5 January). After reading the paper the Prime Minister commented 'we should be getting on with the policy outlined with a view to achieving some results' (Mr Moon to Mr Graham, 1 February).

No. 206

Sir A. Douglas-Home to Sir D. Trench (Hong Kong)
8 January 1971, 3.10 p.m.[1]
Tel. No. 24 Immediate. Confidential (FCO 21/875, FEH 14/1A)

Personal for Governor from Secretary of State.

I have been giving thought to our relations with China and their implications for Hong Kong. The Chinese have now made it abundantly clear that they wish to normalise and improve contacts. By releasing Johnston, they have removed the only serious obstacle remaining from the strictly British point of view.[2]

2. They now see us as having a moral responsibility to respond. They have made it clear what form they consider the response should take—the release of the remaining confrontation prisoners.

3. I and my predecessors have always recognised the need to ensure that releases do not lead to a reduction in confidence in the firmness of the Government of Hong Kong and its ability to withstand Chinese pressure. On the other hand the situation is now calm, three years have passed and the communists in Hong Kong are at present avoiding clashes with your Government. We are therefore at the moment in a position of comparative strength, but if, after the Chinese have played their best remaining bargaining card in releasing Mr Johnston, we make no response, they may feel the need to resort to more hostile measures. They have already hinted to us here that they intended to demonstrate the indignation of relatives in Hong Kong, and I see that this campaign has now started. The Chinese have linked the continued detention of confrontation prisoners with British subjects detained in China, and might conceivably be eventually tempted to take further hostages. They have recently also linked them with the future of branches of British banks in Shanghai. There are unfortunately many ways in which they could extend their pressures and their obvious target for pressure is Hong Kong which is much more vulnerable than the UK. Indeed it is only by maintaining friendly and practical contacts with the Chinese that the Colony can maintain its prosperity.

1 Repeated for information to Peking.
2 There were another four British subjects in China—Elsie Epstein, Gladys Yang, Michael Shapiro and David Crook—either married to Chinese or who worked for the Chinese authorities about whom the Mission had no information despite constant approaches to the Chinese authorities. It was agreed to continue raising these cases with the Chinese without suggesting that their detention was a major impediment in relations (Mr Morgan to Mr Denson, 2 February; FCO 21/850).

4. I should therefore be grateful if you could take these considerations into account in your Review of the Position (Your Telno. 883).³ I see from your telegram No. 183 of 21 March³ that at that time 5 were convicted of crimes of violence, 87 of possession of offensive weapons (either personal possession or being on premises where such weapons were found), and 23 of possession or use of explosives. I imagine the proportion remains much the same. It would clearly be preferable from the point of future Sino-British relations if we could remove this obstacle completely. I fully understand the difficulties in any remission of the 5 actually committed for violence and there may well be others that would present difficulties to you. I would hope nevertheless that you would be able to release under your letters patent well over half of those still detained. Thereafter and in the light of the reactions we could consider a time-table for the release of the rest. If it would help public presentation in the Colony, you may like to consider parallel remissions in respect of persons serving sentences for other crimes not connected with the disturbances, although this would make it difficult to explain the remissions in the case of Confrontation sentences by reference to their original exemplary character.

5. I am very much aware of the difficulties of conscience involved in this matter for you and those who serve on your Board of Review. Nevertheless we here and in Hong Kong have reached a most important stage in our relations with China and in these circumstances I am asking you to consider whether the interests of the long-term future of the Colony would not be best served by making the most of this opportunity to establish more cordial and workmanlike contacts. The Chinese timed Johnston's release for Christmas—it would be particularly felicitous if you were able to time releases for the Spring Festival.

3 Not printed.

No. 207

Sir D. Trench (Hong Kong) to Sir A. Douglas-Home
9 January 1971, 3 a.m.¹
Tel. No. 13 Immediate, Confidential (FCO 21/875, FEH 14/1A)

Personal from Governor to Secretary of State.

Your telegram No. 24.²

Before I reply more directly to the points in your telegram under reference I must report recent reactions to an *Agence France Presse* item which was reproduced in the press here and which speculated that action would be taken in Hong Kong almost precisely along the lines in your telegram.

2. On Tuesday, 5 January, in Executive Council, an unofficial member raised the subject of the press reports and spoke strongly to the effect that there should under no circumstances be any premature releases of confrontation prisoners because

1 Repeated for information immediate to Peking.
2 No. 206.

of recent Chinese attitudes, including the release of Johnston. His view was that Johnston's release resulted from recent moves by the Government of Singapore to restore the situation over the Bank of China there; but, in any case, it was his view that any action of this kind would result in dangerous loss of confidence over this Government's ability to withstand pressure. He spoke vigorously and was supported by all other unofficial members.

3. On Friday, 8 January, The Secretary for Home Affairs[3] reported in his weekly round-up of public opinion derived from sources other than the newspapers that the *Agence France Presse* report had aroused comment from those who had seen it and that while Johnston's release was welcomed there were strongly adverse reactions to the suggestion of amnesties.

4. Press editorials have expressed similarly adverse views. A typical example which may be available to you is the leading article in the *South China Morning Post* of today's date 9th January, which followed upon an announcement we had to make, to quieten public opinion, refuting the *Agence France Presse* report and re-assuring enquirers that these prisoners would be treated no differently from any others.

5. It can be said with certainty, therefore, that any wholesale action on the lines suggested will gravely outrage all strata of local opinion and result in severe loss of confidence.

6. Moreover, since it is inconceivable that any such action would have the slightest effect on essential Chinese attitudes towards Hong Kong (even if some benefits in improved Sino-British relations accrue to Britain therefrom) I must most earnestly ask that we do not depart from our present policy, and that we go no further than our present search for any prisoners who might be released, or have their sentences curtailed, on grounds acceptable to public opinion and not out of line with what would be normal practice for any convicted prisoner. As you are aware there is a group (of very roughly about 20) whose sentences may have contained an excessively exemplary element, and whom we are now looking at.

7. To follow any other course, would, in my firm opinion, have grave long term consequences for security here, quite apart from the high risk of outbreaks of violence in the prisons which might very well result. Even to follow the course we are following has grave dangers unless we proceed with caution.

8. If these views are not acceptable to you, I most sincerely ask for consultations here before we proceed any further.[4]

---

3 Mr (David) Ronald Holmes.
4 Sir A. Douglas-Home commented: 'I do not see how we can go against this advice. The Governor's analysis of Chinese reasoning is probably right.'

No. 208

Sir D. Trench (Hong Kong) to Sir A. Douglas-Home
11 January 1971, 5 a.m.[1]
Tel. No. 17 Immediate, Secret (FCO 21/875, FEH 14/1A)

Personal from Governor for Secretary of State.

My Telegram No. 13.[2]

I have the following further observations on your telegram No. 24,[3] which I ask to be considered and which I would like to put forward as a basis for any further consultations here on which you may decide.

2. It has, of course, been for long an important Chinese objective to secure the release of these prisoners. Local communists promised, in 1967, that the release of all their adherents who were imprisoned would very quickly be effected. That this has not been achieved except at a pace dictated by us, has reflected adversely on the efforts of local Communist leaders to regain adherents and on the credibility of Peking's expressions of support for Hong Kong Communists. In short, it has both bolstered confidence here amongst non-Communists and discouraged Communists. If they prove able, even now, to effect the release of prisoners as they promised (they themselves admitted from about 1968 that it would take several years) they will be able to claim (and will claim) a victory which will demonstrate to their own adherents, and, more importantly, the public at large, that they are indeed able in the end to force us to do what they want. Our only real defence has always been to show clearly that the Communists cannot usurp our essential authority except by the use of a degree of actual violence which will ruin Hong Kong's usefulness to them. To depart from this basic posture is, in my opinion, the most fatal mistake that can be made here and the issue of the prisoners seems to be the ground they have chosen to make us depart from it.

3. As to our moral responsibility to respond, the fact is that our response to more reasonable behaviour by them throughout has been greater than theirs. Nor can I see that the ordinary population of Hong Kong has any moral responsibility, at the risk of their security, for UK citizens unconnected with Hong Kong who are harassed in China. It has by no means been unobserved here that there has been little or no similar concern shown for Hong Kong Chinese abducted or imprisoned in China as there has been for persons of European race.

4. There may be a certain false calm here at the moment, but the Communists continue to make constant and strenuous efforts to gain adherents and strengthen their position generally. In this they are inevitably meeting with some success, and certainly nothing we do will ever persuade them to desist from these efforts. Nor can I see that we are in any special position of strength at this time, other than that we have so far shown that we can be firm enough to cope with pressure short of direct intervention or extreme violence.

5. The Chinese can of course, although it seems very unlikely at the moment, resort to more hostile measures at any time—and are the more likely to do so the

1 Repeated for information priority to Peking.
2 No. 207.
3 No. 206.

more they learn that they can out-pressure and out-bargain us. The 'campaign' by relatives has amounted to one petition (covering 41 of the 74 still in prison) peacefully presented and nothing further has transpired except a continuance of fairly low-key correspondence in the Communist press. It bears no resemblance to the sustained campaign which was undertaken to induce us to re-instate dismissed workers, and which we resisted without much difficulty and which petered out when we stood firm.

6. There is no doubt that the continued detention of prisoners and British in China have become linked, but it seems to me to have been so linked almost as much by us as by the Chinese. My impression is that we have let ourselves get into a unfortunate bargaining position in this matter, and if HMG is indeed now in some moral need, as part of a bargain, to release prisoners, it is quite substantially our own doing.

7. I agree also that they may be eventually tempted to take further hostages, but surely they are all the more likely to do so if the policy proves a successful method of exerting pressure on Hong Kong through HMG.

8. I am not sure how the reference to the future of branches of British banks in Shanghai arises, as I do not immediately recall seeing any such linking by the Chinese but if it relates to their ejection, the Hong Kong and Shanghai Bank, until recently at least (I do not know how the Bank now feels) was only anxious to affect a withdrawal.

9. Certainly friendly and practical contacts with the Chinese are desirable, provided they are coupled with firm refusal at all times to give way unwillingly to pressure.

10. Again, I agree it would in many ways be a relief to be rid of these prisoners entirely. No one would be happier to see the last of them than I, provided this can be accomplished in an acceptable manner, and the search for the suitable grounds for clemency is one in which I am presently personally and closely engaged. The figures in your paragraph 4 do not give a true picture of the violent nature of the actions of these remaining prisoners, who inflicted considerable casualties on the police but were often charged with what could quickly and easily be proved rather than on more serious charges. However, the possibility of some prisoners having been given sentences of an excessively exemplary character is precisely one of the things we are looking at now, as my previous telegram indicated. But nothing will help presentation here if the public smell general amnesties for the sake of a bargain over Europeans.

11. I have some difficulties of conscience, of course, in this matter and some feelings of caution over my relations with the judiciary; but my greatest fears are for the results on the security of the Colony of going for conscious amnesties. We live on confidence here, and to impair gravely, or destroy, local confidence in the Hong Kong government and indeed in Her Majesty's Government's continuing support for Hong Kong seems to me much less and wise in the long run; and I can only advise firmly that at the present time amnesties of the kind being proposed, if I understand your message aright, would have a seriously adverse effect on the confidence which is so very important an element in stability here. It is for these reasons I believe we should not suddenly deviate from our present courses, and go in for purely politically

amnesties, but demonstrate only that we do keep the situation of these prisoners under continual review. One young prisoner was, indeed, recently released early in accordance with the Board of Review's policy on young prisoners, although I do not suggest this is of any importance in the present context.

No. 209

Sir A. Douglas-Home to Mr Denson (Peking), 15 January 1971, 3 p.m.[1]
Tel. No. 29 Priority, Confidential (FCO 21/808, FEC 2/2A)

The new Chargé d'Affaires today paid his first calls on Mr Royle, Sir S. Tomlinson and Mr Wilford.

2. Mr Royle drew attention to the raising of your status and said that we should now like to proceed to exchange Ambassadors. P'ei replied that he welcomed the new suggestion to improve and develop relations on the basis of the Five Principles. He asked where subsequent discussion could take place and Mr Royle said in London. No other topic was discussed.

3. Subsequently with Sir S. Tomlinson P'ei said that China's conditions to an exchange had involved withdrawal of the consulate on Taiwan and removal of our support for the Americans in the United Nations. Sir S. Tomlinson replied that for the first time in recent years a minister had raised the question of exchanging Ambassadors: this was a new situation. Should the considered Chinese reply relate to the points P'ei had mentioned then it would be studied.

4. In his call on Mr Wilford P'ei raised the confrontation prisoners and hoped that speedy steps were being taken to release all 74. The Chinese regarded this as a serious obstacle to further improvement in relations. Wilford said that the memorandum handed to you (Your telegram No. 33)[2] was being studied.

1 Repeated for information to Hong Kong and saving to Washington.
2 Not printed.

No. 210

Mr Denson (Peking) to Sir A. Douglas-Home, 16 January 1971[1]
Tel. No. 42 Priority, Secret (FCO 21/875, FEH 14/1A)

Your Telno 24 and Hong Kong Telnos 13 and 14 to you.[2]

1. I agree that a most important stage has been reached in Sino British relations. The Chinese are looking for normalisation and improvement in all aspects of our relations and have made it clear that they wish to see an end to the situation created by the events of 1967. In this they will regard the actions of Her Majesty's Government

1 Repeated for information Priority for Hong Kong (personal for Governor).
2 No. 206, No. 207 and not printed respectively.

and the Government of Hong Kong as indivisible as they have all along. It is around this question that the comments which follow mainly revolve.

2. In my view the link between British subjects detained in China and confrontation prisoners in Hong Kong has always been implicit in Chinese thinking. They did not at first make it explicit because they probably hoped that by not doing so we should be assisted in carrying out a gradual process of relaxation without specific terms being stated. But after Grey's release they made the link quite clear and it was emphasised during Wilford's visit last April.

3. I find it difficult to understand why if the matter were suitably explained, people in Hong Kong would not acknowledge that they owed something to Britain and to British subjects in China who had suffered in the interests of maintaining law and order in the Colony and hence that now and in the future there could be no complete divorce between their interest and wider Sino-British interests.

4. The present improvement in Sino-British relations is part of a general improvement in relations between China and the rest of the world from which we may benefit to some degree even if problems in Hong Kong remain unresolved. I think, however, that it is unwise to assume that there is unanimity within the Chinese leadership about the way in which relations with individual countries should be conducted. There are reports that there has been disagreement about the recent Chinese condemnation of events in Poland[3] which is said to have been opposed by those in favour of better bilateral relations and championed by those wishing to give all-out support to 'revolution'. The position of Hong Kong is *sui generis*[4] since the Chinese consider it part of China. For this reason a policy of no change there must be correspondingly more difficult to explain and justify. From all available evidence it is clear that the Chinese Government have instructed their supporters in Hong Kong not to make trouble and have criticised their handling of events in 1967 since the outcome showed they did not enjoy popular support. The present policy is to try slowly to build up such support. While I, of course, defer to the Governor's assessment of the present situation and the reaction of non-Communist opinion to further releases, I should have thought that the risk of further Communist recourse to violence or other action which would constitute a threat to security would be less rather than more at a time when they had obtained some satisfaction for their *amour propre*[5] and relations between the United Kingdom and China were seen to be getting better. There would no doubt be some crowing but I do not think it would receive particular encouragements from here. The greater danger seems to me to lie in a situation where local activists become totally frustrated and clamour to be let off the leash. In these circumstances the more moderate elements in the Peking leadership will not be well placed to counsel caution and in the event of another outburst of violence the Chinese Government may not be able (or perhaps willing) to try to control it.

5. If we take the opportunity now offered, I do not, repeat not, think that the Chinese Government will regard it as a sign of weakness but rather a political

---

3 In December 1970, protests occurred in northern Poland due to a sudden increase in the price of food and other everyday items. The protests were quashed by the Polish army and militia resulting in many deaths and injuries.
4 Unique, not like anything else.
5 Self-esteem; self-respect.

sagacity. Progress with release of prisoners would in my view be significant not only in the short term but also in the longer term when the attitude of the Peking Government will be decisive. *Per contra*[6] a totally unyielding attitude now could make matters more difficult at such time as the future of the Colony becomes the subject which has to be raised.

6. I very much hope therefore that it will be found possible to continue to make at any rate some further releases and that as has been suggested the first group might be let out for the Chinese New Year.[7]

6 On the other hand, on the contrary.
7 Sir A. Douglas-Home minuted: 'I would like to have a word about this in the office. I am inclined to think that the balance of interest lies in releasing some prisoners now.'

No. 211

Sir D. Trench (Hong Kong) to Sir A. Douglas-Home
19 January 1971, 4.45 a.m.[1]
Tel. No. 36 Priority, Secret (FCO 21/875, FEH 14/1A)

Peking Telegram No. 42:[2] Confrontation Prisoners.

When risks to the security of Hong Kong are balanced against the chances of improved relations with China it is probable that any Governor will see things differently from any Chargé. I do, however, think the telegram under reference underestimates the risks and overestimates the chances of better relations.

2. Ref. paragraph 3. More thoughtful residents of Hong Kong will see that the future of Hong Kong cannot be wholly divorced from the state of Sino-British relations generally but it is probably impossible to convince many that the wholesale and speedy release of the remaining confrontation prisoners will benefit Hong Kong. It is only too obvious that the morale of the local Communists would be raised and the determination of this Government to enforce its authority brought into doubt. The difficulties of dealing with another local Communist resort to violence or indeed dealing with them on a day to day basis as we have to do, would be increased. For most residents, Hong Kong is their only safe haven and they would inevitably be very quick to feel a weakening at the top. Furthermore, the press are only too likely to do further damage by representing any concession as something forced on Hong Kong by London, with Hong Kong's interests an inconsiderable element in the situation.

3. Although the subject certainly belongs more to the Chargé than to me I can recall no evidence to support a belief that any improvements in relations with China achieved by an amnesty would be either substantial or lasting. Relations have eased over the last three years without an amnesty, and there are other issues here to which the Chinese are equally or more, sensitive e.g. their press and schools. It is therefore difficult to believe that a settlement of the prisoner issue would unlock the door to a

1 Repeated for information priority to Peking.
2 No. 210.

trouble-free era. The available evidence is that the long term policy of China towards Hong Kong would be unaffected and that at the best short term policy could lead to some inconsiderable improvement here. But it is also possible that even the short term policy would worsen if such an important deliberate concession by us encouraged Peking to think more could easily be had.

4. Of course I agree, as I have stated in earlier telegrams (e.g. my telegram number 13)[3] that the existing procedure of the Prison Board of Review should be fully used. I hope that in the next two months or so there will be some results to show on the less serious cases although I remain apprehensive over the Board's reactions. Moreover, I am myself reading through the entire available court records of every serious case and will ask The Board to consider releasing or reducing the sentences of as many as we safely can through this procedure, where there is any justification for it. It should be possible then to let the Chinese assume that we have responded to the gesture over Johnston, although to say too explicitly still seems to me to have dangers. Releases by Chinese New Year next week however are procedurally impossible.

5. In short, it is amnesties as a pure political manoeuvre which I most sincerely fear: not releases at our own pace and for own deliberate and explainable reasons.[4]

---

[3] No. 207.

[4] In a minute dated 19 January, Mr Morgan argued that the Far Eastern Department's considered assessment remained that it was in the long-term interests of Hong Kong for a gesture now to be made to the Chinese and that the moves the Governor contemplated making would not constitute an adequate gesture. The Governor clearly needed some reassurance that the action suggested was based on an assessment of the long-term interests of Hong Kong and Sino-British interests were not viewed in isolation from those. Mr Wilford, in a minute of 22 January, thought the Governor had used 'some extremely strong language.' He was loath to accept his argument believing that, if the Governor got his way, virtually none of the prisoners in jail would be released more than a month ahead of their normal release date. 'We shall get no credit for this from the Chinese and there remains the serious risk that the Chinese will stir up trouble of some kind in Hong Kong'.

No. 212

Letter from Mr Millard (Washington) to Mr Wilford, 22 January 1971
Confidential and Guard (FCO 21/808, FEC 2/2A)

Dear Michael,

Chinese Representation in the United Nations

I carried out on 20 January the instructions contained in John Morgan's letter of 23 December to Anthony Elliott.[1] The interview had been arranged with Marshall Green, but was switched at his request to De Palma, the Assistant Secretary for UN matters. Winthrop Brown was also present.

2. I enclose a record of the interview,[2] which was rather disappointing, particularly in view of informal indications from ACA that the timing of our approach was not bad. De Palma was unable to give us a reply at this stage about the Important

---

[1] No. 204.

[2] Not printed. For the US record of the meeting see *FRUS, 1969–1976, Volume V*, No. 323.

Question Resolution or to promise one before the completion of the US review of policy. Contrary to what we were led to hope earlier, the Americans do not appear to have reached any significant conclusions in their review so far (other, clearly, than a decision to try and keep everyone in play). On the other hand, as De Palma made clear, they will be vexed if we try in any way to jump the gun ourselves. De Palma asked us quite firmly to avoid foreclosing our options until we had discussed the matter thoroughly with the Americans when they themselves were in a position to do so. This, he expected, would be in about five to six weeks. He and Brown particularly hoped that we would not indicate to other Governments meanwhile that our policy was likely to change. I made it clear that such a delay was unwelcome. I hope in practice, however, that it will be possible for us to fall in with the Americans on this point. If in the end we are going to have to face a row on substance, it would be a great pity to have one over procedures as well.

3. De Palma represented to us that until the review was complete no assumptions should be made what the US attitude would be; any approach was conceivable. However, his remarks suggested a preoccupation with two particular points. He gave us a clear warning (paragraph 5 of record) not to jump to the premature conclusion that the Important Question Resolution was no longer taken very seriously by the US. Second, certain other remarks suggested that the Americans were looking particularly closely at the possibilities of 'dual representation'. I made quite clear our distaste for a 'Two Chinas' approach and our belief that a solution of this type was unrealistic. Winthrop Brown claimed to have some evidence of a possible change in Nationalist attitudes, based on a reading of the Taipeh press. De Palma for his part made what was possibly a significant distinction between an 'approach' and a 'solution'. He implied that such an approach would not be a 'Two Chinas' solution in the US view, but if Peking or the Nationalists chose to put this construction on it that would be entirely their own fault.

4. To sum up, we are no further forward, except that we have put on record again, more formally than before, the fact that we are considering a change, and our distaste for delaying devices or a 'Two Chinas' approach. As far as the Important Question Resolution is concerned, the Americans know they cannot necessarily count on us to stand out against the pressure of events, should the scenario next autumn be the familiar one. Meanwhile it is clear that they would be most unhappy if we were to take a decision in favour of a change without further consultation.[3]

Yours ever,
GUY

---

3 Officials in London found the American response disappointing, even confused. Mr Tomlinson noted the letter 'confirms my fears that we are not going to have an altogether easy passage with the Americans on this issue'. Mr Royle noted: 'We must be careful not to push the Americans too hard tho'—I fear they may react by stonewalling.'

No. 213

Mr Denson (Peking) to Sir A. Douglas-Home, 22 January 1971, 3.20 a.m.[1]
Tel. No. 58 Immediate, Secret (FCO 21/875, FEH 14/1A)

Hong Kong Tel. No. 36 to FCO.[2]

At a Reception last night I was tackled by T'ang Hai-Kuang about Hong Kong prisoners. He said that the Chinese Government hoped that we would find it possible for some of them to be reunited with their families for Chinese New Year. I made a noncommittal response and sought to terminate the conversation. But T'ang pursued the question with considerable tenacity and it was clear that what he wished to convey was that we should match the Chinese gesture of releasing Johnston before Christmas with some gesture in Hong Kong. As I have said before, there may well be differences within the Chinese Government about the conduct of relations with us in particular over Hong Kong and that those who favour a policy of détente may be under pressure from those who want greater toughness. T'ang's initiative seems to support this view, and argues in favour of a policy of graduated relaxation.

1 Repeated for information priority to Hong Kong (personal for Governor).
2 No. 211.

No. 214

Minute by Sir L. Monson, 25 January 1971
Confidential (FCO 21/875, FEH 14/1A)

The Private Secretary has said the Secretary of State wishes to discuss this subject at 4.15 p.m. on Wednesday 27th.

2. I supported the general proposition behind the Secretary of State's telegram No. 24[1] that a substantial gesture to the Chinese in these matters was in the long-term interests of Hong Kong and I had hoped that by private consultation with the Governor we could bring him to see that.

3. As things have developed since however I have grave doubts whether such a gesture still remains in the long-term interest of the Colony. I refer to the ill-timed Press speculation on the subject and the self-generated mood of apprehension and opposition that have been created in Hong Kong by this speculation. In the circumstances wholesale releases could easily turn apprehension into panic and in that event it is almost inconceivable that the CPG would not stir up the trouble pot to secure what must be the most desirable policy aim—to reduce Hong Kong to the same state of puppet-like impotence as Macao. It is one thing for the Hong Kong security forces to contain communist disturbances (as they did in 1967) when the population has rallied behind them: it would be quite a different matter if the population were in a state of panic and anxiously hedging their bets.

1 No. 206.

4. If however this view is not accepted, I do not think that the revised draft is calculated to bring the Governor around to the contrary view: there is much in it which he will with greater or less reason resent—especially the statement that the question of confrontation prisoners must be dealt with with[in] the framework of Britain's relations with China. It must be remembered that he has been 'conditioned'

(i) by ten years' experience as a Colonial Governor in which he has been accustomed to exercise the delegated power of pardon 'in his own deliberate judgement' against the background of the general policy, stated in parliament in 1947 and followed since that 'intervention by Her Majesty on the advice of the Secretary of State ... would seriously impair the administration of justice in the Colonies (Mr Creech Jones in the Commons 11 August 1947); and

(ii) by his own views as to the responsibilities of a Governor of Hong Kong—in briefing us on the qualities of a Governor against the background of choosing a successor to himself he set high on the list of priorities that a Governor should be seen to be defending the interests of Hong Kong against all-corners including and perhaps especially the United Kingdom.

5. I would prefer to see something on the lines of the original draft sent with a view to influencing the Governor's judgement towards more and more speedy releases. It could be strengthened by the arguments in the revised draft to the effect that we cannot rely on the Chinese taking a rebuff lying down and therefore a situation very different from 1967 is on the cards. But on the other hand the draft does not take account of the weakness in our position caused by the reaction of the Press speculation.

6. In short my assessment is that whatever we do we run a risk of serious trouble but our chances of containing it are that much better if the bulk of the people of Hong Kong reckon we are standing firm and have not persuaded themselves that we shall give way to pressure. I do not believe that there is any significant 'middle ground' of opinion that can be rallied to us. The bulk of the people will back whom they think is the winner and are likely in that case to determine the issue of the conflict.

L. MONSON

No. 215

Sir A. Douglas-Home to Sir D. Trench (Hong Kong)
28 January 1971, 11 a.m.[1]
Tel. No. 82 Immediate, Confidential (FCO 21/875, FEH 14/1A)

Personal for Governor.
Confrontation prisoners.

---

1 Repeated for information to Peking (personal for Mr Denson).
   The FED were losing patience with the Governor. In a minute dated 3 February, Mr Wilford said the choice was either to accept the Governor's position and say nothing, or 'seek to keep him up to the mark by making some reply which shows that we are not wholly satisfied with what he has said'. While not seeking to provoke the Governor 'by back-seat driving' he favoured sending this telegram stating: 'I do not think it can be said to be provocative in any way and it permits the Secretary of State to have the last word, as indeed he should.'

On my return from Singapore I have been able to reconsider this question on the basis of the valuable advice contained in your telegrams Nos. 13, 17 and 36 and Peking telegram No. 42.[2] I should like you to be in no doubt that I do not see Sino-British relations in isolation from the interest of Hong Kong and that it was primarily my estimate of the long-term interest of Hong Kong which prompted my telegram No. 24.[3] I should also like to assure you that there is no question whatever of being under some sort of obligation to the Chinese to do a deal about the confrontation prisoners. The Chinese have persistently sought to connect this issue with the release of British subjects detained in China. We have, however, retained and still do retain complete freedom of action.

2. Our assessment of the present attitude of the Chinese Government is based on evidence from a variety of sources and is reinforced by Mr Denson's telegram No. 42. There can be no certainty in these matters, but there is a real risk that if there is no sign of movement in regard to the confrontation prisoners the Chinese Government will sooner or later (and probably sooner) begin to cause trouble and in this context trouble means in the first place trouble for Hong Kong. At the same time, the indications are that the Chinese Government want to liquidate this issue rather than to make public capital out of it and are therefore unlikely to crow unduly about it and perhaps even to discourage their adherents in Hong Kong from doing so if we decide that it is in our own best interest to go some way to meet them. This is borne out by the unobtrusive way in which they have made their representations in Hong Kong, coupled with the manner in which they have spoken to us both here and in Peking.

3. I am, of course, giving the most serious consideration to the views which you have urged upon me about the danger to the security of the colony and the strength of feeling of 'all strata of public opinion' if you were to pursue the course set out in my telegram No. 24.

4. At the same time I cannot but be concerned about the threat which the Chinese could, and in my view might well, pose to the Colony if we show that we are unwilling to move other than at a very slow pace. You say in paragraph 2 of your telegram No.17 that 'your only real defence has always been to show clearly that the Communists cannot usurp our essential authority except by the use of a degree of violence which will ruin Hong Kong's usefulness to them'. But must we not recognise that the Chinese Government could put Hong Kong to a very considerable degree of inconvenience without necessarily taking matters to extremes? We must also remember that in 1967/68 the Hong Kong Government benefited from the fact that the trouble-makers enjoyed little practical support or encouragement from Peking beyond newspaper articles and broadcasts. All-out Peking support, or indeed inspiration, of disorders following on rejection of their present overtures would cause problems of a very different magnitude.

5. Against this background I am concerned about the programme contained in your telegram No. 30[4] for the reconsideration by the Board of Review of sentences. We have already passed the Spring Festival date, but could the Board not get down to business forthwith without violating your criteria of releases at our own pace and for

2 Nos. 207, 208, 211 and 210 respectively.
3 No. 206.
4 Not printed.

our own deliberate and explainable reasons? If they did I would hope that it might be possible for you to take decisions within the next month, which would affect the release of as many as possible of the 24 you mentioned as being under consideration because their sentences may have included an exemplary aspect, plus perhaps the female prisoners, plus the one or two who are due out anyhow. I hope that taking into account paragraph 4 above you will feel able to achieve this. The Chinese will be looking closely at our actions and the absence of any response by us at the time of the Spring Festival might well make it harder for the calmer counsels at present in evidence in Peking to prevail. You might perhaps see advantage in arranging your review procedure in such a way that prisoners would be released in a steady stream as their cases were dealt with by the Board. This would help us play the Chinese along, and to keep the temperature down, and to give time for fuller consideration of the future programme of releases.

6. I recognise that you may feel that you will have to take your Executive Council with you on this, but I would hope that by using my arguments you would be able to convince them that the action I propose would in the long-term and wider context be of greater value to the Colony than keeping these people locked up.

No. 216

Sir A. Douglas-Home to Sir D. Trench (Hong Kong)
28 January 1971, 11 a.m.[1]
Tel. No. 83 Immediate, Confidential (FCO 21/875, FEH 14/1A)

My immediately preceding telegram.[2]
Personal for Governor.
Confrontation Prisoners.

I would like to expand on the argument in the first part of paragraph 1 of my telegram under reference. I hope that I may have convinced you that the action I propose is not dictated by the narrow interest of HMG, but is in our view in the long-term interest of Hong Kong also. We must not forget that in international relations Hong Kong is a Crown Colony which has no status at all *vis-à-vis* China except as a dependency of Britain. Relations between Hong Kong and China are therefore an integral part of Britain's relations with China and it is for this reason that I believe that we cannot separate the question of confrontation prisoners from the broader framework. I think that you recognise this in paragraph 2 of your telegram No 36,[3] and, as you say, the more thoughtful residents of the Colony see it too.

2. Secondly, I am concerned at what you describe as the virtually unanimous view of all strata of public opinion which seems to reflect a narrower view of the Hong Kong interest, which I believe carries great danger for the Colony. How can the wider view be put across? As Governor of Hong Kong you have faithfully reflected

1 Repeated for information to Peking (personal for Denson).
2 No. 215.
3 No. 211.

to me the views of the local people, but at the same time as the Representative of Her Majesty you must be the channel through which the views of HMG are represented not only to your official advisers, but to Hong Kong opinion as a whole. The problem, if we are to resolve the issue of confrontation prisoners in the way I suggest, is therefore to put across our point of view to those who help to form public opinion. Our task is to do this in such a way as to convince them that the action which we are taking is in Hong Kong's as well as Britain's best interest. We must expect that some people in Hong Kong and perhaps even the Chinese Government may wish to represent our action as some sort of capitulation to Chinese pressure. However, we know that this is not the case and what we must seek to proclaim publicly, and to convince the residents of the Colony of, is the plain fact that HMG have made no deal, whether explicit or implied, with the Chinese Government on the matter of prisoners.

3. If you are able to fall in with the proposals made in my immediately preceding telegram I should be grateful for any ideas you may have for dealing with this problem of communication. I should, of course, be ready to give you any help which I can.[4]

---

4 For good measure Sir A. Douglas-Home added in FCO Tel. No. 103 to Peking, dated 4 February: 'The Prime Minister has very recently told me that he wants to see results on several issues affecting Sino-British relations which include releases of confrontation prisoners.'

No. 217

Record of conversation with the Chinese Chargé d'Affaires at the Afghan Embassy, 3 February 1971
Confidential (FCO 21/838, FEC 3/548/5)

I asked Mr Pei whether he had yet had any reaction from Peking to the proposal about an Ambassador put to him by Mr Royle.[1] He said that he had conveyed what Mr Royle had said to Peking and awaited their reaction. In the meantime he must point out to me that on the question of confrontation prisoners in Hong Kong he had not seen any action by us. If relations were to be improved it was necessary that HMG should take positive steps. He then said that we should close our Consulate at Tamsui. I then asked if he meant that this was a condition to be met before we could exchange Ambassadors. Mr Pei did not go so far as to say that it was a condition, but he made it clear that without our closing Tamsui to exchange Ambassadors would not be possible. He said this in such a way that I enquired again if the issue of our Consulate was the only matter which would have to be resolved. If this was what he was saying it was an important matter.

2. Mr Pei then raised the question of the UN on which he seemed rather muddled. He said that it was important that we should vote for the Albanian resolution. When I pointed out that we had voted for it for many years he altered his tack and mentioned what he called the American resolution. I said that there was no certainty that the

---

1 No. 209.

important question would be posed in the same form at the next Assembly. Mr Pei then said that the Americans would propose another subterfuge to keep China out of the UN. such as proposing one China-one Taiwan solution. Britain must not support any such subterfuge. I said that without knowing whether the Americans had any such intention all that I would say was that I could not see a one China-one Taiwan solution getting off the ground since neither Peking nor Taiwan would accept it.

3. Mr Pei then reverted to the question of confrontation prisoners. I said that Mr Pei had made quite clear what were the Chinese Government's expectations in this matter. HMG understood the Chinese position. It was true, I said, that we had not been able to make any releases over the Chinese New Year, but Mr Pei must not think that this meant that we were unwilling to do anything. We were sometimes slow workers.

4. In the course of the conversation Mr Pei also raised the question of their desire to rebuild their house in Portland Place. At this point Mr Biggs Davison MP was with us and he joined in explaining to Mr Pei that matters of this kind did not lie within the control of the FCO. Despite what both he and I said Mr Pei persisted in saying that they would rely on the FCO to obtain for them what they wanted.

K. M. WILFORD

No. 218

Mr Denson (Peking) to Sir A. Douglas-Home, 9 February 1971
Confidential UK Eyes Only (FCO 21/850, FEC 14/7)

Sir,

British Subjects Detained in China: The End of a Chapter?

1. Hostage taking is not new in China where the position of foreigners has always been precarious. It is sometimes forgotten that the destruction of the Yuan Ming Yuan (the old Summer Palace) by British and French troops in 1860 so often held up as the supreme example of Western barbarity towards China, was in retaliation for the maltreatment and murder of hostages by the Chinese. One of those seized at the same time was the British envoy himself, Sir Harry Parks, who spent eleven days in chains in an appalling underground cell and was lucky to escape with his life. Happily Chinese methods have softened, but is hostage taking still a policy? With the arrival in Hong Kong on Christmas Day, 1970 of Mr David Johnston, the last expatriate detained, a sorry chapter in our relations with China is almost closed and the moment is therefore appropriate to give some account of what happened to the persons principally involved and the significance of the chapter as a whole.

The Victims

2. Mr Anthony Grey, Reuters correspondent in Peking, detained July 1967 and released in October 1969.

Mr George Watt, an engineer from the firm of Vickers-Zimmer detained in September 1967, tried in Lanchow in March 1968 and sentenced to three years imprisonment, released in August 1970.

Mr Eric Gordon, a former journalist employed by the Chinese. Detained together with his wife and young son in October 1967 and held in a Peking hotel. Released October 1969.

Mr David Crook

Mrs Elsie Epstein (née Fairfax-Cholmondely)

Mr Michael Shapiro

All three had been working in China for some years. They were reported to have been detained in the Autumn of 1967 and nothing has since been heard of them.

Mr Norman Barrymaine, a freelance journalist, arrested in Shanghai in February 1968 when visiting the city as a passenger on a Polish ship. Held in gaol and released in October 1969.

Second Officer Peter Crouch of s.s. 'Demodocus', arrested in Shanghai in February 1968, held in gaol and released in October 1970.

Captain Peter Will of m.v. 'Kota Jaya', arrested in Tangku (near Tientsin) in May 1968. Held in gaol and released in October 1969.

Mrs Gladys Yang, British wife of Professor Yang Hsien-yi working as a translator. Both were reported arrested in the early summer of 1968 and there has been no further information.

Mr David Johnston, formerly Manager of the Chartered Bank, Shanghai. Arrested and held in gaol in that city in August 1968. Released December 1970.

Mrs Constance Martin, a long time resident of Shanghai, employed by the Hong Kong and Shanghai Bank. Arrested in October 1969, held in gaol and released in April 1970.

Mr William McBain, a long time resident of Shanghai, living in retirement. Arrested in October 1969, held in gaol and released in February 1970.

Captain James Ray of s.s. 'Anchises', arrested in Shanghai on 1 March 1970, held in gaol and released on 26 March.

Second Officer Patrick Duff of s.s. 'Glenfalloch', arrested in Shanghai on 9 March, held in gaol and released on 26 March.

3. Memoranda based on researches by Mr Hugh Llewellyn Davies, recently HM Consul in Peking, which give details of the cases of Mr Grey and others detained are annexed.[1] The picture they give is necessarily incomplete in the case of Mr Grey because of the destruction of our archives in August 1967; and in certain other cases also because of the need to restrict the amount of paper held in the temporary Office.

4. Mr Anthony Grey was the first and only clear-cut case of hostage taking by the Central Government and until it was settled there was no real progress elsewhere although a number of Merchant Navy officers, including Chief Officer D. V. Jones, and Captain Pope were released after relatively short spells in gaol in 1967-68. Mr Grey was held in his house for over twenty-six months in retaliation for the arrest and sentencing in Hong Kong of members of the New China News Agency and other employees of Chinese Communist newspapers who were involved in the disturbances of the summer and autumn of 1967. Apart from the physical unpleasantness of Mr Grey's treatment, which he himself has vividly described, the Chinese deliberately prolonged the length of his detention by raising the price of his

---

1 Not printed.

release from the original eight Chinese ultimately to twenty-one. This might have been avoided if it had been possible to take quick and effective retaliatory action. Immediately after his arrest, consideration was given to expelling, or threatening to expel, representatives of the New China News Agency in London. The then Home Secretary[2] was however reluctant to exercise his powers under the Aliens Order as an instrument of foreign policy. The debate was overtaken by events—the burning of the Mission in August, the restriction on staff movements and the denial of exit visas. It was then rightly judged that retaliation against the New China News Agency on Mr Grey's behalf would have been not only pointless but dangerous. At various stages the Chinese showed themselves sensitive to the damage which the Grey case was doing [to] their international image and a desire to see it resolved. But having in December 1968 explicitly stated their terms, namely the release of the remaining thirteen news workers still in prison, they stuck to them. Furthermore, they insisted that Mr Grey could only be visited in exchange for 'official' visits to the Chinese concerned in Hong Kong. These people already received regular monthly visits from their relatives and employers. As a result Mr Grey was seen only three times. The eventual improvement in Mr Grey's conditions took place only after the Chinese knew that, as a result of action by the Prisons Board of Review in Hong Kong, the last remaining news worker would be released earlier than originally seemed likely and hence that Mr Grey himself would be released within five months.

5. Though the Chinese were unrelenting over Mr Grey, there can be no doubt that they were relieved when the case was finally closed. The remarks made to me by Chou En-lai on the evening Mr Grey was freed were evidence of this. Very soon afterwards, the Gordon family, Mr Barrymaine and Captain Will were allowed to leave China. Various explanations have been suggested for this choice—that Messrs Gordon and Barrymaine were journalists, there was intense feeling in the journalistic world and the Chinese preferred to get a bad press all at once; that the Gordons had a young son and Mr Barrymaine was ageing and unwell; that the offences committed were not unduly serious—in Gordon's case taking out notes for a book, in that of Barrymaine taking photographs and being under suspicion as a well-known adventurer who might have his finger in various intelligence pies. This leaves out Captain Will whose conduct was in some respects the most egregious of all and included, according to one report, urinating on a bust of Mao Tse-tung and certainly sailing his ship out of Tangku harbour without permission and with the Chinese frontier guards still on board. The explanation may be more simply that adequate confessions had been extracted from these persons and not from others. But what is clear is that the Chinese decided to make a gesture and they hoped it would be matched by the release of some confrontation prisoners in Hong Kong. While the Grey case persisted the Chinese did not specifically link other British subjects under detention with other prisoners in Hong Kong not connected with the press. But thereafter the link became increasingly explicit.

6. Shortly afterwards the Shanghai security authorities arrested two aged British subjects, Mrs Constance Martin and Mr William McBain, on what turned out after their release to be the flimsiest of grounds which suggests that they acted from vindictiveness because they had been obliged by the Central Government to disgorge

---

2 Mr Roy Jenkins.

Mr Barrymaine and there had been no dividend in Hong Kong. In this as in other fields Shanghai has always been something of an independent kingdom. The Martin and McBain cases were the occasion of the stormiest interview of the many which I had with the Chinese Ministry of Foreign Affairs about British subjects. The Chinese replied in kind to the representations 'in the strongest possible terms' which I had been instructed to make. Beneath the violence of the language lay some embarrassment and the need for self-justification. In the event Mr McBain, who was seriously ill, in prison, was released in February 1970 and Mrs Martin in April. Incidents in March involving two Merchant Navy officers in Shanghai, Captain Ray and Second Officer Duff were quickly settled.

7. It was against this background that Mr K. M. Wilford, Under-Secretary of State responsible for the Far East, visited Peking in April, the first visit by a Foreign Office official since before the Cultural Revolution. In discussion at the Ministry of Foreign Affairs, including a call on Vice-Minister Lo Kuei-po, the Chinese made it clear that an improvement in relations, which they repeatedly stated they wished to see, would be affected by whether or not there were progress on the release of confrontation prisoners. The Chinese set aside reference to British subjects still under detention emphasising the greater number of Chinese still imprisoned in Hong Kong, though no attempt was made to strike specific bargains. They merely told us in as many words that if we moved they would. At this stage the cases preoccupying us were those of Second Officer Crouch and Mr Johnston and the question of remission for Mr Watt. He was in fact released in July 1970 somewhat over thirty-four months after his original arrest, a remission of under two months. Soon after the release of four sick prisoners in Hong Kong, Mr Crouch was put across the border in October, and the release of two further sick prisoners apparently secured an exit visa for Mr Louis Dent, an ailing British subject in Shanghai who had previously not been allowed to leave. This left Mr Johnston and the group of four who had been employed by the Chinese. Very strenuous representations were made on Mr Johnston's behalf and his continued detention was described by the Parliamentary Under-Secretary of State in the House of Commons as a 'serious obstacle to the improvement of relations'.[3] By this time there had been improvements in other directions and the Chinese were becoming generally more active in diplomacy. It had been made clear in various ways that the Chinese Government wished to be dissociated from the action against the Mission in 1967 and to start a new chapter in their relations with us. I was informed on 22 December that it was as a gesture in this direction Mr Johnston would be released, and was presented with a memorandum asking for the release of the remaining seventy-four confrontation prisoners in Hong Kong, the first time the demand had been made in writing.

8. The fate of the four remaining British subjects believed to be detained is unknown. It seems likely they got into trouble during the Cultural Revolution either because they were suspected as foreigners of engaging in some illegal activities or were connected with Chinese who are in disgrace. Inevitably the Chinese have concluded that, while we are not indifferent to their fate, they matter less to us than those whose cases I have been discussing. I think that in due course they will work

---

3 Mr Anthony Royle. *Parl. Debs., 5th ser., H. of C.*, 16 November 1970, vol. 806, cols. 850-1.

their passages, but the Chinese may well decide not to surface them until such time as further releases of prisoners takes place in Hong Kong. There are also two British subjects in Shanghai who are having difficulties over exit permits, but in each case their dependants with whom they wish to leave are of Chinese or disputed nationality.

9. To conclude this section of the despatch, it should be recorded that, except in the case of Mr Grey, no consular access was allowed to any of those detained or imprisoned. Only Mr Watt and Mr Grey were allowed occasionally to receive and send letters. Repeated written and oral representations here and in London elicited no information about the health and welfare of those detained except in the cases of Messrs Ray and Duff. Apart from a press announcement of Mr Watt's sentence on espionage charges, no information was given about the charges preferred against British subjects who were merely said to have offended against the law, broken Harbour Regulations and so forth. Attempts to obtain copies of the regulations failed. In fact it is likely that no corpus of laws was then or is now being applied in China. Mr Watt's trial by a People's Court in Lanchow was a mass trial on standard lines where the howls of the mob and the vituperation of the lady judge replaced any judicial process. With the exception of Mr Watt who has said he was hit with a rifle butt at his trial and subsequently beaten and Mr Grey who was roughly handled when the Red Guards broke into his house, physical violence was not used, either during interrogation or at other times. Those detained, with the exception of Messrs Barrymaine and McBain when they were in hospital and the Gordon family who were kept together in one room, were held in solitary confinement. Food was sparse but adequate, interrogation was rigorous and confessions were extracted in all cases. Mr Watt was submitted to intensive courses of Mao Thought and others received only Communist publications to read but by contrast to two cases in [the] 1950's (Messrs Ford and Bull captured in Tibet)[4] no systematic attempt at brainwashing was made.

Chinese Motives

10. The decision to detain Mr Grey demonstrated China's extreme sensitivity about the Communist press in Hong Kong. The Chinese may also have regarded the members of the New China News Agency as enjoying some form of quasi-official status which entitled them to immunity. Our firm refusal to bow to pressure over Mr Grey in the first instance probably decided the Chinese to raise the price to the maximum. In the atmosphere of the Cultural Revolution when the so-called bourgeois aspects of the former society as well as all things foreign being condemned it was almost inevitable that foreigners should fall victim to the prevailing xenophobia. This is what happened in Lanchow to Mr Watt whose main sin was probably too loose a tongue. With Sino-British relations at rock-bottom and no give on the Grey case, the prospects for other British subjects who might offend the local authorities were far from bright. Excluding Mr Grey and the group working for the Chinese, seven out of the remaining nine were arrested in Shanghai, on the independence of which I have already commented. It is unlikely in the earlier stages that the Central Government wished or would have been able to intervene on their behalf. After Mr

---

4 Mr Robert Ford, a British radio operator, and Mr Geoffrey Bull, a British Christian missionary, were both imprisoned on espionage charges by the Chinese following the invasion of Tibet in October 1950. Bull was released from prison in 1953 and Ford in 1955.

Grey's release they probably did so on behalf of Mr Barrymaine and later on behalf of Mrs Martin, Captain Ray and Mr Duff. At the same time they may have been content to see the remaining British subjects treated as hostages.

11. A factor in the case of Second Officer Crouch was his personal attitude of toughness and intransigence which for a long time prevented him from admitting anything. In order to try to secure some progress, I was authorised to send him a carefully worded letter suggesting he made a suitable apology. In the event it was never delivered and it turned out his was the case in which the Chinese had most real grounds for complaint. Mr Johnston's case still remains the hardest to understand as the evidence on which he was accused of being 'an enemy of the Chinese people' is derisory. So far as we can discover, his detention had no connection with difficulties between the Chartered Bank and the Bank of China in Singapore, though the continued detention of a Belgian banker because of a dispute over blocked funds in the United States indicates that even at this stage the Chinese are capable of a crude form of blackmail against the national of a country with which they are not in relations and which is showing no particular signs of wishing to move towards them. On balance therefore we must conclude that the Chinese pursued a conscious policy of hostage taking in the case of Mr Grey and that they were prepared to use the weapon put into their hands in the form of other British subjects detained but that finally they become somewhat disillusioned with the policy and were prepared to make some gestures in the hope we would respond by removing their major problem in Hong Kong.

The Lessons

12. It remains to examine to what extent the measures which we took to secure the release of those detained were effective and to see if any lessons can be drawn for the future. As I have remarked, consideration was at one time given to taking retaliatory measures to secure Mr Grey's release. Later the feasibility of taking measures of administrative harassment against Chinese nationals in Britain was examined but it was decided they would require a disproportionate amount of effort and would be of dubious value in influencing the Chinese towards greater reasonableness. The possibility of enforcing economic sanctions was also explored. This would have been highly unpopular with the China traders and difficult to enforce. And again it probably would not have worked as other countries would not have co-operated and indeed would have been happy to profit from our self-imposed embargo. It turned out therefore that the only instruments in our hands were diplomatic representations, the publicity generated by public opinion and the press both at home and abroad, and measures of relaxation in Hong Kong, particularly the release of prisoners. For obvious reasons, the last was a matter of great difficulty. The Governor of Hong Kong considered any release of prisoners, for example by means of an amnesty, would affect public confidence in the ability of the authorities to maintain law and order and would amount to capitulation to Communist pressure. Diplomatic representations were maintained at an intensive level and there was continuous Parliamentary interest. Some discussions took place officially about whether publicity would be helpful or otherwise. In the case of Mr Grey, it would in any case have been impossible to stop as he was one of the journalistic fraternity. There is a good deal of evidence that the Chinese were irritated by publicity but none that they were deflected from a course of action because of it. In some cases the employers of those detained, the

Ocean Steam Ship Company in the case of Mr Crouch and the Chartered Bank in the case of Mr Johnston, counselled against it in the hope that the cases could be settled privately, but this did not work out. In general I consider publicity, coupled with diplomatic representations, was valuable in showing the Chinese that detained British subjects could not be swept under the carpet and if they wanted to improve relations something would have to be done about them first. What in the end broke the deadlock was first the Chinese were finally enabled to get off the hook of the Grey case; secondly, that considerable numbers of prisoners were released with full remission in Hong Kong (though the Chinese never accepted this as any form of gesture) and for certain special reasons it was found possible to release others by means of the Review Board procedure. All along I do not think the Chinese were expected [*sic*] the full loaf but only a few slices from time to time. (They could indeed have had the full loaf at any time if they had accepted the proposal of prisoners being 'released to China', but this they refused which demonstrated that political considerations as always took first place.)

13. Leaving aside the iniquity of the whole hostage policy, the inequity of the Chinese seeking to equate British subjects detained in China with convicted prisoners in Hong Kong, the Chinese refusal to grant consular access and so on, given the tumultuous period with which China was going through and the consequent difficulty of exercising central control I think we should be thankful that those unfortunate enough to be detained at Mao's pleasure did not fare worse. After the Grey affair was over the Chinese did make some effort to meet us and thereafter they matched any gesture we felt able to make. In neither the Grey nor the Watt case (the only two in which a terminal date was more or less certain) did the Chinese resort to threats of bringing charges which would result in long terms of imprisonment as did the Russians with Gerald Brooke.[5] This would indeed have been difficult with Mr Grey against whom no charges had been preferred. The revelations made by those detained after their release have apparently been ignored by the Chinese, with the exception of those by Mr Watt which we were particularly asked to curb in the interest of those still in China. This is possibly because by their curious canons of morality they considered that since Watt had been leniently treated because he had made a full confession he had no right on release to bite the hand that pardoned him.

14. We have now emerged from the nightmare period of the Cultural Revolution and with luck there should be no repetition of the chapter I have just described. I nevertheless think that we should remain cautious in the advice we tender to potential travellers to China and that visiting business men should be very fully briefed. It seems unlikely that the Chinese will again wish to see foreigners living for extended periods in the remoter parts of China where they might get into difficulties, and the word has obviously gone down to the local authorities that they are now to be nice to foreigners including ourselves. Nevertheless, xenophobia can well up quickly and the security of any of our citizens in difficulty will largely depend on the state of political relations between Britain and China. The continued detention of American

---

5 Brooke, a British subject, was sentenced by a Soviet court in 1965 to five years imprisonment for alleged anti-Soviet activity. He was released and returned to the UK in July 1969 as part of a spy-swap. See *DBPO*: Series III, Volume I: *Britain and the Soviet Union, 1968-1972* (London: HMSO, 1997).

and other foreigners is testimony to this and to China's continuing inclination to use foreign nationals in China as bargaining counters.

15. I am sending a copy of this despatch to HM Ambassador, Washington and to The Governor of Hong Kong.

I have, etc.
JOHN DENSON

No. 219

Letter from Mr McCluney to Mr Moon (No. 10), 10 February 1971
Confidential (FCO 21/838, FEC 3/548/5)

Sino-British Relations

Your letter of 1 February recorded the Prime Minister's comments on the paper about Sino-British relations.[1] The Prime Minister may wish to know the progress made so far in the implementation of the recommendations in the paper.

On 15 January Mr Royle proposed an exchange of Ambassadors to the Chinese Chargé d'Affaires.[2] The Chargé's initial reaction was receptive and he asked where subsequent discussion could take place. Mr Royle said in London, but the Chinese have not yet come back to us. Indeed on 3 February the Chargé told us that he had not yet received any comment from Peking.[3] As regards confrontation prisoners the Governor has agreed to convene his Prison Review Board on 18 February.[4] His response has not been as forthcoming as might have been hoped, but at least a start has been made in considering the sentences of the remaining 70 odd confrontation prisoners with a view to further early releases. Provided the present exercise goes as the Foreign and Commonwealth Secretary wishes we would very much like to secure the release of all the confrontational prisoners before the new Governor takes office in October. This may, however, be over-ambitious in the circumstances.

Our Chargé d'Affaires in Peking has been instructed to convey an invitation from the Secretary of State for Trade and Industry for the Chinese Government to send a broadly-based trade mission headed by a Minister or Vice-Minister. It is intended that this invitation should be passed to the new Minister for Foreign Trade when Mr Denson makes his first call on him. The Minister has only recently returned to Peking from abroad and the meeting has not yet taken place.

On 20 January the Minister at the Embassy at Washington asked the Assistant Secretary at the State Department for the United States reaction to a change in our vote on the Important Question Resolution at the next General Assembly.[5] The American response was disappointing—even somewhat confused, but suggests that they have in mind to proceed with a 'one China, one Taiwan' type of resolution (whereby the

1 Not printed.
2 See No. 209.
3 See No. 217.
4 See No. 221.
5 See No. 212.

Nationalists would declare themselves the republic of Taiwan and drop the claim to China proper), which the Chinese would undoubtedly see as a subterfuge to put off Peking's occupation of the China seat at the United Nations. They have asked us to wait 5-6 weeks for their considered views. The Embassy have been instructed to tell the State Department that delay beyond that could cause us difficulties. It has also been agreed that Lord Cromer should touch on this subject when he first sees Dr Kissinger.[1]

I. McCLUNEY

1 In a reply dated 15 February, Mr Moon noted that the Prime Minister welcomed the action being taken.

No. 220

Note for the Cabinet Defence and Oversea Policy Committee, Sub-Committee on Strategic Exports, 17 February 1971[1]
DOPO(SE)(71)1 Confidential (CAB 148/109)

Aircraft for China

After the meeting of the DOPO(SE) held on 17 November 1970 the Minister of Trade obtained the agreement of the Ministerial Sub-Committee to the memorandum prepared by the Official Chairman (DOP(SE)(70)3). The Prime Minister then indicated that he agreed with the recommendation contained in the memorandum to authorise the sale of four ex-BUA VC-10's to the Chinese, subject to United States and, if necessary, COCOM agreement.

2. The Caledonian/BUA offer was passed to the Chinese authorities on 27 November by our Mission in Peking. The Americans meanwhile were approached by our Embassy in Washington and, after examination of the list of US-made and US-licensed items of equipment, suggested the removal of the more sensitive of them, including the sole item embargoed by COCOM. Caledonian readily agreed, and on 24 December the Americans told our Embassy in Washington that there would be no difficulty in obtaining formal clearance for the export of American components if the export went through.

3. The Chinese considered the offer for some time and asked our Mission a number of technical questions. Their attitude throughout seemed to be one of suspicion because so few VC-10's were produced. On 29 December the Chinese Commercial Counsellor in London wrote to Mr John Keswick of the Sino-British Trade Council to tell him that the Chinese civil aviation authorities were not interested in 'used VC-10' aircraft. The Chinese Ministry of Foreign Trade confirmed on 23 January that this was their final answer to the Caledonian offer.

4. It seems that the Chinese will buy Russian 1L-62's, possibly for the Peking-Moscow route, and we know that they are still negotiating with the Russians. There is some uncertainty about delivery dates, and it is conceivable that the purpose

1 This note was sent for the information of the sub-committee who could inform their respective Ministers as necessary.

of the Chinese enquiry about VC-10's was only to compare details of performance, price and delivery with those of the 1L-62, and possibly to help force the Russians' hand.

FOREIGN AND COMMONWEALTH OFFICE

No. 221

Sir D. Trench (Hong Kong) to Sir A. Douglas Home
19 February 1971, 09.10 a.m.[1]
Tel. No. 108 Priority, Confidential (FCO 21/875, FEH 14/1A)

Your telegram No. 103[2] to me: Confrontation prisoners.

The Prison Board of Review, which met on 18 February, recommended to me reductions in the sentences on all 24 confrontation prisoners under consideration. I have accepted their recommendations.

2. 22 of the prisoners were due for release on 29 July this year, assuming remission of one-third. The Board of Review recommended that their sentences of six years should be brought into line with sentences of four and five years passed on others who had committed similar offences and that they should therefore be released as soon as convenient. The Board also recommended that sentences on two other prisoners due for release not earlier than 2 June 1972 and 2 September 1972 should be reduced from 7 years to 5 years, resulting in one becoming due for release immediately and the other on about 2 May.

3. In addition, and quite separately from the Board of Review, I have decided that Fung Chun-Sing should be released at the same time on grounds of undue hardship in prison resulting from partial disablement. The earliest release date would have been 9 May 1976.

4. In short, 24 confrontation prisoners will be released next Thursday, 25 February and one other about 2 May, apart from normal releases in the same period on expiry of sentence.

5. I have chosen this date because you will no doubt wish to make arrangements to inform Chinese government of these decisions. I hope you will consider 48 hours notice to them sufficient. If we give them more word would get back to the Communists here in time for them certainly to organise large scale 'welcome home' demonstrations, and possibly to mount an impressive and prior 'free the prisoners' campaign to which the actual release might be represented as a response. I hope you would also be able to avoid any suggestion that these releases are motivated by political considerations and would stress that they follow from the normal and humane procedures of the Hong Kong government.

6. We shall avoid publicity until the releases have taken place. Our information services will then say that as a result of an additional meeting of the Board of Review, recommendations had been made and accepted by me as described in para. 2 above.

1 Repeated for information to Peking.
2 Not printed.

7. The Board of Review will meet again on 18 March when so far about 8 more confrontation prisoners will be considered; but they are more difficult cases than this batch and I do not expect the Board to recommend reductions in sentence in more than a proportion of them. Moreover, reductions of sentence will not necessarily mean very early release (for example, in two cases life sentences were awarded which it is thought might be converted into fixed terms of imprisonment as is not unusual on review by the Board).

8. A list of the names of the prisoners to be released on 25 February follows by bag.

No. 222

Sir A. Douglas-Home to Sir D. Trench (Hong Kong)
22 February 1971, 5.42 p.m.[1]
Tel. No. 164 Immediate, Confidential (FCO 21/875, FEH 14/1A)

Your telegram No. 116:[2] Confrontation Prisoners.

The fact is that whenever we discuss Sino-British relations with the Chinese they invariably mention the Confrontation prisoners. While we shall certainly continue to avoid any public linking of the issues, I think it is quite unrealistic to pretend, in the course of our official contacts with the Chinese, that they are wholly unrelated. Denson will be speaking to T'ang in confidence and I can see no reason why he should not use the language he has proposed and does not in any way suggest we have responded to Chinese pressure. We have spoken similarly to Chinese Chargés here in the past.

1 Repeated for information immediate to Peking.
2 Not printed.

No. 223

Mr Allan (Peking) to Sir A. Douglas-Home, 3 March 1971, 7.05 a.m.[1]
Tel. No. 183 Immediate, Confidential (FCO 21/839, FEC 3/548/6)

MIPT:[2] Sino/British Bilateral Relations.

After preliminary remarks Chou referred to the British Office which, he said, had been burned down in 1967 by 'bad people'. The Chinese Government had been opposed to this, and people led by the Premier himself had broadcast to the mob urging them not to do it. However, these bad people had refused to obey. In the end it was only the PLA which had protected British Officials from harm.

1 Repeated for information immediate to Hong Kong. Shortly before going on leave Mr Denson received a call from the MFA to say that Chou En-lai would like to see him. He was received 45 minutes later, in the Prime Minster's office inside the Great hall of the People, and the meeting lasted two hours.
2 Not printed.

2. The Chargé said that he was glad to hear this from the Prime Minister, and also that Sino-British relations had made great advances since that time.

3. Chou said it was for this reason that the Chinese had sent Officials to attend the celebration of the opening of the new office. We said that the Chinese side would pay the costs of the rebuilding of the burned Chancery building

4. Chou said that Mr Royle and the Chargé had recently informed the Chinese that Hong Kong were releasing 25 imprisoned Chinese in Hong Kong. There were, however, still 49 in jail, and the Chinese Government and people were most concerned about them. The British were also concerned about some British citizens who had committed crimes in China and who were being detained. In order to improve relations between Britain and China, the Chinese hoped that the remaining prisoners in Hong Kong would be speedily released. This had important implications for the improvement of Sino-British relations. The Chargé said that this was a difficult and complicated question, which fell within the purview of the law in Hong Kong. The Board of Review had been used to review prisoners' sentences, which was a set legal procedure. This process would continue. The British Government were well aware of the importance that the Chinese Government attached to this question.

5. Chou asked the Chargé to convey to the Hong Kong authorities during his forthcoming visit the feelings of the Chinese Government. He said that there were many laws in Hong Kong which were of a provisional nature. 'Only he who attached the bell could untie it again'. He believed that the Governor would be retiring towards the end of the year. It would be a good thing if this matter could be completely resolved before his term of office ended. He went on to say that there were some British citizens who had committed crimes in China and whose cases the Chinese authorities were investigating. The Chargé said that this was true, and that we would be very grateful for any details the Chinese Government could give us. We acknowledged that if these people had transgressed against the law in China, then they must be subject to Chinese law. This was also true of Chinese in Hong Kong. However, the process of investigation had taken a long time and relatives and friends of these British subjects in England were anxious.

6. Chou replied that the MFA might be able to tell the Chargé something about these British subjects when he returned from leave. He said the British Government in the person of the Chargé himself and senior officials and ministers in the Foreign Office had constantly expressed a desire to improve relations with China. The People's Republic of China had been recognised by Britain at a very early date. Britain had been the first Western country to do so. However, relations remained at Chargé d'Affairs level, and it would be a pity if Britain was the last Western country to establish relations with China.

7. The Chargé said that we were ready to exchange Ambassadors with the PRC at any time. However, he believed that the Chinese Government felt that there were certain impediments in this. As we understood it, there were 2 problems: One was the question of Chinese representation at the United Nations; the second was the question of Taiwan. Could the Prime Minister confirm this?

8. Chou recalled the history of the establishment of relations at Chargé d'Affairs level. It had been impossible to establish relations at Ambassador level because Britain supported Taiwan in the UN instead of the restoration of Chinese lawful rights. The

United States had a problem in Taiwan, since they were occupying it, and committing aggression in the Taiwan straits. The UK did not have this problem. France had taken a different attitude and therefore her relations with China had developed faster than those with Britain. Why did not the UK have an independent policy?

9. The Chargé said we had no relations with the so-called 'Nationalist Government'. Our Consulate, which was very small, dealt mainly with commercial matters and was accredited to the provincial authorities in Taiwan. At the UN we had voted for the Albanian Resolution since it had first been proposed. We had also voted for the Important Question Resolution since we considered that it was an important question. None of this, in our view, constituted recognition of a second China as opposed to the People's Republic of China. Chou said that we could not put things in that way. The United Kingdom, as a permanent member of the Security Council, had been the first Western country to recognise the CPR Government as the sole legal government representing the Chinese people. Since this was so, how could we believe that the question of Chinese representation was an 'Important' one? This resolution was simply a United States trick.

10. The Chargé said that he did not think that it could be denied that it was an important question. However, he recognised that with the passing for the first time last year of the Albanian Resolution by a simple majority, a new situation had arisen. He was not yet in a position to tell the Premier what our policy would be when the question arose again, but we were actively considering it.

11. Chou said that the Chinese Government found Britain's position illogical in the United Nations, and very difficult to understand. Related to the problem of the United Nations, there was the question of Taiwan. Taiwan was a province of China. If it was not for the protection of the United States, it would by now be an integral part of China. For the British Government to maintain a Consulate in Taiwan was like having '2 feet in 2 boats'. The Chargé said that there was a legal difficulty for us. After the Japanese had relinquished sovereignty over the island we held that the status of Taiwan was undetermined. He knew that the Chinese government did not agree with this view and would never be able to agree with it, but he was grateful to the Prime Minister for making it clear.

12. Later Chou said that the Chinese had always supported the British Government when she had taken an independent policy, such as the Chinese themselves had taken. Improvement and development of Sino-British relations could become possible, but it would be difficult if the UK had to follow the United States on certain questions. The Chargé said every Government pursued the policy which it saw as being in its own national interest. If another Government chose to think that this was following in the footsteps of a third government, this was their affair. However, even if we had to agree to disagree on certain points, perhaps we could still make progress elsewhere.

13. Chou said that the Chinese were not making what he called an independent policy a pre-condition for progress in every field. Each government should have its own independent judgement, and this judgement should proceed from the facts. The Prime Minister, Secretary of State and Chargé had all expressed a desire to improve Sino-British relations. Chairman Mao had also expressed such a desire, and in accordance with this directive the Chinese Government had expressed the desire to improve relations and had taken concrete actions. He had taken this opportunity to

clarify his Government's position, especially in regard to the UN in this question, the initiative did not lie with the Chinese. The Chinese felt that Britain had not followed an independent policy in the UN. There were problems in Sino-British relations but it should not be difficult to put them right. If the UK wished to follow its old policy, that was, of course, its own concern, but the Chinese Government wished to clarify the matter, because it affected Sino-British relations.

14. There was one more question relating to Hong Kong. Should the authorities in Hong Kong contact the Kuang-Tung Provincial Authorities, or the authorities in Peking? Sometimes Hong Kong contacted the Kuang-Tung authorities and sometimes the Peking authorities, via the Office of the Chargé d'Affaires. But there was no official relationship in Hong Kong. Nevertheless we maintained that we must have an official office in the province of Taiwan! This was a contradictory position. The Chargé said he thought that the authorities in Hong Kong dealt with the Kuang-Taung authorities in general on matters which were essentially local, such as the water supply, but on matters which were thought more appropriate to diplomatic level, we preferred to talk through Chargé d'Affaires.

15. Chou, summing up the conversation, said that the first point was the Chinese Government's concern over the Chinese people in Hong Kong who had not yet been released. Discussion of this question had led to discussion of many others.

16. Much of the rest of the discussion about Korea and Indo-China also bears directly on Sino-British Relations, see MIFT.[3]

3 Not printed. In a letter to Mr Graham of 22 March regarding the meeting, Mr Moon reiterated the Prime Minister's view that British policy should be to go ahead with normalising relations with Peking while trying to avoid sacrificing trade interests with Taiwan.

No. 224

Sir A. Douglas-Home to the Earl of Cromer (Washington)
9 March 1971, 10.25 a.m.[1]
Tel. No. 695 Priority, Confidential (FCO 21/808, FEC 2/2A)

Your Telno 776:[2] Chinese Representation in the United Nations.

The Minister[3] at the US Embassy called, at his request, on Mr Royle on 8 March. He spoke along the same lines as Irwin adding informally that the Americans might be in a position to take a decision this week.

2. Mr Royle stressed the importance we attached to an early decision by the Americans, our relations with China had greatly improved. We had different policy restraints from the Americans both because of our relations with Peking and the importance to us of Hong Kong. Chou En-lai had recently summoned our Chargé d'Affaires—the first time any Chinese Prime Minister had done so. Mr Royle

1 Repeated for information to Peking and UKMIS New York.
2 Not printed.
3 Mr Joseph Greene.

said that he had himself raised with the Chinese the question of an exchange of Ambassadors. The Chinese always sited as an obstacle our continued support for the Important Question Resolution. Chou En-lai had again laid great emphasis on this. We had noted President Nixon's recent remarks about China and we saw our improved relations as in our own as well as the US long-term interest. It would be folly for the UK not to take advantage of the new climate of friendship.

3. It would be helpful if the Americans could tell us that they no longer intended to table the Important Question Resolution. We would then be able to assure the Chinese we would not support it in the knowledge that it would not be put. Mr Royle said that we did not doubt the sincerity of the US Government's search for a reasonable and equitable solution. HMG had already made clear that it would not support any 'Two Chinas' solution as this would not be acceptable either to Peking or Taiwan.

4. Greene asked about our attitude to the expulsion of Taiwan. Mr Royle said that in supporting the Albanian Resolution since 1961 we had recognised that this entailed the expulsion of the Nationalists. We nevertheless maintained our links with Taiwan and indeed were endeavouring to increase our trade.

5. Mr Royle assured Greene that we would keep them informed about our attitude to the Important Question Resolution and in particular would not make any public statement on this matter without further discussion.

6. The Parl. Under Secretary of State also informed the US Minister of the discussion between Mr Denson and Chou En-lai.

No. 225

Mr Littlejohn Cook (Bangkok) to Sir A. Douglas-Home
9 March 1971, 3.26 a.m.[1]
Tel. No. 136 Priority, Confidential (FCO 21/839, FEC 3/548/6)

For Morgan from Denson.

1. The following are some points which emerged in conversations with the Governor about my interview with Chou.

(*a*) The Governor was upset by Chou's reported remark that the problem of prisoners should be settled before his term was over, and thought this was an attempt to exert pressure to humiliate him. Since my recollection of the remark differed from this, I undertook to point it out to you and said in any case I did not think this was the intention.

(*b*) The Governor said under the review procedure a few more prisoners could probably be released, and the two life sentences could be commuted in the normal way, to say 14 years. But in the end, probably by the Board in July, we should have got down to an irreducible minimum of 30 or so about whom nothing could be done. He thought that this would be the time to tell the Chinese that the end of the road had come. I pointed out that past experience suggested it was wise not to close doors. This did not help those in China like Chou, who were trying to pursue pragmatic and generally reasonable policies. The Governor said not to do so would

---

1 Repeated for information routine to Peking (personal for Allan).

lead the Chinese to conclude that all that was needed was further pressure to achieve a political amnesty. He remained totally opposed to this and might well resign if it were pressed on him, (for what it is worth my impression from talking to a number of prominent Chinese businessmen and bankers is the recent releases were regarded as a sensible measure further to relax relations with China, and had no effect on confidence. Political Adviser and Trade Commissioner confirm from conversations they have had with Chinese. My meeting with Chou was also taken as a good sign.)

(c) The Governor reverted to the references I made to the release of the 24 prisoners being a contribution to improving relations. I pointed out that we were under no illusions about the limitations on such an improvement and the many areas e.g. Indo-China where we could never fundamentally agree. So no doubt were the Chinese; but their present policy was so far as possible to improve bilateral relations with countries with which they were in relations within their own ideological and political framework. They wanted to do so with the UK and what matters to them most were problems nearest home: Taiwan, the UN and prisoners.

(d) The Governor asked how seriously the Chinese took the question of official representation in Hong Kong to which Chou had referred. I replied that I thought it was not a matter of the first importance—it came almost as an afterthought at the end of the talk, and was possibly a proposal by the local Communists. The Governor said it was out of the question and thought we should again let it drop. At a meeting I had with UMELCO[2] Y. K. Kan[3] also raised the question and the group were unanimously opposed to the idea. I parried an enquiry as to whether Chou had raised it.

2. The Governor told me that he would probably not comment on the Chou conversation unless he was asked to do so. The foregoing should not be taken as his considered views and of course not referred to in correspondence with him. I am afraid he still remains deeply suspicious of HM Government's intentions and the possibility of Hong Kong's interests (as he see them) being sacrificed in pursuit of the false fire of improved Sino-British relations.

2 Office of the Unofficial Members of the Executive and Legislative Councils of Hong Kong.
3 Yuet-keung Kan, Hong Kong banker, politician and lawyer.

No. 226

Sir A. Douglas-Home to Mr Denson (Peking), 26 March 1971, 6.20 p.m.[1]
Tel. No. 182 Priority, Confidential (FCO 21/832, FEC 3/548/2)

MIPT.[2]

P'ei's remarks about an exchange of Ambassadors constitute the formal Chinese reply to Mr Royle's approach on 15 January. The 2 preconditions for an exchange

1 Repeated for information priority to Hong Kong, Washington and Tamsui.
2 Not printed. Mr Morgan had asked P'ei to call to inform him of the latest releases of confrontation prisoners in Hong Kong. He also asked for clarification of Chou En-lai's remarks about an exchange of Ambassadors and added that they were still waiting for a reply from the Chinese government to Mr Royle's question on 15 January (see No. 209).

have now been set out unambiguously. These are an undertaking no longer to support the Important Question Resolution and the withdrawal of our Consulate in Taiwan. It is significant that at no stage in the interview did P'ei refer to our position on the legal status of Taiwan. The implication of his statement seems to be that if we were prepared to take action on the 2 points we could exchange Ambassadors with a formal communiqué.

No. 227

Letter from Mr Denson (Peking) to Mr Morgan, 6 April 1971
Personal and Confidential (FCO 21/833, FEC 3/548/3A)

Dear John,

You will have seen my telegram no. 315[1] about the exchange of Ambassadors which confirms your view that the physical presence of the Consulate at Tamsui is of more concern to the Chinese than our position on the legal status of Taiwan. We have heard from a member of the Soviet Embassy that during a recent meeting between Tolstikov[2] and Chou En-lai, the latter spoke about Sino/British relations saying that the obstacles to improvement were the Consulate at Tamsui and our support for the Important Question Resolution. Again no mention was made of our legal problem.

2. It has seemed to me that there were three main reasons for maintaining the Consulate:

(*a*) to promote British exports;
(*b*) to deal with visa work, particularly visas for Hong Kong;
(*c*) to benefit from the presence of the Naval Liaison Officer.

To start with the last. Having seen the NLO's product during my time in Far Eastern Department, I had always doubted whether he served any useful purpose. Duffy's letter of 11 March[3] amply confirms this view. As to visas work, this could presumably be done by post or through a travel agency as happens in some countries. This is something on which you would no doubt wish to have the views of the Hong Kong Government but I imagine it would not be regarded as a major obstacle to closure if it were decided to go ahead for other reasons. The main value of the Consulate, and presumably the main reason which would be adduced for its retention by the Formosa lobby, is its value in trade promotion. I note that various improvements are now to be made in trade promotion work. Personally I have often wondered whether this work might not be done better if we had no representation at all, given that the Consul and his staff are inhibited for political reasons from having contacts with Central Government Ministers and officials. Other countries like France and West Germany seem to do very well without representation.

3. So far as export promotion is concerned the key man in the Consulate seems to be locally engaged Commercial Officer, Juan Huang. If he could somehow be employed under non-government aegis, say in Taipei in a different office, he could

1 Not printed.
2 Vasily Sergeyevich Tolstikov, Russian Ambassador to China, 1970–79.
3 Not printed.

assist British businessmen and have wider contacts since he had no political affiliations. I am told that if Mr Huang and any supporting staff were taken over by a body such as the Federation of British Industries or the Association of British Chamber of Commerce this would have the disadvantage that Tamsui could no longer be listed in the Board of Trade Journal. However, I think this would be much preferable to other arrangements such as a 'British Commercial Office' which would be registered here as merely a disguised form of Consulate. There are also, I am told, such beings as 'British trade correspondents'. This title would probably be less offensive from the Chinese point of view. But ideally the less official sounding and the less connection with the firm the better.

4. No doubt all these ideas are very much in your mind, but I thought you might care to have our views on record. I need hardly say from our point of view closing the Consulate could do nothing but good, quite apart from the question of an exchange of Ambassadors. When the subject was raised earlier by Arthur Maddocks it was decided, probably rightly, that at that time sacrificing the Consulate would not be sufficient to have a decisive influence on relations at a time when so many other problems were outstanding. The situation has now entirely changed. We have formally proposed that there should be an exchange of Ambassadors and the Chinese have stated their terms. We are at present benefitting from a Chinese desire to improve relations. Now is probably as good or indeed a better moment than any other to decide to go for an exchange of Ambassadors. If we do not do so, I do not think that the problem will get any easier in the future. Indeed our general relations with China might well slip back for one reason or another. Furthermore we shall remain at the disadvantage of having a lower-level representative at a time when China is expanding her diplomatic contacts and showing some disposition to find out the views of others.

5. I am not copying this letter to Tamsui as I do not know how far your thinking has gone, and to what extent and in what form you intend to consult Duffy.

Yours ever,
JOHN

No. 228

Submission from Mr Morgan to Mr Wilford, 6 April 1971
Confidential (FCO 21/833, FEC 3/548/3A)

Exchange of Ambassadors with China

Problem

1. For the first time since 1950 when the United Kingdom recognised the Peking Government the Chinese have clearly stated the actions they consider necessary before an exchange of Ambassadors can take place. These are:

(*a*) that we should no longer support the Important Question Resolution in the United Nations if it were tabled,

(*b*) that we should withdraw our Consulate from Taiwan.

Should we now accept? The Secretary of State is to discuss this at a meeting at noon on 7 April.

Argument

2. Over the last 21 years the Chinese have stated various preconditions to an exchange of Ambassadors with us but never in any precise form and always with the implication that if we met them other conditions would be forthcoming. It was open to the Chinese in the present state of our relations to raise four specific preconditions. These were:

(*a*) the release of the 41 remaining confrontation prisoners in Hong Kong;

(*b*) a change in our view that the status of the sovereignty of Taiwan is undetermined;

(*c*) that we should no longer support the Important Question Resolution in the United Nations if it were tabled.

(*d*) that we should withdraw our Consulate from Taiwan.

In fact the Chinese have chosen to require only the last two of these. Mr P'ei informed me categorically on 26 March that these were the only two obstacles. He also said that only action on our part was now required before an immediate exchange of Ambassadors could take place. It therefore seems likely that we would not require to agree to a formal communiqué which could involve us in a statement on (*b*) above. Communiqués have been required by the Chinese of those countries recently establishing relations such as Canada and Italy. We would be free in our own statements to reaffirm that we continued to regard sovereignty over Taiwan as undetermined.

Important Question Resolution

3. The Americans were warned last October that we would be considering a change in our attitude to the Important Question Resolution. Despite reminders they have not yet formulated any official response to our intention beyond saying 'that they would be glad to talk to us as long as we were still there to listen'. They have, however, made clear that they would hope that we would not take any decision until they have decided what tactics to adopt at the next session of the General Assembly. They are pursuing the idea that representation in Taiwan should be maintained even if Peking occupies the China seat. We can see no basis on which they can produce a workable scheme. Moreover Mr Godber minuted on 8 March that

'We must not let the State Department put an embargo on us . . . We should therefore do no more than undertake to keep them informed of any steps we may be contemplating'.

The arguments in favour of changing our stand have been set out in detail in previous submissions in particular my submission of 11 September.[1] Since then it has become clear that support for the motion will be considerably eroded should it be tabled again in its usual form this year. The Italians have told us they intend changing and the Canadians are also likely to do so. Other countries who have recently recognised are likely to follow suit. Eight countries have recognised Peking in the last six months. It is indeed very likely that the Americans will decide not to table the motion at all.

---

1 No. 194.

4. Irrespective of its implications for the question of an exchange of Ambassadors I would recommend strongly that we did not support the motion this year. Were we to do so in the light of the recent marked improvement in our relations it would have a disproportionate effect on the whole course of Sino-British relations.

5. I recommend that we now inform the Americans that we will no longer support the Important Question Resolution, but that we would not make our decision public. Nevertheless it would almost inevitably be deduced when an announcement of our first Ambassador to Peking was made. The simple fact is that American policy and ours on China are most unlikely to coincide *in toto* given our relations with Peking and our special problem over Hong Kong on the one hand and American ties with Chiang Kai-shek and involvement in Vietnam on the other. In our discussions with the Americans we have told them only that we intend changing our vote but have not specified whether it would be to opposition or to abstention. The latter would be adequate for our purpose with the Chinese and it might soften the blow with the Americans if we were to tell them that we only intended abstaining. In practice, however, the effect on the outcome for the Resolution, if tabled, would be much the same.

6. Mr Royle has suggested that the Secretary of State might wish to take the opportunity of Mr Rogers' presence here for the SEATO meeting (27-28 April) to inform him personally of our decision. We should also inform the Australian and New Zealand Governments, possibly taking advantage of the presence here of Sir K. Holyoake and Mr Bury at the end of April.

British Consulate, Tamsui

7. On 22 March the Prime Minister commented that:

'Our policy should be to go ahead with normalising relations with Peking while trying to avoid sacrificing our trade interests in Taiwan'.

The DTI have been formally consulted by Export Promotion Department. Their preliminary reaction is that the potential for trade is so great with Peking that this should be over-riding. They can produce no evidence to suggest that the Consulate in Taiwan has facilitated any specific export. This is understandable given the restrictions imposed on the Consul by our recognition policy which debars him from contacts with Ministries of the 'Republic of China'. A number of Members of Parliament have an interest in the maintenance of the Consulate and a decision to close it can be expected to arouse criticism. Mr Royle is taking preliminary soundings. It is arguable that if there was sufficient commercial interest to justify unofficial links it would be possible to establish a more business-like relationship with the Central Government authorities. In 1968 (the latest year for which figures are available) West German exports were valued at £14.56 million (20% increase over 1967) without any resident representation or recognition. Ours now amount to some £6 million per annum. Mr Royle asked that the CBI be tentatively approached. The Director General has agreed that, if it was thought there was need for some sort of representation along the lines of the British Business Bureau which is being established in East Berlin, they would be prepared to look at the possibility.

8. There is at present included in the Tamsui Consulate staff a Naval Liaison Officer. The Ministry of Defence have been sounded about their attitude to his removal. They tell us that this officer is able to obtain useful intelligence on mainland Chinese activities from the Nationalist authorities (although we and HM Consul

have yet to see any evidence of this). While they would wish to keep the post so long as the Consulate remains open they would greatly prefer an opportunity to appoint Service Attachés to Peking with far greater[2] potential.

9. The Consulate in Taiwan issues large numbers of visas mainly for Nationalist Chinese visiting or passing through Hong Kong. The easiest way in which this work could be continued would be if the Australian Embassy in Taipei could be induced to take it over. This would however be a heavy burden for them and they would probably have to take over our locally engaged visa staff. We should also need to look into the financial aspect; payment to the Australians and loss of revenue from fees. An alternative solution would be for Nationalists travelling to Hong Kong to apply for visas by post direct to the Hong Kong Immigration Department. This is what has happened in Macau since the closure of our Consulate there. In view of the large numbers involved this is not a solution which will appeal to the Immigration Department, but might make the Australians more ready to deal with the much small number of applications for United Kingdom visas. We should need to consult the Australian and Hong Kong authorities, and also the Government of Singapore on whose behalf the Consulate of Taiwan issues a substantial number of visas, but it should not prove impossible to make adequate alternative arrangements.

The Ambassador

10. Personnel Operations Department have for some time been keeping Mr Addis in mind for the post of Head of Mission at Peking. Subject to the Board so recommending, Personnel Department consider that there should be no difficulty in extracting him from his present post (Instructor at the Royal College of Defence Studies) at short notice.

Recommendation

11. That we propose Mr Addis to the Chinese as Ambassador. In so doing informing them that we will no longer support the Important Question Resolution if tabled and that we are taking steps to withdraw our Consulate from Taiwan. I recommend also that we should inform the Americans of our decision sometime in advance, undertaking to give no publicity to our intentions over the Important Question Resolution. We should also inform the Australian and New Zealand Governments.

12. North American Department, UN (Pol) Department, Export Promotion Department, Hong Kong Department, Personnel Policy Department, Personnel Operations Department, Migration and Visa Department, and PUS Department concur.

Background

13. On 5 January the Secretary of State sent the Prime Minister a paper about Sino-British relations.[3] The Prime Minister commented that we should:

'be getting on with the policy outlined with a view to achieving some results'.

2. The policy and objectives set out in that paper were:

(*a*) To normalise and improve our bilateral contacts.

(*b*) To increase our share of the Chinese market, in particular, in capital goods.

(*c*) To help to bring China into a healthier relationship with the rest of the world, and, in particular:

---

2 A word or words have been retained here under section 3(4) of the Public Records Act, 1958.
3 No. 205.

(i) to useful membership of the United Nations, and

(ii) to participate in international agreements, such as the Nuclear Test Ban Treaty, which are of limited meaning without her.

(*d*) To maintain the peace and prosperity of Hong Kong.

(*e*) To maintain and improve our presence in Peking, which gives us an exceptionally high level of specialist Chinese expertise. This is of outstanding use in the context of intelligence exchanges with our allies.

The paper pointed out that a British Ambassador would be received on a higher level in Peking and could have a greater influence on Chinese thinking. Amongst the conclusions of the paper was 'that we should pursue more actively the possibility of raising our diplomatic representation—eventually to that of Ambassadors'.[4]

J. A. L. MORGAN

4 Sir A. Douglas-Home minuted on 10 April: 'I am more concerned about the Americans than the submission. We want some very important things out of the Administration just now. I will talk to Mr Rogers. My inclination is to (i) drop the 'important question'; (ii) release some more prisoners; (iii) say that Taiwan is a matter for the UN but that Peking should be a permanent member of the Security Council; (iv) say that we would only recognise if they were to opt to be a separate country'.

No. 229

Minute from Mr Logan to Mr Graham, 7 April 1971
Confidential (FCO 21/833, FEC 3/548/3A)

Private Secretary,

Mr Royle agrees with Mr Morgan's recommendation.[1] He thinks however that the following points should be borne in mind:

(*a*) We should be certain that, although we cannot expect to receive American support for our change of policy over the UN vote and Tamsui, we at least have their tacit acceptance of our intentions. It is suggested in the submission that the Secretary of State talks to Mr Rogers when the latter is here for the SEATO Ministerial meeting.

(*b*) We should endeavour to reduce as far as possible the opposition of those Conservative Members of Parliament who have strong connections with Taiwan. We might therefore consider telling the Chinese that it is our intention to change our vote on the Important Question Resolution, and that we recognise the Government of the People's Republic of China as the sole legal government of China. This could meet the Peking Government's point, as the Consulate in Tamsui is accredited to the Provincial Government of Taiwan. If it proved unacceptable to the Chinese we then accept the closure of the Consulate. Mr Royle recognises that there are dangers in such a move; the Chinese might attempt to introduce further conditions, including the question of Confrontation prisoners and the status of Taiwan, but he feels that it might be unwise to meet both the Chinese points straightaway. In this respect Mr Royle has Mr Denson's telegram No. 182[2] in mind.

1 No. 228.
2 Not printed.

2. I understand that the Secretary of State agreed with Mr Royle that he would consider these papers over the recess, and would decide whether he felt it necessary to discuss the matter at an office meeting after Easter.

D. B. C. LOGAN

No. 230

Letter from Mr Maddocks (Hong Kong) to Mr Wilford, 13 April 1971
Secret (FCO 21/833, FEC 3/548/3A)

Sino-British Relations

Dear Michael,

I imagine that you have started a review of relations between Britain and China in the light of John Denson's interview with Chou En Lai (Peking telegrams Nos. 183[1] and 184[2] to FCO of 3 March). We shall be very interested to hear in due course how your thoughts are developing. Meanwhile you may like to have the following comments on how it looks from Hong Kong.

2. Apart from his remarks on Indo-China, which do not concern Hong Kong at all, Chou En Lai raised four subjects:

(*a*) the United Nations;
(*b*) the Consulate at Tamsui;
(*c*) confrontation prisoners in Hong Kong; and
(*d*) possible Chinese representation in Hong Kong.

(*a*) *The United Nations*

3. When Peking obtains the China seat in the UN it seems likely that the increasing respectability and prestige that China will acquire will produce some inconvenience in Hong Kong. Our population are alert to changes in status and quick to move to what they think may be the winning side or at the very least to try to hedge their bets. There is no logical connection between Peking occupying the China seat in the UN and a change in the relations of Hong Kong with China but some people here may think that one is a forerunner of the other. Attention may turn a little more to 1997 with consequences that can only be awkward for the Hong Kong Government.

4. We think that when Peking sits in the UN there will be some development of opinion in Hong Kong in that direction but we do not think that it will get out of hand or present us with problems which are seriously embarrassing. In any case it seems inevitable that China will occupy the UN seat at some date in the next few years and it is not sensible for us to ask you to try to stop the process or even to delay it because of these worries about possible developments in Hong Kong. On the UN issue therefore there are no Hong Kong considerations that need to be taken into account in London.

(*b*) *The Consulate at Tamsui*

---

1 No. 223.
2 Not printed.

5. I assume that it is reasonable to consider the question of withdrawing the Consul from Tamsui as a question on its own, in other words that withdrawal would probably not be associated with any significant deterioration of relations between Taiwan and Hong Kong. As you know, those relations do not exist on any official level but flourish exceedingly on every other level. In 1970 we imported from Taiwan goods worth HK$820 million, Taiwan being our fifth largest supplier, surpassed only by Japan, China, the USA and the United Kingdom, and we sold to Taiwan domestic exports to the value of HK$147 million, Taiwan being our 10th largest market. It seems a reasonable assumption that the Taiwan authorities would not want to disturb trade of that size which is so much in their favour. Hong Kong is also much more important to Taiwan than Taiwan to Hong Kong as a convenient communications centre.

6. On that assumption, our opinion is that the withdrawal of British consular representation from Taiwan would cause us only minor problems. We should not feel the loss of the political and economic reporting of the Consulate. Matters concerning civil aviation, shipping and other communications, which at the moment pass to a small extent through the Consulate, could, we think, easily be handled by commercial channels. The most awkward problem we should have would relate to visas. We should not want to relax the controls we now have over visitors from Taiwan and we should therefore have to make other arrangements for visa applications by Taiwan residents to be communicated to our Immigration Department by travel agencies or other bodies in Taiwan and the actual visa granted on arrival here. We see no insuperable difficulties.

7. There would no doubt be some criticism from the pro-KMT elements in Hong Kong but we would find that quite acceptable, indeed desirable so far as relations with Peking go, and we could in any case blame it on London!

(c) Confrontation Prisoners in Hong Kong

8. Our views are already well known to you. The Board of Review will meet again in June when there will probably be 37 confrontation prisoners still in Stanley.[3] The Board will consider about 13 cases, but we shall be surprised if we get recommendations to reduce sentences in as many as half of them. It is difficult at the time of writing to assess what effect the coincidence of the news of early releases announced in March, and the recent spate of 'bombing', will have on the minds of the unofficial members of the Board. After the June meeting there are unlikely to be any more cases in which the Board will be invited to consider a possible reduction of sentence.

9. We shall, therefore, reach a position after the June meeting when no more recommendations to reduce sentences can be expected from the Board of Review, because the Attorney General and the Governor personally will then have examined the case of every prisoner and the Board will have reviewed every case of every prisoner and the Board will have reviewed every case put forward for consideration. We shall by then still have perhaps 30 or so in prison.

10. It will thereafter be possible to release confrontation prisoners only through a 'political' decision outside our present procedures. I need hardly say that the

---

3 A high-security prison in Hong Kong.

Governor would continue to recommend against any such move and that he does not see anything in Chou En Lai's remarks to make him change that view. Indeed the recent 'bombing' has, if anything, made it more difficult to contemplate any such course of action. It was after all not the Governor who attached the bell but the judges.

(*d*) *Possible Chinese Representation in Hong Kong*

11. The Mission's record of Chou En Lai's remarks on this subject indicates that it was a very small item in the conversation and that no particular proposal was made. But we know . . .[4] that it has been presented to the communists here as being a much more important item and in the form that one of the existing Chinese officials, e.g. the head of NCNA, would be given some kind of quasi diplomatic or consular status.

12. At first sight such a proposal might seem not unreasonable. If China were prepared to have a Consul-General in Hong Kong it might even be regarded as an admission by China that Hong Kong was a separate territory. But in fact we regard the idea with the gravest suspicion. In paragraph 3 above I mentioned the tendency of our population to be quick to hedge their bets. We already see in Hong Kong a nauseating tendency to try to curry favour with the NCNA in the hope of getting commercial or travel favours in China. If the head of NCNA for example were given some more important status this tendency might grow and it would be very difficult to stop especially in later years as the uncertainty of 1997 attracted more attention. I believe Sir Alexander Grantham[5] commented on an earlier version of this proposal by saying that there could not be two Governors in Hong Kong. We therefore consider that we should have nothing to do with any such idea.

13. I think we could reasonably say to Peking that the existing arrangements work satisfactorily, i.e. that on technical matters such as water, post, railways, civil aviation, meteorology, direct technical contacts already exist which could be improved if China wishes, whilst contacts between governments on important matters are appropriate for the diplomatic channel in London and Peking, not in Hong Kong. From our point of view there would be some advantage in telling Peking as soon as possible that we would not agree to any formal Chinese representation in Hong Kong but there may be some practical difficulties in communicating that message in advance of communications on other matters raised by Chou En Lai. There may also be some doubt whether it is advisable to give a firm negative to a question which Chou En Lai put only in rather vague language and which we have seen in clearer language only in secret communications. From the Hong Kong point of view we should like to have a clear negative expressed soon but we can understand that you may see the matter differently.

14. In brief, of the four points mentioned in paragraph 2 above (*a*) and (*b*) give us little trouble but (*c*) and (*d*) we do not like at all.

Yours ever,
ARTHUR

---

4 A word or words have been retained here under section 3(4) of the Public Records Act, 1958.
5 Governor of Hong Kong, 1947-1957.

No. 231

The Earl of Cromer (Washington) to Sir A. Douglas-Home
15 April 1971, 11.02 p.m.[1]
Tel. No. 1299 Priority, Confidential (FCO 21/833, FEC 3/548/3A)

Personal for Head of Far Eastern Department from Millard.
Your letter of 7 April to Denson.
Exchange of Ambassadors with China.

1. Thank you for letting us see these papers.

2. While I have much sympathy with the aims set out in your submission,[2] I have some reservations about the timing, particularly with regard to what we say to the Americans. I do not suggest that Ministers need delay taking a decision in principle on your recommendations, especially in the light of the recent rapid thaw in the Americans' own relations with China, which may make it much harder for the US Government to mobilise effective international support for the kind of alternative UN scenario which they evidently had in mind. However, in deciding how to how to handle with the Americans any ministerial decision on your recommendations you will no doubt wish to take account of the fact that the US Review on Policy on Chinese Representation at the UN is now with the President and there are some indications that a decision will be reached shortly. Though the latest developments in Sino/American relations could lead to further delay, the State Department spokesman has referred to an announcement being expected 'soon'. If the Americans are in fact on the point of being able to give us their views, we might give them unnecessary and avoidable offence by notifying them of a decision by HMG to go ahead on the lines you recommend without at least giving them a further and final indication that time is running out for us. From our point of view it would be greatly preferable to warn them fairly shortly that we have done our best to meet their request to await the results of their own review but that we cannot postpone a decision for more than a few weeks longer. Mr Rogers' presence in London for the SEATO Meeting would, as seen from here, provide an excellent opportunity to put him on notice in this way, leaving a full briefing on our decisions for a later occasion.

3. If by this means we can avoid the appearance of presenting the Americans with a *fait accompli*, it should be much less easy for them to place on us later the onus for a worldwide shift of attitude towards the Important Question.

---

1 Repeated for information to Peking.
2 No. 228.

No. 232

Mr Denson (Peking) to Sir A. Douglas-Home, 16 April 1971, 1.17 a.m.[1]
Tel. No. 356 Immediate, Confidential (FCO 21/823, FEC 3/304/1A)

China/US.
MIPT.[2]

The way the Chinese have played these visits looks to us like a carefully calculated diplomatic manoeuvre. It clearly points up the increased tactical flexibility which the Chinese have shown in recent months, particularly trying to rally support for the admission to the UN this year.

2. The British Team leader here tells us that before the Table-Tennis Championships took place in Japan the Chinese sounded him out in London about the possibility of a visit to China. Feelers were put out to other National teams as well. The speed with which the arrangements were made at Nagoya for the American visit strongly suggests that the Chinese had made careful advance preparations for it.

3. The main target at the moment seems to be the US (which in turn is linked with the UN question). But the Chinese doubtless have their sights on Moscow as well. As seen from here, Chou's latest gestures towards the Americans are designed to undermine those aspects of American policy they dislike by going over the Administration's head to the American people. In his talk with the American team Chou made it clear that their visit marked a new phase in the relations between the Chinese and American peoples, though not between the Chinese and American governments, as we understand some commentators have tried to suggest. There is no indication of any softening toward the Administration as such on Indo-China and Taiwan, though it will be interesting to see how the Chinese react to the five new steps in the travel and trade field announced by President Nixon. Nonetheless in order to convince international opinion of China's reasonableness it would not be surprising if China agreed to the resumption of the Warsaw talks before the UN General Assembly Meeting in the autumn. We should be interested to know if the Americans have had any indications that they might.

4. Some observers here have speculated that the invitation to the US team and US journalists are the first moves in a new policy which could lead to China taking a similar approach towards the US as it does towards Japan—i.e. that it would make considerable efforts to influence US policy by trying [*sic*] establishing extensive contacts with groups favouring the recognition of China, while refusing to normalise relations fully until other outstanding issues have been resolved. The recent Chinese moves certainly seem to be part of a wider policy. Though it is obviously still too early to assess the fuller implications of this 'ping-pong diplomacy'.

---

1 Repeated for information Priority to Washington, Hong Kong, Moscow, Paris and UKMIS New York.
2 Not printed. The telegram reported that Chou En-lai had received table tennis teams from America, Britain, Canada, Colombia and Nigeria.

No. 233

Minute from Mr Graham to Sir A. Douglas-Home, 20 April 1971
Confidential (FCO 21/833, FEC 3/548/3A)

Sino-British Relations

There is an office meeting tomorrow afternoon to consider our policy towards China. You have seen the attached submission and minuted on it on 10 April.[1] The following summary however might be useful:

(i) The objects of our policy, approved by the Prime Minister, are:

(*a*) to normalise and improve bilateral contacts;

(*b*) to increase our share of the Chinese market, in particular, in capital goods;

(*c*) to help to bring China into a healthier relationship with the rest of the world (in particular in the United Nations and in such international agreements as the Nuclear Test Ban Treaty);

(*d*) to maintain the peace and prosperity of Hong Kong;

(*e*) to maintain and improve our presence in Peking which is of particular value in the context of intelligence;

(ii) As a step in this policy we should raise our representation in Peking to Ambassador level;

(iii) The Chinese conditions for this are:

(*a*) that we no longer support the Important Question Resolution;

(*b*) that we withdraw our Consulate from Taiwan;

(iv) The following courses are recommended:

(*a*) that we should propose Mr Addis to the Chinese as Ambassador, in so doing informing them that we no longer support the Important Question Resolution if tabled and that we are taking steps to withdraw our Consulate from Taiwan. We should not in fact initiate action on the latter until *agrément* for Mr Addis had been received;

(*b*) that you might take the opportunity of Mr Rogers' presence in London to put him on notice of our intention. We should propose to take action with the Chinese some 2 weeks later—in mid-May. We should say nothing as yet in public;

(*c*) that we should tell the Australian and New Zealand Governments at some stage in advance;

(*d*) that we should not change our position on the sovereignty of Taiwan;

(*e*) that the question of further release of confrontation prisoners in Hong Kong should be looked at after the next meeting in June of the Hong Kong Prison Board of Review.[2]

J.A.N. Graham

---

1 See No. 228 and note 4.
2 At the meeting Sir A. Douglas-Home agreed to talk to Mr Rogers on 27 April (see No. 235) on the lines of Mr Morgan's submission of 6 April (No. 228).

No. 234

Minute from Mr Darwin to Mr Stratton, 26 April 1971
No classification (FCO 21/808, FEC 2/2A)

Chinese Representation

May I refer to paragraph 8 of the Record of Conclusions of a meeting with Sir C. Crowe dated 19 April 1971.[1] I hope that the Americans will come up with a new line of tactics so that we shall not be put in the awkward position of reversing ourselves on the Important Question question.

2. This will be somewhat easier if political considerations allow us only to abstain rather than to vote against.

3. If we decide to justify a change of vote 'on the lines that it was not our policy to vote in such a way as to obstruct the clearly expressed will of the majority of the General Assembly', we would have to be careful not to put this in a manner which would imply that one should never frustrate the simple majority of the General Assembly. On subjects to which a two-thirds vote applies, the mustering of a blocking third is wholly consistent with the Charter. But I imagine that Sir C. Crowe had this point well in mind and that my concern only arises out of the necessary abbreviation for a Record of Conclusions.

4. Whereas we have argued that the substantive question of Chinese representation is an Important Question, the preliminary question whether it is an Important Question is undoubtedly to be decided by a simple majority (since the substantive question does not fall with the classes out in Article 18 (ii)). We could therefore reasonably say that this was a matter on which we did not now wish to support either viewpoint and would therefore abstain. But this leaves us with the need to invent a reason why we do not wish to influence the Assembly on this question.

5. If we had to give a reason for our change of vote on the preliminary question, two lines of argument have occurred to me. Essentially, we have to show why the achievement of a simple majority for Peking requires a change in our attitude on the preliminary question.

6. The first line might be that we could not continue to maintain the position whereby the Chinese Nationalist authorities which had minority support only in the General Assembly, hold the Chinese seat. Accordingly, we were not prepared to continue to vote that this was an Important Question. But this is not very persuasive since this was always the necessary effect of voting on the preliminary question that the substantive question was important. There may well be political objections against taking a line which points a finger at Taiwan.

7. Secondly, we might argue that now that Peking had a simple majority any decision taken on credentials (by a simple majority) could get out of step with the voting on representation, if the latter continues to be treated as an Important Question. Accordingly, we now think it appropriate to deal with the question of representation

---

[1] Paragraph 8 read: 'In the course of discussion the following main points were made: (*a*) Mr Morgan thought that if the Important Question Resolution were again tabled, a UK abstention would be adequate from the point of view of relations with China. (*b*) If an explanation of our change of vote on the Important Question Resolution were required, Sir C. Crowe thought this would have to be on the lines that it was not our policy to vote in such a way as to obstruct the clearly expressed will of the majority of the General Assembly'.

as not important. But this is not consistent with our past views that the matter ought to be dealt with on the basis of representation and *not* of credentials. And it also comes close to implying that the question of importance depends on a pragmatic decision to the vote of the majority is more appropriate.

8. Altogether, it is clearly going to be difficult to find an argument for changing our vote if the Important Question is the device the Americans favour.

H. G. DARWIN

No. 235

Minute from Mr Graham to Mr Morgan, 27 April 1971
Confidential (FCO 21/808, FEC 2/2A)

Admission of China to the UN

Since I dictated the record of today's discussion at lunch with Mr Rogers, the Secretary of State has told me that in private discussion with Mr Rogers over lunch the latter told him that the Americans' calculation was that even without our vote, the important question resolution would this year be lost by four votes. The Secretary of State added that although he had spelt out to Mr Rogers what was involved for our Consulate in Tai Wan [*sic*] the latter had taken the matter very calmly. The Secretary of State said he would certainly want to put this to DOPC but he was not inclined after his conversation with Mr Rogers to alter his recommendation in any way.

2. I had the impression from what Mr Marshall Green said that the Americans may have in mind a new form of important question resolution. He gave no hint of what that form might be, but without being an expert it occurs to me that it might be possible to draw a distinction between the recognition of the credentials of Government in Peking as the Government of China and as entitled to the Chinese seat, and the expulsion of an existing member called 'The Republic of China'. It might be that the Americans would reckon that a number of states would vote for the latter, in isolation, to be regarded as an important question, who would not do so if it were inextricably linked with the admission of Communist China.

3. The Secretary of State also told me this evening that he hoped to talk again to Mr Rogers about this in the course of the next few days and I will let you know if anything comes out of it.

4. The PUS has suggested to me that in the light of the Secretary of State's implicit acceptance that we should not act before the Americans have reached a decision, you may wish to recast the whole recommendation, since, once the Americans have announced their decision we will not obtain much kudos with the Chinese by switching our vote—although we might still be able to gain kudos by our attitude to any revised resolution that the Americans may devise.[1]

J. A. N. GRAHAM

1 Mr Royle commented on 27 April: 'Although the Americans hope to take a decision within a month, I formed the impression that they will not immediately make a public announcement. If I am correct, our submission for DOP can stand?'

No. 236

The Earl of Cromer (Washington) to Sir A. Douglas-Home
28 April 1971, 11 p.m.[1]
Tel. No. 1469 Priority, Confidential (FCO 21/824, FEC 3/304/1B)

My telegram No. 1452:[2] China-U.S. Relations.

In the course of conversation with Kissinger today, I asked him how the American review of policy on Chinese representation now stood. He said that it was still before the President, and that he hoped we would be able to hold up our own decision on UN tactics until about 15 May. He added that there were some people in the Administration who were coming round to the view that the best solution after all might be for the United States simply to allow itself to be out-voted in the General Assembly.

1 Repeated for information routine to Hong Kong and Peking; and saving to Tokyo, POLAD Singapore, Moscow and Paris.
2 Not printed.

No. 237

Mr Denson (Peking) to Sir A. Douglas-Home, 29 April 1971
Confidential (FCO 21/845, FEC 6/548/9)

Sir,

Trading with China: Review and Prospects

It is generally acknowledged that the Chinese economy has recovered from the losses sustained during the Cultural Revolution, and has entered a new period of growth. At the same time Sino-British political relations have markedly improved, though problems remain.

2. However, British exports to China in 1970 fell from about £54 million (including re-exports) to £45 million. This is explained largely by the fact that our 1969 exports were inflated by a sudden increase in Chinese buying of non-ferrous metals. Chinese demand for these and for industrial diamonds remained high in 1970. Detailed analysis of the 1970 figures has not yet been possible, but it seems likely that shipping problems contributed significantly to the marked fall-off towards the end of the year. We failed to resume higher sales of machinery, chemicals, steel products and scientific instruments. These are commodities which the Chinese undoubtedly want, and which they bought in increased quantities last year from most of our close competitors. The most striking example is Japan, whose exports to China overall increased by 46% to US$570 million, with an increase of 250% in sales of machinery and 45% in sales of steel products. By no means all of this is accounted for by Japan's geographical advantage. Chinese buying of machine tools, transport equipment and chemicals from West Germany, France and Switzerland also rose.

3. Though we have toiled to keep pace with some of our competitors in exploiting the market, there are economic factors beyond our control which have worked against

us. Since last summer, there has been a striking reduction in Chinese buying activity, which has affected all their traditional sources of supply. One important reason for this is probably their concern about their short-term foreign exchange position. By the middle of the year, it was clear that they were running into a hard currency deficit. There is no doubt that they had bought very heavily from Japan, in some cases in excess of their immediate needs and beyond the distribution capacities of the Chinese transport system, which became critically over-loaded. This is now rightly the top priority, after defence, for central Government expenditure. Moreover, the Chinese export earnings did not recover as quickly as the authorities probably hoped (e.g. Chinese exports to Hong Kong rose by only 5% over the previous year). At the same time, the balancing of books at the end of the 3rd 5-year plan and planning for the 4th (which began on 1st of January this year), involving as it must intense competition for scarce resources between different sectors of the economy and their trade representatives (for instance between those who would prefer to import fertilisers and those who want vehicles), probably imposed special constraint on the buying authorities. There is no reason to suppose that this lull in Chinese buying may be coming to an end now that we have entered the period of the Spring Canton Fair.

4. The JIC have recently produced two very useful papers on Chinese economic prospects;[1] and have drawn some general conclusions about the implications for British interests. JIC(B)(70)(N)36 concluded that the 'Chinese economy has entered on a period of steady but unspectacular growth'. On the other hand, a Japanese estimate, published last year, was that the Chinese Gross National Product would rise by about 4% per annum over the next few years (approximately the same as the average over the whole period 1952-68); and similar figures have been used by other observers.

5. In deciding policy we should, I think, remember how tenuous such estimates inevitably are and that despite the existence of an enormous Western intelligence interest in China, we probably know less about this economy than any other. Western experts have generally tended to under-estimate Chinese economic performance throughout the past 20 years: hence the gloomy prognostications for the early fifties, and the exaggerated assessment of the effects of the Great Leap Forward and more recently of the Cultural Revolution. The trend for several years now has been to improve the estimate we made previously; for instance, of Chinese industrial growth in the mid-sixties and the grain harvests of the last 4 years. The JIC papers in question continue this trend.

6. One positive sign that we should not accept too gloomy a view of Chinese economic prospects is the great increase in Chinese foreign aid commitments undertaken in 1970. The JIC estimates give Chinese foreign aid commitments between 1954 and 1969 as US$1059 million Our study of new commitments in 1970 is not yet complete, but I do not think implausible a local Soviet estimate of US$950 million, not including commitments to North Korea and North Vietnam, which are almost certainly greater than ever before. Whilst the content of this aid is largely in commodities and technical assistance, and disbursement will be spread over 10 or more years, such large commitments surely indicate considerable confidence in Chinese economic prospects among the people in a position to estimate them best, the Chinese leadership.

1 Not printed.

7. One further comment on the comparatively pessimistic picture painted by the JIC is that, though no detailed estimates have yet been attempted on the cost of Chinese imports over the next few years, the major components of their present import bill (chemicals, fertilisers, wheat, non-ferrous metals and steel and transhipping) may well become cheaper, at least in the short to medium term.

Britain's interest in the market

8. The JIC concludes that the Chinese market is unlikely to be a significant growth area for the time being, although the paper adds that large contracts could be obtained which would cause great variations from year to year. This might lead us to conclude that there is little the British Government need or can do about trade with China. But this would be greatly mistaken. In the first place, for the past two years about two-thirds of British exports to China have consisted of non-ferrous metals and industrial demands. This trade runs itself without official intervention or contribution. A serious decline in this precarious trade, in volume or value or both, (of which there have strong signs in the first quarter of this year) would throw us back upon commodities which, value for value, are very much harder to sell; and with which official assistance is of much greater importance.

9. Secondly, eighteen months ago there were no signs that the Chinese would buy substantial numbers of railway locomotives or that there would develop a demand for aviation equipment. Yet at this moment, a delegation from Hawker Siddeley is in Peking to discuss a contract for Tridents which is unlikely to be worth less than $20 million and there is reason to believe that further significant contracts for aviation equipment are in the offing. It is virtually certain that within the next few years the Chinese will take delivery of Ilyushin-62 long-range airliners with which they could open an international airline. British exports to China in 1972 and beyond could therefore become much better than ever before.

10. There is no doubt that the official contribution to export promotion in the necessary reserve areas referred to above, and more so in the potential growth areas is at least as important as in any other future export markets, and a good deal more important than most. China is a state trading country whose buyers are used to dealing with official representatives of foreign Governments in an environment essentially dominated by political relations. The classic example of this is our prospective exports of aviation equipment. I think we need not be over-modest in saying that the official contribution to the conclusion of any contracts which may be signed in the coming months has been substantial.

11. Much of the groundwork for sustaining a high level of official assistance to British exporters in China has now been done: but important work remains. One continuing aspect is the need to keep in touch with senior Chinese trade officials. What they have to say is ultimately the only information worth having on British trade prospects in China. It is therefore the task of officials to keep up the pressure by cultivating such officials and extracting the last ounce of information from the perhaps uniquely elliptical and ambiguous conversations which make working with Chinese officials such a joy (for some). It should never be assumed the Chinese do not want to buy something until they have said so.

12. Another aspect of our official contribution to trade promotion in China is that much of the background information on which good decisions about this market

must be based, is available only to officials who have access, denied to businessmen, to a wide range of intelligence on the Chinese economy.

Our competitors and the advantages and disadvantages which we enjoy

13. The competition from our rivals is intensifying. The news of substantial improvements in China's economic performance and policy has spread quickly. In particular there are disturbing prospects of the Japanese becoming even stronger by having diplomatic or quasi-diplomatic contacts and being willing to offer long-term credit facilities. The Chinese see positive advantage in favouring the 'friendly firms' which account for 90% of Sino-Japanese trade; and in keeping open the semi-official Memorandum trade talks which are an effective medium of political communication which helps to surmount the lack of formal diplomatic relations between the two Governments. The French have a political advantage from which they have perhaps so far not derived full commercial benefit. With the establishment of diplomatic relations, the Canadians and Italians should now have better working access to Chinese decision makers; and their exporters are giving the Chinese market increasing attention. Others may follow in the not too distant future; for example Austria.

14. There is also the possibility of further encroachment by the Americans. The American China trade lobby last year became stronger than ever before and will have been encouraged by President Nixon's most recent gestures towards China. Even last year American trade concessions led to Chinese purchase of American equipment through third countries. The political factors which crippled Soviet and East European export promotion in this market for several years have now largely disappeared. It is very unlikely the Chinese will permit a major shift in the present balance of their trade between 'revisionist' and 'capitalist' sources of supply, but the Russians and East Europeans are now equal competitors with us for important individual contracts, particularly for aircraft, machine tools and vehicles.

15. In the face of this competition, we have certain advantages over our rivals:

(*a*) Our official access to trade authorities in Peking is now as good as anyone else's. The Chinese some time ago reinforced their commercial staff in London to a point where it is probably their strongest in Western Europe (and incidentally used by our rivals from Western European countries).

(*b*) Our businessmen are well organised institutionally in the United Kingdom. With official encouragement, the Sino-British Trade Council has become a useful vehicle of trade promotion. Their technical journal in the Chinese language gives it an advantage over its competitors, and we have recently obtained tangible evidence of its impact on the market.

(*c*) The level of interest and professional expertise in the China trade concentrated in a comparatively few firms in London is probably higher than that enjoyed by any other developed country except Japan. This expertise is reflected in our representation at the Canton Fairs, where last autumn we again resumed our position as numerically strongest among West European countries.

(*d*) This expertise extends to our banking and other financial services; and the good relations established with the Bank of China branch in London has conveyed definite advantages, even off-setting to some extent the discriminatory rate adopted last year by the Chinese for supplying their currency forward against sterling. There are however, reports that the Chinese intend soon to open a branch of their bank in Zurich, in line with the very distinct favour with which they at present regard the Swiss Franc.

(*e*) The Chinese Chartering Corporation relies heavily on the expertise of the shipping market in London to arrange the transportation of most of its trade with Western countries.

(*f*) The Chinese in 1970 sent three missions to Britain, giving us a far better exposure in this respect than any of our competitors. We plan to keep up the pace by inviting further missions and have made other promotional proposals at official level.

16. But certain disadvantages can be readily distinguished:

(*a*) Whilst certain differences over major policy matters and the level of our diplomatic representation no longer effect our official access to the Chinese trade authorities, they do limit the frequency with which we exchange trade missions, particularly at the highest level; and they could affect large contracts where the balance of commercial advantage was fine.

(*b*) The recent unhappy period of Sino-British relations still deters major British exporters who might otherwise take a more active interest in this market.

(*c*) Particularly since the withdrawal of the British liner service last year, we suffer disadvantages in shipping delays and costs. Opinions of the extent of the damage so far suffered differ, but we do know of deliveries delayed (textile fibres, steel products, machine tools) and of contracts lost at the last Canton Fair (steel products, industrial products, pedigree livestock). The Chinese Foreign Trade Transportation Corporation rarely misses an opportunity to complain about loading and unloading delays at London and Liverpool docks.

(*d*) There are also purely commercial disadvantages. We have no real grounds for doubting Chinese allegations that our deliveries are peculiarly subject to unexpected delay, and that particular problems result regarding penalties and other contract terms. This is presumably mainly a problem of the British industrial situation; but it may in part be a question of educating British exporters to understand Chinese conditions and to take Chinese demands seriously. They must be able to distinguish between casual enquiries and specific requests, which are often only passed on through official channels.

17. Given the state of the market as outlined above and the current favourable political climate *vis-à-vis* our bilateral relations with the Chinese, I consider this an opportune moment to outline (in greater detail than is possible in publications such as the 'Hints to Businessmen Booklet' and the Board of Trade Journal) the way in which the Chinese organise their trade, to review our official export promotion activities and to make further specific recommendations. This is done in the attached memorandum[2] prepared by Mr J. D. Laughton, who recently completed his tour of duty as my Commercial Secretary. I should like to take this opportunity of expressing my appreciation of his competence and energy which have contributed in no small measure to the improvement in our commercial relations with China. The memorandum has been drafted in a form suitable for showing in confidence to the Sino-British Trade Council. They might be invited to study it in the Department as an example of our desire to collaborate with them in the improvement of our service to British exporters.

2 Not printed.

18. On Mr Loughton's review of Chinese trading methods and of our current official services I have no comment except to point out that it reveals the degree to which any expansion of our trade will depend upon official initiatives. I thus fully endorse his recommendations for further action nearly all of which fall to be carried out either by this Office or by departments in Whitehall. The recommendations can be summarised as follows:

(a) *Action with British exporters and trade groups*

(i) More effective presentation by British exporters of their product and better use by them of market information;

(ii) A wider range of sponsorship by the Sino-British Trade Council and greater collaboration by them with our official export promotion;

(iii) Minimising fruitless competition between the Sino-British Trade Council and the 48 Group, who include in their number several effective and energetic exporting firms.

(b) *Action within the British Government*

(iv) Some assistance to Chinese attempts to export to Britain thus taking account of their disposition to think of their trade with us in terms of balance;

(v) A review of the policy adopted by the Exports Credit Guarantee Department towards the provision of credit for trade with China;

(vi) Consideration of the problems created by the lack of adequate shipping services between the United Kingdom and China;

(vii) The coordination of economic intelligence and trade promotion and the consideration of ways and means to deny the former to our allies who are trade rivals;

(viii) The encouragement of cooperation between British firms who can supply capital equipment to China and the possible extension of such cooperation to include Western European firms;

(ix) A careful watch on changes in the international situation which might affect trade, in particular, changes in American policy towards China which could affect the operation of the strategic embargo;

(x) A better coordination of promotional methods i.e. Sino-British Trade Council journal, BBC overseas service and technical film shows in Peking;

(xi) Consideration of the increased use of the British Trade Commission in Hong Kong for the promotion of trade with mainland China.

(c) *Action to be taken with the Chinese authorities*

(xii) Consideration of the advisability of long-term trading agreements;

(xiii) Visits to China by a Minister from the Department of Trade and Industry after we have succeeded in bringing a Chinese Minister to the United Kingdom;

(xiv) Continuing to invite Chinese specialists to visit the United Kingdom;

(xv) The improvement of telecommunications between Britain and China and the exchange of air-line services.

19. I submit that the above guidelines provide a basis on which we might work to improve the quality of our services to British exporters. If my hopes are fulfilled and we achieve an increase in trading contracts with the Chinese authorities, it may be necessary to increase the strength of the commercial staff in Peking. We have recently appointed a Third Secretary in this Section which will enable us to foster new initiatives while keeping abreast with day to day enquiries. I believe that for the present this staff is adequate but it will be necessary to keep the situation under

constant review and in the future to consider the case for an increase in numbers and the upgrading of the Commercial Secretary's post.

20. I am sending copies of this despatch (without enclosure) to Her Majesty's Ambassadors in Bonn, Paris, Moscow, Rome, Tokyo and Washington, to the High Commissioner in Ottawa, and with enclosure to the Governor of Hong Kong and to the Commercial Relations and Exports Division of the Department of Trade and Industry.

I have, etc,
JOHN DENSON

No. 238

Sir A. Douglas-Home to the Earl of Cromer (Washington)
30 April 1971, 5.40 p.m.[1]
Tel. No. 1232 Immediate, Confidential (FCO 21/833, FEC 3/548/3A)

Sino-British Relations.

I took the opportunity of Mr Rogers' presence for the SEATO Meeting to let him know that we had been considering the recent developments in our relations with China and in particular whether we should now proceed to exchange Ambassadors.

2. In order to achieve this we would propose to submit the name of an Ambassador to the Chinese for agreement, in so doing informing them that we would no longer support the Important Question Resolution if tabled and that we were taking steps to withdraw our consulate from Taiwan. We should not in fact initiate action on the latter until agreement had been received.

3. Mr Rogers said that as regards Chinese representation at the UN the US Government were examining their position and they would hope the President would reach a decision within a month. They would probably announce it then but would in any case tell the British Government. They were thinking in terms of 'dual representation'. If Taiwan were expelled it would have a very severe impact on American opinion quite apart from the effect that it would have on the US's allies in the Far East. They had considerable trouble as it was in obtaining funds for the support of some UN activities, for example the ILO,[2] and the expulsion of Taiwan would produce a considerable disenchantment with the UN in general. The solution they would like to see was one based on the concept of universality with the admission of the Government of China and Taiwan as the Republic of China. Fine distinctions relating to Taiwan's claim to be the Republic of China, would not be understood by American public opinion.

4. As regards the consulate, Mr Rogers took the matter very calmly, Marshall Green told officials that this would not present difficulties for the Americans.

5. I accepted Mr Rogers' request for one month's delay and stressed to him that I and my colleagues had not yet made a final decision.

1 Repeated for information to Peking, Hong Kong, Tamsui and UKMIS New York.
2 International Labour Organisation.

No. 239

Letter from Mr Wilford to Mr Millard (Washington), 4 May 1971
Confidential (FCO 21/824, FEC 3/304/1B)

[No salutation]

1. You will by now have seen from our telegrams the outcome of the Secretary of State's talk with Mr Rogers and of the further talk which took place between officials and Marshall Green on the afternoon of the 28 April. I have just been reading Washington telegrams Nos. 1478-1480.[1] Every day that passes seems to bring either from you or from our newspapers new reports of US views on relations with China or estimates of US intentions—not least those about a possible visit by the President to China. The impression which these reports gives me is one of rapid development of the US position. This, as I see it, is all to the good, but there are certain dangers for us which I wish to make clear.

2. As we told Marshall Green very frankly, one of the dangers which we see is that having made up our own minds about what we should do in our own interest, we have now deferred any approach to the Chinese about an exchange of Ambassadors, because of American preoccupations. What I now fear, and what Marshall Green said makes me all the more fearful since he said that once an American decision was taken it would inevitably leak, is that at some time in the next month the President will take a decision of which you will be informed at the last moment and we shall probably read of it in the newspapers early one morning. Only when we get into the office will we find the report of your conversation informing us of the decision. It would be deplorable if after we have gone out of our way to assist the Americans, we should find the ground cut from under our feet by a Presidential announcement of this kind. There seems little doubt that the Important Question Resolution is not going to be presented in its traditional form this year. If therefore we had gone ahead now against the wishes of the Americans with an approach to the Chinese we should at least have been able to gain credit for saying that it was not our intention to vote in favour of the Important Question Resolution if it was posed. If, before we act, there is an American announcement of which we have inadequate warning which makes it clear that the Important Question Resolution as such is dead, we shall gain no credit with the Chinese for saying that we are not going to vote for it and there is then, in our view, every danger that we shall be faced with some other Chinese condition whether in respect of sovereignty over Taiwan or confrontation prisoners in Hong Kong.

3. But a greater danger to the position we have recommended our Ministers to take is that we shall then be faced with very heavy pressure not to break Anglo-American solidarity. We shall be encouraged to vote for some half-baked American idea which is indistinguishable from a two-Chinas solution which you firmly told de Palma on 11 January would be unacceptable (paragraph 3 of your record).[2] The point which we should like you to put across is that since we have voted for the Albanian

1 Not printed.
2 No. 212.

resolution every year since 1961 any action by us in support of an American ploy will inevitably be less satisfactory to the Chinese and regarded by them as a *hostile* action on our part. We do not of course dispute that the US Government intend their actions to appear *forthcoming* and that from the Chinese viewpoint it may appear that way too although they would be bound publicly to condemn it categorically—but our position as the Chinese see it would be very different.

4. I recognise, of course, that there is no single issue which can be regarded as wholly divorced from Anglo-American relations in their widest sense, but looked at from the narrow point of view of my own responsibilities in the Office it would be the greatest shame if we should lose this opportunity to gain something which in our view cannot do any harm to the Americans and will, conceivably, be as much in their interest as in ours simply to play along with what is another procedural gimmick even if the State Department are not prepared to admit that this is what it is.

K.M. WILFORD

No. 240

Letter from Mr Millard (Washington) to Mr Wilford, 7 May 1971
Confidential (FCO 21/824, FEC 3/304/1B)

Dear Michael,

Thank you for your letter of 4 May about Chinese representation in the United Nations.[1]

2. I can well understand your preoccupations and sympathise with them. It is, as you say, only too likely that we shall be informed of any American decisions at the very last minute and that it will then be too late to protect our interests. I cannot, I am afraid, guarantee that this will not happen. Indeed, on past form the scenario you describe seems quite a probable one, though I should imagine that the more the Americans study this question the more the difficulties must become apparent to them and that the timetable is therefore likely to slip further. It may therefore be rather too pessimistic to assume, in spite of the indications of an impending decision referred to in our telegram no. 1299,[2] that the Americans are likely to face us with some dual representation scheme before the month is up.

3. We have made it clear here on a number of occasions that, having voted for the past ten years for the Albanian Resolution, it would be impossible for us to reverse ourselves now and vote for some form of dual representation. We will do so again, though it goes rather beyond what was said in London, and I do not of course want to give the impression that the Embassy is being tougher than our instructions warrant. I will also take an opportunity to rub in with Marshall Green the point, which you make in your letter and which was made to him by Tomlinson, that support by us for the kind of solution the Americans have in mind would be regarded by the Chinese as a hostile act.

1 No. 239.
2 Not printed.

4. This will not, however, make much impact here unless we are at the same time able to tell the Americans that at the end of the month's grace which we have conceded, i.e. towards the end of this month, we shall have to go ahead and tell the Chinese that we will not this year support the Important Question Resolution (the question of the Consulate in Taiwan is, I think, a subsidiary issue and surely not of direct concern to the Americans).

5. For the above reason, I rather regret that it was not made clearer to the Americans in London that we could not in any circumstances support anything along the lines of their proposed dual representation tactic. This would in effect have amounted to telling them that we would hold off for a time to enable them to complete their studies; but that at the end of that time we should feel free to speak to the Chinese. On looking at our telegram no. 1299 again, I admit that it could have been expressed more clearly that this was the kind of communication to the Americans which we had in mind. Our concern at that moment was that Ministers might announce an act on our decision before the Americans had completed their review.

6. However, it would not be too late now to tell the Americans that if their proposals are what we think they are going to be, then we shall have to go ahead with the action described by the Secretary of State to Mr Rogers last week (your telegram no. 1232).³ This might cause them to have further second thoughts. I personally do not believe that this issue is one of such importance in the wider interests of Anglo-American relations that we should yield to pressure to go along with some half-baked scheme for dual representation, though I have no doubt that if this is what the Americans eventually decide to go for, the pressure will be applied.

7. I am not copying this letter elsewhere.

Yours ever,
GUY

3 No. 238.

No. 241

Memorandum by Sir A. Douglas-Home for the Cabinet Defence and Oversea Policy Committee, 7 May 1971
DOP(71)27 Confidential (CAB 148/116)

Relations with China: Proposals for Improvement

Policy Aims

The objectives of our policy towards China are:

(*a*) To normalise and improve our bilateral contacts;

(*b*) To increase our share of the Chinese market, in particular in capital goods;

(*c*) To help to bring China into a healthier relationship with the rest of the world (in particular the United Nations and in such international agreements as Nuclear Test Ban Treaty);

(*d*) To maintain the peace and prosperity of Hong Kong;

(*e*) To maintain and improve our presence in Peking which is of particular value in the context of trade, intelligence and Hong Kong.

Obstacles to their fulfilment

2. The main obstacles to realising these aims are now:

(*a*) Our voting position in the United Nations and

(*b*) The maintenance of our Consulate in Taiwan

This has recently been made clear by the Chinese Chargé d'Affaires in London, in reply to a formal proposal put to him on 8 February by the Parliamentary Under-Secretary (Mr Royle) that we should proceed to an exchange of Ambassadors, the visible token of improvement in our relations. The Chargé did not refer to two other matters at issue between us—the release of the remaining confrontation prisoners in Hong Kong and our view that the status sovereignty of Taiwan is undetermined. We should therefore be free to maintain our policy in both these matters.

Important Question Resolution at the United Nations

3. In the 1970 General Assembly the substantive resolution to seat Peking and expel the Nationalists was passed by a simple majority for the first time. We have voted for this resolution at every Assembly since 1961. Only the procedural resolution requiring that the question needs a two-thirds majority (the Important Question Resolution) effectively barred Peking's entry. Countries that have voted for it with us in previous years, such as Canada and Italy, have made it clear that they will no longer support it. Eight countries having recognised Peking in the last 5 months, it is most unlikely that the resolution will again succeed (American estimates are that it will fail by 4 votes). If it is decided by its sponsors to put forward the resolution in the same form as last year and if we were to vote for it, we should be left amongst the small band of countries against whom the Chinese would bear a lasting grudge.

The Consulate in Taiwan

4. A note on the position of the Consulate is attached, showing its present limited value to us.

Exchange of Ambassadors

5. If we are to remove the obstacles to the achievement of our policy objectives we shall have to change our position at the United Nations and withdraw our Consulate from Taiwan. The best way of achieving the maximum credit for doing this would be to propose the name of an Ambassador to the Chinese for *agrément*, and in doing so to inform them that we would no longer support the Important Question Resolution if tabled, and that we were taking steps to withdraw our Consulate from Taiwan. An Ambassador would give us greater access to the top level of the Chinese leadership. The better our working relationship with Peking the less likely it is that we will run into difficulties in Hong Kong.

Consultation with Other Governments

6. The State Department were informed last October that we would be considering a change in our vote at the United Nations this year. On 27 April I put Mr Rogers on notice of our intention. He said that the US Government were examining their position and would reach a conclusion in a month.[1] It was likely that if there were a change it would be in the direction of universality of representation in the United Nations, i.e. representation of both Peking and Taiwan; any solution that involved the expulsion of Taiwan from the United Nations, quite apart from its effect on the

1 No. 235.

United States' Asian Allies, would not be acceptable to American opinion. He would let us know their position by 27 May.

7. I myself regard any form of dual representation of both Peking and Taiwan as wholly unrealistic, since both sides are adamantly opposed to it. We have repeatedly told the Americans since 1961 that we could not support any new proposals which amounted to yet another device to delay the seating of Peking nor could we support any 'Two Chinas' approach. The Parliamentary Under-Secretary of State (Mr Royle) repeated this to the American Embassy on 8 March.[2]

8. As regards the Consulate, Mr Rogers did not appear concerned that we would close it.

9. I have not yet consulted other friendly governments but would wish to inform at least those of Australia, New Zealand and Japan before any announcement was made.

Recommendation

10. I recommend that after we have heard again from the Americans, and depending on their response, we should propose the name of an Ambassador to the Chinese for *agrément*; and that at the same time we should inform them that we would no longer support the Important Question Resolution, if tabled, and that we were taking steps to withdraw our Consulate from Taiwan. We should not in fact initiate action on the latter until *agrément* had been received, and we would in any case look into the possibility that it be replaced by a Trade Mission organised through the CBI.

ANNEX

The British Consulate in Taiwan

The Prime Minister has commented that 'our policy should be to go ahead with normalising relations with Peking while trying to avoid sacrificing our trade interests in Taiwan'. In fact our Office is of limited use, as it is accredited to the Provincial Government of Taiwan, and is debarred from contacts with Ministries of the 'Republic of China'. If there were sufficient commercial interest to justify unofficial links it would be possible to establish a more business-like relationship with the Central Government authorities. The Director-General of the CBI has agreed that, if it was shown that there was need for some sort of representation along the lines of the British Business Bureau which is being established in East Berlin, they would be prepared to look at the possibility.

2. There is at present included in the Tamsui Consulate staff a Naval Liaison Officer. The Ministry of Defence consider that this Officer is able to obtain useful intelligence on mainland China's activities from the Nationalist authorities. The Ministry of Defence would, however, greatly prefer the opportunity, which an Ambassador would provide, to appoint a Service Attachés to Peking with far greater intelligence gathering potential.

2 No. 224.

No. 242

Extract from the minutes of a Cabinet Defence and Oversea Policy Committee meeting held at 10 Downing Street, 26 May 1971, 11 a.m.[1]
DOP(71)11th Meeting, Secret (CAB 148/115)

3. *Relations with China: proposals for improvement.*

The Committee considered a memorandum by the Foreign and Commonwealth Secretary (DOP(71)27)[2] proposing that with the aim of improving our political and commercial relations with China we should not only give our customary support at the next United Nations General Assembly to the Albanian resolution for the seating of Communist China and the expulsion of the Nationalists, but that we should cease to support the procedural device ('The Important Question' resolution) whereby the Albanian resolution had hitherto been frustrated, and that we should also withdraw our Consulate from Taiwan.

THE FOREIGN AND COMMONWEALTH SECRETARY said that given the prospect of these changes in policy we should be able to agree with Peking on the elevation of our diplomatic missions to Ambassador status. The consequences would be good for our bilateral political relations, including the stability of Hong Kong, and would also assist our commercial effort, as well as bringing China into a healthier relationship with the rest of the world. Many countries including some of our NATO and SEATO Allies were restive at the annual procedural frustration of the resolution for the seating of Communist China. Even the Americans now calculated that the procedural resolution would be likely to fail this year and there was some doubt whether it would be tried again. The Americans were believed to be seeking to devise a 'two Chinas' solution on the problem, which he considered both illogical and unrealistic. Although we should be prepared to consider any alternative solution whereby Taiwan was allowed to remain in the United Nations the Chinese Security Council seat properly belonged to the Peking Government and no other State should be designated as China. He would very shortly be meeting the United States Secretary of State, Mr Rogers, in Lisbon and if the Committees agreed with his proposals he would wish to explain our intentions.

In discussion it was suggested that notwithstanding the desirability of improving our relations with Peking it would be unwise to embark on a policy which would put us at odds with the United States, Australia, New Zealand and Japan without securing any concrete benefit for ourselves. It was suggested that a change of policy was primarily a matter of timing. Although the United States was still resistant to the seating of Communist China coupled with the expulsion of the Nationalists it was certain that they recognised the reality of the problem and they might well, as in other important fields of policy, decide at any time on a dramatic change of policy towards Communist China. It might be possible to contrive an arrangement whereby the Nationalists remained in the United Nations (but not as a permanent member of the Security

---

1 Those present were: Mr Heath, Sir A. Douglas-Home, Mr Barber (Chancellor of the Exchequer), Mr Whitelaw (Lord President of the Council), Mr Joseph Godber (Minister of State, FCO), Lord Balniel (Minister of State for Defence), Sir G. Howe (Solicitor General), Admiral Sir M. Pollock (Acting Chief of the Defence Staff), General Sir M. Carver (Chief of the General Staff), Air Chief Marshal, Sir D. Spotswood (Chief of the Air Staff) and Sir B. Trend.
2 No. 241.

Council) whilst their Security Council seat was transferred to Peking. The importance of this matter warranted further discussion with the Americans, before we reached a final policy conclusion. As regards the withdrawal of our Consul from Taiwan it was agreed that provided alternative arrangements such as a CBI Trade Mission could be made to maintain our commercial interests there would be no objection to the early implementation of the Foreign and Commonwealth Secretary's proposal.

THE PRIME MINISTER, summing up the discussion, said that the Committee endorsed the general policy aims stated in the Foreign and Commonwealth Secretary's paper. However before reaching a firm decision on the implementation of the recommendation in paragraph 10 relating to the seating of China in the United Nations it was desirable that the Foreign and Commonwealth Secretary should discuss our proposals frankly with the American Secretary of State at Lisbon and seek his reactions.

The Committee could consider the matter again in the light of the Foreign and Commonwealth Secretary's report of his discussion with Mr Rogers. A decision could then be taken with more certain knowledge of American views.

The Committee:

1. Took note, with approval, of the Prime Minister's summing up of their discussion.
2. Invited the Foreign and Commonwealth Secretary to discuss his proposals with the United States Secretary of State and report the outcome to the Committee.

No. 243

Mr Muirhead (Lisbon) to the FCO, 3 June 1971, 11.30 p.m.[1]
Tel. No. 238 Priority, Secret (FCO 21/809, FEC 2/2B)

Following from Private Secretary.

Chinese Representation.

The Secretary of State and Mr Rogers discussed this over lunch today.[2] The Secretary of State said that we were concerned, to improve our relations with China, particularly because of Hong Kong. We wanted to propose the exchange of Ambassadors and in doing so to tell the Chinese Government that we would not vote for the Important Question Resolution and were planning to remove our consulate from Taiwan. He did not think that either of these points should cause the US Administration any difficulty, more particularly because Mr Rogers had told him (in a private conversation before lunch) that the Americans were not in any case thinking of moving the Important Question Resolution this year. We were particularly concerned, however, that the value of this card should not be lost through an announcement of the American policy before we had had a chance to play it.

2. Mr Rogers said that the Administration were thinking over various possibilities and had more or less decided to propose that the People's Republic of China should be seated in the UN; that the Republic of China (Taiwan) should remain a member of the United Nations; and that the expulsion of an existing member of the

---

1 Repeated for information to Washington and UKMIS New York.
2 For the US record of the meeting see *FRUS, 1969–1976, Volume V*, No. 363.

United Nations should be treated as 'An Important Question'. The question of the seat in the Security Council should be left open. Although he recognised that some people would argue that the seat in the Council went automatically with representation in the United Nations, he believed that this was a matter for the Security Council itself. Moreover it would not arise if either the Republic of China (Taiwan) or the People's Republic of China rejected admission on the terms proposed and failed to turn up. His own view was that the People's Republic might not accept admission on these terms for the first year or two, but would eventually come round to it, and that there would be a lot of support for the proposed American approach in principle, although many might argue that it was not practical. When the Secretary of State pointed out that the main obstacle to the success of these tactics was the claim by Taiwan to be the Government of China, and added that at the best the American proposal would cause a lot of confusion, Mr Rogers said that that was his fervent hope.

3. In conclusion, Mr Rogers undertook to let the Secretary of State know, in a fortnight or less, the final American position. He said that he fully recognised that Britain had her own interests to protect and, speaking personally, he did not think that the US Government would see any objection to our going ahead on the lines proposed by the Secretary of State, more particularly if, in speaking to the Chinese Government we said merely that we would no longer vote for a resolution couched in the form of previous Important Question resolutions since whatever the Americans finally decided, their new resolution would take a different form. The Secretary of State repeated the point that we should not wish the Americans to announce their policy before we had acted. Mr Rogers again promised to let the Secretary of State know, within a fortnight, and added that the President did not have it in mind to announce any policy for about six weeks.[3]

3 In a letter to Mr McCluney of 14 June, Mr Moon reported the Prime Minister's view that 'it is essential, if we are to get ahead with our relations with Peking, to avoid becoming embroiled in any new US device at the United Nations, which would be seen as intended to bring about the continued exclusion of Communist China' (FCO 21/834).

No. 244

Letter from Mr Moon (No. 10) to Mr McCluney, 7 June 1971
Confidential (FCO 21/809, FEC 2/2B)

China

Dear Ian,

The Prime Minister has seen Washington telegram No. 1895 of 2 June[1] reporting the extract from President Nixon's Press Conference of 1 June relating to China.

The implication of what President Nixon said would seem to be that the Americans may reach an early decision and the Prime Minister has commented that we had better

1 Not printed. President Nixon said the US was analysing the question of admitting mainland China into the UN in consultation with others. 'After we have completed our analysis, which I would imagine would take approximately six weeks, we will then decide what position we . . . should take at the next session of the United Nations this fall, and we will have an announcement to make at that time with regard to that particular problem'. See *Public Papers: Nixon*, p. 695.

move quickly. With regard to what President Nixon said about liberalising trade with China I should be grateful to know whether this is likely to affect COCOM arrangements.

I am sending a copy of this letter to Manley (Department of Trade and Industry) and Norbury (Cabinet Office).[2]

Yours sincerely,
PETER MOON

[2] The Prime Minister also questioned, following an announcement that Ambassadors would be exchanged between Austria and China, 'how it is that Austria can achieve this result so quickly whereas we cannot do so.' The short answer to the question, minuted Mr Wilford, 'is, of course, that Ministers have not yet authorised us to make an approach to the Chinese. When they do we may get an answer (hopefully favourable!) even more quickly than the Austrians' (Mr Moon to Mr McCluney, 1 June and minute by Mr Wilford, 8 June; FCO 21/833).

No. 245

Submission from Mr Morgan, 8 June 1971
Confidential covering Secret (FCO 21/833, FEC 3/548/3A)

Relations with China: Proposals for Improvement

Problem

1. What attitude should we adopt to a proposal along the lines of that suggested by Mr Rogers (Lisbon telegrams numbers 237 and 238)[1] to secure representation of both China and Taiwan in the United Nations? What should be our next step towards improvement of relations with China? The Prime Minister commented on 7 June that 'we had better move quickly'.[2]

2. We have told the Americans on many occasions since 1961 that we could not support any new proposals which amounted to yet another device to delay the seating of Peking nor could we support any 'two-Chinas' approach. Mr Royle repeated this to the American Embassy on 8 March.[3] Mr Rogers' current proposals are in this category.

3. *I recommend* that:

(*a*) When we have Mr Rogers' promised reply we should leave him in no doubt that we could not support proposals for dual representation such as those outlined in Lisbon. We should tell the Americans that in proposing to the Chinese an exchange of Ambassadors we should say that we no longer intended to support the Important Question Resolution, nor would we support any procedural manoeuvre calculated to delay the seating of Peking in the United Nations.

(*b*) These points should be put to the Defence and Oversea Policy Committee. A draft paper is submitted.[3]

4. Mr Wilford, North America Department, UN (Political) Department and Legal Advisers concur.

Argument

5. Mr Rogers' proposals, as amplified by Mr Pedersen, contain fundamental shortcomings. There are:

[1] Not printed and No. 243 respectively.
[2] No. 244.
[3] No. 224.
[4] Not printed.

(*a*) Peking's opposition to any 'two Chinas' formula is hardening. They will make it clear as soon as such proposals have become known that the Chinese would regard support for them as an unfriendly act.

(*b*) We see no signs of any weakening of the Nationalist claim to represent the whole of China.

(*c*) The proposals are defective on legal grounds as inconsistent with the Charter. They amount to an attempt to bring in a new member without applying Article 4. It would be argued that since Peking was not seeking admission as a new member, the new membership must be that of Taiwan who should therefore seek membership under Article 4. Articles 18(1) and 23(3) lay down that a member state shall have one vote only. Review of the Charter would therefore be needed to make the American proposal legally satisfactory. In general UN members, particularly the Permanent Members of the Security Council, including ourselves, do not wish to embark on this.

(*d*) The China seat was described in the Charter as The Republic of China because it was the title then current. It did not refer to any particular regime or government. The issue is which authorities are entitled to send representatives on behalf of the state of China.

(*e*) Mr Rogers has revealed that 'his fervent hope' was that the proposals would lead to confusion. In our view this would probably work against the Americans. We must assume that the Albanian Resolution will be tabled again and we believe that the majority in favour of seating Peking will ensure the defeat of any procedural manoeuvring designed to put another resolution first or to incorporate in some way a two-thirds majority requirement. Many of the less sophisticated members of the UN already find questions of Chinese representation sufficiently confusing. They may well prefer to act on resolutions they know and on which they have clear instructions.

(*f*) Although the dual representation formula could attract some waverers (such as Belgium and Ghana we think it unlikely that they will be in the sort of numbers the Americans seem to assume. We calculate that, exclusive of a change by ourselves, the Important Question Resolution, if tabled, would probably fail 55-65-5 and possibly 51-69-5. This gives an index of likely voting on a dual representation solution.[5]

J. A. L. MORGAN

---

[5] Sir A. Douglas-Home minuted on 11 June: 'Agreed. Do not delay. But instead of saying that we could not support any procedural resolution designed to seat 2 Chinas could we not say that we would go no further than to hold that the status of Taiwan is undetermined. It is the same thing but is it not less offensive to US, Japan and Singapore?'

No. 246

Memorandum by Sir A. Douglas-Home for the Cabinet Defence and Oversea Policy Committee, 14 June 1971
DOP(71)32 Confidential (CAB 148/116)

Relations with China: Proposals for Improvement
United States' views

1. The meeting of 26 May[1] agreed that I should discuss the proposals in DOP(71)27[2] with Mr Rogers in Lisbon. He told me on June 4 that he would let me know, in a fortnight or less, the final American position, but speaking personally he did not think that the United States' Government would see any objection to our going ahead on the lines proposed.

Exchange of Ambassadors

2. On the assumption that there is in fact no United States objection we should forthwith inform the Chinese Chargé d'Affaires on the lines of the attached paper (Annex). This follows the formula in DOP(71)27 but with the additional phrase, '. . . nor support any procedural manoeuvre calculated to delay the seating of Peking in the United Nations'. This is now necessary as there has been so much well-informed speculation about Mr Rogers' thinking, as confirmed to me, that the Americans are not in any case thinking of proposing the Important Question Resolution this year. In these circumstances a simple undertaking by us not to support it would invite further probing from the Chinese and possible enlargement of their conditions. We should inform the Americans of the terms of our approach to the Chinese.

Action with other Governments

3. At the meeting of 25 May my colleagues referred to the attitude of Australia, New Zealand, and Japan. I should like discretion to decide, in the light of Mr Rogers' reply, when and in what way they should be informed of the action we are taking. In any event there would be no public announcement of our intention until after such consultation had taken place. All these Governments have made moves of various kinds towards Peking and are expected to be understanding of our proposals. I shall also consider informing other Governments that have shown interest in our policy.

Taiwan

4. On receipt of favourable Chinese reply we should initiate steps to remove our Consulate. We should also discuss with the CBI the need for some sort of unofficial commercial representation.

Danger of delay

5. We should endeavour to avoid further delay. Time is not on our side. There are now some dozen countries in various stages of movement towards recognition of Peking. The Chinese will soon see themselves as less in need of our support. There is an increasing possibility that they may introduce further conditions which we would not be prepared to accept—such as release of the remaining 35 Communist prisoners in Hong Kong or a change in our view that the status of the sovereignty of Taiwan is undetermined.

Conclusion

6. I invite my colleagues to agree that I should proceed on these lines.

ANNEX

For the Chinese Chargé d'Affaires

Her Majesty's Government propose to appoint Mr . . . as HM Ambassador at

1 No. 242.
2 No. 241.

Peking and enquire whether this appointment would be acceptable to the Government of the People's Republic of China.

The Chargé d'Affaires should be aware that on receipt of a favourable response, steps would be taken to remove British official representation on Taiwan.

The Chargé d'Affaires should also be aware that Her Majesty's Government do not intend to support the Important Question Resolution on Chinese representation at the United Nations nor any procedural manoeuvre calculated to delay the seating of Peking in the United Nations.

No. 247

Extract from the minutes of a Cabinet Defence and Oversea Policy Committee meeting held at 10 Downing Street, 16 June 1971, 10.45 a.m.[1]
DOP(71)12th meeting, Secret (CAB 148/115)

2. Relations with China: Proposals for Improvement

The Committee considered a memorandum by the Foreign and Commonwealth Secretary (DOP(71)32) proposing that we should now take steps leading to an exchange of ambassadors with the Government of China.

THE FOREIGN AND COMMONWEALTH SECRETARY said that at its last discussion of the subject the Committee had decided to await the outcome of his discussions in Lisbon with Mr Rogers, the United States Secretary of State, before deciding finally on the line which we should take on the seating of China in the United Nations. The Chinese conditions for an exchange of ambassadors were: first, that we should support the transfer of the Chinese seat on the Security Council of the United Nations from the Taiwan to the Peking Government; secondly, that we should not support any procedural resolution which would have the effect of requiring a two-thirds, rather than a simple, majority for the admission of China to the United Nations; and, thirdly, that we should withdraw our Consul from Taiwan. The view which Mr Rogers had provisionally conveyed in Lisbon was that the United States Government would see no objection to our proceeding to an exchange of ambassadors with Peking on this basis. If this view was confirmed he would propose, if the Committee agreed, to put forward to the Peking Government, in the terms of the annex to this paper, the name of our Ambassador for agreement.

In discussion, there was general support for the view that we should seek to bring about an exchange of ambassadors as soon as possible both because of the potential trading benefits and because of the possibility that, as their seat on the Security Council became more certain, the Chinese might raise their terms.

The following additional points were made in discussion:

(*a*) It was likely that the Americans, while abandoning the tactic of the Important Question resolution, would seek by some procedural resolution to ensure that the

---

1 Those present were: Mr Heath, Sir A. Douglas-Home, Mr Maudling (Home Secretary), Mr Whitelaw (Lord President of the Council), Lord Carrington (Secretary of State for Defence), Sir J. Eden (Minister for Industry), Sir P. Hill-Norton (Chief of the Defence Staff), Admiral Sir M. Pollock (Chief of the Naval Staff and First Sea Lord), Air Chief Marshal Sir D. Spotswood (Chief of the Air Staff) and Sir B. Trend.

Taiwan Government could not be expelled from the United Nations (as distinct from being compelled to give up its seat on the Security Council).

(b) It would be desirable to maintain some contact, for commercial purposes, with Taiwan after the Consul was withdrawn. This could probably be achieved by setting up some form of Business Bureau under the auspices of the Confederation of British Industries.

(c) It would be invaluable from a defence viewpoint if the appointment of an ambassador were shortly followed by that of a Defence Attaché. Although it would probably be unwise to mention the point specifically to the Chinese until after the ambassador had been appointed, it would be as well to make some general reference to the need for appropriate supporting diplomatic staff to be appointed to Peking in due course.

(d) The reference to a 'procedural manoeuvre calculated to delay' in the last paragraph of the annex was capable of improvement. It might with advantage be replaced by 'a procedural initiative which might have the effect of delaying'.

THE PRIME MINISTER, summing up the discussion, said that the Committee agreed with the proposals in the Foreign and Commonwealth Secretary's paper and, provided that the provisional statement of United States views made by Mr Rogers was substantially confirmed, action should proceed on the lines proposed by the Foreign and Commonwealth Secretary, subject to the points made in discussion.

The Committee:

1. Took note, with approval, of the Prime Minister's summing up of their discussion and invited the Foreign and Commonwealth Secretary to proceed accordingly.

No. 248

Sir A. Douglas-Home to the Earl of Cromer (Washington)
16 June 1971, 6 p.m.[1]
Tel. No. 1671 Immediate, Confidential (FCO 21/834, FEC 3/548/3B)

Relations with China.

1. My colleagues and I have today again considered our proposals for the improvement in our relations with Peking. I should be grateful if you would now seek an appointment with Mr Rogers for 18 June and inform him that, having heard nothing from him, I assume that he has no objection to our going ahead.

2. You may inform Mr Rogers that Mr Royle intends summoning the Chinese Chargé d'Affaires on 22 June to propose a named Ambassador for agreement. In so doing he will inform the Chargé d'Affaires that we do not intend supporting the Important Question Resolution on Chinese representation at the United Nations nor any procedural initiative which might have the effect of delaying the seating of Peking. He will also say that on receipt of a favourable response we intend taking steps to remove British Official representation on Taiwan. We do not intend revealing to the press the content of Mr Royle's interview. We are still considering whether certain other governments should be informed and, if so, at what stage.

1 Repeated for information to Peking, UKMIS New York, Hong Kong and Tamsui (DEYOU).

3. In informing Mr Rogers you should also leave him in no doubt that we would not be able to support dual representation proposals on the lines outlined in Lisbon telegrams Nos. 237 and 238.[2]

2 Not printed and No. 243 respectively. On 17 June, Sir A. Douglas-Home received a message from Mr Rogers stating that since the UK needed to act expeditiously to raise the status of representation in China, and since it appeared that it was possible 'to proceed in a way that would not necessarily preclude later support for the kind of resolution that we have in mind' there was no need to delay any further an approach to Peking. The qualification in the message was the subject of some debate and the response to Mr Rogers, in FCO Tel. No. 1680 to Washington of 17 June, contained the categorical statement that if the US proposal was designed to seat two China's in the UN: 'I could not hold out hope that we could support it.' For the US side of this exchange see *FRUS, 1969–1976, Volume V*, No. 366.

No. 249

Mr Duffy (Tamsui) to Sir A. Douglas-Home, 19 June 1971, 1 a.m.[1]
Tel. No. 49 Priority, Confidential (FCO 21/834, FEC 3/548/3B)

Relations with China.

I note from telegram No. 1671[2] to Washington that Ministers have decided against any form of representation in United Nations. I trust this does not indicate that we have closed our minds to the possibility of an independent Taiwan. Taiwanese are to Chinese as Australians to Englishmen and have an equal aversion to absorption by the Motherland. A referendum would undoubtedly give overwhelming majority for independence. By any measurement an independent Taiwan would have greater claim to United Nations representation than many countries now represented.

1 Repeated for information priority to Washington, Peking, UKMIS New York and Hong Kong.
2 No. 248.

No. 250

Minute from Mr Wilford to Mr Morgan, 22 June 1971
Restricted (FCO 21/876, FEH 14/1B)

I met the Chinese Chargé d'Affaires the other night at the Pakistan High Commission. He raised with me again the question of confrontation prisoners in Hong Kong mentioning that he hoped the matter would be resolved by the time the present Governor's tour of duty came to an end. I said to Mr Pei that, as he knew, we had the question of confrontation prisoners very much in mind. It was, however, not an easy question to resolve though we knew what the Chinese position was. It was most important for us to proceed within the law or there could be serious problems in Hong Kong. As he knew, releases which had taken place so far had been on the advice of the Prison Board of Review and this we thought was the correct way to proceed.

2. Mr Pei then asked me when Sir D. Trench would be leaving and what Sir M. MacLehose's plans were for taking up his post. I said that Sir D. Trench would be leaving about the middle of October and there would probably be a gap of three weeks to a month between his departure and the new Governor's arrival. I asked Mr Pei if he had ever met Sir M. MacLehose and he said he had not done so. I said that Sir M. MacLehose would be in London from time to time over the next few months and enquired if he would be interested in meeting him if this could be arranged. He did not give me any particular answer to this.

3. I understand that at his meeting with Mr Royle this morning he mentioned our conversation and said that he would like to meet Sir M. MacLehose if this was possible. Mr Royle, I gather, has some doubts whether this would be a good thing suggesting that the Chinese might be able to represent in some way that Mr Pei was giving the new Governor the once over. I recognise that this is a possibility though I rather doubt if the Chinese would take this attitude if indeed a meeting were arranged. I had in mind that if a meeting took place—and this would be dependent in the first place upon Sir M. MacLehose saying that he was agreeable—it should be on a social occasion, e.g. Mr Pei is coming to lunch with me at home on 10 July. In the past there used to be contacts of an unofficial kind between the Governors of Hong Kong and officials in China. For example, I recall Sir A. Grantham paying a visit to the Chargé d'Affaires in Peking in the course of which informal meetings were arranged. For myself I would see no objection to Mr Pei and the Governor-designate meeting informally, but if Sir M. MacLehose or Mr Royle were against this I think that it will not be difficult to get out of the meeting on the grounds that Sir M. MacLehose will shortly be travelling abroad for a month or more and that he will be very busy with final briefing when he is next in London.[1]

K.M. WILFORD

1 Mr Royle was not happy about a meeting taking place immediately and it was decided to look again at the issue in the autumn by which time Sir M. MacLehose, who was not opposed to an informal meeting, would be available.

No. 251

Record of a meeting between Mr Royle and the Chinese Chargé d'Affaires, 22 June 1971, 10.30 a.m.
Confidential (FCO 21/834, FEC 3/548/3B)

Mr Anthony Royle MP
Mr J. A. Morgan
Mr L. V. Appleyard
Mr M. F. Forrester

Mr P'ei Tsien-Chang
Mr Chian En-chu

1. *Mr Royle* began by saying that on 15 January he had proposed to Mr P'ei that discussions should take place in London about the level of our diplomatic representation with the aim of an exchange of Ambassadors.[1] On 26 March Mr P'ei

1 No. 209.

had told Mr Morgan, Head of Far Eastern Department, that discussions were not necessary since only 2 obstacles remained to an exchange.[2] These were first, the UK vote on the Important Question Resolution on Chinese representation at the United Nations, and secondly the presence of the British Consulate on Taiwan. Mr P'ei had confirmed that if action were taken on these 2 points we could proceed to an exchange of Ambassadors.

2. Mr Royle said that he would like to seek *agrément* as HM Ambassador to the Chinese People's Republic for Mr John Addis. Mr P'ei would see from the papers which Mr Royle would hand to him that the conditions which he had earlier proposed had been met fully. He would see that the formula which was used about the vote on Chinese representation in the United Nations was even more forthcoming than he had mentioned. In fact, the formula contained a further undertaking by HMG not to support any procedure calculated to delay the seating of the Chinese People's Republic. Mr P'ei would see that Mr Addis was a most experienced diplomatist. He had already served twice in China and twice as Ambassador in other countries.

3. Mr Royle then read out the *aide-memoire* which was to be handed over to Mr P'ei (copy attached).[3]

4. Mr Royle ended by saying that the British Government had no intention of publicising the contents of the meeting, but would confirm that the meeting had taken place. On receipt of a favourable response from the Chinese Government to the British proposals, an announcement on an exchange of Ambassadors would be agreed.

5. *Mr P'ei* said that he had noted Mr Royle's reply on an exchange of Ambassadors. He wished to make clear that, when he had said to Mr Morgan last time that no negotiations were necessary, he had meant that the questions of principle on both sides were very clear. The Chinese had said they would like to see the British Government withdraw its Consulate from Taiwan. He asked whether the wording in the *aide-memoire* meant that the Consulate would be withdrawn. *Mr Royle* confirmed that this was so.

6. *Mr P'ei* then repeated the Chinese position that there was only one China— the People's Republic of China. Its legitimate seat in the United Nations must be restored. We were aware that US imperialism was adopting a 2-Chinas or one China, one Taiwan policy to delay the seating of the CPR or to deprive it of its seat. He asked whether the phrasing of the paper meant that the British Government no longer supported or approved any form of 2-Chinas or one China, one Taiwan policy.

7. *Mr Royle* said that our position was plain from the fact that we had voted for the Albanian Resolution which called for the seating of the CPR and the removal of the Nationalist representatives. In the past we had supported the Important Question Resolution. In addition we made clear that we would not support any procedural manoeuvre to avoid the seating of the Chinese People's Republic. We considered that the question of the seating of China was so important as to require a two-thirds majority. As the *aide-memoire* explained, we were no longer prepared to support the Important Question Resolution. In addition we made clear that we would not support any procedural manoeuvre to avoid the seating of the Chinese People's Republic.

2 No. 226.
3 Not printed.

8. When *Mr P'ei* repeated his question whether this meant the British Government would no longer support any 2-China or one China, one Taiwan approach, *Mr Royle* confirmed that this was correct and repeated that we would continue to support the Albanian Resolution.

9. *Mr P'ei* said that he would transmit Mr Royle's remarks and the contents of the *aide-memoire* to his government. Mr P'ei agreed with Mr Royle that the press should be told that the meeting had taken place but not the subjects under discussion.

10. *Mr Royle* said that at present there was great interest among MPs about the possibility of visiting China. Winston Churchill MP, the grandson of Sir Winston, would be approaching the Chinese Office for a visa and would like to travel to China in August or September He hoped that it would be possible for the Chinese to agree. *Mr P'ei* said that if any MPs wished to visit China, the Foreign and Commonwealth Office could inform the Chinese Office and this could be discussed. Now that relations between our 2 countries were improving he hoped that there would be increasing cultural exchange. He mentioned that he had been in Cambridge recently where he had met the President of the Royal Society, Professor Hodgkin. *Mr Royle* said that we would welcome an increase in cultural exchanges.

11. *Mr P'ei* said that when he had last seen Mr Wilford, Mr Wilford had suggested that he might meet the Governor-designate of Hong Kong, Sir Murray Maclehose.[4] Mr P'ei said that he would be glad to meet him if this could be arranged. *Mr Royle* said that Sir Murray Maclehose was not in London at the moment. He was going abroad for a few weeks. We would look at his programme to see whether a meeting could be arranged.

4 No. 250.

No. 252

Minute from Mr Wilford to Mr Royle, enclosing a paper on the Future of Hong Kong, 28 June 1971
Top Secret (FCO 40/331, HKK 4/1)

The Future of Hong Kong

1. I attach a paper for consideration by the Secretary of State. It has been seen and commented upon by the two Deputy Under-Secretaries directly concerned as well as by the Planning Staff and by Hong Kong and Far Eastern Departments. In its present form it is agreed by all concerned save only one point, on which I must seek ministerial guidance.

2. We are all in agreement on the text of the paper save so far as the crucial paragraph 12 is concerned. Briefly my preference would be to opt for Course 4(*c*) (ii)—that is to have as our objective extension of the life of the Colony post-1997 because of the dangers I foresee in trying to negotiate a withdrawal, which can only result in abandoning very large numbers of citizens of the UK and Colonies to Communist domination and may be even more uncomfortable for HM than this. Only as soon as it is clear that extension is unattainable should we go for course 4(*c*)

(i)—negotiation of an orderly withdrawal in 1997. My preference does not exclude this as a fall back position. Mr Cradock does not believe that my preference could be a valid option, and both he and Mr Morgan prefer the objective of an orderly withdrawal in 1997. Accordingly two alternative paragraphs 12 are submitted.

3. There is also a procedural issue. A comparable paper, but different in many important respects, was prepared by a committee of officials representing the FCO, Ministry of Defence, Treasury and Board of Trade under Cabinet Office chairmanship under the previous Administration. This paper was never taken by the Cabinet Committee to which it was submitted and therefore lapsed when the Government changed in June 1970. The present paper has been written wholly in the FCO. It has not been cleared so far with any other Department since before it goes elsewhere in Whitehall I believe that we should obtain sanction of our Ministers.

4. If it is approved by the Secretary of State it is for consideration whether a shorter paper summarising its conclusions should be put to DOPC. On the other hand the paper closes no options and its only recommendation is for regular review of the situation. The Secretary of State may feel that no action with DOPC is therefore needed, though he may wish to inform senior colleagues of the consideration which he has given to this thorny question. If, however, the paper is to go to DOPC it would be as well that it should be cleared through DOP(O) Committee first.

5. The text of the paper has not so far been seen by the Governor of Hong Kong, or by the Governor-designate.[1]

K.M. Wilford

Enclosure in No. 252

The Future of Hong Kong

1. In the annexes[2] to this paper are set out details of the physical characteristics of the Crown Colony of Hong Kong, of the legal position in respect of our tenure of it and of the situation there today. In this paper no proposals are made which require immediate decisions, but a number of considerations in relation to the future of the Colony are set out which we must inevitably bear in mind, and the options with which any Government will be faced as time goes on are set out.

2. The present Chinese Government, and probably any Chinese Government in the foreseeable future, see no distinction between the status of those areas of the Colony acquired by Britain by cession under the Treaties of Nanking and Peking and that the New Territories which are held under lease. All, as they see it, are part

---

[1] In a minute of 29 June, Mr Royle indicated that he supported the recommendation to try first for a solution on the lines of 4 (*c*) (ii) or (iii). The new Governor, Sir M. MacLehose, read the paper later in the year. In a minute of 27 October he agreed with the conclusion that the Government should negotiate, at the right time, for the best terms that it could get. He thought it likely that the best they could hope for would be some form of special status for Hong Kong under which sovereignty would return to China, but Hong Kong might be defined as a special administrative district to be managed in a way that would facilitate the continued residence of foreigners. Meanwhile his object was to ensure that conditions in Hong Kong were so superior in every way to those in China 'that the CPG will hesitate before facing the problems of absorption'.
[2] Not printed.

of China and to be recovered at the appropriate time. It is therefore unrealistic for us to think of them differently. For this reason independence as a goal for the Colony is unthinkable and so is any movement towards constitutional progress along conventional decolonisation lines.

3. Secondly, it is very difficult indeed to imagine Hong Kong as viable if the New Territories are detached from it at the expiry of their lease in 1997. The frontier would lie in the middle of a built-up area; Kaitak airport would be in China; so would a substantial part of the industrial area and also the main reservoirs; virtually no food would be grown in British territory. The population remaining in our control would be of the order of 3 million, assuming that there was not a huge influx from the New Territories.

4. The options which appear open to us, though events cannot be said to lie fully within our control, are broadly as follows:

(*a*) Maintain the *status quo*, either on the assumption that the Chinese will be prepared to permit the present situation to persist unaltered after 1997. Or simply because no other course of actions seems feasible;

(*b*) Prepare a voluntary and negotiated withdrawal from the whole Colony as soon as this can be arranged;

(*c*) Maintain the *status quo* for the time being, and take preliminary informal sounding with the Chinese Government at a suitable time nearer 1996 with a view to:

(i) negotiating an orderly withdrawal in 1997;

(ii) securing an indication from the Chinese that they will not interfere with the present arrangements after 1997; or

(iii) securing an indication from the Chinese that they will agree to negotiate new terms for the lease of the Colony.

5. Before deciding which of these options may be obtainable there are certain factors to be stated:

(*a*) There seems no likelihood of any negotiation with the Chinese being feasible during the lifetime of Mao Tse-tung; even afterwards it may not be possible.

(*b*) The nearer we approach to 1997 the greater is the danger of loss of confidence in Hong Kong. This could only result in the breakdown of the administration, but will certainly mean that investment will fall off and the industrial machine will run down. The result, relatively quickly, would be that Hong Kong would become a financial liability to HMG. By the middle 1970s certain decisions will have to be taken, for example on electricity and telephone franchises which could expose HMG's way of thinking, though it should be possible to find ways and means of getting round this problem.

(*c*) There can be no question of a large scale movement of population from Hong Kong elsewhere. The majority, including some 2 million citizens of the UK and Colonies, would, if the Colony became part of China, pass under Chinese Communism against their will.

(*d*) The Chinese have the capability to occupy the Colony by overwhelming force of arms without warning and with no hope of a successful military defence on the part of the Garrison. In these circumstances an evacuation, even of UK citizens, would be a hazardous operation and very few could probably be extricated.

(*e*) In certain circumstances it might suit the Chinese not to permit Britain to abandon the administration of the Colony, but to insist on our remaining in most humiliating conditions with real control in their hands. In this event it would be open to us to call their bluff, although this could almost certainly involve some degree of violence.

6. Although the situation viewed from HMG's position seems thoroughly uncomfortable, ranging from the possibility of major military disaster or humiliating expulsion to a negotiated withdrawal involving at best the transfer of considerable numbers of citizens of the United Kingdom and Colonies into Communist hands, there are certain other factors to be considered:

(*a*) Hong Kong is China's largest trading partner and this trade, both visibles and invisibles, is today worth $580-600 million (US) annually in foreign exchange to the Chinese. This is over one-third of China's total foreign exchange earnings. It more than pays for all her cereal imports. The day Hong Kong returns to China this flow of foreign exchange will cease and China will also have difficulty in finding markets for her farmers who at the moment provide food for Hong Kong at a vastly higher standard of living than exists in China.

(*b*) Hong Kong under Chinese ownership will no longer be the power house it is today. Nor would Hong Kong continue to have access to the markets of the world. Hong Kong would probably sink to the level of Shanghai—and for the same reasons.

(*c*) Hong Kong's tourist and entrepôt earnings would quickly dry up.

(*d*) China is still a very backward country agriculturally, economically and industrially. Even under less doctrinaire leadership than it has at present, it will take a very long time to achieve even modest economic success.

All these factors rationally militate against the Chinese Government taking voluntarily a decision to regain control of the Colony until they no longer need the foreign exchange benefit of it. Nevertheless we should not underestimate the difficulties for the Chinese in agreeing to a prolongation of British rule, since at the time envisaged they are very likely to be a highly nationalistic and revolutionary Government. The Chinese Government may well take the view in 1997, when they will be presented with a clear-cut choice, that for reasons of national prestige and to safeguard their claims to be in the forefront of anti-colonialism they must reclaim the Colony, despite the economic benefits which would then be denied to them.

7. There is, however, a remote chance that the Chinese might be prepared to see Hong Kong remain under our administration, thus enabling them to continue to enjoy the fruits of its Colonial status. At this point in time it would be extremely rash to plan solely on the assumption that the Chinese might renew the present lease or negotiate a contractual agreement for lease on new terms, since this could present the Chinese with unacceptable difficulties in terms of ideology and national prestige. However we are considering a situation many years from now and we should not wholly exclude the possibility that the Chinese might be prepared to give us a tacit and private indication that over an indefinite period they did not propose to reclaim the Colony. But the public uncertainty surrounding such a situation could have an unsettling effect on Hong Kong public morale and business confidence, and might well put the Colony in difficulties. A tacit and private indication on these lines from the Chinese might moreover be coupled with an attempt to enforce a Macao-style solution on us, though in view of our successful resistance to pressure in 1967, the Chinese could hardly expect to get away with this tactic very easily.

8. Although the Chinese Government will be strongly tempted in 1997, and possibly before, to try to enforce a humiliating withdrawal upon us, there are other factors which might sway them in favour of a more reasonable settlement. By then the Chinese should be in the United Nations. They will probably be keen to foster an impression of moderation and responsibility, which would be damaged by an attempt to impose impossible conditions upon us. Minor considerations could be that a quarrel with us would also focus unwelcome attention on Chinese inaction over the years since 1949, and upon the obvious reluctance of Hong Kong Chinese to accept voluntarily Communist rule. For these reasons the odds will not necessarily be overwhelming against the Chinese agreeing to an orderly withdrawal under tolerable conditions, or to some other solution of the kind envisaged. In 1963 the Chinese themselves stated that, as far as Hong Kong, Kowloon and Macao were concerned 'we have always held that, when conditions are ripe, (these issues) should be settled peacefully through negotiations and that, pending a settlement, the *status quo* should be maintained.'

9. In these circumstances the options mentioned in paragraph 4 are hereafter studied in detail:

Course 4(a) [Do nothing]

This appears to have nothing to commend it save in the face of an utterly intractable Government in China, or if China should fall into a state of anarchy. In the first case we should have no option; in the second no one with whom to discuss Hong Kong's future.

Course 4(b) [Prepare a voluntary and negotiated withdrawal as soon as this could be arranged]

Nothing would be possible pending a change of Government inside China. Once a Government which seemed amenable was in power cautious informal soundings might still reveal that a negotiation could not be concluded because:

(*a*) The Chinese wanted to have their cake and eat it by making us continue to administer Hong Kong under their control;

(*b*) Their conditions were so humiliating as to be intolerable;

(*c*) The Chinese preferred to continue to obtain the economic benefits of our administration;

(*d*) It was clear that Hong Kong opinion would not accept a negotiated withdrawal whatever HMG's intentions were;

(*e*) Political feeling within the Conservative Party, and indeed in this country as a whole, might not permit it.

Course 4 (c) (i) [Negotiation for an orderly British withdrawal in 1997]

Subject to the existence of a Government in China with which negotiation seemed feasible it might still be impossible to reach agreement for some of the reasons given under Course 4(*b*). If it became apparent that we were attempting to negotiate and being rebuffed the effect on confidence might be catastrophic. The outcome might be humiliating expulsion from the whole Colony in 1997 at the expiry of the lease. Alternatively it might become clear that, while China was adamant about recovering all her territory in 1997, she was prepared to cooperate in preparing for an orderly transfer of administration and would permit the withdrawal in good order of British troops and expatriates. In this latter case it would be vital however to delay any substantive negotiation to as late a date as possible so as to avoid the danger and panic and disastrous loss of confidence in the Colony.

Course 4(c) (ii) and 4(c) (iii) [Seek to maintain present situation post-1997 or negotiate a new lease post-1997]

If it became apparent following informal soundings which led to the opening of negotiations with an amenable Chinese Government that they would prefer to see Hong Kong's colonial status maintained in the 21st century. They might prefer to maintain the legal *status quo* as we see it, or they might prefer to make a lease on completely new terms. In either case they would require of us certain concessions; these might take one of the following forms:

(*a*) Payment for the lease of the New Territories. The Government of Hong Kong would probably be willing to pay a considerable sum if it were to mean the continuation of their present status. Such a rent could be nominal, fair or exorbitant.

(*b*) We might agree, having retroceded our territory, to pay a fair, or exorbitant rent for the whole territory which we would continue to administer as a Colony.

Solution (*b*) above would be dependent upon radical change in the internal political scene within China of which there is at best a very faint chance only.

10. There would clearly be some advantage from our point of view in remaining in Hong Kong after 1997:

(*a*) This may be the only way of continuing for the time being to look after the two million citizens of the United Kingdom and Colonies who would otherwise pass into the hands of the communists.

(*b*) The chance that if we hang on we might secure better terms later.

(*c*) We should continue to enjoy the advantages of Hong Kong as a Far East base, as a China-watching post and as a bargaining counter in negotiating Air Service Agreements with other countries.

(*d*) Provided the stability of the Colony is maintained it will continue to be a substantial provider of sterling for the reserves and of modest advantage to our balance of payments generally.

11. On the other hand, there are arguments in support of an orderly withdrawal in 1997, if this can be obtained.

(*a*) To remain voluntarily in Hong Kong would be to run counter to one of the principles of post-war British policy, that we should divest ourselves of our remaining colonial responsibilities at a favourable moment.

(*b*) By 1997 we should be fully integrated into the EEC. Hong Kong would be an increasingly embarrassing political anachronism.

(*c*) We should be committed to maintaining economically a territory which could well become a financial liability in the future, particularly after our entry into the EEC, and which could be faced with enormous social problems by 1997. We should also be involved in continuing substantial defence commitment.

(*d*) The problem of Hong Kong would continue to be a severely distorting factor in our relations with China.

Alternative 'A'

12. It will be realised that the choice as to the course which should be adopted does not lie solely in HMG's hands. Nevertheless because of the disagreeable prospect if we are unable to reach some agreement with the Chinese on the future of the Colony because of the distressing circumstances involved for us if we were forced to leave Hong Kong under humiliating conditions, at the appropriate moment we

should be prepared to enter into informal sounding with the Chinese Government. These sounding should be conducted through diplomatic channels in strictest secrecy, which the Chinese would be likely to respect. Our first objective should be to try for a solution on the lines of 4(*c*) (ii) or (iii). In doing so we should have to resist any Chinese pressure to permit us to stay only in Macao-like conditions. Unless assured of indefinite tenure under 4(*c*) (ii) or unless we got a solution on the lines of 4(*c*) (iii) we should have always to bear in mind that, at an appropriate and favourable moment from our point of view, we should have to negotiate with the Chinese Government about the future of the Colony. We must recognise that the Chinese Government retain the ability at any time to expel us and there would be little which we could do to resist. If it is apparent that the Chinese Government will never envisage a solution which leaves us in control of Hong Kong after 1997, then we should have to go for a solution on the lines of 4(*c*) (i).

Alternative 'B'

12. Our first objective should be to try for a solution on the lines of 4(*c*) (i). Only if handover under tolerable conditions in 1997 or earlier seems impossible, should we try to remain in Hong Kong after 1997. In that case we should resist as far as possible Chinese pressure to impose a Macao-style solution on us and hold out for a favourable moment at which we negotiate with the Chinese Government a reasonable settlement. We must recognise that if the Chinese Government is determined to expel us at any time, there is little we can do to prevent this.

13. No immediate action is necessary on the recommendations in this paper except that officials should be instructed to review the situation annually, reporting to the Secretary of State. Any approach to the Chinese Government would need to be very carefully timed and in a form which could, if necessary be disavowed. Ideally this approach should be later rather than sooner to minimise the risk of a damaging leak which might occur if we were negotiating too far ahead. It would also involve less danger of forcing the Chinese to revive their claims, when they might otherwise have been content to let matters rest. But at the same time we must take into account that to drift toward 1997 with no apparent policy would provoke the loss of confidence which could destroy the Colony. Therefore if we have an indication from the Chinese before 1997 that they would be prepared either to provide for our continued occupation of the Colony beyond 1997 or to negotiate an agreement involving a handover on reasonable terms in 1997, then we should consider very seriously a favourable response.

No. 253

Sir A. Douglas-Home to Mr Soames (Paris), 30 June 1971, 4.10 p.m.[1]
Tel. No. 488 Flash, Confidential (FCO 21/834, FEC 3/548/3B)

Relations with China.
On 22 June Mr Royle sought agreement from the Chinese Chargé d'Affaires

---

[1] Repeated for information immediate to Brussels, The Hague, Luxembourg, Bonn, Rome, UKMIS New York; Priority to Oslo, Stockholm, Copenhagen, Tokyo, Peking, Hong Kong; and saving to Ottawa, Canberra and Wellington.

for a named Ambassador to Peking. In doing so he informed the Chinese that we no longer intended supporting the Important Question Resolution on Chinese representation in the United Nations nor any procedure calculated to delay the seating of Peking. He also said that on receipt of a favourable response from the Chinese we would take steps to remove our Official representative on Taiwan.

2. The Chinese have not formally replied but they are now leaking in Peking the news of our action.

3. The Americans, Australians, New Zealanders and Canadians have already been informed.[2] We now intend informing WEU[3] in strict confidence at their meeting in 1 July. In addition we shall inform the Danish, Norwegian, Swedish and Japanese embassies in London.

4. We should be grateful if you would give the Quai d'Orsay advance notice of our intention.

5. There is no objection to other recipients of this telegram informing colleagues of the countries concerned. This should be done in strict confidence and it should be made clear that it is not our intention to seek to influence any other government's attitude towards voting in the United Nations.

6. For your own information we were in touch with the Americans over a period of months before the decision to approach the Chinese was taken. In acquiescing they expressed the hope that our action would not prejudice whatever decisions about Chinese representation in the UN they might take. In this connexion see last sentence of para. 5 above.

2 Having informed the Americans of their intentions, Mr De Palma of the State Department stated they would prefer the British not to widen the circle of people to whom they communicated their intentions with regard to the Chinese issue in the UN. From the US point of view it was preferable that the British attitude remained speculative rather than generally known and raising the issue with other governments was bound to stimulate international discussion of the problem (Washington Tel. No. 2253 of 2 July 1971, FCO 21/810).
3 Western European Union.

No. 254

Mr Denson (Peking) to Sir A. Douglas-Home, 10 July 1971, 3.54 p.m.[1]
Tel. No. 628 Immediate, Confidential (FCO 21/834, FEC 3/548/3B)

Sino-British Relations.

I was summoned tonight at short notice by Vice-Minister Chiao Kuan-hua. He recalled that on 22 June Mr Royle had met the Chinese Chargé d'Affaires in London and explained the British Government's new attitude to this question.[2] More recently on 3 July the Head of Far Eastern Department had made a further explanation to the Chargé d'Affaires.[3] The Chinese wished to express their welcome for this new attitude on our part and to put forward a proposal. This was that the principles for an

1 Repeated for information to Hong Kong, Washington and UKMIS New York.
2 No. 251.
3 Mr Morgan had confirmed to Mr P'ei that the British Government would not support a 'Two Chinas' approach and did intend to support the Albanian Resolution at the next Assembly (FCO Tel. No. 424 to Peking, 12 July 1971).

exchange of Ambassadors should be put into writing in the form of an exchange of notes between the two governments. The Chinese had prepared a draft (see MIFT)[4] to which they sought our consent. After agreement had been reached on the exchange of notes we could proceed to an exchange of Ambassadors. At that time the Chinese would wish the notes to be published.

2. The Vice-Minister then read out the draft note. I said that I could not make any substantive comments but it would be transmitted immediately to my Government for study.

3. I noted that the communication had been made in Peking whereas Mr Royle had proposed that any negotiation on the exchange of Ambassadors should take place in London. The Vice-Minister said that the Chinese wished further discussion to take place in Peking between him and me. I said that I would transmit their views to you.

4. I asked for confirmation that any exchange of notes must precede any Chinese agreement for a named British Ambassador. The Vice-Minister said that this understanding was correct. I pointed out that Mr Royle had also said that only after agreement had been given for a British Ambassador would we take steps to withdraw our official representative from Taiwan. Did the Chinese accept this? The Vice-Minister referred to paragraphs 1 and 2 of the Chinese draft which states that the official British representative in Taiwan should be withdrawn on the same date as both sides decided to raise the level of their Mission in Peking and London. However, he had noted Mr Royle's statement that withdrawal should take place after agreement had been given and said that there was no real difference of substance on this point. The modalities of the question could be discussed later.

5. The Chinese have clearly raised their conditions. The major difference in the Chinese draft is the reference in paragraph 2 to 'China's Taiwan Province', to which the Vice-Minister specifically drew my attention. This is a very fast ball but can probably be played on the lines of the Canadian Formula.[5] The reference to the United Kingdom's support of the People's Republic of China as 'one of the five permanent members of the Security Council of the United Nations' will presumably also require study.

6. I shall send comment on the draft note after further reflection.

[4] No. 255.
[5] In the joint communiqué establishing diplomatic relations between Canada and China in 1970, the Canadian Government 'took note' of the Chinese Government's reaffirmation that Taiwan was an inalienable part of the territory of the PRC.

No. 255

Mr Denson (Peking) to Sir A. Douglas-Home, 10 July 1971, 4 p.m.[1]
Tel. No. 629 Immediate, Confidential (FCO 21/834, FEC 3/548/3B)

MIPT.[2] Following is text of Chinese draft.
Begins.

[1] Repeated for information to Hong Kong, Washington and UKMIS New York.
[2] No. 254.

1. Both confirming the principle of mutual respect for sovereignty and territorial integrity, non-interference in each other's internal affairs and equality and mutual benefit, the Government of the People's Republic of China and the Government of the United Kingdom have decided to raise the level of their respective official missions in each other's capital from the office of Charge d'Affaires to Embassy as from . . . and the two sides will exchange Ambassadors within . . . months.

2. The Government of the United Kingdom has decided to remove the official representation of the United Kingdom in China's Taiwan Province on . . . (the same date as specified in paragraph 1).

3. The Government of the United Kingdom recognised the Government of the People's Republic of China as the sole legal government of China in the United Nations. The Government of the United Kingdom supports the restoration of all the rights of the People's Republic of China in the United Nations, including its rights as one of the five Permanent Members in the Security Council of the United Nations, opposes any procedure calculated to delay the restoration of the above-mentioned rights of the People's Republic of China and favours the expulsion of Chiang Kai-shek's representatives from the United Nations and all its subordinate organisations. The Government of the People's Republic of China appreciates the above stand of the Government of the United Kingdom.

Ends.

No. 256

Mr Denson (Peking) to Sir A. Douglas-Home, 12 July 1971, 8.05 a.m.[1]
Tel. No. 636 Immediate, Confidential (FCO 21/834, FEC 3/548/3B)

Telno. 629:[2] Sino/British Relations.

The Chinese proposal for an exchange of notes is a development which you will no doubt consider, as I do, unfortunate, but I feel it would be unrealistic to try to dissuade the Chinese from proceeding. The raising of China's conditions is a disappointment after their clear statements both here and in London though it is as you know a development I feared all along. I am afraid that the Chinese will not now agree to an exchange of Ambassadors unless a public announcement of the terms is made. At the same time it will be open to us to argue about the language to be used in the note and indeed the Chinese will expect us to do so. If Italian and Canadian experience is any guide it may take some time to hammer out a formula acceptable to both sides.

2. I do not wish in any way to prejudge the tactics you may now wish to adopt, but on the assumption that you will wish to discuss the draft exchange further with the Chinese you may find it helpful to have the following comments on the text as I see it.

3. The first paragraph contains the ritual preamble which was included with appropriate variations in the Canadian and Italian communiqués. It is no doubt

---

1 Repeated for information to Hong Kong, Washington and UKMIS New York.
2 No. 255.

otiose, but the language seems fairly harmless. Unless it in fact contains anything objectionable from the legal point of view their might be tactical advantage in not contesting it and saving our fire for the passages which follow.

4. Chiao made it clear that he realised the reference to 'China's Taiwan Province' would be point of particular difficulty. Indeed in view of para 2 of your Telno. 374[3] I take it that you would find it altogether unacceptable in its present form. If we were to get round it at all we should presumably be obliged, as that telegram indicated, to settle for a 'Canadian type' formula possibly incorporating in some form a reference to our decision to remove our Consulate in Taiwan. If this approach were agreed we would not, I imagine, wish to present a redraft to the Chinese ourselves because it would contain a statement of the Chinese position which only they themselves could put forward but we might indicate in discussion that we would be willing to consider a 'taking note' formula.

5. Previous communiqués have not contained any reference to the United Nations, and the fact that this draft does so illustrates the importance the Chinese now attach to their campaign for entry on their own terms and underlines the significance they attach to the British attitude to the legal aspects of it and to the impact our decision would have on others. The reference to China's 'right' as one of the 5 Permanent Members of the Security Council is probably designed to tie us—and others—down over Charter revisions particularly in view of the possibility that at some stage there might be pressure from Japan to become a permanent member of the Security Council.

6. On re-reading the last two sentences of paragraph 1 of my telegram No. 628[4] I realise that they may seem ambiguous though they record accurately what Chiao said. What he clearly meant was that the exchange of notes should be published as soon as it had been agreed and we should thereafter proceed to an exchange of Ambassadors within a stated time.

[3] Not printed.
[4] No. 254.

No. 257

Submission from Mr Morgan to Mr Wilford,[1] 13 July 1971
Confidential (FCO 21/834, FEC 3/548/3B)

Relations with China: Proposals for Improvement

Problem

How should we respond to the Chinese proposal for an exchange of Notes relating to the exchange of Ambassadors (Peking telegram No. 629 as amended by No. 632)?[2]

Argument

2. Although we would not ourselves have proposed such a detailed public

[1] Also sent to Sir S. Tomlinson and Mr Logan.
[2] No. 255.

announcement it can be used as a basis for negotiation. A counter draft is attached.[3] Apart from the phrase 'China's Taiwan Province' the rest of the Chinese draft does not present us with great difficulty. However by including this phrase they are in effect posing a third precondition by asking us to change our view that the status of the sovereignty of Taiwan is undetermined. The Chinese Chargé said on the 26 March that there were only 2 obstacles to an exchange of Ambassadors and that negotiation was not required.[4] They must now calculate that they are no longer in such need of our support at the United Nations and can raise their terms.

3. Paragraph 1 of our draft contains only minor amendments to the Chinese.

4. Paragraph 2 contains the most contentious point. It is for consideration whether we should at this stage include the phrase I have put in brackets:

'The Government of the United Kingdom take note of the position of the Government of the People's Republic of China that Taiwan is a province of China.'

Paragraph 4 of Peking telegram No. 636[5] suggests that we should leave it for discussion. The disadvantage of producing it now is that it is likely to be our final position and would not leave room for manoeuvre. On the other hand it would be unreal to ignore Chinese preoccupations on the subject. Moreover, time is not on our side; as China's international position becomes stronger they will be less ready to compromise. My inclination would be to present the draft to the Chinese including the passage in brackets.

5. I consider that the 'taking note' formula would be the most likely to be acceptable to the Chinese. There are other variants such as 'remove its official representation which has existed on Taiwan since it was a province of China' but this would be likely to lead to even lengthier negotiation. The Canadian and Italian formulae provide precedents for 'taking note'.

6. The re-draft of paragraph 3 is shorter and in effect meets all the Chinese points. It seems from UKMIS New York telegram No. 743[6] that the Albanian Resolution will this year cover all the issues raised by the Chinese. If this is so we could simply refer to the Albanian Resolution without spelling out our attitude towards the Security Council or the expulsion of Taiwan. I have asked New York to telegraph the text as soon as it has been tabled.

7. In a reply to a question by Mr Denson the Chinese proposed that further negotiations take place in Peking. Mr Royle originally proposed London. I understand that Mr Royle would like to continue and on balance I consider there are advantages in so doing. I do not think that we need make heavy weather over this and when Mr Royle hands Mr P'ei our suggested revised text he could say that we did not mind whether further discussion took place here or in Peking. The advantages for Peking might be greater accuracy of transmission and slightly faster communication. The advantages for London are that it makes it harder, although only slightly, for the Chinese to slide out from the original 'only two obstacles' stand set out by Mr P'ei himself. It would also serve to reinforce the

---

3 Not printed.
4 No. 226.
5 No. 256.
6 Not printed.

impression that we wished to give that it is not our intention to engage in a lengthy drafting haggle.

8. I recommend that we take the opportunity of Mr Rogers' visit to London next week to inform him of the present position. I also recommend that we do not reveal the detail of the Chinese reply or our response to any other governments. If asked by those we have so far taken into our confidence we should limit ourselves to saying that discussion on an announcement is continuing.

Recommendation

9. I recommend that we agree to the Chinese proposal for an announcement and that Mr Royle give Mr P'ei a revised version on the lines of the attached draft.

10. United Nations (Political) Department, North America Department and Legal Advisers concur.[7]

J. A. L. MORGAN

---

[7] There was agreement amongst senior officials and Ministers to negotiations taking place in Peking in order to expedite matters and on the wording regarding Taiwan.

No. 258

The Earl of Cromer (Washington) to Sir A. Douglas-Home
16 July 1971, 1.56 a.m.
Tel. No. 2412 Flash, Confidential (FCO 21/826, FEC 3/304/4A)

Secretary Rogers telephoned from California to inform me that the President is accepting an invitation to visit Peking before May next as a result of a visit to Peking by Kissinger 9/11 July. Rogers said that whilst this did not fundamentally change US relations with China at this time he hoped it would open the door to peace. He would have communicated direct with S of S but for time differential.

Top Secret until publicly announced probably on TV by President at 2230 EST tonight.[1]

---

[1] In his television address, Nixon said he had accepted an invitation to visit China in order to seek the normalisation of relations and because of a 'profound conviction that all nations will gain from a reduction of tensions and a better relationship' between both countries. See *Public Papers: Nixon*, p. 819-20.
In a telegram sent later in the day, Washington Tel. No. 2435, The Ambassador reported that President Nixon's announcement of his visit to Chinese 'clearly came as a total surprise not only to press and public but also to official circles here in general'. Only those at the highest level in the State Department appear to have been aware. Nixon had spoken in April of a visit to China in his lifetime but his comments 'were hardly taken seriously.'

No. 259

Letter from Mr Graham to Mr Moon (No. 10), 16 July 1971
Confidential (PREM 13/988)

Dear Peter,

President Nixon's Visit to China

Thank you for your letter of 16 July to Ian McCluney.[1]

You also asked on the telephone about the timing of the handling of this matter. Washington telegram No. 2412[2] reached the FCO Resident Clerk at 3.15 a.m. on 16 July. This was only a very short time before the President was about to speak. We authorised the News Department here to comment that we had been informed by the Americans before President Nixon's broadcast, that we welcomed his intention to visit Peking and that we ourselves had been taking steps to improve our relations with China over the past 18 months.

Our present information on the extent of US consultation with other governments is limited. Our impression is, however, that none were consulted much in advance. The Japanese, who were given similar notice to ourselves in Washington, have told us here that they were upset.

We know little of the evolution of the President's China policy nor the circumstances of Dr Kissinger's visit. There was an obvious reason for avoiding a leak of any kind until the visit had been finally agreed with the Chinese, and this could account for the American's silence. Equally the White House does operate in this secretive way even vis-à-vis the State Department. It is likely therefore that the final decision was taken very late—as Mr Rogers' message to us implies.

As far as HMG are concerned it is legitimate to feel a little hurt that the Americans did not see fit to give us real advance notice of the President's decision particularly in view of the trouble we have taken to keep the Americans informed of the development in the thinking of our own China policy. Regrettably this is not the only example of a somewhat cavalier American attitude to consultation with allies: Sterner's last visit to the Middle East was sprung on us at the last minute despite the fact that we are in almost daily touch with the State Department about Middle Eastern affairs, and as you know, we have felt it necessary to put down markers about consultations in the SALT context.

It is too early for a balanced assessment of the reasons for the President's decision in American domestic political terms. It will undoubtedly cause a considerable stir in the United States and should be viewed in the perspective of next year's Presidential Election. The timing of the intended visit, extending to next May, seems at first sight to be connected more with the Presidential primaries than with the urgency of any specific issue in the Far East. The decision could also be an attempt to introduce a new issue into the whole presidential election campaign and to distract attention from the two main current issues of Vietnam and the economy which have to some extent gone sour on the Administration. Moreover a success in the Far East, particularly if

---

[1] Not printed. The letter requested a preliminary assessment of President Nixon's announcement and the fact that the Americans gave no advance warning of their decision.

[2] No. 258.

it contributed to a satisfactory ending of the Vietnam War would pay a handsome dividend domestically.

In the international field the most profound impact must be on the Chinese Nationalists. We do not yet have their considered reaction, but this move by their principal ally has fundamentally affected their future status.

The second most important international consequence is undoubtedly in the United Nations. It would seem now to be virtually impossible for President Nixon to announce any policy on Chinese representation which would have the effect of delaying Peking's entry or of a kind which Peking could describe as a 'Two Chinas' policy. Were he now to do so he would need to give up any thought of visiting China. (This emphasises how little we know of what has been going on in the President's mind since our last information suggested that he was being recommended to try precisely for some sort of two Chinas solution). The end result in our view is that it is highly probable that Peking will be seated at this year's General Assembly in place of the Nationalists.

As regards Vietnam the Chinese invitation may reflect a willingness on their part to take a more helpful line instead of continuing to advocate a protracted struggle. But this does not necessarily follow and we would not wish to encourage any premature euphoria.

The role of the Pakistan Government is of particular interest. They must have been closely involved at an early stage in the arrangements for Dr Kissinger's visit. This may go some way to explain American unwillingness to take any action or make any statement over recent weeks which might cause offence in Islamabad.[3]

You spoke, in your letter, of our own bilateral relations. The present limitations in our own exercise of exchanging Ambassadors with China are of our own making and no longer related to American susceptibilities. The sole remaining obstacle is, in effect, our view that we cannot recognise Taiwan to be a province of China. This concept has been included in the Chinese draft for an exchange of Notes. The Foreign and Commonwealth Secretary has today instructed our Mission in Peking to say that we should be prepared to consider a formula, similar to the one used by the Canadians, such as 'the Government of the People's Republic of China stated their view that Taiwan is a province of China. The Government of the UK took note'.[4]

Yours ever,
JOHN

[3] This is likely to be a reference to the ongoing military action taken by Pakistan, following the declaration of independence by Bangladesh (then East Pakistan) in March 1971.
[4] In Washington, Lord Cromer thought a personal message from the Prime Minister to the President on his initiative would be well received but Mr Heath declined to send one (FCO 21/826).

No. 260

Submission from Mr Morgan to Sir S. Tomlinson, 21 July 1971
Confidential (FCO 21/834, FEC 3/548/3B)

Sino-British Relations in the Post Kissinger Era
1. On 15 January Mr Royle formally raised with the Chinese Chargé d'Affaires

the question of an exchange of Ambassadors.[1] At that time it was far from certain that China had an adequate majority for entry to the United Nations this year. We, as in 1950, had been among the first Western countries to be receptive to the changes in China. An announcement of the appointment of a British Ambassador this spring would have been a major development which would have served China's purpose in demonstrating their return to greater international acceptability.

2. The Chinese conditions for an exchange of Ambassadors set out in March were generally reasonable and definitive.[2] If we had responded then I suspect that we should have an Ambassador in Peking by now. Our delay, in deference to American wishes, has put us in a different negotiating position. The Chinese now see their admission to United Nations this autumn as a virtual certainty. The announcement of the appointment of a British Ambassador now would have greatly reduced international significance overshadowed by the American Presidential action.

3. In this situation it is not altogether surprising that the Chinese should harden their terms. Their sights are now set on a post United Nations entry situation where their major foreign policy objective seems likely to be recognition that Taiwan is part of China. From what Vice-Minister Chiao Kuan-hua said to Mr Denson in Peking it seems unlikely that the Chinese will compromise on any 'take note' formula.[3] They have prepared a case that we are in a special position as signatories to the Cairo and Potsdam Declarations[4] to justify this additional requirement for us over and above the terms they agreed with the Canadians and Italians. Mr P'ei's case to Mr Royle on 20 July is clearly specious that 'the essence' of their 2 earlier pre-conditions was sovereignty of Taiwan.

4. It could be that we are soon to be faced with a clear choice between accepting the 3 words 'China's Province Taiwan' in the exchange of notes or give up our proposal to exchange Ambassadors.

5. The advice I have given throughout on the submissions on this subject has been that there are impeccable legal grounds for our view that the status of the sovereignty of Taiwan is undetermined and that this should not be negotiable.

6. Mr Godber has commented that officials told him for many years that it was unthinkable to change our policy on the Oder-Neisse line[5] as the legal arguments were overriding.

7. If we now decide to stand firm on rejection of 'China's Province Taiwan' we should do so recognising one or two consequences:

(*a*) it may be a long while before we are again so close to an exchange of Ambassadors—it has taken us 21 years to get this far;

(*b*) other countries are showing unexpected flexibility—it is now possible that an American President will be in Peking before a British Ambassador; it could even be that an American Ambassador will be;

---

1 No. 209.
2 No. 226.
3 No. 254.
4 The Cairo Declaration of 27 November 1943, issued by President Truman, Winston Churchill and Chiang Kai-shek, and reiterated by the Potsdam Declaration of 26 July 1945, stated that after Japan's defeat Formosa would be restored to China.
5 The basis of the international border between Germany and Poland devised by the Allied powers at the end of the Second World War.

(*c*) China will be in the United Nations and we shall need to have wider dealings on many more subjects than before. We will not be helped by second-class status;

(*d*) the signature of a £25 million contract for British aircraft can be expected shortly. This could increase commercial pressures for raising our representation—a point the Chinese could exploit.

8. For us now to accept the Chinese formula would have the following consequences:

(*a*) it would amount to a reversion of a soundly-based and frequently-repeated legal position. Our view has been held since before the Communist take-over—indeed we had informed Chiang Kai-shek's Government in 1946 that we regarded the status of the sovereignty of Taiwan as undetermined;

(*b*) Peking would be highly grateful to us and we would start off our new relationship in the best possible light;

(*c*) adverse reaction from the Nationalists, and even the Japanese, would be infinitely less in the aftermath of President Nixon's announcement.

(*d*) if in the future Taiwan were ever to declare itself a separate country we would have a new situation with 2 states fulfilling our usual conditions for recognition. This could mean that it would be theoretically possible for us to alter our view and recognise Taiwan—although a decision to do so would have profound effect on relations with Peking;

(*e*) whatever we do will not affect the occupants of Taiwan. The insertion of the 3 words in our communiqué will not alter the reality of Chinese Nationalist control of the island nor limit any of the options open to the leadership.

Conclusion

9. We are not yet faced with the choice between accepting 'China's Province of Taiwan' or giving up an exchange of Ambassadors. If the Chinese wish to be forthcoming to us after our genuine efforts to meet them they can do so without loss of face. For the present I recommend that we should continue to hold out against this wording although time is not on our side. We should defer our decision until the Chinese have disclosed more of their hand. Meanwhile I should welcome any comment on the factors we shall need to take into account.[5]

---

6 In a minute from his private secretary, Mr Royle agreed with Mr Morgan's recommendations. He went on to say that if the Nixon initiative had not taken place he would propose rejecting the suggested three words 'China's Province Taiwan' and stand on the legal position that the Government had taken for so many years regarding the status of Taiwan. 'But the situation has changed. Mr Royle thinks therefore it would be politically very difficult for us now to allow our talks with Peking to founder on this issue. But he believes it is important to consider hinting to the Chinese that if Taiwan were ever to declare itself independent, we might, whether we liked it or not, be obliged to say that the island fulfilled our conditions of recognition'.
Sir A. Douglas-Home noted he would like to see the whole text again: 'There must be some way of expressing our intention without using the word "Province"'.
Meanwhile Mr Overton of the North American Department, in a minute dated 29 July, thought the US position needed to be taken into account. 'If they have not yet reached an understanding [with China over Taiwan], a decision on our part to consider Taiwan as part of China would make it more difficult for the Americans to work out with the Chinese Government a solution to the Taiwan problem ... If they have reached agreement, it is likely to involve a compromise of some sort which we ourselves could probably accept ... it may be that the American policy will no longer be a drag upon the improvement of our relations with China but a spur to it' (FCO 21/824). Mr Crowson, acting head of FED, in a minute of 30 July, generally agreed with Mr Overton but noted: 'since we have consistently agreed to American requests for delay on the Chinese representation issue, I do wonder whether the Americans were in any position to complain about a change of policy on Taiwan'.

No. 261

Letter from Mr Denson (Peking) to Mr Wilford, 27 July 1971
Personal and Confidential (FCO 21/835, FEC 3/548/3C)

Dear Michael,

Sino/British Relations

1. You will have seen my telegram number 695 of 26 July.[1] I am afraid that as a result of the Chinese decision post-Kissinger to place particular emphasis on the status of Taiwan, we may be in for a sticky time. The next round of discussions with the Chinese may show whether they are willing to come any of the way to meet us. Now that they have got what they want over the United Nations, they could take a very hard line and try to squeeze another concession out of us. If so, I think tactically we should be prepared to play it cool and long. The more eagerness we show to get an Ambassador here, the more likely the Chinese are to turn the screw.

2. If progress turns out to be slow, I trust we shall not feel bound by any particular timetable for the Ambassador's arrival. I do not think it would be right to rush him out before 1 October if, for example, we do not get agreement until the beginning of September. I should also like to reaffirm my view that he should wait until the house is ready. We shall be lucky if this is before early October. All other new Ambassadors have gone at once into permanent accommodation. Peking hotels are not impressive and for our first Ambassador to put up in one would not, I think, be dignified, convenient or very comfortable.

Yours ever,
JOHN

1 Not printed.

No. 262

Letter from Mr Samuel (Peking) to Mr Hervey, 27 July 1971[1]
Confidential (FCO 21/826, FEC 3/304/4/A)

1. Though we, like all the other diplomatic missions in Peking, except the Pakistanis, were taken completely by surprise by the announcement of Kissinger's visit, we have gleaned a certain amount of background information since, some admittedly speculative, which it may be worth reporting for the record.

2. K. M. Kaiser, the Pakistan Ambassador, has confirmed to the Chargé d'Affaires that he had known since earlier this year what was afoot. Indeed he claims to have dropped several heavy hints, though if he did they were so delphic as to be unrecognisable as such. We can take it that very few people in the Pakistani Embassy were aware of what was going on. A number of visitors to Peking appear to

1 Copied to Mr Boyd in Washington, Mr Howells in Hong Kong and the Chancery at Paris.

have been used, at least unconsciously, as channels through whom the United States administration could indicate to the Chinese at a high level that they were interested in bringing about an early improvement in relations. We doubt if Tillman Durdin,[2] for example, was let into the secret, but he spoke to Kaiser about the Administration's desire for greater contact and Kaiser says he urged him to stress the point in his conversations with the Chinese. This and similar remarks by correspondents like Seymour Topping[3] would have helped to confirm the impression that American intentions were serious.

3. The Danish Embassy tell us that their Ambassador to Washington who visited Peking for a few days from 13 June onwards was received before his departure by President Nixon. Kissinger was present. They discussed the Ambassador's forthcoming visit to Peking and though, apparently, no suggestion was made of Kissinger's mission it was indicated that the Ambassador could convey to the Chinese the American desire for an improvement in relations. It seems quite likely that apart from the journalists, other unconscious 'agents of influence' may have been used by the Americans both in Peking and elsewhere to reinforce the message.

4. We still have no evidence that the Romanians were in on the act. At the time of Ceaucescu's visit we reported our doubts about them playing an intermediary role, and conversations with Romanian contacts since the announcement was made tend to bear this assessment out.

5. We are intrigued by the apparent involvement of the Chinese Ambassador in Paris, Huang Chen. Kissinger was, we understand, in Paris on 12 July on his way home from the Far East and French contacts believe that he was in touch with Huang that afternoon. Huang was due to dine with M. Schumann[4] on 15 July but cancelled the engagement on 12 July and left for China the following day. This perhaps suggests that Kissinger told the Chinese in Paris that the President was prepared to go firm on a visit. Kissinger might also, having consulted Washington from Pakistan on his way out of China, have been able at the same time to clear the text of the joint announcement. At all events Huang arrived in Peking rather suddenly, turning up half-way through the French National Day Reception on the evening of 14 July direct from the airport. I happened to be standing close to Chou En-lai when Huang came out on to the verandah. Chou leaped up, wreathed in smiles, to shake his hand, but was unable to exchange more than a few words because the seats nearby were occupied by visiting French parliamentarians. Before the Acting Foreign Minister had a chance to reply to the French Ambassador's long and florid speech on Sino/French relations Chou and Huang made their excuses and departed as unexpectedly as Hung had appeared. By Peking standards this was unusual, though at the time no-one had any explanation for it. If Huang's only purpose had been to be present for the parliamentary visit it seems odd that he should have made a dinner date with M. Schumann right in the middle of it which he knew he would have to break.

2 Frank Tillman Durdin was a foreign correspondent for *The New York Times*.
3 Foreign correspondent and editor for *The New York Times*.
4 Maurice Schumann, French Foreign Minister, 1969-73.

6. Looking further back there were one or two high-powered Pakistani visits, notably that of the Army Chief of Staff, Abdul Hameed Khan, in March and later the visit of the Foreign Secretary's private secretary, Ahmad Kamal, at the end of May, which might conceivably have played some part in the preparations. But, as is obvious from the reactions in many other capitals throughout the world, the security of the operation was exceptionally good and there were no hints which could lead anyone here to expect the bombshell announcement of 16 July. We have reported separately the steps the Chinese took in Peking to tip off their Asian friends shortly before the news was made public.

Yours ever,
RICHARD

P.S. I cannot help remarking, rather ruefully, that little of the foregoing speculation would be necessary if the Americans took us as much into their confidence as we have made a practice of taking them . . .

No. 263

Minute by Sir S. Tomlinson,[1] 30 July 1971
Confidential (FCO 21/835, FEC 3/548/3C)

Sino-British Relations

The formulation which we have consistently used in regard to the legal status of Formosa was adopted on purely legal grounds. There was no element of expediency in it. We were told by our lawyers that it was a correct statement of the position. It is a formulation that has been repeated in public, in the General Assembly, in the Security Council, in Parliament and in other places by senior representatives of successive British Governments on an extremely large number of occasions.

2. In so far as this formulation coincided with the requirements of the policy, it was for a reason that the Peking Government ought to (but certainly will not) give us credit. We wanted to resist any suggestion that Chiang Kai Shek's position in Taiwan should be given any sort of formal recognition and that the mere act of occupation was in itself a fulfilment of the Cairo Declaration. It was, if I remember rightly, largely because of the British attitude that Japan was required, in the Treaty of Peace, to renounce sovereignty over Taiwan but not to renounce it in favour of anyone else. Mr Dulles would doubtless have preferred that Japan renounce her title in favour of 'the Government of the Republic of China', i.e. Chiang Kai Shek. It was at the

---

[1] Copied to Mr Cradock, Mr Crowson, Mr Logan, Mr Renwick, North American Department, United Nations (Political) Department and Legal Advisers.

time of this Treaty of Peace that the then Legal Adviser said that Taiwan's status in international law was *res nullius*.[2]

3. If we now ourselves use the phrase 'China's Province Taiwan' we shall be seen to be publicly renouncing a firm, clear, long-held, and the Legal Advisers would doubtless say, still correct, legal position on grounds of expediency. The reasons why it is suggested that we should contemplate doing so are of the highest importance and may indeed be thought overriding. But there seems to me to be some risk of weakening the credibility of future British official assertions about the sanctity of law. Perhaps the Legal Advisers can be considering how we can make the change, if it becomes inevitable, with the least damage to our position from this point of view.

4. The immediate effect on our relations with Peking would obviously be good. There could be less agreeable consequences in the longer term. If the Chinese see that by resolute pressure they can push us off positions of principle, they might draw inferences which could affect their attitude in any future confrontation over Hong Kong.

5. The parallel with the Oder-Neisse Line is not a good one in one important respect. The Oder-Neisse Line represents the *de facto* position, but in fact Taiwan is certainly not now being administered as a Province of China. It is said that our use of the words 'China's Province Taiwan' will have no effect on the factual position in the Island. I think that this is a little too strongly stated. Obviously it would have no direct or immediate effect. But we should be making our contribution to a process which could lead in the end to major changes for the inhabitants of the Island. It is not long since the Australians were arguing that if we were to acquiesce in the unseating of the present 'Republic of China' representatives in the UN, we should be making a contribution to the eventual Communist takeover of the Island. I certainly do not want to exaggerate this point. But equally we must not, I think, maintain that our attitude is totally without any possible relevance to the fate of the Taiwanese.

6. If the Government of Taiwan were to stop calling itself China and to claim to be nothing more than the Government of the Island of Taiwan we should be in an embarrassing position. If we were to give the Chinese any hint that in this eventuality we might have to recognise Taiwan as Taiwan, I think that they would call all bets off.

7. I have no very constructive suggestions to offer. I think we should do our very best to get the Chinese to accept some kind of 'taking note' formula. If this fails, perhaps there are other formulae, possibly based on some form of unilateral reaffirmation of our adherence to the principles of the Cairo Declaration. There are no doubt other variants.[3]

F.S. TOMLINSON

---

2 Nobody's property i.e. a thing with no owner.
3 Sir A. Douglas-Home noted on 2 August: 'I am by no means happy about this 'Province of China' formula. To give way on a legal interpretation which we have supported for a long time is very weak. The Chinese won't forget when it comes to Hong Kong.'

No. 264

Minute from Mr Overton to Mr Crowson, 3 August 1971
Confidential (FCO 21/835, FEC 3/548/3C)

Taiwan

1. At the meeting with the Secretary of State on 2 August[1] two points affecting the United States were raised during discussion about the consequences of moving towards the Chinese formula on Taiwan: i.e. that it is a province of China. It was argued:

(*a*) that, despite the legal difficulty of changing the UK attitude without any substantial change in circumstances, a formula might be devised to the effect that the status of Taiwan is an internal Chinese affair.

(*b*) that, in the light of their change of policy on China and President Nixon's electoral commitment to better US/China relations, the US will be bound, at least in the long run, to abandon Taiwan.

2. On (*a*) the formula suggested presents three main difficulties:

(i) It would amount, I am advised, to admitting that Taiwan was a province of China since it would imply that the Chinese Government's view was binding as in any other Chinese 'internal affair'.

(ii) It would imply acceptance of Peking's assertion that the existing United States Defence Treaty with Taiwan and the presence of US troops in Taiwan are illegal. It would also imply acceptance of Peking's right to control shipping in Taiwan territorial waters (and perhaps the Pescadores[2]). Peking would then expect us to support any resolution which might be moved in the UN—by the Albanians or the Chinese themselves—demanding the withdrawal of US troops from Taiwan and condemning the US for interference in Chinese internal affairs by having dealings with Taiwan. (Political action on these lines seems more likely than a Chinese attempt to change the status of Taiwan by force, though the latter cannot be ruled out in the long term).

(iii) The formula would establish an embarrassing precedent for anomalous recognition situations elsewhere. (Mrs Denza's minute of 30 July).[3]

3. On (*b*), President Nixon's new China policy has clearly put the US Government before an embarrassing dilemma, but it cannot be assumed that they will decide to abandon Taiwan. There is evidence to suggest that the new Two China policy declared by Mr Rogers, even if it fails at the UN (as seems likely) may be applied to the *de facto* situation, and that the US Government may continue to support the independence of Taiwan even if (which is not sure) the Chinese government decide to make total abandonment of Taiwan a breaking-point for President Nixon's visit to Peking. The evidence, admittedly incomplete, is as follows:

(i) A US Government spokesman seems to have tried to make a distinction in principle between sovereignty over Taiwan and the Pescadores ('an unsettled question

---

1 At this meeting Sir A. Douglas-Home instructed officials to produce a form of words which might bridge the gap between the two sides.
2 An archipelago of 90 islands and islets in the Taiwan Strait, between Taiwan and the Chinese mainland.
3 Not printed.

subject to future international resolution'), and the 'legitimate authority' over the area exercised by the Nationalists (Washington telegram No. 2589).[4]

(ii) The President continues to distinguish firmly between his policy on better relations with the Chinese Peoples Republic and a sell-out of the Republic of China, and has specifically underlined the continuing validity of the US-Taiwan Mutual Security Treaty.

(iii) There are indications that the Americans may have done a 'deal' with the Chinese Nationalists over UN recognition; this must involve some undertaking to give the Nationalists continuing practical support.

(iv) The Nixon Doctrine of 1969 declares the President's firm intention to keep US Treaty Commitments to the countries of East Asia, partly as a means of permitting them to maintain their independence. Even in the present US mood of disillusion about overseas involvement, reneging on a clear Treaty commitment to Taiwan could become an electoral liability.

(v) Abandonment of Taiwan would have a dangerous effect upon other US allies in the area, notably Japan, South Korea, South Vietnam and Thailand. The US Government cannot afford to ignore this.

4. A decision by HMG to accept now the Chinese formula on Taiwan or any formula to the same effect would therefore contain the seeds of serious future trouble with the US.[5]

H. T. A. OVERTON

[4] Not printed.
[5] Mr Godber minuted to Sir A. Douglas-Home on 3 August that what was not determined at the meeting was the line to take in the UN in the light of the American announcement that they will produce a resolution to attempt to maintain a two China posture of some kind. 'I presume that they will try to persuade us at least to abstain on such a measure but I feel that we cannot do other than oppose any step of this kind.' The Secretary of State replied on 4 August: 'We would have to oppose anything which could be said to be a two China policy. What would be much more difficult would be if Taiwan decided to go it alone and ask for membership as an independent country.'

No. 265

Mr Denson (Peking) to Sir A. Douglas-Home, 5 August 1971, 4.57 a.m.[1]
Tel. No. 743 Immediate, Confidential (FCO 21/835, FEC 3/548/3C)

My Telno. 740:[2] Exchange of Ambassadors.

The meeting went much as I expected (My Telno. 707).[3] There was no sign of give in the Chinese position and Ch'iao pointedly did not respond to hints which I threw out that a compromise formula might be acceptable.[4]

2. What Ch'iao said about the situation changing fast seemed to indicate that at an earlier stage the Chinese might have accepted an exchange on the original

[1] Repeated for information routine to Washington, UKMIS New York and Hong Kong.
[2] Not printed.
[3] Not printed.
[4] In Peking Tel. No. 753 of 7 August, Denson reported that the Chinese were 'cock-a-hoop diplomatically' and taking a hard line on Taiwan: 'Now is therefore a particularly difficult time to persuade them to compromise.'

conditions. His argument that recognition of the Chinese position on the status of Taiwan was implicit to the other two conditions was not convincing but I saw no point in rubbing this in. The hardening of the Chinese position is probably due mainly to the need to reconcile in private the present public emphasis on the cardinal importance of Taiwan in the context of the Nixon visit and the UN. (It may not have been entirely coincidental that on 10 July when the Chinese handed over their draft and drew particular attention to the Taiwan point, Kissinger was in Peking.) The Chinese will also wish to get as many countries as possible to recognise their position against the time when Taiwan might claim independent status, and if we could be persuaded to change our position in public the effect internationally would be considerable.

3. In spite of these considerations, I think it is still possible that the Chinese might accept a 'taking note' formula but it is clear that we shall have to propose the wording. On the assumption that we are not (repeat not) prepared to change our legal position I think that the correct tactics now would be to delay a reply to the Chinese for at least two or three weeks. If we appear too eager this will only encourage them to put on the pressure. Though I recognise that having asked for agreement for a named Ambassador we naturally wish to avoid undue delay I am convinced that if there is any hope at all of reaching a compromise we must be prepared to play the negotiations slowly.

4. The Chinese amendments to paragraph 3, in particular the substitution of 'support with reservation' for 'intend voting for' and the substitution of 'oppose' for 'not support' seem designed to ensure that we do not abstain on any resolution designed to prevent the expulsion of the Nationalists. Whatever our own interpretation of our undertaking to the Chinese might be, they would certainly interpret such a move as a breach of faith. I trust therefore that we shall not consider doing this in deference to American susceptibilities or indicate in any public statement before then that it might be possible. You will have noted the sharp Chinese reaction to Mr Rogers' statement[5] of 2 August.[6]

---

5 Mr Rodgers announced that the US would support action at the UN General Assembly calling for seating the PRC but at the same time the US would oppose any action to expel the Republic of China or deprive it of representation in the UN. The US Ambassador called on Sir A. Douglas-Home on 2 August to convey a message from Mr Rogers giving advance notice of his statement in which he expressed his 'great appreciation for the advice and assistance which you and your Government have given during our past consultations on this exceedingly difficult problem'. Nevertheless the Secretary of State took the opportunity to point out to the Ambassador that Britain had 'suffered' by agreeing to Mr Rogers' request to delay agreement on an exchange of Ambassadors as Peking had now 'put the price up' (FCO 21/824)
6 Sir A. Douglas-Home noted on 5 August: 'I wonder if the position will be so hard if the Americans back Taiwan in the UN. We need not be in a great hurry.'

No. 266

Minute from Mr Overton to Sir S. Tomlinson, 6 August 1971
Confidential (FCO 21/824, FEC 3/304/1B)

China and Taiwan

1. I hope that you will not mind if I put to you direct a point which has not yet been seized directly and argued out in the recent learned minutes and submissions which I have seen. This point relates to the timing of any new decision by HMG to advance our China policy.

2. President Nixon's recent decision has discredited past American policy on Chinese representation etc. and thrown the US Government into confusion. Whether this was the object of Mao's agreement with Nixon, he will certainly exploit the result, and there is every sign that the Chinese Government are doing this. Using the Nixon visit as a deadline they will clearly put all possible pressure on the Americans to agree to abandon Taiwan before the visit takes place—though it is not clear that the Chinese Government are prepared, in the last resort, to make abandonment of Taiwan an absolute pre-condition for the visit. The Americans, on the other hand, have to decide between now and next May at the latest whether they are prepared to abandon Taiwan, or whether they must ultimately insist upon the *de facto* independence of Taiwan even at the cost of abandoning the visit, if the Chinese insist. In practice this dilemma is rapidly becoming more acute, and a decision will be precipitated by all the argument at the UN about Chinese representation there.

3. Whatever comes out of this imbroglio will decisively affect one way or another not only the future pattern of US-Chinese relations, but also China's relations with other countries. If the Chinese win their point and the Americans agree to abandon Taiwan a new situation will be created, because the American decision will have far reaching effects, not only on Taiwan, but throughout the Far East. In particular, it will be apparent to all that Taiwan has no long term hope of survival, and all countries will be wise to adapt their policies accordingly. If the Americans win their point on Taiwan there will be a good chance that Taiwan will survive for a while at least, and other countries will be wise to adapt to this fact. If neither the Chinese nor the Americans carry their point on the substance, but both nevertheless agree that the Nixon visit to Peking should take place, there will be a fluid situation. The Chinese will nevertheless have lost some face, and there will be a better chance for the Americans to carry a '2 Chinas' policy *de facto* though not in the UN.

5. [*sic*] In this highly uncertain situation, with the heat on the Americans and decisions imminent, prudence offers many advantages for other Governments less directly engaged. There is a strong *prima facie* case for waiting to see what comes out of the US-Chinese squabble, and not adopting lines of policy which may embarrass if the outcome is not what we expect. Having been without an Ambassador for some years, are the arguments in favour of pressing on in the hope of making our own limited deal with the Chinese on this front really powerful enough to counterbalance the evident dangers of finding ourselves offside later on? There were arguments six months ago, certainly, but the whole situation has now been changed by the Nixon decision, which has shifted the argument from a question of *representation* to a question of

independence. I suggest, in short, that if the Chinese are adamant in refusing to agree to a formula on Taiwan which would not allow for self-determination, we should postpone a decision on whether to accept the Chinese view or not until the outcome of the US-Chinese imbroglio is clearer.[1]

H. T. A. OVERTON

No. 267

Sir A. Douglas-Home to Mr Denson (Peking), 12 August 1971, 4.15 p.m.[2]
Tel. No. 516 Priority, Confidential (FCO 21/835, FEC 3/548/3C)

Your Tels. Nos. 743 and 753:[3] Exchange of Ambassadors.

I am not willing to accept any formula which would be a manifest breach of our consistent practice in regard to recognition. A statement that Taiwan is now a province of China would constitute such a breach.

2. It may be useful to restate briefly this practice. It is to accord recognition, whether of states, governments or acquisition of territory, when and only when we are satisfied that certain conditions are fulfilled. On this point we differ from the US which regards the according of recognition as a matter of policy. You were correct in maintaining (paragraph 1 of your Tel No 740)[4] that the fact that we participated in the Cairo Declaration does not distinguish our legal position from that of non-parties to it since the Declaration was only a statement of intention.

3. Although it would obviously be better if you could avoid arguing the point, it is not the case that China could only acquire sovereignty over Taiwan by a peace treaty or other formal diplomatic instrument. The 1946 exchanges referred to in para. 6 of Morgan's submission of 14 May[3] took place at a time when it was confidently expected that a Treaty of Peace with Japan would not be long delayed and would in fact regulate this question.

4. We regard the status of Taiwan as being undetermined because:

(i) The Japanese Peace Treaty was not in itself effective to transfer sovereignty over Taiwan, since all that Japan did under it was to renounce her own title and she did not formally cede the island to China.

---

1 In a minute of 10 August, Mr Crowson thought that there was no indication that the Americans would 'abandon' Taiwan 'so the dilemma foreseen by Mr Overton may not in fact become more acute'. He also cautioned against following 'in the wake of the Americans' adding: 'We have to recognise that our interests as regards China exist independently of those of the US. It is the failure to act on this that had led to the difficulties in which we now find ourselves. This is not to suggest that we should not keep in touch with the Americans. Clearly we should, and are doing. But we must be careful to put our own clear interests first.' Responding on 11 August, Mr Overton agreed the UK should put its own interests first but pointed out: 'The fact that "following in the wake of the Americans" on that occasion worked to our disadvantage . . . does not mean that it would necessarily be a mistake in our own interests to wait on the Americans in the new situation which now exists.'
2 Repeated for information priority to Washington, UKMIS New York, Hong Kong (personal for Governor), Tokyo and Canberra.
3 No. 265 and not printed respectively.
4 Not printed.

(ii) Sovereignty over Taiwan was not in our view acquired by China on the relinquishment of title by Japan, because the island was not under the effective control of the only Government of China recognised by us and sovereignty was not acquired by any other means.

(iii) There has been no change in the situation since then justifying on any legal basis our recognition of the acquisition of Chinese sovereignty over Taiwan.

5. The Chinese analogy with the position of Manchuria (para 3 of your Tel. No. 740) is false. Manchuria was never ceded by treaty to the Japanese. The puppet state of Manchukuo set up by the Japanese in 1932 never received any general international recognition. Following the Japanese surrender in 1945, *de facto* control reverted automatically to China no *de jure* rights needed to be transferred since Manchuria had continued to be regarded as an integral part of China.

6. I have been considering whether some form of words can be found to which the Chinese might be persuaded to agree. I should be grateful for your advice on some formula on one of the following lines which are listed in order of preference:

(i) The Government of the PRC, having regard to their position that Taiwan is a province of China, have noted the decision of the Government of the United Kingdom to remove their official representation from Taiwan on . . .

(ii) The Government of the United Kingdom, in recognition that the position of the Government of the Chinese People's Republic is that Taiwan is a province of China, have decided to remove their consulate at Tamsui;

(iii) The Government of the United Kingdom have decided to remove their official representation on Taiwan on . . . They recognise that the future of Taiwan is one solely for the Chinese people to decide;

(iv) The Government of the United Kingdom have decided to remove their official representation on Taiwan on . . . In the Cairo declaration of 1943 the government of the United Kingdom stated that Taiwan should be restored to China. It remains their view that the question of Taiwan is one for the Chinese people to resolve;

(v) The Government of the United Kingdom reaffirm their declaration at Cairo in December 1943 that Taiwan should be returned to China, and have decided to remove their Consulate at Tamsui.

7. The first two formulae put the words 'Taiwan is a province of China' into Chinese mouths alone. Admittedly neither goes further than a 'take note' formula but the Chinese may marginally prefer one of our versions. The third formula seems the most likely to appeal to Peking. The fourth and fifth formulae restate our Cairo Declaration position. My present feeling is that it might be unwise to resurrect this Declaration. It might also be alleged that the fifth formula ignores the view that we have expressed that the wishes of the inhabitants of Taiwan should be taken into account. I should therefore be reluctant to authorise you to make use of it, although we would welcome your comments on it.

8. As regards the Chinese amendments to paragraph 3 of the draft in my Tel. No. 443[5] I agree to the substitution of 'support without reservation' for 'intend voting for'. As for the substitution of 'oppose' for 'not support', I would propose you should give the Chinese a private oral undertaking that we shall oppose any

---

5 Not printed.

procedure intended to delay the seating of Peking and that we shall vote against any 'reverse Important Question' resolution e.g. the lines of those set out in Washington Tel. No. 2637.⁶ However I would propose you should tell the Chinese that I would not be prepared to express our specific voting intentions in a published exchange of documents: to do this would be inconsistent with long-established practice particularly where we do not know the exact terms of the resolutions we are likely to be voting for. We should not take the initiative to inform other governments of our position but will clearly have to do so if asked.

9. I should be grateful for your comments. Meanwhile you should of course take no action with the Chinese until instructed to do so. I agree that it would be wise not to reply immediately to the Chinese. I should like you to approach them again on about 23rd August. I should welcome any further views you may have about the tactics of such an approach. It would seem prudent to emphasise the difficulties which the Chinese attitude causes us but at the same time to tell them that we would be prepared to consider a compromise formula. I would leave it to your discretion whether or not at that stage to propose any of the first three formulae suggested in paragraph 4 above.

10. If an approach on or about 20 of August is, for any reason, unlikely to be possible please let me know by telegram. I shall then consider whether the exchange should be continued with the Chinese Chargé d'Affaires here.

6 Not printed.

No. 268

Sir D. Trench (Hong Kong) to Sir A. Douglas-Home
16 August 1971, 1.15 a.m.[1]
Tel. No. 568 Immediate, Confidential (FCO 21/835, FEC3/548/3C)

From Denson.[2]

Your telegram No. 516[3] to Peking: Exchange of Ambassadors.

I am grateful for the clarification of our legal position on Taiwan which will be helpful if the argument is pursued. But I doubt if anything is to be gained by our initiating another full-scale discussion, as, however impeccable the grounds for our position, the Chinese will not be moved from their belief that in this, as in everything, politics are or should be 'in command'.

2. As regards the formulae proposed in your paragraph 6, I agree that it would be unwise to put the fourth or fifth as this would stimulate more fruitless discussion on the Cairo Declaration, and the fifth would also be open to the other objection you cite. The third might possibly have some attraction for the Chinese, but it is somewhat vague and does not refer to the Chinese position on status which is a current obsession with them. Furthermore is there not also a danger from our point of view that, like the fifth formula, it might be construed as ignoring our declared intention of taking into account

1 Repeated for information immediate to Peking; and routine to Washington, UKMIS New York, Tokyo and Canberra.
2 Mr Denson was visiting Hong Kong for medical treatment.
3 No. 267.

the wishes of the people of Taiwan, since not all of these could be included within the normally accepted meaning of the term 'the Chinese People'? It is true that apart from the Chinese who come from the mainland, the majority of the rest (with the exception of some Aboriginals) are ethnic Chinese, but they no more constitute 'The Chinese People', with its essentially mainland connotation, than say the Chinese in Malaysia or Canada. They are part of the people of Taiwan. If a formula containing this sort of ambiguity were the only way of doing the trick, the risk would be worth taking. But I doubt if it is, and if this formula is put there is another risk that the Chinese might retort that 'the Chinese People' have already decided the future of Taiwan, and if our position is as stated, all we have to do is accept the original wording of the Chinese draft. After that further discussion would be very difficult.

3. On balance, I think the second formula would have greatest attraction for the Chinese since it is the United Kingdom which is *recognising* the Chinese position and as a consequence removing the Consulate at Tamsui. This might appear in public in some quarters as a greater success for the Chinese than the third formula would.

4. On tactics, I agree that we should again emphasise the difficulty the Chinese attitude causes us. I have of course done this twice already, and to add weight on the next occasion I should like to say that personally I see no hope of progress if the Chinese persist in trying to force us to accept their position. We have recognised their problems, they should do something towards recognising ours. In order to make progress we are prepared to consider a compromise. Are the Chinese willing to do so? Depending on the reply, I might say that the type of compromise we had in mind was on the lines of your first and second formulae which I would rehearse in general terms without reading out the actual form of words. I would add that if the Chinese were willing to consider something on these lines, I would shortly submit precise formulations. If the Chinese in the course of discussion indicated any preferences or gave any indication of what they would accept this could be taken into account when the formulae were submitted.

5. At the same time I would explain your views on the UN vote as set out in your paragraph 8, on which I do not expect difficulty. After reporting back to you, a meeting could then be arranged to discuss a new draft incorporating all our changes in paragraphs 2 and 3 which could be submitted to the Chinese in advance.

6. Grateful for any comments from Peking.

No. 269

Sir A. Douglas-Home to Mr Samuel (Peking), 19 August 1971, 2.35 p.m.[1]
Tel. No. 532 Priority, Confidential (FCO 21/835, FEC 3/548/3C)

Your Telegram No 733:[2] Exchange of Ambassadors.

I agree that our tactics should be as Denson suggests in paragraph 4 of Hong Kong telegram No 568.[3] I leave it to discretion how far to go in rehearsing the

---

[1] Repeated for information priority to Hong Kong; and routine to Washington, UKMIS New York, Tokyo and Canberra.
[2] Not printed.
[3] No. 268.

historical and legal considerations (paragraph 1 of your telegram under reference). It could be that adequate time has already been devoted to this aspect.

2. A decent interval has now elapsed since the Chinese reply and I hope that Denson will be sufficiently recovered to take action in Peking during the week beginning 23 August. Should Denson's return be likely to be delayed you should act as soon as convenient. (P'ei is returning to Peking for consultations on 23 August).

3. The aim in the next round of talks should be to put us in a position to assess definitively whether there is likely to be any readiness on the Chinese side to accept anything less than 'China's Province Taiwan'.

4. I do not think that we can delay our assessment much longer. The United Nations General Assembly will be upon us in a few weeks. Particularly in the light of UKMIS New York telegram No 905[4] it is conceivable that Chinese representation could be raised at an early stage. For this issue to be resolved while we are still negotiating our exchange of Ambassadors would considerably reduce China's incentive to reach an agreement with us.

4 Not printed.

No. 270

Mr Samuel (Peking) to Sir A. Douglas-Home, 26 August 1971, 2.50 p.m.[1]
Tel. No. 825 Flash, Confidential (FCO 21/835, FEC 3/548/3C)

Your Telno 542: Sino/British relations.[2]

1. Vice-Minister Ch'iao Kuan-hua received me this evening. After brief discussion of paragraph three of the draft exchange of notes (about which I had the impression there should not be much difficulty) I went on to rehearse our position on paragraph two at some length. I emphasised that I did not believe we could make progress unless the Chinese were prepared to take account of the firmness of our legal position on the status of Taiwan.

2. I asked if the Chinese would be prepared to consider a formula for paragraph two which would meet our difficulties. Ch'iao said that although his government stood firm on their principles, he would be ready to discuss an alternative formula. That, he said, was what the negotiations were about. He suggested that we officially put forward our own form of words for consideration and asked what sort of language we had in mind. He made it clear that he would like to see something in writing soon. I outlined the first two formulae in paragraph six of your Telno 516,[3] without however reading them out in full. From Ch'iao's reactions it was clear that something on the lines of version two was more likely to be acceptable. He pointedly observed that the Chinese continue, despite our disclaimers, to regard us as being in a different category from countries like Canada and Italy: consequently the 'take note' formula such as was used in their cases would not be appropriate in ours.

1 Repeated for information priority to Hong Kong.
2 Not printed.
3 No. 267.

3. I said I would report back and let him have a text shortly. I assured him that we would go as far as we could consistent with our own stand to meet the Chinese position but urged him when studying our proposals to remember what our difficulties are.

4. It seems clear that the Chinese want to make early progress. I will send a fuller account of the meeting tomorrow morning with considered comments.[4]

[4] On 11 September Mr Denson was summoned at short notice to see Qiao Guanhua who said it had been agreed that they should seek a formula for the wording of the second paragraph which expressed the 'principled stand' of the Chinese side but was also acceptable to the UK side. The current wording was not acceptable and he suggested the British put forward another draft exchange of notes (Peking Tel. No. 900). On 25 September, in an attempt to break the deadlock, Qiao Guanhua proposed alternative wording for the joint statement and asked that the Government to give an 'oral assurance' that the UK would no longer promote or support the 'fallacy' that the status of Taiwan was 'undetermined' (Peking Tel. Nos. 969/970). To avoid further delay British ministers accepted the Chinese draft, which allowed Britain to acknowledge China's position on Taiwan without stating its own, and agreed to give a private assurance but they refused to give up the freedom, if asked, to tell Parliament that their legal position on Taiwan remained unchanged (Letter from Mr Grattan to Mr Moon, 7 October 1971).

No. 271

Letter from Mr Grattan to Mr Roberts (No. 10), 3 September 1971
Confidential (FCO 21/810, FEC 2/2C)

[No salutation]

Chinese Representation in the United Nations

The Foreign and Commonwealth Secretary has been considering what our response should be to the inscription in New York by the Americans of a new item on representation of China in the United Nations and you may like to have this account for the Prime Minister's information.

The explanatory memorandum attached to the American item amounts to a proposal for a 'two-Chinas' solution, and may be followed later on by an American draft resolution. They are unlikely to circulate this until they have a clearer idea of the support they could obtain for a 'two-Chinas' approach. This is a clever move on the Americans' part. They have given us no advance warning in relation to it and it seems designed to make things awkward for those of their friends whom they think might be persuaded at least to support the inscription of the resolution, even if they voted against it, and thus give an early impression of greater support for the American position than is really the case.

We should certainly have to oppose the resolution when it came before the full Assembly. If we voted at any earlier stage for the inscription of the item in the General Committee on the grounds that it was logical to hear the arguments, there is little doubt that in the United Nations context this would be construed as supporting the American position.

Sir Alec Douglas-Home has therefore concluded that it would be better to make clear from the start that we are not prepared to support any move designed to forward a 'two-China' policy, and that we should vote against the inscription of the American item from the outset. Our decision is unlikely to come as a great surprise to them.

For their part, the Chinese would almost certainly regard our undertaking 'not to support any procedure calculated to delay' the seating of Peking as requiring a vote against inscription. They have not yet specifically referred to this point in our negotiations over an exchange of Ambassadors. Our Chargé d'Affaires in Peking has been told to refer for instructions should they do so.

If we are to tell the Americans of our intention to oppose inscription it is probably better done fairly soon. Nevertheless there is no great urgency and there would be advantage in waiting to see whether the Chinese raise it in the next round of talks in Peking. This could take place next week. In the light of developments there we can consider how best to inform the Americans. The Foreign and Commonwealth Secretary's present inclination is to send a short personal message to Mr Rogers. The alternative would be to inform them through Sir Colin Crowe in New York.[1]

P.H. Grattan

1 In a reply dated 6 September Mr Roberts stated that the Prime Minister agreed with the views of the Foreign Secretary. In UKMIS New York tel. No. 992 of 8 September, Sir C. Crowe noted that it was by no means certain that the inscription of the American item would be pressed to a vote and the normal practice in cases not involving intervention in domestic jurisdiction was to support inscription. In light of this fact, on 13 September Sir A. Douglas-Home noted; 'I think we need not and should not stick out our necks and unnecessarily incur Mr Rogers' wrath. If the Chinese were to show positively that this was a factor in an immediate appointment of an Ambassador that could be different—but they have not shown much sign of wanting to be helpful. I think we had better play this by ear for a bit longer. I cannot see why abstention in the committee would be interpreted by the Chinese as "support" for the American proposition. It is our usual practice' (FCO 21/811).

No. 272

Letter from Mr Millard (Washington) to Mr Wilford, 10 September 1971
Personal and Confidential (FCO 21/811, FEC 2/2D)

Dear Michael,

You will have observed that I have not intervened further from here in the argument about whether we should or should not oppose the inscription of the American item on Chinese representation.

2. I can well see that the question is a difficult one for the delegation in New York, in view of the line which we have taken in the past over inscription in cases which do not involve intervention in domestic jurisdiction. But whatever the difficulties at the United Nations, I do not feel that the question is one of great importance in Anglo-American relations. The Americans must have quite a bad conscience where we are concerned over policy towards China. We have voted consistently, over the years, at the expense of our own interests, in favour of the Important Question Resolution and at their request we held off for months telling the Chinese we would not support it this year. Although the Americans finally gave us the go ahead in June, this communication seems to have been too late to make much impact on the Chinese. And the Americans then arranged Kissinger's journey to China, followed by the announcement of the President's visit to Peking, without a word of warning to us, although the result has been to cause the Chinese to raise their terms. I am very conscious that this scenario is more or less the one which you outlined in your letter to me on 4 May[1] and which I said at the time seemed to me only too probable.

1 No. 239.

3. In view of all this, I do not really think that the Americans can make much of our failing to support them over inscription, and if they did we should have a very good answer. Of course they will not like it, and they would prefer us to abstain than to vote against. But I do not feel that this Embassy has a case for asking you to reconsider the decision.

4. I agree that when the time comes to inform the Americans of our decision a personal message from the Secretary of State to Mr Rogers would be a good way of doing it.

Yours ever,
GUY

No. 273

Sir A. Douglas-Home to Sir C. Crowe (UKMIS New York)
20 September 1971, 4 p.m.[1]
Tel. No. 633 Immediate, Confidential (FCO 21/811, FEC 2/2D)

Your Telno. 992:[2] Chinese Representation in the United Nations.

I have decided that on balance it would be preferable for you to inform the Americans in New York of our decisions on their item on Chinese Representation.

2. I should therefore like you to take an early opportunity to inform them that:

(i) We should have to vote against both the Resolutions set out in Washington Telno. 2637[2] (with the addition reported in my telno 2366[2] to Washington);

(ii) We should have to vote for priority for the Albanian Resolution.

3. I have also decided that should it come to the vote, we should have to oppose inscription of the American Item in the General Committee. Although it now seems that the matter may not be pressed to a vote (Your Tels Nos. 1033 and 1038),[2] you have discretion, should you think it necessary, to tell the Americans of this decision on the following lines. While we understand the reasons for their move they will realise that our position is totally different from their own. It is only right to let them know that although we shall not take any initiative and although we believe that the question is in fact unlikely to be pressed to a vote, we should probably feel obliged to vote against the inscription of this item should it come to a division in the General Committee with voting along 'Chinese Representation' lines. In such circumstances this would be an exceptional case where our basic policy considerations must override our normal practice regarding inscription of items. Support for inscription would be seen by the Chinese as going against the spirit of the undertakings we have given them in Peking in the context of our exchange of Ambassadors. You should inform the Americans that if events turn out this way we shall not speak except to make a brief explanation of vote after the vote on the lines of paragraph 3 of your telegram under reference. We would say that their item is in our view inappropriate since it aims at a result which would be incompatible

1 Repeated for information immediate to Peking; routine to Washington.
2 Not printed.

with the Charter and that, in any case, there is already an item on the agenda which allows full scope for discussion of Chinese representation.

4. In any event please reaffirm to the Americans that it is not our intention to make their task any more difficult. We shall not publicise in any way how we propose to vote although, once the Americans have been informed, if specifically asked in private by those countries with whom we co-operate more closely we shall have to tell them of our intentions on all the above points except inscription. On inscription we would only state our position once it became clear that there was to be a vote.

5. I think it advisable that, because of the complexity of the possible votes, discussion with other Governments on this matter should only take place in New York. We intend to advise any foreign missions who might raise this with us in London that their delegation should keep in touch with yours.[3]

3 On hearing these voting intentions Mr Bush, who had made a strong pitch for maximum support for the US initiative, was said to be 'ashen with dismay.' He said the reaction of the State Department would be one of surprise in view of the UK's undertaking to do nothing that would make the US task more difficult. Later in the day, the State Department telegraphed Ambassador Annenberg in London and urged him to meet with Sir A. Douglas-Home at the earliest opportunity (see No. 274) to seek to persuade him to vote for inscription of the US item. See *FRUS, 1969–1976, Volume V*, No. 410.

No. 274

Sir A. Douglas-Home to Sir C. Crowe (UKMIS New York)
21 September 1971, 5.30 p.m.[1]
Tel. No. 644 Flash, Confidential (FCO 21/811, FEC 2/2D)

My telegram No. 633:2 Chinese representation and the inscription of the American item.

The United States Ambassador called this morning on instructions to say that Mr Rogers was dismayed by our decision of which he had heard through Bush, to vote against the inscription of the American item on Chinese representation. He said that this would be the first time to American knowledge that Britain had voted against inscription of an item and would place us clearly in opposition to the Americans. He fully understood my reasons for not voting with the Americans on the substance of the matter, but to oppose inscription would be to deny the Assembly the right to discuss the issue under a neutral heading. He hoped therefore I could see my way to voting for inscription and that as regards priority I should hold my hand until I see him in New York on 1 October.

2. I told Mr Annenberg that I could not see the purpose behind the American wish to inscribe a separate item since in my opinion they would be entirely free, as they had been in the past, to discuss the whole question of Chinese representation and to introduce whatever resolutions on the subject they wished, under the Albanian item. For this reason and because of the memorandum that had accompanied their proposal for the item I could only regard it as an attempt to bring about a two-Chinas

1 Also sent flash to Washington; repeated for information immediate to Peking.
2 No. 273.

solution which I had told Mr Rogers I could not support. However in view of Mr Rogers' personal request to me I would look at the matter again.

3. I should of course very much like to meet Mr Rogers on this if I can, but American tactics (which, as I told Mr Annenberg, had been adopted without prior notice to us) do not seem to me to be very well judged since they have the effect of producing what promises to be a polemical debate on the agenda, in addition to the debate in the substance. Nevertheless in deference to his plea I am prepared to modify the instructions I have given you as follows:

I. If you judge that voting on inscription will be solely on procedural lines with no Chinese representation connotations, you should vote in favour of the inscription;

II. If however you judge that the voting pattern is going to be along 'Chinese representation lines' you should vote against inscription;

III. Assuming that voting takes place on a proposal to amalgamate the American item with the Albanian item you should vote against amalgamation, on the assumption that the 'pro Peking' vote will be against amalgamation;

IV. If there is a vote on priority of any kind between the American and the Albanian items you should vote for priority for the Albanian item;

V. If you have to speak in explanation of a vote against inscription, you should do so after the vote (in order to make as little trouble as possible for the Americans) drawing on the material we have already given you. If you vote for inscription you should give an explanation before the vote, stating that it is our normal practice to vote for inscription, that such a vote in no way prejudices our view on the substance of the question, and that the United Kingdom will oppose any resolution which would have the effect of delaying the seating of the representatives of Peking in the United Nations.

VI. In so far as we have influence you should work to avoid a vote altogether.

4. I should be grateful if Lord Cromer would tell Mr Rogers that I am afraid that this is really as far as I can go to meet him. I am sorry if my decision causes him difficulty in the event of a vote, but I hope he will understand my difficulties on the other side. I still hope there will be no vote.

No. 275

Sir C. Crowe (UKMIS New York) to Sir A. Douglas-Home
22 September 1971, 3 a.m.[1]
Tel. No. 1112 Immediate, Confidential (FCO 21/811, FEC 2/2D)

Your telegram No. 644:[2] Chinese Representation.

1. The debate was confused, but it was clear from the outset that discussion would be substantive rather than procedural. The confusion was due partly to the weakness of the Chairman Malik, who has made a disappointing start, and partly to the American tactic of getting in first, ostensibly on a point of order, with the proposal to combine their item and the Albanian under a neutral hearing. The point of

1 Sent at 3 a.m. on the 23 September. Repeated for information Immediate to Washington, Peking and Hong Kong.
2 No. 274.

order was soon lost sight of, but it served the purpose of allowing the sponsors of the Albanian item to blow off steam on the substantive issue while excluding from debate the question of inscribing the American item. It soon became clear that there would be a majority against combining the items. The Americans accordingly refrained from pressing it to the vote first, possibly in the calculation that a defeat would have reduced the chances of a favourable subsequent vote on inscription for their item by itself.

2. On learning that the French intended to abstain on inscription, and in the light of the Private Secretary's telephone call to Jamieson[3] subsequent to the instructions in your telno. 644 I sought and obtained authority by telephone to abstain likewise. In the event these two abstentions were probably crucial in that a switch to two negative votes would have caused the American item to fail to be inscribed. Bush, whom I had not informed in advance, was most grateful for our help in saving the Americans from what would undoubtedly have been seen as a complete and humiliating defeat.

3. As regards our relations with Peking, I hope that my explicit reservations in my explanation of vote will suffice to allay any dissatisfaction with our abstention on inscription. We might also make use privately of the point in Kosciusko's explanation of vote, that in practice the Albanian item will now be taken first: if the Albanian resolution is passed unamended the American item will become academic. It is perhaps useful also to have had one relatively respectable African abstention (Sierra Leone).

4. Two minor surprises in the voting were the votes cast against the Americans by Finland (who had been expected to follow France on inscription) and Burundi's vote in favour of inscription of the American item.

3 The Minister at UKMIS New York, Mr Jamieson, contacted the resident clerk to obtain permission to abstain. This was granted after discussion with Mr Graham and Mr Parsons, it not having been possible to contact the Secretary of State.

No. 276

Minute from Mr Stratton to Mr Parsons, 7 October 1971
Confidential (FCO 21/811, FEC 2/2D)

Chinese Representation

1. I have never doubted that the Americans were in earnest over Chinese representation; the information you brought back from New York last week confirms this impression. But, although it is not strictly my business, I suggest that the time has come for us to tell the Americans that we have had an earful of their lectures about what we should or should not say to the Bahrainis, Qataris and Omanis—or anyone else for that matter. In particular we should make it clear that we do not need any further proposals, such as made by Mr Oplinger,[1] that we should make blinding suggestions of the obvious to these three governments. American homilies on this subject are getting beyond a joke.

1 Mr Oplinger, Second Secretary at the US Embassy, London, had visited the FCO to request that the three new members of the UN be left to decide for themselves how they should vote on the various resolutions relating to Chinese representation and that Britain should not to seek to influence them against the US position. He also pressed the point that the US Government had every intention of fighting for a continued representation for the Nationalists. He said the US had gained the impression that the British thought they were putting up a 'sham fight' but this was not the case.

2. In my opinion the Americans have no grounds for making these admonitions. Dr Kissinger's visits, past and prospective, to Peking were arranged without forewarning let alone consultation. They have delayed our exchange of Ambassadors with the Chinese by several months. Our undertaking to them was that we would not lobby other governments to support our views on Chinese representation. We made it clear from the start that we should feel free to express these views, and our intentions, in reply to questions from our friends and allies. Still less are we obliged, as the American Embassy seem to imagine, to pretend to the three new members of the UN that we hold no views on the subject at all.

3. In short I suggest that if they come at us again the Americans should be quietly told to 'belt up' and leave us alone.[2]

R.J. STRATTON

[2] Mr Parsons noted: 'I think that we have all been taking a pretty firm line with the Americans. I certainly did in New York. But I'm afraid they just won't "belt up"!'

No. 277

Mr Denson (Peking) to Sir A. Douglas-Home, 19 October 1971, 8.30 a.m.
Tel. No. 1076 Immediate, Confidential (FCO 21/855, FEC 22/11)

Personal for Wilford from Denson.

My Telno 1075: Mr MacDonald's meeting with Chou En-lai.[1]

1. Mr MacDonald has given me a fuller account than that recorded in his telegram to John Morgan (whom I discover on checking will still be out of the office). Chou En-lai indicated that the Chinese thought that in maintaining that the status of Taiwan was undetermined we might (*a*) wish to be free to recognise an 'independent' Taiwan which might be set up by the US and Japan after the expulsion of the Nationalists from the UN; (*b*) we might fear that if we acknowledged China's sovereignty over Taiwan this would have an effect on the standing of Hong Kong. Chou said emphatically that there was no, repeat no, parallel to be drawn between Taiwan and Hong Kong. China had no intention of seeking to get Hong Kong back until the expiry of the New Territories lease. Mr MacDonald said speaking personally that he did not think that China's fears about our possible future attitude to Taiwan were justified and also discounted any connection in British minds between the position of Taiwan and Hong Kong.

2. Mr MacDonald gave as his strong personal advice that the Chinese should go ahead on the basis of the agreement so far reached. This would have several advantages for China if the announcement were made in the course of the next

[1] Mr MacDonald, a former politician and diplomat, was travelling round China as a private individual. He was trusted by the Communist regime and able to act as an unofficial intermediary between the UK and China. Before leaving he was fully briefed by the Government about negotiations for an exchange of Ambassadors and the various formulae considered. His late night meeting with Chou En-lai on 18/19 October continued for nearly four hours until 3.15 in the morning.

few days while the UN debate was still in progress. The switch of the vote and withdrawal of our Consulate while the Assembly was in session would have a powerful effect on opinion within the UN which could only work to China's advantage. It would represent a serious blow to Taiwan's claim to represent the whole of China and again speaking personally he did not think that having removed the Consulate the British Government would ever think of sending it back again.

3. I think the line Mr MacDonald took was most helpful. Let us hope that it will do the trick. It is now up to the Chinese to summon me again and I see no advantage in our making any move before then. If at the next meeting they make another attempt to get us to change our position or to give the sort of private assurance which it will not be in our power to honour, e.g. that we will say nothing in public about our legal view, I assume that you would wish me to take a very robust line, to deplore what appears to be a hardening in the Chinese position since the last meeting and to urge settlement on the present terms. If the Chinese raise the question of what our attitude would be towards an independent Taiwan I could reply that this was a hypothetical question but I would raise the matter with you. Would we in fact be prepared to give any indication of what our position might be? The question of independence is a matter which is clearly very worrying to the Chinese. A point I could make to the Chinese is that if the talks break down, we shall be obliged to inform Parliament and that the question of the status of Taiwan is bound to come up. This may have the effect of airing the idea of an independent Taiwan even if it is not intended to, which is precisely what the Chinese want to avoid.

No. 278

Sir A. Douglas-Home to the Earl of Cromer (Washington)
21 October 1971, 4.45 p.m.[1]
Tel. No. 2701 Immediate, Confidential (FCO 21/812, FEC 2/2E)

Chinese Representation.

The American Minister and Counsellor[2] called on Mr Royle on 21 October to raise, on instructions, the question of our vote on a motion for priority for the American Resolution. Mr Sohm said that while he understood HMG's attitude to the substantive votes he hoped that it would be possible to go along with the Americans on this one procedural aspect. He expressed appreciation for the fact that we had taken no initiative in lobbying. Mr Galloway added that the possibility of the expulsion of the Republic of China was attracting more attention in Congressional circles. If it was thought that the Americans had not been able to have a 'clear shot' procedurally it would inhibit the ability of the United States to work towards strengthening the United Nations and other International Organisations.

1 Repeated for information immediate to UKMIS New York; routine to Peking and Hong Kong.
2 Mr Sohm and Mr Galloway respectively. Instructions from Mr Rogers for this meeting can be found in FRUS, 1969-76, Volume 5, No. 423.

2. Mr Royle said that there could be no question of our reversing our decision. Mr Godber had made it clear to Mr Bush as recently as 12 October that we would vote against the American proposals both procedural and substantive. We had made our position clear throughout. Sadly the Americans had not kept us in touch with their views. We particularly regretted that we had not been advised of Dr Kissinger's intention to visit Peking although he had been in London 10 days earlier. This had made our task with the Chinese more difficult in particular with regard to our negotiations for an exchange of Ambassadors. Mr Royle regretted the American attitude particularly bearing in mind that we had gone out of our way to keep in close touch with the Americans on Chinese affairs.

3. Mr Galloway said that there was a feeling in the State Department that they had not been kept fully informed about the negotiations for an exchange of Ambassadors. Mr Royle replied that they had indeed been kept informed from the outset, and, moreover, that the Americans would be the first to be informed should agreement be reached.[3]

---

3 UKMIS New York tel. No. 1364 of 12 October noted: 'There is mounting evidence that the Americans are now really waging a no-holds-barred campaign to get the votes for their dual representation proposal, characterised by a surprising degree of emotional commitment and an almost reckless disregard for the longer term consequences.' Sir C. Crowe reported that not only had the Americans accused the British of lobbying against them, but were not above misrepresenting the position of other delegations to attract waverers and implying that the result might have implications for future US financial support for the UN. He concluded that it was 'only too likely that there will remain a legacy of resentment at the strong-arm tactics now being employed, and they will inter alia leave the Americans in a weaker position to protest about the Soviet attitude towards the UN and its finances' (FCO21/811).

No. 279

Sir C. Crowe (UKMIS New York) to Sir A. Douglas-Home
26 October 1971
Confidential (FCO 21/814)

Chinese Representation in the United Nations

Sir,

The debate was disorderly in every sense of the word, primarily owing to the weakness, incompetence and inaudibility of the President, Malik. As you know the Americans had originally thought that a certain degree of confusion might work to their advantage but there was altogether too much and if anything I suspect it had the opposite effect. In the later stages the crude and vindictive exultation of the Albanian co-sponsors, notably the Africans, at the discomfiture of the Americans and the Chinese must have won some sympathy for the latter especially the Chinese, though it came too late to find expression in votes. But the Americans brought part of the trouble on themselves by their rough tactics.

2. By the beginning of the final meeting, even those Delegations which had consistently predicted an American defeat were beginning to be affected by the confident claims of the United States Delegation and evidence that last minute arm-twisting was delivering certain critical votes. Among countries which had been expected to

vote against or abstain on the Important Question Resolution, Argentina, Ghana and Tunisia had reportedly been won over, Italy and Senegal (the latter after a telephone call from President Nixon to President Senghor) looked like abstaining and there were strong rumours that Bahrain, Qatar and Oman had been persuaded to vote in favour after all. The Canadians for example privately estimated that the resolution would be passed by about one or two votes. It was generally assumed that time was on the side of the United States and the fact that a preponderance of their co-sponsors were inscribing themselves to speak before the vote was clear evidence that the Americans, with this in mind, were aiming to postpone voting until the following day. These tactics seemed likely to succeed, for whereas the American Delegation, reinforced by Pedersen and de Palma of the State Department, constantly patrolled the floor of the Assembly keeping their supporters up to the mark, there was little sign of the Albanians exerting themselves to rally the opposition.

3. It was likewise universally assumed that Baroody's[1] new Draft Resolution and the three Tunisian Draft Resolutions had been cooked up with the Americans and represented a further delaying tactic. This suspicion was reinforced when Baroody intervened to propose a postponement of voting on all, repeat all, Resolutions until the following day. Although he received the support of Japan it seems that Baroody was acting on his own initiative rather than at the behest of the Americans (it is incredible that he could be anyone's chosen instrument). In any case the defeat of his motion for postponement was due in part to general resentment at the insolent manner in which he presented it and impatience with his persistent long-winded and egocentric interruptions at the expense of serious debate. On the other hand while this vote had no substantive significance it represented a psychological set-back for the United States in that the first vote of the evening went in favour of the Albanians. To have got away with postponement would probably have served to reinforce the impression that things were going the Americans way, as well as giving time for further pressure on waverers. The subsequent success of the American motion for priority for the Important Question Resolution had been taken for granted and did little to offset that effect, especially as Baroody had further muddied the waters by demanding priority for his Draft Resolution.

4. After the decisive voting on the important question (55-59-15) the outcome was a foregone conclusion, though not exactly an anti-climax. The President was in the process of bringing the Assembly to the vote on the Albanian Resolution and appeared to be saying that the original Saudi amendments should, as amendments, be put to the vote first, when Bush intervened to propose deletion of the second part of the Albanian Resolution calling for the expulsion of Taiwan. After strenuous objections from Iraq and Tanzania on the grounds that voting had started the President eventually ruled that the amendment was not receivable. Ironically this ruling, the sole positive intervention by the chair during a debate when the behaviour of speakers cried out for firm rulings on points of order, was in our view questionable in that it was not clear whether he had in fact announced the beginning of voting in the sense of Rule 90. However Bush succeeded later in putting essentially the same proposal, calling under Rule 91 for separate votes on the two parts of the Albanian Resolution. In between there had been

---

1 Jamil Baroody, Saudi Arabia's representative to the UN.

a disgraceful episode in which Baroody declared that in retaliation for being denied postponement of voting he would insist on roll call votes, paragraph by paragraph, on each of his original amendments, and got half way through this process before giving way. This too may have affected the voting on Bush's motion for separate votes, on which he might have expected to do at least as well as on the important question. The fact that the Albanian Resolution in the event obtained a two-thirds majority was of course due to the band-wagon factor, some of the switches in favour, notably Israel, Mexico and Portugal produced a storm of cheers.

5. As regards the decisive vote on the important question, the result came very close to our prior assessment and those of friendly Delegations (including incidentally those of Australia and Japan) but the Americans seem to have been genuinely taken by surprise and are correspondingly dejected. Bush has said publicly that the Americans had been given certain promises which were not honoured. We hear that the Delegation has drawn up a list of guilty men comprising Belgium, Cyprus, Oman, Qatar, Trinidad, Morocco, Tunisia, Ireland, Ecuador, Laos and Botswana, all of whom abstained except Ecuador, Ireland and Trinidad who voted against and Oman who were absent. American bitterness is understandable in that if only three or four of these countries had come up to scratch the Important Question Resolution would have passed. I find it difficult to believe, however, that the Americans could have had positive undertakings from all these States, and I fear they are to some extent the victims of self-delusion (for example they knew Laos would abstain because Pedersen had upbraided me for your allegedly persuading Prince Souvanna Phouma[2] to abstain). As far as the United Kingdom is concerned I think things are smoothed down with Bush but I suspect there is soreness down the line especially on the part of Pedersen and de Palma. We are doing what we can to pour oil on the waters. The trouble is that a number of Delegations congratulated us and say how our stand helped them.

6. In addition there can be little doubt that the strong-arm tactics of the Americans had some counter-productive effect, especially with Delegates who had any flexibility in their instructions. The Cyprus Foreign Minister for example was incensed to be told by Pedersen that he must vote in favour as the Americans had a promise from Makarios. The wrigglings of the Tunisian Representative were painful to watch. Even Finland and Denmark received scarcely veiled threats of retaliation if they voted against postponing the vote. Dr Kamel[3] of Qatar told us he simply could not bring himself to vote in accordance with his instructions. These American tactics were only made more obvious by the absence of any effective lobbying (other than strident cold war speechifying) by the Albanian Delegations, of whom it can confidently be said that they achieved victory in spite of themselves. According to the New Zealand Representative the American tactics suffered particularly from the stage management of Pedersen and de Palma, who virtually took over the operation from the United States Mission and their co-sponsors without having the necessary familiarity with the immediate situation here or with the personalities involved.

---

2 Prime Minister of Laos.
3 Dr Hassan Kamel, Qatar Permanent Representative to the UN, Minister of State and Adviser to the Qatar Government.

7. In sum, I think the main lesson of this debate has been to demonstrate beyond all doubt that no great Power by itself can any longer control events at the United Nations. The manner in which the Africans gloated over the American defeat made an ugly spectacle which may have ominous implications for future patterns of behaviour at the United Nations. However to a large extent the Americans brought this reaction upon themselves, and it was only among the more moderate Delegations that the restraint and dignity with which they and the Chinese accepted defeat was able to evoke respect.

8. After the passage of the Albanian Resolution (and a decision by consensus not to vote on the substantive American Resolution A/L 633), the Secretary General sent a message to Peking inviting the Chinese People's Republic to send a Delegation to the United Nations. There is naturally much speculation as to how and when the Chinese Government will react, and I shall be grateful for any news on this point from Peking.

9. As a tailpiece, I might mention that Baroody began his last intervention by denouncing the Swedish Ambassador for having allegedly remarked that there ought to be a Resolution to expel Baroody from the United Nations. Rydbeck's denial was put neatly in perspective by the Canadian Ambassador who 'confessed' from the rostrum that Baroody had in fact overheard a private conversation. There would be unanimous sympathy for any such Resolution, for Baroody's antics throughout the debate aroused universal derision. Is it too much to hope that King Feisal will get the message?

I have, etc.,
C. Crowe

No. 280

Sir A. Douglas-Home to Mr Denson (Peking)
29 October 1971, 12.45 p.m.[1]
Tel. No. 772 Priority, Confidential (FCO 21/832, FEC 3/548/2)

MIPT[2] (not to all).

1. During the course of his call on the Head of Far East Department on 28 October Chinese Chargé d'Affaires expressed thanks of Chinese Government to HMG for our votes in the UN.

2. Pei then referred to Mr Malcolm MacDonald's meeting with Chou En-lai (Peking Tels no. 1075 and 1076).[3] Mr Pei provided some additional information about this meeting. Chou En-lai had apparently spoken at great length of the importance he attached to the Prime Minister's speech at the Conservative Party conference. Mr Pei understood that Chou's comments were very important. Chou had said that Mr Heath's references to 'A New World' and Britain finding 'A New

---

1 Repeated for information to Washington, UKMIS New York, Hong Kong and Canberra; repeated saving to Tokyo.
2 Not printed.
3 No. 277.

Place' reflected the British Government's view that the era in which two super powers dominated the world was at an end. Chou had said that British entry into the EEC reflected the fundamental aspirations of the British people. It was the first time he had read such a speech since the end of the Second World War. He set great hope on this speech. He said that Mr Heath recognised that the world situation had changed. Chou had also said that the disintegration of the British Empire was a new birth for Britain and in some senses an emancipation because Britain was now able to get away from the past.

3. He went on to say that the present Government's attitude to China was clearer than that of any other British Government.

4. Mr Pei also touched on Chou's references to Hong Kong. He said that of course Hong Kong is a place which will be returned to China, but the Chinese Government had not raised this and it would not be raised for a long time. The lease of Kowloon expired in 1997. Chou wished to assure the British Government not to think of this in connection with Taiwan. Mr Pei repeated several times however that the Chinese Government could not understand why, if we were prepared to undertake not to seek to persuade others nor publicly advocate our view of the status of Taiwan, we nevertheless insisted on the reservation, which he termed a 'vestige' that we should if publicly asked state that our legal view was unchanged.

5. Morgan emphasised that Ministers considered we had already gone a long way to meet the Chinese. We had moreover amply demonstrated our attitude by the clear vote in the United Nations. If the Chinese now hoped that we would be prepared to remove what Mr Pei described as a 'vestige' he thought Ministers would find the greatest difficulty in going any further. He hoped that the terms which were put to Chiao Kuan-hua would soon be agreed.

No. 281

Letter from Mr Denson (Peking) to Mr Wilford, 2 November 1971
Personal and Confidential (FCO 21/845, FEC 6/548/9)

Dear Michael,

Sino/British Trade

Before departure I should like to put down some thoughts about our efforts to increase exports to China. The figures for 1971 are not encouraging but there are particular reasons for this. First, they probably reflect the low level of Chinese buying during 1970 which was the final year of the previous Five Year Plan. Second, there has been a very marked drop in the sale of non-ferrous metals and industrial diamonds which in the past have given a somewhat false impression of the position as they are in fact nearly all re-exports. If we exclude these the figures have improved over those of 1970. Furthermore I am sure that the signature by Hawker Siddeley of a contract worth £20 million for the supply of Tridents[1] is not only excellent in itself but represents a breakthrough which should benefit us in other directions.

---

1 A British airliner produced by Hawker Siddeley.

2. In my dispatch of 29 April[2] I reviewed the prospects for Sino/British trade and made some recommendations. I have never received any substantive comments on these nor have I been told whether, as suggested, the memorandum enclosed with the dispatch was discussed with the Sino-British Trade Council. Some of the recommendations have been overtaken by events. I think it might be therefore be useful at this stage to look at them again and see what is still relevant. I accordingly enclose a paper[3] which discusses the recommendations originally set out in paragraphs 18 of the dispatch. The paper is in a form which may be discussed with the SBTC and I hope that this will be done. The remainder of this letter raises other questions which, as will become clear, are not suitable for discussion with them.

3. Let me first consider the general question of how we organise our services at the London end. We are beginning to get a steadily mounting stream of enquiries from British firms attracted to the China market by the prominence given to things Chinese by the news media over the past six months. Some of this has, of course, being stimulated by articles in the DTI's publication 'Trade and Industry' and by the Sino-British Trade Council. With our limited commercial staff we are just able to cope with these enquiries but it is proving difficult to transfer some of the bread and butter work to the Export Services Division of the DTI because few people in that Division have any experience of the peculiarities of the Chinese market and can do little more than hand out the titles and addresses of the trading corporations. Now that the 1971 addition of the 'Hints to Businessmen' booklet on China has been published, the task of Export Services Division should be easier but invariably our correspondents ask for some background which can only be given by someone who is fully conversant with the whole of the Chinese scene. We receive excellent cooperation from Commercial Relations and Export Department in the DTI and from Far Eastern Department but Export Services Division seems to have no central point into which we can feed our reports on the market as a whole. It seems to me that consideration might be given to setting up a co-ordination point in Export Services Division with whom we can maintain the kind of day-to-day contact which we have with CRE.

4. Alternatively, we should try to make better use of the expertise and specialisation of the Sino-British Trade Council. We do our best to maintain good working relations with John Keswick, Norman Webb, the Secretary General, and Peter Marshall, the Chinese Secretary who visits China twice a year to cover the Canton Fair. But we have a feeling as a result of recent conversations with Marshall that the SBTC feel, however unjustly, that they are not being taken fully into the confidence of the DTI. I know that the DTI and the FCO are represented at senior levels at the Council Meetings of the SBTC and that John Keswick keeps in regular contact with the two departments often at ministerial level. However Marshall has suggested to Derek March that he should prepare regular reports to the SBTC or actively send them sanitised versions of his reports to the CRE. This seems to be a waste of time and the needs of SBTC could be met by regular informal get-togethers in CRE to ensure that the SBTC do not feel cut off from the information

2 No. 237.
3 Not printed.

which is being fed into London by my Commercial Section. The monthly Council Meeting of the SBTC is not an appropriate occasion; it is too large and too high level for the kind of informal exchange which I have in mind. Could we not arrange for Marshall and Webb to have regular meetings with Cochlin and representatives of Export Services Division in order to be told the gist of our bread and butter reporting on trade developments.

5. This brings me to the question of the future of the SBTC. John Keswick will probably wish to give up his presidency sometime in 1972. I have seen a copy of a letter from Peter Marshall to Keswick suggesting that Norman Webb should be appointed to take his place. Frankly I do not think that Webb would be a good choice. He is not an impressive personality and he does not have sufficient personal standing to speak convincingly on behalf of the many leading British firms who are now becoming interested in trade with China. In the past most of our trade with China has been conducted by middlemen represented by large emerging firms including those based in Hong Kong. I believe that in the future it will be important to demonstrate to the Chinese that the SBTC is also fully representative of major British manufacturing industry, e.g. such firms as GEC, ICI,[4] the two major aircraft companies, Shell, BP, etc who do not need to operate through agents or merchants. It would therefore be best for the next President to be unconnected with the old China trading houses, the memory of whose privileged position and at times overbearing methods (in some cases at variance with the political aims of HMG) is repugnant to the Chinese. It would also be desirable to have an uncommitted President who does not seek continually to further the interest of his own company. I fear that John Keswick is more often than not regarded by the Chinese as a representative of Jardine Matheson.[5] During his visit here in May he rarely lost an opportunity to ask whether Jardines could have 'their share of the cake' and we know that, acting as the agent for British Aircraft Corporation, he could well have wrecked the chances of the Hawker Siddeley Trident deal by intervening at a difficult juncture in the negotiations with a counter offer for the BAC 1-11 and secondhand VC10s. Moreover he has an unfortunate tendency to reveal in public information which has been given him in confidence and even to represent such information as the fruits of his own efforts. I have in mind particularly the frequent references he makes to *his* initiative in arranging for a British trade promotion in Peking in March 1972. As you know this proposal was put forward by us in an aide memoire which I delivered to the Chinese Minister of Foreign Trade in February this year and we are telling the Chinese firmly that this will be a British Government promotion (which is what they want) although we shall naturally enlist the help and support of the SBTC. If it were merely a question of who took the credit, it would not matter if the SBTC took it all, but the Chinese do distinguish between HMG and SBTC and still retain some prejudice against the latter.

6. I think the complaints of Webb and Marshall to which I have referred are often based on the misapprehension that more is being withheld from them than

---

4 General Electric Company and Imperial Chemical Industries respectively.
5 One of the original Hong Kong trading houses, founded in 1832.

is in fact the case and that there are large untapped resources of information which do not actually exist. But a large part of the problem is human: they wish to be favoured and courted, to be invited to discuss problems, inspect reports and exchange ideas rather than being put in the position of having to seek the audience of government mandarins, as they see them. Many of their complaints are indeed groundless and the persistent repetition by Keswick of the need to raise the level of commercial representation in Peking in order to draw level with more fortunately endowed countries such as France and Italy, (who in fact lag behind us their efforts here) is tiresome and graceless. But some further effort on the personal relations side would, I think, pay off.

7. I believe that the SBTC has a very important role to play at the London end. They cheerfully take on all the hard work of looking after the needs of Chinese missions visiting Britain. They are geared to do so and I believe do it very well. I think we should recognise this role and make as much use as we can of the ability to act as a coordinator of our trade promotion efforts. If they can be brought to work much more closely with the official services, it would to some extent compensate for the lack of geographical organisation in Export Services Division. Ideally this would involve the SBTC being prepared to work on behalf of British firms even including members of the 48 group.[6] As you know there has been some correspondence with you about the attitude to be taken to the group. While I fully recognise that some members of it are not politically very desirable, and in the past they may have been unhelpful to us, I doubt whether in overall terms they do any more harm to British interest in China than the buccaneering activities of Jardines, who in the present circumstances would be quite likely to switch their interest from British to American goods if they think there is a market.

8. To sum up I think we ought to look very closely at our relations with the SBTC and do what we can to ensure that the next President is more representative of British industry as a whole. We should also try to bring the hard-working members of the SBTC secretariat more closely in touch with government thinking and policy in order to ensure that we reduce as much possible the friction which I fear may be creeping into relations with them.

Yours ever,
JOHN DENSON[7]

6 An organisation dedicated to the promotion of trade with the PRC. Named after a British trade delegation of 48 businessmen who travelled to China, in 1954, to establish trading relations between the two countries.
7 In a letter to Mr Wilford dated 17 November 1971, Mr Blackwell, the Senior Trade Commissioner in Hong Kong, agreed with Mr Denson about choosing a president from outside the main circle of the old China trading houses. 'These firms . . . are associated in the Chinese mind with the bad old days of opium trading, foreign concessions, gun boat diplomacy etc and it has always amazed me that the present Chinese Government has been prepared to do business with John Keswick who to them must represent the old order. It says much for their pragmatism and for their wish, or need, to trade with us'.

No. 282

Sir C. Crowe (UKMIS New York) to Sir A. Douglas-Home
15 November 1971[1]
Tel. No. 1626 Priority (FCO 21/814, FEC 2/2G)

Chinese Representation.

1. Today's Plenary Meeting of the General Assembly spent the whole day listening to speeches welcoming the representatives of the People's Republic of China. I did not speak since it had been agreed that Fack[2] (Netherlands) should speak on behalf of the West European and Others Group. Although the opening speeches were made by Chairmen of Regional Groups they were followed by a procession of delegates from individual states regardless of the fact that their Regional Chairman had already spoken on their behalf. In the end 55 Delegations spoke. From WEOG France spoke early in the debate, as did Italy and Austria: Denmark spoke on behalf of the Nordic Group. The Russians and the Indians were among those who did not inscribe themselves until late in the afternoon.

2. Bush (US) made a short and dignified speech as Host Country Representative. Otherwise the speeches were undistinguished and echoed the China debate. A few African countries defended their right to 'dance in the aisles' if they wished, denied that they had been crowing over the United States and criticised the American Press for misrepresenting their behaviour on 25 October. The Hungarian went one up by making his speech in Chinese. The Chilean recited one of Mao's poems. At the conclusion of the debate Ch'iao Kuan-Hua, Vice Minister for Foreign Affairs, expressed the thanks of the Chinese delegation for the many speeches of welcome and made a long and uncompromising statement with frequent references to the bullying policies of 'one or two Super Powers'. (Extracts in my two immediately following telegrams and in UKMIS Geneva in New York's's Telno 154[3]. Full text by Bag.)

[1] Sent at 1.30 a.m. on the 16 November. Repeated for information to Peking, Hong Kong, Ottawa, Washington, Moscow and Paris.
[2] Robbert Fack, Netherlands Permanent Representative to the UN.
[3] Not printed.

No. 283

Letter from Mr Denson (Peking) to Mr Wilford, 15 November 1971[1]
Secret and Personal (FCO 21/820, FEC 2/11)

Dear Michael,

At the time of my interview with Chou En-lai on 2 March[2] you will recall that I took issue with the Embassy in Washington about the fullness of the report

[1] Copied to Mr Elliott in Washington. See No. 306 for his reply.
[2] No. 223.

which they gave the Americans which, in my view, went beyond what I agreed to. Washington expostulated (Millard's letter of 7 April to you)[3] saying that 'it was fully in the spirit of customary exchanges' to be quite frank with the Americans on Sino/British matters. I did not at that stage see any point in carrying on the battle since, in any case, the communication had been made and those concerned in London seemed content. But in the light of subsequent events I wonder whether we would not have been wiser to have said less to the Americans and not to have delayed so long over the Ambassadorial negotiations in deference to their susceptibilities when we must have known that in the end we could not agree with them on the Chinese representation question. We certainly seem to have received little thanks for our trouble.

2. At the time that I was seeing Chou the Americans were already considering, if not planning, the first Kissinger visit and at the time when Mr Rogers made his appeal to the Secretary of State at the Lisbon NATO meeting in June[4] for a further delay in making known our position in the context of an exchange of Ambassadors with China (Peking Tel No 1178),[3] the Kissinger visit was very imminent. I am forced to the conclusion that the hardening in the Chinese line on Taiwan which is causing us so much difficulty stems at least in part from considerations of future relations with the US and the Chinese desire not to show any weakness to another signatory of the Cairo and Potsdam Declarations. We have been very frank with the Americans about our relations with the Chinese; they have been quite the reverse about theirs. I note from the record of the recent Anglo/American talks Marshall Green said there was nothing very much to tell about Sino/US relations!

3. As regards the Ambassadorial negotiations the damage has probably been done and by the time you receive this letter my interview with the Vice-Minister may well have shown just how much. In the light of the way the Americans have behaved should we not consider whether our exchange with them on China should continue unchanged. I am of course not fully in the picture in Peking about exchanges of certain kinds which may be of great intelligence value and in which the Americans are able to help us. But as seen from here the Americans get a good deal and give little in return. It is true that some of the product of the US Consulate General in Hong Kong is useful, particularly on the economic side, and no doubt you receive papers from the CIA and elsewhere which we do not. My general impression remains however that while we are frank and comprehensive the Americans are cagey and restrictive. Since we cannot assume that our interests are necessarily going to remain parallel—and this applies particularly in the commercial field and the application of the strategic embargo—a greater circumspection in what we say about any subjects where there might be a conflict of interest would surely be prudent.

4. In some communications to the Americans in London and Washington I have detected a very natural chagrin on our part about the handling of the Kissinger visits by the Americans. I do not know what the feeling now is nor do I wish to make

3 Not printed.
4 See No. 243.

things difficult. For this reason I am not making any recommendations but merely addressing you personally in the hope that you will take the matter up if you think this would be profitable.

Yours ever,
JOHN

No. 284

Mr Denson (Peking) to Sir A. Douglas-Home
18 November 1971, 6.50 a.m.
Tel. No. 1177 Priority, Confidential (FCO 21/836, FEC 3/548/3D)

Personal for Morgan.

My telegrams numbers 1171 and 1172:[1] Sino/British Relations.

The interview with Han Nien-lung was disappointing but not really surprising. I am somewhat puzzled by what the Chinese really want. On the one hand they seem prepared to recognise that we cannot change our position but they profess not to understand that we will be obliged to state it in some form. I think we will have to hammer away on this point. On the other hand they may still hope that under pressure we will give way. The decision to send Addis as Chargé d'Affairs was in one respect a useful indication that we were not too worried about having an ambassador. Unfortunately, as indicated in my telegram up to the Chief Clerk I have doubts about whether Addis will be accepted in this capacity. I certainly think that the matter should be further [text corrupted] the Chinese, perhaps in London, before consideration is given to sending any formal communication.

2. Finally, I should like you to know that despite the difficulties in the negotiations the Chinese have treated me with the greatest courtesy and cordiality in these last days. There was a very good representations of Chinese officials both political and commercial at the farewell party we gave on 16th November, the first and alas the last time that we could use the new residence. Last night Chang Wen-chin and Han Hsu jointly gave a dinner to which the diplomatic staff were invited and very kind things were said. The Scottish Export Mission is also receiving excellent treatment. I therefore leave disappointed that the negotiations could not be brought to an end but not too downhearted.[2]

---

[1] Not printed. In Tel. No. 1172 of 17 November, Mr Denson reported: 'The atmosphere of the meeting was cordial and the door is still open, but the message is clear. Unless we are prepared to go further than we have already the Chinese will not agree to exchange Ambassadors.'

[2] Mr Royle noted: 'It underlines that it would be unwise to change our position.'

No. 285

The Earl of Cromer (Washington) to Sir A. Douglas-Home
18 November 1971, 9.24 p.m.[1]
Tel. No. 3854 Routine, Confidential (FCO 21/836, FEC 3/548/3D)

China.

1. During my discussion with Kissinger (my telno 3850,[2] not repeated to Peking) I mentioned that the Chinese were still playing it very slow on the exchange of Ambassadors and, as we felt that our negotiation position had in no way been helped by our acquiescence to American requests, the whole subject of relations with China was one that sooner or later should be discussed at a high level.[3]

2. Kissinger asked whether it was still the juridical problem of Taiwan and was obviously well informed on the issue. I asked him how he knew about all this and he told me that it had been mentioned to him in Peking. He said that Chou En-Lai had gone out of his way to speak in highly complimentary terms of the Prime Minister and in particular his speech to the Conservative Party Conference.

3. Kissinger said that he would not for a moment presume to proffer advice but that in his own dealings with the Chinese he had found that in several cases when he thought that he had got three quarters of the way to agreement they would introduce all sorts of difficulties. He had found that if he then suggested that it was clear that the Chinese were not ready to accept the normal conventionalities of Western diplomacy they then in the end climbed down.

4. This was in the course of a conversation which was wide ranging and in no way formal but I feel it is possibly nonetheless worth reporting.

1 Repeated for information to Peking.
2 Not printed.
3 In early November the FCO prepared, at Mr Heath's request, a chronological account of negotiations with the Chinese over the exchange of Ambassadors. In a reply dated 15 November, Mr Moon noted that the Prime Minister felt it brought out 'pretty clearly that we have put ourselves at some disadvantage out of consideration for the Americans'.

No. 286

Submission from Mr Morgan to Sir S. Tomlinson, 18 November 1971
Confidential (FCO 21/836, FEC 3/548/3D)

Exchange of Ambassadors with China

Problem

1. How to respond to the Chinese request that we should reconsider our attitude to the status of Taiwan (Peking telegrams Nos 1171 and 1172).[1]

Argument

2. Mr Denson is in a better position to judge from the context of the conversation

1 Not printed. See No. 284.

but in my view I think it now most unlikely that the formula he proposes in paragraph 3 of Peking telegram No 1172[2] will commend itself to the Chinese. Indeed anything using the words 'status of sovereignty ... undetermined' appears to me to be ruled out. The Vice-Minister seems to be saying this and it is now a regular theme of Chinese public statements. Nevertheless the formula Mr Denson suggests would present no problems for us and there is no harm in trying it if the Mission think it a possibility.

3. I have discussed with Sir V. Evans whether we could find a formula which means that we regard the status of Taiwan's sovereignty as undetermined but avoids actually using those words. Sir V Evans agrees that a passage on the following lines would be acceptable for the joint statement.

> 'The Government of the United Kingdom recognise the Government of the People's Republic of China as the sole legal Government of China and have done so since 6 January 1950. Moreover they still accept in principle the Cairo Declaration of 4 December 1943 that "all the territories Japan has stolen from the Chinese, such as Manchuria, Formosa and the Pescadores, shall be restored to the Republic of China." They do not recognise any State other than China as having a valid claim to Taiwan.
>
> The Government of the United Kingdom, acknowledging the position of the Chinese Government that Taiwan is a province of the People's Republic of China, have decided to remove their official representation in Taiwan on (date of signature).'

4. We should also need to assure the Chinese that if asked what is our present view of the status of Taiwan's sovereignty we should limit ourselves to referring to the terms of the statement. If asked whether the statement constitutes a change in our position we could say that it clearly did so by recording our decision to remove our official representation on Taiwan. I think that something on the lines of the above 2 paragraphs might well succeed in bridging the gap with the Chinese.

5. The Chinese delayed 6 weeks in replying to us and we do not wish to appear over eager by returning too promptly. Nevertheless, unfortunately, there are now no pressures on the Chinese to compromise. Indeed they have every reason to hold out for the full demand that we recognise Chinese sovereignty over Taiwan. Meanwhile there are several matters of interest to us which our Mission have recommended should not be pursued further while the question of Ambassadorial exchanges is outstanding. These include such subjects as BOAC rights in China, a visit by the Chinese Minister of Foreign Trade, the future of British banks in Shanghai and the Hong Kong/Canton telex link. I do not think therefore that it would be prudent for us to delay our reply unduly.

Recommendation

6. I recommend that our Chargé d'Affaires in Peking be given authority to negotiate on the basis of both these formulae (paragraph 3 of Peking telegram No. 1171 and paragraphs 3 and 4 above), neither in fact involving a change in our basic position.

---

2 'The British Government's view is that the status of Taiwan is juridically undetermined because they consider the Cairo Declaration was not in itself an instrument constituting a transfer of sovereignty. Nevertheless they still stand by it in principle. Its implementation is a matter for the parties concerned. They have moreover made it clear that they regard the government of the CPR as the sole legal government of China and they have decided to remove the Consulate in Taiwan to demonstrate their acknowledgement of the Chinese stand.'

We shall then be able to judge whether a compromise over China's sovereignty over Taiwan is in fact going to be possible.³

J.A.L. MORGAN

3 Sir S. Tomlinson minuted on 19 November: 'I really do not think that every time the Chinese refuse to accept what we offer we can go on offering just a little bit more, thereby getting steadily closer to the total erosion of our original position. I am afraid the Chinese still do not or will not understand that our attitude in regard to the status of Taiwan is based on a doctrine and a practice which are very far from being something we have elaborated simply in the Taiwan context. They certainly show no sign of understanding that for us to "change our view on Taiwan" would be to act in breach of a doctrine which must be either universally applied or lose its value altogether. However, I am far from convinced that there is much to be gained by further legal discussion with the Chinese either in Peking or anywhere else'.

Mr Godber minuted on 22 November: 'I shall certainly be happy to discuss this with you and others, if you wish, but my present view is that "Enough is Enough", and that having made a genuine effort over past months we should now call a halt, and stand on our present position. If the Chinese want to exchange Ambassadors they know our terms. If they do not, then we continue as we are'.

No. 287

Mr Denson (Peking) to Sir A. Douglas-Home, 18 November 1971
Confidential—UK Eyes Only (FCO 21/859, FEC 25/10)

China, 1969-71: Mr. Denson's Valedictory Despatch

Sir,

The most remarkable year of the three which I have just spent in China has been 1971, particularly the last six months: ping-pong diplomacy, the visits of Dr Kissinger, China's entry into the United Nations and a major leadership upheaval. In this valedictory despatch, however, I do not wish to anticipate more considered assessments of these developments but to put down a few thoughts of a more personal kind about some aspects of domestic affairs, living here and our relations with China.

2. But it would be impossible to pass over completely the leadership problem which has a critical bearing on where China will go in the future and how far the experiments in this unique political and social system will work. Evidence mounts that Lin Piao, his wife (also a Politburo member), the Chief of Staff and two of his assistants have been disgraced after an attempt to wrest effective power from Mao Tse-tung and Chou En-lai. In this they may have been associated with another member of the top five, Chen Po-ta who has been in disgrace for some time. The crash of the Trident aircraft in Mongolia, which may have had Lin and his entourage aboard, adds a touch of the fantastic to the whole story but may well turn out to be true. Chou En-lai has once again emerged unscathed, his policies apparently triumphant and his standing enhanced. He remains with Mao the only important member of the Politburo to survive since the demotion of Liu Shao-chi in 1966. The reasons for the move against him and Mao are still unclear. They could affect the role of the army in the country or his foreign policy line. The situation appears to have been held. A new army figure has emerged in the veteran Marshal Yeh Chien-ying and we must assume that the army is generally solid. But the disappearance at one blow of one-third of the Politburo when added to earlier Cultural Revolution casualties must

give some ground for doubt. The greatest misfortune for China and probably for the rest of the world would be the disappearance of Chou En-lai for whom no possible successor is in sight. Indeed the ageing and dwindling top leadership was already posing a problem before the recent developments.

3. While the leadership convulsions were going on in September there were no outward signs of difficulty. Foreign Ministry officials continued to behave with their now normal civility and friendliness. Chou and his immediate associates showed remarkable *sang froid*[1] in dealing with foreigners including Mr Wedgwood Benn[2] and Mr Malcolm MacDonald. The struggle was presumably going on at a very high level and the attempt to wrest power may have been scotched early enough to prevent serious repercussions in the provinces. It seems to me unlikely that an attempt was made actually to remove Mao since his prestige and Thought is so important a political cement in China today. It is more likely that his opponents wished to supplant Chou and manipulate the old man.

4. The fact that this episode passed off on the surface so quietly may also be of testimony to the degree of normalisation which has been attained in the last three years. For the foreigner this is clear in a number of ways: by the attitude of the people in the streets who are willing to smile and talk, by the freedom to photograph, by the opening of certain ancient monuments like the Forbidden City and some of its museums, the revival of old restaurants, the greater availability of consumer goods, the restoration of games playing, the diminution of the cult of Mao, the possibility of some dialogue with officials and the increased opportunity to travel. But let us make no mistake, this is a Police State, people (including our local staff) disappear without warning and to be on the wrong side of the law which is governed by politics must remain highly unpleasant.

5. The situation also compares unfavourably with the early fifties in some respects. It is still impossible to buy any except political and technical books. The dead hand of Madame Mao lies on revolutionary operas and films though there are welcome signs that the Chinese are beginning to rehabilitate their past which could lead to a less rigid attitude to the present. The education system had been drastically revised with shortened courses and an emphasis on combining work with study. University entry depends on class worthiness and all students have to work in factories or on the land before they can do higher education. But it is stressed that this is experimental. In the institutions of higher learning like the Chinese Academy of Sciences there are indications that work is going on as usual and that Mao has given his blessing to theoretical as well as practical research. It is therefore possible that some balance will be struck and the worst excesses of proletarianism avoided.

6. In the rather limited sphere in which a foreign diplomat moves it seems that many of the old faces are returning. The calibre of the officials we meet is impressive. All the newly appointed Ambassadors are career members of the Diplomatic Service. Now that the demand for diplomatists is increasing others will presumably have to be retrieved from May 7 cadre schools[3] where they are atoning for past sins by physical labour. The greatest losses have been in the higher ranks of the Party

1 Ability to remain calm in a dangerous or difficult situation.
2 The British Labour politician, better known as Tony Benn.
3 Chinese Labour Camps established during the Cultural Revolution in order to 're-educate' intellectuals, including by them having intensively study the ideology of Mao.

where life is presumably more exciting and more dangerous. Even in a country as large as China there must remain a shortage of qualified people in all fields. We may therefore expect the rehabilitation process to continue.

7. What then has the Cultural Revolution achieved except to purge certain individuals and to sterilize somewhat the intellectual atmosphere? It is too early to say for certain but one thing it has attempted is to lessen the gap between the ruling and the ruled, to purge the mandarin mentality, to involve ordinary people in some way in the processes of government and to minimize material incentives and status as the springs for social and economic development. The more cynical might claim that this has been done merely by institutionalizing 'mass' representation as one of the three strands in the administrative unit, the revolutionary committee, which now controls all organisations. In the provincial revolutionary committees it is true the real power resides with the officials and the army and the popular heroes who sprang up during the Cultural Revolution have largely taken a back seat. But even to the foreign observer it appears that at lower levels and in everyday matters the ordinary person does have a greater voice, provided of course that he stays within the framework of Maoist orthodoxy. I have for example seen a lengthy debate following a minor traffic accident in which those involved argued their case in front of a large crowd, citing the Great Helmsman,[4] and the police were unable to settle the matter until the disputants had talked themselves to a solution. Some years ago it would have been settled summarily without discussion. As time goes on I think that bureaucracy will assert itself but that a continual effort will be made to keep contact with the grass roots, and between the various age groups—young, middle-aged and old—which now form a parallel strand in all organisations. Periodical physical labour for officials has become a permanent feature. In their own way therefore the Chinese are tackling a major problem of our times: communication.

8. As to the abolition or near abolition of material incentives and status as a means of driving society forward I am less sanguine than some foreign observers. The commune system is certainly impressive and the benefits of group labour particularly on very large projects ('a million men with tea spoons' as Ritchie Calder[5] once described them) must have convinced most of the peasants that it is preferable to individual work in small groups. The Government has however been careful not to try to re-institute the more radical features of the first commune system such as the removal of private plots, completely communal living and so on. What they are trying to do is limit private labour and private gain while allowing a minimal increase in the standard of living coupled with improved medical and social services. Exaggerated claims have undoubtedly been made for the success of barefoot doctors, native Chinese medicine and particularly Chinese medical techniques such as acupuncture. The absence of contact between China and the rest of the world in this and other fields must have a detrimental effect. But overall the medical services have probably improved and if the atmosphere further liberalises foreign contacts may resume. I think, however, that the tendency to denigrate the professional classes,

---

4 A Chinese honorific title, most commonly referring to Mao Tse-tung.
5 Lord (Peter Ritchie) Calder was a Scottish socialist author, journalist and academic. He was quoted saying this during a Parliamentary debate on industrial relations on 3 May 1967. See *Parl. Debs., 5th ser., H. of C.*, vol. 282, col. 1057.

which is reflected for example in the very low wages paid to many doctors and teachers, cannot be helpful to society nor can the exclusion from higher education of the children of those considered to come from undesirable backgrounds. In the same way the attempt to remove material incentives altogether cannot to my mind work. Neither Rousseau, Marx nor Mao has demonstrated that man is perfectable in an ideal environment let alone the environment we are dealing with in China today. One anthropologist has suggested that the three requirements for the human being are security, status (*i.e.* identity) and stimulus and they will react strongly against their opposite insecurity, anonymity and boredom. The Chinese have gone some way to provide security militarily, economically and socially but the lack of fulfilment of the other two could store up trouble in the future if the screws are not gradually loosened. The frugality, industry, patience and intelligence of the Chinese aided by an incorrupt bureaucracy may enable the present kind of social experiment to go on longer than it could anywhere else. The system is certainly not exportable.

9. In this despatch I do not propose to discuss China's external relations as we have fully reported on these elsewhere and in the United Nations we shall have to wait and see how the Chinese behave. Suffice it to say that the Chinese are delighted to be in New York but also surprised to be there this year and probably bemused by many of the problems this represents. At the moment they have not the resources of manpower or experience to cope comprehensively with many United Nations problems. In certain fields they may therefore take things quietly but they will be quite uncompromising in others.

10. Sino-British relations have happily shown a steady improvement since I arrived. In February 1969 there were 13 British subjects detained in China and the 'confrontation' prisoners in Hong Kong (some 350 at the beginning of the year) were raised on almost every occasion I had official dealings with the Chinese. The most difficult case was Anthony Grey who was being held as a hostage for Chinese newspaper workers arrested in 1967. His release in October after more than two years was the first watershed. Thereafter, there were other releases of British detainees (as well as the unaccountable arrest of two aged British subjects in Shanghai). Finally, the last expatriate, David Johnston of the Chartered Bank was released at Christmas 1970, according to the Chinese as a token of their desire to improve relations. After that it was decided to raise my status to that of Chargé d'Affaires *en titre*[6] which the Chinese recognised as a move in the same direction on our part. We are now left with only four British subjects detained all of whom previously worked for the Chinese Government. I think that in the end they will also be released but I doubt if our representations on their behalf will have much effect as the Chinese know that we do not regard them as being in the same category as the others.

11. The negotiations for the exchange of Ambassadors which came as a result of our initiative in London in January this year, to which Chou En-lai responded when he saw me in March, have been slow and frustrating. It appears from my last meeting yesterday that we may have run into an impasse because of our legal position that the status of Taiwan is undetermined and the need for us to restate it in public if asked. At the preceding meeting in early October it seemed that we had reached agreement

6 Official.

by means of a formula to be used in a public announcement of the exchange which linked the acknowledgement of China's position with the closure of the Consulate in Taiwan together with an oral assurance that we would not promote our view. Since then the Chinese attitude has hardened and they seem to be making another attempt to force us publicly to change our position as the price for an exchange. The reasons for this are not clear, but they may be connected with United States relations with China since we and they both signed the Cairo and Potsdam Declarations which expressed the intention that Taiwan should be returned. This puts us in the Chinese view in a different category to other countries who hold similar views about Taiwan's status.

12. The remaining confrontation prisoners (35 by mid-1971) were not made an element in the negotiations for Ambassadorial relations and though the Chinese will undoubtedly revert to them, they and other Hong Kong problems which loomed large earlier are no longer a major obstacle to the development of relations. The Chinese have indeed indicated positively that they have no intention of disturbing the status quo.

13. Looking back over the period since my meeting with Chou En-lai I feel convinced that had we been willing to settle for the original terms proposed *i.e.* full support for China's entry into the United Nations and the closure of the Consulate the matter could have been fairly speedily settled since at that time it would have been an advantage for the Chinese to have secured our assistance, which could have been made public, that we would support them in the United Nations. But since for various reasons, including our relations with the United States, we delayed giving our assent until late June, the whole question may then have become entangled with United States/China relations since the Kissinger visit was in prospect. In fact I held my first meeting with Vice-Minister Ch'iao Kuan-hua while Kissinger was in Peking, though we did not then know it. Thereafter the Chinese took a progressively harder line about Taiwan which they have since maintained. Having secured our support in the United Nations and been voted in there is less reason for them to make what they would regard as a concession on a point to which they attach major importance. It is, I think, possible that after this last attempt to put pressure on us to change our legal view, if they see that this does not work and we are not visibly perturbed by the sight of many other countries sending Ambassadors before we do—a point on which they continually harp—then they might settle for something like the terms we offered in October.

14. Though the absence of an Ambassador is a disadvantage it is not a tragedy. We have succeeded over the years, including my extended tenure as Chargé d'Affaires, *a.i.*,[7] in conducting business satisfactorily with the Chinese. There has been no sign that the failure to exchange Ambassadors has adversely affected the expansion of trade to any extent, though some British traders think so and say it (rather too frequently) in public. The Chinese seem decided to give a cut of the commercial cake to as many countries as possible and thus never become dependent on one or a few. I am sure that with our commercial organisation here and in London both official and otherwise we are as well equipped as anyone to take advantage

---

7 *Ad interim.* Meaning an office or arrangement held or made temporarily.

of the opportunities that exist. The recent sale of Tridents by Hawker Siddeley and the presence in Peking now of the large Scottish Export Mission are examples of this. The Trident sale was also important to the Chinese because it indicated there had been a relaxation in our attitude about the export of advanced and previously embargoed equipment. At a time when American relations with China may improve to some extent, and American businessmen will be quick to exploit the change, we should be on our guard not to be left behind and should weigh very carefully the extent to which we defer to American wishes. Recent experience suggests that the Americans are not inclined to pay much heed to the susceptibilities of their allies where their own relations with China are concerned.

15. As regards relations of other kinds, I think that there are limited possibilities in the cultural and scientific fields; but here the fault of the Chinese, like that of the Dutch, 'is of giving too little and asking too much'. That is to say they will wish us to accept their so-called cultural manifestations for their own political reasons, they may also wish to make use of our science and technology, but they will not allow us to penetrate very far within their cultural and social Great Wall. Contact of any kind is of course useful and in the long run may bring about changes in China and the Chinese attitude to the outside world. But we should not expect too much too soon nor be disappointed if we do not succeed.

16. In the political field we can look for an increase in exchanges over a wide variety of subjects particularly those in which China will be involved in the United Nations. Chinese interest in Europe will increase. The Chinese have expressed warm support for our entry into the Common Market which they regard mainly as an assertion of political independence vis-à-vis the United States and mistakenly as the movement towards a more Gaullist world view-point. Fundamentally, however, they have no sympathy with most of our aims and policies, they will continue to attack us vigorously on a wide variety of questions and fish in the troubled waters of industrial relations, Northern Ireland and Colonial questions. In this context the presence of an Ambassador would undoubtedly lend weight to what we have to say to the Chinese but we are still very far from the point where the Chinese are willing to consult in our sense of the term with European countries (or perhaps with any others). The French, who are in some ways China's favourites in Western Europe, have received some painful shocks by Chinese attacks on certain of their policies and I doubt if their advice will have any substantial effect on the Chinese at this juncture.

17. Personally it has been a great privilege and much of the time a pleasure to head this Mission, and to see the physical and psychological scars of 1967 heal. The repairs to the Chancery were finally completed at China's expense in the autumn of 1970 and we moved in in February of this year. After my interview with Chou En-lai the Chinese expressed willingness to rehabilitate the Residence, which had served as a temporary office, for a modest sum. Failure to accept the estimate immediately caused a delay of some months and as a result it is only now only more or less ready for occupation. Our farewell party was the first and last social engagement we were able to hold there. As in the case of the Chancery there have been a series of administrative delays, muddles and various forms of incompetence on the part of the Department concerned on our side, which underlines the desirability of

our undertaking, as Duncan[8] recommends, a far greater control of the management of our own property. In other respects the situation has radically improved and my successor should have a better environment in which to live and work than any since the move from the old compound in 1959. The period of administrative cold war with the Chinese is ended and we now receive from the Diplomatic Service Bureau help and cooperation as good as that enjoyed except by the most favoured nations. This does much to mitigate the effects of what is still a very limited environment where a good deal of patience and resilience is required to survive and prosper. Fortunately this has been possessed in ample measure by those who have served here with me and I am grateful to them for having made my task so much easier and more enjoyable than it might have been.

18. It is always hard to form a balanced view about China whether one is inside or outside. There have been times in the past three years when I would have been very pleased to leave and happy never to come back. When the Chinese decide to be unhelpful their officials can act with a degree of coldblooded unpleasantness, arrogance and self-righteousness which is unparalleled in my experience. Equally when things are going well they have charm, gaiety and a capacity for something like friendship. Ordinary people in so far as one meets them and as the political atmosphere permits are friendly and well-disposed. Some foreigners who have been in China in the old days look back on it with intense nostalgia which probably increases with time while they look upon the present régime with an equally intense distaste because they think it has betrayed their conception of what China was and should continue to be. There is also a current generation of lovers of the New China who are equally in the other direction. I hope that we may be entering a period when it will be possible both for individuals and some Governments (unrealistic about China) to form a more just view of this country and its people, to get rid of the exaggerated feeling of guilt which still assails some because of Chinese treatment by foreign Powers in the past which the Chinese play on and at the same time to avoid overpraise. At the very moment of departure I feel that I should like to return and many Chinese officials have been good enough to say that they would like to see me back. Whatever happens I shall continue to follow Chinese affairs with the greatest interest and attention.

19. I am sending copies of this despatch to Her Majesty's Ambassadors at Washington, Paris, Moscow, Tokyo, Seoul and Ulan Bator; the British High Commissioners at Delhi, Islamabad, Canberra and Wellington; to the United Kingdom Permanent Representative to the United Nations, New York; and to the Governor of Hong Kong.

I have, etc,

J.B. DENSON

---

8 Report of the Review Committee on Overseas Representation 1968-1969, Chairman Sir Val Duncan, (London: HMSO, 1969) Cmnd. 4107.

No. 288

Mr Samuel (Peking) to Sir A. Douglas-Home
24 November 1971, 12.45 a.m.[1]
Tel. No. 1202 Immediate, Confidential (FCO 21/836, FEC 3/548/3D)

Mr Denson's Tel. No. 1172.[2]

We have just received specific evidence that the Chinese are now using our commercial relations as a lever in the context of the Ambassadorial negotiations.

2. During the visit of the Scottish Trade Mission Mr E. Jamieson, sales manager of Ferranti Ltd,[3] told the Commercial Secretary that on 19 November a possible cooperation agreement had been blocked by the Chinese on the grounds that 'political relations between Britain and China were not developing as quickly as had been hoped'.

3. Jamieson had discussed Chinese manufacture of electronic equipment with the Director of General Administration of Telecommunications who recently visited the Ferranti works in Scotland. It emerged that the Chinese were having problems with Microflex systems and equipment for use in very low temperatures. Chung asked if Ferranti could help with insulation problems which led to Jamieson suggesting a cooperation agreement to help with the installation of microwave links throughout China. Chung expressed great interest, said he would like to consult with other people concerned and invited Jamieson to a banquet that evening.

4. It was at the banquet that Chung said that after discussing the morning's proposals with his colleagues it had been decided there were political obstacles to an agreement. He subsequently mentioned the problem of Taiwan and the need for a change in our attitude before large scale cooperative agreements could be negotiated with British firms. He invited Mr Jamieson to bring this to the attention of 'those concerned in Britain'.

5. A similar message was given to Mr Tam Dalyell MP on the same day during an interview with the Director of West European and American Department of the MFA. Chang said that though Sino/British trade would continue to develop real progress on major projects such as the motor industry would have to await the solution of the Ambassadorial problem.

6. I understand that Neville Maxwell was also told by Chou En-lai on 19 November that he did not expect Sino/British relations to develop further for some time because of our stand on the Taiwan question.[4] According to Italian colleagues Chou developed the same theme at length and with some vehemence in conversations on 11 November with Pietro Nenni, former Italian Foreign Minister and on 22 November with Vittorino Colombo, President of the Italian-Chinese Institute for Economic and Cultural Exchanges.

7. All the indications are thus, unfortunately, that the Chinese policy has become very rigid. I do not think we shall get anywhere at our next meeting if we confine

1 Repeated for information to Hong Kong, Washington, Canberra and Tokyo.
2 Not printed. See No. 284, note 1.
3 UK electrical engineering and equipment firm.
4 See No. 290.

ourselves to saying that we have already made enough concessions and that the next move is up to the Chinese. This does not necessarily mean that it is all or nothing but it may come to that in the end. Tactically our best hope is, I believe, to convince the Chinese that our intentions are right even if our juridical position is wrong (from their point of view) and that if as they say they are not seeking to embarrass us they should accept something on the lines suggested in the telegram under reference.

No. 289

Note by Far Eastern Department, 24 November 1971
Confidential (FCO 21/836, FEC 3/548/3D)

Possible consequences of a breakdown in our negotiations with the Chinese on an exchange of Ambassadors

The Chinese have many ways of making difficulties for us, whereas we have no scope in return. If negotiations for an exchange of Ambassadors fail, our unique position in maintaining representation in both Peking and Tamsui would provide an incentive for the Chinese to put pressure on us to close the Consulate and to emphasise the second-grade status of our Mission in Peking. This at a time when after China's admission to the United Nations we need to have wider dealing on many more subjects than before.

2. In recent months the Chinese have made no reference to the confrontation prisoners in Hong Kong. If the negotiations cease, they would certainly do so. This would present difficulties, particularly so soon after the appointment of the new Governor.

3. Our Mission in Peking have recently reported (Peking telegram No 1202)[1] that the Chinese are using commercial relations as a lever in the context of the Ambassadorial negotiations. One British firm has been told that there are political obstacles to the conclusion of a major contract, which they had previously been encouraged to pursue. The Director of the West European and American Department of the Chinese Ministry of Foreign Affairs has told Mr Tam Dalyell MP that real progress on major projects will have to await the solution of the Ambassadorial problem.

4. Our Mission in Peking have recommended that we defer raising the following subjects of interest to us while negotiations are continuing.

(*a*) The proposed BOAC mission to China to negotiate air traffic rights;

(*b*) Outstanding exit visa applications for the British community in Shanghai;

(*c*) The future of British banks in Shanghai;

(*d*) Chinese Ministerial visit to the United Kingdom;

(*e*) Hong Kong/Canton telex link;

(*f*) Hong Kong/Macao helicopter service;

(*g*) Outstanding claim against China.

1 No. 288.

No. 290

Mr Samuel (Peking) to Sir A. Douglas Home, 1 December 1971, 2 a.m.
Tel. No. 1215 Priority, Unclassified (FCO 21/836. FEC 3/548/3D)

My Telno 1214:[1] Sino-British relations.
Following is text:
Maxwell: What is your view on Sino-British relations?
Premier: Britain is one of the earliest Western countries to recognise China, but up until now it is still not possible for the two countries to exchange Ambassadors, because the British Government clings to its untenable logic. It can agree publicly to acknowledge the position of the Government of the People's Republic of China that Taiwan province is an inalienable part of the territory of the People's Republic of China. What this means should naturally be very clear. Yet, it further stated that if it was asked the British Government would say that Britain's position maintaining that 'Taiwan's status remains undetermined' remained unchanged. This is really absurd. I discussed this matter with Mr MacDonald[2] and said to him that this was the doing of your civil service system. He said that it was done by some people in the Labour and the Conservative cabinets who studied law. They said it had been stated in the past that 'the status of Taiwan remains to be determined', and since it had been so stated, it could not be changed now. Isn't this ridiculous? I said, your British policies have undergone many changes, why couldn't this policy be changed? Weren't Chamberlain's policies changed by Churchill? Yet it insists on making this reservation. In the recent voting in the UN General Assembly, Britain kept its word by voting for the Albanian Algerian Resolution and against the US Resolution. But its reservation is completely unreasonable. Does it mean that the British Government would recognize Taiwan if other big Powers should some day concoct by scheming an 'independent state' of Taiwan? The British dare not make any reply. We do not agree to such act of theirs. Because they have retained a tail, and a very long one at that.
Maxwell: What if the British Government completely adopts the wording of the Sino-Canadian joint communiqué on the establishment of diplomatic relations?
Premier: Britain is different from Canada. It is a signatory to the Cairo Declaration and the Potsdam Declaration and has committed itself to the return of Taiwan to China. We are firmly opposed to the fallacy of 'undetermined status of Taiwan'. What is more, this fallacy is a British creation. Having lost China, the Americans were deeply distressed and tried to shift the blame on each other. Acheson's White Paper was made public, in which the US Government cursed the Chinese Communist Party and blamed Chiang Kai-shek at the same time and made it appear as if it had always been correct. Truman made a statement in January 1951 saying that Taiwan was already returned to China and that the United States had no predatory designs on Taiwan or on any other Chinese territory. The Cairo Declaration was already very clear, and moreover Taiwan was returned to the motherland. And now the United States also

1 Not printed. It informed London that the Mission in Peking had obtained the official text of an interview on 19 November with Chou En-lai by the journalist Neville Maxwell. It appeared in *The Sunday Times* on 5 December 1971.
2 See No. 277.

recognizes that there is only one China. To help the United States create some excuse, however, Britain began to resort to legal quibbling in 1951. The San Francisco Peace Treaty was deliberately worked to state only that Japan gives up such and such territories, including Taiwan and other places, without specifying to which country these territories belong. This is a loophole. Moreover, the idea was spread that the problem would await relaxation of tension in the Pacific region. The San Francisco Treaty was not signed by the Soviet Union, nor does it specify to which country should Southern Sakhalin belong. Then why don't they say that the status of Southern Sakhalin is also undetermined? The southern half of the island was ceded to Japan after the 1904-05 Russo-Japanese War only ten years later than the 1894 Sino-Japanese War, by which Japan annexed Taiwan. After Japan surrendered, a Chinese administrative official accepted the Japanese surrender of Taiwan. So the status of Taiwan was settled long ago. The British theory is therefore utterly untenable. It was painstakingly worked out by the then British Labour Government. The United States had by then occupied Taiwan and the Taiwan Straits, and Britain wanted to help the United States.

Maxwell: This presents no problem to the Chinese side. Only there will be no exchange of Ambassadors.

Premier: This is nothing to us, but it is disadvantageous to Britain. Britain has recognized us for 22 years, but other countries which recognized us later have all exchanged Ambassadors with us.

Maxwell: Its purpose is not to go back on statements made by past Governments.

Premier: That is only a façade. In essence, Britain wants to leave a tail behind, so that it may recognize Taiwan if ever Taiwan should declare 'independence'. Although Britain is your country, I must criticize the traditional British policy. It always leaves a tail behind wherever it goes. You are well aware of this because you have studied the South Asian sub-continent. For example, Jammu and Kashmir, East and West Bengal, East and West Punjab, etc. Wherever Britain quits, it always leaves some trouble behind. Now the British Prime Minister says that Britain is returning to Europe. Since you are returning to Europe, you should let the Asians relax somewhat and make things easier for the Asians. Mr Denson may have the wrong impression that we are all dull and pliable. We do not conceal our views, and we dare to admit our mistakes. You know the burning of the office of the British Chargé d'Affaires was done by bad elements in total violation of Chairman Mao's policy. At that time there was a conspiratorial reactionary clique, called the 'May 16 corps'. It incited a group of people to encircle the office of the British Chargé d'Affaires. We asked them by means of a loudspeaker on a car not to break into the compound under any circumstances. The British Chargé d'Affaires heard this and he knew about our policy. Later on we had their building repaired for them and expressed our regret for the incident. It seems to me that Britain has got the wrong impression that the Chinese people are pliable. It is not so simple. We will always stand firm on principles.

Maxwell: Three weeks ago, a diplomatic official from a certain country told me that a break-through had been made in the Sino-British negotiations and Ambassadors would soon be exchanged.

Premier: If Ambassadors are to be exchanged between China and Britain, Britain must chop off that tail.

Ends.

No. 291

Mr Samuel (Peking) to Sir A. Douglas-Home
1 December 1971, 8.15 a.m.[1]
Tel. No. 1220 Priority, Confidential (FCO 21/836, FEC 3/548/3D)

My Telno. 1215:[2] Sino-British Relations.

Chou's key phrase is of course 'If Ambassadors are to be exchanged between China and Britain, Britain must chop off that tail (the publicly expressed reservation that the status of Taiwan remains to be determined)'.

2. By going over his negotiators' heads in such categoric terms Chou will I am afraid have deprived them of most if not all of their remaining 'pliability'. His observation that failure to agree would be disadvantageous only to us also implies a preparedness to hold out for Chinese demands indefinitely.

3. As the interview falls outside the framework of our negotiations, the formal position nevertheless remains as it was left with the Vice-Minister on 17 November.[3] A further meeting would no doubt be required in order to clarify the position now reached.

4. Whatever decision may be taken on the 'Glossing' formula (Our Telno 1172)[4] we should I think at the next meeting point to the contradiction between:

(i) Chinese willingness to accept a compromise formula earlier and their stated desire not to embarrass us, and

(ii) their insistence that we accept their views in full and go on to ascertain if in their view any possibilities for compromise remain. The reaction would no doubt indicate either that it is all or nothing or that, Chou's remarks notwithstanding, some room for manoeuvre still exists (which however I now rather doubt).

5. On the assumption that the views set out in your Telno 516[5] are not open to further consideration, we would then be faced with the need to say either

(*a*) that the Chinese reply appeared to close the door for the time being, or

(*b*) that, in a final effort to reach agreement, we would, with great reluctance, be prepared to consider taking one final step towards the Chinese position (A 'Glossing' Formula).

6. Chou's rhetorical question about the possibility of our recognising an independent Taiwan heightens the probability that discussion arising from 5(*b*) above would provoke a specific enquiry about our attitude. A vague reply would I am afraid confirm the Chinese in their suspicions and in their eyes deprive the compromise formula of much of its value. In any case they may turn it down out of hand.

7. If the Chinese repeat Chou's intransigent line at the next meeting and it becomes necessary to suspend the talks we will probably have to accept that further development of relations will be inhibited in various ways if not halted at the present level. It would be unreasonable of them to penalise us deliberately for coming part of

1 Repeated for information to Hong Kong and Washington.
2 No 290.
3 No. 284.
4 Not printed.
5 No. 267.

the way but not all of it but they may decide they have nothing to lose by turning the screws a bit more e.g. in the commercial field. This would be regrettable but could prove inescapable if the talks break down. I doubt if we have anything to lose by seeking clarification now on the lines of our paras 4 and 5 above.

No. 292

Sir Colin Crowe (UKMIS New York) to Sir A. Douglas-Home
1 December 1971[1]
Tel. No. 1880 Immediate, Confidential (FCO 21/836, FEC 3/548/3D)

UK/Chinese Relations.

Minister of State had a long meeting with the Chinese Vice Foreign Minister (Chiao Kuan hua) this morning. The tone was very relaxed and friendly. Chiao began by expressing his Government's thanks for HMG's support for the seating of China.

2. After discussion of other matters (please see MIFTS)[2] Chiao enquired about the present state of negotiations concerning an exchange of Ambassadors. Mr Godber said that we were far from happy with the situation which had now been reached. We had tried to meet the Chinese position in a number of respects, we had given full support to the seating of China at the UN. We had also indicated that we were prepared to withdraw our Consulate from Taiwan. We were however, obliged to maintain our view that the status of Taiwan was 'undetermined', largely because of legal consideration.

3. Chiao said that he shared our regret that these negotiations had not yet been brought to a successful conclusion. But the proposition that the status of Taiwan was undetermined was, of course, totally unacceptable to China. He understood that it would be difficult for HMG to state that its position had changed in this regard. He wondered, however, whether it was necessary for us to reiterate in public our view on the status of Taiwan. Our Chargé in Peking had told him that if a question were asked in Parliament, we should be obliged to state that Britain's position remained unchanged. He suggested that HMG should not allow its policies to be 'dictated by lawyers'.

4. It was agreed that formal discussions would continue in Peking. But Chiao gave the impression that he would like these negotiations to be brought to a successful conclusion if a way round this problem could be found.

---

1 Sent at 12.10 a.m. on 2 December. Repeated for information immediate to Peking.
2 Not printed.

No. 293

Letter from Mr Elliott (Washington) to Mr Wilford, 2 December 1971
Secret and Personal (FCO 21/820, FEC 2/11)

Dear Michael,

Liaison with the Americans on China

As you may know, John Denson sent me a copy of his Secret and Personal letter of 15 November[1] to you on this subject.

2. We certainly have much sympathy with John's frustrations in Peking over the lack of advance warning from the Americans about the President's new China policy and over the slow progress of our own negotiations aimed at an exchange of Ambassadors. We cannot, however, go along with the conclusion which he seems to draw—namely that we should stop being so frank with the Americans in our exchanges on China.

3. John is quite right to say that 'as seen from [Peking] the Americans get a good deal and give little in return'. But he would, I am sure, agree on reflection that it is the worldwide picture that is important. It is quite natural that in some geographical areas we should be the providers—indeed, it is because this is so that we can stake a strong claim with the Americans for special consideration in other respects. It is not necessary for us to be frank and to the point of damaging our central interests, to realise that we must make the maximum use of our sources (especially where, as in Peking, they are unique) in order to ensure the continuation of the benefits we receive from the incomparably greater US effort world-wide. There is little doubt that if we were to close down on the Americans about China this would be noticed and would react adversely on the quality of the overall exchanges.

4. However, even in the strictly China context we believe that John Denson draws the wrong conclusion. While it is certainly true that the White House were less than frank with us earlier in the year when they were planning the Kissinger visit to Peking at a time when the State Department were asking us to delay our own negotiations with the Chinese, this applies much less to ACA with whom, as you well know, the majority of our exchanges are conducted. ACA were themselves almost as much in the dark as we were about what was being planned.

5. In any event, before we act in the way John Denson implies that we should, I think we must consider what we would hope to achieve by so doing. I do not think it can convincingly be argued (and it may well not be John's intention to argue) that our frankness with the Americans contributed to the hardening of the Chinese conditions for our own exchange of ambassadors. It was of course highly irritating to be asked to hold our hand so long, but as seen from here it is not absolutely certain that we should have fared any better if we had been able to tell the Chinese at an earlier stage that we would not have voted for the Important Question Resolution again. They might still have wanted ultimately to use our wish to exchange ambassadors as a lever with which to weaken the position of the United States on the relationship of the Cairo and Potsdam Declarations to the current status of Taiwan.

1 No. 283.

6. My own belief is that Kissinger is now very conscious of our irritation at being kept so much in the dark about the planning of the Peking visit and, though it would be rash to prophesy, it may well be that the President will have something substantial to tell the Prime Minister about his plans for the visit when he meets him in Bermuda; you may have noticed that the White House's suggested agenda for the talks (our tel. No 4009 of 30 November)[2] includes 'Relations with PRC including President's trip to Peking'. In any event it seems highly improbable that any obvious restriction on our exchanges on China with the Americans (except where justified on grounds of commercial competition) would have the effect of persuading the Administration to be more frank with us in future. Indeed, if we do not wish to raise further obstacles to our being kept as fully informed as possible by the Americans, I am sure it is important that we should be seen to continue our own willingness to share our information with them. As seen from here, we lose nothing by this, and though we may not get as much as we would like (in political terms) in return, our continued readiness to help the Americans in this way contributes to creating a general atmosphere from which we have much more to gain than to lose.

7. In short, while we are very willing to use any suitable opportunities to rub in the difficulties caused for us by lack of frankness on the part of the Americans, we have to remember that a great many high American officials were equally in the dark. We also think that to react by being deliberately cagey with the Americans would do us more harm than good in this and other fields.

8. I hope that these points will be borne in mind in connection with any briefing on this subject that may be in preparation for Bermuda.

Yours ever,
ANTHONY ELLIOTT

2 Not printed.

No. 294

Mr Samuel (Peking) to Sir A. Douglas-Home, 7 December 1971, 4.30a.m.[1]
Tel. No. 1233 Immediate, Confidential (FCO 21/845, FEC 6/548/9)

Personal for Morgan.
Our Telno 854:[2] Sino/British Relations.

1. It is difficult to quantify the potential upper limit for British exports to China if the 'vestige' is removed or to assess accurately possible damage to them if we do not. While the vestige remains the Chinese will always claim that it is hampering our trade relations. Nevertheless the Chinese are now going all out to prevent the emergence of an independent Taiwan, and since our attitude has considerable relevance to the Sino/US dialogue they may attach more importance to a change in our stand than

1 Repeated for information priority for Hong Kong (personal for Governor).
2 Not printed.

they would have done in the past. We are therefore likely to find ourselves subjected to increasing pressures. The Ferranti episode looks like a pointer.[3]

2. In spite of past references by Chinese officials to 'our losing out on our competitors', the facts show that in 1970, excluding purchases of wheat from Canada and Australia, our exports to China were exceeded by only two free-economy countries, Japan and West Germany, neither of whom have diplomatic relations with China. Although our exports for 1971 are likely to reach only £30 million (i.e. approximately £14 million down on 1970) the drop is more than accounted for by a decrease of £19 million in China's purchases of non-ferrous metals and industrial diamonds, neither of which are indigenous British exports.

3. In relation to the size of China's domestic economy, her foreign trade is statistically a marginal activity, albeit vital for the purchase of essential imports. Industrial and agricultural development will therefore be slow and geared to the ideological concept of 'self-reliance'. It is doubtful if China has the capacity rapidly to expand her imports. Unwilling to accept aid or credits from abroad, she aims to strike a rough annual balance between her imports and exports, and the increase in exports will be correspondingly slow. Thus China will not in the foreseeable future present a rapidly expanding market for heavy plant and machinery. Furthermore the Chinese aim to balance their bilateral trade with individual third countries and thus our export potential is limited by our capacity to buy Chinese products (at present £40-50 million per annum) and Chinese concern to allocate a share of the market to our rivals. Neither the French, nor more recently the Italians, can claim an especially favoured position in the Chinese market: the Japanese do so entirely on prices and deliveries which we can rarely beat.

4. But as China's economy expands, though slowly, we would have several advantages over our West European rivals if our political relations were on an equal footing. These are Chinese familiarity with English as a technical language, the good reputation of leading British firms such as Hawker Siddeley, Rolls Royce and ICI, our own long experience of the China trade: they have commented on various occasions that we are 'serious' people with whom they find it relatively easy to do business. This might enable us to obtain more than our share of the market by winning 'once off' orders for plant, equipment, machinery and electronic equipment. We shall need to be in the most favourable position to take advantage of any relaxation of COCOM restrictions especially if the Americans get a foothold in this market.

5. There are a number of fields in which we can probably satisfy Chinese commercial requirements better than our competitors and in these it would not be in their own interests to put the brakes on. But they have shown in the past that politics is 'in command' in trade as in everything else and that they are prepared to switch or block trade contacts if political considerations seem to require it. Outstanding examples were of course the switch of grain purchases from Australia to Canada and more recently the abrupt break-off of high level talks [text corrupted] Peking with Toyota after the Japanese Government decided to co-sponsor the American reverse Important Question Resolution.

---

3 See No. 288 for background.

6. MIFT[4] lists five existing commercial projects whose progress may in various ways depend on a Chinese political decision, though not all may be relevant because of concrete progress already achieved or because they fall within a permissible 'ceiling'. Other deals (either 'once off' or larger cooperative agreements) may on the other hand be affected in future and we shall watch closely for indications.

7. I realise that it would not be right to overestimate the importance of Sino/British trade in the context of our trade interests worldwide. It might also be felt that if the Chinese could make us 'back down' on Taiwan they might be encouraged to use trade relations as a weapon every time political issues brought us into conflict—as will presumably happen increasingly in the UN context. But I believe the Taiwan question to be in Chinese eyes in a different category from other issues. If the wider considerations allow it, our assessment here is that an ambassadorial exchange soon would enable us to exploit more fully the opportunities presented by China's requirement for advanced technology. The exchange would also put a bit more warmth into our political relations, though there are obvious limits to this: the chief short term advantage would be the boost it would give to the settlement of outstanding bilateral issues.

4 Not printed.

No. 295

Memorandum by Sir A. Douglas-Home for the Cabinet Defence and Oversea Policy Committee, 13 December 1971
DOP(71)83 Top Secret (CAB 148/117)

The Future of Hong Kong

1. This paper sets out the options open to us with regard to the future of Hong Kong.

2. The New Territories lease expires in 1997, but Hong Kong Island, together with three other small islands and Kowloon peninsula, were ceded to Britain in perpetuity. However, we consider Hong Kong would not be viable if the New Territories were detached. 1997 therefore remains the crucial date.

Chinese Policy

3. We must recognise that if the Chinese Government is determined to expel us at any time there is little we can do to prevent this. The Chinese Prime Minister, Chou En-lai, told Mr Malcolm MacDonald on 19 October[1] that of course Hong Kong is a place which will be returned to China, but the Chinese Government has not raised this and it would not be raised for a long time. He referred specifically to the fact that the New Territories lease expired in 1997 and that the Chinese had no intention of seeking to get Hong Kong back before the expiry of the lease. A future Chinese Government might nevertheless not feel themselves bound by Chou En-lai's statement.

4. Over one third of China's total foreign exchange is earned through her trade with Hong Kong. A decision to take over Hong Kong would therefore have most serious economic consequences for her. For this reason, the Chinese might prefer to see

1 See No. 277.

Britain continuing the administration of Hong Kong in humiliating circumstances without real control—a Macao-type solution. But we should not underestimate the possibility that before 1997 national pride will overcome economic realism. If the Chinese decide to take over we consider that although they may be tempted to expel us in humiliating circumstances they will more probably honour their 1963 statement that 'when conditions are ripe (these issues) should be settled peacefully through negotiations and that pending a settlement the *status quo* should be maintained'. Nevertheless, negotiation with China about Hong Kong will probably be impossible while Mao Tse-tung lives, and may not be possible even after his death.

British Policy

5. There would be both advantages and disadvantages for us in remaining in Hong Kong after 1997. Among the disadvantages are that to stay would run counter to our post-war colonial policy, and our membership of the EEC might make Hong Kong an increasingly embarrassing political anachronism. Furthermore Hong Kong might become an economic burden, particularly if confidence should become eroded, as well as a defence commitment and could continue to be a disturbing factor in our relations with China. The advantages include the maintenance of our commitment to the 2 million inhabitants who are citizens of the UK and Colonies, who would otherwise pass under Chinese rule, Hong Kong's use as a base and as a source of intelligence and its modest advantage to our balance of payments.

6. In the face of these conflicting factors the options open to us are broadly:

(*a*) To maintain the *status quo* without taking any further action.

(*b*) To prepare a voluntary and negotiated withdrawal as soon as possible.

(*c*) To maintain the *status quo*, and take preliminary informal soundings with Peking nearer 1997 with a view to:

(i) negotiating an orderly withdrawal in 1997;

(ii) securing an indication from the Chinese that they will not interfere with the present arrangements after 1997;

(iii) securing an indication that they will agree to negotiate new terms for a lease.

7. Of these options, (*a*) has nothing to commend it, save in the face of an intractable government or a state of anarchy in China. (*b*) could be impossible for a number of reasons including Chinese reluctance. Opinion in Hong Kong might not accept a negotiated withdrawal whatever HMG's intentions were.

8. I accordingly seek the concurrence of my colleagues in proceeding on the lines of alternative (*c*) (ii) or (iii), which would lead to similar practical results. At an appropriate moment nearer 1997 we should be prepared to enter into informal soundings with the Chinese Government in the strictest secrecy. We must recognise, however, that the Chinese will more probably feel bound not to allow us to remain in Hong Kong after 1997, in which case we shall have to go for a solution on the lines of (*c*) (i).

9. I intend instructing officials to review the situation annually.[2]

---

2 Mr Heath noted: 'This hardly seems a high priority at present' but agreed that the situation should be reviewed annually (PREM 15/1626).

No. 296

Memorandum by Sir A. Douglas-Home for the Cabinet Defence and Oversea Policy Committee, 31 December 1971[1]
DOP(71)93 Confidential (CAB 148/117)

Exchange of Ambassadors with China

Our negotiations with the Chinese over an exchange of Ambassadors have reached a decisive stage with the Chinese insistence that we should give up our view that sovereignty over Taiwan is 'undetermined'. Our position on this has been consistent and legally correct—China resumed the administration of Taiwan in 1945 in accordance with the Cairo and Potsdam Declarations, but did not acquire sovereignty. Japan renounced her title in 1951 by the Peace Treaty, but (at US insistence) the Treaty did not transfer sovereignty to China. The Chinese People's Government has never exercised effective control over the Island by which means they could have acquired sovereignty. Hence sovereignty over Taiwan remains undetermined.[2]

2. ...[3] there are the following arguments against changing our position on sovereignty over Taiwan:

(*a*) Title is a legal matter recognition of which carries legal consequences;

(*b*) If we accept Taiwan as a province of China we could not dispute that matters affecting it are an internal matter within the meaning of Article 2(7) of the UN Charter.

(*c*) Our position would be more embarrassing if Taiwan were successfully to declare its independence. Nevertheless this would constitute a new situation which would give us grounds to reconsider our view.

(*d*) The Chinese might conclude that we were prepared to sacrifice law to political expediency.

(*e*) Our doctrine on questions of recognition generally would be weakened.

3. There are the following arguments in favour of making a further effort to reach agreement with the Chinese:

(*a*) Our Mission in Peking report that commercial relations are being used as a lever by the Chinese to get us to change our position. In the present unemployment situation we might come under heavy pressure from firms who hope to achieve contracts. If the Chinese choose to discriminate against our exports (£45 million in 1970), we should have no means of retaliation.

(*b*) Good relations with China in the context of Hong Kong are of paramount importance to us and justify our going beyond the position of other friendly countries.

(*c*) China's entry into the United Nations now necessitates access for us to her rulers at the highest level which can only be achieved by having an Ambassador.

(*d*) A number of current issues are held up pending resolution of this dispute, including the possibility of our traffic rights for BOAC, exit visas for the remaining

---

1 In a letter from Mr Moon to Mr Barrington dated 29 November, Mr Heath asked Sir A. Douglas-Home to circulate a paper to DOP setting out the position reached so far over negotiations to exchange Ambassadors, 'with the pros and cons of conceding on the Taiwan point and the possible degrees of concession' (FCO 21/836).

2 A sentence is here omitted.

3 A phrase is here omitted.

British community in Shanghai, Hong Kong/Canton telex links, Hong Kong/Macao helicopter service, etc.

Recommendation

4. I recommend that we should make a further effort to reach agreement with the Chinese on the basis of a compromise formula. We should offer once more to use in the joint announcement the form of words already agreed with them,[4] as follows:

'The Government of the United Kingdom, acknowledging the position of the Chinese Government that Taiwan is a province of the People's Republic of China, have decided to remove their official representation from Taiwan on . . . '.

We should however add that when challenged in Parliament or elsewhere to explain our position further, we should reply as follows:

'Both the Government of the People's Republic of China and the authorities in Taiwan maintain that Taiwan is a part of China. We held the view both at Cairo and at Potsdam that sovereignty over Taiwan should revert to China. That view has not changed but we think that it is for the Chinese people themselves to settle this matter'.

5. This formula is legally acceptable since it does not commit us on the present status of Taiwan. It avoids the phrase 'sovereignty . . . is undetermined' to which the Chinese have taken exception. On the other hand it is sufficiently clear for us to stand on its terms without further elaboration. We could indicate that taken with our withdrawal of our Consulate from Taiwan it did indicate a change of attitude. It is not inconsistent with the statements we have frequently made in public that the wishes of the inhabitants of Taiwan should be taken into account in any settlement. It would cause no embarrassment in the event of a declaration of independence by Taiwan.

6. We should inform the American and other interested Governments of the action we propose to take.

7. I hope the procedure which I propose will be accepted by my colleagues without the need for a meeting. In the absence of any comment by 7 January, I will seek the Prime Minister's approval to act accordingly.

4 See No. 270, note. 4.

No. 297

Minute from Mr Wilford to Sir S. Tomlinson, 4 January 1972
Secret (FCO 21/981, FEC 3/304/1)

US Relations with China

We were told that one of the main purposes of President Nixon's meetings with heads of Government in recent weeks would be to inform them of his thinking about his forthcoming visits to Peking and Moscow. Our own 'summit' meeting with President Nixon is now a fortnight old and I have so far seen no report whatsoever on what passed on this question, though I have heard from the PUS of one outcome of the Bermuda meeting which could affect the decision to be taken by Ministers on the basis of the Secretary of State's paper for DOP Committee about HMG's position on sovereignty over Taiwan.¹

2. Would it be possible for the PUS to press Sir B. Trend or the PS to press the PS at No. 10 for an account of what passed on China? It is extremely difficult for us to formulate policy or indeed brief Mr Addis or our mission in Peking if we are kept in the dark like this.²

K.M. WILFORD

1 No. 296.
2 Sir S. Tomlinson minuted on the same day: 'I feel the same frustration as Mr Wilford and have no idea what might have been said about China in Bermuda. I hope Mr Kissinger has not successfully insisted that the game should be played according to Kissinger rules in Whitehall as well as in Washington.'

No. 298

Sir A. Douglas-Home to Mr Addis (Peking), 24 January 1972, 12.20 p.m.¹
Tel. No. 30 Immediate, Confidential (FCO 21/986, FEC 3/548/1A)

Washington Tel. No. 232:² Sino-British Relations.

I should now like you to seek an interview with Mr Chiao Kuan-Hua and speak on the lines set out in paragraph 2 of FCO Tel. No. 106 to Washington.³ If you prefer to ask to see Mr Chi Peng-Fei by all means do so, but it is our impression that Chiao is better disposed towards us.

2. You should emphasise that I see this as a further genuine attempt on our part to meet the Chinese position and that I consider we have gone a great deal further in meeting their views than they have in meeting ours. In the course of the last 2 years we have consistently shown a forthcoming and friendly approach in all our dealings with the Chinese authorities. The fact that we are now prepared to give up using the formula 'sovereignty over Taiwan is undetermined' and to withdraw our official representative has, we trust, removed the last obstacle to an exchange of Ambassadors.

3. You have discretion to omit the first sentence of the Parliamentary explanation if it is clear that the reference to the 'authorities in Taiwan' would be a stumbling block. Nevertheless we should need to use it ourselves to put the matter in context in any Parliamentary reply.

4. If it is necessary you also have discretion to reaffirm to the Chinese that we had no intention of seeking to persuade other Governments to accept a position similar

1 Repeated for information to Washington and Hong Kong.
2 Not printed. In FCO Tel. No. 106 to Washington of 17 January, Sir A. Douglas Home stated he was going to make a further effort to reach agreement with the Chinese, once the new Chargé reached Peking at the end of the month, on the basis of a compromise formula laid out in paragraphs 4 and 5 of DOP(71)93 (No. 296). He instructed the Earl of Cromer to relay this intention to the Americans. Replying in Washington Tel. No. 232 on 22 January, the Ambassador stated: 'Kissinger has told me today that, whilst the US administration is not exactly enthralled at the prospect of our proposed approach to the Chinese, they understand our position and will raise no objection.'
3 This was the same formula set out in paragraph 4 of the memorandum to the DOP Committee (No. 296).

to ours. This would be equivalent of the Assurance in 2(*c*) of FCO Tel. No. 691 of 1971 to UKMIS New York.[4]

5. At your discretion you may reaffirm that we consider the request for your own Agrément to be outstanding.

4 Not printed.

No. 299

Planning Staff Paper on 'The Asian Quadrilateral' for the Permanent Under-Secretary's Planning Committee, 2 February 1972[1]
PC(72)1 Confidential (FCO 49/383, RS 3/5A)

The outlook on the eve of President Nixon's visit to Peking

1. President Nixon is to visit China from 21-28 February 1972. His immediate purpose is to improve his electoral prospects at home, though he also hopes to establish a new American relationship with China and exploit to American advantage the triangular rivalry of Moscow, Peking and Washington. But the very fact that a visa to China is now both possible and popular shows how the climate has changed both internationally and in the United States. After a decade of relative stability, power relationships in Asia and the Far East, particularly those among the four key countries—China, Japan, the Soviet Union and the United States—are becoming fluid. The Nixon visit may thus mark the beginning of rather an unpredictable era.

The stability of the Sixties

2. The Asian Quadrilateral was relatively stable in the 60s because:

(*a*) China was self-absorbed and relatively inactive in the region;

(*b*) The Sino-Soviet dispute, which claimed some of the energy of both countries, resulted in deadlock;

(*c*) Japan, still absorbed by her own economic expansion, adopted a low profile in international affairs;

(*d*) The United States had negligible contact with China;

(*e*) Korea and Taiwan—the major territorial issues of concern to all four powers—were in effect frozen;

(*f*) A strong and continuing United States military presence in the area was taken for granted and the credibility of the US nuclear commitment to Japan was unquestioned.

The Factors for Change

3. Today the factors for change are:

Japan

(i) The dramatic growth in Japanese economic strength has opened up new possibilities of a major political, conceivably even a military, role for Japan;

China

(ii) Peking's increasing emergence onto the world stage; her more flexible and

1 A covering minute from Mr Goulden, the committee secretary, dated 2 February 1972, stated the paper was intended to sketch in the foreign policy backdrop to President Nixon's visit to Peking and was the sole topic on the agenda for the committee's meeting 8 February.

pragmatic policies. (A return to the chaos and extremism of the 'Cultural Revolution' cannot be discounted, but seems unlikely in spite of the recent power struggle.)

The USSR

(iii) Soviet anxiety about Chinese policies and China's emergence as a nuclear power; greater Soviet involvement (including naval deployment) in Asia;

The USA

(iv) American military disengagement from Vietnam and elsewhere in accordance with the 'Nixon doctrine'. And the new American conception of China as a major and possibly maneuverable factor in the world balance of power;

Taiwan

(v) The new uncertainty surrounding the long term future of Taiwan, whose future rulers might ultimately see greater security in an understanding with the mainland than in continued American protection.

The problems of the Seventies

4. The four major powers may well therefore be faced with difficult policy problems in the longer term on the following lines:

(*a*) *China*

Chinese objectives tend to conflict and carry considerable potential dangers (e.g. the revival of militarism in a more independent Japan, or a flare-up in Sino-Soviet relations). Peking will want to keep the Soviet Union and Japan (her most dangerous potential enemies) well apart; to exploit the renewal of American interest while continuing to combat American influence in Asia; to pursue her claims on Taiwan and to border settlement with the Soviet Union; and to loosen Japanese links with the United States to China's advantage. China will also be concerned to prevent any rapprochement (even tactical and temporary) between the US and the Soviet Union, who will eventually have a common interest in persuading China to join in arrangements for strategic arms limitation and nuclear non-proliferation.

(*b*) *The USSR*

While the US will remain formally the main enemy, Moscow will continue to be at odds with Peking and simultaneously alarmed by, and tempted to cultivate, the growing power of Japan. The Soviet problem in containing China is likely to be aggravated both by American military disengagement and by any reduction in Sino-American hostility. It will be difficult for the Soviet Union to achieve a satisfactory balance of power within the quadrilateral.

(*c*) *Japan*

Japan's first priority will remain a close relationship with the US; and she would prefer to avoid choosing between China and the Soviet Union. Japanese suspicion of the Soviet Union is deep and, if other things were equal, the claims of good relations with China would probably prevail. This would be particularly true if a settlement between China and Taiwan removed that obstacle to closer Sino-Japanese relations. But the Soviet Union is the more promising economic partner for Japan. Nevertheless the greatest potential factor of change for Japan is the possibility of an American military withdrawal or some other major shift in US policy which might undermine the credibility of the Mutual Security Treaty. This would not only increase the importance of Japanese relations with China and the Soviet Union, but might prompt Japan to consider the acquisition of nuclear weapons. Japan will in any case probably be obliged to do more for her own conventional defence, e.g. in Asian sea lanes. In principle China, the Soviet Union and the US have a common interest in discouraging Japan from going nuclear, but may in practice find any agreement on this issue difficult to achieve.

(d) The United States

Ideally the United States might like to see China and the Soviet Union keeping one another in check and Japan holding the Asian balance, but none of these three powers will be easy to manipulate. Unless the United States are ready for major concessions on Taiwan, for instance, the Chinese are unlikely to give President Nixon much more than, by accepting his visit, they have already. Admittedly any degree of Sino-US rapprochement constitutes some constraint on the Soviet Union; but the US cannot go too far in this direction without imperiling such understanding as has so far been reached between the two super powers and without further upsetting Japan. Equally, a powerfully armed and more independent Japan could help to balance both China and the Soviet Union; but could in turn prove a major threat to US interests.

Long term Outlook

5. With all four Powers alert to the possibility of new combinations, the Asian kaleidoscope could shift more than once in the Seventies, not least because the Soviet Union and the United States have wider interests, to which the Chinese already—and the Japanese may ultimately—aspire. Developments in the Middle East or Europe could so modify US-Soviet relations as to change their attitude to Asian problems as well; China and Japan might seek new spheres of influence. The final pattern is unpredictable.

6. What is clear, however, is the special importance of Japan, whose long term options are the most extensive. This is partly because Japan's present political and military efforts are so much less than her economic strength can support and partly because of the ambivalence inherent in Japan's present relationship with both China and the United States. It is arguable that President Nixon has already shifted United States policy in Asia almost as far as it can go without causing a critical loss of Japanese confidence in the United States. If he can, President Nixon will doubtless try to consolidate the present American position in Asia and will try not to alienate the allies of the US by further disengagement or by concessions to China at their expense. Although many other variations are possible, the major forks in the road ahead are likely to be initiated in Washington and could include the following:

First Fork

(*a*) The reductions in American commitments in Asia already effected by President Nixon prove enough to satisfy American public opinion and enable future US Administrations to maintain a continuing commitment which preserves their influence in the region and the confidence of Japan.

(*b*) Isolationism in the US forces the next President to continue disengagement, thus losing influence in Asia and forfeiting the confidence of Japan.

Second Fork (i)

(*c*) Japan continues on her present path.

(*d*) Japan becomes rather more self-reliant military, but remains non-nuclear and a cooperative member of the Western camp.

Second Fork (ii)

(e) Japan rearms, goes nuclear, remains in the Western camp, but tends to follow her own line.

(f) rogue-elephant Japan.

Short term outlook

7. In the short term, and assuming no major shift in US policy, the prospects for the Asian Quadrilateral are much less dramatic. Each of the four countries is anchored by its own traditions, past policies, alliances, domestic preoccupations and other distractions. There will be some uncertainty; and changes in US policy will undoubtedly have an initially unsettling effect. But these changes seem unlikely to be superficial. The following factors will help to delay modification of the status quo in the immediately foreseeable future:

(i) The continuing US military presence, which cannot be conjured away overnight (South Korea, Taiwan, facilities in Okinawa, permanent bases in Guam, the existence of the Seventh Fleet, etc); and the continuing close interest of the US Administration in Asian matters.

(ii) The probable caution and conservatism of Chinese diplomacy (though the deaths of Chiang Kai-shek and Mao Tse-tung could occur now and change existing attitudes considerably).

(iii) The opposition of Japan to any substantial rearmament programme.

(iv) The caution imposed on the Soviet Union by continued Sino-Soviet hostility and their simultaneously uneasy relations with the United States.

(v) The perceived importance in Washington and Tokyo of good US/Japanese relations.

8. To a considerable extent the international impact of President Nixon's visit has already occurred and it is unlikely that anything of comparable significance will be agreed between the President and the Chinese leaders. The establishment of full diplomatic relations, for instance, is unlikely. At most the Chinese might accept a resident American representative to discuss the problem. Nor are the Chinese capable of delivering a Vietnam settlement. But the effects on President Nixon and on American opinion could be more important. The traditional American belief in their unique capacity to understand and influence the Chinese is not dead. A flattering Chinese reception, even one that brought little concrete agreement, could revive this old belief and encourage the newer hope that Chinese hostility to the Soviet Union might somehow be exploited to reduce the burden of American defence postures. The significance of the Nixon visit is that it could—particularly if the President is re-elected—influence American aspirations and colour American policy in Asia for years to come. Both in Moscow and in Tokyo it is American reactions to the visit that will be scrutinised with anxiety and suspicion.

The British interest

9. The UK has important, but not vital, national interests in Eastern Asia and the Far East. We are primarily concerned by the impact which developments in this area might have on US support for Europe and on the Soviet threat to Europe. Less important, but by no means negligible, is the stability of the area itself and, in particular:

(*a*) The continued viability and good order of Hong Kong;

(*b*) The promotion of trade (principally with Japan, but also with China);

(*c*) British investments in South East Asia and the Indian sub-continent;

(*d*) The security and prosperity of Australia and New Zealand.

10. The relative stability of the Asian Quadrilateral in the Sixties served British interests well and we have no reason to wish major changes, though the normalisation of US/Chinese relations is healthy and welcome. In the longer term in particular, the dangers of upsetting the present equilibrium seem likely greatly to outweigh any possible advantage. In the medium term we should like to see (but may not, of course, get):

(*a*) A China that has settled the dispute with Taiwan and remains ready to encourage trade and tolerate Hong Kong;

(*b*) A continued off-shore US military presence, and maximum stabilising US political influence;

(*c*) A non-militaristic, non-nuclear and Western-aligned Japan with whom to trade and cooperate in world economic and political terms;

(*d*) A Soviet Union still deeply divided from (but well short of war with) China and sufficiently confident of relations with the United States to react by seeking détente in Europe.

11. Britain acting on her own will not be able to exert a decisive influence on the relationship among the members of the Asian Quadrilateral or on the resulting balance of power. It would, of course, be useful to establish full diplomatic relations with China, but this would not make China any more amenable to our influence than is the Soviet Union. British influence on the United States administration is at present the main instrument available to British policy in the Far East, but this influence is more likely to decline than to increase. It will scarcely be supplemented by British influence on Japan, to whom we will be important primarily as one of the leaders of Western Europe. Indeed our best hope lies in the emergence of a coherent and purposeful European policy, which could make a more united Europe a factor of major and increasing importance to at least Japan, the Soviet Union and the United States; perhaps even to China. In the long term, if Europe can maintain an understanding and equal relationship with both the United States and Japan, this will help to lessen the danger of divergence between American and Japanese policies and also strengthen the European position vis-à-vis China and the Soviet Union. Initially, however, the success of British policy in Asia and the Far East will depend on our ability to encourage the United States to pursue a middle course in Asia which will neither frighten Japan into dangerous options, nor diminish American support for Europe.

No. 300

Sir C. Crowe (UKMIS New York) to Sir A. Douglas-Home
3 February 1972
Confidential (FCO 21/971)

Sir,

China's Long March to the United Nations

In a supplementary despatch I propose to report on the initial Chinese performance in the United Nations up to and including their performance at the Security Council meetings in Africa. But in order to see this in perspective I felt that I should first describe how it came about that a Government which came to power in the end of 1949 was debarred from sending its representatives to the United Nations until the end of 1971. Future historians will no doubt speculate on the effects on an already xenophobic people of being excommunicated for all these years from the world community. The saga of Peking's twenty-two year long struggle for representation is unique in the annals of the United Nations. It was the subject of many paradoxes; over the years alliances shifted and yesterday's friends became today's deadliest foes. When the battle was finally decided the two antagonists China and the United States were to find themselves almost immediately backing the same side in the Security Council debate on the India/Pakistan war.

2. On the 18th of November 1949 Chou En-lai in his capacity as Foreign Minister, had sent a telegram to the Secretary-General, Mr Trygve Lie, announcing the formal establishment since the 10th of October of the Central People's Government of the People's Republic of China as the 'sole legal government representing all the people of the People's Republic of China.' A telegram conveying similar information was sent to the President of the General Assembly. The General Assembly was in session at the time, but since the credentials of the Chinese representatives had already been approved no immediate action was required and none was taken. It was not until 22 years later that the credentials of the representatives of the government of the People's Republic of China were accepted enabling them (having already taken their places in the General Assembly on the 15th of November) to take their seats in the Security Council on the 23rd of November 1971, thus completing the final step in what the Chilean Representative in his welcoming speech in the General Assembly aptly described as China's Long March to the United Nations.

Initial Chinese Reaction to the United Nations

3. The Chinese Communist reaction to the founding of the United Nations had been favourable. In April 1945 Mao Tse-tung wrote:

'Respecting the establishment of an international organisation for the maintenance of world peace and security, the Chinese Communist Party completely agree with the Dumbarton Oaks proposals and the Crimea decisions concerning this problem. The Communist Party welcomes the UN Conference in San Francisco. It has sent its own delegate to join the Chinese delegation to San Francisco, as a means of expressing the will of the Chinese people.' (*On Coalition Government*)

4. Since the Kuomintang and the Communists were ostensibly co-operating at this period the Communists had been allowed to appoint one of the five Chinese delegates to the San Francisco Conference. The delegate sent by Mao was the veteran Communist Tung Pi-wu who was later to take over most of the formal duties of Chairman of the People's Republic of China after the fall of Liu Shao-chi. According to Dr Chai, a former Chinese member of the Secretariat who was an adviser to Dr Wellington Koo the leader of the Chinese Delegation at San Francisco, the arrangement worked surprisingly well. He has told us ruefully that Tung Pi-wu and his two advisers (Chang Han-fu, later First Deputy Foreign Minister, and Chen Chia-kang later Ambassador in Cairo) were in fact the only members of the Chinese Delegation who did not cause Dr Koo any problems. Thus, although the Chinese Communist leaders, like other Communists, no doubt had reservations about the

'bourgeois' character of the projected new organisation they appear to have recognised its potentiality as a political forum and were anxious to be present at the birth. In approaching the United Nations immediately upon coming to power in 1949, the Chinese Communist leaders again showed a desire to participate in the world organisation. Such participation would incidentally have set the seal on their legitimacy as successor state to the Chiang Kai-shek Government and encouraged those states which still hesitated to recognise the new Government.

Action by the Security Council

5. The General Assembly having failed to act on Chou En-lai's telegram in 1949 the subject was next raised in the Security Council in January 1950, where a Soviet proposal calling for the rejection of the credentials of the representatives of Nationalist China, was defeated by six votes to three with two abstentions (including the United Kingdom). Following this defeat the Soviet Representative withdrew announcing that he could not participate in the Security Council until the Nationalist Chinese representative had been excluded. On the 9th of March the then Secretary-General Trygve Lie, who actively campaigned for a change in Chinese representation, circulated a memorandum he had commissioned from the UN Legal Department which said *inter alia* that voting for representation of a regime did not entail diplomatic recognition of the regime by the country so voting; and that when two governments claimed to represent the same state, the question at issue should be which of the two was 'in a position to employ the resources and direct the people of the state in fulfilment of the obligations of membership.' The Soviet Representative did not return until August, by which time his providential absence had enabled the Security Council to authorise UN military action to repel the North Korean invasion of South Korea. On resuming his seat in the Security Council, the Soviet Representative (who was President for the month of August) attempted to rule that the Chinese Nationalist Representative was not entitled to participate, but his ruling was challenged and over-ruled (eight votes against, including the UK, and three in favour).

6. A few months later Chinese 'volunteers' on a massive scale were fighting UN forces in Korea so that support for the People's Republic of China inevitably diminished and the subject of Chinese Communist representation in the United Nations became academic and remained so for some years. It was raised briefly in the Security Council in 1951 and twice in 1955, but no action was taken. Instead on 31 January 1955 the Security Council adopted a US resolution 'not to consider any proposals to exclude the representation of the Government of the Republic of China, or to seat representatives of the Central People's Government of the People's Republic of China.' Thereafter action was confined to the General Assembly. (Statements for the record were made in the Security Council by Algeria in 1968 and by Somalia in 1971 in the context of credentials. Both statements caused a flurry of interest at the time, but neither stimulated any action in the Council.) Although the Russians have never again risked absenting themselves from meetings of the Security Council, their seat was normally left vacant whenever the Chinese Nationalist Representative intervened in the debate. Latterly it became customary to avoid, where possible, convening the Security Council during a month when the Chinese was President owing to the difficulty of conducting negotiations with a Nationalist Chinese Representative in the Chair.

Action in the General Assembly

7. The General Assembly, when it met in the autumn of 1950 (by which time the Korean War had broken out) established a Special Committee to consider the problem of Chinese representation. But the Special Committee failed to agree on any recommendations and the General Assembly merely 'took note of its report.' For the next ten years the General Assembly successfully avoided discussion of the issue by a 'moratorium' procedure. By 1960, however, the majority in favour of this procedure was so small that in 1961 no attempt was made to prevent a debate on Chinese representation. From that time on, except for the abortive 19th Session, there has been an annual debate in the General Assembly and each year a resolution (known latterly as the Albanian resolution) has been tabled calling for the restoration of the lawful rights of the People's Republic of China and for the expulsion of the representatives of Chiang Kai-shek. In 1961 and in the years 1965-70, a procedural resolution sponsored by the United States and others, the so-called 'Important Question' resolution (which declared the substantive resolution 'important' within the terms of Article 18 of the Charter, requiring a two-thirds majority) was also tabled and adopted. The latter resolution was invariably criticised by the supporters of Peking as a procedural device designed to prevent the seating of Chinese Communist representatives. But although this was indeed its intent, it was not until 1970 that the Albanian resolution calling for the seating of the representatives of the Chinese People's Republic obtained a simple majority. When this happened there was at once a strong feeling among many previous supporters of the Important Question resolution that this procedural device was no longer appropriate and should be re-considered. It was not tabled in this form again, (see paragraphs 16-18), so that in practice the Important Question resolution only served to delay the seating of Chinese Communist representatives for one year.

Attitude of China to the United Nations during the Years of Exclusion

8. During the Korean War, representatives of the People's Republic of China briefly visited the United Nations in 1950 to attend the debate in the Security Council on their complaint charging the US government with the invasion of Taiwan. But there was no prospect of their securing the necessary support to seat their representatives in the United Nations while Chinese Communist forces were fighting UN forces in Korea. Moreover, their maltreatment of UN prisoners and their propaganda fabrication that the United Nations had used 'germ warfare' in Korea were not calculated to further their cause with the UN membership.

9. There was an ironical postscript to this first Chinese appearance at the United Nations. When they finally took their seats in the Security Council twenty-one years later Ambassador Malik,[1] the Soviet Representative, in welcoming the Chinese delegation reminded them unctuously that he was the self-same Soviet Representative who had fought unceasingly on their behalf in 1950 and had been primarily responsible for overcoming resistance to their participation in the deliberations of the Security Council at that time. However, recollection of past favours did not subsequently deter the Chinese either from attacking Malik personally (they described him in ECOSOC[2] as a clown), or from denigrating the Soviet Government on every possible occasion.

---

1 Yakov Alexandrovich Malik, Soviet Permanent Representative to the UN from 1948-52 and 1968-76.
2 United Nations Economic and Social Council.

10. After the conclusion of the Geneva Armistice Agreements in 1954 and in the spirit of euphoria which pervaded the period of the Bandung Conference,[3] China's prospects might have been expected to take a turn for the better. But owing to what Chinese propaganda justifiably described as American manipulation of its 'automatic voting majority' this was not to be. Deprived for ten years by the 'moratorium' of an opportunity even to get their case heard, Chinese propaganda derided the United Nations as an instrument of American policy. In September 1965 Chen Yi at a press conference listed his much publicised conditions for Chinese participation in the world organisation. These were that:

' ... the UN must free itself from the control of the USA, rectify all its mistakes and undergo a thorough reorganisation and reform. To expel the elements of the Chiang Kai-shek clique is an indispensable step ... The UN must also resolutely condemn US imperialism ... and cancel its slanderous resolution condemning China and the Korean Democratic People's Republic as aggressors, and all its other erroneous resolutions. The UN Charter must be reviewed and revised by all countries of the world. Its membership must include all independent countries to the exclusion of all imperialist puppets.'

Peking also supported at the time President Sukarno of Indonesia's still-born proposals for the establishment of a rival world organisation which would be truly revolutionary and not susceptible to US manipulation. However, when the vote eventually went in their favour they quietly dropped the more extreme conditions listed earlier. The only condition upon which the Chinese appear to have insisted throughout their twenty-two years in the wilderness was that the representatives of Nationalist China must be excluded and therefore, that any form of Two Chinas solution was unacceptable.

11. From 1968 onwards as the Cultural Revolution abated and the tide appeared to be turning in China's favour in the United Nations, signals began to be received from Peking hinting that they were now definitely interested in taking their seat in the world organisation. In 1969 African leaders visiting China were praised and thanked for their support for the restoration of China's legitimate rights in the United Nations. During the 1970 General Assembly both Mr Sharp, the Canadian Minister for External Affairs, and M. Schumann, the French Foreign Minister, reported that they believed China now wished to participate in the United Nations and similar reports emanated from Norwegian diplomatic sources in Peking.

Attitude of the General Membership

12. The attitude of member states of the United Nations on the question of Chinese representation has also fluctuated. Thus India and the Soviet Union, the two states which between 1950 and 1960 had most zealously promoted the Chinese cause, both later had reason to regret their earlier enthusiasm although neither openly admitted to a change of heart. In 1960 India, by then engaged in the Sino/Indian border dispute, no longer proposed the inclusion on the agenda of an item on Chinese representation. In 1963 the Soviet Union, whose doctrinal dispute with Peking was leading to an open rift, dropped from the co-sponsors of the resolution on Chinese representation leaving Albania to mastermind the Chinese cause in the

3 See No. 27, note 2.

United Nations from then on—a task which they undertook with more zeal than skill (see paragraph 29). Although India and the Soviet Union continued dutifully to vote for the seating of representatives, they otherwise showed a marked lack of enthusiasm, sometimes not even bothering to speak in the debates. In present circumstances they may well regret having given even this limited support.

13. The influx of new members from developing countries in the early nineteen-sixties brought new sympathy and support for Communist China which reached a first peak in 1965 when there was a tie-vote for the Albanian resolution (47 in favour, 47 against, 20 abstentions). But in the next three years support again declined owing to disquiet over the excesses of the Cultural Revolution and the hostile tone of China's public statements about the United Nations. China's support for rebel movements also cost them the goodwill of some African countries, several of which changed their vote on Chinese representation as a result. (All these points were effectively exploited in US and Chinese Nationalist speeches in the General Assembly).

14. The United Kingdom followed a consistent policy throughout the period 1961-70. We always voted for both the Albanian and the Important Question resolutions and in speeches in the General Debate and/or in the debate on Chinese representation we advocated the seating of representatives of the People's Republic of China while reserving our position on the status of Taiwan which we described as 'undetermined'. Even the year that our Mission in Peking was burned down we continued to support and vote for Communist China's participation in the United Nations as well as voting for the Important Question resolution.

15. During 1968-70 the attitude of the general membership began to change once again and this time decisively in Peking's favour. Straws in the wind were the changing attitude of Canada and Italy which culminated in their recognition of Peking. Both had already in 1968 put forward proposals designed to break the log-jam but these had in neither case won wide support. Mr Paul Martin, the Canadian Minister for External Affairs had suggested a 'Two Chinas' interim solution giving the China seat, including permanent membership of the Security Council to Peking, but seating Nationalist China as the representative of Taiwan and 'other islands over which it exercised jurisdiction . . .' the Italians had for three consecutive years proposed the setting up of an *ad hoc* committee to ascertain the views of Peking on UN representation.

16. In the 1970 debate on Chinese representation Italy, while voting for the Important Question, gave warning that if this resolution continued 'to frustrate the will of the Assembly' they might not do so again; the representative of Ireland also gave the first hint of his Government's subsequent defection from the American ranks by urging that a solution should be found to a problem which had 'stalemated' the General Assembly for twenty years; and the emergence for the first time in 1970 of a majority vote in favour of the Albanian resolution, although it was nullified by the Important Question resolution, was psychologically a major break-through. Between October and the end of December 1970 five new countries recognised the People's Republic of China (Canada, Equatorial Guinea, Italy, Ethiopia and Chile) and many more Member States were to do so in 1971. Others indicated, more or less openly, that they were re-considering their position on the question of Chinese representation in the United Nations. Even the Latin American bloc was showing signs of erosion.

The New American Line

17. That the Americans themselves were contemplating a change in their China policy at the United Nations had been hinted at in their speech in the 1970 debate on Chinese representation. For the first time they had expressed more interest in keeping the Nationalists in than in keeping the Communists out. Their Deputy Permanent Representative[4] had described his Government as actively seeking to 'move from an era of confrontation to an era of negotiation with Peking.' They were as interested as anyone, he said, in seeing the People's Republic of China 'play a constructive role in the family of nations', provided this was not achieved at the expense of Nationalist China.

18. Early in 1971 both HM Government and the Italians informed the Americans in confidence that we were not prepared to vote for the Important Question at the next General Assembly and it seemed evident that the Canadians would do likewise. (The French had voted against the Important Question ever since President De Gaulle recognised the Government of the People's Republic of China in 1964 and the Scandinavians—except for Iceland—had always done so.) During the Anglo-American talks in the end of April 1971 the Americans told Sir Stanley Tomlinson that they had conducted informal soundings with the Australians, Canadians, Japanese, New Zealanders and Nationalist Chinese on future tactics in the China debate and all, even the Chinese, were agreed that the Important Question resolution was doomed and could not be used again.

19. Meanwhile, it was becoming clear to all that the new American policy towards China would also lead to a modification of their previous policy on Chinese Representation at the United Nations. On the 21st of March Ambassador Bush admitted on TV that the question of Chinese Representation was under review at a high level and that President Nixon had 'expressed a certain flexibility'; in April there was the much publicised visit of the American ping-pong team to China:[5] on the 15th of July President Nixon disclosed that Dr Kissinger had secretly visited Peking a few days earlier and that he himself would visit China before May 1972; and finally on the 2nd of August Mr Rogers announced that the United States would support action at the General Assembly for seating the People's Republic of China (while continuing to oppose any action to 'expel' the Republic of China or 'otherwise deprive' it of representation in the United Nations). On the question of the Security Council seat Mr Rogers said that the United States were 'prepared to have this question resolved on the basis of a decision of members of the UN.'

20. Throughout these developments the Americans showed a lack of sensitivity to the feelings—and indeed the interests—of their friends and allies, failing to take them into their confidence until the very last minute. This behaviour was undoubtedly resented and may have contributed to their subsequent defeat in the United Nations. It also caused genuine difficulties; (c.f. the domestic reaction in Japan to President Nixon's projected visit to Peking and the effect on our own negotiations for the exchange of Ambassadors of American urgings that we should delay informing Peking of our decision no longer to support the Important Question resolution

---

4 Mr William Tapley Bennett.
5 See No. 232.

as they were re-thinking their policy. Mr Denson, in his valedictory despatch has commented on the damaging consequences of this delay.)[6] There was undoubtedly a suspicion among UN members that the Americans had done a deal with China during the Kissinger visit and were merely going through the motions of supporting Nationalist China in the United Nations for domestic consumption and in order not to alarm their other Asian allies. These fears were also given wide currency in the American press. In these circumstances many previous supporters of the United States on Chinese Representation were understandably reluctant to go down with the sinking ship and although Ambassador Bush and other members of the US Mission repeatedly denied that their Government had any such intentions the inherent inconsistency between their policy of rapprochement with China and their policy at the United Nations undermined their credibility. (It will be recalled that Dr Kissinger was actually in Peking on his second visit at the time the vote was taken in the United Nations. The local wits claimed that he had offered the Chinese Communist delegation a lift back in the Presidential aircraft.)

The new American Resolutions

21. Given the difficulties, the Americans left very little time for the detailed planning of their tactics in the United Nations. The day after Mr Rogers' 2nd August announcement a meeting of all delegations who held views similar to the United States on this issue was held in the US Mission. Two draft resolutions were presented by the Americans as a basis for discussion (and afterwards leaked to *The New York Times*.) The first was a substantive resolution which 'having regard for the existing factual situation' affirmed the right of both Chinas to be represented in the United Nations. The second was a procedural resolution which reversed the procedure followed in the Important Question Resolution of previous years and designated any proposal 'depriving the Republic of China of representation', rather than for the seating of the representatives of the People's Republic of China, as an Important Question under Article 18 of the Charter. This second and key resolution thus became known as the Reverse Important Question resolution. These two resolutions were the subject of lengthy negotiations between the Americans and their allies, some of whom, notably the Australians and New Zealanders, were not prepared to co-sponsor unless the substantive resolution specified that the People's Republic of China should have the permanent seat on the Security Council. The Americans were slow to concede this, although they did so in the end. They also had difficulty with the Japanese who had reacted strongly to the American failure to give them adequate prior warning about President Nixon's projected visit to Peking and were under domestic pressure not to co-sponsor. They only agreed to do so at the eleventh hour.

22. Because of these difficulties the Americans lost out on priority which is a matter of some importance in the United Nations since resolutions relating to the same question are taken up in the order in which they are submitted unless the General Assembly decides otherwise. (There is in general a built-in advantage for the resolution which is taken first because of the tendency of delegations to prefer to vote for, or abstain rather than cast a negative vote.) Thus the request by Albania and its co-sponsors for inscription of an item entitled 'The Restoration of the Lawful Rights

6 No. 287.

of the People's Republic of China in the United Nations' was dated the 15th of July and included in the Provisional Agenda, whereas the Americans only put in their letter requesting the inscription of an item entitled 'The Representation of China in the United Nations' on the 17th of August and did so without waiting to round up co-sponsors. Because it was submitted so late the American item only appeared in the Supplementary List of Agenda Items. The Albanians and their co-sponsors also got in first with their resolution which was dated the 25th of September whereas the two resolutions co-sponsored by the United States and its allies were not tabled until the 29th of September. (The text of these two resolutions are in my Tel 1092).[7] This put the Americans at a disadvantage from the start since the onus was on them to persuade the General Assembly to reverse the normal order of procedure. They took the precaution of tabling their two resolutions under the Albanian item as well as under their own in case they failed to get their own item inscribed. Although this particular fear was not realised, it was well that they did so since the Albanian resolution was passed before their item was reached so it would not otherwise have been possible to vote on their resolutions. (After the Albanian item had been disposed of the General Assembly decided not to discuss the American item.)

The Battle for Inscription

23. The first round took place in the General Committee, the day after the 26th Session opened, in the context of adopting the Agenda. The American aims were first: to secure the inscription of their item; and secondly to have it amalgamated with the Albanian item as two sub-items under the neutral title 'The Question of China'. They succeeded over inscription by a narrow vote (11 in favour, 9 against (including Finland), 4 abstentions (including the UK and France) but their proposal for amalgamation was defeated. (We were among those who voted against.)

24. When the report of the General Committee was taken in plenary on the 24th of September inscription of the Albanian item was approved without objection, but the US item was again only approved by a small majority. (65 in favour, 47 against (including the Nordic States, Guyana and Peru), 15 abstentions (including France and the UK) and 3 absent.) Although the Americans purported to be pleased with the result, this was a Pyrrhic victory which in no way foreshadowed success on the substantive issue since many states, including ourselves, are traditionally reluctant to oppose inscription of an item. We abstained on this occasion because of our serious doubts whether dual representation was compatible with the Charter: in explaining my vote in the General Committee I stated further, on your instructions and for the first time in public, that the UK would 'oppose substantive resolutions or procedural motions which would have the effect of delaying the seating of the representatives of the People's Republic of China in the United Nations.' In fact the slender US majority on inscription was seen by many as the first indication that in 1971 the Americans would be defeated.

'Ants on a Hot Pan'

25. Between the vote on inscription in plenary and the opening of the debate on Chinese representation on the 18th of October, there was theoretically a pause, but in practice the subject of China was to dominate the Session from its opening

---

7 Not printed.

until the final vote in plenary on the 25th of October and even after. Most of the speakers in the General Debate included passages on Chinese representation in their speeches and the 'China watchers' in UN Missions and in the world press seized on and tried to interpret these often delphic utterances. Further evidence was provided in the speeches in the debate on Chinese representation which opened on the 18th of October. Head-counts were taken and revised in the light of new clues, or rumours; and information was exchanged with friendly missions so that the atmosphere was more reminiscent of a race-course than a political forum. Meanwhile, the Americans were, in the words of the Peking *People's Daily* 'like ants on a hot pan' in their feverish efforts to cajole and coerce reluctant delegations into supporting them. Capitals were repeatedly lobbied, in many cases at Head of State and Prime Minister level, and in New York Ambassador Bush, the US Permanent Representative, personally called on almost every mission sometimes two or three times to explain the American position and to solicit support. Rumours proliferated that various small states had been 'bought' (my tel. 1476 paragraph 2);[8] for example the Americans were said to have either bribed or threatened (perhaps both) on import quotas for Mauritian sugar to secure their vote.

26. When the Americans first tabled their two resolutions they pointed out to us and others that they had referred to the '*Right of Representation* of the People's Republic of China' and the '*Continued Right of Representation* of the Republic of China', thus avoiding a controversial reference to expulsion. However, as the time of the vote approached the Americans and their allies, probably because this was the only argument in support of their case which evoked any sympathy, increasingly asserted that the Albanian resolution called for the expulsion of a Member State from the United Nations and would thus set a new and undesirable precedent. They were at pains to obscure the fact that this was a question of representation and not one of the expulsion of a state; or to the fact (frequently cited in the debate) that there have been of course many previous cases in the United Nations where representatives of member states have vacated their seats because the governments they represented had ceased to exercise authority.

27. We were careful not to lobby in view of your undertaking to Mr Rogers on the 4th of August that we would do nothing to make their task more difficult. But even so we did not escape criticism. We were, for instance, falsely reported as having advised Bahrain and Oman (both new members) against supporting the American resolution. We were also accused of damaging American chances of victory by privately forecasting their defeat. Here again we had made no public predictions although we perforce exchanged views in confidence with other friendly missions (my tel 1452).[8] (Incidentally head-counts by two of the chief co-sponsors of the American resolutions, Australia and Japan, which we had been shown in confidence, had also predicted defeat.) But this almost hysterical approach was typical of the American attitude at this time. It was reflected in an increasingly reckless use of pressure tactics as the critical moment approached. Yet, as I reported in my tel. 1482[9] the reinforcement of the US Mission by two senior Under-Secretaries from the State Department, Mr Pedersen and

---

8 Not printed.
9 Not printed.

Mr De Palma in order to stage-manage the proceedings probably contributed more harm than good to the American cause. To anticipate a little, these strong-arm tactics reached a crescendo the night of the vote. The brusque manner in which Mr Pedersen demanded of Mr Kyprianou[10] that he vote for the Americans undoubtedly lost them the Cyprus vote despite a commitment they had secured from Archbishop Makarios. (My tel. 1482 paragraph 6 and my letter of 28th of October paragraph 2(iv)).[9] We were also informed by the Scandinavians that Finland and Denmark had considered supporting the Americans on postponing the voting (see below paragraph 30), but when the Nordic Ambassadors whose Governments had already been told much to their annoyance that a vote against the Reverse Important Question resolution would be regarded as an unfriendly act and that they had better think of their relations with the United States, were jointly lectured and threatened with retaliatory measures if they did not do as they were told, they were all so incensed that it was decided to demonstrate Nordic solidarity and vote as a bloc against postponement. In other cases the Americans appear to have overestimated their powers of persuasion and to have believed that they had secured firmer promises of support than the other parties believed they had given. Thus, up to the time of the vote they were not only publicly predicting victory, but they appear to have succumbed to their own propaganda so that they seemed genuinely surprised and shocked by their defeat.

28. The Americans played a lone hand in all this making much less use than they might have done of their allies. The Australians privately complained at the general confusion and lack of tactical planning. They told us that the Americans would not even discuss the possibility of defeat on anything and therefore would make no contingency plans. This confusion among their supporters was evident the night that the voting took place. For instance there was an obvious lack of co-ordination on who should make which procedural move.

29. In contrast to the Americans the Albanians, who were responsible for tactics on the other side, were almost inert. They made their usual propaganda speeches in support of Peking but gave little evidence of lobbying or concerting tactics with their allies. It was not for instance clear why they did not press for a vote on the Friday evening or even Saturday, since it was known that the Americans were trying to delay the proceedings in order to round up a few more waverers. The Algerians were particularly critical of the Albanian performance, but it is said that the latter were acting on Chinese instructions. Peking, it seems did not wish to appear to be making any special effort in case they were once more defeated. Such lobbying as did take place was the work of the Yugoslavs and the Pakistanis presumably on their own initiatives. The latter were probably more concerned than any other member of the United Nations to see Peking seated; theirs was the most effective speech made by a co-sponsor of the Albanian resolution, and they played a leading role in the various procedural moves when voting took place.

The Night of the Vote and the Post Mortem

30. The voting took place on the evening of Monday the 25th of October. The vote as I have said could have been taken the previous Friday evening but the President had adjourned the meeting early, probably at the suggestion of the Americans who

---

10 Cyprus Foreign Minister, 1960-72.

had told the Secretariat that they would prefer to postpone the vote. So that when on Monday afternoon Tunisia and Saudi Arabia respectively introduced new resolutions, which were variations on the two China's theme and when the latter proposed postponing the voting on all resolutions until the following day to enable the new resolutions to be studied, this was generally believed to be an American manoeuvre. (Whether the Americans inspired Ambassador Baroody as well as the Tunisian is debatable. They certainly failed to control him.) Consequently when the proposal for postponement was challenged by the Albanian co-sponsors and voted down the result was seen as a first defeat for the Americans. Although they won the next round, the vote on a motion for priority for their procedural Reverse Important Question resolution, this had been expected and so did not cause undue despondency to the other side. The next and key vote was on the Reverse Important Question resolution itself and when this was defeated 54-59-15 it was clear that the Americans had lost. No-one doubted that the Albanian resolution would win the simple majority which was all it now required. The Americans in a last ditch attempt to save the day requested separate voting on the two substantive paragraphs of the Albanian resolution on the not unreasonable belief that a number of states which were prepared to vote for the resolution as a whole would have preferred to abstain, or even vote against, the second paragraph which called in insulting terms for the expulsion of the Chinese Nationalist representatives. But at this late stage, with no advance preparation and poor presentation by Ambassador Bush the manoeuvre carried no conviction and was defeated by a substantial margin. The Chinese Nationalist after a brief and dignified intervention, then withdrew with his delegation. Immediately afterwards the Albanian resolution was put to the vote and adopted by 76-35 with 17 abstentions; i.e. more than the two-thirds majority which would have been required had the Reverse Important Question resolution been adopted, (for details of voting see my tel. 1476).[11]

31. I have already described in my letter of the 28th of October to Mr Parsons the emotional and undignified reaction of some delegations at the moment of victory. It must have been a distasteful spectacle, particularly to American television audiences, but it was I think unfortunate that Americans from the President down chose to treat the jubilation as a personal slight on the American Government and people. There was, of course, an element of *Schadenfreude*[12] at this proof that even a super-power could not 'go it alone', but satisfaction that the Americans had been unable to manipulate the General Assembly against the wishes of the majority was not in itself an ignoble reaction. And what the Americans failed to recognise much less admit was that the majority of members voted as they did, not to annoy the Americans or to please the Communists, but because they had come to believe that the People's Republic of China should be represented in the United Nations and that the procedural devices hitherto used to keep them out were no longer tolerable. The Americans on this issue were isolated from most of Western Europe including NATO allies, from their northern neighbour Canada and, ironically, from the mother countries of the three main ethnic groups in New York: Ireland, Israel and Italy.

11 Not printed.
12 Pleasure derived from another person's misfortune.

32. As I reported in my telegram referred to above, the Americans were not only surprised by their defeat, they were also bitter over their 'betrayal'. In a typical comment Ambassador Bush hoped that the United Nations would not 're-live this moment of infamy'—echoing infelicitously President Roosevelt's description of Pearl Harbour. Both he and Mr Rogers castigated certain states which had allegedly gone back on firm commitments to support the Americans. However, as noted above, the degree of firmness of some of these commitments is debatable. The Permanent Representative of Ireland,[13] which had been listed among the offenders by US official spokesmen, forced Mr Bush in a sharp exchange of letters to concede that Ireland had made no prior commitment on voting. Trinidad and Tobago and Botswana, two other states accused of duplicity, were equally adamant that they had not deceived the Americans as to their voting intentions. We were not among those cited since we had made our voting position clear from the outset.

The Chinese Arrive

33. Immediately after the vote the Secretary-General sent a telegram to Chi Peng-fei, the acting Minister of Foreign Affairs of the People's Republic of China, informing him of the result and inviting Peking to nominate a delegation. The Chinese replied that their delegation would be led by Chiao Kuan-hua, Vice Minister for Foreign Affairs, and that the Permanent Representative would be Huang Hua. (For further details of the delegation see my tel 1520.)[14] The Chinese delegation arrived in New York on the 11th of November and have installed themselves in the Hotel Roosevelt until suitable accommodation can be found. During the first few days their every movement was the subject of almost morbid interest and curiosity in the American press. They might have been Martians judging by the way in which even their breakfast menus and table manners (good) were deemed worthy of report in normally serious papers. It was one of the many paradoxes of this strange period that while US leaders fulminated over the result of the vote, New York stores publicised displays of goods from mainland China and American dress designers were inspired by Chinese fashions. While most of the latter bore little relation to the drab unisex suits worn by the members of the Chinese delegation, purists were offered authentic Mao suits with washing instructions enabling them to achieve the faded appearance of the originals.

34. The Chinese delegation formally took their seats in the General Assembly on the 15th of November when the whole day was spent in effusive speeches of welcome (my tel. 1626).[15] They participated for the first time in the Security Council on the 23rd of November when it met to consider a complaint by Senegal against Portugal. The occasion was something of an anti-climax. The Americans having accorded the Security Council seat to the People's Republic of China in their own draft resolution could hardly object, even if they had not been on record in 1950 as regarding the question of Chinese credentials as procedural and thus not subject to the veto. And the Chinese Nationalist delegation by its withdrawal spared the Council the final embarrassment of dealing with an attempted Nationalist veto which

---

13 Mr (Cornelius) Con Cremin.
14 Not printed.
15 No. 282.

had earlier seemed a possibility. In the event the Secretary-General reported to the President that he considered that the telegram appointing Ambassador Huang Hua and his deputy provided adequate provisional credentials (S/10382) and the subject was not even formally raised in the Council at the beginning of the meeting.

35. The United Nations in voting at long last to seat the representatives of the People's Republic of China took a step that was both right and overdue. It could not be regarded as a world organisation so long as China, a nuclear power with a population amounting to nearly a quarter of the world's population was debarred from its deliberations. Moreover, the absence of the People's Republic of China had imposed limitations on the United Nation's ability to deal with certain subjects, for example disarmament and Vietnam. But whether the Chinese advent will in general help the conduct of business at the United Nations is another matter—and one on which I shall be reporting separately. They will certainly do their best to make life more difficult for the two super powers and especially for what one of the Chinese Mission's recent press releases described as 'Soviet revisionist social-imperialism whose ferocious features can never be camouflaged by any flowery words of Malik.'

36. I am sending copies of this Despatch to Her Majesty's Ambassadors in Washington, Paris, Moscow and Tokyo; Her Majesty's Chargé d'Affaires Peking; the British High Commissioners at Ottawa, Canberra and Wellington; the United Kingdom Permanent Representative to the Office of the United Nations at Geneva; and to the Governor of Hong Kong.

I have, etc,
C. T. CROWE

No. 301

Mr Addis (Peking) to Sir A. Douglas-Home, 4 February 1972, 10.20 a.m.[1]
Tel. No. 77 Immediate, Confidential (FCO 21/986, FEC 3/548/1A)

Your Tel No. 30.[2]

1. Ch'iao Kuan-Hua received me this afternoon. I said that since the last meeting with Vice-Minister Han Nien-Lung ministers had undertaken a very full and thorough review of the whole question. Great progress had been made in the talks already and the difference between us had been narrowed down to the text of a supplementary oral statement to be used by the British Government in Parliament and elsewhere in answer to questions about our position on Taiwan and to one phrase in that statement. Ch'iao did not comment but indicated assent.

2. I then informed him that because they sincerely desired to improve relations and remove the last remaining obstacle to agreement the British Government were prepared in future no longer to use the formula that the status of Taiwan was

1 Repeated for information to Hong Kong and Washington.
2 No. 298.

undetermined. I said that instead we would use the formulation given in paragraph two of your telegram No. 106 to Washington,³ explaining that the two principal points were the reaffirmation of the Cairo and Potsdam Declarations and the statement that we consider the question of Taiwan to be a matter for the Chinese people themselves to settle and that the first sentence of the formula was by way of introduction to those two main points. We thought this, together with the closure of the Consulate would be seen to indicate a change of attitude on our part. Even if pressed we would not elaborate on the proposed new formulation. I then handed over the text of the new formula in writing.

3. Ch'iao said the Chinese Government would study my communication and reply as soon as possible. He asked about what he called the 'promotion' of the Vice-Consul at Tamsui⁴ in Duffy's place and was told that he had simply remained in charge after Duffy's departure. We stood by our intention to remove the Consulate as part of the agreement. Ch'iao appeared to accept this.

4. The meeting was brief and businesslike. Ch'iao was personally very cordial. He listened most attentively throughout and clearly took in every single point but he did not reveal by the least sign what his reactions were. His only comment of any possible significance was 'Your intention is good, but as many British understand the Chinese adopt a very careful attitude to this question. I believe that a reasonable settlement should be found as a result of common efforts on both sides.' I replied that on our side we were indeed making a very great effort.⁵

---

3 This was the same formula set out in paragraph 4 of the memorandum to the DOP Committee (No. 296).
4 Mr Joseph Featherstone.
5 Mr Addis was summoned at short notice by Vice-Minister Chiao Kuan-hua on 18 February to be told that although the Chinese Government welcomed the commitment to no longer publicly stating that the status of Taiwan was undetermined, the proposed revised formula for an oral statement could 'easily lead to misconceptions'. They proposed a revision to this formula, the final sentence of which read: 'We think that the Taiwan question is China's internal affair and it is for the Chinese people themselves to settle it'. Chiao stated that if the British believed the question of Taiwan was for the Chinese people to decide, then 'it necessarily and logically followed that the question of Taiwan was China's internal affair'. Commenting on the meeting, Mr Addis thought they could now 'clinch the deal at once' by accepting that the Taiwan question is China's 'internal affair'. He thought there was force in the Chinese argument and it was significant they were being given a chance to reach an agreement before the visit of President Nixon, after which there was a risk that the Chinese terms may harden (Peking tel Nos. 116 and 119, 18 February 1972). Sir A. Douglas-Home accepted the formula except for the one word 'internal' in the last sentence, which he said should be omitted or rephrased to read: 'We think that the Taiwan question should be settled internally by the Chinese people' (FCO tel. No. 98 to Peking, 18 February 1972).

No. 302

Mr Addis (Peking) to Sir A. Douglas-Home, 19 February 1972, 9.05 a.m.[1]
Tel. No. 120 Flash, Confidential (FCO 21/986, FEC 3/548/1A)

Your Tel No. 98:[2] Ambassadorial Negotiations.

Ch'iao received me at 11 this morning. I told him that Ministers had given careful consideration to the formula proposed at the last meeting and that they were prepared to accept it in its entirety with the exception of one difficult phrase, namely the reference to the Taiwan question being China's internal affairs. I said the word 'internal affair' seemed to us to have legal implications and come too close to a reversal of our previous position on the judicial status of Taiwan. To use these words would therefore embarrass us, which Ch'iao had assured us the Chinese had no wish to do.

2. We would be prepared to accept the Chinese formula without the word 'internal'. The 'China's affair' would be practically the same as 'China's internal affair' but would avoid the strictly legal implication. Alternatively we could retain the word 'internal' but with the sentence recast in a different order and I handed Ch'iao the form of words given in para two of your telegram under reference.

3. Ch'iao said he was grateful for our prompt reply. We now offered 2 possible alternatives but he was bound to say frankly that he regarded neither version as appropriate. He did not think it was very tenable to say that to except 'internal' would come close to reversing a previous position. Ch'iao had done some study in logic and was not convinced by the reasoning of our lawyers. He went on to say that the Chinese formula had been put forward in a spirit of willingness to reach agreement. If it was not acceptable he was frankly disappointed. The same argument applied to the second variant. Since I had asked whether either of these 2 alternatives was acceptable to the Chinese government, he was bound in frankness to say that he would it would be very difficult.

4. Ch'iao said he would like to leave aside the text for the moment and say something about his personal impressions. In his dealings with British friends, Mr Denson, Lord Trevelyan,[3] Mr Godber and Mr MacDonald, he had always been perplexed why it should be that the British Government should insist so hard on a so-called legal position on a question which was so easy to resolve. He hoped that I would report these comments of his fully to the British Government and he wished to reaffirm the Chinese desire to seek agreement acceptable to both sides, but they could not consider the 2 alternatives as they stood.

5. I said that on the legal position I had at our last meeting informed him of an important change. By giving up a formula on the undetermined status of Taiwan we were prepared to allow a change of attitude to be seen. I understood this change of attitude to mean that we were shifting our position from a purely legal view of the question to a broader political standpoint. This represented a big step for us. In

---

1 Repeated for information immediate to Washington; and routine to Hong Kong (personal for Governor).
2 Not printed. See No. 301, note 5.
3 Humphrey Trevelyan, British Chargé d'Affaires, Peking, 1953-55.

making this change we could not take a stand which would run counter to our previous position. We could make a shift but not a reversal of our position.

6. Ch'iao then said with some passion that in the first paragraph of our exchange of notes we had agreed that we respected China's sovereignty and territorial integrity; we acknowledged China's position on Taiwan; we agreed that the government of the People's Republic of China was the sole legal government of China; we reaffirmed that our views on the Cairo and Potsdam Declarations had not changed; furthermore we agreed that the Taiwan question was a question for the Chinese people themselves to settle. But we stopped short of agreeing that Taiwan was China's internal affair. The implication of saying that the Taiwan question was China's internal affair was that interference by foreign countries would not be permissible. So our refusal to use that phrase obliged the Chinese to reflect why we were so insistent on this point. Ch'iao said that as a student of logic, but never of law, he believed that on the basis of stated facts and reason, our stand was untenable.

7. He went on to say that the Chinese side were willing to continue the discussions. He had today stated their views very frankly and hoped that the British Government would give them serious consideration. He again repeated their desire to reach agreement.

8. I then asked him whether we might together, by discussing the texts before us, be able to find a form of words which might be acceptable to both sides and I suggested 'the question of Taiwan is China's own affair' or 'the question of Taiwan is China's affair to be settled internally by the Chinese people themselves'. I emphasised that I offered these suggestions by my own responsibility and said I would be glad to consider any proposals from his side. Ch'iao said he did not think either of these two new formulations could answer the questions he had just put but that he did not wish to repeat what had already been said. He was not saying that we had made no concessions and he referred to our change of position on 'the undetermined status of the Taiwan'. He said with regard to the words 'internal affair' the Chinese side insisted on their stand, and had stated their reasons. I said that I hoped that he would give further consideration to the two alternatives which you had instructed me to make and see if they might form an acceptable basis for an agreement. Ch'iao said that they did not agree with our revisions but the Chinese never refuse to continue to consider proposals. Our relations should be put on a clear-cut and unambiguous basis. The Chinese could not make any concessions on the phrase 'Taiwan is China's internal affair'. Mr Heath had recently said the world is changing. Why should we allow the lawyers to dictate our policy?

No. 303

Mr Addis (Peking) to Sir A. Douglas-Home, 19 February 1972, 9.45 a.m.[1]
Tel. No. 121 Flash, Confidential (FCO 21/986, FEC 3/548/1A)

MIPT.[2]

We have come to the end of exploring this particular avenue. We can have agreement now by accepting the Chinese formula that the Taiwan question is China's internal affair. But I see no hope of devising some variant formula to get around the difficulty.

2. The choice I must put before you therefore is the plain one between agreement to the Chinese wording and accepting an indefinite postponement of an exchange of Ambassadors.

3. The only alternative for us now might be to go back to the original Chinese proposal for an acknowledgement of Taiwan as a province of China, in which case no supplementary oral statement would be required, but I presume that this would be no easier for us than to except the Taiwan question as China's internal affair. I cannot conceive of any fresh line of approach to the problem which could remove the difficulty. So much ground has already been covered in these discussions that we would be certain to come back to the same central pocat [*sic*]even were it framed under another form of words. The formula 'China's internal affair' is certainly the most innocuous from our point of view that we are ever likely to get.

4. Ch'iao was genuinely unable to see why we cannot accept the Taiwan question as China's internal affair if we are prepared admit that it is a matter for the Chinese people to settle themselves. I pressed the legal objection as hard as I could but he really could not see it at all. There is a conceptual difficulty for the Chinese here. It is not in their tradition to be bound by purely legal considerations. Furthermore they attach real importance to the form of words and do not find it easy to get round a genuine difficulty by altering the wording.

5. I have a great deal of sympathy with Ch'iao's position on this. Like him I was trained as a logician and not a jurist. If the Taiwan question is for the Chinese people themselves to settle surely it is also China's internal affair?

6. You will note that in putting our case I was careful not to represent it as a final and inalterable answer but as a step in a continuing frank exchange of views. There would thus be no embarrassment at this end if after further consideration you accept the Chinese formulation.

---

1 Repeated for information immediate to Washington, and routine to Hong Kong.
2 No. 302.

No. 304

Sir A. Douglas-Home to Mr Addis (Peking), 19 February 1972, 11.35 a.m.[1]
Tel. No. 100 Immediate, Confidential (FCO 21/986, FEC 3/548/1A)

Your telnos. 120 and 121: Ambassadorial negotiations.

Is our understanding correct that Ch'iao Kuan-hua is not giving further consideration to our formula and that it is for us to take the next step?

2. It will clearly now take some time to consider further instructions for you.

1 Repeated for information to Washington and Hong Kong (personal for the Governor).

No. 305

Mr Addis (Peking) to Sir A. Douglas-Home, 21 February 1972, 3.55 a.m.[1]
Tel. No. 123 Immediate Confidential (FCO 21/986, FEC 3/548/1A)

Your Tel. No. 100: Ambassadorial negotiations.

It was only for tactical reasons that towards the end of our discussion I asked Ch'iao to consider our proposals further. Thus if they do have second thoughts they can come back with further comments. But we can take it as virtually certain that they will not. The next move is clearly up to us.

1 Repeated for information routine to Washington and Hong Kong (personal for the Governor).

No. 306

Mr Morgan (Lima) to Sir A. Douglas Home, 23 February 1972, 2.30 p.m.
Tel. No. 33 Priority, Confidential (FCO 21/986, FEC 3/548/1A)

From Renwick.

Your Telno. 22: Exchange of Ambassadors with China.

1. Minister of State is sorry that the Chinese have raised this further very narrow point when we have come so near to agreement. However he feels that the latest Chinese demand presents no political as opposed to legal problem and that having swallowed a fairly substantial political camel it would be a pity to strain at a relatively small legal gnat.

2. Mr Godber would like to be kept informed of developments.

No. 307

Minute from Mr Morgan to Mr Wilford, 24 February 1972
Confidential (FCO 21/986, FEC 3/548/1A)

Exchange of Ambassadors with China

1. Peking telegrams nos. 120 and 121.[1]

2. I have looked again at the Chinese version of the key sentence (Peking tel. No. 117,[2] last sentence) in the Chinese formula. Instead of translating this as 2 propositions it can equally well be put as one. Thus instead of:

'We think that the Taiwan question is China's internal affair *and it is for the Chinese people themselves to settle it*', it could be translated as:

'We think that the Taiwan question is China's internal affair to be settled by the Chinese people themselves.'

3. I have put this to Mr Addis who agrees (Peking tel. No. 133).[3] Although the text was given to us by the Chinese in English as well it would be entirely unreasonable for them to turn down a version in our own language of their unaltered draft.

4. This slight variation makes it easier for us to argue that the significance we attach to the words 'China's internal affair' must be seen in the context of the sentence as a whole as meaning no more than that we regard the question as one to be settled by the Chinese people themselves.

5. The Prime Minister undertook at Bermuda to keep in touch with the Americans in this matter.

6. A draft telegram to Washington is submitted.

7. Sir V. Evans and North America Department concur.[4]

J.A.L. MORGAN

1 No. 302 and No. 303 respectively.
2 Not printed.
3 Not printed.
4 Mr Royle noted: 'Mr Morgan has done well. Let us hope it will work.'

No. 308

Sir A. Douglas-Home to the Earl of Cromer (Washington)
25 February 1972, 11.25 a.m.[1]
Tel. No. 469 Immediate, Confidential (FCO 21/986, FEC 3/548/1A)

Peking telegrams numbers 120 and 121:[2] Ambassadorial negotiations.

1. On balance I consider that we should now be prepared to accept the Chinese formulae as set out in Peking telegrams numbers 117 and 118.[3] Our English translation of the Chinese text given in the last sentence of Peking telegram number 117

1 Repeated for information immediate to Peking, Lima (for Mr Godber) and routine to Hong Kong.
2 No. 302 and No. 303 respectively.
3 Not printed.

would however be: 'We think that the Taiwan question is China's internal affair to be settled by the Chinese people themselves.'

2. If we are asked in Parliament or elsewhere to explain what significance we attach to the words 'China's internal affair' we would say that they must be seen in the context of the sentence as a whole as meaning no more than that we regard the question as one to be settled by the Chinese people themselves.

3. I should like to instruct Mr Addis to inform the Chinese of our agreement after President Nixon's departure from China.

4. I should therefore like you to give the Americans a full account of Mr Addis's two recent conversations with the Chinese and tell them our intention. In doing so, we should be grateful to learn about what discussion of Taiwan and other matters took place with the Chinese during the President's visit.[4]

4 In Washington Tel. No. 734 of 1 March, Lord Cromer confirmed that the President, Mr Kissinger and Mr Rogers were all aware of, and agreed with, how the Taiwan issue would be handled in the negotiations. They were also grateful that the Government had delayed action in Peking until after the departure of the Presidential party (FCO 21/987).

No. 309

Mr Addis (Peking) to Sir A. Douglas-Home, 4 March 1972, 6.15 a.m.
Tel. No. 168 Immediate, Confidential (FCO 21/987, FEC 3/548/1B)

Your Tel No. 138:[1] Ambassadorial Negotiations.

1. Ch'iao Kuan-Hua received me this morning. I spoke as instructed. Ch'iao said he did not think our revised rendering of the last sentence made any difference to the Chinese text. But since the Chinese Government attached considerable importance to the question, he would need a little time to consider and report to his Government.

2. We nevertheless went on to review all the technical procedures which would require decision. Ch'iao agreed that an announcement could be made at 1530 GMT (23.30 hours Peking time) to enable you to make the announcement in the form of statement in the house. The Chinese themselves would broadcast the communique at 2330 and carry it in the following day's newspapers.

3. Ch'iao said the Chinese had no strong feelings about the form agreement on the joint communiqué would take. He suggested that both sides prepare both an exchange of notes and a simple statement. I said we did not mind either and we agreed we would decide which to use at the next meeting. I gave him for consideration the text of the communiqué with formal topping and tailing as in your Tel. No. 701 of 1971.[2] Ch'iao also asked if I would write him a letter, which he would acknowledge, setting out the oral assurance. He confirmed that this would remain a confidential exchange between the two Governments.

1 Not printed. In FCO Tel. No 132 to Peking, dated 2 March, Mr Addis was instructed to take action on the lines of FCO telegram 469 (No. 308).
2 Not printed.

4. I then raised the question of my own *agrément*. Ch'iao said that the Chinese would be happy to accept my nomination but formal reasons would like to have a written request for it. I said I would bring it to our next meeting. He may have forgotten the Chinese had already received this in the aide-memoire given to Mr Pei Tsien-Chang by Mr Royle on 22 June 1971. I will nevertheless give Ch'iao in writing the first sentence of the aide memoire to which he can reply on the date of signature. We agreed that the words 'and Ambassadors will be exchanged within . . . months' should be omitted from the communiqué.

5. We arranged to meet again on Monday 6 March when he would tell me the result of his reference to higher authority. Assuming it was favourable we would then go on to settle the practical arrangements. Ch'iao proposed that we meet thereafter on Monday 13 March for signature and agreed that an announcement could be made at 15:30 GMT on that day. Ch'iao explained that the Chinese side also have their own procedures to go through.

6. I do not see anything sinister in Ch'iao deferring his final concurrence until Monday 6 March. It is just that on this matter he cannot agree even the smallest change in an approved text on procedure without reference to Chou En-lai.

7. I should be grateful to know by 2200 GMT 6 March if what we have provisionally agreed is acceptable.

No. 310

Mr Addis (Peking) to Sir A. Douglas-Home, 6 March 1972, 10.05 a.m.
Tel. No. 174 Immediate, Confidential (FCO 21/987, FEC 3/548/1B)

Your Telno 141:[1] Exchange of Ambassadors.

1. Chiao Kuan-hua received me this afternoon and informed me without any preliminaries that the Chinese were content with the English version of the oral assurance. We could therefore proceed to a formal agreement to be signed on 13 March. I told him that this would also be acceptable to you.

2. We agreed that rather than exchange notes we would both sign copies of the joint statement in English and Chinese, the final text which is in MIFT.[2] We agreed that we would omit the reference to the period within which Ambassadors would be exchanged. We also agreed to meet on 13 March in the afternoon (Peking time) to sign the communique before the announcement at 15.30 GMT. The communiqué would be entitled 'Communiqué on the Agreement between the Government of the People's Republic of China and the Government of the United Kingdom and Northern Ireland on an exchange of Ambassadors.' I handed over the request for my own *agrement*. Chiao said that this was agreed but that he would give me a formal reply on 13 March. I also handed over to him, in the form of a letter, the oral assurance (see my Telno 176).[3]

1 Not printed.
2 Not printed.
3 Not printed.

3. I said that I was glad that we had reached this point after much hard work. Chiao replied that our final agreement was something that we should both be happy about. I said that as he had himself pointed out at an earlier meeting the real point of our negotiations was not so much an exchange of Ambassadors as an improvement in the state of relations between our two countries. Chiao replied that he hoped that the agreement would mark the beginning of a development in our relations. I said that this was both our hope and our intention.

4. It would be useful if I could let the Chinese know soon when my credentials can be expected to reach Peking.

5. I will send a Flash telegram immediately after signature. In the meantime I should be grateful for a copy, Immediate, of your telegram informing other interested posts about the agreement: it would also be helpful to know if you intend to make the statement in the House yourself and, if so, for a verbatim report immediately after the announcement has been made.

No. 311

Sir A. Douglas-Home to HM Representatives Overseas
9 March 1972, 12.05 p.m.

Guidance Tel. No. 269 Immediate, Confidential (FCO 21/987, FEC 3/548/1B)

Exchange of Ambassadors with China

1. We have now reached agreement with the Chinese for an exchange of Ambassadors. This will be announced by the publication of an agreed statement at 1530 GMT on 13 March. At the same time the name of our Ambassador Designate at Peking will be announced. For your own information at this stage, our Ambassador will be Mr J. M. Addis the present British Chargé d'Affaires. The Chinese have not yet proposed the name of their Ambassador.

Instructions for Use

2. The whole of this guidance is confidential until the publication of the agreed statement. We are informing some countries in confidence before publication (see paragraph 3 below): no action in advance is required of posts unless specifically instructed. After publication you may draw as appropriate on paragraphs 1, 4, 6, 7, 10 and 11 (attributable). You should not volunteer anything about Australia's agreement to look after residual British interests on Taiwan or the CBI agreement about trade assistance (paragraphs 8 and 9) but the information may be used unattributably in answer to questions. Paragraphs 3 and 5, are for your own information only. Paragraph 12 may be used unattributably with suitable contacts.

3. Before publication we shall be informing the High Commissions or Embassies in London of the following countries: United States, Canada, Australia, New Zealand, Japan, Sweden, Norway and Denmark, and members of the WEU. In addition I am sending a personal message to Mr Rogers and Mr Royle is sending messages to Signor Angelo Salizoni, Italy; Herr Karl Moersch, Germany; and M. Jean de Librowski, France. The Prime Minister, will send a short personal message to Chou En-lai expressing pleasure that the negotiations have been satisfactorily concluded.

The Joint Statement

4. The statement (text in MIFGT)[1] contains an undertaking we have given to the Chinese that we shall withdraw our official representative from Taiwan. We have not subscribed to Peking's claim that Taiwan is a province of China. The statement in 'acknowledging the position of the Chinese Government that Taiwan is a province of the People's Republic of China' does not imply acceptance of the Chinese claim.

5. We have however privately agreed with the Chinese that we shall no longer express in public the view which we have long held that sovereignty over Taiwan is undetermined. We have held this view since the Japanese Peace Treaty provided for the relinquishment of sovereignty by Japan in 1951 and believe that it remains legally correct. Nevertheless the Chinese made it clear during the course of our discussions that they would not agree to an exchange of ambassadors unless we undertook not to continue to maintain this view in public (see for instance Neville Maxwell's interview with Chou En-lai in *The Sunday Times* of 5 December 1971).[2] It has therefore been decided that in answer to any future questions about our attitude to the status of Taiwan we should limit our reply to the wording given in paragraph 12(*c*) below. We will refuse to be drawn further. In reply to questions you should act similarly. You should not go beyond this form of words. If pressed you should explain that they speak for themselves and that you have nothing to add. If asked in Parliament or elsewhere what significance we attach to the words 'China's internal affair' we would say that they must be seen in the context of the sentence as a whole as meaning no more than that we regard the question as one to be settled by the Chinese people themselves.

6. The Consulate at Tamsui and the office of the Consulate at Taipei will close for business 7 days after the date of the announcement. The withdrawal of UK-based staff will take longer, but we expect the process to be completed and the staff to have left Taiwan within six weeks.

7. The issue of visas for Hong Kong and other countries and Colonial Territories was one of the Consulate's busiest tasks. Arrangements are now being made for the issue of visas by the Immigration Department in Hong Kong to Taiwanese wishing to visit Hong Kong and the UK. Applications for visas will be ferried to the Immigration Department (which will also process applications to visit the UK) by the sea and air carrier companies with whom the applicant proposes to travel.

8. The CBI have agreed to consider how any necessary assistance to British firms wishing to do business with Taiwan can be given following the closure of the consulate. It should be borne in mind in this connection that many of our trade competitors such as the West Germans whose trade with Taiwan is larger than ours have no form of resident representation.

9. The Australian Government has undertaken to assume informal responsibility for the protection of our remaining interests in Taiwan.

Historical Background

10. On 6 January 1950 HMG was the first Western government to recognise the PRC. The Chinese continued to insist on various preconditions to proposal for the establishment of diplomatic relations. Discussions have been held at sporadic

---

1 Not printed.
2 See No. 290.

intervals since 1950 but no progress was made until 1971. Our respective Missions are not Embassies and the Heads of the Missions are Chargés d'Affaires. Early in 1971, following the improvement in relations after the release of most of the British subjects detained in China, we proposed the resumption of discussions. We made it clear that there were no obstacles on our side to an exchange of ambassadors. Discussions have been protracted because of Chinese insistence on introducing new elements into the negotiations at successive stages.

11. British consular representation in Taiwan dates from 1860. It continued during the period of Japanese rule from 1895 until the Second World War. In 1946 the Nationalist Government moved there from the mainland. Exequaturs[3] have not been sought from Nationalist authorities since this would have implied recognition. British consuls did business only with the local provincial authorities and have had no dealings with the Nationalist 'Government' in Taipei.

Unattributable Answers to Questions

12. (*a*) What will be the benefits of an exchange of Ambassadors? The presence of an Ambassador in Peking will give us greater access to the top level leadership of the Chinese Government and will place our diplomatic representation on a level with that of other countries. It will mark a further step in the continued improvement of our relations with China, and should lead to increased commercial, political, and cultural exchanges.

(*b*) Are we abandoning Taiwan? There is no question of our having 'abandoned' Taiwan. We do not recognise the Nationalist authorities on Taiwan and have not done so since 1950. The continued presence of our consulate did not imply recognition. Since 1961 we voted for the substantive (Albanian) resolution calling for the seating of Peking at the United Nations and the expulsion of the Nationalist representatives. We believed that the exclusion of the Chinese People's Republic made more difficult the solution of many pressing world problems. We therefore welcomed the General Assembly's decision in October 1971 to seat the representatives of Peking. In our view the exclusion of the representatives of 14 million inhabitants of Taiwan is a lesser evil than the continued exclusion of the representatives of 750 million Chinese.

(*c*) What is HMG's view of the status of Taiwan? The Government of the United Kingdom acknowledges the position of the Chinese Government that Taiwan is a province of the People's Republic of China. Both the Government of the People's Republic of China and Taipei maintain that Taiwan is a part of China. We held the view both at Cairo and Potsdam that Taiwan should be restored to China. That view has not changed. We think that the Taiwan question is China's internal affair to be settled by the Chinese people themselves.

(*d*) Has our view of the status of Taiwan changed? The statement above reflects the reality of the position. The expression 'The Taiwan Question is China's internal affair' must be seen in the context of the sentence as a whole as meaning no more than that we regard the question as one to be settled by the Chinese people themselves.

---

3 Official recognition by a Government of a consul or other representative of a foreign state.

No. 312

Mr Addis (Peking) to Sir A. Douglas-Home, 13 March 1972, 8.45 a.m.[1]
Tel. No. 201 Flash, Confidential (FCO 21/987, FEC 3/548/1B)

My Telno 109[2] (not to all): Exchange of Ambassadors.

1. Ch'iao Kuan-Hua and I signed copies of the communiqué in English and Chinese at 4 p.m. Peking time today as previously arranged. I also handed over the text of our oral assurance and received Ch'iao's acknowledgement. Ch'iao repeated for the record that the Chinese Government were happy to accept my formal nomination as Ambassador.

1 Repeated flash for information to Hong Kong (Personal for Governor) and for information immediate to Washington.
2 Not printed.

No. 313

Sir M. MacLehose (Hong Kong) to Mr Addis (Peking)
13 March 1972. 9.30 a.m.[1]
Tel. No. 13 Routine, Restricted (FCO 21/987)

Personal for Addis from MacLehose.
Your telegram number 201 to FCO.
Heartiest congratulations. It was a slow start but a fast finish.

1 Repeated for information to the FCO.

APPENDIX

Joint Communique on the Agreement Between the United
Kingdom of Great Britain and Northern Ireland
and the People's Republic of China
on an Exchange of Ambassadors

1. Both confirming the principles of mutual respect for sovereignty and territorial integrity, non-interference in each other's internal affairs and equality and mutual benefit, the Government of the United Kingdom and the Government of the People's Republic of China have decided to raise the level of their respective diplomatic representatives in each other's capitals from charges d'affaires to ambassadors as from March 13, 1972.

2. The Government of the United Kingdom, acknowledging the position of the Chinese Government that Taiwan is a province of the People's Republic of China, have decided to remove their official representation in Taiwan on March 13, 1972.

3. The Government of the United Kingdom recognize the Government of the People's Republic of China as the sole legal government of China.

The Government of the People's Republic of China appreciate the above stand of the Government of the United Kingdom.

J. M. Addis

Representative of the Government of the United Kingdom of Great Britain and Northern Ireland,
Charge d'Affaires to the People's Republic of China

乔冠华

Representative of the Government of the People's Republic of China,
Vice-Minister of Foreign Affairs

中华人民共和国和大不列颠及
北爱尔兰联合王国关于互换
大使的联合公报

一、中华人民共和国政府和联合王国政府一致确认互相尊重主权和领土完整、互不干涉内政和平等互利的原则，决定自一九七二年三月十三日起将本国派驻对方首都的外交代表由代办升格为大使。

二、联合王国政府承认中国政府关于台湾是中华人民共和国的一个省的立场，决定于一九七二年三月十三日撤销其在台湾的官方代表机构。

三、联合王国政府承认中华人民共和国政府是中国的唯一合法政府。

中华人民共和国政府对联合王国政府的上述立场表示欣赏。

J. M. Addis

中华人民共和国政府　　　　大不列颠及北爱尔兰
代　　　　　表　　　　　　联合王国政府代表
外交部副部长　　　　　　　驻中华人民共和国代办

乔冠华

一九七二年三月十三日于北京

INDEX

Aden 41
Addis, John xx-xxi, 412, 419, 444, 493, 516, 538, 540-41; Ambassador designate to Peking 543; interviews at Chinese MFA 534-37, 541-43
Afghanistan 47, 307
Albania *see also* United Nations 293, 302, 306, 308, 314, 321, 526, 528-29, 531-32
Algeria 25, 210, 249, 531
Allan, James 318, 357, 402
Allen, Sir Denis 155, 159, 199, 230, 234, 240, 244, 246, 249, 266, 269, 349
Annenberg, Walter 478-79
Appleyard, Leonard 82, 314, 330, 333, 348, 363, 443
'Asian Quadrilateral' 517-21
Atomic energy/weapons 24; non-proliferation 24; Test Ban Treaty 25 373, 413, 419, 431
Australia xviii, 63, 264, 313, 411-12, 439, 452, 511, 521, 543; admission of PRC to UN 355-356, 370, 465, 485, 527-28, 530; Taipei Embassy 412, 543
Austria 353, 359, 425, 491; exchange of ambassadors with China 437

Bahrain 481, 484, 530
Bandung Conference (1955) 44-5, 525
Bank of China 33, 110, 194, 232-33, 267, 270, 425; restrictions on London staff 54, 63, 66, 73, 119-20, 122, 136, 138-39, 146, 150, 156-57, 232, 253; Singapore branch 379, 397
Bank of England 233
Baroody, Jamil 484-86, 532
Barrass, Gordon 357
Barrington, Nicholas 514
Barrymaine, Norman xiv, 143, 145, 148, 151, 160-61, 266, 393-95, 397
Beamish, Sir Tufton 367
Belgium 353, 366, 438, 485
Benn, Anthony Wedgwood 497
Bennett, William Tapley 527
Bettencourt, André 352, 354
Biafra 270
Biggs-Davison, John 392
Blackwell, John 490
Blishen, Anthony 49, 81-2, 126, 187
Bolland, Edwin 24, 28, 34, 104-6

Botswana 366, 485, 533
Bottomley, Arthur 12, 42
Bowden, Herbert xxi, 12-13, 39-40, 42, 63-4, 101-3
Boyd, John 262, 289, 315, 327, 369, 371; China-US relations 361-65
Bray, Raymond 274, 277, 327
Brewer, Frank 126, 290, 315
Brezhnev, Leonid 320
BBC 10, 17, 58, 224; *Panorama* visit to China 374
British Council 340
British Missions in China *see also* UK relations with PRC ix-x, 17, 37-8, 93-4, 125, 142, 148, 155, 195-6 413, 419, 504, 514; Peking attacks on/burning xi, 56-60, 64-9, 77-82, 84, 87, 93, 95, 97, 99, 106, 111, 228, 230, 293, 338, 394, 402, 526; behaviour of Chinese staff 2, 16, 27, 58, 67, 78; commercial staff 427; communications disrupted 62, 64, 73, 92, 102; demonstrations 2, 14-16, 25-8, 54-5, 149, 154, 253; diplomatic offensive against Chinese restrictions 196-9, 204-5, 209-11, 217, 223, 227, 257-58, 260-61; exit visas xiv-xv, 66, 83, 100, 102, 107, 119-23, 126-27, 131-36, 143, 145-46, 148, 153-55, 157, 181, 185-86, 190, 196-97, 208-10, 213, 219, 223-24, 230, 234, 238, 250, 257-58, 262, 394; 'foreign friends' 26, 154; 'Operation Effigy' 48-9; press campaign against Mission 263-64; Queen's Birthday Party (1967) 26-7 (1970) 345, 354; Queen's Messengers 92, 102; residence 58, 64-5, 81, 501; restrictions on Mission staff xiii, 17, 95, 107, 109, 130-31, 135, 253, 292, 324, 326, 332-33, 335, 337, 394; staff morale 64-5, 147, 158, 190; Shanghai ix, xi, 2, 4, 8, 14-15, 161, 335; attacks on compound 3, 28-30; Chinese staff 31; closure of mission 31-3; demonstrations 2-3, 6-7, 12; exit visas 143, 161-62, 185, 202, 204-5, 303, 504, 514; Tamsui (Taiwan) ix-x, xvii, 274, 276-77, 343, 350, 354, 356-58, 367, 374, 382, 391, 404, 408-9, 411-12, 414, 421, 431-34, 444, 535; intelligence value 354, 411, 433, 492; Naval Liaison Officer 408, 411, 433; withdrawal of Consulate 409-10, 412, 414-15, 419, 428, 433-35, 439, 441, 444, 453, 455, 471, 473, 500, 508, 544
Brooke, Gerald 398

Brown, George xii, xiv, 24, 34, 37-8, 42, 53-4, 84-6, 90, 92, 94, 101-3, 121, 139; letter of support to British Mission in Peking 98; messages to Ayub Khan 63-4, 66, 90; messages to Chinese Foreign Minister 8, 10, 15, 76-7, 98, 105, 127, 135, 139, 145, 150, 168, 254; minutes to PM 106-8; protest to Chinese Chargé (May 1967) 7-8; resignation (March 1968) 142; speech in House of Commons (July 1967) 44; speech in UNGA 105
Brown, William 364
Brown, Winthrop 385-86
Bulgaria 27
Bull, Geoffrey 396
Burma 44, 47, 210, 304; Chinese communities 45; Communist Party 321; Peking Mission 102
Bury, Leslie 411
Burundi 480
Bush, George H.W. 478, 480, 483-85, 491, 527-28, 530, 532-33
Bush, Ronald 83

Cabinet (11 July 1967) 37, (9 Nov 1967) 107; Cabinet Office 282, 446; DCP Committee xiii, xviii, xxi-xxii, 12-14, 40, 84-91, 183-84, 400-1, 421, 431-33, 437-42, 446, 512-16; Ministerial Committee on Hong Kong xxii, 37, 39-43, 91, 103, 184, 282-86, 328-30
Cairo Declaration (1943) xix, 355, 460, 463, 465, 470-72, 492, 495, 500, 505, 509, 514-15, 535-36, 545
Calder, Lord Ritchie 498
Callaghan, James 12, 42, 90, 183-84
Cambodia 47, 99, 112, 270, 307, 319, 321, 342, 359, 363; Peking Mission 102
Canada xviii, 63, 187, 327, 452, 463, 473-74, 505, 511, 543; PRC representation at UN 370, 372, 410, 432, 484, 486, 526-27, 532; recognition of PRC xviii, 260, 264, 266, 307, 311, 353, 359, 410, 425, 453-54, 456, 459-60
Canton Trade Fairs 2, 100, 107, 112, 326, 331, 423, 425-26
Carrington, Lord 440
Carter, William 333
Cater, William 142, 229-30, 244-46, 250-51, 271-72, 286, 297-98
Central African Republic 359
Central Intelligence Agency (CIA) 492, 355, 363
Ceylon 187, 270, 310, 319
Chalfont, Lord 272
Chang Wen-chin 493
Channon, Paul 160
Chao Tse-min 105

Ch'en Po-ta 96-7, 496
Ch'en Yi xii, 8-10, 15-16, 20-3, 27, 45-6, 76, 83, 94, 98, 101, 105, 118, 127, 139-40, 144, 150, 168, 254, 525
Chiang Ch'ing (Jiang Qing, Madame Mao) 96-7, 111, 291, 301, 497
Chiang En-chu 348, 443
Chiang Kai-shek ix 10, 357-58, 366, 411, 454, 460, 465, 505, 520, 523, 525
Ch'iao Kuan-hua (Qiao Guanhua) xviii, xx-xxi, 452-53, 460, 468, 474-75, 487, 491, 500, 516, 533-37, 541-43
Chile 491, 526
Chinese Nationalists (KMT) see also Taiwan, United Nations 20, 178, 274, 320, 368, 372, 386, 400, 404, 412, 415, 438, 459, 461, 463, 480, 522-23, 527, 533, 545; US support 411, 467, 528
Chi Peng-fei 516, 533
Chou En-lai (Zhou Enlai) x, xvii-xviii, 20, 22-3, 46, 69, 81, 97-8, 101, 138, 142, 145, 149, 244-45, 251, 267, 293, 297, 301, 310, 315, 324, 394, 402-5, 408, 414-15, 418, 481-82, 486-87, 491-92, 494, 496-97, 499, 503, 505-6, 542-44; announces establishment of PRC (1949) 522; atomic weapons 301-2; Hong Kong xii, 142, 272, 512; meeting with Kosygin 320; regret for burning of British Mission xvii, 81, 96, 111, 402, 506; Taiwan xx, 505-7
Cockburn, David 154
Colombo, Vittorino 503
Commonwealth Office xiii, 177, 222, 237, 269; Hong Kong dept xii, 103, 333; Labour adviser 13; merger with FO xiii, 240-41, 271; statement on Hong Kong riots 6;
Confederation of British Industries (CBI) 411, 433, 435, 439, 441; agreement on trade assistance 543-44
Cradock, Percy xii, xv-xvi, 67-9, 82, 119, 127-28, 153-55, 190-92, 212, 227-28, 234, 251-52, 265-66, 268-6, 271-72, 286, 344, 350, 446, 463-64; interviews at Chinese Ministry of Foreign Affairs 179-80, 185-86, 246-48, 275-76, 281; Taiwan 276-77; visa war 252-62
Cremin, Con 533
Cromer, Lord xviii, 400, 417, 422, 441, 457, 459, 479, 482, 494, 516, 540-41
Crook, David 393
Crouch, Peter xiv, 142, 160, 266, 335-36, 338-39, 341, 349, 393, 395, 397-98
Crowe, Sir Colin xix 242, 365-66, 420, 476, 479-80, 483-86, 491, 508; China's Long March to the UN 521-34

551

Crowson, Richard 461, 464, 466, 470
Crozier, T.R.K. 31, 266, 272
Cyprus 485, 531
Czechoslovakia 270, 308, 321

Dalyell, Tam 503-4
Darwin, Henry 420-21
Davies, Emrys 97, 126
Davies, Hugh Llewelyn 357, 393
Day, Derek 272
Dayan, General Moshe 26
Defence Review Working Party 89, 282
de Gaulle, Gen Charles 249, 309, 527
de la Mare, Arthur xi, 3-4, 9, 24, 52-3, 59, 69, 92, 95, 98, 108; relations with Chinese 61-3
Demodocus, SS 142-43, 145, 148, 151, 158, 160-61, 393
Denmark 452, 491, 531
Denson, John xv, xvii, xix-xx, 47, 59, 67, 104, 153, 19, 198, 212, 296, 301-5, 315-16, 330-31, 336, 341, 345, 354, 356, 377, 387, 389, 399, 402, 456, 473-74, 481-82, 486, 491-94, 503, 506, 509, 536; British detainees 392-99; Chinese foreign policy 304-11, 337, 418; hosts Chinese officials 357-38; consultations in London (Apr 1970) 334; impressions of China 290-94; interviews at Chinese Foreign Ministry 281-82, 322, 452-53, 460, 467-68, 475; interview with Chou En-lai 402-7, 414, 491, 500-1; PRC representation at UN 360-61, 418; Sino-British relations 322-27, 382-84, 452-55, 462, 493; Tamsui Consulate 408-9; trade with China 422-28, 487-90; valedictory despatch 496-502, 528
Dent, Louis 395
Denza, Eileen 466
De Palma, Samuel 385-86, 429, 452, 484-86, 531
Department of Economic Affairs (DEA) 90
Department of Trade and Industry 376, 411, 437, 488
Douglas-Home, Sir Alec xvii-xviii, xx, 360, 366-67, 377, 412-13, 419, 434, 438, 440, 461, 466-68, 477, 535; becomes Foreign Secretary 345; confrontation prisoners 388-91; exchange of ambassadors 514-16, 540-41, 543-45; Hong Kong policy 377-82, 384, 387, 512-13; meetings with William Rogers 421, 428-29, 431, 435-36, 439; PRC representation at UN 477-79; relations with China 431-33, 438-39, 441-42, 475-76
Duff, Patrick 393, 395-97
Duffy, Thomas 409, 442, 535
Duncan Review (1969) 502

Ecuador 485
Equatorial Guinea 359, 526
Elliott (Thomas) Anthony 100, 155, 371, 385, 491, 509-10
Epstein, Elsie 393
Ethiopia 526
European Economic Community (EEC) 321, 337, 373: UK entry 487, 501, 513
Evans, Sir (William) Vincent 156, 464, 495, 540
Ewart-Briggs, Christopher 104
Export Credits Guarantee Department (ECGD) 331, 427

Fack, Robert 491
Featherstone, Joseph 535
Federal Republic of Germany (West Germany) 12, 63, 85, 308-9, 543; trade with China 411, 422, 511, 544
Finch, John 132, 155
Finland 480, 531; Peking Mission 80
Ford, Robert 396
Foreign Office: Export Promotion Dept 411-12; Far Eastern Dept xiii, xv-xvi, xix, xxi, 65-7, 240, 319-23, 330, 342-43, 385, 388, 408, 417, 444-45, 452, 461-62, 486, 504; Hong Kong Dept 332-33, 347, 412, 445; Information Research Department (IRD) 111, 266, 290, 315; memo on internal events in China 21-26; Migration and Visa Dept 412; News Dept 224, 349, 458; North America Dept xix, 343, 350-51, 368, 412, 437, 457, 461, 464, 540; Permanent Under-Secretary's Dept (PUSD) 290, 315, 412; Permanent Under-Secretary's Planning Committee 517; Personnel Operations Dept 412; Personnel Policy Dept 412; Planning Staff xvi, 240, 249, 344, 351, 445, 517-21; Research Dept 290, 327; UN (Political) Dept 343, 351, 359, 368, 412, 437, 457, 464
Formosa *see* Taiwan
France 12, 315, 452, 491, 543; admission of PRC to UN 343, 355, 480, 527, 529; aircraft for export 312; Air France 58, 376; Peking Embassy xii, 56-8, 80, 92-4; protest at treatment of British 62; relations with China 308, 322, 326 337, 501, 527; trade with China 422, 491, 511

Gallagher, M. 185, 263
Galloway, William 482
Galsworthy, Anthony xvi, 125, 222, 248, 357
Galsworthy, Sir Arthur 203, 239, 249

Gandhi, Indira 310
Garside, Roger xvi, 228, 266, 275, 302; impressions of China 289-90
Gass, Sir Michael 174
Geneva Conference on Indochina (1954) x, 214, 294, 327, 336, 525
Ghana 366, 438, 484
Gleysteen, William 364
Godber, Joseph xx, 410, 434, 460, 467, 483, 496, 508, 536, 539-40
Godden, Charles 277, 316
Gordon, Eric 393-94
Gore-Booth, Sir Paul 249
Government Communications Headquarters (GCHQ) 62
Graham, John xviii, 377, 405, 413, 419, 421, 458-59, 480
Grattan, Patrick 475-76
Green, Marshall 361, 364, 385, 421, 428-30, 492
Greene, Joseph 405-6
Greenhill, Denis xviii, 112-13, 355, 369, 421
Grey, Anthony ix, xii, xiv, 51-4, 58, 62, 77, 85, 120-25, 127, 130, 134-35, 137, 139-40, 143-45, 150-51, 154, 157, 160, 168, 177-80, 195, 205, 209, 214, 220, 225-28, 231, 239, 241, 243-44, 250-51, 261, 263-64, 266, 268-69, 275-77, 281-82, 286-88, 295, 296-98, 344, 392-93, 396, 398, 499; arrest 39; consular access 130-31, 138, 148, 162-63, 165, 168, 175, 181, 192; British journalists raise issue 272-73, 287; exchange discussions 147, 172-75, 246, 271-72; publicity campaign for release 243-44, 251-52; publishes book 337; release xvi, 288-89, 296, 300, 302-3, 316, 324, 332, 383; visits by officials xv-xvi, 170-71, 252, 275, 278, 394
Griffiths, Eldon 160
Guyana 366, 529

Han Nien-lung 493, 534
Han Hsu 493
Hart, Judith 12, 39, 42; Parliamentary statement 17
Healey, Denis 12, 39, 42, 183-84
Heath, Edward xvii, 366, 371, 373, 377, 391, 399-400, 404, 434-35, 440, 459, 475-76, 506, 510, 513-14, 537; becomes PM 345; Bermuda conference (1972) 540; Party Conference speech 1971 xvii, 487, 494; Sino-British relations 412-13, 436, 441, 543; Taiwan 433
Heath, John 155, 191
Hewitt, Peter xi, 2-3, 8, 14-15; family abused 3, 4-5, 15, 31-2; leaves China 15; report on attacks on Shanghai mission 28-33

Hibbert, Reginald 126, 290, 315
Ho Chi-Minh 104, 304, 310
Holroyd, Frank 82, wife 155
Holyoake, Sir Keith 411
Home Office 9, 38, 41, 50, 53, 61, 66, 147, 153, 155-57
Hong Kong *see also* NCNA, PRC ix, xv, 7, 12-14, 17, 45, 73-4, 83-4, 86, 88-91, 98, 103, 109, 120, 124, 129-34, 136-37, 139, 150-51, 153, 163-65, 168-69, 196, 212, 234, 252, 273-74, 299, 336, 339, 346-47, 373, 377-78, 411-12, 419, 431, 465, 472, 487, 495; arrested 'newsworkers' 50-1, 53, 59-60, 77-8, 88, 93, 130, 145, 147, 162, 177-80, 209, 220, 226, 229, 243, 257, 268, 273, 277, 279-81, 286, 294, 393; Bank of China xv, 45, 110, 297; Border Agreement (1967) 201, 209, 215, 219; border tensions 43, 208; Chinese propaganda 20, 37, 60, 93; Chinese representation 414, 416; Chungwah School 192, 199-201, 203-4, 228, 237, 246, 251, 258, 303; Communist activities/leadership 23, 59 67, 113, 116-17, 120, 135, 142, 172, 337, 375, 380; Communist press xii, 5, 50-1, 53, 59, 78, 88-9, 110, 114, 125, 129, 142, 144-45, 245, 258, 381, 396; Communist/'confrontation' prisoners xii, xvi, 120, 124, 130, 133-35, 140-41, 145-46, 154, 164-65, 171-72, 175, 181, 189, 192-93, 212, 215, 217, 222-27, 235, 239, 248, 256, 260, 275-76, 282, 294-95, 299, 323-26, 330-32, 334, 336, 339, 341, 344, 347-48, 373, 375-78, 380-85, 387-92, 394-95, 399, 401-3, 406-7, 410, 413-15, 419, 429, 432, 439, 442-43, 499-500, 504; Communist schools 110, 192-93, 199, 200-01, 212, 218-19, 238, 246-48, 279, 303-4, 339, 375, 384; contingency planning for British withdrawal xxii, 42-4, 61, 103-4, 133, 137, 282, 284-86; costs to UK 184, 283; Cultural Revolution xi, 18, 144, 212, 282; demonstrations/disturbances xi, xxi, 1, 7, 12, 14, 18, 20, 25, 29, 40-1, 113-14, 116, 141, 203, 215, 238, 258, 278, 328, 383; economic value 6, 12, 18, 21, 23, 40-1, 93, 113, 232, 283-84, 338, 344, 375, 513; emergency powers 13; Executive Council 13, 192, 378, 390; garrison 91, 183-84, 283; Government xi, xvi, 5-6, 130, 183, 215, 221, 284, 294, 296, 300, 323, 330, 347, 375, 389, 408; Gurkhas 36; Immigration Dept 412, 415, 544; impact of attacks on British Missions in China 67-9; informal UK contacts 153, 164-65, 244-46, 269, 271-72, 296-99; intelligence value 19, 283, 344, 373, 492, 513; KMT activities 115; Kowloon

disturbances xi, 5, 14, 129; law and order 91, 129, 103-4, 141-42, 245; Legislative Council 13; local conditions 60-1, 208; Local Intelligence Committee 135; 'mosquito broadsheets' 91; New Territories/Kowloon lease (exp 1997) 13, 40-1, 86, 112, 116, 282, 284, 298, 328, 376, 414, 446-48, 481, 487, 512; planning for possible UK withdrawal 14, 40, 86; police 6-7, 13-14, 116-17, 279, 304, 449-51; population 114, 116; press/propaganda 206-7, 212, 219, 238, 273, 378-79, 384; refugees 19, 89, 118, 339; Prison Review Board xvi, 287, 295, 325, 332-33, 339, 375, 378, 382, 385, 389-90, 394, 398-99, 401-3, 406, 415, 419, 442; Security Forces 114, 387; Shau Tau Kok incident xxi, 35-6; sovereignty/status 12-14, 18, 93, 113, 115, 280, 284-85, 298, 328, 375, 384, 446, 481; terrorism 118; trade xv, 60, 245, 297, 427, 512; Trade Unions 13, 114, 246, 271, 303-4, 324; UK long-term policy 42-4, 61, 89, 103-4, 137-38, 184, 241, 249, 282-86, 328-30, 373-77, 384-85, 388-91, 445-51, 512-13, 520-21; US interests x, xxii, 13, 116, 182, 283-84; visits by US warships xv, 6, 19-20, 41, 43, 178, 181-82, 186, 189, 191, 193, 196, 239, 257

Hong Kong and Shanghai Banking Corporation 17, 161, 381, 393

Hopson, Donald xi-xii, xiv-xv, xxi, 54-5, 64-8, 72, 76, 82, 92-3, 95, 98-100, 105-7, 109, 118-19, 121-23, 135-37, 140, 142, 146, 149, 151-55, 163, 170, 175, 179-8, 194-95, 197, 200-1, 205, 211, 213, 222-23, 225, 233-3, 238, 240, 248, 282; account of 1967 disturbances 14-17, 25-8; application for exit visa 189-9, 198, 202, 223, 226, 239, 258; burning of British Mission 77-82; Chinese policies towards Hong Kong 17-21; Grey 177-80; impact of Cultural Revolution 44-7; interviews at Chinese Foreign Ministry 50-2, 73-4, 83, 109-11, 126-31, 139, 150-51, 153, 164, 167-69, 182, 202, 213, 257; leaves Peking (Aug 1968) 227, 262; message from Secretary of State on arrival in London 263; Operation Effigy 48-9; proposes diplomatic pressure on PRC 186-8, 198, 204-5, 223; proposes publicity for Chinese treatment of British staff 133-34, 189; protest at attacks 65; reports attack on Peking Mission 56-9, 64-5; talk with PUS 249; visa row 121-34, 157-58, 186-88

Hsieh Fu-chih 96

Hsueh [?] 50-1, 78, 83, 98, 109-10, 127, 130-31, 223, 246-8, 254-55

Hsueh P'ing 122, 172, 226, 229-30, 242-43, 250-51, 266, 268-71

Huang Hua 533-34

Hungary 491; 1956 uprising 308

Hunter, Alistair 80

Hurd, Douglas x

Hussain, Mian Arshad 224

Iliffe, Pat 53, 81, 97, 190

India 24, 27, 62, 68, 187, 211, 293, 310, 313, 491, 526; border clashes with China 97, 525; Communist Party 44; Peking Mission 81, 97, 335; relations with Soviet Union 322; Sino-Indian agreement on Tibet 293; war with Pakistan 522

Indochina 405, 407, 414, 418

Indonesia 41, 99, 211, 261, 310, 525; abortive coup (1965) 45; attack on Peking Embassy 48, 96, 102; attacks on Chinese mission in Djakarta 68; Chinese communities 19, 45; Communist Party 44-5

Intelligence *see* British Missions, Hong Kong, UK relations with PRC

International Labour Organisation 428

Iraq 25, 484

Ireland 366, 485, 526, 532-33

Israel 27, 463, 485, 532

Italy 63, 327, 474, 490-91, 503, 511, 543; PRC representation at UN 410, 526, 532; recognition of PRC 311, 353, 359, 410, 425, 454, 456, 460

Jamieson, Kenneth 480, 503

Japan 12, 24, 60, 63, 85, 187, 362, 368, 433, 438-39, 452, 455, 458, 461, 467, 481, 484, 517-18, 543; aircraft 312; defence 518-20; economy 310, 517, 519; Peace Treaty (San Francisco Treaty, 1951) xi, 355, 463, 470, 506, 514, 544; PRC admission to UN 517-18, 521, 527-28, 530; relations with China 321, 418, 519; surrender of Taiwan (1945) 355, 463, 471, 506, 514; trade with China 415, 422-23, 425, 511; US nuclear commitment 517

Jardine Matheson 489

Jay, Douglas 12, 42

Jay, K.C. 297-99

Jenkins, Alfred 361, 363, 371

Jenkins, Roy 12, 37-8, 42, 50, 53-4, 72, 90, 108, 157, 183, 232, 394

Johnson, President Lyndon B. 26

Johnston, David xvii, 265, 270, 339, 349, 395, 397-98, 499; imprisoned for espionage xvii, 335-36; release 375, 377-79, 385, 387, 392-93

Joint Intelligence Committee xxii, 21, 103, 312, 423-24; threat to Hong Kong 112-18
Jones, D.V. x, 160-61, 393

K'ang Sheng 46, 96-7
Kao Shih-k'un 110, 120-1, 126, 128, 132, 153-54, 185-86, 190, 202, 255, 257-58
Kenya 99, 187, 270; Peking Mission 102
Keswick, Sir John 153, 315-18, 400, 489-90
Khan, F-M Ayub 63-4, 66, 84, 90, 138, 149
Kissinger, Henry xviii, 362, 400, 422, 459, 462, 494, 510, 516, 541; visits to China xvii, 457-58, 468, 476, 481, 483, 492, 496, 500, 527-28
Korea 405, 467, 517, 520; Korean War ix, 242, 352, 362, 523; North Korea 60, 301, 319, 321, 423
Kosygin, Alexei 310, 320
Ksilopolski, M. 32
Kuwait 359
Kyprianou, Spyros 531

Laos 310, 321, 485
Laughton, John 317, 426
Levin, Herb 364
Li Choh-chih 174, 178, 244, 267-68, 271-72
Lin Piao 21, 46, 101, 301-2, 304, 306, 311, 496
Littlejohn Cook, George 406
Liu Shao-chi 19, 21-2, 46, 496, 522
Lo Kuei-po 8, 18, 45, 73, 76, 83, 126-35, 138-39, 143, 145-46, 150, 152-53, 158, 161, 167-69, 171-72, 177, 181-82, 185-86, 190, 193, 202, 253, 256-57, 341, 345, 354, 395; 'half-relations' with UK 327
Logan, David 413
Long, Gerald 156-57, 170, 226, 269, 288-89
Longford, Earl of 12, 42
Loseby, Francis 104
Lo Yu-ho 172, 226, 229-30, 243-44, 251, 269
Luo Guibo xvii, 1
Luxembourg 353

Macao *see* Portugal
McBain, W. 316, 324, 331-32, 336, 338, 393-95
McCluney, Ian 366-67, 436-37, 458; Sino-British relations 399-400
MacDonald, Malcolm xxii, 210, 481-82, 436, 505, 512, 536
Ma Chia-chun 119, 288-89, 348-49, 352
McKearney, Philip 126
McLaren, Robin 192, 265, 290, 315
Maclehose, Sir Murray xxi, 443, 445-46
Maddocks, Arthur xiii, xvi, 228, 327, 332-33, 343-44, 409; Hong Kong policy 345-47,

Sino-British relations 414-16; Taiwan 273-74, 276-77
Maitland, Donald 153
Makarios, Archbishop 485, 531
Malaysia 116, 135, 183, 310, 359, 473
Malik, Adam 480, 483, 524, 534
Manac'h, Étienne 327, 341
Mao Tse-tung (Mao Zedong) ix-xi, 3, 21-2, 26, 34, 46-7, 85-6, 89, 96, 101, 272, 290, 294, 301, 306-7, 345, 394, 398, 404, 447, 469, 496, 506, 513, 520; 'Little Red Book' 126, 291; personality cult 291-92, 497; Thoughts/writings 15, 30, 115, 127, 129, 133, 162, 166-67, 193, 200-1, 247, 291, 302, 304, 320, 396, 491, 497-98, 522
Marshall, Peter 489-90
Martin, Constance 316, 324, 331-32, 336, 338, 393-95, 397
Martin, Paul 526
Mason, Robert 222
Maxwell, Neville xx, 503; interview with Chou En-lai 505-6
Melhuish, Ramsey 155, 192
Metropolitan Police 108, 157, 253; Special Branch 72, 108
Mexico 485
Middle East 519; Six-Day War, 25, 27
Millard, Guy 385-86, 417, 430-31, 476-77, 492
Ministerial Committee on Hong Kong *see* Cabinet
Ministry of Defence 184, 411-12, 433, 446
Ministry of Technology 312; on export of civil aircraft to China 312-14
Mongolian People's Republic 14, 68, 99, 210; attack on Peking Mission 96, 102; incidents in Ulan Bator 23; Trident crash 496
Monson, Sir (William) Leslie 387; release of Hong Kong prisoners 387-88
Moon, Peter xviii, 366-67, 377, 399-400, 405, 436-37, 458, 494, 514
Moreton, John 280, 289, 304
Morgan, Hugh 539-40
Morgan, John xvi, xix, xxi, 342-43, 345-47, 355-57, 361, 377, 385, 406-7, 419, 421, 442, 446, 452, 481, 510; exchange of Ambassadors 409-13, 494-96, 538-40; meetings with Chinese Chargé 348-49, 443-45, 486-87; PRC representation in UN 359-60, 368-72; Sino-British relations 349-55, 437-38, 455-57, 459-61; visit to US (1970) 356, 361
Morocco 485
Morphet, David 34-5
Muirhead, David 435-36

Mulley, Fred 12, 42, 272-73
Murray, James 108-9, 119, 154, 155-59, 191, 211, 213, 225, 228, 249, 272, 280, 303, 316-18, 322; British mission in Peking 196-98; Chinese view of their image 111-12; covert contacts with Chinese 296-99; economic pressure on China 230-34; Grey 266-69; Sino-British relations 134-39, 143-49, 163-65, 234-40, 244-46, 335-40

Nanking, Treaty of (1842) 446
Nepal 44-5, 47, 270, 310, 321
Netherlands 63, 327, 353, 491; affair of the Chinese welders 253; detention of Chargé (1966) 187; Peking Mission 81
New China News Agency (NCNA) xii, xiv, 9, 14, 25, 45, 53-4, 96, 112, 114, 169, 171, 230, 245, 264, 266, 272, 288, 297, 307, 314, 396, 415; article protesting visit of USS Enterprise 178, 180; restrictions on London staff 37-8, 41, 50, 52-3, 63, 66, 119-20, 122-24, 132, 134, 136, 138-39, 146, 148, 150, 153, 156-58, 232, 253, 255-56, 270, 394; staff detained in Hong Kong xiv, 51, 88, 130-31, 144-45, 147, 163, 165, 172-73, 175-76, 17, 195, 198, 239, 243, 246, 248, 267-68, 393
New Zealand 264, 313, 370, 411-12, 419, 433, 439, 452, 485, 521, 527-28, 543
Nixon, President Richard ix, xviii, 310, 342, 350-51, 356, 371, 418, 422; China policy 362-64, 406, 425, 436-37, 458-59, 466, 469, 484, 509; Guam speech 320; Nixon Doctrine 518-19; visit to China (1972) xviii, 429, 457-59, 461, 467-69, 476, 510, 515, 517-21, 527-28, 535, 541; visit to Moscow 515
North Atlantic Treaty Organisation (NATO) 308, 337, 373, 532; Lisbon meeting 435, 492
North Vietnam 104, 301, 306, 319, 321, 423
Norway 326, 452, 543; transmits messages from Peking 59

Oman 481, 484-85, 530
Oplinger, Gerald 481
Organisation of African Unity (OAU) 306
Overton, Hugh 461, 466-67, 469-70

Pakistan 17, 104, 112, 138, 140, 145, 150, 187, 224, 275, 306, 310, 459, 531; East Pakistan (Bangladesh) 459; Pakistan International Airways 58, 63, 66, 340, 376; policemen killed in Hong Kong 36-7; relations with China 62, 270, 321; war with India 522
Palestine 302, 306

Palliser, Michael 272-73
Parliament (UK) xiv, xx, 17, 107, 133, 140, 151, 159-60, 162, 318, 332, 341, 353, 395, 397, 464, 482, 498, 515-16, 534, 541; Foreign Affairs debate (July 1968) 258
Parsons, Anthony 370, 372, 480-81, 532
Paye, Lucien 92-4
Peck, Edward 242
Pedersen, Richard 437, 484-86, 531
P'ei Tsien-chang (Pei Jianzhang) xvii, 382, 391-92, 407-8, 410, 442-45, 452, 456-57, 460, 474, 486-87, 542
Peking, Treaty/Convention of (1898) 446
People's Republic of China (PRC) *see also* Bank of China, British Missions, Hong Kong, New China News Agency, Taiwan, UK relations with PRC, United Nations ix-x, xvii, 290-92, 522; 20th Anniversary Celebrations 301-2; Academy of Science 497; accusations of British imperialism 110, 115, 331; Anwhei 111; Communist Party x, 115, 293-94, 304, 307, 319; Cultural Revolution ix-x, xii, xxi, 1, 11-12, 18-19, 21-3, 33, 44-8, 89, 101, 108, 112-13, 115, 140, 144, 147, 150-51, 162, 187, 214, 218, 221, 236, 291-93, 304, 306, 310, 319, 322, 335-36, 340, 342, 376, 395-96, 398, 422-23, 496, 498, 518, 525; Cultural Revolution Group (CRG) 46, 101; establishment (1949) 422; foreign aid 423; foreign policy 23, 4, 46, 93, 216-17, 305-11, 319-22; Honan 23; Hong Kong policy xxii, 11, 17-26, 52-3, 112-18, 126, 134-36, 142, 150-51, 181, 187, 217, 224-25, 238, 242, 273-74, 283-84, 304-5, 343, 380-82, 448-49, 512-13; internal situation 100-1, 108-9, 487, 497, 511; Kansu 101; Kiangsi 101; Kwantung 22, 43, 60, 85-6, 89, 100-1, 129; Manchuria 471; Ministry of Foreign Affairs xi, 1, 16 18, 20, 23, 26, 39, 50-1, 68, 108, 127, 151, 158, 165-66, 170, 179, 196, 210, 242, 252, 272, 275-76, 294, 336, 341, 395, 403, 497, 504; Ministry of Foreign Trade 317, 345, 400, 489; Mission in London xi-xii, xvii, 8, 34-5, 54, 66-7, 72-4, 107-8, 146, 155-59, 333; nuclear weapons 24-5, 301-2, 312, 373, 413, 534; People's Liberation Army (PLA) xii, 22-3, 47, 57, 67, 69, 89, 101, 402, 496; ping-pong diplomacy 418, 496, 527; police 68; Politburo 46, 336, 496; press/propaganda 16, 18, 22-3, 95-6, 111, 154, 293, 307, 314, 324, 335; proposal for exchange of Notes (1971) 453-57, 459, 475; protest at US naval visits to Hong Kong 182, 257; Red Guards x, 21-3, 30, 33,

46-7, 67, 78, 81-2, 89, 94, 101, 108, 111, 118, 170; rejection of 'two Chinas' 438, 525; Revolutionary Rebels 21; Shanghai 15 22, 299, 336; Shantung 101; State Council 96; statement on Hong Kong/'Five Demands' (May 1967) 1, 3, 5, 9-11, 16, 18, 20, 23-4, 56, 83, 135, 144, 149, 177, 300, 382; statement on Sino-British relations (March 1968) 127-31, 135-36, 139-43, 152, 158, 161, 163-64, 167, 169, 256; students x, 101, 340; support for Asian insurgencies 321; Szechwan 23, 100; Tibet 100; trade ix, xxii, 318-21, 335, 343, 415, 420-28, 448, 488-90, 511-12; ultimatum on Hong Kong (Aug 1967) 53, 59, 68, 77-8, 83, 88, 96; Transport Monopoly 28; use of troops in Hong Kong 36-7

Peru 529

Peters, Theophilus 2, 7, 82, 99, 185, 187, 190; return to UK 263; visa for wife 155

Pickard, Sir Cyril 63

Poland 308; Oder-Neisse line 460, 465; unrest (1970) 383

Pope, Captain R.V. 181, 393

Portugal xi, 533; British consulate in Macao 7; Macao as model for Hong Kong settlement xxi, 6, 12, 18, 40, 44, 88, 93, 113-14, 116, 132, 140, 142, 146, 152, 215-16, 218-19, 235, 387, 448, 450, 504, 513; Macao riots (1966) 5

Potsdam Declaration (1945) 460, 463, 482, 500, 505, 509, 514-15, 535-36, 545

Qatar 481, 484-85

Quirie, Mabel 185

Raghunath, Krishnan 27

Ray, Capt James 393, 395

Reilly, Patrick 92-4

Renwick, Robin 464, 539-40

Reuters ix, 39, 51, 58, 62, 77, 107, 127, 143, 156-57, 170, 214, 226, 252, 266, 269, 286, 289, 296; suspension of Chinese operations 324, 331

Rhodesia 149, 154, 463

Roberts, Christopher 475

Rodgers, Sir John 366; Taiwan 367-68

Rodgers, William xiv, 9, 10-11, 37, 39, 94-5, 111, 139-40, 150-51, 153 198; interviews with Chinese Chargé 161-63, 165, 181-82; on restrictions against Chinese in UK 49-50, 159-61; speech in House of Commons (28 Mar 1968) 160

Rogers, William 411, 413, 417, 419, 428, 431-33, 435, 437, 439, 441-42, 457-58, 467, 476-79, 482, 492, 527-28, 530, 533, 541, 543

Roosbroeck, Frank van 32-3; disappearance from Shanghai 191

Royal Society 340

Royle, Anthony xvii-xviii, xxii, 160, 349, 368, 382, 391, 395, 399, 403, 407, 411 421, 432-33, 437, 441, 443-46, 456-57, 493, 540, 542-43; meetings with Chinese Chargé 443-45, 451-53, 459-60; PRC representation in UN 405-6, 482-83; Sino-British relations 356-57, 413-14

Rumania 306, 308, 315, 321

Rusk, Dean 362

Samejima, Keiji 191

Samuel, Richard 111, 473-75, 504-05; Sino-British relations 505-8, 510-12

Sato, Eisaku 310, 321

Saudi Arabia 484, 532

Seaby, John 59, 64, 81, 83

Secret Intelligence Service (SIS) 102, 104, 298

Security Service (MI5) 63, 66, 147, 156

Senegal 533

Shackleton, Lord 39, 183

Shapiro, Michael 393

Sharland, (Edward) John 266

Shen P'ing 3-4, 34-5, 39, 52-3, 56, 76, 161-63, 181-82, 277-80, 288

Shepherd, Lord 272; Grey 286-88; meeting with Chinese Chargé 277-78; meeting with Keswick 315-18

Sierra Leone 480

Singapore 41, 43, 116, 135, 183, 241, 310, 379, 412, 438; CinCFE 17, 28

Sino-British Trading Council xxiii, 233, 315, 331, 335, 400, 425-27, 488-90

Soames, Christopher 451

Soekarno, Dr I. 45

Sohm, Earl 482-83

South East Asia Treaty Organisation (SEATO) 411, 413, 417, 428

Soviet Union 19, 25, 44, 62, 89, 210, 293, 306, 310, 321, 337, 362, 373, 483, 491, 517, 521, 525; Aeroflot 58; aircraft for China 400-1; attacks on Peking Mission 99, 102; border tensions with China 19, 301, 304, 307, 310, 319-20, 322, 363, 518; Sino-Soviet hostility 301, 304, 360, 320, 518-20; threat to Europe 520

Spendlove, Roy 126, 265, 290

Sterner, Michael 458

Stewart, Michael xiv, xxii, 12, 42, 90, 150, 152-53, 155, 161, 183, 270, 282; appointed Foreign Secretary 142; Grey 275, 279; Hong Kong 328-30

557

Strategic Arms limitation Talks (SALT) 320, 458
Stratton, Richard 420, 480-81
Suez Canal 60
Sukarno, President 525
Sweden 309, 452, 486, 543; Peking Embassy shelters British staff 59
Switzerland 205, 422
Sykes, Bonor 241
Syria 307

Taiwan (Formosa) *see also* British Missions, Chinese Nationalists, United Nations ix-x, 19, 184, 242, 352, 400, 403, 405, 407, 436-37, 503, 517, 524; Chinese policy xx, 328, 414, 418, 466-67, 469-70, 492; 386; sovereignty/status xviii-xx, 276, 351, 354-56, 358, 367, 374, 408, 410, 413, 419, 429, 438-39, 442, 453, 455-56, 459-65, 470-72, 481-82, 487, 494-98, 505, 514-16, 526, 534-41; UK policy xvii, xix, 236, 331, 336, 350-51, 356, 366-68, 459, 461-62, 469-72, 474, 499, 504, 507-8, 514, 534, 537-38, 543-45; UK representation 273-74, 350, 354, 367, 439-40, 495, 545; UK trade 354, 367-68, 405, 408-9, 411, 415, 433, 453; US Defence/Mutual Security Treaty 466-67; US troops 466; US policy xix, 274, 309, 320, 352, 364-65, 368, 404, 415, 463, 505, 509
T'ang Hai-kuang 280-81, 324, 341, 357-58, 387, 402
Tanzania 112, 210, 270, 306, 322, 484
Thailand 302, 467
Thomas, George 59, 90; situation in Hong Kong 59-61
Thomson, George 53-6, 61, 66, 140, 174, 183-84, 199, 224-25
Thornton, Ernest 13
Tolstikov, Vasily 408
Tomlinson, Sir (Frank) Stanley. 159, 296, 382, 430, 459, 469, 496, 515-16, 527; Sino-British relations 464-66
Treasury 40, 90, 233, 446
Tregilgas, William 185; visa for wife 155
Trench, Sir David xiii, 6, 35-7, 42, 102-3, 145,199-200, 211, 233, 271-72, 282, 316, 333, 377, 443; Communist prisoners in Hong Kong xv-xvi, 137, 146, 173, 175-77, 225-26, 287-88, 303-5, 325, 375, 378-82, 384-5, 388, 397, 401-2, 406-7; exchange of ambassadors 472-73; Grey 125, 17, 195-6, 228-30, 250; Hong Kong defences 184; UK policy on Hong Kong 203-4, 206-7, 237, 383-84, 406-7; Sino-British relations 140-42, 158, 234-35, 248, 295-96; proposal for reply to Chinese statement of Mar. 1968 164

Trend, Sir Burke 12, 42, 90, 183, 434, 440, 516
Trevelyan, (Lord) Humphrey x, 536
Trinidad and Tobago 366, 485, 533
Tunisia 366, 484-85, 532

United Arab Republic (UAR) 25
United Kingdom (UK) relations with PRC *see also* British Missions, Hong Kong, Sino-British Trading Council, Taiwan, United Nations, United States: ix, 11-12, 37-8, 53-5, 58, 61-3, 84-91, 94-5, 102, 105, 126-31, 137-49, 151-53, 162-65, 205-9, 213-22, 224-25, 234-42, 271-74, 276-77, 299-300, 322-27, 330-33, 335-41, 343-47, 349-56, 371-77, 382-84, 391-92, 399-400, 402-5, 419, 428, 435-36, 438-40, 499-500; agreement on representation (1954) 8; 'Battle of Portland Place' xii, 34-5, 72-3, 96, 102, 105, 253; British banks in Shanghai 221, 232, 270, 375, 377, 381, 393, 397, 495, 504; British business interests 41, 84, 102, 208, 374; British community in Shanghai 205, 214, 262, 265, 270, 303, 336; British subjects detained in China xiv, xxii-xxiii, 62, 85, 109, 132, 149, 159-60, 162, 188, 205, 214, 216, 219, 221, 225, 231, 236-37, 254, 261, 265-66, 270-71, 276-78, 280-81, 294, 296, 299, 303, 316, 322, 325-26, 330, 334-36, 349, 374, 377, 383, 392-99, 499, 545; Chinese accusations of espionage 188-89, 205, 261, 292; claims against China 317-18; clemency for Hong Kong prisoners xv, 175, 218-20, 226-27, 235, 239, 241, 248, 381-82, 397, 406-7; COCOM 313, 400, 437, 511; defence against Chinese attack on Hong Kong 41, 112-18, 153, 183-84, 216, 241, 285-86, 384; direct telephone link 334, 340, 349; East of Suez policy 310; economic sanctions xiv, 137, 144, 148, 15, 194, 203, 211, 232, 236, 337, 397; exchange of ambassadors ix-x xvii-xix, xxi, xxiii, 274, 327, 345, 350, 354-55, 358, 367, 375-76, 382, 391, 399, 403, 406-13, 417, 428, 432, 435, 437, 439, 443-44, 453-56, 460-61, 467-68, 470-74, 476-77, 481, 483, 492-94, 496, 499, 506-8, 512, 516, 527, 535, 537-45; Guidance telegrams 100-2, 209-10, 543-45; informal contacts with Chinese Communists 229-30, 244-46; intelligence value of China 413, 423, 431; proposal for trade mission (1971) 399; protests against Chinese treatment of British missions xi, 188, 190; recognition of PRC (1950) 367, 403, 409, 463, 505, 544; rejection of 'Two Chinas' policy x, xix, 274, 352, 358, 372, 386, 429, 431, 433,

437, 442, 445, 452, 467, 475; restrictions on Chinese Mission in London xii, 37-8, 54, 56, 61-2, 66, 72-3, 91-2, 102, 106-9, 119-21, 134, 139, 144, 145-46, 148-50, 155-63, 166, 169, 185, 189-90, 196, 209, 217, 252, 254, 259; retaliation against Chinese in UK 49-50, 106, 397; sales of aircraft to China xxii-xxiii, 312-14, 317, 334, 340, 345, 349, 376, 400-1, 424, 461, 488, 501; Scottish Export Mission 493, 501, 503; shipping 63, 3, 194, 231, 337-38, 398, 422; Sino-British statement (March 1972) xx-xxi, 496-98, 505, 515-16, 535-44; trade xxii-xxiii, 11, 63, 85, 126, 137, 140, 194, 208-9, 211, 214, 221, 231-32, 271, 278, 303, 316-18, 334-36, 339, 344-46, 367, 376-77, 411, 422-28, 431, 487-90, 493, 500-1, 503-4, 510-12, 514; visas for Chinese citizens in UK xiv, 100, 119-23, 126, 128, 131-36, 138-39, 190; visits to UK by Chinese ships 94-5, 232

United Nations (UN) xix, 284, 352, 483; Albanian Resolution xvii, 342, 350-51, 353-54, 357, 359-61, 365, 369, 371-72, 391, 404, 406, 429-30, 434, 438, 444, 452, 456, 466, 477, 479-80, 484-86, 505, 524, 525, 529-30; Charter 86-7, 351, 420, 438, 455, 464, 478, 524-25, 529; Disarmament Commission 25; ECOSOC 370, 524; expulsion of Chinese Nationalists xix, 358-60, 364, 366, 368, 370, 406, 420, 428, 432, 441, 444, 454, 456, 459 468, 481-84, 532; General Assembly xix, 64, 87, 314, 353, 365-66, 368, 370, 372, 374, 418, 420, 422, 432, 434, 452, 459, 464, 468, 474-75, 478, 484, 505, 522, 524, 527, 533, 545; Important Question Resolution xvii-xviii, 87, 342, 350-53, 355-57, 359-61, 366, 368-72, 374, 386, 399, 404, 408-12, 417, 419-21, 428, 431-32, 434-37, 439-41, 444, 452, 472, 476, 484-85, 509, 511, 524, 526-28; PRC admission/representation x, xvii, xix, 47, 84, 86-91, 293, 311, 314-15, 336, 342, 345-46, 350-61, 364-66, 368-72, 382, 385-86, 399, 403-10, 413-14, 418, 420-23, 428-31, 434-37, 440, 444, 449, 452-53, 460-61, 475-76, 479-86, 496, 500, 504, 522-34, 545; Reverse Important Question Resolution 528, 531-32; Secretary-General 486, 488, 522, 533-34; Security Council 232, 368, 370, 372, 404, 413, 436, 438, 440, 453-55, 464, 521-23, 526, 533
United States *see also* Hong Kong, Japan, Taiwan, Vietnam: xviii, 19, 25, 135, 178, 326, 366, 373, 543; aircraft 312-13, 400; Asian strategy 518-19; China policy xviii-xix, 312-13, 342-43, 350, 352-53, 356, 361-65, 371, 411, 417-18, 422, 429-30, 466, 492, 500, 505, 509-10, 515-18, 528; Chinese attitudes 44, 111, 114, 206, 245, 302, 307, 309, 320, 327, 331, 337; Congress 352, 365, 369, 371, 483; domestic pressures 363-64, 458, 519, 528, 533; Guam Doctrine 352; House Foreign Affairs Committee 361, 363-64; PRC representation in UN 361-65, 369-71, 385-86, 399-400, 405-6, 410-11, 417, 420-21, 428-32, 435-36, 452, 460-61, 469-70, 476-78, 482-86, 526, 528-33; Presidential election (1972) 458; relations with Japan 517-21; relations with UK 346, 351, 371-72, 412, 417, 429-30, 432, 492, 509-10; State Dept xviii, 356, 361, 364, 371, 399, 410, 417, 430, 432, 452, 457-58, 478, 483-84, 509; trade with China 425, 427, 437, 501; Two Chinas policy 366, 372, 399, 429-30, 433, 435-38, 444, 459, 466-67, 469, 475-76, 479; US subjects detained in China 399; USS *Enterprise* xv, 178, 180-82, 185-86, 191, 196-97, 239, 257; views on Hong Kong 112, 283-84, 299, 371; Warsaw talks with PRC 309, 319, 331, 352, 363, 418; White House 356, 362, 364, 371, 458, 509-10

Vickers-Zimmer 102, 142-43, 147, 161, 233-34, 392
Vietnam *see also* North Vietnam 44, 47, 93, 135, 218, 302, 309, 375, 534; Paris peace talks 180, 307; South Vietnam 467; US forces 13, 25, 118, 182; US policy 236, 352, 411, 518; Vietnam War x, 14, 19, 114, 178, 214, 241, 282, 311, 321, 362, 458-59, 520

Walden, George 262-65, 314-15
Warner, Frederick 351
Warsaw Pact 308
Watt, George xiv, 143, 145, 151, 158, 160-61, 163, 236, 303, 325, 395-96, 398; imprisoned for espionage 102, 147, 154, 162, 181, 335; release 348, 392
Webb, Norman 489-90
Western European Union (WEU) 452, 543
Weston, John xi, 4, 78, 82, 154, 290, 315
Whitelaw, William 434, 440
Whitney, Ray 9, 14, 28, 31, 48, 55, 81-2, 95-7, 126-27, 185, 187, 191, 196, 202, 212

Wigg, George 12, 42, 90
Wilford, Michael xvii-xviii, 100, 342-43, 347, 349, 355-5, 359, 368, 370, 382, 385, 388, 391-92, 409, 414, 429-30, 437, 442-43, 445, 462, 476, 481, 490-91, 515-16, 538-40; future of Hong Kong 445-51; visit to China (1970) xvii, 341, 383, 395
Wilkinson, Peter 111, 121, 133, 143, 149, 163, 189, 198, 212-13
Will, Capt Peter 393-94
Wilson, A.N. 160-61
Wilson, Colin 17, 21, 33, 111, 126, 277, 318; Sino-British relations 330-33
Wilson, David 95, 126
Wilson, Sir Duncan 308
Wilson, Harold xi, 12, 42-3, 59, 72, 90-1, 102-3, 108, 183-84; effigy in Peking 48-9; Grey 272-73, 275; Parliamentary statement (5 May 1970), 342
Wong Chak 287

Yang Hsien-yi 383; Gladys Yang 393
Yemen 307
Yen, C.K. 364
Yugoslavia 307-8, 321, 368, 531

Zambia 187, 270, 306, 322